V+2 CON

6/he

HISTORY OF GUELPH

1827~1927

HISTORY OF

GUELPH

1827-1927

Leo A. Johnson

Commissioned and Published
by the
GUELPH HISTORICAL SOCIETY
GUELPH, Ont.

June 1977

ISBN 0-9690594-0-X
Printed and bound in Canada

Managing Editors: Ruth and Eber Pollard
Designer: Helmut Weyerstrahs

Printing and Binding: The Hunter Rose Company
Typeface: Baskerville
Paper: No. 1 Oxford Opaque
Cover: Tanolin 10

Financial assistance provided by—

The City of Guelph,
New Horizons,
Wintario.
Bank of Montreal,
Bank of Nova Scotia,
Canadian Imperial Bank of Commerce,
Royal Bank of Canada,
Toronto Dominion Bank,
Canada Trust Company,
District Trust Company,
Fidelity Mortgage and Savings Corporation,
Royal Trust Company,
Victoria and Grey Trust Company.

Contents

Foreword

This book is dedicated to the past, the present, and the future. It is dedicated to the past because we owe so much to those great pioneers who came before us. They left us with a heritage of which to be proud.

It is dedicated to the present because we have a responsibility to learn from the past so that we might better enjoy our day and age.

It also is dedicated to the future. Hopefully, the citizens of another one-hundred-and fifty years will look back at us with kindness. When they write their history book of Guelph may we be remembered as a city where people came first.

So let us learn from the past, enjoy the present, and plan for the future. If we have the zeal, the will, and free spirit exemplified by so many individuals written about in this book, including our founder John Galt, we will have a bright future indeed.

Norm. Jary

Norm Jary, Mayor,
City of Guelph.

Preface

This book was undertaken by the Guelph Historical Society and myself three years ago in recognition of Guelph's sesquicentennial in 1977. When I was approached by the Executive of the Society to write the History of Guelph, I suggested that it should be a joint enterprise, as otherwise it would not be possible to complete the task in the time available. It was agreed that the Society would research any and all material available in the Guelph area, while I researched the Archives in Ottawa and Toronto, and the resulting material would greatly enlarge the Society's archives. The result is a collection which today comprises over 20,000 research cards.

This history attempts to provide answers to a number of questions: why did Guelph grow and develop when other centres such as Rockwood, Georgetown or Hespeler remained much smaller? Why, on the other hand, given the strenuous efforts of the business community to promote Guelph's growth, did it never achieve the size and dominant position to which its leaders aspired? What were the ideologies, strategies, and consequences of growth and the failure of dominance? Finally, what were the periods and nature of the development of Guelph's major social institutions and organizations. In a word, what I have tried to achieve is an outline of Guelph's development upon which other historians could build a broader and more refined understanding of Guelph's social history.

Due to limitations of time and space, this undertaking has resulted in some major and ofttimes painful compromises, and many interesting and important subjects have been merely touched upon or omitted entirely. Moreover, because the research and writing was a shared undertaking with sometimes divergent goals, the book is neither exactly what the Society wanted nor what I had hoped to achieve. Nevertheless, the opportunity to work closely with a local historical society in this way has been most interesting and rewarding for me, and an experience which I can recommend to other professional writers of local history. I owe a particular debt of thanks to Ruth and Eber Pollard who were indispensable in the conception and carrying out of every aspect of this book, as well as to all those who helped in any way to make this book a reality.

April 18, 1977.   Leo A. Johnson

Acknowledgments

The History of Guelph—a project to commemorate the 150th anniversary of the founding of Guelph in 1827 by John Galt, initiated and sponsored by the Guelph Historical Society—involved many people in many ways.

To those people the Guelph Historical Society extends their most heartfelt thanks and appreciation—to the members of the History workshop who turned out faithfully twice a week for two years to research books, pamphlets and newspapers; to read and correct manuscript and galley sheets, and the numerous other details connected with the publishing of a book; to the ladies who typed manuscript tirelessly for several months; to the kind and generous people of Guelph who donated or loaned their precious records, pictures, scrap books and other historical items; a special thanks to the Guelph Public Library, without whose wealth of knowledge and generous use of historical material, this book could not have been written, to the editors of the Guelph Mercury for their enthusiastic coverage of our project; to the Guelph Civic Museum, the Guelph City Hall and Wellington County Offices for the use of their records; and to the Archives at Toronto and Ottawa.

We would also express our appreciation to Norm Jary, the Mayor of Guelph, for his interest and encouragement; to Leo A. Johnson, the author, who taught us how to research and who spent endless hours writing the manuscript.

The shortness of time and the limitations of space governed the content of the History, and we hope that any errors or omissions will be overlooked, as they were purely unintentional.

We hope that in some small way we have contributed to Guelph's anniversary, and that all who read our History will enjoy reading it as much as we have enjoyed working on it.

Ruth Pollard, President,
Guelph Historical Society.
April 18, 1977.

To the people of Guelph who carried on
John Galt's grand design with ingenuity and
untiring zeal, and to Carolyne,
whose encouragement and support have
helped to make this work possible.

L.A.J.

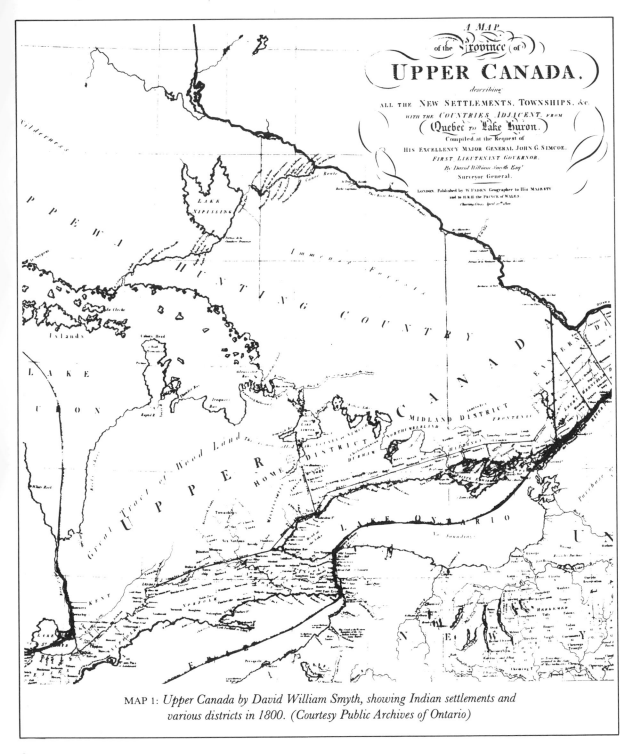

MAP 1: *Upper Canada by David William Smyth, showing Indian settlements and various districts in 1800. (Courtesy Public Archives of Ontario)*

I

John Galt's Grand Design

Prior to the coming of white settlers to North America, the region surrounding Guelph lay in a neutral zone generally unoccupied by any aboriginal nation. To the north, the Hurons had developed an advanced commercial and agricultural society which traded over half a continent. To the west, lay the regions inhabited by the Petun and Neutral nations, whose economics were entirely agricultural, and who were forced to pay tribute to the Hurons.

To the south-east, across Lake Ontario, resided the Iroquois Confederacy, the chief rivals of the Hurons. The Iroquois economy, like that of the Hurons, was based upon a combination of agriculture and trade. Thus when European contact began along the Atlantic coast, the Hurons and Iroquois competed vigorously for dominance of the main commodity, fur. It was not long before alliances were formed between the French and Hurons on the one hand, and the Iroquois and British on the other, and warfare began. This struggle culminated in 1649-1650 with the defeat of the Hurons and their Indian allies, and their dispersal amongst other Indian nations. A few Hurons settled amongst the French in Quebec.

Joseph Brant, from a portrait by Romney in 1776. (The Picture Gallery of Canadian History).

3

After the destruction of the Huron, Petun and Neutral nations by the Iroquois-British alliance, a period of relative calm occurred during which several small bands of Algonkian-speaking Indians moved into the region. These bands, called variously Ojibwa, Chippewa and Mississauga, however, established no permanent villages. Their economy was based upon hunting, trapping, fishing and gathering fruit and wild grain, and with only a little farming or gardening. The difference in economic activities between the Hurons and Iroquois, and the Algonkian-speaking Indians would have a very important consequence: whereas the former groups, because of their agricultural orientation placed a high value on land, and fought fiercely to retain ownership of it, the more nomadic Algonkians lacked the same sense of ownership, and, once white settlement began to push into Upper Canada, were much more easily persuaded to sign away their rights in treaty negotiations.

It was not until 1792, however, that major changes began to occur in the Guelph region. As a result of the American Revolutionary War (1776-1783) British Loyalists and their Indian allies, the Iroquois, were driven north into Canada. In order to retain the loyalty of the Iroquois, the British had promised to replace any lands that they might lose. The American colonies having won their independence, it was now Britain's duty to make good that promise. After long negotiations, it was decided to grant the Iroquois a strip of land twelve miles in width, lying on both sides of the Grand River, running from its mouth to its source.

To satisfy Iroquois claims and to obtain land for white settlement adjacent to Lake Erie and Lake Ontario, the British authorities negotiated a treaty with the local Mississaugas for a tract of land, roughly triangular in shape, reaching from Burlington Bay to the headwaters of the Grand, then south-west to Port Burwell on Lake Erie. This huge area, which includes present-day Guelph, was surrendered by the Mississaugas on December 7, 1792, for the sum of £1,180.7s.4d. sterling. Then, in 1793, the Grand River tract, including the area north and west of Guelph Township, was granted to the Iroquois. As a result, that area, now comprising Nichol, Pilkington, Wilmot, Waterloo and Dumfries Townships, passed into Iroquois hands.

The rest of Wellington County lying northwest and north of Nichol and Pilkington, was surrendered by the Mississaugas at a much later date.[1] It was not until 1818, under two separate treaties, that Eramosa, Erin, West Garafraxa and West Luther Townships were surrendered. In 1825 Maryborough was made part of a treaty, and finally, in 1836, Minto and Arthur were surrendered.

The primary reason for the long delay in signing treaties for the northern areas was that the land was not required for white settlement. With millions of acres available closer to Lake Ontario, and immigrants arriving at a slow rate, there was a huge surplus of vacant land. It was only when the older areas close to the lakes began to fill up that the government needed to acquire the more northerly regions.

Although Guelph Township had been acquired by the government in 1792, it would be another thirty-five years before settlement would begin. This delay was entirely the result of government policy. In 1791, as a means of supporting a "Protestant" clergy and of financing government expenditures, the Colonial Office and the Government of Upper Canada had decided to set aside one-seventh of all land as Clergy Reserves, and an additional one-seventh as Crown Reserves. These reserves, it was hoped, would be leased by new settlers and the revenue would support both church and government.

In areas where settlement had not yet begun, the reserves were laid out throughout the townships in a checker-board pattern, so that their value would be representative of the average value of the townships involved. For those regions already settled by Loyalists and other immigrants, this pattern could not be followed. It was decided, therefore, that whole townships would be set aside in new areas to make up for the lack of reserves in settled areas. Thus it was, that in order to compensate for the lack of reserves in Lincoln County, the entire Township of Guelph was set aside as a Crown Reserve, and Puslinch was named a Clergy Reserve. As such, both Townships were closed to settlement for those who hoped to buy land of their own. Such would remain the situation until the Canada Company came upon the scene.

The creation of the Canada Company arose from two sources: the failure of the Crown and Clergy Reserve leases to raise significant revenues, and the desire by a number of British capitalists to find an opportunity for profitable land speculation. In 1823 both goals began to come together. The chief protagonist for the sale of the Crown and Clergy Reserves was John Beverley Robinson, Attorney-General of Upper Canada. It was Robinson's belief that the reserves, and if possible all Crown lands,

should be converted to cash so that a permanent sinking fund could be created. Such a fund would, he believed, prevent the elected Legislative Assembly from forcing the voters' will upon the Governor and Executive Council by the Assembly's capacity to cut off tax revenues. Although there was general agreement amongst the Executive Council of Upper Canada that some such step was necessary to shore up the government's position against the growing demands of the Legislative Assembly for a share of power, no satisfactory method to achieve fiscal autonomy immediately presented itself.

Meanwhile, a second proposal for the sale of the reserve lands in Upper Canada was brewing. During the War of 1812, many Upper Canadians had experienced large financial losses, not merely from American soldiers who burned and pillaged, but also from the British troops who were stationed amongst them for the defence of Upper Canada. The latter requisitioned homes, seized grain and produce, slaughtered livestock for food, and, as armed mercenaries often do, showed little concern for the property of those they were defending. Although the more prominent sufferers quickly received compensation, the great majority of citizens who had experienced losses received nothing. In spite of long and bitter complaints to the British authorities, and years of fruitless petitions to the British Government, nothing was done. Finally, in 1822, a group of these "Canadian Claimants" banded together to hire the Scottish novelist, John Galt, to pursue their case at Whitehall. It was their choice of Galt that would set into motion the chain of events that led to the settlement of Guelph.

John Galt was, by all accounts, a most unusual person, a novelist of Scottish tales, world traveller, poet, author of a popular biography of the poet, Lord Byron, and man of affairs. Galt, as he says of himself, aspired as well to become a successful promoter and business-man.[2] It was the latter aspect of Galt's career (as well as his reputed influence over some sixty members of the British House of Commons) that drew Galt to the attention of the Canadian Claimants.

Initially, in spite of his influence, Galt had little success in representing his clients to the British authorities. During 1822, he was passed back and forth from office to office, meeting everywhere with frustration and delay. Galt made proposal after proposal on behalf of his long-suffering employers, but without result.[3] The British Government simply refused to consider any kind of a cash settlement. In the face of this refusal, Galt gradually evolved the idea of selling the vacant lands of Upper Canada to compensate his clients.

In 1823, Galt began to put his scheme into motion, but by now, in his fertile mind, it took on larger and larger dimensions. Not only would he propose to sell the "Reserves" in Upper Canada to satisfy his clients, but he would also create a gigantic land speculation and settlement company in the hopes of profiting personally. The scale of the enterprise, as he imagined it, was breath-taking. He would raise a million pounds and contract to buy all the unsold lands of Upper Canada. Although the Canada Company ultimately fell short of these goals, it would still be the largest enterprise of its kind in Canadian history.

During 1823, Galt undertook a vigorous promotional campaign to sell his idea to British investors. The company, he proposed, was to be a purely commercial venture, with a nominal capital of £1,000,000. John Galt

John Galt, the founder of Guelph.

would be hired as its manager. Within the year, he was able to dispose of enough shares to raise sufficient money to begin operations.[4]

The charter of the Canada Company, passed by the British Parliament, gave it enormous powers. It could purchase, hold, improve, settle and dispose of waste or other lands, make advances of capital to settlers, and open or make improvements to roads through the lands to be opened for settlement.[5] The Company was granted the right to import and export goods free of duty, provided that such articles were brought in to be used for the cultivation and improvement of its lands, or exported for the common good of its settlers. The right to own lands elsewhere in the British Dominions was also allowed.

The Company's charter provided for the appointment of a Governor, Deputy-Governor, sixteen Directors, four auditors and a secretary. Those elected as officers and Directors (soon to have their names commemorated by townships named after them in the Huron Tract) were: Governor, Charles Bosanquet; Deputy-Governor, William Williams; Directors, Robert Biddulph, Richard Blanshard, Robert Downie, John Easthope, Edward Ellice, John Fullarton, Charles David Gordon, William Hibbert, Jr., John Hodgson, John Hullett, Hart Logan, Simon McGillivray, James McKillop, John Masterman, Martin Tucker Smith, and Henry Usborne.[6] With his Company incorporated, Galt was now ready to deal with the various governments.

During his British negotiations, Galt dealt primarily with the Under Secretary for the Colonies, R. Wilmot Horton. In December, 1823, Galt was ready with his proposal: a commission should be established to travel to Upper Canada, both to assess the value of the re-

serves and remaining crown lands, and to recommend a method of disposal so that the war losses of the Upper Canadians could be satisfied. Naturally Galt suggested strongly that he should be one of the commissioners.

During the spring and summer of 1824, Galt worked hard to sell the Canada Company idea to prospective shareholders. By August he had managed to persuade investors to subscribe to all the shares, although only a small first subscription of capital was paid in. Nonetheless, it was enough so that, when the time was right, operations could begin. Meanwhile Galt had been successful in getting his commission idea accepted. As a result John Galt and William McGillivray were appointed to represent the Canada Company, Francis Lockburn and John Harvey represented the British authorities and those of Upper Canada, and John Davidson was chosen by the other commissioners to make up the commission. The commissioners were instructed to report to the Lieutenant-Governor of Upper Canada at York, which they did in March, 1825. In all, they were to report on the value of some 2,200,000 acres of reserve lands.

The negotiations concerning the actual purchase and price would drag on for almost another year. Ultimately, Archdeacon John Strachan, objecting to the low price offered for the Clergy Reserves, had them withdrawn from the agreement. In their place the Canada Company was offered 1,000,000 acres in the Huron Tract. Moreover, those Crown Reserves already under lease were withdrawn from the deal and turned over for the support of Upper Canada College. Remaining to be included in the sale were all Crown Reserves still unleased in townships surveyed before March 1, 1824. In all, these amounted to 1,322,010 acres, in-

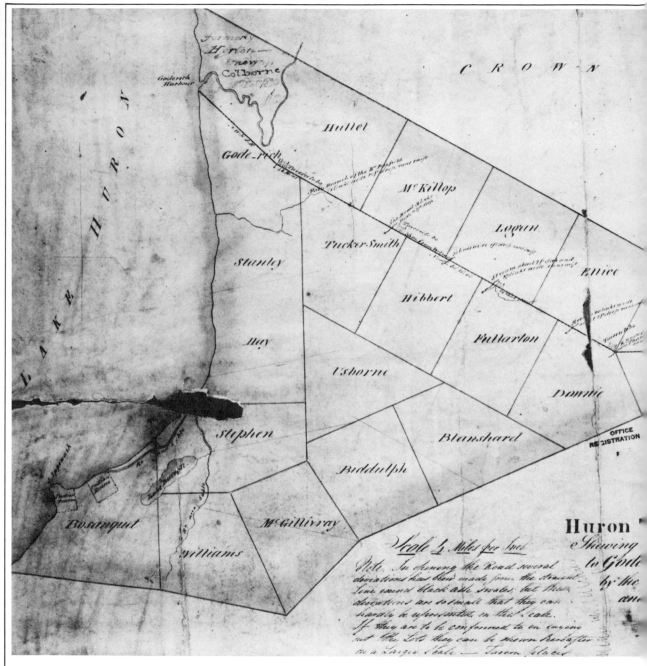

MAP 2: *The Huron Tract. (Courtesy Public Archives of Ontario)*

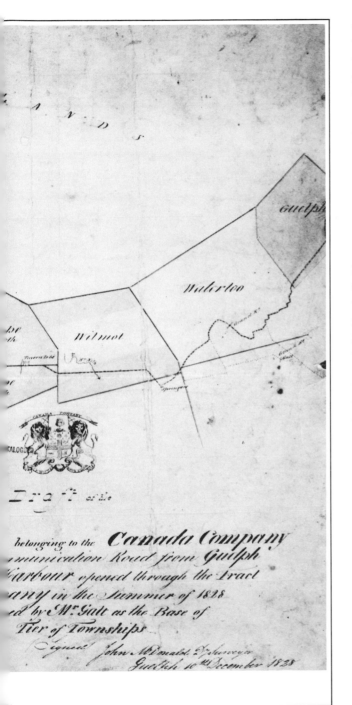

cluding the Township of Guelph. In addition the Company received the 1,000,000 acres in the Huron Tract. These lands were to be paid for at the rate of 3s. 6d. per acre over a twenty-year period. The total purchase money was to amount to £2,484,413 sterling. Aside from the simple land-jobbing of vacant Crown Reserves in long-settled areas, the first major undertaking of the Canada Company under Galt's direction, was the settlement of Guelph Township.[7]

The Canada Company's choice of Guelph for its first major development was a logical one. Not only was Guelph one of the largest vacant blocks of land remaining within trading distance of York, but settlement was already well established on both sides of it. To the west, the Iroquois had long since sold off Dumfries, Waterloo, Wilmot, Pilkington and Nichol Townships to land speculators, and Waterloo had received its first settlers in 1800. To the east, Erin and Eramosa had begun to receive settlers by 1820. Thus Guelph was now clearly in the path of settlement.

When John Galt arrived in Upper Canada in January, 1827, to take up permanent residence as manager of the Canada Company, he had already formulated his strategy for the project's success. Whereas most land jobbers were content to sell off wild lands cheaply as demand arose while spending as little as possible, Galt intended to maximize profits through large-scale capital investment and extensive advertising and promotion. Rather than have settlers trickle into an ever-widening frontier, he would present them with a ready made settlement with a town, good roads and such social necessities as a school, market and shops already in place. Not only would such an approach speed the rate of settlement, but it would greatly increase the value of farm lands to potential settlers. Upon Galt's arrival he was greatly encouraged to find that good lands were becoming relatively scarce and a strong demand existed. Indeed, within the first few weeks of his arrival he received nearly three hundred offers to purchase lots. The Guelph project, then, seemed to promise every likelihood of success.

Once Galt had set up his land sales office in York, recruited a staff and got sales of the scattered Crown lots moving, he was able to turn his attention to the Guelph project. His orderly and business-like approach is revealed in his instructions to his lieutenant, Dr. William "Tiger" Dunlop, regarding the selection of the Guelph townsite:

York, 19th March, 1827

Sir,—As the business of the company calls me away and I may not have the power of communication with you for some weeks, I leave with you the following instructions for your guidance during my absence, or until I shall have instructed you to the contrary.

You will proceed tomorrow to Ancaster and acquaint Mr. Prior and Mr. Tiffany on your arrival. You will receive from them whatever information they may have collected concerning the Guelph block additional to, or explanatory of, the regular report, a copy of which is subjoined.

You will then proceed, with these gentlemen, and Mr. Ewart, whom I have desired to accompany you, to the proposed site of the City of Guelph, which site you will carefully and diligently examine, and should it appear to you that it is inconvenient or ineligible you will make a tour of the Guelph block for the purpose of selecting one better adapted for the offices and public buildings of the company.

But should it appear to you that the situation is well fitted for such purposes you may request Mr. Ewart to make his arrangements for procuring building materials without loss of time.

As it is absolutely essential that a road should be cut into the block as a preliminary step to any permanent improvement, you will carefully examine the country between the settled parts of the townships bounding on the company's lands and run a blaze between these and the company's boundary in the line which can be cut with the least expense to the company, but after passing the company's limits you will run your road along the most convenient line that the general face of the country points out, without having any reference to regular straight lines or angles.

Having set the business of the Guelph block in train, you will then turn your attention to exploring the Huron territory. . .

I am under the necessity of leaving much to your own discretion in this matter, allow me to beg of you, continually to bear in mind that whenever you incur an expense on account of the company it is to be done with a reasonable prospective view to a profit equivalent to the risk incurred, and that you are never for a moment to imagine that any object of a mercantile company is to be carried through coûte que coûte—this caution I deem necessary on intrusting you for the first time with a discretionary power, from the mode of proceeding I have uniformly seen adopted in this Province and elsewhere by men whose modes of thinking are habitually military. . .[8]

Three weeks after Dunlop had received his instructions, the *Gore Gazette* of Ancaster noted that matters in Guelph were proceeding as planned. On April 14, the *Gazette* reported that the "Canada Company commence active operations cutting roads from Galt through their 40,000 acre tract in Halton [District] and in selecting a *scite* for a town".[9]

Meanwhile, Galt's business, which had taken him to New York, was completed, and he was ready to take active command of the Guelph project. Galt's strategy to make the most of the undertaking, and thereby to in-

Dr. William "The Tiger" Dunlop,
Warden of the Forests in the Huron Tract.

crease the enthusiasm of both the employees and prospective buyers for it, was revealed in his autobiography:

When the causes which induced me to visit New York were adjusted, I returned to Upper Canada and gave orders that operations should commence on St. George's Day, the 23rd of April. This was not without design; I was well aware of the boding effect of a little solemnity on the minds of most men, and especially of the unlettered, such as the first class of settlers were likely to be, at eras which betoken destiny, like the launching of a vessel, or the birth of an enterprise, of which a horoscope might be cast.

The founding of a town was certainly one of these, and accordingly I appointed a national holiday for the ceremony, which secretly I was determined should be celebrated so as to be held in remembrance, and yet so conducted as to be only apparently accidentally impressive.[10]

Travelling from New York via Dundas, Galt met a party of Canada Company officials there, and then proceeded to the village of "Galt", as Shade's Mills had been renamed, in his honour. On the morning of the twenty-third, the Canada Company party were ready for their journey to the proposed site of Guelph. Robert Thompson, one of Guelph's early residents, then a child living in Galt, remembered their departure:

In the spring of 1825, my father, with his family, came to reside in the Town of Galt. He purchased a lot on the west side of the Grand River, and erected a house where we resided for about two years. Galt was at that time a place of about 70 to 80 inhabitants, with one store, one tavern, grist and saw mill, a cooper's shop, a distillery, and about ten dwelling houses. [One] morning. . .my attention was arrested by a small group of men and ox teams on the opposite side of the river. I was then a boy of about ten years, and possessing, as I believed I did, a fair share of full-fledged curiosity in seeing and knowing all that was going on around me, I hastened to the spot, and very soon gathered from the conversation that the party was preparing to start for a place they called the Block, somewhere east of the Township of Waterloo. So far as memory serves me the party were as follows:- Mr. Galt, Dr. Dunlop, Charles Prior, John McDonald (late Sheriff of Goderich), William Goodin of Galt, and some eight or ten axe men and chain bearers—four of whom I knew—as Harry and Curtis Lambert, Stace and Ira Holdin, all residing in or near Galt. The teams belonged to Absalom Shade, and were loaded with pork, flour, whiskey, etc. The easterly part of Waterloo through which they had to pass was at that time thinly settled, and only one settler in the entire Township of Guelph; this was a man named Rife, who had about two years previous squatted near the westerly limits of the Township, about five and a half miles from the town, the creek running through his farm is still known as Rife's Creek. The distance to be travelled from Galt was about seventeen miles, and for the most part was over a rough and newly-made bush road. The cortege left Galt at eight o'clock in the morning, and reached their destination about five o'clock in the afternoon.[11]

Galt's trip from Galt to Guelph proved to be particularly unpleasant. Galt had remained behind the main party, and no sooner had he and "Tiger" Dunlop, his "Warden of the Forest" set out than they missed the blazed track and became lost in the forest. Galt described their situation as follows:

I was excessively angry, for such an incident is no trifle in the woods; but after "wandering up and down" like the two babes, with not even the comfort of a blackberry, the heavens frowning and the surrounding forest sullenly still, we discovered a hut, and "tirling at the pin," entered and found it inhabited by a Dutch shoemaker. We made him understand our lost condition, and induced him to set us on the right path. He had been in the French army, and had, after the peace, emigrated to the United States; thence he had come to Upper Canada, where he bought a lot of land, which, after he had made some betterments, he exchanged for the location in the woods, or as he said himself, "Je swapé" the first land for the lot on which he was now settled. With his assistance we reached the skirts of the wild to which we were going, and were informed in the cabin of a squatter that all our men had gone forward. By this time it began to rain, but undeterred by that circumstance, we resumed our journey in the pathless woods. About sunset dripping wet, we arrived near the spot we were in quest of, a shanty, which an Indian, who had committed murder, had raised as a refuge for himself. . .We found the men under the orders of Mr. Prior, whom I had employed for the Company, kindling a roaring fire. . . .[12]

In spite of the rain and dark, Galt was determined to have his ceremony. Galt continued his narrative as follows:

After endeavoring to dry ourselves, and having recourse to the store basket, I proposed to go to the spot chosen for the town. By this time the sun was set, and Dr. Dunlop, with his characteristic drollery, having doffed his wet garb, and dressed himself Indian fashion, in blankets, we proceeded with Mr. Prior, attended by two woodmen with their axes. It was consistent with my plan to invest our ceremony with a little mystery, the better to make it remembered. So intimating that the main body of the men were not to come, we walked to the brow of the neighboring rising ground, and Mr. Prior having shewn the site selected for the town, a large maple tree was chosen; on which taking an axe from one of the woodmen, I struck the first stroke. To me at least the moment was impressive,—and the silence of the woods that echoed to the sound was as the sigh of the solemn genius of the wilderness departing for ever. The Doctor followed me, then, if I recollect correctly, Mr. Prior, and the woodmen finished the work. The tree fell with a crash of accumulated thunder, as if ancient nature were alarmed at the entrance of social man into her innocent solitudes with his sorrows, his follies, and his crimes. I do not suppose that the sublimity of the occasion was unfelt by the others, for I noticed that after the tree fell, there was a funereal pause as when the coffin is lowered in the grave.[13]

It was "Tiger" Dunlop who put an end to the air of solemnity which pervaded the darkened glade. Pulling a bottle of whiskey from among his blankets, Dunlop proposed a toast to the future of Guelph and the prosperity of the Canada Company. After drinks all around, the little party returned to the cabin to undertake the actual labour of founding the Town on the morrow.

Galt's ceremony had its desired effect. Later the maple stump would be levelled and a sun dial fixed upon it to commemorate the event. As time went on the "romance" of Guelph's beginnings would displace its purely commercial origins in the residents' minds, and John Galt would be credited with almost supernatural vision. In this, at least, Galt succeeded far beyond his expectations.

There can be little doubt but that as a promoter and land salesman, Galt was a genius. At every step of Guelph's development he utilized the necessary capital expenditure in such a way as to maximize public visibility and investor interest. These aims were foremost in his mind when he chose the name for the prospective Town. The name Guelph (or Guelf) goes back to mediaeval times when two parties called the "Guelphs" and the "Ghibellines" contended for dominance in Italy and Germany from the eleventh to the fourteenth centuries. Descendents of the leaders of the "Guelph" party ruled as crowned heads of many of the small German states, and eventually, one of these princelings, George Louis, Duke of Brunswick, Lunenburg and Zell, Elector of Hanover, became George I, King of England. As John Galt noted, the name Guelph was chosen for the Town "in compliment to the Royal Family, both because I thought it auspicious in itself, and because I could not recollect that it had ever been before used in the king's dominions."[14]

Perhaps Galt's greatest success in combining practical investment with a publicist's eye for promotion was in the building of the road from Waterloo Township to the site of Guelph. It was his aim to use the road both to raise the price of land in Guelph Township and to make his project famous. He succeeded in both. Galt explained the road in this way:

The works, being on a grand scale were now becoming objects of curiosity. Not being restricted in any means which could be employed in the country, I certainly did indulge myself in the rapidity of creation. . .The glory of Guelph (the Waterloo Road) was unparalleled, but like all earthly glories, it was destined to pass away. It consisted of a glade opened through the forest, about seven miles in length, upwards of one hundred and thirty feet in width, forming an avenue, with trees on each side, far exceeding in height the most stupendous in England.

The high road to the town lay along the middle of this babylonian approach, which was cut so wide as to admit the sun and air, and was intended to be fenced of the usual width, the price of the land contiguous to be such as to defray the expense of the clearing. . . .

But the imagination forbears when it would attempt to depict the magnificent effect of the golden sun shining through the colossal vista of smoke and flames;—the woodmen dimly seen moving in "the palpable obscure," with their axes glancing along in the distance. A Yankee post-boy who once drove me to Guelph, on emerging from the dark and savage wood, looked behind in astonishment as we entered the opening, and clapping his hands with delight, exclaimed, "What an Almighty place."

By doing speedily and collectively works which, in detail, would not have been remarkable, these superb effects were obtained. They brought "to home" the wandering emigrants, gave them employment, and by the wonder of their greatness, magnified the importance of the improvements. This gigantic vision did not cost much more than the publication of a novel.[15]

So spectacular was the result, that, for a time, it rivalled Niagara Falls as a tourist attraction, and both wealthy travellers and government officials came to view the fruits of Galt's grand design.

It was in the development and promotion of the Town itself, that Galt managed his greatest success as an innovator and salesman. Galt's main interest in the development of the Town of Guelph was the sale of agricultural land in the surrounding township. Under ordinary conditions in Upper Canada, agricultural settlement tended to spread slowly inland from the good natural harbours on the Great Lakes. As inland settlement increased, small villages gradually appeared where a local stream provided a good site for a primitive saw or grist mill, or where main roads met. Eventually other suppliers of goods and services to the farming community such as blacksmiths, coopers, distillers, tanners, carders and weavers set up shop, and the village prospered. This growth, however, was entirely dependent upon the presence of a large, prosperous farming community which provided the economic base for the town. Berlin, for example, developed in exactly that pattern.

Once such a village had developed, other farmers were attracted to the area by the ready market and many conveniences offered, and the resulting competition for land drove prices well above those demanded for land distant from a village. Such a pattern of mutual growth and economic interdependence between village and countryside usually continued until all available farm land was settled and cultivated, then growth slowed, and the community settled into comfortable stability.

Galt's plans, however, were aimed at exactly reversing this pattern. By utilizing the large capital resources of the Canada Company, he intended to create a town containing all the necessary goods and services demanded by an advanced agricultural community, and which would provide a ready market for the locally grown produce. By creating instantly an advanced community, Galt hoped that farm land prices would rise, and the Canada Company would reap the benefits that usually came only after a long period of growth. The first step, therefore, was to create the Town.

The main difficulty he faced, from Galt's point of view, was that although the site had some useful assets, such as good land and several excellent mill seats, it possessed no advantage over its potential rivals that guaranteed its success as a great commercial centre. Even Galt, when later defending his choice of the site could offer no characteristic that was not shared by virtually every other local village:

It may appear ludicrous to many. . .but in truth I am very serious; for although Guelph is not so situated as ever to become celebrated for foreign commerce, yet the location possesses many advantages. It will be seen that it stands almost in the centre of the tableland which separates four of the great lakes, namely, Ontario, Simcoe, Huron and Erie, and though its own river Speed, as I named it, is not large, yet at the town it receives the Eramosa, and at a short distance flows into the Grand River, which may be said to be navigable from the bridge at Galt to Lake Erie.[16]

Galt's method of promoting Guelph was to plunge ahead, spending money in the early stages in a grand manner, and all the time proclaiming that Guelph's future was assured. From the first he confidently called Guelph a city—and laid it out as though it actually was. As Galt explained his method:

In planning for the city, for I will still dignify it by that title, though applied at first in derision, I had like the lawyers in establishing their fees, an eye to futurity in the magnitude of the parts. A beautiful central hill was reserved for the Catholics, in compliment to my friend, Bishop Macdonell, for his advice in the formation of the Company; the centre of a rising ground, destined to be hereafter a square, was appropriated to the Episcopal Church for Archdeacon Strachan; and another rising ground was reserved for the Presbyterians. Education is a subject so important to a community that it obtained my earliest attention, and accordingly in planning the town I stipulated that the half of the price of the building sites should be appropriated to endow a school, undertaking that the Company in the first instance, should sustain the expense of the building, and be gradually repaid by the sale of the town lots. The school house was thus among the first buildings undertaken to draw settlers.[17]

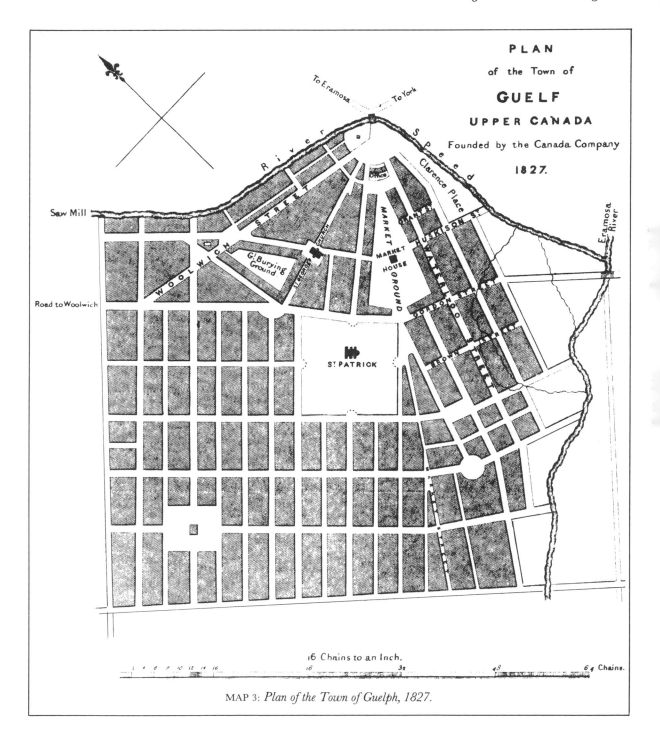

MAP 3: *Plan of the Town of Guelph, 1827.*

Galt ordered the Town to be laid out roughly in the shape of a fan, with the streets converging upon the ceremonial tree stump. This arrangement gave easy access from all directions to the best mill seats and to the large plot that Galt had reserved for a market square. Considerable care was taken to leave several large parks and open spaces. In keeping with Galt's determination to convey a feeling of optimism to prospective settlers, the Town was laid out to accommodate several thousand inhabitants—a population larger than would be achieved for decades to come.

For all of Galt's enthusiastic promotion, it is doubtful that Guelph would have grown so rapidly had he not poured men and money into the preparation of the townsite. By paying good wages Galt attracted workmen and their families to Guelph.[18] Because the influx of workmen caused a housing shortage, Galt used Canada Company funds to construct log houses, then sold the houses and lots to the workmen on credit. By such methods Guelph was given the appearance of a successful booming centre and more workmen were attracted there. Thus, as long as Galt continued to pour large amounts of capital into Guelph, thereby ensuring jobs and creating an artificial prosperity, rapid population growth was assured.

In addition to building houses for his workmen, Galt moved ahead quickly in the development of public works. Gordon and Waterloo Streets were cleared and levelled, and the market square was cleared of trees as well. Among the first buildings erected was the market house, which consisted of a cottage roof supported by twelve sets of double posts of squared timber.

The most imposing building erected that first summer was a large log building called by Galt "The Priory" after its builder, Charles Prior. The Priory stood on elevated ground on the banks of the Speed, about a hundred yards from the ceremonial tree stump. The main structure, built of natural logs, measured about 50 by 33 feet, with a lean-to wing on either end, and a rustic porch facing the river at the front.[19]

As was the case with most of his undertakings, Galt had a larger end in view when he ordered the Priory built. He says:

I had some reason to hope that Mr. Weld of Lulworth Castle (now Cardinal Weld of Rome) would come to Upper Canada, and probably make it his residence. Being desirous to allure him to Guelph, I had this in view in converting the receiving house into a habitation.

Having in some sort a kind of taste in architecture, it seemed to me that the house could be made into a comfortable ecclesiastical abode, and accordingly, although it was only ten feet high in the ceiling, I employed my best skill in laying it out. The reader will be pleased to recollect, that it was but a cottage of one storey and formed of trunks of trees; as I have said, however, before, it was of its kind very beautifully constructed by Mr. Prior, externally. I only added a rustic portico to it, of trees with bark, but illustrative of the origin of the Ionic order: it did not cost five pounds. The interior was planned for effect, and on entering was imposing, but the hall and two principal rooms were only twenty feet some inches square.[20]

Although Galt failed to persuade Weld to come to Guelph, the Priory served both as a residence for Galt and the Canada Company commissioners during their stay in Guelph and as a receiving house for new immigrants.

In order to speed Guelph's growth as a commercial centre, Galt undertook the establishment of a wholesale depot at Burlington and a retail general store in Guelph. The Guelph store was intended not only to sell a wide variety of goods to townspeople and farmers, but also, once farming was established, to buy and export local grain and produce. Like most retail stores of the period it operated on a two-price system: one price for cash and a much higher price for items bought on credit. Of course, Galt intended that the store and warehouse should make a profit. Galt says:

Among the inducements held out to obtain the reserves at a moderate price, was the vast advantages which would arise to the province from having an opulent ·company interested in promoting its improvement. One of the most obvious modes of accomplishing this, was, as it appeared to me, to receive payments in produce, and to undertake the sale of it on consignment. By an arrangement con-

templated, in the event of the directors agreeing to this, I conceived that the commissions on the consignments of wheat would defray all the official expenses, and a stimulus would be given to the prosperity of the Province, which would soon compensate the country for all the profit that might be drawn from it in consequence of the Company's speculation.[21]

In addition to the workmen who were attracted to Guelph by the high wages, two other types of immigrants arrived in 1827, a group of craftsmen and a few independent businessmen. Between them these immigrants began to provide the nucleus of commercial activities necessary to attract farmers to Guelph Township.

While Galt was in New York in March, 1827, he had arranged with the British Consul, James Buchanan, to seek out and forward

The Priory as it appeared circa 1864.

skilled tradesmen whose crafts would be useful in a rural commercial centre. These tradesmen began to arrive in Guelph shortly after the work of development had begun. Thus John Owen Lynch, blacksmith; Thomas Stewart, shoemaker; William Gibbs, baker; William Holmes, wagon maker; and William Collins and James Anderson, carpenters, were among the first to arrive in Guelph. They immediately set up small workshops and began manufacturing to meet local needs.

The most important of the independent businessmen to arrive in Guelph in 1827 were David Gilkison (eldest son of Captain William Gilkison, a cousin of John Galt) and William Leaden, his partner. The firm of Gilkison and Leaden announced the opening of their general store in the *Gore Gazette* on August 18:

NEW STORE IN GUELPH
D. Gilkinson and Co., announce to the Inhabitants of *Guelph*, Waterloo, Dumfries, Eramosa, Esquesing and the other Townships in that Vicinity, that they have opened a Store of *Goods*, in the Town of *Guelph*, and that they will dispose of them on reasonable terms, for prompt payment.
Guelph, Aug. 18, 1827.[22]

In addition to their store, Gilkison and Leaden proposed to Galt that the Canada Company should build a grist mill which they would lease with an option to purchase. This proposal was rejected. A resolution passed by the directors of the Canada Company on August 3, 1827, states the reasons:

RESOLUTION VIII.—That Messrs. Gilkison and Leading's [*sic*] proposal for renting and ultimately purchasing a grist mill to be built by the company is entirely inadmissable. That if a grist mill is necessary or wanted, it will in all probability soon pay itself, and therefore if the company is to build a mill, that it be supported at the company's expense until it can be let or disposed of to advantage, but that it

is considered a more eligible plan to grant a mill seat, and even to advance a moderate sum of capital as a loan to parties who may be induced to build a grist mill at their own risk and charge.[23]

The Canada Company having rejected their proposal for a grist mill, Gilkison and Leaden decided to build a saw mill. Purchasing a mill seat and twenty-five acres of land on August 12, 1827, (for 7s. 6d. per acre, a total of £9. 7s. 6d.) they built a dam and erected a saw-mill. Until then, there had been a serious shortage of sawn lumber, and the mill operated day and night to satisfy the local demand. For the first time, frame buildings could be erected and the interior of log cabins could be improved.

In addition to Gilkison and Leaden, several other businessmen set up establishments. Taverns were opened by Philip Jones and John Read, and in August this advertisement for Guelph's first "manufacturer" appeared in the *Gore Gazette*:

Guelph—James Livingston, Taylor & Habit-Maker, respectfully calls upon the Inhabitants for their custom.   Guelph, Aug. 18, 1827.[24]

Not all these businessmen and tradesmen, however, were used to working under the difficult conditions imposed by the pioneer environment. Acton Burrows recounts one such incident with amusing results:

In September Mr. Samuel Wright arrived here and opened a bakery on the Dundas Road, near the river. The bakery was in the open air, built of limestone, and not being accustomed to such ovens, and, indeed, being a miller by trade, not having a very large experience in baking at all, he one day heated the oven so hot that he transformed it into a miniature limekiln, and it crumbled into dust before his eyes.[25]

By midsummer, Galt could report that in

general outline the town was taking shape. Between May and August, 1827, no less than thirty lots had been sold, and most had some form of habitation built upon them. Acton Burrows gives this list of purchasers:

Lot	1	Jas. D. Oliver	Aug. 11
Lot	2	Allan McDonnell	Aug. 12
Lot	3	Alex. Elder	May 20
Lot	4	Thomas Leigh	—
Lot	5	Thos. Kelly	May 31
Lot	6	Aaron Anderson	May 15
Lot	8	Edward Worswick	May 27
Lot	9	Nancy Riffe	May 27
Lot	10	Bernard McTague	May 31
Lot	11	Bernard McTague	May 31
Lot	12	Jas. Thompson	May 31
Lot	13	Jas. McLevy	May 31
Lot	14	Robert McLevy	May 27
Lot	15	David Gilkison	May 27
Lot	16	Chas. Boynton	May 17
Lot	17	Philip Jones	May 17
Lot	19	Andrew McVean	May 19
Lot	20	Wm. Elliott	May 16
Lot	21	Wm. Leaden	May 16
Lot	22	Wm. Leaden	May 16
Lot	23	Wm. Reid	May 16
Lot	24	James Smith, Jr.	May 28
Lot	25	Geo. Abbott	June 1
Lot	27	Geo. Dobbies	May 19
Lot	29	Wm. Reid	May 16
Lot	35	Thos. Butler	June 2
Lot	42	Jas. Corbet	July 10
Lot	47	Geo. Whiteside	June 9
Lot	53	Wm. Goodwin	June 2
Lot	71	Chas. Armstrong	Aug. 12

Of these purchasers, J.D. Oliver, lot 1, built the first stone house in Town, and was given his lot free by Galt as a reward for his confidence in Guelph's future.[26]

On August 1, 1827, Galt wrote Dr. Moir, the editor of many of his works, describing the progress made in developing the village:

I have been engaged in the interesting task of. . . laying the foundations of a city at this place—at the ceremony of which, if I had no vultures to omenate wars and conquests, thousands of pigeons came in flocks. . . The town thrives amazingly. Upwards of a hundred and sixty building lots are engaged, and the approach to it, on one side, is probably the finest avenue in the world, being upwards of seven miles in length. . .I have not had a book in my hand, save an old magazine, for the last six weeks; but I am laying the foundation of an academy, the Company having allowed me to reserve one half of the money arising from the sale of the land in the town for that purpose, by which I have already upwards of two thousand pounds in store. I have got a school already opened in a shed—three taverns filled with boarders—a khan after the Turkish fashion, which accommodates eighteen families. I am about to begin a church, having received £100 from the Bishop to begin with. We have a regular mail-coach twice a week, a post office, and they speak already of getting up a newspaper, and a bank agent; all this since the 23rd April, at which time the site of the market place was in the centre of the wood, some miles from any habitation.[27]

Galt's self-satisfaction at the progress was well deserved.

In contrast to the rapid settlement and commercial development of the village, Galt had only limited success in settling the agricultural community around it. High among Galt's priorities in developing the Township was the creation of a network of good roads. These roads, Galt hoped, would not only open the farm lands for settlement, but also attract the trade of older settled areas to Guelph. Thus, as soon as Absalom Shade, the contractor for the Waterloo Road, had completed that work, he and his men were set to work clearing the Dundas Road through Puslinch Township. In addition the Elora Road was opened to the Township line. Work on both these roads, and others, would continue as long as Galt directed the affairs of the Canada Company.

In spite of extensive road building and advertising, only one significant group of settlers took up farm lands in 1827. These were known as the La Guayran settlers. The La Guayrans were a group of fifty-seven men, women and children who, in 1825 had been persuaded to leave Britain by the lavish promises of the Columbian Company, a South American-based competitor of the Canada Company. The La Guayrans had sailed to Caracas, but finding that the glowing promises of easy wealth were false, had attempted to return to England. In April, 1827, they reached Philadelphia, and being destitute, appealed to the British Consul for help. That gentleman, being aware of the existence of the Canada Company, but apparently failing to appreciate its purely commercial aims, forwarded the La Guayrans to Guelph as objects of charity looking for free land.

When they arrived in Guelph, the La Guayrans presented a pitiful spectacle. Because of their poverty, the unhealthy climate of their Latin American residences, and the long and difficult journey, several of the men and many of the women and children were in a weak and unhealthy condition. What was Galt to do when faced by this ragged and emaciated group? Clearly the La Guayrans ought to have been the responsibility of the British government, and Galt had neither the spare funds nor the authority of the Canada Company to spend money on their behalf.

Galt's decision was typically decisive. He made the assumption that government authorities would accept responsibility for the La Guayrans, and withheld a portion of the government funds in his hands to pay for their care. Those capable of labour, he put to work clearing the Elora Road. The government, however, refused to accept responsibility for the La Guayrans, and ordered Galt to immediately forward the money that he had held back to pay their expenses.

In the meantime, the La Guayrans had recovered their health and strength, and by their industry and thrift had demonstrated to Galt that they were likely to become desirable settlers. Galt, therefore, allotted each of them fifty acres of land, at the usual price, but allowed them to defer the down payment, with the understanding that they were not only to pay for their land and supplies, but also the cost of their upkeep during their illness, all at six per cent per annum interest.[28]

From Galt's point of view, the affair, while provoking, turned out well in the end. The La Guayrans, to their credit, fulfilled their obligations to the Canada Company to the penny. But many and bitter were the memories retained by them and their descendents of the interest charged and the high prices exacted for goods bought on credit at the Canada Company store.[29]

Among the La Guayrans were many who would contribute much to Guelph's development. Mrs. B.S. Kennedy, one of their descendents recorded some of their names for posterity: Alex McTavish, Donald Gillies, Alex. Reid, —McFie, Peter Butchard, Angus Campbell, —Holliday, Joseph McDonald, Capt. McDonald, Jas. Stirton, Jas. McQuillan, Wm. Patterson, —Rose, —McCrae, John Dean, Jas. May, Thos. Knowles, Thos. Daly, three families of Kennedys, M. Sweetnam, and others, settled on the Elora Road in what was later called the Scotch Block. Although a number of the La Guayrans sold their farms

On Board an Immigrant Ship in the Thirties. (Courtesy Public Archives of Canada)

after making improvements, those who stayed and struggled through the first difficult years eventually became prosperous farmers.[30]

In order to publicize Guelph's auspicious beginnings, Galt decided to hold a gala celebration to which he invited influential people from all over the province. His choice of August 12 was typical of Galt's strategy:

I appointed the 12th of August as a kind of fair in the new town, invited a number of friends, and gave a public dinner in the market-house to the inhabitants; for it required not the wisdom of Solomon to see that occasional amusements were necessary to promote content, and I have always had a peculiar enjoyment in the hilarity of others. But the 12th of August was not chosen without design: it was the King's birthday, celebrated in the first town of the family name; the anniversary of the day on which the Canada Company was instituted; the anniversary also of my father and mother's wedding; the birthday of one of my sons, and within six hours of being the anniversary of another.[31]

The celebration, by all accounts, was a great success, but Galt would remember the occasion with considerable unhappiness.

As described by George Gurnett, editor of the *Gore Gazette* in the issue dated August 13, 1827, the day began on a festive note:

THE CITY OF GUELPH

In proportion as the operations of the Canada Company, and the magnitude of their plans for bringing into active usefulness the vast tracts of uncultivated forests, developed themselves, the public feeling in this section of the country becomes more extensively and deeply interested in the successful prosecution of these operations. It is to this feeling—after making due allowance for the attractions of a roasted ox, etc.,—to which we should principally attribute the presence of so large a number of persons, (not less than 500) at Guelph yesterday, who had assembled from different parts of the district, to witness the ceremony of laying the corner stones of two Public Buildings now erecting in that town by the Canada Company. The corner stone of the 'Seminary' was laid about one o'clock p.m. by Mr. Galt, assisted by the Rev. Mr. Sheed, who delivered an address appropriate to the occasion. . .The corner stone of the office of the Warden was next laid by Dr. Dunlop. Two or three newspapers, (an Albion, a York and a Gore Gazette) together with one or two Colonial Bank notes, were deposited in the cavity prepared for the purpose in the corner stone, which was then covered by another of the same dimensions, when Dr. D. ascended the stone and gave three cheers for the King and Canada Company in which he was heartily joined by the spectators.[32]

In addition to the founding of the Guelph "seminary" as the school was called, the celebration was noteworthy for the creation of an agricultural society aimed at serving the interests of west-central Upper Canada. The *Gore Gazette* described this event:

During the evening it was proposed by Mr. Galt, and assented to by the gentlemen present, that an agricultural society should be forthwith established in this part of Upper Canada. Mr. Galt expatiated at considerable length upon the advantages which had resulted to the agricultural and breeding interests at home from the institution of such societies, and anticipated equally valuable results from their introduction into this Province, in which, as yet nothing of the kind had been projected. It was subsequently,

Resolved: That a society, to be called the 'Agricultural Society of Upper Canada,' be now established, and that the gentlemen present, who may affix their signatures now entered into, to constitute the members of that society, with powers to add to their numbers.

That John Galt, Esq., be the President of said society.

That the Hon. W. Dickson, Geo. Hamilton, Esq., and John Brant, Esq., be a committee to manage the affairs of said society, with power to add to their numbers, and that John Brant, Esq., be secretary of the same.

That T. Coke, Esq., of Norfolk, J.C. Curwen, Esq., of Cumberland, and Sir John Sinclair, of Ulster, be elected honorary members of said society.

That a meeting of the officers above named shall be held on an early day, for the purpose of drafting a constitution, which shall be submitted to the members of the society, for their scrutiny and approbation.

That an annual meeting of the Agricultural Society of Upper Canada shall be held at Guelph, on the 12 August in each succeeding year.

The resolutions were signed by the greater part of the gentlemen present.[33]

The centre piece of the celebration was the two feasts prepared: a roast ox for the public and a formal dinner for the invited gentry. The *Gore Gazette* gave this description of the meals:

About two o'clock a very excellent dinner, consisting of the ox which had been roasted whole, and consequently cut up in joints, for the occasion, and a great variety of other excellent dishes, was served up in the market house, and partaken of by the farmers, and their wives and the lads and lasses from the neighboring Townships of Eramosa, Waterloo, Esquesing, etc.—the workmen employed by the company, and many other of the inhabitants of the town, to the number, we are informed, of three hundred persons. Messrs. Martin and McDonnel, and two other gentlemen connected with the company, presided at the different tables, and waited on the company during the dinner, after which, wine and liquors passed freely round, and a number of loyal and patriotic toasts were drunk; while a small band of musicians performed a number of appropriate airs without the building. A rustic dance succeeded the more solid enjoyments above mentioned, and continued till the declining sun summoned the lasses and their swains from the scene of festivity to their distant homes.[34]

In contrast to these rustic entertainments, the dinner for the invited guests was much more formal:

In the evening about forty gentlemen sat down to an elegant dinner of two courses, in the company's large hall, at which Mr. Galt presided, supported by Hon. Mr. Dickson and the Rev. Mr. Sheed. Dr. Dunlop acted as vice. After the cloth was removed the following toasts were given:

The King—three times three.

Song, God Save the King.

Duke of Clarence and the Navy—three times three.

Song, Hearts of Oak.

Duke of Sussex and the rest of the Royal Family—three times three.

Song, Hail! Star of Brunswick. . .

The memory of his late Royal Highness the Duke of York—drank in solemn silence. . .

Lord Dalhousie and the British Army in North America—great applause—three times three.

Air—Blue Bonnets over the Border.

The chairman next proposed the health of Sir Peregrine Maitland, and the Province of Upper Canada. He stated that although there must be, in so large an assembly, persons whose opinions might be at variance with regard to some of the Lieutenant-Governor's political measures, there could be no two opinions with regard to the purity of his motives, as His Majesty's representative, or his private virtues as a man. After enumerating the many public works for the improvement of the Province which have been begun under his Excellency's administration, he proposed the toast which was drunk with three times three.

Air—Grenadiers' March.[35]

It was ironic indeed that after such a long and fulsome toast to Sir Peregrine Maitland that Galt would soon find himself deeply involved in a bitter quarrel with Sir Peregrine, Canada Company officials and the British Colonial Office over a supposed slight to Sir Peregrine at the dinner. Galt described the controversy this way:

The first toast after dinner was of course the King, the next, the rest of the Royal Family. The army and navy were certainly intentionally omitted, because the list of public toasts was long enough without them, but in their stead were the governor-in-chief of the provinces, and the lieutenant-governor of Upper Canada. In giving the former, I took occasion to mention that I had a particular pleasure in proposing it, as I regarded myself personally indebted to the Earl of Dalhousie. The next was Sir Peregrine Maitland, which I prefaced with strong assurance of the alacrity with which my every wish had been met by his Excellency; no more than the truth; and it was in consequence drunk with marked approbation. But will it be credited, that an occasion of mere festivity was converted into one that served to justify detraction? It was said that I had omitted to drink the health of Sir Peregrine, and that I had seized the opportunity to abuse the clergy corporation. The matter taken by itself was trivial, and but for the assurance that it gave of my being an object of malevolence, would have been disregarded.[36]

No sooner had Sir Peregrine Maitland heard of the supposed slight, than he wrote to the British Secretary of State, Mr. Huskisson, who passed the complaint on to the board of directors of the Canada Company. They, without investigation or giving Galt a chance to explain, assumed Galt to be guilty, and wrote him, reprimanding him and stating that they altogether disapproved of his behavior.

To say the least, Galt was chagrined and angered by the injustice of the accusations. He sent a letter to London offering his resignation, but Charles Bosanquet, the Governor, refused to accept it. As Galt rightly remarked, the whole incident in itself was both trivial and vexatious. Unfortunately, the willingness of the Canada Company officials to believe the worst was symptomatic of deeper problems developing within the company. Within the year these problems would result in an open break between Galt and his employers.

In the meantime, all appeared well in the bustling community. In the euphoria of the moment, the editor of the *Gore Gazette* exclaimed:

Each individual present appeared happy and joyous—he was pleased at the generous hospitality and affability of his host—pleased to see all around him as happy as himself—and as a patriot he was pleased at the brilliant prospects of national prosperity, which the scene of enterprise and industry before him justified. . .We do think it impossible for any individual—not absolutely a stoic—to look upon such a scene as that which presented itself upon this occasion—upon the extensive improvements—in clearing land, cutting out spacious streets and public roads, and in erecting dwelling houses and public buildings—the result of only about three months labor—wlthout indulging in some feelings of gratification at the prospect. . .[37]

For Galt, this day was probably the high point of his Canadian career.

The balance of the summer and fall passed off uneventfully. A few more settlers came, but the necessity of completing houses before the onset of winter meant that most immigrants arrived in a rush in the spring and early summer. The main occupation, therefore, was completing those buildings already begun. For the inexperienced settler, as James Innes pointed out, this was no easy task:

As there was no such thing as a cooking stove, the providing of suitable fire places was a most arduous undertaking. Exorbitant prices were charged by the initiated for the performance of very moderate services and as all the settlers were comparatively poor, very moderate accommodation had to suffice. Many of the first houses had nothing but the cold earth for a floor. Some hewed basswood planks with their axes and others more experienced brought the whip saw into operation. The chimneys were for the most part of the most primitive character and it was really surprising that more fires did not occur during the first year or two when the protection against it was generally of such a flimsy character.[38]

In addition to completing their houses, several additions were made to Guelph's commercial life. A post office was opened under the supervision of John Reid in one wing of the Priory, and the first livestock was imported to the Town when John O. Lynch brought in a horse and cow. By fall there were three teams of horses in the village: one team owned by John Galt, one by the firm of Gilkison and Leaden, and the third by Benjamin Harrison who used them to draw loads of merchandise from Niagara. Finally, following the offer of a house and lot to the operator of the first loom in Guelph, James Hodgert imported a loom and wove the first cloth in the winter of 1827-1828.

This winter also saw the birth of Guelph's first white children, Letitia Brown, daughter of Galt's "grog boss" who received a free lot, as the first born, and Thomas Lynch, son of John O. Lynch, the blacksmith, the first male child.

In addition to the settlers already named, Robert Thompson gives a list of those first-year immigrants still living on Guelph's fiftieth anniversary. These were:

Jas. Lynch, Hugh Henry, Robt. Thompson, Jas. McQuillan, Mrs. Jas. McQuillan, Felix Hanlon, Mrs. Michael Allen, Mrs. Ann Keough, D. Stirton, Donald Wallace, Hugh Wallace, Alex McDonald, Walter McDonald, Alex Kennedy (teacher), Thos. McBride, Mrs. McBride, John Gillis, Mrs. Charles McTague, Mrs. John McTague, Mrs. Peter McTague, Mrs. Soden, Mrs. Bickiers, Mrs. Tobin, Rory McCrae, Wm. McCrae, Henry Foster, James Benham, Mrs. Macdonald (widow), mother of Alex Macdonald; Mrs. McCrae (widow), mother of Wm. and Rory McCrae; Wm. Croft, Miss F. Harrison, Mrs. Henry, Alex Campbell, Thomas Daily.[39]

For Guelph, its founder and its residents, the year ended full of hope and optimism. From a wilderness tract a village had been created and a society begun which promised much for the future. If they were poor now, Guelph's residents expected, if not wealth, at least comfort would be theirs in the future. As for John Galt, not only had he accomplished the first major step of the Guelph project, but he had successfully begun the sale of lands in other areas as well. The only cloud on the horizon remained the continued uneasiness of the Canada Company Directors at Galt's ambitious and expensive undertakings.

From an oil portrait of John Galt by Joshua Smith, R.B.A.
This painting was presented to the City of Guelph by the descendants of Mr. Galt
on April 23rd, 1927, in honour of their centenary celebrations.

II

Galt's Departure and Aftermath

In 1828, with the opening of the spring season, activities in Guelph commenced where they had left off the previous fall. With Charles Prior away in the Huron Tract, Galt hired Samuel Strickland to manage Canada Company affairs in Guelph. Under Strickland's direction, Galt's policy of aggressive capital expenditure and development continued.

When Strickland arrived in Guelph to take up duties there, he found that the "City" consisted of some thirty log houses, an equal number of shanties, a large frame tavern (likely Robert Elder's) not yet completed, a store (Gilkison & Leaden), and the walls of two stone buildings (the "seminary" and Dr. Dunlop's headquarters).[1] Thus it fell to Strickland to complete the works begun by Galt in 1827, and to undertake the construction of several new projects.

Amongst the undertakings ordered by Galt in 1828 was the construction of a third stone building. It was Galt's intention to spur Guelph's growth by temporarily moving the headquarters of the Canada Company to Guelph, thereby greatly increasing local economic activity. This building was also intended as the premises of a bank, and it was

Early harrowing. Frame and teeth of wood. (Courtesy Public Archives of Canada)

erected with iron doors and a strong stone vault. Unfortunately, this building was never used for either of these purposes. When Galt was forced out of the Canada Company, that institution's enthusiasm for Guelph wained, and the "bank" became a very expensive warehouse, occasionally used as an immigrant depot. When the Honourable Adam Fergusson visited Guelph in 1831, the "bank" was pointed out to him by J.D. Oliver who remarked, "there stands the bank that never stopped—since it never commenced."[2]

The most important of Strickland's undertakings in 1828 was the continuation of street clearings and the erection of bridges over the river on the Eramosa and Dundas Roads. The Dundas Road bridge over the Speed River was a substantial affair, built on piles and constructed of squared timbers. Since a considerable number of early settlers had taken up land in the southern part of the township and had hitherto been forced to ferry themselves across the river on a crude raft, the bridge was a great convenience. During the summer Wyndham Street was cleared to the point where it met Woolwich Street, while improvements continued on the Scotch Block, Eramosa, Waterloo and Dundas Roads.

Settlers arriving to take up land found that with the community developing, Galt had raised prices in order to begin recouping on the Canada Company investment, and had established new, tougher regulations to ensure prompt payment. In Guelph, the flexible terms which had been offered the La Guayrans would not again be repeated. An advertisement in the *Gore Gazette* of October 27, 1827, laid down the new terms:

CANADA COMPANY
The following are the terms on which the Canada Company will sell lands in the Township of Guelph, from this date until notice to the contrary is given by public advertisement.

1st. Town Lots, 40 dollars in cash. Purchasers are required to commence preparations for building, within three months, and to have their houses finished within 12 months from the date of purchase.

2nd. Farm Lots of 25, or 50, or 100 acres, paid in cash, 2 dollars per acre. On credit (that is, one fifth in advance, and the remainder in four equal annual instalments, with interest), two and one half dollars per acre.

3rd. Farm Lots of from 100 to 200 acres, two dollars and a half per acre; one third in advance, and the remainder in two years, with interest; or two dollars and a quarter cash.

4th. Persons purchasing Farm Lots are not required to purchase Town Lots. Nor are purchasers of Town Lots required to purchase Farm Lots.

5th. Purchasers of Farm Lots are required to commence improvements thereon within 12 months from the date of purchase. Those who have purchased Town Lots are not required to build houses on their farms, but they must, where the lots front the road, enclose them with a complete fence. Those who have not purchased Town Lots are required to commence preparations for building houses on their farms, within three months, and to have them finished and inhabited within 12 months from the date of purchase.

Guelph, 25th Sept., 1827.
Thomas Blair Husband, Clerk[3]

Of course, these new terms made it more difficult for poor immigrants to buy land. Nonetheless, Canada Company advertising argued that although land prices had risen considerably since the previous year, the advanced state of settlement made Guelph an attractive site for the settler who possessed some capital. A Canada Company prospectus, issued on February 1, 1828, put it this way:

On the largest of the [Crown Reserve] Blocks, situated in the county of Halton, and district of Gore, and containing above 42,000 acres, a town, now called *Guelph*, has been laid out in a central position, to which roads from the adjoining Townships have been opened at the expense of the Company; and the progress made by the Town and the settlements in its vicinity has exceeded expectation, and is understood to be without precedent in Canada.

This Town is situated on a branch of the Ouse, or Grand River of Lake Erie, called the River Speed, which is a considerable stream, with falls in the vicinity of the Town sufficient to afford sites for fifteen or twenty mills. Limestone, easily quarried, and which makes excellent lime, is found in the immediate vicinity of those falls, and clay well adapted for making bricks is plentiful; the land is found covered with heavy timber, so that all materials for building were abundant, and no time was lost in improving these advantages. The operation of clearing ground for the Town Plot was commenced on the 23rd of April; the first building erected was a large house for the reception of settlers on their arrival; and, as an encouragement to the early settlers, it was promised, on behalf of the Company, to set apart one-half of the prices obtained for Town Lots as a fund for building a school-house, and maintaining a schoolmaster; while sites for churches and burying-grounds were given gratuitously to all religious denominations applying for the same. As a further inducement to early settlers, the price at first fixed for Town Lots of a quarter of an acre each, was twenty dollars, with the privilege to purchasers to take up farms in the vicinity, of fifty acres each, at 7s. 6d. currency, or one and a half dollars per acre. These prices, however, being insufficient to pay the expenses incurred by the Company, were subsequently raised, first to thirty dollars, and then to forty dollars for Town Lots, and to 10s. and 12s. per acre for the Farms, and at these different prices, according to the respective dates at which the contracts were made, above 200 Town Lots, and 16,000 acres of land had been engaged previously to the 1st of October; at which period seventy-six houses were built, or building—a saw-mill was in operation—a brick-kiln was actually burning—a grist-mill was in progress—a market-house, two taverns, and several stores have been opened—several tradesmen and

mechanics had established themselves, and found advantageous employment—a temporary school-house was regularly attended by above forty children, and the foundation of a stone building for a permanent school-house has been laid—a printing-office was in preparation—and, in short, if the progress of this Town may be assumed as a criterion for other settlements to be opened by the Company, it is considered to afford abundant evidence of the encouragement given by the Company to settlers on their lands.[4]

In sum, the advertisement promised that, "an agriculturalist of industrious habits may in all cases, and more especially if he have some capital wherewith to begin, look forward to the possession, in a few years, of comfort and independence as a landed proprietor. . ."[5] In order to emphasize the fact that the Company wanted only those settlers with sufficient capital to make a substantial beginning at farming in Guelph, the advertisement firmly asserted that "The Company will not defray, or contribute towards defraying, the expense of embarking emigrants from the United Kingdom, or of conveying them to their place of location in Canada."[6]

Although these higher prices and tougher regulations appear to have reduced the flow of settlers to Guelph, still considerable growth occurred.[7] Guelph lay directly in the path of the advancing agricultural frontier and shared in the general population growth thus created, as shown in Table I.

As in 1827, most of these settlers were poor in everything except spirit, and depended for their livelihood upon wages earned by working for the Canada Company. Of particular interest were the first settlers to take up land in the third concession, Division B of Guelph Township—part of the area which became known as the "Paisley Block"—named after

Table I
Population of Townships in the Guelph Area, 1825-1840[8]

Township	1825	1830	1835	1840
Guelph	—	703	1,854	2,290
Puslinch	—	*	1,017	1,617
Nichol		53	397	1,002
Eramosa	284		631	863
Erin		267	963	1,256
Garafraxa	—	—	169†	284
Amaranth	—	—	—	—
Waterloo	1,640	2,016	2,791	4,223
Wilmot	—	—	1,101	1,901
Woolwich**	—	325	506	939
Wellesley	—	—	—	—
Dumfries	1,330	2,397	4,306	5,764
Beverley	728	858	1,477	2,573
Total	3,982	6,619	15,212	22,712

* Not given.
** Includes Pilkington.
† Average of 1834 and 1836 figures.

the place of origin of many of the settlers. These settlers—John McCorkindale, Sr., William Alexander, Nathan Ferguson and James Craig—had previously settled in the Huron Tract with their families, but a shortage of provisions and widespread ague amongst them, had caused the Canada Company to shift them to farms in the Guelph area.[9] Among the settlers arriving in 1828, those listed by Robert Thompson as being still living in 1877 were:

Wm. McCuen, Saml. McCuen, Mrs. Ann Mitchell, Mrs. Jane Ritchie, Martin Duley, Isaac Lenix, Mrs. Mannie, William Patterson, Robert Patterson, Mrs. Charles McWilliams, Mrs. Laird (widow), Thomas Lynch, Joseph Margin, Wm. Logan, Arch. McCorkindale, John McCorkindale, John Drew, Jas. Keough, Wm. Benham, Bernard McTague, Sarah McTague, Robert Knowles, Mrs. Fields, Janet McKersie, William McKersie, John McKersie, David McKersie, Gavin McKersie, Robert McKersie.[10]

For these settlers, most with little or no capital and few assets, life was indeed difficult. The shelter provided for newcomers by the Canada Company—Galt's self-styled "Khan"[11] was little better than a log barn. With eighteen or twenty families crowded into this receiving house, all household tasks, such as cooking and laundry had to be performed outdoors, rain or shine, over open fires. While the wives and children waited in these squalid surroundings, their husbands laboured clearing the Huron Road in order to earn enough money for the down payment on a lot in town or a fifty-acre bush lot in the country.

Even when settlers had sufficient money to buy a farm for cash, life remained difficult for the first few years. Adam Fergusson, for example, described the situation of first year farmers in Guelph Township, as follows:

Chopping or clearing land, ready for sowing, will cost sometimes 12 dollars, or £3 per acre; the first return will be 15 or 20 bushels of wheat, worth at present 5s. [$1.20] per bushel. The usual mode of clearing timbered land is to cut down and burn all the wood of one foot in diameter, and under that. The larger trees were only girdled. Clearing, in this way, costs about 8 dollars, or 40s. per acre. When this is done, a crop of wheat can be harrowed in, to be followed by two or three years of pasture or hay, when the plough may be used, and, during which time, the girdled trees are either cut into fencing stuff or burnt.[12]

James Innes gives this description of the pioneer farmers' difficulties:

Paisley Block Pioneer Group. TOP ROW: *Arch. McCorkindale, Jas. Laidlaw, Sr.; Jas. Elliott, Jas. G. Wright, John I. Laidlaw, Wm. Whitelaw.* BOTTOM ROW: *John J. Hobson, Wm. Dunn, Robert Brydon, Robert Boyd, Thos. Laidlaw. (Historical Atlas of Wellington County, 1906)*

They had neither means nor experience—two very important elements of success—to assist them in their first start in the woods. They could do little individually in the way of erecting the most humble habitation for their wives and little ones, and the ability to pay for more experienced labor was out of the question. Then, again, very few could make the raise of a yoke of oxen of the most common kind. We can therefore well understand the difficulties which the poor settler must have labored under in such trying circumstances, and as a proof that this state of things continued—as it naturally must have done—for several years, we would state that in the whole Scotch Block settlement containing some 26 settlers, there was only one yoke of oxen, on the whole line of road during the first year, two yoke during the second year, three in the third year, and

not till the fourth year was there anything like a supply of teams. . . . Such being the indigent state of the settlement, we can easily imagine that very little progress was made for the first few years in the clearing of the forest. A large portion of the poor settler's time was taken up in raising and conveying the necessary feed for his family.

It was no uncommon sight in those early days of the settlement to see the care-worn head of a family carrying the fruits of his labor, in the shape of a bag of flour, even as far as 20 miles for the support of his wife and little ones.[13]

There could be little doubt that the greatest hardship facing these farmers was the lack of a grist mill in Guelph. Although the Canada

Company advertisement of February 1, 1828, proclaimed that "a grist mill was in progress",[14] in fact, the closest mills were in Berlin, Dundas or Galt, and required a journey of at least two days to have a bushel of wheat ground into flour.

In spite of these hardships, settlers were eager to take up life in the forest clearings. What the forest offered to the British working class immigrant was hope—hope that had been destroyed by the industrial revolution. For them a Canadian bush farm offered their only chance to achieve a respectable status in life. In James Innes' words:

Their's was a hard lot, but the prospect was also cheering and certain. An independent position in society, and a home of his own creation, was a glorious prospect and well worth contending for.[15]

In addition to the agricultural settlers, in 1828 several important additions were made to Guelph's commercial life. Among these were two new grocery stores, situated on the south side of the Upper Market Square, owned by Thomas McVane and Charles McCrae.[16] Perhaps the most ambitious commercial addition was the establishment of a semi-annual stock show and sale to be held on the first Mondays of May and November. In order to encourage the improvement of livestock and the use of Guelph as a marketing centre, prizes were given for the best animals shown. The first of these fairs, held in May, 1828, was something of a commercial failure, but apparently a social success. Although only three cows and two yoke of oxen were shown, the fair would long be remembered. Robert Thompson described the "main event":

It was a rare thing in those days for gatherings of this sort to pass off without a few fights. On this occasion it was Irishmen pitted against Yankees. Two

James Innes, Editor and part owner
of the Guelph Mercury, circa 1863-1898.

brothers named Sullivan appeared to have been the principal actors on the Yankee side. A row commenced in a newly-opened tavern called the "Horn of Plenty" kept by Charles McTague, resulting very unfavourably for the poor Yankees. As soon as that affray was over one of the bystanders hurried off up town to Jones' Tavern, where a number of Irishmen were collected, and told them that the Yankees had gouged out a bushel of Irishmen's eyes. This of course was the signal for a general onslaught on the perpetrators.[17]

The "Yankees", badly outnumbered, took to their heels, and only narrowly escaped the rage of the pursuing mob. Apparently, social life in pioneer Guelph was not for the faint of heart.

None of the events of 1828 would more deeply affect the future of Guelph than the growing quarrel between John Galt and the

Canada Company Directors concerning the management of that concern's financial affairs. At the heart of their differences was one concerning the strategy to be pursued in extracting a profit from the company's operations. On the one hand, Galt saw maximum profit and the greatest social benefit arising from his policy of large scale capital investment by creating the kinds of community services which would allow the rapid increase of land prices in the developed agricultural community. This policy, while it took some time to realize a profit, would in the long run return the greatest total wealth in proportion to the original investment. In contrast, the Directors appeared to be much more interested in speculating in the shares of the company than they were in operating it as an ongoing business. They wanted to minimize expenses, dump the land on the market for what it would bring in the short run, and pay the largest possible immediate dividends so that the price of shares would rise on the London stock exchange—thereby allowing them to sell their shares and realize an immediate profit. The two views, of course, were incompatible. In his *Autobiography* Galt gave his analysis of the situation:

It had been clearly understood as an inducement to Government to sell the Reserves to the Company, that the province was to be greatly benefitted by its operations, and that it was not to be a mere land-jobbing concern. I therefore estimated the expenditure, one thing with another, equal to the price of land, and I received a paper of calculations made by the gentlemen who acted in my absence, by which he shewed himself of the same opinion. But without this consideration, there were circumstances in the state of the times by which the shares of all joint-stock companies were affected. Nevertheless, though I was, to use a familiar figure, only building the house that was afterwards to produce a

rental, it was said my expenditure had tended to lower the Company's stock.[18]

The lack of a common agreement in goals and methods appears to have led to a mutual mistrust almost from the beginning. No doubt some of the problems arose from the fact that Galt felt a strong proprietorial interest in the Company that he had created, and he appears never to have become used to the fact that he was merely the hired servant of the stockholders and board of Directors. For example, when Galt informed the Canada Company Directors in early 1827 that he had named the town Guelph, the Directors immediately ordered him to change the name to Goderich in honour of one of England's most influential politicians. Whether wisely or not, Galt took the occasion to assert his independence in the management of Company affairs. As Galt said:

In reply, I endeavoured to justify what had been done, and as the same could not be altered, I called another town, founded about this time at Lake Huron, by the name of his Lordship.

But instead of giving any satisfaction, my letters of justification drew a more decisive condemnation of the name of Guelph. The manner in which the second disapproval was couched, set me a-thinking, and laying different things together, I drew the conclusion that there was somewhere a disposition to effect my recall. That I knew could be done without assigning any reason, but it was a step that required a pretext to take, and there I determined to make a stand.

Strictly according to rule and law, I wrote back that the name of the place was not a thing that I cared two straws about, but as it had been the scene of legal transactions, it was necessary to get an act of the Provincial Parliament before the change could be made, and that therefore if the Court [the board of directors] would send me the preamble for a bill, I would lose no time in applying for it. I heard however nothing more on the subject, and thus a most contemptible controversy ended; but I cannot yet imagine how a number of grave and most intelligent merchants ever troubled their heads about such a matter.[19]

Whatever Galt might have gained by his triumph in the name-change quarrel, he clearly lost much more in the trust and confidence of the Directors. After all, if Galt refused to obey orders in so trifling an affair as the name of the town, could he be depended upon to take orders in more substantial affairs? From the point of view of the Directors, things were dangerously out of control in Upper Canada, and henceforth they would react nervously at every rumour of Galt's doings.

In 1828, by now deeply concerned by news of vast public works, the extension of credit to prospective settlers, and lavish expenditures on offices and houses for Canada Company personnel, the Directors sent across the Company's accountant, John Smith, to take charge of the books and accounts, and to manage the Company's financial affairs. Initially, Galt seems to have been of the opinion that the accountant had been sent out of England as a means of getting rid of him, while speculators drove the stock down in order to buy it cheaply on the market. Indeed, Galt's confidence in his own managerial capacities and the future prosperity of the Company was so great that he could think of no other explanation for the fact that the accountant's "emoluments seemed. . .greatly beyond an adequate payment for the duties to be performed", and "that the excessive emoluments of the accountant were bait to allure him out of the way, and to enable him to meet the exigencies to which he might be exposed, when the machination should take effect."[20]

It was not long, however, until the truth began to dawn. Smith, far from being the dupe of the machinations of a group of speculators, was in fact sent out by the Directors to regain fiscal control of the Company's affairs, even at the cost of offending so talented a promoter as John Galt—and offend Galt he apparently did. Smith's insulting attitude, his fault-finding and criticism of Galt's management of the Company's affairs, and above all, Smith's attempts to prevent the expenditure of funds by interfering with and countermanding Galt's orders to subordinates, all revealed that in Smith's eyes at least, Galt had to be replaced as manager of the Company's affairs. After a violent quarrel over Smith's behaviour, during which Smith apparently threatened to report Galt's "misbehaviour" to Company officials, Galt decided to resign, and wrote at once to London stating his intentions and demanding a full investigation into his management of the company.[21] Even here Smith forestalled Galt by departing for England without notice, leaving Galt behind to manage Company affairs, while he, Smith, poured his complaints into the Directors' ears.

Now the crisis became acute. The Directors, apparently thrown into a panic by Smith's reports and without adequate consideration of all the possible consequences of their actions, ordered the Bank of Upper Canada in York to freeze Canada Company funds, and to refuse to honour any drafts drawn by Galt. Galt now faced a difficult and potentially disastrous situation. Acton Burrows puts the matter succinctly:

Notwithstanding this harsh and unaccountable treatment on the part of the Directors, Mr. Galt stood manfully to his post, and determined, if possible, to save the Directors, in spite of themselves, from the effects of the suicidal policy they were pursuing. He accordingly sent Mr. Dunlop to Montreal, to endeavor to procure money from the agents of the Company, or from some of the correspondents of the leading shareholders, a payment of £8,000, being soon due to the Colonial Government. No success whatever attended this mission, and matters were in a desperate condition, as, if the payments to the Government were not made when due, the public credit of the Company, against which not a word could be said hitherto, would be irretrievably injured. . . .To avert this. . . ., he took a step which under other circumstances he would not have presumed upon. He had in the bank £10,000 worth of government debentures, which seemed to have been forgotten by everybody but himself. He accordingly waited on the receiver-general, whom he had himself obliged on more than one occasion, and after stating the circumstances, offered, if he would endorse his bills on the Company for the payment to government, to hand over the debentures as security. The proposition was a startling one, and required time for consideration; but, the matter being submitted to Sir John Colborne [the Lieutenant-Governor], his assent was secured, and the transaction effected in a very few days, thus tiding over what was, perhaps, the most momentous crisis in the history of the Company. . . .[22]

Having managed to solve the crisis created by the lack of foresight of the Directors, Galt spent the rest of the fall putting Company affairs in order so that he could return to England to offer a defence concerning his management of the company.

One strategy of defence that Galt hit upon was to solicit testimonials from managers of American land companies as to his good work. One of these, Joseph Fellowes, manager of the Pulteney Estates in New York, offered a glowing account of Galt's management:

Guelph, Upper Canada,
February 4, 1829.

Gentlemen:
    At the request of John Galt, Esq., Supt. of the concerns of the Canada Company, I have visited this place, viewed the improvements in the village, and examined the roads contiguous to it, made under his orders.

Considering the short period of time that has elapsed since the village was founded, and that it is only eighteen months since it was an entire forest, the number of buildings and the population are proof of uncommon industry and enterprise.

I have perused with attention a report made to Mr. Galt by Mr. Charles Prior of the different improvements made by him on the lands of the Company, under the direction of Mr. Galt, and I have the pleasure of expressing to you my most decided opinion that all the proceedings of Mr. Galt and Mr. Prior have been exceedingly judicious; that the improvements have been indispensable to the sale and settlement of the Company's lands, and the outlay for mechanics' and labourers' wages are as moderate as is usual in a new and unsettled country; for it is impossible in such a country to get good hands without the allowance of high wages as an inducement to submit to the inconvenience incident to labouring in the wilderness, remote from settlements, where many privations must be endured and the health greatly exposed. Mechanics' and labourers' wages are uniformly higher than they are after a more general improvement of the country.

I am of the opinion that the sales thus far made have been at good prices, and the cash payments larger than is usually received from the first settlers in a new tract of land.

I have examined the books in which sales are entered, and also certificates and contracts to purchases, finding all well adapted to exhibit correct and accurate views of the affairs of the Company. . . .

Upon the whole, I beg leave most respectfully to state to the Company my decided opinion that Mr. Galt's agency has been conducted with sound judgment, a proper regard to economy and the interest of the Company, that his proceedings have promoted their best interests; and I believe the Company cannot more effectually promote their own views than by delegating to him the most ample discretionary powers. I am, Gentlemen, your most humble servant.

(Signed) "Joseph Fellows".[23]

In a similar vein, Robert Troup, a New York land agent wrote:

From all I have learned of the operation of Mr. Galt's agency, I have reason to believe that he is eminently worthy of the confidence of his friends, and that he has laid a solid foundation for future profits. To realize these profits, however, will necessarily be a work of time, from the extraordinary difficulties ever attending the settlement of wild lands, and from the scanty resources with which the settlers generally commence the cultivation of their farms. . . .[24]

Armed with such expert testimony Galt prepared to return to England in April, 1829.

When the residents of Guelph realized that Galt was leaving—perhaps forever—they rallied to support him; for if Galt were replaced as general manager, it might mean a severe reduction in local capital expenditures and consequently in employment and wages. At a large public demonstration held at the Priory, Galt was presented with an address signed by almost the entire adult male population. It read:

Sir: We, the undersigned inhabitants of the town and township of Guelph, learning that you are about to leave us, beg to express our sincere regret that we should be deprived of your presence, and the satisfaction and pleasure it has ever afforded us. We trust and hope that your absence from amongst us will not be of long duration, and that you will accomplish the objects of your journey, whatever these may be. We would wish to express to you the obligation which you have conferred upon us, in the prosperity which has flowed upon us ever since we became united with you and the Canada Company—many of us having come here in dependent circumstances, who are now in a fair way to become independent, and all having improved their condition under your fostering care. By the measures you have adopted, our lands in many instances have, in the space of eighteen months, doubled or tripled their value; and we do not look on our obligations as the less, that the Canada Company has shared in the advantage. You have set an example to the Province in the formation of proper roads and bridges, and showed by what means the progress of the settlement of the colony can be accelerated an hundred-fold by your measures, which have created this town and township. Finally, we beg you to accept our best wishes for your happiness and prosperity, wherever you may be; and we request you to thank the Canada Company for all the benefits they have conferred on us, and the greatest of these we consider their having sent you amongst us.

(Signed by 144 heads of families)[25]

In the meantime, the Canada Company had dispatched Thomas Mercer Jones to Canada to take Galt's place.

Galt arrived in York on April fifth on his way to London, where he read to his surprise in a short item in the Montreal *Gazette* that:

Mr. Galt, the author, who has hitherto acted as Manager for the Canada Company has been dismissed from his office by the Directors. Mr. Galt's character is unimpeachable, but it appears he was too fond of having his own way, and this gave offence.[26]

Galt still had not heard from the Directors.

Galt's return to England was a good deal less auspicious than his departure from Guelph. Arriving home in May, he met a cold and hostile reception from Company officials. They were, they made it clear, determined to change the direction of the Company, even if it meant breaking it up. In their eyes, Galt's sheaf of testimonials as to the excellence of his management was meaningless. Galt had been allotted £4,000 to develop the Township of Guelph and £4,700 had been spent—with more still required to complete the job. Galt had quarrelled with important officials. He had refused to obey orders. He had overdrawn his salary of £1,500 per year by no less than £529. 16s. 5d. On and on the list of charges and complaints ran.[27] Finally, recognizing the futility of further argument, Galt accepted his dismissal. The Directors granted him the munificent sum of £50 to defray the cost of his passage home "in consideration of his totally destitute condition."[28] His replacements, Thomas Mercer Jones and William Allan, were presumably more amenable to direction from London.

Galt's problems did not, however, end with the loss of his position. Deeply in debt, he was thrown into prison as a pauper where he remained until rescued by his friends. He spent the rest of his life writing furiously to recoup his fortunes. He died April 11, 1839, without again returning to Canada. But before his death, he had the painful pleasure of seeing his plans come to fruition and his judgment vindicated. In his *Autobiography* written in 1833, he noted that:

The population [of Guelph Township] now exceeds, I am informed, a thousand souls; mills projected have been built, a respectable bridge constructed, several taverns and a ball-room, and as a mark of the improved society, there are, I have heard, several harps and piano-fortes in the town. . . .
Before the foundations of the town were laid, land was valued by the magistrate in quarter sessions at 1s. 3d. per acre, and the settled townships around at three-fourths of a dollar; when I left the place the lowest rate of land sold was 15s., and the price in the neighbouring townships was estimated at 10s.
Nearly, if not all the land in the township of Guelph is now sold, and all the houses which I ordered to be constructed, have also been at prime cost.[29]

Moreover, the rise in the price of land had resulted in huge profits for the Company. By 1833 on an initial investment of £170,000, something over £300,000 had been paid out in dividends.[30] As Galt noted, the Canada Company shares were:

now the highest priced vendible stock in the market; only seventeen pounds are paid, and the price with premium is fifty-five per cent, and there has been no change in the system established by me.[31]

It was, however, cold comfort to a poor and dying man.

With Galt's departure as manager of the Canada Company, a new regime of severe austerity was imposed. Capital investment virtually stopped in Guelph, and a good deal of unemployment and individual hardship resulted. James Hodgert, long-time clerk of the municipal council remembered that depressed period as follows:

In [1827] and the succeeding year, a great deal of money was laid out in Guelph by Mr. Galt—so much so indeed that that gentleman, in 1829, was recalled by the Directors in St. Helen's Place, for his alleged extravagance. His successor, immediately on his arrival, proceeded to undo all that Mr. Galt had done; the office was ordered back to little York, and the dark days of Guelph succeeded, and brooded o'er the land for three years, during the currency of which, a mad bull might have rushed through the streets of Guelph without the risk of hurting many people; in truth, every person that could, left the apparently doomed locality.[32]

Another resident of Guelph in 1829, Doctor J.C.W. Daly remembered that "with three exceptions none of his patients had anything wherewith to pay him. Bread . . . . became scarce, and potatoes dear."[33] With the future of the Canada Company still in doubt, Waterloo farmers refused to honour orders drawn on the Canada Company's credit. Absalom Shade of

Galt, perhaps better aware of the true condition of the Company's finances, bought up all the orders which he could get at fifty percent of face value and realized a huge profit as a result. The upshot of these difficulties was, as Dr. Daly says, that "for months many families had nothing to eat but potatoes and turnips."[34]

Illustrative of the impact of the Canada Company's new policy, was the history of the firm of Gilkison and Leaden. After its rapid expansion in 1827, the firm operated its sawmill during 1828. In 1829, however, with the market for lumber in a state of collapse, the firm's creditors seized its assets and threw it into bankruptcy.

In 1832 David Gilkison's father, Captain William Gilkison, founder of Elora, attempted to rescue the sawmill from the hands of the trustees. Two entries from his diary tell the story:

July 23rd, 1832. Tomorrow Mr. Crooks [Hon. James Crooks of Crooks' Hollow, near Greenville] proposes to convey me to Guelph, that I may see where my dear son, David, has toiled for many a day. My object is to induce his return [to Guelph] by settling with his creditors, on condition that they shall deliver the estate of D.G. and Co. to me. . . . If I shall interfere in this affair either David or Jasper [another son who eventually became a leading Hamilton businessman] must go to Guelph at some future period. . . .

Sunday, 29th July, 1832. Last Wednesday I went to Guelph, a distance of 30 miles, and slept there. Looked at the sawmill which had been built by David. It has made no profit since he left it three years ago, but it is valuable in its way—perhaps

Table II
Acres Occupied in the Guelph Area, 1831-1845[37]

Township	Total	Acres Occupied				
		1831	1834	1836	1840	1845
Guelph	46,664	13,950	24,762	29,275	34,237	37,444
Puslinch	60,990	NA	22,438	32,706	39,924	51,701
Eramosa	46,030 }	22,995	16,509	20,684	22,838	28,943
Nichol	26,445 }		17,722	28,604	27,905	20,906
Erin	74,143	11,662	24,452	25,576	27,431	36,767
Garafraxa	94,377	—	5,430	1,012	7,563	13,318
Amaranth	66,261	—	—	—	—	3,061
Total	414,910	48,607	111,313	137,857	159,898	192,140
Waterloo	104,667	58,854	67,066	73,876	76,771	83,253
Wilmot	64,586	19,715	36,940	37,345	46,172	55,001
Woolwich & Pilkington	90,838	15,766	21,241	23,664	26,023	35,803
Queen's Bush*	141,753	—	—	—	—	1,426
Total	401,844	94,335	125,247	134,885	148,966	175,483

* Includes Wellesley and Peel Townships.

worth £500, though no one could be found to offer more than £320 for it, though it has 10 acres of land in the town and on the river bank.[35]

Gilkison apparently failed to effect the rescue, because in 1833 it was sold by the trustees to Captain Henry Strange who built a residence upon the property.[36]

The problem facing the Town was that from an economic standpoint it was an artificial creation. Under the rapid infusion of capital during Galt's management, it prospered. But the rural areas, which it was intended to serve, simply had not—and could not—develop at the same rate. With new capital projects restricted or halted, the Town had no economic base. For those residents who stayed (and as James Hodgert noted, many village residents did not) the process of building an economic base would be long and difficult.

In spite of the state of the village's economy, the process of rural land settlement and agricultural development continued unabated. As tables II and III show, farmers continued to move into the area without interruption, with the most rapid periods of settlement for the whole area occurring between the years 1831-1834 and 1840-1845. During the severe depression and rebellion activities of 1836-1839, land sales were lower although in Guelph Township sales continued at a uniform rate. By 1836, most of the longer settled Townships—Guelph, Puslinch, Eramosa and Nichol, Waterloo and

Table III
Percentage Occupied of Total Acreage in the Guelph Area, 1831-1845[38]

Township	*Percent of all Acreage Occupied*				
	1831	*1834*	*1836*	*1840*	*1845*
Guelph	29.9	53.1	62.7	73.4	80.2
Puslinch	NA	36.8	53.6	65.5	84.8
Eramosa	31.7	35.9	44.9	49.6	62.9
Nichol		67.0	108.2*	105.5*	79.1
Erin	15.2	33.0	34.5	37.0	49.6
Garafraxa	—	5.8	1.1	8.0	14.1
Amaranth	—	—	—	—	4.6
Overall	11.7	26.8	33.2	38.5	46.3
Waterloo	56.2	64.1	70.6	73.3	79.5
Wilmot	30.5	57.2	57.8	71.5	85.2
Woolwich & Pilkington	17.4	23.4	26.1	28.6	39.4
Queen's Bush	—	—	—	—	1.0
Overall	23.5	31.2	33.6	37.1	43.7

* Township boundaries were later realigned.

Wilmot were about fifty percent settled, while significant settlement had occurred in Erin and Woolwich. On the other hand, and this factor would greatly retard the commercial development of both Guelph and Berlin, the increase in acreage occupied by farmers does not tell the whole story. Because many of the original farmers were poor, they lacked the means to make their farms productive. As Table IV shows, in 1836, some nine years after settlement in Guelph Township had begun only 5,365 acres had been "improved", that is, converted into pasture, fields or garden. In other words, if one assumes that the average sized farm contained one hundred acres (their approximate size in 1851), then the average farm in 1836 contained only 18.31 improved acres, barely enough to grow produce for the house-

hold, let alone have much to sell. Given the same assumptions, in 1845 the average farm would contain 36.09 improved acres, or almost double that of 1836, but still not sufficient to allow a large scale sale of agricultural products.

The assessment rolls for Wellington District confirm this impression of slow agricultural growth. As tables V, VI, and VII show, in 1836 the 1,854 residents of Guelph and Guelph Township (See Table I) (including 565 males over 16 years of age) occupied approximately 293 farms and had only 97 horses, 393 oxen and 569 milk cows. In 1845, when the population had increased to 3,400,[43] of whom approximately 374 were farmers, they owned 447 horses, 572 oxen and 949 milk cattle. In other words, in 1845 the average farmer still pos-

Table IV
Acreage Under Cultivation in the Guelph Area, 1831-1845[39]

| Township | Acreage Improved | | | | |
	1831	1834	1836	1840	1845
Guelph	1,224	3,841	5,365	8,959	13,500
Puslinch	NA	1,348	2,641	5,704	15,345
Eramosa	1,033	2,110	3,064	4,734	8,352
Nichol		492	1,132	3,266	5,933
Erin	1,656	2,338	3,231	5,175	8,852
Garafraxa	—	186	372	617	1,638
Amaranth	—	—	—	—	351
Total	3,913	10,315	15,805	28,455	53,971
Waterloo	13,660	16,858	18,816	23,601	32,282
Wilmot	1,619	3,986	6,166	12,033	17,901
Woolwich & Pilkington	2,990	3,435	4,512	6,346	9,489
Queen's Bush	—	—	—	—	1,426
Total	18,269	24,279	29,494	41,980	61,098

Table V
Horses per Township in Wellington District, 1831-1845[40]

Township	Horses				
	1831	1834	1836	1840	1845
Guelph	11	54	97	249	447
Puslinch	NA	0	16	87	285
Eramosa	11	28	48	101	217
Nichol		3	19	38	151
Erin	24	47	74	141	250
Garafraxa	—	5	8	7	34
Amaranth	—	—	—	—	20

Table VI
Oxen per Township in Wellington District, 1831-1845[41]

Township	Oxen				
	1831	1834	1836	1840	1845
Guelph	86	301	393	594	572
Puslinch	NA	167	240	478	733
Eramosa	107	157	204	265	394
Nichol		66	149	273	324
Erin	98	162	194	245	393
Garafraxa	—	25	40	48	164
Amaranth	—	—	—	—	22

Table VII
Milk Cows per Township in Wellington District, 1831-1845[42]

Township	Milk Cows				
	1831	1834	1836	1840	1845
Guelph	154	399	569	860	949
Puslinch	NA	226	331	641	910
Eramosa	151	210	307	424	616
Nichol		61	186	364	467
Erin	188	239	330	553	733
Garafraxa	—	34	61	82	233
Amaranth	—	—	—	—	47

sessed only one horse, two oxen and three milk cows. With such a slender economic base, it is little wonder that the village grew slowly in its first years.

The single most important barrier to productivity amongst the Guelph area settlers stemmed from lack of capital necessary to buy land without the burden of debt and interest payments, to have it cleared, to build the necessary buildings, and to buy the machinery, tools, livestock and necessities of life required while the farm was brought into production. With land selling from two dollars to two dollars and fifty cents per acre in its wild state, and costing from nine to twelve dollars per acre to clear, a one hundred acre farm, half cleared, was worth at least six hundred and fifty dollars. In addition, Adam Fergusson gives this list of prices for necessities in 1831:

Prices of Live-Stock, Upper Canada

Horses	£7. 10.0	to	£10.0.0
Oxen, pr.	15. 0.0		17.0.0
Milch Cows	3. 15.0		5.0.0.

Implements, Etc.

Waggon for a pair of horses	£20. 0.0
Harness for a pair of horses	10. 0.0
A plough	3. 0.0
Brake-harrow	2. 0.0
Long chains to drag trees, each	1. 5.0
Double horse-sleigh	7. 0.0
Common ox-sleigh	2. 0.0[44]

With these prices, it was generally assumed that a settler with £100 could put a down payment on a lot and support himself from its proceeds.

Although these prices appear small in today's currency, they were not cheap in 1830. Guelph's first settlers were mainly of the labouring classes, and as such their wages averaged about three shillings, sixpence per day if they kept themselves, and about £2. 10s. 0d. per month if they were boarded by their employer.[45] Assuming that in the latter case an immigrant could save half of his wages, it would require almost seven years to save the minimal £100 and seventeen years to save £250. As a result, most of Guelph's early settlers, such as the La Guayrans, were forced to work away from home much of the time, leaving their wives and children to look after their few animals and acres.

For those farmers with £250 or more, the situation was quite different. Tiger Dunlop, for example, in his *Statistical Sketches of Upper Canada* stated that:

A farmer who commences with some money, say £250, ought, in the course of five or six years, to have all his capital in money, and a good well-cleared and well-stocked farm into the bargain, with the requisite dwelling-house and out-buildings on it, besides having supported his family in the meantime.[46]

With the depression after 1829, many of the poorer farm settlers were unable to find labouring jobs, and being without capital, could not keep up payments on their farms and were forced to sell them so as not to lose their original investment and improvements. William Cattermole, an author of promotional books for emigrants, described the attractions of Guelph for the immigrant with capital in 1831:

Settlers, with capital, who prefer establishing themselves on land, on which partial clearings have been made, and log-houses erected, will generally find lots with such improvements, for sale. This arises from persons going originally in very destitute circumstances, or rather dependent on the Company's assistance, who, having succeeded on their lots, are willing to sell their land, with a reasonable profit, to newcomers, at from 4 to 6 dollars, with the improvements on the same, houses, barns, etc. These individuals generally remove further westward, having acquired sufficient knowledge of the country, and purchase on the Huron tract, which is equal in quality, at from 7s. 6d. to 10s. per acre.[47]

Just how profitable a farm could be when one had the capital to clear the land and stock it properly is illustrated by a letter from an anonymous farmer in Eramosa Township who described his position after having farmed for five years:

ERAMOSA, AUG. 15, 1830.
. . .This is my sixth year on my new farm, being five miles from the town of Guelph. . . .Our crops look remarkably well, we have 94 bushels of seed-grain sown of all sorts, 20 acres of good meadow land to cut, 2½ acres of potatoes, 2 acres of turnips, and 1/2 an acre of flax. Our stock consists of 30 head of horned cattle, 62 sheep and lambs, 30 hogs, a pair of young horses, you wished me to give you a statement of last year's crop, as we had not done thrashing when you went away, it was our fifth year's produce, we had 1,329 bushels of all kinds of grain, mostly wheat and barley; we killed 2,400 lbs. weight of pork, a good fat beeve for Christmas, sold 2 yoke of fat oxen, some fat sheep, etc., cut 35 tons of hay, at £3 per ton, for all we could spare. . . .[48]

Unfortunately, as the assessment figures show, very few of the farmers in the Guelph region reached this level of productivity and prosperity before 1845.

The almost total collapse of the village's economy and the consequent outflow of village residents posed a serious problem for the Canada Company. With only about a third of the farm lots sold in the area, something had to be done to stimulate the local economy. Moreover, only a small proportion of village lots had been taken up, and many which had been previously sold were now thrown back on the market as their owners left town. Thus there was a real danger that land prices would fall rather than continue to rise. The Company officials hit upon two strategies to overcome the problem. First, it undertook a few new capital expenditures to stimulate the local economy, and second, it sent experienced Guelph residents to Quebec to meet the wealthier immigrants as they got off the boat in order to convince them that Guelph was an ideal location for immigrants with capital.

The major capital expenditure decided upon was the erection of a grist and flour mill. Until 1830, Guelph Township farmers had been forced to transport their grain to Dundas, Galt or Waterloo to be ground, and as most mercantile transactions were on a credit basis against each year's crop, they did much of their commercial business there as well. Such a loss of trade, of course, served to undercut Guelph's economic situation even further.

In the winter of 1830, a contract was let by the Company to Horace Perry of Port Hope to build a grist mill, and on April 28 he arrived with his workmen to begin construction. The site chosen for the mill was on the west bank of the Eramosa, close to where the present C.N.R. bridge is located. For the times, it was an imposing structure. Built of wood, it cost some £2000 to erect. William Lyon Mackenzie in 1831 described it as containing "four run of stones; two for merchant flour, one for country flour, and one for oatmeal."[49] Perry's workmen laboured to such good effect that the mill was ready for operation by December 10 of that

The Canada Company's Mill. (Courtesy Public Archives of Canada)

year. For the next two years it was operated for the Company by a Mr. Elgie, an Englishman. With the mill's opening, Guelph's fortunes began to revive.

Horace Perry did not, however, end his connection with Guelph with the completion of his contract. While building the Canada Company mill he apparently became excited about the area's economic potential. As a result in 1831 he bought a lot on the Waterloo Road, and built a small saw mill for himself. Again built of wood, Perry painted it red, and the "Red Mill" it was called thereafter.[50]

Perhaps even more important in the return of economic viability to the town was the success of the greatly expanded advertising and recruitment of immigrants which had been undertaken. Pamphlets were circulated widely in England praising the merits of Guelph as an

The Red Mill,
from a water colour by David Allan.

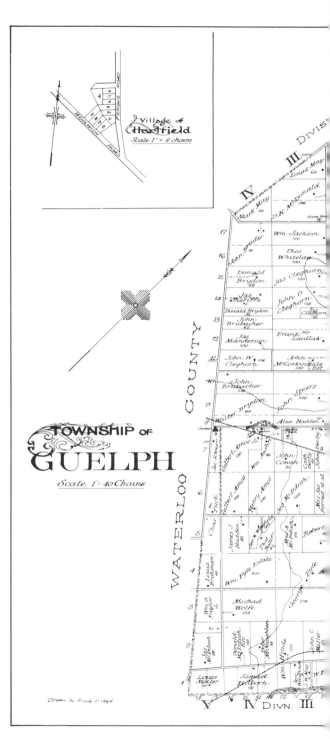

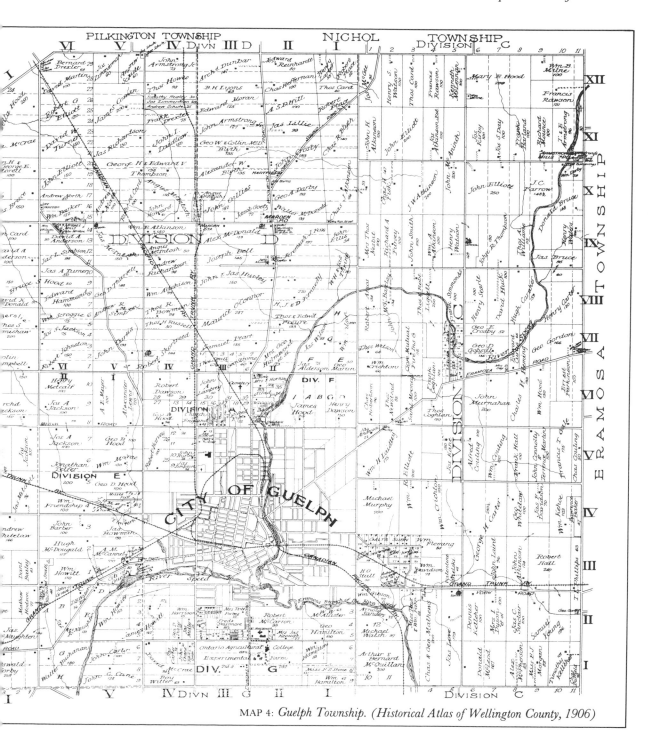

MAP 4: *Guelph Township. (Historical Atlas of Wellington County, 1906)*

attractive location for "men of capital," and James Corbett, an early settler of Guelph, was stationed in Quebec City to meet incoming immigrants. The point of the whole exercise of course was to obtain the largest price possible for land. For example, Tiger Dunlop who had been sent to Montreal in 1829 to meet immigrants, made the excellent catch of forty families in a group. In announcing his good fortune, Dunlop urged that:

As they have money I would advise that they be sent to Guelph and as a shipload more of them is hourly expected they will follow them. In the event of the first party going there I would recommend that the price of land should be raised at least one shilling and threepence per acre, it would be given just as readily as not.[51]

As a result of these efforts a considerable number of well-to-do English immigrants were persuaded to take up residence in Guelph. Acton Burrows describes this success:

In the summer of 1832, however, a fresh impetus was given by the arrival of a large party of immigrants from England, who had chartered the ship "Caroline" to bring them out. Among them were, Messrs. John and James Wilson, Edward Murton, Wm. Neeve, Edmund and Osmond Huntley, Josiah McKelkan and others, the entire party consisting of nearly a hundred persons. All of them were in comparatively affluent circumstances, some of them keeping servants in livery, and their arrival was the signal for a general revival of business, guineas being very plentiful with them, and they were not in any way niggardly in spending them. Houses sprang up on all sides, and a period of general prosperity commenced, the influence of which was never entirely lost in the town. . . .

Besides this party of wealthy immigrants, there were a few others, who came from Ireland. A number of gentlemen had decided on coming to Canada, and formed a party by themselves, chartering a vessel. Among them were the late Chancellor Blake [father of Edward Blake, later Premier of Ontario,

A full-rigged Brig of 1843.
(Courtesy Public Archives of Canada)

leader of the Liberal party, and Irish nationalist], the late Archdeacon Brough, Dr. Robinson, afterwards well known as an eminent physician, the late Justice Connors, Rev. Edward Blake, Rev. Arthur Palmer, Mr. Samuel Crawford and Mr. R.M. Richardson. All of these were in good circumstances, and all men of education and position, everyone of them holding a B.A. degree. The three last named came to Guelph. . . .

In the fall of the same year, several other well-to-do immigrants arrived, including Captain Poore and Mr. Rowland Wingfield.[52]

Suddenly Guelph boomed again as it had in 1827 and 1828. New buildings of a much better description were erected on a large scale, provisions of all kinds were once again in demand, and work at good wages was available. James Hodgert remembered that with the arrival of the *Caroline* immigrants:

Sovereigns then were plentiful, and champagne bottles strewed the streets, and although the former soon changed masters, still that they were not lost was soon apparent in the numerous buildings which sprang up, and the extensive clearings that gladdened the eye. Indeed, the rich stream irrigated the whole locality. . . .[53]

Among the original log buildings now appeared substantial taverns, merchant shops, churches, and homes built of frame, brick and stone. Tables VIII and IX drawn from the assessment rolls demonstrate the rapid rate of growth in the Town and Township as these wealthy settlers set about recreating their comfortable British life style. Although this prosperity was, like that in 1827 and 1828, created by the expenditure of capital rather than by the increase of agricultural production, it would help to ensure that Guelph became the focus of local economic activity as over-all productivity increased.

Prominent among the new wealthy settlers who took up residence in Guelph in 1832 was William Allan, cousin of the future transportation magnate, Hugh Allan of Montreal. William Allan was born at Killochan, Ayrshire, Scotland, in September, 1789, and had lived at Leith near Edinburgh where his son, David, was born in 1808.[56] Accompanied by his family he went to Sweden in 1818, where he built and supervised mills for the great milling firm of Dixon, Dudgeon & Co. of London, England, and Gottenborg, Sweden. In 1830 he returned to Leith, and from there emigrated to Canada. Their trip was typical of the hardships and difficulties facing even the wealthiest immigrants. A note written by him or a member of his family reads:

After being at Trolhatten [Sweden] 11 years, we left it on the 29th of May, came to Gottenburgh [sic] on the 30th, and left Sweden on the 27th of June 1830, and arrived at Leith 3rd July, 1830; left Leith the 8th of June (1831) in the brig "Magnet", of Bourness, Captain P. Wallace. We touched Newfoundland for some water and provisions; were 11 weeks and 4 days, when we arrived at Quebec.[57]

Table VIII
Guelph Township, Merchant Shops and Mills, 1831-1836[54]

	1831	1834	1836
Merchant Shops	3	7	10
Store Houses	0	0	0
Grist Mills	1	1	1
Additional Run of Stones	1	1	2
Saw Mills	1	1	1

Table IX
Guelph Township, Taxable Houses, 1831-1836[55]*

	1831	1834	1836
Squared Log Houses:			
1 storey	4	0	5
Additional Fireplaces	0	0	2
Framed Houses:			
1 storey	9	17	52
Additonal Fireplaces	3	0	12
Squared Log Houses:			
2 storeys	1	1	0
Additional Fireplaces	0	0	0
Brick or Stone Houses:			
1 storey	0	0	2
Additional Fireplaces	0	0	0
Framed, Brick or Stone:			
2 storeys	3	7	26
Additional Fireplaces	2	0	22

* It should be remembered that the poineer "shanty", built of round logs, was not taxed.

After residing at York for a year, Allan bought the mill in Guelph which had been built by the Canada Company, and he and his descendents remained important figures in Guelph's commercial life for decades to come.

During this burst of prosperity, a number of new merchant shops and craft industries were begun. Among the new merchants were Thomas Sandilands, Captain Lamprey, and Dr. Robert Alling who operated a druggist and chemist shop in addition to his medical practice. In addition, James May began the manufacture of fanning mills, Robert Crowe opened a blacksmith shop and built a small cupola furnace where he could smelt and cast iron; and in 1834 Robert Armstrong began to build waggons, buggies and carriages, while George W. Allan set up a one-man chair-making business.

Once again the residents of Guelph were swept up with visions of rapid growth and future prosperity. Thomas Rolph, no doubt, expressed their spirit of optimism when he wrote in 1836:

During the past year no less than 16 frame and two brick houses made their appearance in our streets, and there are at present two large taverns in progress, a chapel, and seven or eight frame houses building or contracted for in the town, and building of all sorts and descriptions daily rising out of the wood, if I may use the expression, in the country. Almost the whole of the land that is at all available is disposed of, and is under cultivation and settled on, with the exception, I believe, of from two to 3,-000 acres out of 48,000 which compose the township, with a large and daily increasing proportion of Town Lots, also disposed of and built upon. We have breweries and distilleries who give us the highest market price for our grain in cash.

Stores, seven or eight in number, hotels, taverns, watchmaker, saddler, chairmaker, and mechanics of every description. This vicinity is greatly cele-brated for the quantity and quality of Barley grown—and sleighs well laden with it, are brought during the winter months to the respective breweries for sale.[58]

In their enthusiasm, however, the merchants and businessmen of Guelph had overlooked one important consideration: they were in the long run completely dependent upon the productivity of the farmers for the prosperity of the Town. With the lack of roads into the potential market area to the north, the slow rate of northern agricultural settlement, and the shortage of capital, farm productivity had failed to keep pace with the rapid development of the Town. Of all those who described the development of Guelph, only Adam Fergusson appears to have appreciated the underlying weakness of Guelph's economic development:

When farms become numerous and a mill is erected in a convenient situation, a town soon grows up; but here the town has been hurried forward, in the hopes of settling the land. A vast deal of capital has been expended upon roads, etc., which must have so far benefited labourers, and tended, in some measure, to enable them to purchase lots; but, at present, a very desolate complexion marks Guelph, as a city which may be very thankful to maintain its ground, and escape desertion.[59]

What had been true in 1831 when Fergusson made these observations remained true in 1836.

The years 1836-1838 dealt a staggering blow to Guelph's economy. First of all, the harvest of 1836 was almost entirely ruined by continuous rain which sprouted wheat in the sheaf and rotted crops in the ground. During the winter large quantities of flour had to be imported at greatly inflated prices.[60]

No sooner had the results of the crop loss been partially overcome, than the effects of a world wide depression reached Canada in 1837, and the Rebellion of 1837-38 further disrupted local trade. The result was chaos. As James Innes remembered the dark days of 1838, in Guelph:

For months the young men and mechanics of the place were without employment, quite a number joined the incorporated batallions for the permanent defence of the province, and those who stayed at home might be seen whiling away their time or amusing themselves at cricket and other sources of amusement or recreation. The state of things in the whole province assumed such a threatening aspect that many families returned home or removed to the States and many more would have gladly done so had they possessed the funds or could have realized on their landed property.[61]

This situation appears to have continued until the return of international prosperity in 1839 and 1840.

Meanwhile, as Tables II to VII show, the slow process of agricultural development had continued. Land was cleared; live stock increased; and the area of settlement slowly expanded. As general commercial prosperity returned Guelph's businessmen found that their market area had been placed upon a firmer foundation than had previously been the case, and with the increased purchasing power of the farmers, Guelph's manufacturing production expanded as well. A considerable number of skilled tradesmen set up workshops (generally in a room or shed attached to their houses) and began to manufacture goods for the local market. By 1843 Guelph could boast of four distillers, three bakers, two saddlers and harness makers, a coach maker, four wheelwrights, six blacksmiths, a tinker (maker of tin ware), three butchers, two coopers (barrel makers), two tanners, a watch maker, eleven boot and shoemakers, a confectioner, twenty carpenters and builders, three brewers, two painters and glaziers, four cabinet makers, four chair makers, eight tailors, seven dressmakers, and two nurserymen and gardeners. For a village of only seven hundred people, there was available, therefore a wide range of locally made products.[62]

Despite the renewed prosperity and growth after 1840, mercantile trade was severely hampered by the lack of good roads. Although John Galt had spent a considerable amount of money on the Dundas, Waterloo, Eramosa and Elora Roads, none of these were more than rough, treacherous dirt tracks, easily passable in only the best of times. Thomas Rolph, for example, in 1836, stated that the Dundas Road was "through a dense pine wood, extensive cedar swamps, with very few clearings until within seven or eight miles of Guelph. It is but 24 miles, admirable travelling when frozen up in winter, but almost impassable in the spring and autumn months, and but little improved in the midst of summer. The horrible causewayed roads, most clumsily put together, and occasionally broken, renders the more circuitous route by Galt far preferable".[63]

A.D. Ferrier's experiences on the Dundas road were probably typical of the times:

The next day I started in the stage, a common lumber wagon, for Guelph, and an awful shaking we got. One of the passengers put a bottle of whiskey in the pocket of his swallow-tail coat, but, alas, it was smashed before we had gone a mile. There was an English gentleman—who afterwards settled near Guelph—in the stage, and when we got a mile or two out of Dundas he and I resolved to walk. The woods looked so high and dismal that we each hunted up a good big staff in case of meeting a bear. The travelling through the pine woods then was bumping against a stump or the big roots, and then thump into a hole, with a pleasing variety of a little steep gravel and sandy knolls now and then, especially after getting into Puslinch. I never travelled that road in a wagon again, except once, and then it was because I had cut my foot, so I could not help it. The crossways, too, were numerous and bad.[64]

While another traveller, Colonel Saunders, remembered that:

The roads between Hamilton, Dundas and Guelph were sufficiently bad to make it a journey of toil rather than of pleasure. Travellers were often obliged to come round by Galt, the [Dundas] road being impassable after sleighing ceased. By the former route it took two days to reach Guelph to say nothing of the risk run of being thrown out of the wagon into a mud hole by the jolting.[65]

On one such occasion, Colonel Saunders, a child he was holding in his arms, and his Irish driver were all thrown out of the wagon into the mud.

Discomfort and inconvenience, however, were not the major problems created for Guelph by the bad state of the roads. The main trouble was caused by the high cost of transportation which placed the Guelph merchants at a competitive disadvantage in comparison to those centres which enjoyed better roads. In the early days before railroads, everything had to be conveyed by wagon, and in Guelph a considerable number of teamsters made regular journeys from Guelph to Hamilton. One historian noted that:

The teamsters would start on Monday morning from Guelph to Hamilton and get back home again if the roads were good, on Wednesday morning. If the roads were in a bad state, they would probably not arrive home until Wednesday evening or Thursday. Some concerns, such as the distillery and the mills, kept their own teams. Among the general teamsters were Messrs. Jas. Wright, Francis Marriott, David Martin. . ., John Caulfield. . ., and Mr. McHardy. . .Even in this rough trade and in these early days the competition of women had to be feared, for a Mrs. Burrows started up in the business, and, before she retired, had three teams on the road. . . .[66]

As James Innes stated:

The principal part of all the necessary importations had to be brought by the circuitous route past Galt, and the cost of teaming was a most important consideration in the minds of our merchants and mechanics. One dollar per hundred weight was the regular charge for teaming goods from Hamilton and Dundas to Guelph and for heavy goods, such as salt, iron, etc., the increase on the regular cost was very considerable.[67]

For Guelph's businessmen, however, the problem began to be particularly acute in the late 1830's and early 1840's. As settlers began to spread into the northern townships, merchants in rival towns began to cast covetous eyes upon their trade. Thus in 1837, innkeepers and merchants in Dundas, Flamborough, Beverley, Dumfries, Galt, Preston and Waterloo joined together to persuade the government to undertake the creation of a first class road from Dundas to Berlin, and in the succeeding year, merchants in Berlin and Waterloo created a joint stock company to build a bridge across the Grand River in order to remove the last major barrier to cheap and easy transportation from Hamilton to Berlin and Waterloo.[68] By 1840, with improved transportation facilities, Berlin and Waterloo's millers, merchants and craftmen could offer cheaper merchandise and better prices for grain to the farmers in Pilkington, Nichol, Garafraxa and Amaranth, than could their rivals in Guelph.

With the creation of the Bronte Harbour Company in 1840[69] and the Trafalgar, Esquesing and Erin Road Company in 1846[70] which threatened to draw off Guelph's trade to the east as well, the point of crisis had been reached. If Guelph failed to respond to these challenges, its future would, at best, be that of a quiet country town. The question was, what could be done, and what would the residents of Guelph decide to do?

Scene on the River Speed, Guelph, Canada.

View of Guelph in 1830, from a water colour by Effie Smith
based on a lithograph which appeared in Fraser's Magasine, November, 1830.

III

Local Government and Politics

For Upper Canada, the period 1830-1850 was one of deepening conflict and bitter struggle. At no level of government and society was this more apparent than in the transformation of the local municipal system from authoritarian rule to limited democracy; and in the political sphere from fragmentation and antagonism to co-option and co-operation. Guelph, being in the early stages of development, remained generally on the sidelines of these events. Although even here few persons escaped some direct involvement in either the tragic events of 1837-1838 or the social and administrative changes that followed.

In 1827 when Guelph was founded, there were three general levels of municipal administration; the district which was the largest and most important, being the unit of both municipal and judicial administration; the county which was a subdivision of the district, being the basis for provincial elections and militia administration; and the township which was the least important, being the basis of land surveys and local appointments. So rapidly would the roles and functions of these units change that by 1851, none but the townships would be easily recognizable, and even their powers and

Alfred A. Baker, First Division Court Clerk, embracing all Wellington County, 1844-1889.

functions would be completely changed.

When Lieutenant-Governor John Graves Simcoe created the counties in 1792, it was his intention to unite the functions of the districts (which had been established in 1788) with those of the counties, as was the case in England. Local opposition from the already entrenched district officials, however, made him change his mind, and as a result he established the counties as subsections of districts to carry out the limited functions of electoral district and militia units. Until 1838 for electoral purposes Guelph was part of Halton County, a subsection of Gore District. In general, Halton covered the present-day areas of Halton, Waterloo, Wellington, Grey and Durham Counties, although most of the northern area was as yet unsettled.

In 1838 the original Halton County area was divided into two areas, one including the present-day Halton County and the Townships of Puslinch and Dumfries, while the remaining region was designated as Waterloo County. In 1840, before an election could be held, the region was redivided and the Townships of Garafraxa, Nichol, Guelph, Woolwich, Waterloo, Eramosa, Dumfries and Puslinch were renamed West Halton. Table X gives the names of the members elected to the Legislative Assembly from 1825 to 1849.

As Table X shows, Halton and West Halton were "swing" constituencies which alternated fairly regularly between Reform and Tory representatives. This was not true, however, at the township level. For example, Dumfries and Waterloo generally voted strongly for Reform candidates, while Guelph remained Tory. In those days, voting was in itself a test of individual fortitude. There was only one polling place in each constituency, and electors were required to travel long distances to reach it. Thus up to 1840, if they wished to vote it was necessary for electors to travel to Nelson Township, while after that date the polling place for West Halton was in Guelph. Elections were protracted affairs, lasting up to ten days in each riding.

The most important characteristic of elections in those days, one which profoundly affected the practice of politics at all levels, was the custom of open voting. At elections voters were required to step forward individually and declare their qualifications. The prerequisite of owning sufficient property, free and clear of mortgages or encumbrances

Table X

Members of the Legislative Assembly representing Guelph and Area, 1825-1849[1]

Date elected	Politics	Members
1825	Reform	Richard Beasley and William Scollick
1828	Reform	George Rolph and Caleb Hopkins
1830	Tory[2]	James Crooks and William Chisholm
1831	Tory	Absalom Shade*
1834	Reform	Caleb Hopkins and James Durand
1836	Tory	William Chisholm and Absalom Shade
1841	Reform	James Durand
1844	Tory	James Webster
1848	Tory	James Webster — unseated
1849	Reform	Adam J. Fergusson — declared elected

* Elected to replace James Crooks who was appointed to the Legislative Council.

which, if rented, would generate an income of forty shillings per year, would exclude about three-quarters of the adult males—females were not allowed to vote. Then publicly in front of the assembled crowd, they had to declare to the clerk the name of the person for whom they were voting. In a society where almost everyone was deeply in debt to the few wealthy individuals who dominated economic life in places like Galt, Berlin or Guelph, it was a brave man indeed who voted against the wishes of the man who held his notes. Moreover, open voting made bribery very effective and intimidation common.

The political crisis shaking Upper Canada in the 1820's and 1830's had its roots in two fundamental revolutions that were occurring in England and Canada. In England the industrial revolution had brought to the fore two new and expanding classes; the capitalists whose wealth and importance stemmed from their ownership of the great new industrial and trading firms, and the industrial workers whom they employed. Their struggles against the entrenched power of the wealthy landowners and bureaucratic government resulted in political turmoil and threatened revolution in England during that period.

In Upper Canada a similar fundamental conflict was developing. Farmers and small businessmen who, in Britain had been servants and labourers, now dreamed of achieving independence. They also demanded a complete transformation of government and all its structures. A central element in the rise toward independence and equality was the removal of the social controls which bound them while in Britain. Susanna Moodie, who had migrated to Canada in the early 1830's, wrote as follows:

[Of] all follies, that of taking out servants from the old country is one of the greatest, and is sure to end in the loss of the money expended in their passage, and to become the cause of deep disappointment and mortification to yourself.

They no sooner set foot upon Canadian shores than they become possessed with this ultra-republican spirit. All respect for their employers, all subordination is at an end; the very air of Canada severs the tie of mutual obligation which bound you together. . .

Why they treated our claims to their respect with marked insult and rudeness, I never could satisfactorily determine. . .Then I discovered the secret.

The unnatural restraint which society imposes upon these people at home forces them to treat their more fortunate brethren with a servile deference which is repugnant to their feelings, and is thrust upon them by the dependent circumstances in which they are placed. . .But let them once emigrate, the clog which fettered them is suddenly removed; they are free. . .[3]

For those well-to-do Englishmen in Guelph who had fled England looking for a tranquil home where the old values and social structures would be preserved, while those in England were being destroyed, the rising Reform movement in Canada threatened everything they held dear.

For the first few years of its development, the leading force opposing reform in Guelph was the Canada Company. The high prices charged for land, foreclosures on delinquent purchasers and its monopoly of wild lands (practices all made much more extreme after John Galt's departure) soon drew the attention and active opposition of leading Reformers such as William Lyon Mackenzie, who describes his first encounter with the Company's power as follows:

I visited the Canada Company's Town of Guelph on the 5th of September, 1831. It is the seat of the Canada Company's monopoly and was intended at first as the centre of operations. Mr. Galt's plans were injudicious, if the company was meant to be what it is now, a scourge to a new country, a drain to its means. . .

The Company's schoolhouse, taught by Mr. Matthews, is capacious, and also of stone. Mr. Matthews adjourned his school to make room for the meeting to petition for more liberal institutions. Mr. Akin, merchant, Guelph, took the chair and the late James Keough, clerk of the township, acted as secretary. The York proceedings were adopted and it was resolved, among other things, that the Canada Company as constituted for the gain of a few, was a great evil. Jones, the company's agent in York, was enraged at the whole proceedings and threatened Mr. Akin and others with the vengeance of the monopoly, on his visit to Guelph some time after. This had the effect of inducing the farmers who are in debt to the agents to exercise caution, lest their opinions might cause their ruin. The Guelph's, however, addressed the King, and sent their petition with the others.[4]

With the arrival of the English immigrants in 1832, however, leadership in opposition to the Reform movement was assumed by Captain John Poore.

As the Reform movement developed political bitterness deepened. The election of 1834 in Guelph provides a rather amusing illustration of that bitterness. In Halton riding the main contest was between the sitting members, William Chisholm and Absalom Shade, and their Reformer opponents, Caleb Hopkins and James Durand. In Guelph, two local candidates, Captain Poore and Rowland Wingfield, a Reformer, entered into a struggle of their own. As James Innes said:

There was not at that time more than 150 voters within the whole limits of Wellington, and yet neither of these gentlemen could control a vote outside it.

The result of the election was, as might have been expected, the defeat by a large majority of both these local contestants, as well as their finan-

MAP 5: *Townships in Upper Canada in 1821.*

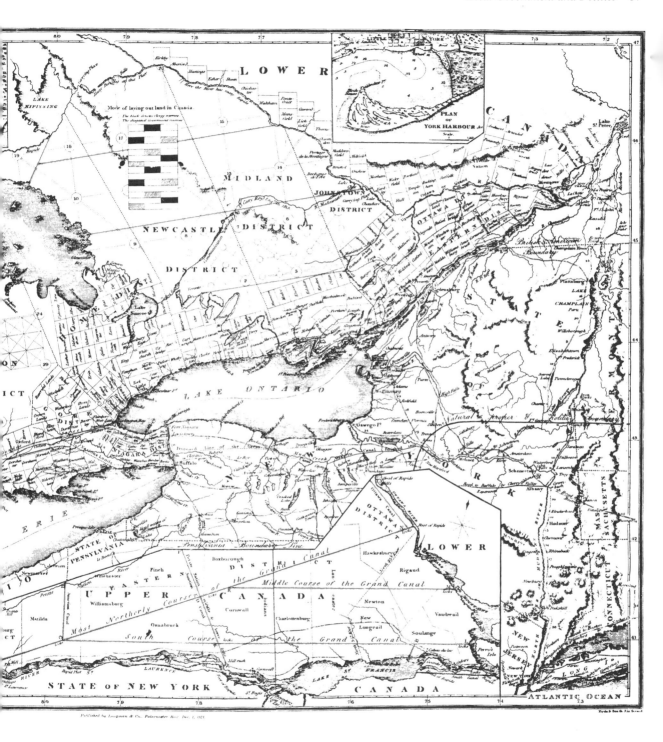

Published by Longman & Co., Paternoster Row, Dec. 1, 1821.

cial ruin, for notwithstanding the certainty of their defeat, they expended a large sum of money during the canvass and while the polling was going on.[5]

Frustrated by his election loss and made even more fearful by the Reform triumph both locally and across the province, Poore turned to creating a bulwark against the feared revolution to come. Acton Burrows describes the response of Guelph's Tories to the Reform victory:

In 1835, however, considerable anxiety began to be felt as to the probable result of the agitations which were then beginning to be heard, more especially with regard to the faction headed by William Lyon Mackenzie. This was an opportunity eagerly seized upon by Captain Poore, and during the summer he formed a [volunteer rifle] company some sixty strong, which met for drill every Saturday, on a portion of Capt. Poore's farm. . .[6]

In the election of 1836 the Tories were triumphant, with William Chisholm and Absalom Shade being returned for Halton. The Guelph Tories were beside themselves with joy. In honour of the newly elected members, a "Grand Constitutional Dinner" was given in what the Toronto *Patriot* called "the loyal and patriotic village of Guelph." The ballroom of Morgan's Hotel was "tastefully decorated" with boughs, banners, artificial flowers, and "transparencies with appropriate devices." Over the head of the chairman hung a large transparency bearing the inscription, "Sir Francis Bond Head, the pilot who weathered the storm." At each end of the room hung banners inscribed, "Fear God and Honour the King" and "The loyal men of Gore." After a splendid dinner and many toasts, William Chisholm addressed the crowd striking the Tory chords which delighted his audience.[7]

In spite of the Tory (Family Compact) triumph in 1836, the succeeding months produced even greater concern. The continued agitation on the part of the Reformers and the economic collapse of 1837 combined to cause a growing unrest among the farmers and tradesmen throughout the province. By the fall of 1837 rumours abounded that Mackenzie's followers, too, had begun to drill. All of this, no doubt spurred Captain Poore and his associates to redouble their own military preparations.

The news that Mackenzie's followers had assembled at Montgomery's Tavern on December fourth for an attack on Toronto reached Guelph apparently the same day, and on the fateful seventh Captain Poore's forces were ready to move. The Guelph militia was split into two groups; one to join the provincial militia, and the second to remain in Guelph for defensive purposes.

On the seventh, sixty-two armed militia left Guelph for active service. Lead by Captain Poore, Lieutenant Thompson, and Ensign Grange, a brother of G.J. Grange; with John Thorp, James Armstrong and James Marshall as sergeants,[8] the Rifle Company marched to Dundas where it joined Allan MacNab's command. The popular sentiment against the government was displayed by the reception given the Guelph Company. As Acton Burrows says:

On arriving at Dundas the company put up for the night at Bamberger's hotel, and the town being somewhat of a rebel hot-bed, a warm reception was given to the Guelph volunteers, stones being thrown at them, and a sort of intermittent fire of such missiles being kept up throughout the night, at the hotel, in which the company were soundly sleeping, mostly on the floor and tables. None of the men were hurt, however, beyond a few slight bruises, and the next morning they marched to Hamilton, where they were heartily welcomed by the majority of the citizens, though there were quite a number who looked upon them with anything but friendly eyes.[9]

The Guelph Rifle Company remained in Hamilton for three days, quartered in the Court House, then with the other militia units went "on campaign" in Brant, Oxford, Middlesex and Norfolk Counties, marching as far west as Ingersoll. While in Brantford, a report reached MacNab's headquarters that rebels were manufacturing bullets and pikes at Scotland, a small town in Burford Township. Eager for action the militia forces marched there, only to discover nothing more threatening than a busily operating little cider mill. Now, tired and obviously frustrated at finding no resistance from such a "notorious" rebel area, MacNab's troops wrecked their revenge. James Innes gives this version of the events:

It was well on in December when the company got orders to march to Hamilton. From there they proceeded to Ancaster, thence to Brantford, and from that to little Scotland in Burford.

Here was the headquarters of the Rebels, who [had] mustered 500 strong under Dunscombe [*sic*]. Here a great many prisoners were taken. The company then marched to Sodom—better known as Norwich—and the rebels in that section, numbering some hundreds, gave themselves up as prisoners after Dunscombe's flight.[10]

The facts of the matter were, however, that what few active rebels there might have been had long since fled, and the vast majority of those arrested were innocent of any crime other than opposing the despotism of the Tories. In the long run, almost all of those arrested were freed, but only after weeks of mistreatment and suffering. After better than a week of marching the militia returned to Hamilton for a few days rest, and on Christ-

mas day were dispatched to the Niagara frontier to meet Van Rensellaer's invading army. Except for the raid on Navy Island and the burning of the *Caroline*, the Guelph company's stay at Niagara was uneventful. Acton Burrows describes that campaign as follows:

The corps which left Hamilton was 1,300 strong, besides about 500 Indians, and upwards of 450 sleighs were employed in conveying them. In consequence of the energetic action taken by the authorities against the steamer "Caroline," and the insurgents stationed on Navy Island, the corps of which the Guelph men formed a part were not called into action, their duty consisting of the more arduous, if less glorious task of preserving peace in the outlying country, and defending the approaches to the scene of action. They were away about six weeks, and when they returned they separated, but were not disbanded, each man going to his own home.[11]

In the meantime, that portion of the Guelph Rifles who had stayed at home under the command of Colonels Lamprey and Young had been busy as well.

When the rebel force under William Lyon Mackenzie had been crushed on December seventh at Montgomery's Tavern, the leaders attempted to escape to the United States to continue activities there. The escape route followed by two of these, William Lyon Mackenzie and Samuel Lount, crossed the Guelph area. One story is told that Mackenzie actually spent the night at the residence of a Guelph farmer named Keough:

In those hospitable days neither the gate nor the front door were ever locked. Every evening Mrs. Keough placed a lighted lamp in the window of the south gable that travellers might be guided from the highway and find shelter for the night.

One evening in December, Mrs. Keough was returning from the barn with a full pail of milk in each hand. When she opened the cabin door she found a strange man warming himself by the fire.

He had a wan, haggard appearance and his face was scratched by the undergrowth of the forest. When Mr. Keough entered some time later, the man was still there staring into the fire.

"Who are you, my friend?" inquired the good-hearted Irish farmer.

"I must trust you," said the man. "I am William Lyon Mackenzie. As you know there is a price of $5,000 on my head. Any one found harbouring me is liable to imprisonment if not death. Nevertheless, I ask you to take me in and give me food and shelter for the night."

"Mr. Mackenzie, you have fallen among friends," said the Irishman. "We are devoted to the same cause, and I will willingly run these risks to help you to safety."[12]

Another story has Samuel Lount spending the night of December ninth in the home of David Oliphant, a Reformer who lived in Eramosa Township.[13]

In the midst of the extreme tension produced by the Yonge Street uprising and the constant search for the escaped leaders, some of the local militiamen took the opportunity to settle old scores. Squads of undisciplined men roamed the countryside abusing the residents and exacting tribute from them. One Eramosa resident, James Peters, remembered those forays:

Guerilla parties from headquarters at Guelph used to scour the township at night, search the houses for firearms, take them away when they could get them, arrested a great number of the heads of families, took them to Guelph, and compelled them to give bonds to appear when called upon.

There was one thing they never seemed to forget, viz: in all cases to bleed them in the pocket according as they were able to bear it, some to the tune of $4 each.—Some got off for $3. Others paid two, and when two could not be got, they took one. I know of one who was a countryman of the operator, who got clear by paying 50 cents. I think this was the commencement of the cash system in Guelph. . . .

The patience of the people was exhausted, and it would have been no wonder had some of the midnight marauders lost their lives, the people were so exasperated, and determined to put a stop to these unlawful proceedings.[14]

For all the turmoil that these raids created only eight men, Robert Armstrong of Guelph and seven of Eramosa Township's leading farmers, James Benham, Calvin Lyman, James Butchard, William Armstrong, James Peters (the Township Clerk), James Parkinson and Hiram Dowlan were ever sent to trial.

Although most of those arrested were allowed to return home upon giving bond or posting bail, Peters, James Benham and John Butchard were consigned to jail in Hamilton without examination or formal charge being laid. There they were held for the next six weeks without hearing, before they were released on bail. Peters tells of the prisoners' treatment:

When we arrived at Hamilton we were taken to a place called headquarters. Geoffrey Lynch of Guelph appeared to be master of ceremonies that night and a jolly set of fellows we were under his command. Lynch ordered us up to the Court House and we were soon provided with quarters in the cells for the night. Before being penned up I requested Mr. [George J.] Grange to use his influence to prevent us from being put into the company of felons.[15]

The commandant, Lynch, responded to Grange's request by locking the prisoners in the unheated, dark Court House basement without blankets, bedding, or heat of any kind. The next morning, however:

Mr. Grange got us out of that dungeon and put us in the debtors' room. Here we had a stove and a blanket each, comforts for which I have been grateful ever since.[16]

On March 8, 1838, the Grand Jury composed of nineteen well-known Tories met in Hamilton to decide whether there was sufficient grounds to charge the Guelph area prisoners with treason. This was the first time that the prisoners had met any of the court officers or heard the nature of the charges against them. Not surprisingly, given the composition of the Grand Jury, true bills were found against nineteen of the prisoners (including Robert Armstrong and the Eramosa seven) and they were given just ten days to prepare a defence. The Eramosa prisoners were the first to face trial. The true bill against these prisoners set the tone for the prosecutor's case:

UPPER CANADA. DISTRICT OF GORE, to wit:

The Jurors of Our Sovereign Lady the Queen, upon their oath, present that James Benham, late of the township of Eramosa, in the district of Gore, yeoman, Calvin Lyman, late of the same place, yeoman, James Butchard, late of the same place, yeoman, William Armstrong, late of the same place, yeoman, James Peters, late of the same place, yeoman, James Parkinson, late of the same place, laborer, and Hiram Dowlan, late of the same place, yeoman, being subjects of our Sovereign Lady Victoria, by the Grace of God, of the United Kingdom of Great Britain and Ireland, Queen, Defender of the Faith, not having the fear of God in their hearts but being moved and seduced by the instigation of the devil, and entirely withdrawing the love, and true and due obedience which every subject of our said Lady the Queen should, and of right, ought to bear towards our said present Sovereign Lady the Queen, and wickedly devising and intending to disturb the peace and public tranquility of this province, on December 8, in the first year of the reign of our said Sovereign Lady the Queen. . .[and]. . .with force and arms, unlawfully, wickedly and traitorously, did incite, encourage, exhort, move, induce and persuade divers of the subjects of our said Lady the Queen unlawfully,

wickedly and traitorously, to levy war against our said Sovereign Lady the Queen. . ., her Crown and Dignity, and also against the form of the Statute in such case made and provided.

(signed) Wm. H. Draper
Solicitor General.[17]

James Peters describes the trial and its outcome:

Miles O'Reilly, Esq., was engaged as our counsel, at $10 each, or $70 for the job. Perhaps your readers may think we were spending money faster than we had been making it lately, and it was so, but there was no help for it.

The late Sir Allan McNab [*sic*], and the Solicitor General, now Judge Draper, were Queen's Counsel, and if we did not get our necks stretched it was not their fault. Judge Macaulay presided, and the Hon. James Crooks, late of Flamboro West and another gentleman supported the judge.

We were all ready for trial at the time appointed [March 18th]. They were 80 petit jurors summoned, namely 57 Tories to the backbone and 23 Reformers. . .

The witnesses for the Crown were William Campbell of Eramosa. Walter King, who now presides in your ticket office at the market house, Guelph, and the third and last one was Robert Grindell of Eramosa. . .

The evidence was so much in our favor that we told our counsel we were willing to submit our case to the jury without examining any of the eight witnesses we had on our behalf.

The crafty Queen's Counsel would not consent to this arrangement, probably expecting to get something out of our witnesses they could not get out of their own, but after examining three of them they gave it up for a bad job.[18]

The jury took just eight minutes to find all seven not guilty, and soon after Robert Armstrong was freed as well. Peters, in summing up the whole affair, no doubt reflected the feelings of the hundreds of people who stood up to the political domination of the Tories:

It is now 29 years since these troublesome times, but my mind has not changed. I believe we did right, and if the same was to take place again, and such an Autocrat [Sir Francis Bond Head], surrounded by such a family compact, was misgoverning the province, I would go into the dungeon again rather than shoulder a musket to keep them in power, in order that they might grind the despised Reformers to dust.[19]

If Robert Armstrong and the Eramosa prisoners had become heroes to the local Reformers, the Tories had their heroes as well. The veterans of the Niagara Frontier campaign were soon followed into the hearts of their supporters by a second company of volunteers raised by Captain Poore in the fall of 1838. These men enlisted for a specific time period (November 1, 1838, to May 1, 1840). This company was stationed in Hamilton in the first week of November, 1838, and remained there during their entire enlistment period.[20] By the time they returned home, the tradition was well established that Guelph was a community that, when called to arms, would respond without delay.

It would be ironic, indeed, that although the Tories would triumph in suppressing the rebellion in Canada, the overthrow of their compatriots' power in England would ultimately lead to their defeat in Canada as well. After an initial period of shocked reaction in Britain, during which a strong repression of suspected rebels was carried out in Canada, Britain's Liberal leadership decided that, if Canada was to be preserved as a colony, fundamental changes had to be made in the structure and method of government. Thus John Lambton, Lord Durham, was sent to Canada to examine the situation and to recommend necessary changes. His harsh denunciation of the Tory ruling class was almost classic in its vigor and completeness. According to Durham, Tory rule must be smashed in Upper Canada if Britain intended to keep the colony content and British. Misrule had brought rebellion, and a key component of that misrule was the total control that was exercised by the Family Compact, its followers and its favorites over local municipal government. The revision of the local municipal system which followed Durham's report would profoundly affect the lives of every citizen.

Following the American Revolutionary War and the signing of the treaty in 1783, Great Britain faced the necessity of providing an administrative structure for the newly settled western areas of Quebec lying along Lake Ontario and Lake Erie. Initially these areas were treated as extensions of Quebec, but under pressure from both the Loyalists and British interests Upper Canada was divided from Quebec by the *Constitutional Act* of 1791, and separate municipal institutions were established soon after. *The Parish and Town Officers Act* of 1793[21] provided the basis for the form of municipal government that existed when Guelph was founded, and that form would remain generally intact until 1841.

Under the 1793 Act the basic unit of local administration was the district. In 1788 Sir Guy Carleton had divided the western regions of Quebec (i.e., Upper Canada) into four administrative districts which were called Luneburg (later Lunenburg), Mecklenberg, Nassau and Hesse, which within a year or so were renamed Eastern, Midland, Home and Western districts. The Guelph area was included in Home District. In 1798 these districts were divided into eight with the names Johnstown,

Newcastle, Niagara and London being added. Subsequent further divisions would raise that total, so that by 1840 some twenty districts existed. In 1827 the Guelph area was part of one of these new divisions, Gore, which had been created in 1816. The seat of administration for Gore district was Hamilton.

The administration of the districts was one which had the advantages of being cheap and easy to establish, but at the same time had the disadvantage of being authoritarian and irresponsible—a situation typical of the provincial government as well. All decision making was placed in the hands of a few Justices of the Peace, "Magistrates" as they were called, who met four times a year in Quarter Sessions at the district town. The office of Justice of the Peace was a very old one, being established in England during the reign of Edward III, and through the centuries had been given very large powers. The magistrates were appointed for life "during good behavior", and were in effect, except in unusual circumstances, responsible to no one. Singly, the magistrate could try minor infractions of the law and settle local disputes, but when two or more of them met in the Quarter Sessions they wielded enormous magisterial, legislative and administrative powers. They could try all kinds of criminal cases, legislate any local by-law not in contradiction of provincial or imperial statutes, and administer local affairs and spend local taxes pretty well as they pleased. The local inhabitants had absolutely no voice or control over any of these affairs.[22]

A partial list of the administrative matters under the control of the magistrates will give some idea of their capacity to affect the lives of the residents: building and repairing roads and bridges; erection and management of court-houses, gaols and asylums; making assessments for highways, the wages of members of the assembly and for local purposes; appointment of district and township constables; fixing the fees of gaolers, town clerks and pound-keepers; the appointment of street and highway surveyors; inspection of weights and measures; the granting of licenses to sell liquor, and to ministers or clergymen of "dissenting" congregations authorizing them to solemnize marriages; etc.[23] Equally important was the fact that they had complete control over all the locally elected township officers.

It is not surprising, however, that such wide discretionary powers, concentrated in the hands of a few men who did not have to face an electorate, was open to abuse, or that these powers were wielded to reward friends and punish enemies. Appointments to retiring army officers, wealthy landowners and political favorites became the rule, and all too often these figures neither sympathized with nor cared about problems outside their immediate interests. In particular the granting of money to build or make repairs to roads and bridges brought outcries of partiality and arrogance from residents of areas distant from the district town.[24]

The chief advantages of such a system as seen from British eyes was that it inhibited the development of both democracy and republicanism among the "common people"—the democratic New England town meeting being one of the elements blamed for the American Revolution. Moreover, because Justices of the Peace were unpaid, the system was cheap to operate and easy to establish, requiring little more than the swearing in of two or more residents of an area to bring both judicial and local administrative institutions into being.

With the power of appointment lying in the hands of the Governor, such magistrates were of course chosen for their loyalty to the Crown and established institutions and traditions. In a colonial setting such as Upper Canada, they were intended to be, and were, a chief bulwark against political change.

The first magistrates appointed in Guelph in 1827 were similar in background and politics: Tiger Dunlop, Charles Prior, James Hodgert and Colonel George Lamprey were all "men of considerable education and ability".[25]

As James Innes pointed out:

Guelph formed part of the old District of Gore, the County Town of which was Hamilton.—All such cases as are now disposed of by Courts of Assize, County and Quarter Sessions, were then adjudicated upon at Hamilton. Our jurymen were all compelled to attend at that place and Sheriff's and Bailiff's expenses were exceedingly high, on account of the distance travelled.

Then again all such business as is now disposed of by our municipal councils was then transacted by the magistrates assembled in Quarter Sessions at Hamilton, and in consequence of the distance, coupled with the bad state of the roads, seldom or ever was there a fair representation of magistrates from this section, and, as might be expected, much of the business which came before them was either untouched or not done to the satisfaction of those interested.[26]

In contrast to the sweeping powers and wide latitude of discretion given to the Quarter Session and the magistrates, the township and its locally elected officers were given virtually none. The debate in the Legislative Assembly in 1791 illustrates the division of opinion between the Reformist and Tory elements concerning the extent that local residents should participate in local government. The first bill "To Authorize Town Meetings for the Purpose of Appointing Divers Parish Officers", was ordered postponed after the second reading, and another bill "To Authorize Justices of the Peace to Appoint Annually Divers Public Officials" was introduced. Neither bill, however, could gain a majority at that time.[27] Although Lieutenant-Governor John Graves Simcoe agreed with the Tories that encouragement of local town meetings was dangerous and unwise, still he was concerned about giving the power of appointment of township officers to the Justices of the Peace.

The Parish and Township Act of 1793, therefore, attempted to balance the two evils; while still paying lip-service to the desire of the Loyalist immigrants to retain the democratic town meetings which many of them had enjoyed in the American colonies, it still left the township officials under the control of the magistrates. As Simcoe put it, "It was therefore thought advisable not to withhold such a gratification to which they had become accustomed, it being in itself not unreasonable and only to take place one day in that year."[28] By the act, any two of "His Majesty's Justices of the Peace" were enabled to authorize by their warrants, the constable of any "parish, township, reputed township or place" to assemble the inhabitants on the first Monday in March (later changed to January) of each year to choose for the following year a parish, town or township clerk, two assessors, a collector, a number of overseers of highways, a pound-keeper and two town wardens. These officers, however, were not responsible to the local inhabitants but took their orders from and reported to the magistrates. If nominated for and elected to a local office, the person elected could not refuse to accept the position on penalty of a fine.[29] Alfred A. Baker, who served for nine years as the Township Clerk in Guelph gives this description of the Guelph Township meeting:

The meetings were held at the old Market House if the weather permitted, if not an adjournment took place to the long room of the Suffolk Hotel. These meetings were held on the first Monday of the year.

It was the duty of the clerk, on the morning of the meeting, to post an account of the place of meeting and also at the post office, of all monies come into his hands during the year last past, and exhibit vouchers for the expenditure thereof.

The first duty of the meeting was to elect a chairman, which usually was filled by one of three gentlemen who have passed away, the late John Inglis, Benj. Thurtell, and Geoffrey Lynch, Esqs.; this done, the appointment of pathmasters, poundkeepers, township wardens, fence viewers, was proceeded with.

The farmers made it a point to attend, and many a wordy war was fought by pathmasters to obtain more labor on their particular roads than they were entitled to.[30]

The insignificance of the township meeting was accentuated by the fact that only two minor pieces of legislation came under its control: what constituted a legal fence, and which animals would be allowed to run at large on the roads and streets. As minor as these matters were, as Alfred Baker pointed out, even these produced sharp differences between town and township residents:

One of the great features at these meetings, was whether or not horses and pigs should be free commoners. One party was often headed by Dr. Orton, and the other by "Old Jack Horning." Parties were divided in opinion, which usually ended in a poll being demanded—the clerk being returning officer.

Sitting astride upon the Suffolk Hotel gate, opened sufficiently wide to allow one person to pass between gate and post, the returning officer counting heads as they went through. By hook or by crook "Jack" was invariably successful, the day's proceedings generally terminating in good will and sundry glasses of "Allan's Old Rye."[31]

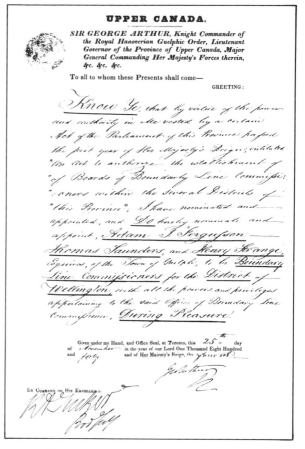

Document dated the 25th November, 1840, appointing Boundary Line Commissioners.

As settlement spread north, the inconvenience experienced by settlers continued to increase. It was not long, therefore, before a strong agitation developed to create a new district out of the northern parts of Gore. Guelph had two reasons to want Gore District divided. Not only would a division mean greater convenience for the residents of the more northern townships, but whichever town became the new district's administrative centre would receive a huge bonus in the form of increased trade and greatly improved facilities. With all the towns in the area suffering the effects of the depression of 1836-1837, rivalry was keen. As James Innes noted:

Before the passing of this act, not a little intriguing was resorted to by the inhabitants of both Galt and Fergus for the honor of being appointed the [district] town but Guelph carried the day.[32]

Acton Burrows gives this version of the events:

A movement had for some time been on foot for the division of the Gore District, which then included the whole of what are now the counties of Wellington, Waterloo, Grey, Bruce, and the district as far as the shores of Lake Huron. As the result of the agitation which was vigorously carried on, an act was passed in 1837, 7 William IV., chap. 18, providing for the division of Gore District, and for the erection of the District of Wellington, as soon as a jail and court-house could be erected, and other necessary preliminary arrangements made. Among provisions of the act were, that the jail and court-house should be situated in the Town of Guelph; that a District school should also be erected, the teacher's salary to be £100, to be paid out of Provincial funds, as also the sum of £250 for the support of common schools. . . .The justices were empowered to borrow £6,000 for building the jail and court-house. . . .[33]

Needless to say Guelph's rivals were not content to have that town win so easily. In Woolwich Township a meeting of the inhabitants was held on February 20, 1837, to protest the division of Gore district. Resolutions were passed stating that the meeting was "dissatisfied to find that a Bill for the division of the District of Gore had been passed through both Houses of Parliament without the inhabitants being apprised that such a measure was contemplated," and "that Guelph has been most injudiciously chosen as the site for the new district town."[34] For the

residents of Woolwich it made little difference, on account of distance, whether the district town was Hamilton or Guelph.

For Berlin and Galt, which had much more to gain, the wave of protest was even greater. Both towns were older and larger than Guelph, and both were feeling the spur of economic necessity created by the depression. A.E. Byerly describes part of the protest movement:

On March 22, 1837, the inhabitants of Waterloo Township met in Berlin. William Scollick was appointed chairman and H.W. Peterson, secretary. These two gentlemen, with John Erb and Adam Ferrie, Jr., were appointed a committee to draft a memorial to the King asking that Royal assent be not given to the division. The committee to obtain signatures consisted of Jacob C. Snider, Jacob S. Shoemaker, John Bechtel, William G. Millar, H.W. Peterson and Adam Ferrie, Jr.[35]

Their protests were without avail, however, and the division was permitted to stand.

As soon as royal assent was given the magistrates who lived within the newly-designated district met and appointed a building committee for the construction of the court-house and jail, composed of A.J. Fergusson, George J. Grange, William Hewat, William Thompson, Thomas Saunders and Robert Alling. Saunders was appointed Chairman; Alling, Treasurer; and James Hodgert was the clerk. Thomas Young was hired as the architect and Alfred A. Baker was named Clerk of the Works.[36]

Due to the outbreak of the rebellion in December, 1837, and the subsequent period of unrest and instability, nothing was accomplished for the next two years towards erecting the necessary public buildings. Finally, in 1839 the contracts for the jail and court-house were let to William Day and William Allan respec-

Court House and Jail. (The Canadian Illustrated News)

tively. The jail was completed in 1840 but as the new court-house would not be ready for some time, alternative arrangements had to be made. The first court therefore was held in the British Coffee House, now the Royal Hotel, on Carden St. In August, 1841, it was decided that better accommodation was required and a room was rented from Mr. Dyson in his new brick building on Gordon Street, then known as the Red Lion Tavern, but later as the Fountain House. In 1843 the new court-house was ready for use and it included space for the offices of the Wellington District.[37]

As soon as the jail and court room were ready for use, evidence of this was furnished to the Government of Upper Canada, and on June 18, 1840, a proclamation was issued officially setting apart the District of Wellington, and in July the officials of the new District received their appointments. George J. Grange was named Sheriff, A.J. Fergusson, Judge, Thomas Saunders, Clerk of the Peace, and James Hodgert, Inspector of Licenses.[38]

Scarcely had the new District been established than the whole basis of its existence began to be revolutionized. Although the rebellion in Upper Canada had failed in its main purposes, it had stirred the British authorities to take a new look at Upper Canadian institutions. To accomplish this new look, John Lambton, Lord Durham, was despatched to Canada to report on the causes of the rebellion, and to recommend methods of preventing a recurrence. His report, two volumes in

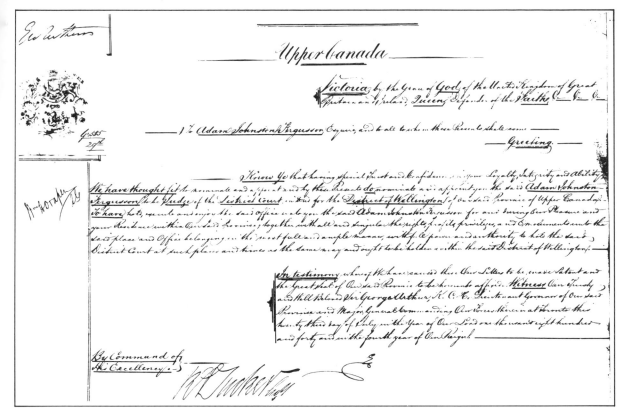

Document appointing Adam Johnston Fergusson Judge of the
Wellington District Court, July 29th, 1840.

length, contained a stinging attack upon the ruling class in Upper Canada. Lord Durham said:

The establishment of a good system of municipal institutions throughout these provinces is a matter of vital importance. A general legislature, which manages the private business of every parish, in addition to the common business of the country, wields a power which no single body, however popular in its constitution, ought to have—a power which must be destructive to any constitutional balance. The true principle of limiting popular power is the appointment of it in many different depositories, which has been adopted in all the most free and stable states of the Union. Instead of confiding the whole collection and distribution of all the revenues raised in any county for all general and local purposes to a single representative body, the power of local assessment, and the application of the funds arising from it, should be entrusted to local management.[39]

Charles Poulett Thomson, later Lord Sydenham, was sent to Canada after Durham's departure to bring Durham's recommendations into operation. In particular, he was anxious to see the municipal reforms take place. As he wrote to the Colonial Secretary, Lord John Russell, "The establishment of Municipal Government by Act of Parliament is as much a part of the future scheme of Government for the Canadas as the Union of the two Legislatures, and the more important of the two."[40] His suggestions to the Legislative Assembly of Upper Canada that it should pass such legislation were, however, rejected by the Tory majority. In Lower Canada where the assembly had been suspended, Thomson was able to have the Special Council pass an ordinance in September, 1840, which provided for elective municipal institutions. It was necessary to wait until the Act of Union came into effect in 1841 before similar legislation could be passed in Upper Canada.

When the assembly of the newly-united Canada opened its first session in Kingston on June 15, 1841, one of the first subjects dealt with was the establishment of municipal institutions in Upper Canada. The bill, introduced by Provincial Secretary, Samuel B. Harrison, was essentially the same as the ordinance passed earlier in Lower Canada. In spite of a storm of protest from both Tory and Reform factions, the *Act for Better Internal Government*[41] was passed by the narrowest of margins—at one point the chairman's vote was required to defeat an amendment. On the one hand, the Tories objected to the election of district councillors to replace the magistrates, while on the other, the Reformers strongly opposed the restrictions that were placed upon that council's freedom of action. The resulting act was a compromise between the two positions.

According to the Act, the district councils were to be a combination of elected councillors and appointed officials. A township with less than 300 voters elected one councillor, while a township with 300 or more voters elected two. Table XI gives members of the Wellington District Council elected from Guelph Town-

Table XI
Members from Guelph Township Elected to the Wellington District Council, 1842-1849[42]

1842	John Howitt	Benjamin Thurtell
1843	"	"
1844	"	"
1845	James Wright	"
1846	"	"
1847	"	"
1848	"	William Clarke, M.D.
1849	"	"

ship for the period 1842 to 1849, during which this statute was in force.

Members of the district council were elected for three years with one-third retiring each year. Those elected were required to be residents of the township they represented, and possess real estate in that or an adjacent district valued at £300 over and above all encumbrances.[43] In addition to the monetary restrictions on elections, a large number of other controls were built into the structure of the council. The warden, treasurer and district clerk were all appointed by the Governor, and responsible only to him. Moreover, all by-laws had to be reported to the Governor, and could be vetoed by the Governor-in-Council within thirty days after receipt.

There were, in addition, checks imposed on the amount and purpose of the expenditures undertaken by the councils. No public work could be undertaken until reported upon by the district surveyor, and if it cost more than £300, by the provincial Board of Works.

Within these limits, considerable powers were given to the district councils, although unlike the old Quarter Sessions, these powers were strictly enumerated. They included the assumption of most of the administrative powers of the Quarter Session, as well as its assets and liabilities which were transferred to the district; jurisdiction over roads and bridges, the purchase and sale of real estate, the administration of schools, the fixing of district and township officers' salaries and fees, as well as the responsibility of defraying the cost of administration of justice. The chief limiting factor in these areas was a strict ceiling on taxation upon real and personal property of two pence on the pound of assessed value—and the old statutory rates of assessment were retained. In addition the district was permitted to levy tolls on users of public works. As table XII shows, given the wide duties imposed upon the

Table XII
Assessed Value of Property in Wellington District, 1840-1848[44]

Township	1840	1843	1845	1848
Guelph	£32,569	£40,229	£44,285	£54,028
Puslinch	18,845	26,767*	32,048	43,079
Nichol	15,115	14,484	16,479	22,604
Eramosa	12,568	16,902	20,839	26,288
Erin	14,680	18,777	23,797	32,327
Garafraxa	2,680	4,265	6,207	10,821
Amaranth	—	919	1,295	2,210
Peel	—	—	—	11,357
Arthur	—	—	—	10,025
Waterloo	74,263	89,683	94,759	106,472
Wilmot	28,054	26,326	43,552	57,548
Woolwich	16,200	20,364	22,315	25,192
Wellesley	—	1,923	2,884	23,883
Sydenham	—	—	—	12,495
Derby	—	—	—	7,294
Glenelg	—	—	—	3,878
Egremont	—	—	—	3,683
Normanby	—	—	—	3,153
Holland	—	—	—	3,615
Sullivan	—	—	—	2,899
Bentinck	—	—	—	3,701
Melancthon	—	—	—	1,061
Total	£214,974	£270,639	£308,460	£477,613

* Estimated value.

district council, the fiscal limitations arising from the low assessed value of local property and the two pence per pound limitation on taxation, meant that little in the way of public improvements could be done. For example, in 1839 when Guelph's residents had considered building a macadamized road to Dundas, the cost had been estimated at more than £31,000, whereas the total assessment of the townships which would be served by such a road amounted to only £51,414. Thus as the northern townships began to open for settlement and Guelph's businessmen strove to establish markets there, they found themselves severely hampered by lack of public funds.

Finally, it should be made clear that except for the election of the district councillor, no additional powers or controls were given to the township meeting. Its main function remained to produce the local servants who would carry out the orders of the district council.[45] Without a capacity to tax its residents or to undertake public works, when local needs developed the most that could be done was to get up a petition begging the district council to act on behalf of the local inhabitants. Municipal improvements, therefore, were generally out of the question at a critical time in Guelph's development.

Until 1849 every change in municipal status required a separate act of the Provincial Legislature. Thus as Guelph village began to grow in the 1840's, the question of persuading the Government to grant incorporated status to the centre began to be seriously discussed. In advocating the incorporation of Guelph as a village, the *Guelph Advertiser* said:

We have long been of opinion, and frequently expressed it, that the incorporation of Guelph would be of great advantage, and. . .we believe the majority of the inhabitants have this week been convinced that any effort on their part for the promotion of its peace and prosperity will prove comparatively useless until such is the case. At present Guelph is in precisely the same position as any other part of the District either in regard to its judicial or municipal business, and, in consequence, the only body to which we can apply for redress or improvement is the Quarter Sessions on the one hand and the District Council on the other. Acting on this principle, three applications were made to the Bench at the last Session,—The first being from the Fire Company. . ., the next was a petition for some action to be taken toward the cleansing of the Town and making necessary preparations for the expected visit from the Cholera. . ., [and] the third application to the Court, and of the treatment this received we have the principal cause to complain and which induced us to make these observations, was a petition to the magistrates to take such steps as they might see fit, to preserve the peace of the town on Fair and Cattle Show days—prompted doubtless by the unenviable character of our town, and the fact that on a late Fair Day a serious disturbance took place.[46]

Not only had the Quarter Sessions not dealt with these petitions to the satisfaction of the *Advertiser*, but in the latter case the magistrates led by Doctor Clarke, had apparently insulted the petitioners who were led by several of the Town's clergymen, and told them in effect that if they didn't like the sight of drunkenness, they should stay out of taverns at late hours.[47]

At this point the *Baldwin Municipal Act* of 1849 was passed,[48] and the municipal system was placed on a completely different basis than had been the case previously. Whereas until 1849 the basic unit of municipal government was the district, in the Baldwin Act the unit of government was the township, and incorporated village. By the act, the district was abolished, and a new municipal unit, the county, was substituted. This latter operated as a committee of townships and villages with interests in common extending beyond their boundaries. In addition, the county was given jurisdiction over matters which were of general concern. Under this system, towns were in effect large villages which required additional powers in order to manage their more complex affairs, while they still remained under the general umbrella of the county. Cities, on the other hand, were structurally equal to the counties, not under the county umbrella and held even wider powers. In addition, the act provided an orderly method whereby a growing urban centre could acquire the powers necessary for its good government. Thus, as a village grew and reached a certain population, it could apply for the next higher status, becoming in turn an incorporated village, town and ultimately, a city. From a structural aspect, the 1849 *Municipal Act* would remain the basis of municipal government in Ontario until regional government was introduced in the 1960's.

According to the *Municipal Act*, the ratepayers were to elect five township councillors annually, who would elect from amongst themselves a chairman and executive officer called the reeve. When a township contained more than five hundred freeholders and householders, the councillors elected a deputy-reeve as well. The duties of the township council included building and maintaining the common schools; erection and maintenance of animal pounds, concession roads, lanes and bridges within the township; the appointment of poundkeepers, fence viewers, and road surveyors and overseers; the regulation of taverns, inns, eating places, joint stock road and bridge companies within the municipality, animals at

large, travelling shows, etc., enforcing or compounding statute labour; and the right to raise taxes, tolls and to borrow money for township works.

Incorporated villages were established as municipalities with a status roughly equal to that enjoyed by townships. When a "convenient area" reached a population of one thousand or above, the local inhabitants could petition the government to be designated as an incorporated village, with the government setting its limits by order-in-council. As in the township, the voters annually elected five councillors who in turn named a reeve and deputy-reeve from amongst their ranks. In addition to those duties and rights given to township councils, the village was given jurisdiction over all aspects of roads, bridges, harbours, docks including the right to prohibit the injury or fouling of them; the right to regulate markets in all forms, weights and measures, vehicles, assize of bread, observance of the sabbath, vice, cruelty to animals, victualling houses, billiard tables, bowling alleys and all other places of amusement, gambling, horseracing, vagrants, drunkards, vagabonds, exhibitions, carnivals, theatres and circuses. They had the right to prohibit all manner of public nuisances including privies, slaughter houses, gas works, tanneries, distilleries, ringing bells, blowing horns, shouting, firing guns, fireworks, washing or bathing the person in public waters in or near villages, chivaries, indecent exposure, profane language, and immoderate driving. In addition, the village was required to make provisions for fire prevention and fighting, interment of the dead, and public health. To enforce these powers, the townships and villages were allowed to attach penalties to by-laws not exceeding ten days in the public lockup. Named as villages in the 1849 act were Chippawa, Galt, Oshawa, Paris, Richmond (Carleton County) and Thorold.[49]

When a village reached a population of three thousand or more, its council could petition for it to become a town with the wider powers and duties attached to that rank. Again, the provincial government named the boundaries. Several aspects of the election of the town council set it off from that of township and village councils. In order to vote, an elector was required to be the proprietor or renter of property valued at £25. To become a candidate for town council, a man was required either to own or lease property valued at £300, or to pay or receive rentals of £40 per year. For electoral purposes, towns were divided into a minimum of three wards, and three councillors were elected from each ward. In addition to the usual reeve and deputy-reeve, the town councillors elected a mayor from amongst their number. The mayor was not only the town's chief executive officer, but on occasions when the police magistrate was absent, the mayor presided in court as the Justice of the Peace. In addition to the powers possessed by townships and incorporated villages, towns could establish and regulate a police force, alms house, work house and industrial farm; construct street lighting; regulate and license livery stables and public conveyances; sweep and water streets; and assess real estate for special improvements. Fines of £5 or jail terms of ten days could be imposed. Included in Schedule B of the act which enumerated the towns were: Belleville, Brantford, Brockville, Bytown, Cobourg, Cornwall, Dundas, Goderich, London, Niagara, Peterborough, Picton, Port Hope, Prescott and Saint Catharines.[50] In addition, Hamilton, Kingston and Toronto were named as cities.[51]

The County councils were made up of the reeves and deputy-reeves elected in the townships, incorporated villages and towns, and in effect operated as a committee of these municipalities. In addition to having control of such obvious common interests as roads lying along township boundaries, bridges which crossed such boundaries and similar mutual works, the county council was responsible for providing a county court-house, jail and shire hall, the erection and maintenance of a county grammar school, and the building and maintenance of main thoroughfares through the county. Of particular interest to Guelph's residents was the power given to counties to regulate and own stock in joint stock road and bridge companies, and to loan or give money to them. Although such public works as a county might undertake were on a much larger scale than those which a town, township or village might erect, the county council possessed little autonomous power. Because its members were elected by and responsible to the township councils, in general those smaller bodies called the tune.

For Robert Baldwin and the other framers of the 1849 *Municipal Act*, places such as Guelph created a difficult problem. Although these villages had been made district seats of government, had courts established in them, or had in some other manner acquired the status appropriate to towns (for example, had been inadvertently designated as a town in some provincial statute), many of them had no municipal government of their own, and none had achieved a sufficient population to require the elaborate and expensive structure and facilities which the *Municipal Act* gave to towns. The solution was eminently practical: these villages would be given the title of "Town" but would have none of the powers associated with that status. As the Municipal Act spelled it out:

Be it therefore enacted, that the several Towns mentioned in the said Schedule, with such limits and boundaries as shall be established and declared for such Towns respectively. . .shall be and continue to be Towns as heretofore, but neither the provisions of this Act applicable to Towns only, nor any Act, nor any of the provisions of any Act to be passed this Session, or at any time hereafter referring to Towns generally, shall thereby extend or be construed to extend to any such Towns.[52]

Thus Amherstburg, Chatham, Guelph, Perth, Simcoe and Woodstock were to be separated from the townships surrounding them and established for all intents and purposes as incorporated villages, but be given the honorary title of town for legal purposes. A second group of villages, Barrie, L'Original, Queenston and Sandwich, were also designated as "Towns" for the same reasons, but these were so small that they were not separated from the townships for municipal purposes. There was, however, an unexpected complication to this whole affair. When the official version of the *Municipal Act* was printed, Schedule D listing the affected villages was omitted from the Bill in error. Thus to the surprise and consternation of Guelph's residents, they had to wait an additional year in order to achieve separate municipal status. In 1850 a second Municipal Act was passed,[53] confirming Guelph's dual status. On January 1, 1851, the new "Town" of Guelph came into being.

To no one's surprise, the changes introduced by the Baldwin Municipal Act caused consid-erable dissention. With the incorporation of Guelph as a village, and because the Municipal Act redrew district boundaries, other neighbouring towns saw an opportunity to seize from Guelph much of the territory which had come under Guelph's administrative control in 1840. At stake were not only the fees and salaries of the various municipal officials, but the increase in trade generated by farmers, businessmen and settlers who were forced to visit Guelph to conduct their affairs.

Of the challenges presented to Guelph, two were most serious: that of Owen Sound which wished to create a new district out of the northern townships of Wellington and the western townships of Simcoe; and that of Galt which wanted to create a district to be called "Bruce" from portions of Wellington, Gore, Brock and Talbot districts.[54] The Galt proposal was particularly galling to Guelph. Not only did Galt propose to incorporate the Townships of Brant, Burford, Blenheim, Dumfries, Waterloo and Wilmot into the proposed Bruce district, but it also demanded that Puslinch be added as well. The *Guelph Advertiser*, already unhappy at the proposed loss of Waterloo and Wilmot was furious at the suggestion that Puslinch should be detached from Wellington District. In its best ironical tone the *Advertiser* editorialized:

DIVISION OF THE DISTRICT
Great are the exertions put forth by property holders and *expectant* office-holders, in various parts of the Province, to obtain divisions of Districts, and none seem more industrious than the inhabitants of the neighbouring village of Galt. Although only 14 miles from Guelph, the inhabitants anticipate being the centre of a new District in a few months, but to enable them to obtain a sufficient population to make even a pretension to such a position, they purpose taking to themselves the fairest portion of

our own; and not content with claiming such Townships as Wilmot and Waterloo, they actually propose coming within some three miles of this Town, claiming the supervision and protection of a considerable portion of Puslinch.

We admire industry and perseverance, and to this extent cannot but approve of the efforts of that enterprising village to elevate itself and increase its importance, but we cannot commend the evident wish to raise themselves on our ruins, which would be the case were they to succeed in their endeavours. . . .Already the village of Sydenham (Owen Sound) anticipates being a District Town, taking from us quite a number of Townships; and if Galt should succeed, we do not see why Fergus or Elora should not next put forth their claims, leaving this Town, perhaps, the Township of Guelph and Eramosa only.[55]

Guelph's civic leaders, of course, immediately undertook an active campaign to frustrate Galt's expansionary designs. A series of meetings were proposed to rally public support and to raise the funds necessary for a vigorous defense of Guelph's interests. These meetings were highly organized with speakers, motions and arguments carefully prepared in advance. Typical of these was the meeting held on December 26, 1848, in the Guelph Court House. The report in the *Guelph Advertiser* sets the tone:

In compliance with a Requisition, the Sheriff called a Public Meeting of the Inhabitants of the District, to take measures for opposing the division of the District, contemplated by the Inhabitants of Galt and neighbourhood, which was held in the Court House, on Tuesday last. This notice was very short, but under the circumstances the attendance on the occasion was much more numerous than expected; whilst nearly every man in the neighbourhood was present, and all showed a determination to resist the encroachment attempted on our limits in that direction. Dr. [Henry] Orton introduced the subject in a speech in which he explained the objects aimed at by the Bruceites, and the unenviable position in which we should be placed by seeing a new

District start up and take from us one-third of our present population, and approach within about two miles of the District Town. He was by no means inimical to the prosperity of Galt, and if it could obtain the rank of a District Town, without injury to others, he had no objection; but he protested against its being done at the expense of Guelph. Mr. Allan looked upon the attempt of the people of Galt as the greatest piece of impudence and presumption that he ever knew; and felt quite satisfied that no Government would comply with such a request. . . . The various speakers supported their resolutions in a manner that showed they not only understood the subject, but also meant what they said; and if we may look upon the meeting as an index to the feelings of the District, the separatists have a labour to perform, before they accomplish their object, which may yet surprise them.[56]

A series of resolutions were then passed condemning Galt and the District of Bruce, pledging the residents to untiring opposition to the proposal, and setting up a committee to draft a counter-petition against the separation. In addition a standing committee composed of George J. Grange, William Dummer Powell, Charles J. Mickle, J. McLean, Alfred A. Baker and John Smith was established and given the power to "add to their numbers, to collect subscriptions and to take such other means as they may deem necessary to carry out the objects of this Meeting."[57] In all some £49. 13s. 10d. was raised to conduct the fight.[58]

In contrast to the strength of feeling against Galt's proposals to create "Bruce District," there was considerable sympathy for the needs expressed by Owen Sound for a more convenient seat of government. No doubt two important considerations helped stimulate this sympathetic attitude: first, the whole northern half of the district, thinly settled as it was, created less business for Guelph than did the single township of Puslinch; second, the rapid expansion of population inland from Owen Sound and Georgian Bay would inevitably create a demand for costly roads, bridges and services which would bear heavily on the wealthier southern townships. Thus although not promoting the separation of the northern part of the district, there was little incentive for Guelph to fight for its retention. Therefore the same meeting which so strongly opposed the creation of "Bruce", approved of the creation of the district of "Owen Sound." A resolution to this effect was proposed by John Howitt and seconded by C. Davidson.[59] The *Advertiser* commented that "A frank acknowledgment was made that no opposition would be offered to the North-Western Townships being set off, whenever they thought themselves able to bear the necessary expenses. . ."[60]

Although the Court House meeting was a resounding success, disquieting rumours began to circulate. Galt, it was said, had the support of several influential members including Francis Hincks, M.P.P. for Oxford, and a petition was being circulated by Galt's leaders which, it was claimed, had been signed by no less than 25,000 ratepayers and householders in the proposed district.[61]

Immediately counter-petitions were written up, and a number of residents hired to take them around to the various townships to obtain signatures.[62] In January a delegation from Guelph lead by John Smith travelled to Toronto to discover the mood of the legislators concerning Galt's proposals. They were able to report, with considerable relief that there appeared to be little general sentiment in Galt's favour.[63] Later in January and again in March, Smith journeyed to Montreal (which since 1844 had been the seat of Parliament) to continue Guelph's fight to retain its territorial

control. In spite of the early optimism of the Toronto visit, the Montreal trips revealed disquieting news.

When Robert Baldwin decided to complete the transformation of local municipal government from rule by Quarter Session to self-government by locally elected councils, he took the concept of community autonomy one step further than had hitherto been contemplated. In order to give local regions the greatest voice on both the municipal and provincial levels, he decided to break the large districts up into smaller units of roughly equal population and to base the provincial electoral system on these smaller units.

When John Smith travelled to Montreal in March, 1849, to oppose the creation of "Bruce" he found that although the Galt-proposed division had not been acted upon, a much more sweeping dismemberment of Wellington District was contemplated. Smith despondently reported to the *Advertiser* that:

The Counties Division Bill. . .will eventually enable the Galt people to accomplish all that we oppose, and all they can desire.—This measure contemplates the division of this District into the Counties of Waterloo, Wellington, and the United Counties of Grey and Peel. These will remain united for judicial and municipal purposes, till such time as any county wishes to be set apart. The County in which the Court House, etc., is situated, is to be called the senior county, and the others junior counties.[64]

Galt's businessmen, however, not content to wait for the three years required by the various Acts to achieve separation of their area, pushed forward the bill to create the County of Bruce. It was soundly defeated, not even being allowed to be presented as a private member's bill. The *Guelph Advertiser* took the occasion to have the last word:

For two years the [Galt] *Reporter* has made strenuous efforts to injure Guelph, by the most unfair means, but we conceive that the moral state of a community may be best judged of by the character of its journals; and if such be the case, the falsehoods and scurrilous language of the *Reporter* has done more to injure the place that supports such a publication than anything that journal may say of another community,—As a specimen of the style adopted by our contemporary, we copy the following from the article to which we have been referring:—

"They who, like our friend of the Guelph *Advertiser* exhibit the exquisitely decent sympathy of

Adam J. Fergusson, first Judge of the Wellington District Court.

rejoicing over our defeat, may yet have occasion to repeat the whine of past times, when, like a dog with a pan to his tail, he was sent home howling from Montreal, and screaming along the road that Guelph was abandoned by God and man, and has nothing left but the *Advertiser*, which belonged to neither.[65]

Unfortunately, from Guelph's point of view, Smith's worst fears were quickly realized. Almost immediately after the new County of Waterloo (as Wellington District was renamed) came into being, agitations for separation were begun in all the junior counties. In 1852 the process of separation was far enough advanced that the county's name was changed from Waterloo to the United Counties of Wellington, Waterloo and Grey. When Waterloo completed its necessary buildings that year it was allowed to separate, and the remaining region was called the United Counties of Wellington and Grey. In 1853 Grey's buildings were completed and it separated as well. Thus on January 1, 1854, the present County of Wellington, with minor changes, came into being. The one consolation in the whole process was that Galt, Guelph's hated rival, had failed in its bid to acquire the county seat of Waterloo; Berlin had acquired that honour.

With the dismantling of Wellington District went a significant part of Guelph's income and trade from the outlying townships. Not only were the salaries and fees of Guelph's officials greatly reduced as settlers went to Berlin and Owen Sound to transact their business, but lawyers, innkeepers, doctors, merchants and craftsmen lost the trade that resulted when residents came to town for official purposes. In order to counteract these losses, Guelph's residents turned wholeheartedly to the politics of roads and railways.

Toll-Gate at Dundas, C.W. (Courtesy Public Archives of Ontario)

IV

Roads and Toll Gates

Guelph's transformation from a backwoods village of some seven hundred residents in 1843 to a bustling commercial and industrial town fifteen years later was the result of good fortune and a concerted effort by the people of Guelph to make their town the centre of commerce in Wellington District. One important element in that struggle was a combination of government subsidization and private investment to create the network of roads and railways necessary for the achievement of that goal.

Economic development was greatly aided between 1843 and 1856 by the settlement of the area north of Guelph. As Table **XIII** illustrates, population grew rapidly, and not only did the old townships—Erin, Puslinch and Guelph—double and triple their population but six new townships received their first settlers.

At the same time there was a rapid increase in agricultural production, particularly in the longer settled townships. Table **XIV** shows that acreage under cultivation increased by fifty percent between 1841 and 1843 and an additional fifty percent between 1843 and 1847. Large scale immigration after 1847

(Courtesy Public Archieves of Canada)

79

brought about the opening of new areas, and for the first time, provided a significant number of labourers. Thus cleared acreage virtually doubled between 1847 and 1851, and Table XV indicates that livestock production followed an almost identical pattern during the decade.

Table XVI points out both the strength and weakness of agricultural development in 1851. On the one hand, the rapid expansion of population, acreage under cultivation and livestock, meant that at last Guelph's commercial stability was assured. On the other hand, in spite of the establishment of a livestock fair and sale in 1828, farmers had not as yet oriented themselves to cash crop production.

Although the farmer was perfectly willing to trade produce for a wide variety of services and goods in the village, this trade was much more characterized by the variety of services than by its volume. Businessmen with money, therefore, found that no single enterprise could absorb all their capital but that it was necessary to enter a wide variety of businesses in order to put their money to work. Thus William Allan was owner-manager of a grist mill, a distillery and a carding mill, in addition to being a building contractor. Despite this, he had no distinct advantage over his competitors who had much less capital but concentrated their energies on a single enterprise.

Nevertheless, in spite of these problems, Guelph could point to some considerable achievements. The successful struggle to divide Gore District and to make Guelph the capital of Wellington District had brought about a

Table XIII
Wellington County, Population by Township, 1840-1851[1]

Municipality	1840	1851
Erin	1,256	3,590
Puslinch	1,617	3,862
Guelph	2,290	2,879
Guelph Town.		1,860
Nichol	1,002	2,450
Pilkington		1,990
Garafraxa	284	2,083
Eramosa	863	2,350
Peel	—	2,435
Maryborough	—	994
Minto	—	
Arthur	—	1,803
Luther	—	
Amaranth	—	500
Total	7,312	26,796

Table XIV
Wellington County, Acres Under Cultivation, 1840-1851[2]

Municipality	1840	1843	1847	1851
Erin	5,175	6,925	9,830	19,950
Puslinch	5,704	11,489*	16,805	25,850
Guelph	8,959	11,925	14,737	18,456
Nichol	3,266	4,819	7,168	10,666
Garafraxa	617	1,054	1,973	5,749
Eramosa	4,734	6,405	9,334	16,241
Peel	—	—	—	6,993
Maryborough	—	—	—	1,693
Minto	—	—	—	
Arthur	—	—	—	4,611
Luther	—	—	—	
Amaranth	—	292	522	1,718
Pilkington	—	—	—	7,154
Total	28,455	42,909	60,369	119,081

* Estimated

spurt of immediate growth. Table XVII shows that in just three years the population of Guelph doubled and other aspects of economic life kept pace. By 1846, however, this growth had begun to taper off.

In deliberations concerning the factors which contributed to its economic weakness, Guelph turned again and again to the problem of transportation. As matters stood, roads were impassable much of the year and with shipment by road and water expensive and difficult, it was not worth the farmers' effort to expand cash crop production beyond what was necessary for an exchange for local services.

A long editorial in the *Guelph Advertiser* of March, 1847, pointed out the severe hardships created for the inland businessmen and farmers:

Table XV
Wellington County, Milk Cows by Township, 1840-1851[3]

Municipality	1840	1843	1847	1851
Erin	553	637	839	1,445
Puslinch	641	802*	1,029	1,444
Guelph	860	951	1,098	1,155
Nichol	364	440	518	670
Garafraxa	82	147	249	593
Eramosa	424	539	700	1,066
Peel	—	—	—	697
Maryborough	—	—	—	198
Minto	—	—	—	
Arthur	—	—	— }	464
Luther	—	—	—	
Amaranth	—	36	60	156
Pilkington	—	—	—	515
Total	2,924	3,552	4,493	8,403

* Estimated

The ice-bound condition of the harbours of our great Lakes, and of the River St. Lawrence during the winter season, renders our situation for five or six months of the year completely isolated, and we are completely cut off from commercial communication with the ocean and with Europe. The consequence of it is that our farmers suffer severely in the diminished price for their grain, to which they are obliged to submit during one half of the year; the season too when many of them are compelled to sell; and when prices rule high at New York, Boston, London and Liverpool. The Canada merchant who buys during the season must deduct from the New York prices five or six months' interest for his money, during which time he must store the grain till the opening of the navigation. When he buys in the beginning of the winter, he does so with a trembling consciousness of the extremely hazardous character of the speculation. . .At this moment, wheat which sells for more than a dollar and a half a bushel in New York market, will scarcely fetch a dollar a bushel in Toronto. This deduction from the price of the grain which our farmers have to submit to, arises, in great measure, from our want of means of communication. . . .[1]

Not only did farmers in the interior townships bear the burden of the general difficulties caused by poor transportation, they also suffered from the particular difficulties of the inadequate roads of Wellington District. For example, one pioneer family, the Tuckers of Bosworth, reported that when they moved to the area in the 1840's:

The townships of Peel, Luther, and Maryborough were solid bush. Their journey thence included boat from Toronto to Hamilton, the Brock Road from there to Guelph, and through unbroken bush from Elora to Bosworth. Brock Road itself was but a mud highway, and when the team hauling the Tucker belongings stuck on a hillside, neighbours had to be called on to assist in pushing the wagon to the top. A wagon was used as far as Elora, but after that a jumper was all that could be hauled through the bush. . . .At the beginnings of the life

Table XVI
Wellington County, Agricultural Development, in 1851[5]

Municipality	Farms, 20 Acres and up	Estimated Acres Cultivated	Acres Cultivated per Farm	Acres Wheat per Farm	Bushels Wheat per Farm	Bushels per Acre
Erin	490	19,350	39.5	9.1	127.6	14.0
Puslinch	496	25,690	51.8	11.5	183.4	15.9
Guelph	343	18,176	53.0	10.9	215.6	19.7
Nichol	221	10,626	48.1	9.7	156.4	16.1
Garafraxa	332	5,529	16.7	6.7	82.8	12.4
Eramosa	319	15,761	49.4	10.3	204.9	19.9
Peel	398	6,813	17.1	5.7	61.3	10.7
Maryborough	167	1,693	4.1	3.8	32.4	8.5
Minto Arthur Peel }	328	4,511	13.8	3.7	32.1	8.6
Amaranth	85	1,708	20.1	4.5	76.1	16.8
Pilkington	255	7,034	27.6	7.6	125.4	15.8
Total	3,434	116,891				
Average			34.0	8.2	126.3	15.4

on the bush farm, it cost a dollar a barrel to have flour hauled from Elora to Bosworth.[6]

The lack of good transportation facilities in Canada was aggravated by the fact that the main source of provincial funds came from tariffs on imports, and, with trade so severely hampered, there was little money to spend on the importation of goods. What money there was in the provincial treasury was quarrelled over endlessly by the elected representatives, eager to get as much as possible for their own constituency. The inevitable result of such a situation was that major undertakings were virtually impossible and the small amount of funds forthcoming were spent in patching up roads that had deteriorated almost to the point of uselessness.

At the local level, the situation was even more hopeless. The primary source of road improvement was the statutory labour which every adult male was required to perform each year. This varied according to the amount of assessment on each person's property and was fixed by statute. In 1837 the rates of statute labour shown in Table XVIII were in effect.

Of course, the wealthier inhabitants hired someone to do this work for them. Although statute labour did contribute significantly towards the development of local roads, residents objected strongly to working away from their neighbourhood when their own roads were still inadequate.

The main difficulty in building trunk roads was the incapacity of the district councils to

Table XVII
Town of Guelph: Growth from 1843 to 1847 [7]

	1843	1846	1847		1843	1846	1847
Gaol & Court House for the Wellington District				Stone Masons	15	18	21
				Bricklayers & Plaisterers [sic]	7	11	13
Population	700	1357	1480	Watch Makers	1	2	1
Houses	234	342	374	Gun Smith	—	1	1
Grist Mills (13 runs of Stones)	3	4	4	Iron Foundry	—	1	1
Saw Mills	1	2	2	Boot & Shoemakers	11	19	25
Distilleries	4	4	4	Confectioners	1	1	2
Churches with Spires	3	3	3	Carpenters & Builders	20	31	37
Plain Chapels	2	3	4	Breweries	3	3	2
Stores general asst. of goods	14	19	22	Painters & Glaziers	2	3	3
Bakers	3	4	4	Private Classical School	—	1	1
Saddlers & Harness Makers	2	3	3	Dist. Grammar D	1	1	1
Coachmaker	1	1	1	Common Schools	2	5	5
Wheelwrights	4	5	6	Bank Agencies	—	2	2
Blacksmiths	6	6	7	Mutual Fire Insurance Co.	—	1	1
Tinware Factory	1	1	1	Hook & Ladder Company	—	1	1
Butchers	3	5	6	Printers & Book Sellers	—	2	3
Lawyers	2	4	4	Well Sinkers & Pump Makers	—	2	2
Surgeons	4	4	4	Cabinet Makers	4	4	11
Druggists	1	2	2	Chair Makers	4	6	
Taverns	9	7	9	Nurseryman & Gardeners	2	1	1
Coopers	2	4	4	Tailors	8	11	13
Tanneries	2	4	4	Dressmakers	7	9	9
Weekly Newspapers	—	1	2	Milliner	—	—	1
Daily Royal Mail (4 horse coach)	—	1	1	Hair Dresser	—	1	2
Daily covered Stages	—	3	2	Auctioneers etc.	—	2	2
Livery Stables	—	1	1	Ironmongers	—	1	1
Reading Room	—	1	1	Carding Machine etc.	—	1	1
Book Club	—	1	1	Cricket Club	—	1	1
Brick Yards	1	2	2	Circulating Library	—	1	1

Table XVIII
Statute Labour

Value of Assessment in £	Days of Labour Required
Up to 25	2
25 to 50	3
50 to 75	4
75 to 100	5
100 to 150	6
150 to 200	7
200 to 250	8
250 to 300	9
300 to 350	10
350 to 400	11
400 to 500*	12

* With each increase of £100 in assessment above £500 requiring an additional day's labour.[8]

raise large sums of money from taxation. With a limitation of two pence per pound on the statutory assessment, money was not available for lare-scale development. With so little cash crop production, higher taxation would have created extreme hardship for the subsistence farmer. Thus there was strong opposition to laws that would open the door to more direct taxation.

In general, what money the district councils had available for road and bridge building was seldom used to undertake such works directly. Rather, these funds were used to encourage local initiative on the part of the inhabitants most directly affected by the public work. To have a bridge built those most interested in the project would get up a petition asking for money for the materials required. Upon the receipt of petitions from all parts of the district,

the councillors, at the Quarter Session, negotiated amongst themselves for a division of the money available. If the area's district councillor had managed to have funds allocated to the projected bridge, a by-law would be passed. In most cases, the labour necessary was supplied by the local residents as part of their statutory labour. After the bridge was completed to the satisfaction of the district surveyor, he reported to the district council and the money was paid out to the supplier of the materials. This was cumbersome and inefficient, although it did reduce the outlay of that scarcest of all commodities—cash.

In spite of these difficulties, Guelph had attempted to have the Dundas Road improved to the point of usefulness. Acton Burrows describes one such attempt and its failure in 1838-1839:

During 1838 a movement was commenced for improving the road between Guelph and Dundas, much inconvenience being felt in consequence of the difficulties in travelling between the two points. . . . Several meetings were held to consider the matter but nothing definite was done until 1839, when a public meeting was called, Mr. Henry Strange being in the chair, and Mr. Thos. Saunders acting as secretary. It was then proposed that a survey should be made, for a road direct to Dundas, instead of going round by way of Waterloo. Subscription lists were opened to defray the expense of the survey, which was entrusted to Mr. R.W. Kerr, of Flamborough West. The estimated cost was £31,159. 17s.7d. or £1285. 16s.8d. per mile. . . . Soon after this had been done, Mr. Henry Strange, who had been the prime mover in the matter suddenly died, and no further action was taken for some time. . . .[9]

In the face of Guelph's failure to improve the Guelph and Dundas road, the success of the merchants and businessmen along the Dundas and Waterloo road in persuading the government to take it over as a public work, was particularly galling. In 1838, Absalom Shade and James Crooks, the local elected members to the Legislative Assembly (both of whom were mill owners with property along the Dundas and Waterloo road) had managed to have a substantial sum of money voted for its improvement. The road was made a government work and the major businessmen along the route were named trustees, responsible for its management and the collection of tolls from its users.[10]

By 1846, so successful had the road's trustees been in the improvement of the road with money received from the collection of tolls and from further government grants, that the *Guelph Advertiser* could report, somewhat enviously, that:

The formation of a mile and a half of new macadamized road, through the swamp between Galt and Dundas, is now proceeding rapidly, under the contractor, Mr. Merigold. When this is completed, little more than three miles of this dismal portion of horse-murdering road will remain to be completed. The trustees deserve every praise for their exertions. They have saved the whole of the sum necessary to complete this improvement out of their income from the tolls besides keeping the road in complete repair; and having on hand a large quantity of broken stone. Mr. Merigold's contract for the work is £998. . . .[11]

As long as the Guelph and Dundas Road was in a poor state, improvements to the Dundas and Waterloo road south of Galt helped to reduce the cost of goods in Guelph. Improvements north of Galt, however, gave the Berlin and Waterloo merchants and millers a distinct advantage over those of Guelph when competing for the trade of the northern townships. Nor were Berlin's merchants blind to that fact. For example, in 1838 a group of businessmen

from Berlin and Preston incorporated the Waterloo Bridge Company to build a first class bridge over the Grand River, thus removing the last major barrier to traffic between those villages.[12] With a capital of £750, it not only improved transportation but by charging tolls, made a profit for its owners as well.

Not only was Guelph falling behind Galt and Berlin in its competitive position in the 1840's, but a second threat began to develop for control of its market area, this time to the east of the village. In 1840, as a first step toward developing a road system into Esquesing and Garafraxa, the leading merchants in Bronte incorporated themselves as a harbour company and undertook to raise £5,000 for the improvement of harbour facilities.[13] Although considerable improvements were made to Bronte harbour, scarcity of money prevented any rapid improvement of the Bronte road.

In 1846, however, Guelph's businessmen faced a much more serious threat from the same direction. The Chisholm interests and their associates in Oakville undertook to open a major traffic link between Oakville and Owen Sound which would cut directly through Guelph's developing market area. The project, as envisioned by the Oakville interests, sought to combine a privately owned toll road from Oakville to Fergus, with a government subsidized road running north from that point to Owen Sound. Capitalized at £20,000, the Trafalgar, Esquesing and Erin Road Company provided a formidable threat.[14]

The significance of this road project to Guelph's future was not lost on Guelph's business community.[15] In order to stave off ruin, Guelph attempted to fight fire with fire. If transportation systems created the threat, then the answer must come from the creation of a Guelph-based system capable of ensuring its dominant position. The problem, of course, was money. The first solution sought—because it was based upon British shareholders' money—was the promotion of a railroad from Toronto through the Guelph area to Lake Huron.

In 1836, a group of Toronto businessmen had chartered the Toronto and Lake Huron Railroad Company[16] which proposed to build a railway from Toronto to some point on the navigable waters of Lake Huron within the Home District. Its proposed capital of £500,000 was, of course, far beyond the resources of Upper Canada, even when the government promised to lend the company £100,000. Thus the project collapsed quickly when the depression of 1837-1838 began to be felt. Even more fanciful was the Huron and Ontario Railroad Company chartered in the same year. Capitalized for £350,000, that company proposed to build a railroad from "Wellington Square, Burlington Bay or Dundas" to Goderich.[17] Needless to say, it collapsed before the Lieutenant-Governor's signature was dry on its charter. For the next few years, the whole idea that railways might be profitable enterprises in Canada became so improbable that these and several other projects were allowed to lapse.

Although the Toronto and Lake Huron project caused a good deal of interest and support in Guelph, a number of local businessmen were beginning to realize that whether or not the railway was built, good roads were still going to be necessary to bring the produce to market. What was needed, they decided, was a first class stone (macadamized) or plank road running from Dundas, through Guelph to

Owen Sound. Faced with the fact that the Provincial Government consistently refused to build such a road, the only alternative was to form a joint stock company and build it themselves. It was an undertaking of major proportions, but should Oakville's road to Fergus be built first, they were faced with almost certain ruin. Having reached that conclusion, in October, 1846, they announced their decision. The *Guelph Advertiser* carried this advertisement:

NOTICE

An Application will be made to the Provincial Parliament at its next session, to incorporate a Joint Stock Company for the purpose of improving the direct Road leading from the Town of Guelph to the Macadamized Road in the Township of West Flamborough by planking or Macadamizing the same.

Dated, this 4th day of October, 1846.

G.S. Tiffany, Benjamin Thurtell, Wm. Notman, William Armstrong, Jas. B. Ewart, James Hodgert, R. Juson, George J. Grange, W. Leslie, Wm. Clarke, James Wright, T. Sandilands, Al. Dingwall Fordyce.[18]

A similar notice a few weeks later announced that an application would be made to incorporate a second joint stock road company from Guelph to Arthur.[19]

In July, 1847, the Provincial Government finally passed the bills incorporating the two road companies. The incorporators named in the acts represented the most important businessmen in the area. For the Guelph and Dundas road they were James B. Morden, Walter Colcleugh, John Weir, William Miller, William McKindlay, George S. Tiffany, William Notman, James Bell Ewart, Richard Juson, James Leslie, James Wright, Benjamin Thurtell, James Hodgert, George John Grange, William Clarke, Thomas Sandilands, Alexander D. Fordyce and Adam J. Fergusson.[20] For the Guelph and Arthur road the incorporators were: George J. Grange, Adam J. Fergusson, Benjamin Bobington, Daniel MacNab, Alexander D. Fordyce, William Hewat, William Clarke, Thomas Sandilands, James Hodgert, William Mutch, Thomas Webster, Alexander Drysdale, John Watt, George Jardine, Gilbert Hunter, Samuel Broadfoot, George C. Hamilton, Alex. Harvey and John McNaught.[21]

In addition to having received the charters for the two road companies, Guelph received a second piece of good news in August, 1847. The Provincial Government, under pressure from James Webster, the local member of the assembly, had voted its first significant subsidy to the Guelph road system—the sum of £500 for the Guelph and Dundas road and an additional £1,500 for the Owen Sound road. The *Guelph Herald*, its spirits buoyed up by this news, waxed eloquent about Guelph's future prospects:

It is alike due to Mr. Webster, and the constituency which he so ably represents, to state that the people of the Wellington District are indebted to his exertions for the improvement of the Owen's Sound Road, the establishment of a weekly mail on that route, and also for £500 to be applied to the improvement of the Brock Road, and the incorporation of a Company for macadamizing the said road. . . . With the Brock Road once finished, and the Owen's Sound Road in a tolerable condition, we need entertain no fears for the future prosperity of Guelph.[22]

In spite of the optimism displayed by the *Guelph Herald*'s editor, the promoters of the road company found that potential investors in the company's stock were most reluctant to risk their savings in such an untried project. Although all the local businessmen vocally supported the project and unanimously pro-

claimed its necessity, after nearly a month of intensive salesmanship only about £2,000 worth of shares had been subscribed in Guelph.[23] When the sales campaign was extended to Dundas and Hamilton, it met with a stony refusal by investors. As a private enterprise, the Guelph and Dundas Road Company was a failure.

Under these conditions, the challenge to Guelph by the Trafalgar, Esquesing and Erin Road Company took on crisis proportions. However the leading public figures in Guelph and Dundas, the merchants and millers, held virtually all of the local public offices, being magistrates, public officials and district councillors simultaneously. As such, they not only controlled most of the private capital in the area, but the public purse as well. Having decided that the Guelph and Dundas Road Company represented too great a risk for their private investment, they now turned to the district treasuries for the solution to their problems.

The technique of transforming the Guelph and Dundas Road project from a private enterprise to a public work was simple; it was only necessary to persuade the two district councils involved, Wellington and Gore, to buy all the shares. However, the political problems presented were considerably more difficult. The farmers in townships like Erin, Eramosa, Nichol or Garafraxa were not concerned as to whether the improved road into their area ran ultimately to Oakville or Dundas. In either case they would benefit.

In October, the *Guelph Advertiser* printed a series of anonymous letters signed "Aliquis" (a favorite device of editors to put forth controversial opinions) outlining the advantages of road-building on a large scale cash basis rather than relying on statute labour supplemented by an occasional government or district council grant. The first major advantage of the cash approach, they argued, was that not only could good roads be created immediately but, by charging tolls, it would be possible to have the users pay, and the actual cost to the farmer would be greatly reduced.[24]

The second part of "Aliquis' " proposal was even more controversial, because it required the subsistence farmers to move towards a cash-crop economy and required all farmers to pay a cash tax for roads rather than performing statute labour—a duty which was generally done during periods when farm tasks were minimal. The argument for increased money taxation was rather complex: higher cash taxes would allow the district councils to borrow more money. With this enhanced borrowing power, local roads could be improved immediately rather than awaiting the slow progress from statute labour.[25]

But how would the farmers benefit from the removal of their option of a right to perform their statute labour themselves? "Aliquis", for the sake of analysis, divided them into two classes:

Farmers who have considerable clearances, or are in easy circumstances, are quite aware that their presence at home is worth more than 2s.6d. per diem (the wages of a common laborer) that they are often called out to the roads at inconvenient seasons, and that their waggons and implements are generally more exposed to injury there than elsewhere. . . .There is, however, another, and perhaps more numerous section of this class, to whom money is of more value than what we are in the habit of considering its equivalent—time; and to whom the idea of paying an additional dollar of tax would be anything but agreeable. Well, in addition to the benefit this body would derive in common with others from the improvement of our common

thoroughfares, I would anticipate that it would be also the recipient of the funds disbursed. The work to be periodically accomplished being offered to public competition, in moderately small portions, such persons having a part of their labor to dispose of, would find a ready market by uniting in small parties to take up the contracts, to be implemented in their respective neighborhoods, and thus, if considering themselves aggrieved by a money rate, they would have an opportunity of reconverting their money into labor, and replenishing their exchequer by contract.[26]

Where the poorer farmers were to get the specialized equipment and capital to undertake successfully such contracting, "Aliquis" did not say.

The most revolutionary aspect of these proposals, and one which would be heard more and more frequently over the next decade, was that, contrary to general belief, debts, particularly public debts, were good things. If public works had a future as well as a present public value, "Aliquis" argued, why should present users be the ones to pay for them. If the residents of Wellington District borrowed money to build high quality public roads, on ten, fifteen or twenty-year debentures, present users would escape the high capital cost such works entailed.[27]

The doctrine that one should spend money now and leave it for future generations to pay the cost was novel indeed in a farming community. Nevertheless, whenever proposals for major public works came up, both the *Herald* and the *Advertiser* would hereafter invariably justify these expenditures on the grounds that future users should pay.

Finally, whenever strenuous objections were raised to such proposals, the promoters of the road would retreat to proclaiming that the question of debt and who should pay was purely speculative. The roads would surely not only pay for themselves, but produce a large profit for the taxpayers. In the face of such vehement assurances by the area's civic leaders, objections soon melted away and public enthusiasm for the projected road was reported from all quarters.

In October, 1847, the first formal step towards the conversion of the Guelph and Dundas road from private enterprise to a public work was taken when a series of meetings was arranged between the members of the Gore and the Wellington District Councils. The *Guelph Advertiser* of October fifteenth carried this note:

The Warden read a letter from John O. Hatt, Esq., expressing his regret at not being able to attend this sitting of the [Wellington District] Council; and inviting them to send a deputation to the Gore District Council at its sitting next month, to confer respecting the improvement of the Brock Road.[28]

The Council agreed that such a delegation should be sent.

Businessmen in Hamilton and Dundas were as anxious as those in Guelph to keep the trade of Wellington District flowing through their towns. One local paper, the *Dundas Warder*, made these arguments in favour of the Gore District Council making a major investment in the road:

The people of this town are largely interested in its completion. Dundas is the natural depot for the reception of the products of this fine country, stretching from Flamboro' to Owen Sound. . . .Nor are the inhabitants of this portion of the Gore District one atom less interested. It is to be hoped, therefore, that the ensuing session of the District Council will not be permitted to close without something being done to *amend the ways* of the Brock road. . . .[29]

The November meeting of the joint councils

was successful when the Gore District Council agreed to purchase £9,000 worth of shares, enough to construct the road from the Dundas and Waterloo road to the Wellington District boundary line.[30]

As soon as the delegation from Guelph reported that the Gore District Council had agreed to purchase £9,000 worth of shares, a special meeting of the Wellington District Council was called for December 15, 1847, to discuss the road proposal. By then, however, the result was a foregone conclusion. With very little debate, the Council agreed to issue debentures to the amount of £9,000 in order to purchase their share of the road stock. Guelph's future, everyone agreed, was now assured.

Having made the decision, the Wellington District Council moved with despatch. Within days, this advertisement appeared:

£9,000 WANTED

The Council of the Wellington District having passed a By-Law for the construction of the Brock Road, in conjunction with the Gore District Council, which By-Law authorizes the Warden of this District to borrow the sum of £9,000, bearing interest at 6 per cent, payable half yearly, in Debentures of £5, £10, £15, £20, and £25, each, on the credit of the District and, the Tolls arising from the said Road,—Persons having funds at their command, and being anxious to facilitate so desirable an object, can apply (if by letter post paid) to

James Wright,
Guelph, Dec. 16, 1847.   Warden[31]

The Wellington District bonds found a ready market locally and the entire £9,000 issue was taken up by Guelph residents as follows: Alexander Drysdale, £2,000; Thomas Sandilands, £3,980; George J. Grange, £600; Frederick Marcon, £1,680; Ann Stevenson,

£40; J. Foster, £300; and Mrs. Lamprey, £400.[32] What was lacking in Guelph, it is clear, was not capital but risk capital—and leading merchants and millers clearly preferred to put their money into their own enterprises rather than into an untried venture such as a road company. On the other hand, those persons who purchased the bonds were not businessmen but investors who were looking for a safe and assured income from the interest they would receive. The district bonds provided such an opportunity.

In addition to the merchants and millers of Guelph and Dundas, a second group of investors anxiously awaited the completion of the Guelph and Dundas road. These were the land speculators whose holdings would be enhanced by local urban growth. Thus as soon as it became clear that the road would be built, plans for new sub-divisions in Fergus, Elora and Guelph were rushed to completion and advertisements were placed in newspapers throughout the province, explaining why potential investors should immediately rush to Guelph, Elora and Fergus to benefit from the coming boom.

In Guelph, the largest of these developments was on the east side of the Speed River bounded by Eramosa Road, Metcalfe Street and Budd Street. This huge area was the first significant extension of Guelph since 1827, and Map 6 shows the location as drawn by Donald McDonald in October, 1847. In July, 1848, this advertisement (which would run unchanged for years) appeared in the local newspapers:

300 TOWN LOTS FOR SALE IN GUELPH
At a moderate upset price, and liberal credit or liberal discount on the purchase money down. The Subscriber offers

THREE HUNDRED TOWN LOTS
for sale, as shown by a new plan of the Town of Guelph, in the possession of Francis Kerr, Esq., who will state terms, point out the Lots on the ground and procure letters of occupation of Title deeds for parties purchasing.

John McDonald[33]

The second major development in Guelph was that of George S. Tiffany, a leading Hamilton businessman and one of the main promoters of the Guelph and Dundas road. In April, 1848, this advertisement appeared:

40 TOWN LOTS FOR SALE IN GUELPH

The Subscriber offers for Sale, Forty TOWN LOTS, fronting on Woolwich and Strange Streets, in the survey lately made by F. Kerr, Esq., for him.

The contemplated improvement of Woolwich Street will much enhance the value of these Lots, and render them among the most desirable for private residences in Town.

The terms are five years for the principal, interest payable half yearly. . . .

Geo. S. Tiffany.[34]

Meanwhile, the promoters of the Guelph and Dundas road were able to proceed with officially organizing the company. On January 3, 1848, the nominal shareholders (including the wardens of Wellington and Gore Districts) met at the British Hotel in Guelph to elect a board of directors to manage the road's affairs. At the meeting, George S. Tiffany, Samuel Clarke, William Millar and John O Hatt, all of Hamilton or Dundas, and James Wright, Adam J. Fergusson and Dr. William Clarke of Guelph, were elected directors.[35] At a subsequent meeting, George S. Tiffany was elected president.[36]

On April 21, 1848, the *Guelph Advertiser* reported the following progress:

We have heard from good authority, that at the

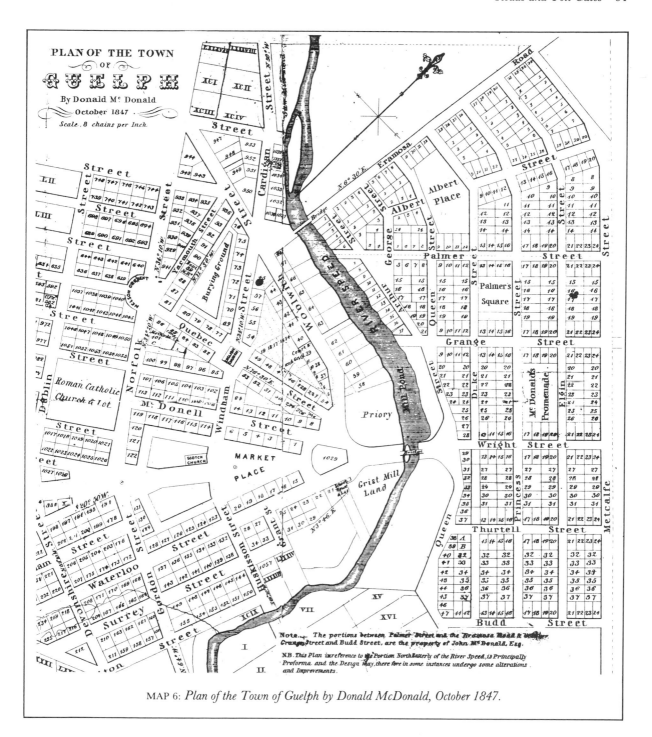

MAP 6: *Plan of the Town of Guelph by Donald McDonald, October 1847.*

meeting of the Directors, held here last week, the necessary steps were taken for laying off the whole road as soon as possible in sections, ready for tenders, and that there is a satisfactory prospect of the work being proceeded with at once; and we have to state, on like authority, that it was also resolved that the money on debentures advanced on the part of this District, shall be expended from Guelph to Freel's Inn, and the surplus (if any) below Freel's.[37]

Tenders for construction were called in June, and on July 13, 1848, the *Guelph Advertiser* announced joyously that:

. . . .we are able to announce the letting out of the contract for gravelling or macadamizing the road last week. . . .

On Friday last the arrangement was finally entered into by the Directors and a Mr. Cook, formerly a contractor on the Welland Canal. From seven to eight miles of the distance is to be macadamized at the rate of £1,230 per mile, and the remainder gravelled at £420 per mile. There is to be a bridge at each end of the road, of wood or stone, which have yet to be contracted for. We may expect to see some *200* men busily employed on the line next week, and the culverts are to be placed and the road graded during the present year, and the whole to be completed by September, 1849. It is anticipated that the whole of the road, including the toll-gates, etc., will not cost more than £20,000.[38]

The official sod-turning on the "Brock" road (the title "Guelph and Dundas" now generally was dropped by the local newspapers), which was set for July 21, 1848, gave local businessmen and public officials the opportunity to indulge themselves in the fulsome public oratory so dear to the civic booster's heart. The *Guelph Advertiser* printed this description of the event:

More than 200 persons assembled on the occasion, and we are informed that the procession was more than one fifth of a mile long, presenting a very animated appearance, with several banners fluttering in the breeze. After proceeding in this order along the Brock Road for four or five miles, they were met by the President of the Company, the Warden of the Gore District, Mr. Williamson of Stoney Creek, the contractor, the Gore District Surveyor, and John Wetenhall, Esq., M.P.P. On returning, the procession halted at Hamilton's Tavern, when the President, G.S. Tiffany, Esq., proceeded to a convenient place on the road, accompanied by the Directors, Committee, etc., and preceded by two persons carrying a pick and spade; when, after a short address on the importance of the undertaking, and the satisfaction he felt at the interest evinced by the inhabitants of the neighbourhood, he commenced the important ceremony by the use of both tools, and after a few words more, the company returned to their conveyances, and proceeded towards Guelph.[39]

The sod-turning was followed by a gala public dinner at Thorp's Hotel, where speeches and merriment lasted well into the night.

The actual construction of the road, which required the best part of two years, was noteworthy for only one event—after the completion of the bridge near Kerr's mills in Flamborough Township, the workmen took the night off to celebrate the event. While the festivities were progressing, the stone bridge fell, delaying the opening of that part of the road until 1850.[40]

In contrast to the relatively smooth progress of construction, the financial aspects of the road continued to create difficulties: first, the contractor ran into financial trouble; and second, £20,000 proved to be insufficient to complete the road. In the fall of 1848, Cook found himself short of cash, as money which he had expected from work on the Welland Canal failed to materialize. To get out of the difficulty Cook decided to pay the workmen in small denomination debentures of five shill-

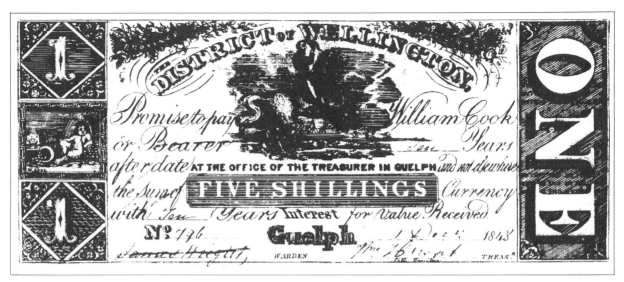

Wellington District Debenture.

ings, which he hoped would be treated as cash by the local storekeepers. On his request, Wellington District issued these debentures, which were then put in circulation by the workmen.[41]

The problem with this form of payment was that local storekeepers and banks had little interest in tying up their money in debentures and severely discounted them. After a sharp exchange between the Guelph and Hamilton newspapers, the notes were apparently withdrawn from circulation.[42]

The second problem, the shortage of funds to complete the road, was more serious. When Benjamin Thurtell assumed office as the Warden of Waterloo County in January, 1851, he discovered that not only had the entire £20,000 authorized capital of the Road Company been spent, but it was in debt, and the road was still incomplete. On March 18, 1851, he called a special meeting of the County Council to deal with the situation.

What was required, Thurtell believed, was

an amendment to the Act incorporating the Guelph and Dundas Road Company which would allow the Company to increase its capital by £2,000 and would also turn the road over to the County Councils so that closer supervision could be exercised over future expenditure. The Councils agreed, and in August, 1851, the Counties of Wentworth, Gore and Waterloo took over direct management of the "road.[43] With the increase in capital of £2,900, the road was rapidly completed and toll houses erected at three points along the route. In place of the old Board of Directors, eight Commissioners were appointed by the County Councils to manage the road.

Once the toll booths were in operation, however, a conflict arose in establishing the rate of tolls on the road.[44] The Waterloo County Council (which included present-day Wellington and Grey Counties) was concerned that no advantage be given to the millers and merchants of Galt and Berlin. In December, 1850, the Council passed a motion:

That this Council recommend, that the Directors of the Guelph and Dundas Road Company should cause the tolls to be collected at the several gates, to be as near as may be in proportion to the tolls collected upon the Galt and Dundas road, but not to exceed a reasonable rate.[45]

Based on this, whenever the Commissioners of the Dundas and Waterloo road raised or lowered their tolls, the Commissioners of the Guelph and Dundas road were quick to follow suit.

The problem of setting a rate of toll for the Guelph and Dundas road was complicated by an additional factor. It was desirable to collect tolls on a flat rate basis, whenever possible, in order to reduce debate and bad feelings between toll gate keepers and teamsters. Thus at

Toll Gate.
(Courtesy Public Archives of Canada)

first a rate of four pence per gate was set for teams and wagons. Unfortunately, such a flat rate encouraged overloading and soon caused severe damage to the road. In consequence the road Commissioners imposed a higher toll on heavy wagons in order to encourage lighter loads. Twelve barrels of flour were declared a "load", and teamsters were charged an additional penny per barrel over twelve up to fifteen. Over fifteen barrels, an additional charge of two pence per barrel was made. The millers and flour dealers of both Guelph and Dundas were furious.[46]

Shortly thereafter a delegation of millers from Guelph presented a petition to the Wellington County Council requesting that the tolls of flour be reduced:

The petition of the undersigned Millers of the Town of Guelph humbly sheweth,
That your petitioners view the making of good roads as one of the surest signs of the progress of the country, and hail the completion of the Road from Guelph to Dundas as one of the greatest improvements that has been effected in favor of this Town and County.

That it was anticipated the opening of the Road would place Guelph in a more favorable position than hitherto; would insure in the place a good market for agricultural produce, and especially for wheat; and induce more local manufacturers by the facilities presented for the same being conveyed more readily to the seaboard.

That your petitioners have done their utmost to meet these reasonable expectations in regard to a Wheat Market, and an increase in the manufacture of Flour, but find their efforts partially counteracted, and a tax imposed upon Milling and Wheat buying, by the additional tolls imposed upon flour—and flour alone—in passing over the aforesaid Road. . . .

Your petitioners therefore pray that. . .you may please. . .relieve your petitioners and others from the burden now imposed upon them.

And your petitioners will ever pray, etc.

David Allan,
J.C. Presant,
27th Jan., 1851.   Smith, Lynd & Co.[47]

The millers were successful in their petition. Two weighing machines were placed upon the road so that tolls could be collected according to weight. But, rather than penalize overloaded wagons, the rate of tolls was set up in such a way that heavy loads paid a much lower toll per 100 lbs. than did light loads. Thus a wagon driven empty or carrying a load up to 1,000 lbs. would pay four pence per gate, while wagons loaded with 3,500 lbs. might pay as little as six pence.[48]

From a fiscal standpoint, the new scale of tolls was a disaster. They never produced enough revenue to cover repairs, interest and to repay the debentures. For example, in June, 1851, the concessions to collect tolls on the Guelph and Dundas road were auctioned off for a year for a total of £1,079. The successful bids were: Gate 1, next to Dundas, Thomas Dickson, £397; Gate 2, middle gate, Thomas Ingram, £302; and Gate 3, near Guelph, William Clinton, £380.[49] On the other hand, interest on the £22,000 debt amounted to £1,320, and repairs, commissioners' fees and improvements, cost a total of £443. 1s. 3d. in the 1851 calendar year.[50] Thus total operating loss of 1851, making no provision for repayment of the debt, amounted to approximately £680. Indeed, in order to cover losses of the road as well as to retire a small part of the debentures, the Waterloo County Council was required to transfer £667. 12s. 2d. from county funds to the road[51] and Wentworth and Halton were required to contribute an equal amount.

In 1852 the County Councillors, unhappy at the mounting losses of the Guelph and Dundas road, forced that road's commissioners to increase the tolls substantially. With the only bridge in Town across the Speed River owned by the Guelph and Dundas Road Company, the townspeople had no choice but to pay the tolls or go miles out of their way to reach Dundas.

To counteract these charges, a public meeting was called by the Town Reeve where the following resolutions were passed:

3. That this Meeting are of opinion that the Council of the Town of Guelph will be justified in taxing the Municipality the Sum of £150 for the purpose of erecting two bridges over the River Speed, such being imperatively required by the recent increase in tolls on the Guelph and Dundas Road.

4. That the following gentlemen be a committee to assist the council in procuring subscriptions, and otherwise forwarding the object of the foregoing resolution, with power to add to their number, Messrs. Fred'k George, Peter Gow, I.J. Tracy, James Armstrong, Wm. Stevenson, David Allan & John Sauvey.[52]

The purpose of the bridges, of course, was to break the road company's monopoly by opening the way for teamsters to use the township concession roads whenever weather allowed. Within this week this advertisement appeared in the Guelph papers:

NOTICE

To parties willing to give gratuitous labor in erecting the New Bridges

THE TOWN COUNCIL, in conjunction with the Committee appointed by the General Meeting of the Inhabitants, having decided that the site of the lower of the two Bridges about to be erected on the Speed, shall be at the point where Wellington Street abuts on the River—all persons willing to give gratuitous labor in the constructing of said Bridge, or of the road leading thereto, are requested to assemble at 7 o'clock on Monday morning [June 28, 1852], at the junction of Wellington and Gordon Streets, where Overseers will attend to direct the operations.

James Hough
Town Clerk.[53]

Guelph, June 22nd, 1852.

In addition to the pressure exerted upon the Guelph and Dundas road Commissioners by Guelph's bridge building program, newspapers in both Guelph and Dundas undertook a vigorous campaign against the Commissioners involved. Not only was their integrity attacked (for example, the *Guelph Herald* claimed that Benjamin Thurtell of Guelph Township was in collusion with Jacob Hespeler to divert Guelph's grain trade to the latter's mill),[54] but they found fault with their economic theories as well. Higher tariffs would reduce revenue, not increase it, the papers argued.[55]

These theories were taken up by local businessmen who incorporated them into their campaign to force a reduction in the toll rate. At a public rally on June 28, 1852, held at Freel's tavern, the following motion was passed:

Resolved—That the tariff of tolls established at the last meeting of the Board of Directors, is not only an unjust tax upon those who travel the said road, unprecedented upon any road in the Province, but also calculated to drive the travel off said road, and thereby decrease instead of increase the revenue of said road, and materially injure the trade of those in business on the line of the said road and the towns of Guelph and Dundas.[56]

In the face of these concerted attacks, the Guelph and Dundas road Commissioners decided to beat a strategic retreat. On the day following the public meeting at Freel's tavern, the road Commissioners met in an emergency session to deal with the issue. The new toll rates established demonstrate the effectiveness of the flour dealers' campaign. Not only were the new tolls rescinded, but they were reduced well below the level established the previous year—a level which had been in effect when the large losses of 1851 had been incurred. (See Table XIX).

The road Commissioners, however, in order to shift responsibility from themselves in making such a controversial decision made these changes conditional upon the lessees of the toll gates accepting the new toll rates while continuing to pay to the road commission the full rate of their lease. By this means the gatekeep-

Table XIX
Rates of Toll per Gate for Wagons Drawn by Two Horses on the Guelph and Dundas Road[57]

Load	April 1 1851		June 29 1852		Percent Decrease
1,000 lbs.	0s.	5d.	0s.	4d.	20
2,000	0	7½	0	7	7
3,000	1	0	0	9	25
4,000	1	6	1	0	33
5,000	2	0	1	3	38

Sheep-washing at Gow's Dam on the Speed River. (Courtesy The College on the Hill)

ers were made responsible for the decision as to whether or not the new lower tolls would be implemented and they would bear the losses if any were created by the change. The Commissioners justified their actions on the grounds that they and the gatekeepers were bound by the terms of the leases, but that if the gatekeepers voluntarily decided to reduce the tolls during the life of the lease, they should be allowed to do so.[58]

Under such pressure from the road Commissioners and the press, two of the gatekeepers, Thomas Ingram and William Clinton (gates one and two) agreed to reduce their tolls to the June 29 rate, but William Card, the lessee of gate three, near Guelph, absolutely refused to accept any revision.

Urged on by the local press, public meetings were held, resolutions passed and delegations appointed—all aimed at forcing Card to

change his mind. A delegation, consisting of three Town Councillors, W.S. Knowles, George Sunley and Dr. Henry Orton, and four businessmen David Allan, W.J. Brown, John Pipe and Fred George, met William Card at Freel's tavern, and the following exchange was reported:

Mr. Card, the lessee of the Guelph Gate, met the deputation at Freel's; and had some conversation relative to the reduction of the tariff of tolls upon which he became lessee. Our readers will recollect that he leased the gate at a rent of £500. He now states, that according to the rates he has collected during the first month—usually the month of least travel—he will make £950 in total, or £450 profit, under his present tariff; and he refuses to adopt a lower tariff, without an amount of compensation such as can not be given.[59]

When it is remembered that William Card's expected profit of £450 would buy, clear and stock two large farms, it is not surprising that he clung so stubbornly to his contract. After reviewing the failure of the Guelph delegation, the *Advertiser* commented that:

The people of Guelph have therefore no alternative but to vigorously push forward the construction of the new bridges and roads into Puslinch, or to stand by and see their milling and wheat buying business ruined and their general commerce seriously injured. The contracts for the bridges have been already let out; the bridge at the foot of Wellington street, and the approaches to it will be completed by the 1st of October, and the line of road thence into Puslinch will be put in good order in the interim; so that loads of any weight may be sent by that road out of Guelph, and the millers and wheat buyers by that means be able still to give about two cents per bushel above New Hope prices. . . .[60]

In the meantime, Card's opponents had decided upon a second avenue of attack. They now undertook to test the legality of the higher tolls in the local courts. The *Guelph Advertiser* gives this outline of the test case, and its outcome:

MAGISTRATES' COURT, GUELPH

Present,—B. Thurtell, Esq., Chairman, and A.A. Baker. *David Martin*, Teamster, appeared to a summons at the suit of Wm. Card, Keeper of the Toll Gate near Guelph, in the Brock Road, for refusing to pay toll. The Prosecutor [Card] stated, that on the 2nd of July, the defendant came to the Toll Gate with a loaded waggon, weighing 60 cwt., the rate of toll which amounted to 3s.2½d. A demand for this sum was made; but the defendant refused to pay more than 1s. 3d. [the revised toll of June 29th]. Prosecutor objected to receive that sum, and defendant passed on with his team.

The Defendant said that sometimes Mr. Card had demanded 4s. 9d. cy, sometimes 6s. 3d. and other sums. Defendant offered him 1s. 3d. each time and believed that that sum was as much as he had any right to pay.[61]

The complexity of the case arose from the fact that Benjamin Thurtell, the Chairman,

Gow's Bridge and Mill.

was one of the road Commissioners who had set the toll, while Alfred A. Baker, the second Magistrate, was Clerk of the Division Court and a political and social associate of Dr. William Clarke, Guelph's leading mill owner. Upon hearing the case, Thurtell voted to convict Martin while Baker argued that under the General Road Act, the Guelph and Dundas road tolls were illegal. Thus deadlocked, the case was adjourned to be heard by a full panel of local Magistrates.[62]

On July 17th, the Martin case came before the Guelph Magistrates' Court again. This time it was heard by Benjamin Thurtell, David Allan (operator of Allan's Mill, owned by his father, William Allan), Dr. William Clarke, and two close associates of Allan and Clarke, John Harland and John McCrea. This time Thurtell again voted to convict Martin, but Allan, Clarke, Harland and McCrea voted to acquit.[63] Not surprisingly, given the composition of the Bench, A.J. Fergusson, M.P.P. and County Solicitor, advised William Card to appeal to a higher court. Card agreed and continued to collect the higher tolls.

Not all of the delegations which visited Card, however, were as polite as that official town group which had met him at Freel's tavern. Five days after that meeting and two weeks after Martin's acquittal, Card received a second visit. The *Guelph Advertiser* describes the event:

THE BROCK ROAD TOLLS

Outrage at the Guelph Gate

On Tuesday night last [August 3, 1852] a serious outrage was committed at the Toll Gate, near Guelph, the particulars of which we have learned from the lessee of the Gate. About midnight, the gate-keeper heard several persons advancing towards the house, and almost immediately after-

MAP 7: *Part of Map of Township of Guelph by Hobson and Chadwick, 1858, showing location of Toll gates south and north of Guelph, at what is now College Avenue and Speedvale Avenue. (Courtesy Public Archives of Ontario)*

wards a large stone was thrown at the bedroom window breaking the glass, and part of the sash; and passing near the head of Mrs. Card, who had just entered the room. Mr. Card then went to the door, but on trying to open it found it held firmly by some person on the outside. Immediately afterwards he heard some person breaking the weighing apparatus of the weighing machine; afterwards followed a parting salute with a volley of stones at the bedroom window and at the glass portion of the door. The parties then went off. It is almost unnecessary to add that a very considerable amount of damage was done.[64]

Although the *Advertiser* rejected such methods of persuasion, it did little to ease Card's nerves when it warned that such conduct, if repeated, "may lead to a grievous amount of suffering, and, perhaps, loss of life."[65]

Finally, Card had clearly had enough. The weigh scales broken beyond repair, the gate house severely damaged and his family, no doubt, in a state of terror, he abandoned his lease and no more tolls appear to have been collected at the Guelph gate that year.[66] Henceforth, under the lower rate of tolls, the Guelph and Dundas road would continue to lose money. In 1854 Wellington County's share of the losses was £477. 10s. and by 1856 these losses amounted to £168. 15s. 11d. on the current account, and £1,451. 10s. on the debenture account as the road debentures began to fall due.[67] Guelph's interests had clearly triumphed.

In contrast to the anxiety felt by Guelph's businessmen to complete the Guelph and Dundas road, the building of the County's northern road network was carried out at a much slower and more cautious pace. On August 10, 1848, the *Guelph Advertiser* put the matter in perspective:

Our prosperity depends entirely upon the means of communication with the lands to the north and north-west of us. The improvement of the Brock Road was a step absolutely necessary to prevent our retrogression, and the gravelling of the roads hence to Fergus on the one hand, and Elora on the other, will give a fresh impetus to this place, and mutually benefit those villages and Guelph.[68]

The Guelph and Arthur and the Guelph and Elora roads, therefore, were initially left in private hands. For some reason, the Guelph and Elora Road Company's charter which had been applied for in 1847, failed to be passed at that time, an oversight which caused considerable consternation. The *Guelph Advertiser* gives this explanation:

Now that the Act of Incorporation for the formation of a road hence to Arthur, has come in to operation, and a considerable quantity of the Stock already taken up there is one clause in the Act which required the immediate consideration of all interested in the road, and which may eventually affect the welfare of the town itself. Notice was duly given that at the late Session of Parliament two Acts would be applied for, one to incorporate a Company for the formation of a road hence to Arthur, and another from Guelph to Elora; and as both would require to go over the same ground for a distance of four and a half miles, to avoid strife it was thought advisable that there should be a clause authorizing the District Council to take this portion of the road into their own hands any time within three years, by which means the roads to the rising and competing villages would branch different ways from Card's Corner. Unfortunately, the Elora bill was neglected, and the other was so altered as to allow the company to take up the road from the limits of the town of Guelph unless the Council take immediate action in the matter. . . . We are inclined to think that it would serve the interests of the Council to exercise the privilege still left them by the Act, and to do so at the coming Session.[69]

From Guelph's point of view, if tolls on the Guelph to Card's Corners section of the road

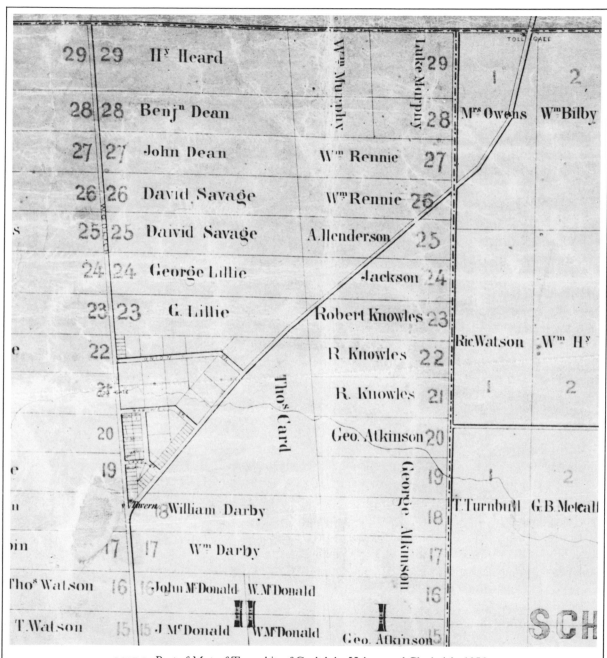

MAP 8: *Part of Map of Township of Guelph by Hobson and Chadwick, 1858, showing location of Toll gate at Card's Corners. (Courtesy Public Archives of Ontario)*

were set too high, Elora's trade might go to Berlin.

To forestall such an event a petition was quickly circulated requesting that the District Council take over the section of road from Guelph to Card's Corners.[70] This proposal was strongly opposed by the company's stockholders and the editor of the *Guelph Herald*. It was their contention that the whole purpose of the petition was to delay the Guelph and Arthur project.[71]

On December 6, 1847, the initial shareholders' meeting of the Guelph and Arthur Road Company was held. At it, A.D. Fordyce was elected president and A.J. Fergusson, William Clarke, Mr. Hogg, Thomas Webster, Samuel Broadfoot and John Watt were named directors. It was decided at the meeting not to make any call upon the shareholders until the District Council had made a decision as to whether or not it would build the road from Guelph to Card's Corners.[72]

On February 4, 1848, the District Council met to consider the issue. Leading the discussion were William Clarke of Guelph, James Cowan of Waterloo, A.D. Ferrier and Charles Allan of Nichol and John Frost of Sydenham. Frost was the strongest opponent of the road. It was his belief that the debenture debt of £9,000 incurred for the Guelph and Dundas Road Company was as much as the District could bear. The gravelling of the four miles to Card's Corners would require another £2,000 and he doubted that the money could be raised.

As the *Guelph Herald* reported, Dr. William Clarke was quick to supply the answer:

Dr. Clarke said, this was only a part of a great District undertaking, which was to connect the waters of Lake Huron with those of Lake Ontario, and he felt satisfied that the Road would amply repay both the interest and principal of the money expended in constructing it. The Act gave the Council the power of constructing the road, and if the Council did not assume it now it would remain forever in the hands of a private Company. . . . Dr. Clarke would have no hesitation in securing the Council in the undertaking to the amount of £500. . .then stated that himself and Messrs. Grange, Powell and Fergusson were willing to become security for £1,200, and he thought there would be no difficulty in getting the remaining £800 taken up.[73]

A by-law was then passed by which the District took over the road and appointed a Commission to supervise its management.

Little more was done during the next twelve months, but in October, 1848, tenders totalling £1,903. 8s. 8d. were let for the road's construction. In addition, the contract to build a toll house on the north corner of the Scotch glebe was let for £124. 10s. At the same time, the Commissioners began collecting tolls.[74] The *Guelph Advertiser* in August, 1849, reported:

It is. . . .with pleasure we lay before our readers the following statement respecting the four miles of road opened last Fall, leading from Guelph northward:

GUELPH AND ARTHUR ROAD

Tolls received from the commencement, 23rd October, 1848, to 10th July, 1849, being 38 weeks, averaging per week, £3. 16s. 0d.		£149. 8s. 9d.
Suppose the same for the 12 months		£197. 12s. 0d.
Interest on cost of Road per annum	£120.	
Expenses of same, about	£75.	£195. 0s. 0d.
		£ 2. 12s. 0d.

It should be borne in mind, that the thousands of barrels of flour, oatmeal, etc., which generally pass through Guelph during the Winter and Spring from Fergus and Elora have this year been sent

Eramosa Bridge, Guelph. (The Canadian Illustrated News, 1874)

northward to supply the deficiency caused by the failure of the crops in that direction, otherwise the receipts would have been much larger.[75]

Unfortunately, these calculations proved to be much too optimistic. In 1859, the treasurer of Wellington County summarized the total income and expenditure of the road since its commencement in 1848. According to the treasurer, a total of £4,116 had been paid out while £2,883 had been received from tolls.[76] In spite of constant promises by the urban leaders that these roads would not only repay their

builders but would make a handsome profit as well, the opposing goal—to retain the market area and to increase the volume of trade—prevented tolls being set high enough for profitable operation on the publicly owned roads.

If the publicly owned roads, occupying the most travelled sections, could not make a profit, the privately owned road companies were even less successful. The Guelph and Arthur Road Company provides a case in point.[77]

The primary reason for the failure of this

road was not lack of traffic but the conflicting interests of many of its directors and large shareholders. In the County Council debate about the likelihood that the Company might raise its tolls to a very high level if no controls were kept upon it, George Jackson, the reeve of Bentinck Township, pointed out that the Directors had every reason to keep the tolls as low as possible.[78]

One Guelph shareholder, William Day, at the 1850 annual meeting denounced the management of the road and declared that he now recognized that the enterprise had been "damned in the beginning."[79] He said that while the directors, being the largest shippers, might be satisfied with the road's operation, "nine-tenths of the stockholders think differently".[80]

With the largest part of the road to Fergus and Arthur remaining unimproved, residents and businessmen along its route were anxious to have the Road Company complete the work undertaken in the charter. With the Road Company holding a legal monopoly on the road, including all the improvements which had been previously made by the district and the statute labour expended in the past, local residents refused to spend local tax money or statute labour on it when such improvements would inevitably result in the imposition of tolls. On the other hand, with continued losses on the improved section, the company was in no mood to sink further capital into a losing proposition. Finally, the Township Council of Nichol took matters into its own hands. It agreed to lend £10,000 to the Road Company on security of the works so that the road could be completed through the township. In turn, in order to get a better price for its debentures, the Township requested the County Council to

issue £10,000 in county debentures and, with the proceeds, purchase the township bonds.[81] On the basis of this loan, work on the road was completed to Fergus. Unfortunately, the road never came close to paying the maintenance, interest and principal of its loans.

In January, 1864, the Directors of the Guelph and Arthur Road Company approached the County Council with an offer to sell the concern. The County committee established to examine the offer made the following recommendation:

While they are aware of the importance of the County owning all the gravel roads in said County, provided they could be obtained at such terms as would not subject the County to any loss, they are of opinion that the said Company asks more for their road than it is worth, and your Committee could not recommend any action to be taken on said offer. From all the information your Committee could obtain, they think that an offer of ten thousand dollars might be made to the Company for the whole road, toll gates and everything with it payable in Debentures at such terms as the County Council may see fit to direct.[82]

This report provided the basis for the eventual purchase.[83]

With improved transportation, settlement within Guelph's potential market area was greatly accelerated, and cash crop farming encouraged by the easier access to markets and the necessity of farmers to have cash for the new money taxes. Having built the basic road system, Guelph's commercial role and economic base was considerably strengthened. In 1853, John Smith, the editor of the *Guelph Advertiser* discussed the significance of these changes, putting into perspective the acquisition of both district town status and the building of the gravel road system:

During the Spring we have repeatedly felt disposed to take a stroll round the town for the purpose of noting its progress and giving the readers of the *Advertiser* the result of our observations. . . . In commencing our remarks it is only proper to state, that a rural town, depending entirely upon a new country with a scattered and comparatively poor population, cannot be expected to make the same progress, or exhibit the rapid changes so frequently evidenced by manufacturing or commercial places, in a new country. With such Guelph does not pretend to vie. . . .

The census of 1843 showed a population of 700, and when we first set foot within the place, in the summer of that year, the rustic simplicity of the people in dress and other respects, gave us anything but a favorable impression of its future progress and importance. Well, it progressed notwithstanding, for in four years its population had doubled, and at the present time it numbers upwards of 2,000 inhabitants. . . . Guelph has not availed itself of the immense water-power within its limits, to the extent frequently witnessed in other towns, and until of late years its prosperity was more dependent on the incomes of the town and neighborhood, derived from other sources, and the circumstances of it being the county seat, than on its manufacturing industry or commercial enterprise. Fortunately that spirit is rapidly dying away before the energy and perseverance of her sons.[84]

As Smith rightly concluded, the era of gravel road-building provided the first step towards the development of Guelph as an important commercial centre.

The Circuit Rider. (Courtesy Public Archives of Canada)

V
Establishment of Churches

For some decades following its founding, life in Guelph was greatly influenced by the pioneer environment and the racial, religious and economic origins of its inhabitants. Thrown together by circumstances, in alien and sometimes threatening surroundings, far from home, family, and friends, economic security and group identity emerged as the early settlers' basic needs.

In Guelph, as in all frontier settlements, the primary component of individual and group identity was country or place of birth. In almost every contemporary document, individuals are spoken of as "Englishmen", "Scotchmen", "Irishmen", "Yankees" or "Dutchmen". Locations such as the "Scotch Block", the "Paisley Block" and "the Dutch Settlement" maintained their identification for generations, while street names such as London, Yorkshire, Cambridge, Essex, Surrey, Edinburgh, Glasgow, Cork and Dublin, recalled to the residents memories of their distant places of birth.

Except for the original "Yankees" sent by Mr. Buchanan, the British Consul at New York, at John Galt's request, most of Guelph's early settlers were of British origin. These peo-

St. Andrew's Presbyterian Church, 1832, from a drawing by David Allan.

ple, however, were by no means as homogeneous as a similar group would be today. England had not yet undergone the tremendous social integration of the industrial revolution and as a result, "British" immigrants to Guelph had great diversity, except where this had been overcome by the effects of a good "British" education. Thus Scots like Dr. William Dunlop, John Galt or William Allan had much in common with Englishmen such as Henry Strange, George J. Grange and Dr. Henry Orton, or Irishmen like Dr. William Clarke or the Rev. Arthur Palmer. All shared a common upbringing, education, and social station, all were men of wealth and high cultural attainments.

Although there is no accurate census by ori-gin for Guelph before 1851, most commentators prior to 1840 described the Township as being settled by roughly equal numbers of English, Irish and Scottish immigrants, with the well-to-do settlers of 1832 being prominent in the village.[1] In 1845, W.H. Smith commented upon the number of "respectable families from the old country, principally English, many of whom came from Suffolk and Norfolk".[2]

While there was a huge influx of immigrants from Ireland into the area in 1847 due to the famine, many of these settled in the new townships to the north. Tables XX and XXI give the population of Wellington County in 1852-1853 by numbers and percentages, according to country of birth. It should be remembered in examining these tables, that

Table XX
Wellington County, Population by Country of Birth, 1852-1853[3]

Municipality	Total	England and Wales	Scotland	Ireland	British Canada	U.S.A.	Other
Erin	3,590	212	685	508	2,040	96	49
Puslinch	3,862	286	961	449	1,941	57	168
Guelph	2,879	537	402	559	1,306	35	40
Guelph-Town	1,860	507	200	392	722	34	5
Nichol	2,450	202	980	304	912	30	22
Garafraxa	2,083	152	336	630	923	40	2
Eramosa	2,350	330	251	458	1,233	78	0
Peel	2,435	280	131	738	1,131	141	14
Maryborough	994	158	71	296	436	31	2
Minto Arthur Luther	1,803	88	342	623	715	21	9
Amaranth	500	45	2	212	227	13	1
Pilkington	1,999	708	523	464	108	5	82
Total	26,796	3,505	4,884	5,638	11,694	581	494

most of the persons designated as being born in Canada were children of immigrant settlers. Almost two-thirds (335 out of 494) of those described as "other" were of German descent, while 87 were born in Nova Scotia, New Brunswick and Prince Edward Island.

In contrast to most inland pioneer settlements, organized religion in Guelph developed more quickly than was usually the case. Whereas many new regions for years had no more than an occasional religious service conducted by a lay preacher or itinerant minister, the rapid influx of families, and the confidence generated by the capital expended in Guelph, first by John Galt and later by the 1832 set-

tlers, allowed a more rapid development of formal religious institutions. Indeed, as part of Galt's promotion of Guelph as a major urban centre, he had made grants of land and gifts of money to religious groups in order to encourage the establishment of houses of worship.

The first church to be formally organized in Guelph was St. Andrew's Presbyterian Church, which was a part of the Church of Scotland in Canada. Like the Anglican Church, the Presbyterians were officially established as a "state" church, and thereby eligible to receive funds from the Clergy Reserve lands.

St. Andrew's Presbyterian congregation had an auspicious beginning on August 12, 1827, when the Reverend Mr. Sheed, a Church of

Table XXI
Wellington County, Population, Percent by Country of Birth, 1852-1853[4]

Municipality	England and Wales	Scotland	Ireland	British Canada	U.S.A.	Other
Erin	5.9	19.1	14.2	56.8	2.7	1.4
Puslinch	7.4	24.9	11.6	50.3	1.5	5.9
Guelph	18.7	14.0	19.4	45.4	1.2	1.4
Guelph-Town	27.3	10.8	21.1	38.8	1.8	.3
Nichol	8.2	40.0	12.4	37.2	1.2	.9
Garafraxa	7.3	16.1	30.2	44.3	1.9	.1
Eramosa	14.0	10.7	19.5	52.5	3.3	—
Peel	11.5	5.7	30.3	46.4	5.8	.6
Maryborough	15.9	7.1	29.8	13.9	3.1	.2
Minto Arthur Luther	4.9	19.0	34.6	39.7	1.2	.5
Amaranth	9.0	.4	42.4	45.4	2.6	.5
Pilkington	35.4	26.2	23.2	5.4	.3	4.1
Total	13.1	18.2	21.0	43.6	2.2	1.8

Scotland minister was invited by John Galt to preside over the King's birthday celebrations, and to lay the cornerstone of the "academy". That morning a small deputation had waited on Rev. Sheed, with a petition signed by 59 residents requesting him to celebrate divine services in Guelph until a resident clergyman could be obtained from Scotland.[5] These services were held in a log house owned by Benjamin Harrison. Later, when the stone school was finished, it was used as a place of worship.

For the first few years, services took place only on an occasional basis, and local residents desiring to worship, seized whatever opportunities were offered to them. Acton Burrows notes that:

The people were very catholic at that time, and minor differences of creed were not allowed to cause strife and contention among them, the privilege of being able to assemble together for worship being too highly prized to permit of their dividing on points of doctrine, such as Apostolic succession, election, immersion or the final perseverance of the saints. So long as the Gospel was preached, however much they might in their own hearts cherish the tenets of their different forms of faith and church constitution, they were, for the time, satisfied, and consequently, whether the preacher happened to be an Episcopalian, a Presbyterian, a Methodist or a Baptist, so far as availing themselves of the privilege of worship together was concerned, it was all one. This harmonious and, under the circumstances, most commendable state of things, continued until 1832, when, as will appear hereafter, they were justified in asserting each his own views, and forming themselves into different religious communities, for the practice and perpetuations of the doctrines and forms of worship in which they had respectively been taught to believe as most in accordance with Scriptural direction.[6]

In August, 1828, the local Presbyterians took their second step towards formal organization when, under the leadership of James Buchanan, who was in Guelph visiting his friend and relative, John Galt, a Presbyterian Sunday school was established and sixteen children were formally enrolled.[7] During 1829, Mr. J. Carruthers, Catechist, took charge of services in Guelph, and the congregation grew rapidly.

The first Board of Trustees of St. Andrew's Church was composed of James Corbett, William Alexander, James Hodgert, John Mitchell, Andrew Ritchie and David McKerzie[8], all well known and well educated men.

On October 11, 1831, a call was issued to the Reverend James Smith, a resident of Scotland[9], and immediately afterwards on November twenty-second, a contract was let to John Thorp for the erection of a frame church which would seat approximately 200. The induction of the Rev. James Smith in 1832, was reported as follows:

On the 8th day of February. . .the Presbytery of York met in the old stone school house to induct the Rev. James Smith as pastor of the Guelph congregation. The members of the Presbytery present were: Rev. Mr. Sheed, Moderator; Rev. Mr. Rintoul, York; Rev. Robert McGill, Niagara, and Rev. Alexander Ross, Aldboro'. The salary of Mr. Smith was £63 currency—exclusive of the Government allowance, or Clergy Reserves, and the use of the Glebe belonging to the congregation, which was at that time covered with forest. Before Mr. Smith could officiate as a clergyman in full standing he had to appear before the Quarter Sessions at Hamilton and take the oath of allegiance to the Government, notwithstanding his being a natural born British subject.[10]

St. Andrew's Church was opened in September, 1832, and the first Elders were John Inglis, Charles Julius Mickle, Hugh Wilson, Thomas Sandilands, and William Elliott.[11]

Rev. Robert Torrance,
first minister of the United
Presbyterian Congregation.

Rev. James Smith,
first minister of St. Andrew's
Presbyterian Church.

Rev. J.G. MacGregor,
first pastor of Knox
Presbyterian Church.

The first Communion was held on November fourth, and membership at that time was 103.[12]

The Presbyterian congregation in Guelph flourished from the first and its members, particularly its ministers, were among the strongest proponents of good education in the township and county. At every educational activity, whether it was the semi-annual visitors' days or the election of trustees and school commissioners, Presbyterians were prominent in their advocacy of educational advancement. They, with the Methodists, were particularly active in the promotion of the common schools, whereas the Anglicans' interest lay primarily with the grammar school.

In the early 1840's there was a split among Scottish Presbyterians. Some members favoured the idea that the State should be associated with the Church. Others believed that the Church should be free of political implications and that religion must not merely be taken to, but controlled by the members of the Church.[13] Thus, when the Free Church movement reached Canada, it was seized upon eagerly by many of the Guelph congregation. In Guelph, these differences resulted in splitting the local group into three during 1843 and 1844—the original St. Andrew's, the United or First Presbyterian and Knox "free church". These latter two erected their own churches, the United Presbyterian being built in 1844 at the corner of Cambridge and Dublin Streets, and Knox Church in 1847 on Yarmouth Street, on lots provided by the Canada Company.[14]

Robert Torrance, the first minister called by the United Presbyterian congregation, had been born in Ireland and received a Bachelor of Arts degree from the Royal Academy College in Belfast, as well as a degree in Theology from Edinburgh University, and had been licensed to preach at the age of 22. In 1845, he came to Canada in answer to a call from a church in Toronto, but found himself dissatisfied with the rigidity of the congregation. He then spent a year doing missionary work throughout western Upper Canada, riding horseback from Toronto to Goderich in his circuit. In 1846 he was invited to the new Guelph church, where he remained an active and aggressive preacher until his retirement in 1882. By this time, the social and political causes which had contributed to the split in the Presbyterian church in the 1840's had healed sufficiently so that upon Torrance's retirement, the United Presbyterian congregation dissolved itself, and its members joined other churches.[15]

The first minister of Knox Church, Rev. John G. MacGregor, was born at Alva, Sterlingshire, Scotland, in 1799. He took his Arts course at Glasgow University, and from there went to Edinburgh Theological College, where on graduation he was licensed to preach. In 1836 he came to St. John, New Brunswick, where he remained until his call to Guelph. On June 23rd, 1847, he was formally ordained and inducted into the Ministry of Knox Church.[16]

During the same period that the Presbyterian Church was being organized in Guelph,

The first Knox Church, Yarmouth Street, Guelph.

Father Joseph Campion, a Jesuit missionary stationed at Niagara began to include Guelph on a circuit that stretched from Niagara to Chatham and Windsor. Acton Burrows gives this rather poetic description of Campion's first visit to Guelph:

His district extended as far west as Chatham and Windsor, and it usually occupied him about three months to make all his pastoral visits, which he did alone, braving all dangers, which at that time were neither few nor small. . . .His first visit to Guelph was in August, and during his stay religious services were held by him, sometimes in the leafy groves adjoining the clearing, and sometimes in some lowly shanty, but generally, and for nearly four years afterwards, the services were held in the house of Mr. John O. Lynch. Just as he was about to leave his little flock the first time—it is said after he had mounted his horse,—he was called back to perform a pleasant duty, the celebration of the first marriage in the new settlement. Christopher Keogh, an employee of the Canada Company, and a fair maid named Kitty Kelly, had been plighted lovers in Dundas, and arrangements had been made for their union at some future time, when they could be married by a priest, but neither of them thought the auspicious time would arrive so soon; so that when the priest arrived the young man was all anxiety to have the knot tied at once, but the lady, with maiden coyness, demurred, and it was not until the priest was just about leaving that her friends prevailed upon her to give her consent, and the expectant bridegroom was just in time to stay the depature of the priest to effect the union of two loving hearts. . . .All the settlers, from Mr. Galt down to the resident of the humblest shanty, turning out to do honor to the occasion, and that day, the 26th of August, 1827, was remembered for many years as one of the pleasantest spent in the early days of Guelph.[17]

In several aspects, the position enjoyed by the Roman Catholic Church in Guelph was remarkably different from that which it enjoyed in the rest of Upper Canada. This situation was due entirely to the efforts of John Galt. Galt, it will be remembered, was a close friend of Bishop (later Cardinal) Weld, and for some time hoped that Weld could be persuaded to move to Guelph, thereby making it an important episcopal seat. In addition, Bishop Macdonell had been very helpful to Galt during his first visit to Canada. In appreciation, Galt said, "a beautiful central hill was reserved for the Catholics, in compliment to my friend, Bishop Macdonell, for his advice in the formation of the Company".[18] Bishop Macdonell visited Guelph at least twice, and took an active interest in the growth of the town.

In 1829, Father John Cassidy was sent to Guelph to form a new mission with Guelph as its centre. Its boundaries stretched from London to Georgian Bay, and required that Father Cassidy be away from Guelph for long periods. In spite of this, the Guelph congregation grew rapidly, and in 1832 a small frame building was erected on the hill and opened the same year.[19] In 1838, Father Thomas Gibney

became the first resident priest at St. Patrick's, as the little church was called.[20] Prominent among Guelph's early Catholic residents were C. Donahue, J. Butler, Joseph Daly, James Mays, Donald Gillies, Bernard McTague, Thomas Kelly, Michael Lennie, Patrick McGarr, James Beirnes, Stewart Coghlin and John Owen Lynch.[21]

The Hon. and Right Rev. Alexander Macdonell, the first Catholic bishop of Upper Canada, and a friend of John Galt.

Although the Anglican Church in Guelph was founded a little later than the Presbyterian and Roman Catholic congregations, it was greatly helped by the influx of wealthy communicants in 1832. Among the well-to-do settlers who arrived that year was an Anglican clergyman, the Rev. Arthur Palmer, who was born near Galway, Ireland, on July 4, 1807, and received his education at Trinity College, Dublin. On his arrival in Guelph he at once organized a church, meeting for the time being in the stone schoolhouse, and at the same time, aided by his congregation, took up the task of building St. George's Church on the plot in the centre of St. George's Square which had been allocated for that purpose by John Galt. The church was fully paid for before it was finished in the spring of 1833. "We learn that a grant was made by the Canada Company towards the building, one by the Bishop of Quebec, and also help from Mr. Bosanquet of the Canada Company, as well as from some of Mr. Palmer's friends in the British Isles".[22] Acton Burrows describes the church as follows:

It was a very substantially built frame structure, said to have been the most solidly and strongly put together building of its kind ever erected in Guelph, and stood as one of the most conspicuous objects in the town. . . .[23]

In addition to the yearly grant which the Anglican Church received from the Clergy Reserve funds, in 1836 Lieutenant-Governor Sir John Colborne issued an Order-in-Council to build a parsonage for St. George's Church from public funds.[24]

The order for the consecration of the church was made by Bishop Mountain of Montreal on September 10, 1838. In the thundering tones of the Old Testament, this order read:

IN THE NAME OF GOD—AMEN
Foreasmuch as the Canada Company hath granted to the Lord Bishop of the Diocese and his successors—a piece or parcel of ground in the Town of Guelph, County of Halton, and District of Gore, for the erection of a Church of the establishment of

The first St. George's Church on the Square, 1833-1851.

*Rev. Arthur Palmer, first minister
of St. George's Anglican Church.*

the Church of England, composed of the centre part of St. George's Square in the Town of Guelph. . . ., a substantial & decent Church called St. George's Church has been erected thereon & the said Church is provided with a reading-desk, Common Prayer Book, Bible, Pulpit & other appendages for the decent performance of divine worship; and whereas George John Grange, William Henry Parker, Robert Alling, Thomas Saunders & John Neeve, have, in behalf of the Parishioners of the said Church, humbly requesting us George Jehoshaphat, by divine permission, Lord Bishop of Montreal, to consecrate the said Church, with which petition we being favorably disposed & freely consenting, do decree that the consecration of the said Church should be proceeded with.

Therefore know all men both now and hereafter, that we George Jehoshaphat by divine permission, Lord Bishop of Montreal, having invoked the name of Almighty God & having first implored His aid and blessing, do, by our ordinary and Episcopal authority separate & set apart, for ever, this Church so appropriated, completed & furnished from all common uses, & do dedicate & consecrate it, *for ever,* for divine worship & the celebration of divine ordinances & to the honor of God & for the use of the Congregation aforesaid. . . .[25]

In 1846, Mr. Palmer acquired from Henry Tiffany, that tract of land, still known as the Palmer survey, and lying between Grange and Palmer Streets, and Metcalfe Street and the

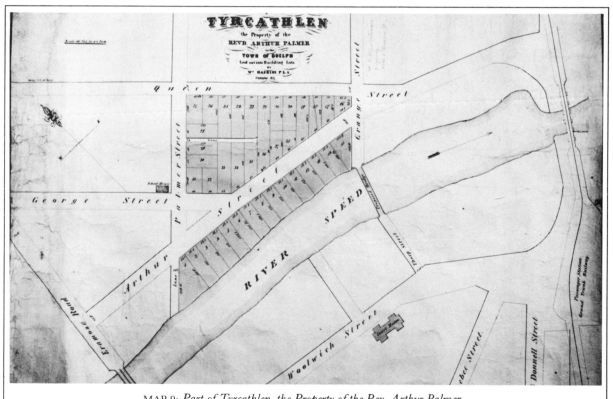

MAP 9: *Part of Tyrcathlen, the Property of the Rev. Arthur Palmer in the Town of Guelph, by Wm. Haskins, P.L.S. 1855.*

River. Here on the brow of the hill in 1855 and 1856, he built the beautiful stone Rectory, known for seventy-five years as "Tyrcathlen", from a design prepared by Sir Charles Barry, F.R.I.B.A., the Architect of the Houses of Parliament in the City of London.[26] The Reverend Arthur Palmer would serve St. George's Church for more than forty years.

In addition to the Presbyterians, Roman Catholics and Anglicans, three other religious groups, the Baptists, Congregationalists and Wesleyan Methodists, had been organized by 1845—the latter two having built "plain Chapels" by that date.[27] Although it is believed that the Baptists held meetings on a regular monthly basis between 1827 and 1850, the local church grew very slowly. In 1853 it consisted of only seventeen members, nine men and eight women.[28]

In contrast, the Congregationalists and Methodists grew much more rapidly. In 1833 three or four Baptists and two Congregationalists met together to read the Bible and to preach the Gospel in a freer and more spontaneous manner than that presented by the organized congregations developing in Guelph.[29]

"Tyrcathlen" later known as "Ker Cavan", the home of the Rev. Arthur Palmer.

The Reverend George H. Knighton, the last minister to serve the Guelph Congregationalists, supplied this description of that church's early days:

In January 1834 Mr. Samuel Wright appointed part of his house for the Public Worship of God when Mr. Ellworthy preached twice on each Lord's Day. The persons assembled were mostly of the Baptist and Independent denominations, joined by a few families who had separated from the Scotch Presbyterian Church.

In 1835 the Rev. E. Parkin was called to the pastorate of the little church. Its membership consisted of eight persons, two of whom, Mr. C.J. Mickle and Mr. T. Hodgskin, were deacons.[30]

The survival of the Congregational Church in Guelph was aided greatly by the efforts of the London Missionary Society, which sent both money and ministers. The Reverend Hiram Denny succeeded the Reverend Parkin in October, 1836, on a temporary basis, and it was not until the arrival of the Reverend W.P. Wastell, a former Congregational minister in Hackney, London, England, that the church was put on a more permanent basis. Wastell was apparently dissatisfied with a number of practices and methods of the local congregation, and immediately reformed it. As a result, membership was reduced to the sixteen who were able and prepared to sign an agreement that "We consider it a duty binding on every individual member jealously to guard against any infringement of Congregationalism".[31] Under Wastell's leadership the congregation grew rapidly, and a small stone chapel was built on Quebec St. E. in 1839-40. It was dedicated on February 5, 1840.

The story of early Methodism in Guelph is best told by quoting from the Centenary Souvenir (1836-1936) of Norfolk United Church:

One of the first, if not the first, of the Methodist families in Guelph was that of Hezekiah Hall, a carpenter and builder, whose house was at the service of the early Methodist circuit riders for meetings. Mr. Thomas McBride, whose family came to Guelph in 1828 remembers being sent four or five miles out the Eramosa road to the Lowrys, and to other families to acquaint them that a Methodist preacher would hold service in Guelph on a certain date. One of Mr. Hall's rooms was sufficient to hold the little company that gathered. Miss Fanny Harrison used to gather a few of the children together at her home, to teach them to read in the New Testament.

The influx of further English immigrants, in 1832-1834 gave encouragement to Dr. Orton, J.H.P. Maddock, John Kirkland, the Days, and others to form a society and to send, about 1835, to Nottingham, England, from which most of the English Methodists in and around Guelph came, for Samuel Fear, a weaver, and local preacher to come to Guelph and preach for the newly-organized society. Mr. Fear and his brother-in-law, Mr. James Hough, for so many years a bulwark of the Church, came out, and for two years, 1836-7, Mr. Fear ministered acceptably to the Methodists of Guelph and district in a little red chapel on Dr. Orton's lot on Nottingham Street, though he was not recognized as an ordained minister until 1847.

Congregational Church, Quebec Street, Guelph, 1840.

In December, 1837, the present lot on the corner of Norfolk and Cork Streets was granted by the Canada Company to the Wesleyan Methodists, and in the following year a frame chapel was erected thereon by the congregation. In that same year the society was reorganized by the Canada Conference and Rev. Benjamin Nankeville was stationed in Guelph. In 1840 the Canada Wesleyan Conference was rent in twain, after a union of seven years, by the religious issues of the thirties. The great majority of the Guelph Church, being English people, held to the British Conference, and the Church property was, in December, 1840, re-deeded to a larger Board of Trustees under the model trust deed of the British Conference, Rev. Ephraim Evans, acting as the Conference representative. Messrs. J.W.B. Kelly, H. Hall, Thos. McBride, Wm. Heather and others, however, held to the Canada Conference, which did most of the pioneer work for Methodism in Upper Canada. The Canada Methodists, as they came to be called, worshipped for seven years in the old school house near Allan's Mill and in the Priory, afterwards the C.P.R. station. The Canada Company granted them the lot on the Norfolk-Cork Street corner, directly opposite the Norfolk Street Church, for a church site but it was not used for that purpose as the local congregations were reunited in 1847.[32]

Table XXII gives church affiliation in 1840 and 1851. It should be noted that while the population had expanded rapidly during this period, the ratio of affiliation between the various religious denominations remained remarkably uniform.

Looking back more than a century later, it is difficult to understand the depth of feeling generated by religious and racial differences. Locally, the rise of the Orange Order and the striving for political power by Doctor William Clarke would create an explosive and tragic situation.

Dr. Clarke was born in Queen's County,

Table XXII
Religious Affiliation in Guelph, 1840-1851[33]

	1840	1851	
	Town and Township	Town	Township
Church of England	762	559	937
Church of Scotland	540	378	360
Other Presbyterians	62	120	469
Roman Catholics	357	193	647
Methodists	278	392	270
Baptists	34	19	57
Congregationalists	216	191	114
Quakers	35	5	2
Menonites & Tunkers	—	—	10
Other (incl. not known)	2	3	13

Ireland, in 1813. He gained a medical degree at Dublin, and while there, had apparently become deeply involved in Orange politics, the Orange Order then being illegal in the British Isles. When, in 1835, the British government undertook an investigation of the secret Orange associations,[34] Dr. Clarke, apparently fearing the results of any investigation of his association with this movement, fled to Canada. Doctor Henry Orton, in his *Memoirs*, says of Dr. Clarke:

He had left Ireland, he said, from taking an active part in a political association called the Spottiswood Association, (I recollect seeing in the papers mention of this Spottiswood Club); and he was in danger of being called up before a committee of the House of Commons.[35]

Dr. William Clarke.

When Dr. Clarke arrived in Canada, he undertook a medical practice in Eramosa township but had little success. In 1837, he negotiated a partnership with Dr. Orton in Guelph. Hardly had Dr. Clarke begun his medical practice there, than his extremely ambitious nature caused him to return to politics again. As his partner, Henry Orton, described the situation in Guelph, there was little room for an "outsider" like Dr. Clarke in local political life:

He [Clarke] had always a strong penchant that way [for politics] but could not well edge in. Public matters were then managed by the Family Compact, as they were termed. At Guelph Dr. Alling and a few British officers on half-pay—Colonel Young, Capt. Lamprey, Captain Hewatt and Capt. Poore. Mind, they had only been lieutenants in service. No matter. They were in the militia or localities of that rank and they with a few select families here and there engrossed all public offices

and had sole direction and influence until after the Rebellion. Dr. Clarke, though a professed Conservative, versant in public business and general politics far beyond the employer and privileged, could gain no admission.[36]

The reforms arising out of the Durham Report gave Dr. Clarke his opportunity. Following his arrival in Upper Canada, Lord Durham had ordered that new magistrates be appointed, and among these was Dr. Clarke. Dr. Henry Orton was named Coroner.[37] The introduction of elected district councillors opened the door even further. Dr. Orton commented on the result:

From this period all public business became open business on the model of the States, municipal arrangements throwing open and committing to the public the entire management of their affairs. Before this it was done by the Governor in Council and the Family Compact. A general jostle ensued. The ambitious and the capable, whatever their peculiarities, had now an open field and a like chance, not always fair play.[38]

Whereas other opponents of the local Family Compact, could and did join the Reformers to take advantage of the new political opportunities, such an avenue was not open to Dr. Clarke. Dr. Orton writes:

A more ambitious or more capable man was scarcely to be met than Dr. Clarke. Yet his ambition was of a peculiar kind. He had really an aptitude above his fellows and an impelling something that seemed irresistible to exercise it in public affairs and public business. He was a very Napoleon in the sphere of his orbit, rapid as lightning, a universal talent. . . .In public meetings he always pushed up and demanded and took the lead in everything or rather took without demanding and kept it and almost engrossed it. . . .But others of course differed continually. . .then was manifested his peculiarities. He. . .had no patience with the infirmities or crudities of others. To require deference, courtesy and elementary explanation before his views could be accepted, was to him stupidity or perverseness. Then followed cutting sarcasm with sharp repartees, menaces and defiances with most rapid, often brilliant expressions of language that ruffled the temper and kindled the passions of meetings, and ended in a veritable row. This was so generally the case in all the public meetings that Dr. Clarke was present at, and few took place without him being there, that Wm. Howitt used to say, "It was not possible for Dr. Clarke to take anything in hand without spoiling it". This continued for years.[39]

Although an Irish Protestant, Dr. Clarke for a long time exercised considerable influence over the Irish Catholics in Guelph. Dr. Orton commented:

From his own countrymen he would not hear a word of contradiction. "Down with them" he used to say to me, "Set your foot on them. They have been used to it and nothing else will do for them". And notwithstanding that he fully acted on it himself, he was their very idol. . . .William Day, his bitter political opponent, used to say, "Dr. Clarke can do anything he likes with the Irish. He can either Bully or Blarney them just as it suits and lead them wherever he likes". He generally could bully them. If in a passion, which was pretty often, he would threaten, abuse and vent such torrents of boiling anger and overwhelming sarcasm with exaggerated statements that it was a perfect scene. He allowed no response, gave no chance for reply. His rapidity and fury confounded everything.[40]

Backed by the powers of his office as magistrate, Dr. Clarke's fury must have seemed awesome indeed to his Catholic countrymen.

Bishop Strachan's anti-Catholic and anti-Reform campaign spread and in 1843, encounters between Irish Catholics and their Orange counterparts became more and more frequent. On October ninth, news reached Guelph that Daniel O'Connell, the Irish reform leader, had been freed from prison. Local Irish Catholics, having recently suffered under the Irish landlord system, "Manifested their joy around a great bonfire on the public square. Some of the non-participants promised a bigger blaze the following night. Next evening the church on the hill was completely demolished by fire, and all records were destroyed".[41]

This incident caused a province wide outcry from Catholics, and the Governor-General, Lord Metcalfe, issued the following proclamation:

Whereas, on the night of Thursday, the tenth day of October, now last past, the Roman Catholic

Dr. Henry Orton, Sr.

Church, situated in the Town of Guelph, in the district of Wellington, of our said Province, was destroyed by fire, and there is reason to suspect that the said fire was not occasioned by an accident, but was the work of an incendiary or incendiaries; now know ye, that a reward of fifty pounds, of lawful money of our said Province, will be paid to any person or persons, not being the actual offender or offenders, who will give such information as will lead to the discovery and conviction of the perpetrator or perpetrators of the said crime, and a free pardon will be granted to any accomplice therein giving such information.[42, 43]

In spite of the offer of a reward, no arrest was ever made.

Between 1844 and 1847, the antagonism between the Orange and Catholic elements grew rapidly worse. Urged on by the extreme language of their leaders, local violence between Protestant and Catholic elements increased rapidly and physical attacks became more and more frequent. Most commonly mentioned, in the local newspapers, as being involved in these assaults, were two families living on the Eramosa Road, the Coghlins and the Olivers. Acton Burrows described the mounting feud as follows:

About two miles out of town, on the Eramosa road, lived two families named Oliver and Coghlin, between which a longstanding religious feud had existed, the Olivers being Orangemen and the Coghlins Roman Catholics. Whenever any members of these families met, high words, and frequently hard blows, were exchanged, the young men especially evincing great bitterness towards each other. . . .the disputes generally resulted from excitement through drink.[44]

Quarrels between members of the two families frequently resulted in court cases. When tried before the presiding magistrate, Doctor William Clarke, Clarke apparently found for the Olivers on every occasion.[45] As a result of these judgments, Dr. Clarke's popularity among the Irish Catholics quickly waned.

In January, 1847, nearly a dozen men were fined for assault and bound over to keep the peace, but apparently to little effect. In March, the situation came to a head. As well as the events can be reconstructed, on Saturday, March twentieth, Thomas Coghlin and a party of his friends were returning home from Guelph at about eight o'clock in the evening. Upon passing John Oliver's house, Coghlin and his friends "called on him to come out of his house, leaned on his rails, etc., but nothing serious occurred".[46] For these actions, Thomas Coghlin was ordered to pay a fine of five shillings and costs of fifteen shillings, nine pence.

Two days later, on March twenty-second, at about four o'clock on a Monday afternoon, William and Richard Oliver (brothers) were proceeding home when they met Thomas and John Coghlin, and a violent quarrel resulted. William Oliver claimed that he and his brother, Richard, had been beaten about the head with a stick by the Coghlins, while both Thomas and John Coghlin, at their trial for these assaults, claimed that they had been stabbed several times about the hands and face by a bayonet wielded by Richard Oliver, but the presiding magistrates, Benjamin Thurtell, J. Parkinson, J. Harland and Richard F. Budd found them guilty of assault. The Coghlin brothers were fined five shillings and one pound respectively.[47]

To this point, the affair was apparently little different than those which had occurred several times previously. Now, however, things took a tragic turn. William Oliver's testimony concerning the events of Mar. 23, 1847, was as follows:

In about a quarter of a mile we met Robert [Oliver,

the third Oliver brother] in the sleigh. I did not notice prisoner [here referring to Charles Coghlin, the third Coghlin brother] till we were in the sleigh, though I looked back once and saw four or five persons after us. It was over a quarter of a mile when Richard said to Robert, the horses are tired, and I will jump out and walk a piece. After walking a little while we looked and saw those fellows, when Richard turned round and said to prisoner, "what are you chasing us for?" Prisoner replied, "I will quickly let you know". He then put his hand to his breast and pull[ed] out something like a dagger or a knife, and made a jump at Richard and stabbed him.—Richard staggered back a little, and recovered himself saying, "Oh, you stabbed me". Prisoner replied, "yes, and I meant to do it". He [Richard Oliver] then got into the sleigh, and we drove on. He attempted to speak, but appeared unable. I saw he was dead, and put my arms round him to hold him up.[48]

Richard Oliver's death created a sensation, and even the normally staid *Guelph Advertiser* devoted pages to the subsequent events and made it clear that drastic action by the authorities was necessary to prevent further outbreaks of violence. In particular, Dr. William Clarke took the lead in demanding at the inquest that Charles Coghlin be tried for first degree murder instead of a lesser charge.

Charles Coghlin's trial for murder was held on May 29, 1847, and was filled with contradictory evidence. The key points of contention were whether or not Richard Oliver was in possession of a bayonet when he was stabbed by Charles Coghlin, and whether or not it was Oliver who had inflicted the wounds to the head and hands of John and Charles Coghlin. In the end, the Jury found Coghlin guilty of murder, and he was sentenced to be hanged on July first.[49]

Immediately after Coghlin's trial, Catholics in Guelph circulated two petitions asking the Government to commute his sentence to life imprisonment. These petitions were "numerously signed" by local Catholics who believed that, at most, Coghlin should have been charged with manslaughter.[50] In June, their hopes were raised when an order came from the Government that the execution should not be carried out until further notice, but two weeks later these hopes were dashed when a second letter followed ordering Sheriff Grange to carry out the execution.

As the day for the hanging approached, tension mounted. William Richardson, the original contractor for the building of the gallows was threatened, and refused to carry out the contract. A second contractor, James Clarvise took it only after having discussed the situation with Coghlin's family, and having been reassured by them that no ill feeling would be held if he completed the job.[51] The *Guelph Advertiser* describes the preparations for the public execution:

As the time drew near when Coghlin was to be hanged for the murder of Richard Oliver, it was deemed advisable that such precautions should be made as would prevent the possibility of the peace being broken, or any inconvenience being suffered in carrying the law into effect. For this purpose the space between the jail and court-house was strongly barricaded and planked twelve feet high, and the recess between the two towers in front of the court-house was similarly defended, from an upper window of which the drop was placed. . . .For some days some little excitement was felt, caused primarily by the fact of no execution having previously taken place in Guelph, and perhaps some little through the peculiar circumstances of the case. On Tuesday [June 29th] about sixty special constables were sworn in for three days' service, instructed to muster at six o'clock on Thursday morning.[52]

As the date for the execution dawned, hundreds of people from far and near began to gather in front of the court-house. The *Guelph Advertiser* described the scene:

Soon after five o'clock on the morning of July first, people were collecting in front of the Court House, and about seven o'clock nearly a thousand were present, which number afterwards increased to up- wards of fifteen hundred at the lowest computation, a considerable number being women and children. It was at first intended that the execution should take place at eight o'clock, but the time was after- wards altered to ten. At the latter hour a cloth in front of the window was removed, and the criminal, with the sheriff and hangman appeared in view, and the former stepped on the drop outside the court house and addressed the assembled multitude during twenty minutes or half an hour.[53]

Coghlin's speech, delivered calmly, but in a firm, loud voice was a sensation. After asking the forgiveness of Richard Oliver's widow, and requesting that his friends not attempt to avenge his death, Coghlin then delivered a stinging denunciation of the quality of justice that he and other Catholics in Guelph had re- ceived, and in particular singled out Dr. Wil- liam Clarke as the source of much of that in- justice. These are a few excerpts from his statement as reported by the *Guelph Advertiser*:

Fellow Christians,—I am now about to appear be- fore the Great Judge who can neither deceive nor be deceived, and I trust in the unbounded mercies of that Judge to pardon all my offences, and with the assistance of my Savior who shed the last drop of his precious blood on the cross for mankind, that I will and do from the bottom of my heart forgive all my enemies, and I also pray to God to pardon them and convert them to his own wish. I will now proceed to give the public a statement of what brought me to this unhappy end, and shall leave to the public to judge whether I got justice or not. It is now about two years since I left my native home, and little did I think that I was coming to America to be hanged for murder,—but a murderer I am not. Unhappily for myself and my friends we settled

near to those unfortunate Olivers. Many years be- fore they quarrelled with us they were disturbers of the public peace and several quarrels took place be- tween the Olivers and us, and tried before the Magistrates in Guelph, and I am sorry to say that I never got justice done me from first to last.[54]

Here Coghlin denounced Dr. Clarke's brand of justice, but the *Advertiser* refused to print his statements. All the paper would say was:

The statement here proceeds to charge Dr. Clarke with neglect of duty in his magisterial capacity, etc., the publication of which would render us lia- ble to an action at law, and, besides, being a mere matter of opinion unconnected with the facts of the case, we do not consider that we should be justified in publishing that portion.[55]

Other area newspapers, however, were not so reticent. The *Galt Reporter* apparently car- ried such a strong attack on Dr. Clarke that both Guelph papers immediately rallied to his defence.[56]

Coghlin continued:

The day that Oliver was killed it is well known that they gave my brother Tom an unmerciful beating. I went to Guelph to buy shingles, which I did and was returning home late in the evening, myself and two or three others. Opposite Mr. Hewat's, or thereabouts, I met my brother Thomas. I enquired what happened to him, he said he met Richard and William Oliver on the hill and they butchered me in the manner you see. I then threw off my coat and followed the Olivers. I overtook the Olivers be- tween what is called Mitchell's hill and James Gay's. I asked Richard Oliver why he stabbed my brother in the manner he did. He made no reply. His brother Robert was on the ground in a sleigh. William Oliver struck me with a stone, at the same time Richard had a bayonet in his hand and struck me. I received several wounds at that time from said weapon. . . .The Olivers got into the sleigh and went towards home. I was greatly irritated at the time and pursued the Olivers again, but never once thought of killing any person. I followed with the intention of giving a good thrashing or getting one. I thought that they could not give me much until my brothers would be up to my assistance. I overtook the Olivers convenient to Murray's, the weaver, when I was within about thirty yards Richard and William Oliver jumped out of the sleigh and came to meet me. Richard had a bayonet in his hand. We met, and Richard made a blow at me with the bayonet. I cried out to him to stand back; he struck me several times, and wounded me. I told him to throw by his bayonet and not to murder, and fight with his hands and feet like a man. . .I recollected I had a knife in my trousers pocket—an old jack knife. I took it out. I again told him to stand back, or he should take it; he did not, but still struck at me. I made a rush at him and gave him a stab, but where I struck him I cannot tell; but with no attention [sic] to kill. . ., when I heard that Richard Oliver was dead, I did not believe it; if I had entertained the remotest idea that he was dead from the blow that I gave him I would not be here to-day; I had plenty of time to escape.

This statement, my fellow-Christians, you may depend on being correct; at this moment I would not tell a wilful lie for a thousand worlds. Farewell, good people. Remember me in your prayers to the Throne of Mercy.[57]

A cap was then drawn over Coghlin's head, and he stepped on the drop. The drop was cut, and he died almost instantly.

With his manner and speech, Charles Coghlin immediately became a hero to Guelph's Irish Catholics. The *Guelph Advertiser* described his funeral, held on July fourth:

On Saturday last, the body of this unfortunate man was committed to the earth, in the Roman Catholic burying ground. We had previously been informed that great preparations were making for a general turn out amongst those who held the same creed, but the attendance far exceeded our expectations; there being a procession which reached from the gate of the burying ground through the Market Square, around Brock's corner, and some distance down Woolwich Street, the numbers being stated to us variously at from 400 to 650, in waggons, on horse back, and on foot.

The assemblage on the occasion would rather have induced us to suppose that one of our greatest benefactors had died, or some martyr had evidenced the truth of the Gospel by his death, than that a culprit was about to be buried; but we believe that almost every Roman Catholic viewed him as a sacrifice, and not as a murderer.[58]

The funeral, however, was only the beginning of the Catholic reaction to Coghlin's execution. Night after night, in the darkness, men would gather around his grave, then fire a volley of shots, shattering the peace of Guelph's sleeping residents.[59] Mysteriously, the house belonging to James Clarvise, the man who had built the gallows, caught fire and burned, and threats of future burnings were made to others.[60] Both of Guelph's newspapers wrote strong editorials attacking those who were carrying out these disturbances, and praised Dr. Clarke for having done no more than to fulfil his duty. Dr. Clarke, however, undid whatever good impression the papers might have made by levelling a bitter attack against Thomas Heffernan, one of the leading Irishmen in Guelph. Clarke accused Heffernan of fabricating Coghlin's statement, and of attempting to foment further strife in Guelph.[61] Heffernan denied these charges, and warned that "it would be a deal wiser of Clarke to keep silent and let things be as they were, because, if he had made enemies for himself, his last letter in the Guelph papers will not make the number one less".[62]

The continued public outcry by Catholics against the apparent injustice of Coghlin's hanging, and the increasing agitation against the "oppression" of Catholics by Orangemen and the courts, threw the local newspapers into a mutual feeling of despair. For once, both editors found themselves upon common ground. What was being attacked, they argued, was not merely the actions of one man, Doctor Clarke, but the whole structure of justice, and the economic future of Guelph itself. The *Guelph Advertiser*, long an opponent of Doctor Clarke, expressed its uneasiness this way:

Really, distant readers must have a strange impression of the state of lawlessness and ill-feeling which appears to exist in our usually quiet town. The trial of Coghlin and the circumstances attending it. . ., the execution, and the speech of the dying man was one of the most singular for a person in his position which we have ever heard of. . . .Next comes a house burning. . . .Coghlin's friends firing guns around the grave. . .

A glance at these circumstances will naturally produce the reflection, that dreadful must be the state of a community where a person finds it necessary to disclaim having any connexion [sic] with the carrying out of the law; or most unrighteously must the law have been administered, which would call forth even an approach to a general feeling against any one connected therewith. Yet such is not the case in reality, and but for some dozen individuals we should be as peaceable and quiet as any part of the Province, or perhaps more so. We therefore hope, that from this time all feelings respecting the past will be forgotten; so that we may not be stamped as a community of Heathens, in the midst of gospel light and Christian privileges.[63]

Within two weeks, the worst fears of Guelph's editors were fulfilled.

If Doctor Clarke intended to heed Thomas Heffernan's warning to "keep quiet", that decision came too late. On August sixth, at about three a.m., the dreaded cry of "Fire!" rang through Guelph's streets. The fine new "Wellington Mill", only recently completed by the partnership of Doctors Orton and Clarke,

was ablaze. Within hours the building was reduced to ashes, the total loss amounting to £5,500 of which only £3,050 was covered by insurance.

The wave of shock which ran through the community as a result of this attack upon private property was far greater than that which had resulted from Richard Oliver's death. After all, however unfortunate the fact may be, as both newspapers pointed out, men were by nature weak and given to such excesses. The legal structure, however badly managed, was designed to contain these excesses, and represented the highest form of mental and social constraint upon individual weakness. If it were to be attacked, however just the individual complaints may be, the whole foundation of public order would be damaged. The shock, however, ran even deeper than the fears about the legal system. By burning the mills, private property, the basis of society, social order, and economic life had been threatened. The initial report of the *Guelph Advertiser* showed the depth of this response:

We cannot express the regret with which we sit down to relate an occurrence which is of greater importance to Guelph than any which has hitherto befallen it. The hopes and expectations of the inhabitants were justly elevated by the erection of the Wellington Mills, as giving increased facilities to farmers for the disposal of their produce, and as being a means of increasing the business and prosperity of the Town. The extensive building was completed so recently as February last, furnished with six run of stones, and finished off in the most complete manner.

But the demon of revenge, as is generally surmised, could not let so noble a structure, so great an acquisition to the neighbourhood, continue in this position long, and it falls to our lot to announce its complete destruction.[64]

The *Guelph Herald* put the connection between the sanctity of private property and the preservation of public order in even plainer terms:

From events which have recently transpired in this town and neighbourhood, there is but too good reason to suppose that the destruction of this valuable property has been the work of a most diabolical and wicked Incendiary, as there had been no fire in the premises for some days, at least, previous to the fire, and a person in the employment of Dr. Clarke, examined the Mill about ten o'clock the same night, in order to ascertain if all was right. Taking these things into consideration with the feelings of certain parties towards Dr. Clarke, engendered in consequence of his zeal in the public cause, there is not the slightest reason to conclude otherwise, than that the hand of some fiend; in human shape, applied the torch which consumed the valuable property.

The owners of the Mill are not the only sufferers by this calamity, but the public generally, especially the Farmer has sustained a very great loss.[65]

In response to the burning of Clarke and Orton's mill, the Town's leading property holders undertook an extensive campaign to rally public support for the magistrates. On the ninth of August, a large public meeting was called by Sheriff Grange at which leading citizens such as Judge William Dummer Powell, John Harland, Doctor Clarke, James Wright, Richard Fowler Budd, Thomas Sandilands, James Wilson, A.J. Fergusson, James Hodgert, J.W.B. Kelly, T.R. Brock and Benjamin Harrison took prominent roles. A statement by A.J. Fergusson set the tone of the meeting:

Mr. Fergusson observed, that he thought the tendency of such conduct, was to reduce the value of property in the District, not certainly to all equally, but all would suffer. It was time that the Magistracy should be supported, and that all should step forward and assist them.[66]

The meeting passed several resolutions condemning the arsonists, offering sympathy to Doctor Clarke, getting up a reward, and petitioning the government to reimburse losses of those who were made to suffer because of their

BRITISH AMERICA
FIRE AND LIFE
ASSURANCE COMPANY.
ONE HUNDRED POUNDS
REWARD.

WHEREAS the Grist Mill and Granary known as the WELLINGTON MILLS, in the Town of Guelph, belonging to, and in the occupation of Messrs. Clarke & Co., upon which a large sum had been Insured with this Company, were totally destroyed by Fire on the morning of the 6th of this present month of August. and whereas, information on oath has been furnished to the Company, such as to leave no reasonable doubt that the said Fire was caused by some evil and maliciously disposed person or persons, to injure the said Clarke & Co., and the Insurance Companies who share their loss.

NOTICE IS HEREBY GIVEN, that a Reward of ONE HUNDRED POUNDS will be paid by the above Company, on conviction of the offending party or parties, or for such information as will secure the said conviction.

By order of the Board,
T. W. BIRCHALL,
Managing Director.

British America Assurance Office, }
Toronto, 28th August, 1847, } 10d

(Guelph Herald)

"devotion to duty". At the meeting £250 was subscribed on the spot for a reward for the discovery of the arsonists.[67] Later this reward was increased to £630 by additional private subscriptions, plus £100 posted by the British American Insurance Company and £250 by the Provincial Government.[68]

The rewards were offered in vain: the culprit was never caught.

After several weeks of province wide discussion, the tragic events in Guelph gradually faded from the public view, but the effects in Guelph ran deep. How could such events be explained in "one of the most quiet and peaceable towns in the Province"?[69] One solution offered in the newspapers was education through the formation of a Mechanics' Institute.

The series of events which culminated in the burning of the Wellington Mill, did, apparently, have an effect upon Dr. Clarke. Having married the widow of Captain Poore and dissolved his partnership with Dr. Orton, he now devoted himself to his business interests, and would re-emerge in the railway promotions of the eighteen-fifties.

"Rosehurst", the residence of Dr. Wm. Clarke, later the home of Thomas Goldie.

The Wellington District Grammar School.

VI

Early Schools and Social Institutions

As the primary educational system evolved in Upper Canada, it contained two Government-subsidized parallel systems; the district grammar schools, created as a better quality system to train the future leaders of society; and the common schools which were intended to provide the rudiments of an education to the general public.

According to the Grammar School Act passed in 1807,[1] a portion of the revenues from Crown lands was set aside to create a fund to support the grammar schools. From that fund, each district town was to receive £100 per year towards the salary of the schoolmaster. In addition, the district was allowed to contribute whatever additional funds were necessary from general taxation revenues, and the schoolmaster was allowed to charge fees for each child taught. Teachers were required to have university degrees (many held M.A.'s) and to swear to uphold the articles of faith of the Church of England. The grammar schools taught all grades (called forms) from primary to university entrance, and the curriculum included, as a matter of course, subjects such as Greek, Latin and Rhetoric, necessary for entrance to the best British universities.

Arthur Cole Verner, B.A.
(Courtesy The High Schools of Guelph)

The Common School Act was not passed until 1816,[2] and schools established under this act differed somewhat from the grammar schools. It provided that when a "competent number of the inhabitants" of any "Town, Township, Village or Place" had built or provided a schoolhouse, had guaranteed to provide twenty or more pupils, and had provided, in part, for a salary for a teacher, they could then call a meeting to select three trustees who were empowered to appoint a British subject as a teacher. The Government maintained a large measure of control over these local school boards through a Government-appointed district board of education, which was empowered to specify what books might or might not be used, to rescind or alter local rules, and to remove the teacher should he or she prove unsatisfactory for any reason. In addition, in 1824, these district boards were given the power to license teachers as well. The Act of 1816 set aside £6,000 annually for common school support, but this provided very little to the individual schools. Thus they were almost entirely dependent on the fees collected by the teachers from the parents. When a teacher had taught for six months, he or she would apply to the local trustees for a "certificate of acceptable service" which was then presented to the district treasurer. If the certificate was satisfactory, the teacher would receive a share (a maximum of £25 per year) of the district's portion of the £6,000. In 1823 an additional degree of centralization was added when a "Central Board of Education" was established, headed by John Strachan, to which the local trustees were required to report at regular intervals. This change provided greater control over the curriculum used in the school system. Such

was the situation when John Galt founded Guelph.

The first school in Guelph was typical of most common schools of the time. In June, 1827, Galt built a shed adjoining the Priory, and an American immigrant named Davis took it over as a private school supported by fees paid by the parents of his students. Acton Burrows says of Davis that he was:

A fair type of the dominie of the period, whose intellectual acquirements did not go much beyond the "Three R's," and who had a deeply rooted conviction that there was no better mode of instilling knowledge into the minds of the rising generation than by the medium of a good sound birch rod.[3]

On more than one occasion, Davis apparently came close to receiving a little of the same "education" at the hands of irate parents. When patronage at this school quickly declined, Davis departed, and a number of village women taught the children until a better school and schoolmaster could be obtained.

The first school building to be erected in Guelph resulted from the decision to set aside half the purchase price of every town lot as an endowment for the support of education. As Galt noted on August 1, 1827:

I am laying the foundation of an academy, the Company having allowed me to reserve one half of the money arising from the sale of the land in the town for that purpose, by which I have already upwards of two thousand dollars in store. I have got a school already open in a shed.[4]

Among the formal ceremonies which marked the August 12, 1827, celebrations, was the laying of the corner stone of Galt's proposed "seminary" at which the Reverend Mr. Sheed delivered the address. James Innes reports:

Mr. Sheed, in the course of his remarks, congratulated the assembly that the first act of the Canada Company, in forming a new colony in the wilderness, was tending to secure, by a diffusion of knowledge, the prosperity and stability of the establishment.

He hoped that the Seminary might prove not only the means of diffusing a knowledge of those things that concerned this life; but might enlighten the minds of the rising generation with an understanding of their higher interests in a world beyond the grave. . .[5]

This school, known for generations as the "Stone School," was a one room building capable of accommodating forty pupils. Its first teacher was Mr. Wiley, followed by David Matthews, who took up the position in 1828 and held it for fifteen years.[6] Among the first pupils were William McCrea, Robert Thompson, James Thompson, Gordon Matthews, Frank Matthews, and Christina Matthews.[7] One writer remembered school life of the time as follows:

In those early days, the compensation of the teacher was in accordance with the circumstances of the settlers. If the fee of 25¢ per month could not be paid in money, the teacher was willing to take its equivalent in flour, pork, wood, or other trade. Attendance was voluntary, the teacher making his own arrangements with the parents. The subjects taught and the methods of instruction were primitive. Writing was carefully taught, but the only text books used were the Bible, the English Reader, spelling book and arithmetic.[8]

In general, education in Guelph did not alter greatly until 1840.

The first major advance over the one room stone common school came with the creation of Wellington District. Upon being named the District Town, the unincorporated village of Guelph automatically became eligible for a grant of £100 to pay the salary of a grammar school teacher. In 1841 a grammar school was opened in rented premises on Huskisson Street with Arthur Cole Verner, B.A., as master, who served in that capacity for the next six years. During 1841 and 1842, a permanent grammar school was erected on Waterloo Avenue, and Verner moved his classes to that building in 1842. Built of frame and plaster, the Waterloo Avenue building was described as being "fitted up in a superior manner,"[9] and continued in use until 1854.[10]

The District Grammar School fees may have been beyond the reach of most of the area's residents. In any event, attendance before 1850 never exceeded thirty pupils, and, at times, the number dropped below ten.

In 1847, Verner resigned his position and was replaced by George Elmslie, a Scottish immigrant and classics scholar who, like John Galt, had come to Canada originally as the employee of a land settlement company. Although Elmslie apparently found that his attempts to farm and teach at the same time were too exhausting to continue (he retired as master after two years) the school appears to have flourished under his charge.[11] An advertisement for the grammar school appeared in the *Guelph and Galt Advertiser*, April 2, 1847, as follows:

Mr. Elmslie begs to intimate that the District Grammar School was opened on the 15th Inst., in the building behind Mr. Armstrong's Tavern, Waterloo Road.

The hours of attendance are from 9 o'clock A.M. to 12 o'clock noon, and from half-past one to four P.M.

The fees as fixed by the Trustees are for the usual branches of English Education: 12s. 6d. per Qr.

Latin, Greek, Algebra, etc. 20s. per Qr.

Mr. E. has room for three or four additional BOARDERS, as to whose intellectual and moral training unremitting care will be devoted.—The dwelling-house is comfortable and commodious, with a large play ground.

                    Guelph, 24th March, 1847.[12]

By late summer, the school's trustees could report:

The Wellington District Grammar School being about to be reopened on the 1st of September, after the usual summer vacation, the Trustees who were present at the half-yearly examination deem it but just to the Master to express their satisfaction at the efficient state in which they found the institution on the occasion referred to. On Mr. Elmslie's entering on his duties in March last, eight pupils presented themselves for instruction, and in the short period that has elapsed, the number of pupils has increased to twenty-six, twenty-five of whom appeared at the late half-yearly examination, whose general progress was most satisfactory.—Their answers in the various branches of instruction clearly indicated the pains that Mr. Elmslie had taken to make them understand the meaning of what they had read, and to accustom them to those habits of analysis which every sound teacher of youth will desire to form. The Trustees were agreeably surprised at the rapidity and accuracy with which the pupils solved the questions in arithmetic, that were proposed to them, and the general state of order and discipline, obtained their entire approval, and they feel no hesitation in recommending the Wellington District Grammar School to the confidence and support of the inhabitants of the Distrlct.

                    Guelph, August 25th, 1847.[13]

For those able to afford the higher fees, the Guelph grammar school provided a good preparatory education.

As a companion piece to the *Act for Better Internal Government* in 1841, the Legislature passed an important new *Education Act*[14] which made great strides towards improving the quality of education in the common school system.

The *1841 Education Act* created a Common School Fund, which was to be financed and sustained by the sale or lease of public lands set aside for that purpose. The income from this fund was to be made up to £50,000 per year by additional grants, and this amount was to be divided among the districts on a per capita basis comprising all children between the ages of five and sixteen years. The district council was made into a "board of education" and in order to receive the provincial grant was required to raise an equal amount from local taxation, all of which they were then required to apportion among the various townships.

Local administration of schools was placed in the hands of township commissioners (five to seven in number depending on the population of the township) who were elected at the annual township meeting. It was their duty to divide the township into school districts, purchase school sites, make estimates of the cost of necessary buildings and repairs of schools, appoint and remove teachers, regulate the local course of study, establish the school rules, determine what books were to be used, and be responsible for a host of other duties connected with the local schools.

At the annual meeting of Guelph Township in 1842 the following school Commissioners were elected: the Reverends Arthur Palmer, James Smith, William P. Wastell and Thomas Gibney; Doctor Henry Orton, Thomas Sandilands and Charles J. Mickle. At their first meeting held on May 11, 1842, the township was divided into seven school districts: No. 1, York Road; No. 2, the Town of Guelph; No. 3, Waterloo Road; No. 4, Paisley Block; No. 5, 4th Concession, Division D; No. 6, Woolwich Road; No. 7, Eramosa Road. The teachers

The Paisley Block School.

employed in 1842 were: Paisley Block school, William Cowan; Guelph town school, David Matthews; Division D school, William Hiscock; York Road school, Cornelius Sheehan; Scotch Block Road school, (Woolwich Rd.) A. Kennedy; Eramosa Road school, George Mimmack; and Waterloo Road school, Mr. Foley. Alfred A. Baker, the Township Clerk, acted as Clerk of the Commissioners.[15]   In 1843 this system was given a more formal structure through the appointment of district superintendents of schools appointed by the district council.[16] In addition to apportioning school funds, and making reports to the provincial Superintendent of Education, the district superintendent in conjunction with the township superintendent, was responsible for the examination of teachers. Thus there was

produced a formal structure of officers, duties and powers which reached from the township to the provincial government. The Provincial Superintendent was charged with supervising the whole system, and making reports and recommendations to the government. The heart of the system was the required reports and inspections and while the school system was given a form of local control, central authority was ensured by dependence upon government funding. Parents, however, were still required to pay fees for children attending the common schools.

Under the new Act, Dr. Henry Orton was appointed Superintendent of Schools in the Town and Township of Guelph, and Trustees for the Town were David Allan, James Hough and Dr. Clarke.

The new school legislation had an immediate beneficial effect upon school building and attendance. Many of the local schools, which had depended upon student fees and volunteer aid, were in poor condition and several had to be replaced over the next few years.[17] With the district council responsible for raising grants to match those made by the provincial authorities, a steady flow of funds into the school districts resulted. Table XXIII shows the amount of money flowing to the local schools from provincial and district sources.

There was, as can be seen, a wide variation in the grant per school among townships, and in the case of Nichol, among school districts. This was due to the distribution of the grant being based upon the number of school-aged children residing in the township, and not upon attendance or need. This system was not changed until 1852 when attendance would be made the basis for grants.

No description of the Guelph school system in the 1840's would be complete without some recognition of the role played by private schools. With all schools dependent to some degree upon fees, private schools which could demonstrate some special value attractive to the well-to-do families, could expect to receive a significant number of students. The fact that the Guelph grammar school catered exclusively to boys meant that there was a constant demand from wealthier families for a private school where their girls would receive a similar training in letters and social deportment. One such school was opened in Guelph in 1843 by a Miss Idington and her sister, Mrs. Worsley.[19] In 1848 a second such school was advertised:

Mrs. and Misses SANDERS, beg leave to announce to the Inhabitants of Guelph and its vicinity, that they purpose [*sic*] opening a SCHOOL in the Town of Guelph, after Midsummer vacation, for the Instruction of Young Ladies, in the usual Branches of an English Education, viz: Reading, Writing, and Arithmetic, Grammar, History and Geography, with Plain and Fancy Needle-work, Music and Drawing.

Guelph, May 2nd, 1848.[20]

In 1847 a different type of specialized school was opened in Guelph for teaching children too young to attend the grammar or girls' schools. In March, this advertisement appeared:

WILLIAM NEEVE

Having been induced, on the recommendation of several friends, to establish a *School* in the Building adjacent to the English Church; hereby informs the Public that he will commence on *Monday*, the 15th of March, when he hopes, by the unceasing atten-

Table XXIII
Distribution of the Common School Grant in Wellington District, 1843[18]

Township	No. of Schools	Amount of grant per school, from school fund and school assessment		
Waterloo	20	£19	13s.	10d.
Wilmot	6	32	1	8
Erin	9	13	9	10
Eramosa	5	16	7	10
Woolwich	7	13	0	0
Garafraxa	5	7	11	2
Guelph	7	27	0	0
Nichol, S.S. No. 1	1	26	9	7
Nichol, S.S. No. 2	1	14	19	6
Nichol, S.S. No. 3	1	10	8	2
Nichol, S.S. No. 4	1	21	3	8
Nichol, S.S. No. 5	1	20	5	5
Queen's Bush	1	22	1	6

tion which he will be enabled to give a limited number of children, *of both sexes*, to merit the approbation of those parents who may be disposed to encourage him.

Terms, Two Dollars per Quarter.

Guelph, March 12, 1847.[21]

While only a limited number of parents could afford to send their children to special schools, common school events, particularly the formal public examinations, loomed large in the social life of the town. Not only were these examinations attended by parents and trustees, but by a considerable number of the public as well—and they were reported upon at length in the local newspapers. This report, of the fall term examinations in December, 1849, was typical:

SCHOOL EXAMINATIONS

On Monday, the 24th ult., the examination of Mr. Blake's School in this Town, took place, commencing at 10 o'clock A.M. The forenoon was taken up examining in Spelling, Reading, Arithmetic, Geography, and Biblical History, which were gone through in such a way that all present were satisfied that the Teacher had not spared pains, or the children application. The afternoon was occupied in the examination of the elder scholars in Grammar. After the Teacher, the Rev. Mr. Torrance, put a number of questions to the pupils, and expressed himself well pleased with the knowledge they displayed of this very important study. . . .We were highly pleased with the deportment of the pupils during their lengthy exercises [exams were also given in Arithmetic, Geography and Astronomy to the senior pupils]. The Revds. Messrs. Torrance, Spencer, Braine, and Fish, were present during part of the examination. After some remarks from the Teacher, the Rev. Mr. Braine addressed the pupils. . . .The pupils returned thanks. The audience then dispersed, (the pupils and a few others remaining) the teacher treated his School to a good repast of bread and butter, cakes, and confectionery. At about seven o'clock, a series of recitations

commenced, both amusing and instructive, in which the scholars displayed a confidence truly surprising. Ignorance, vanity of dress, oppression, cruelty, avarice, drunkenness, and other evils, were shown up, and stripped of every covering that is used to deceive. Two of the beautiful dramas of Hannah More were performed in such a manner, that Mr. Braine stated, after all was over, that he never saw them better performed in his own School. These were Moses in the Bulrushes, and David and Goliath. A number of temperance, and other hymns, were sung during the evening by the children, in a very pleasant and correct manner; the last was, "Good night my Christian friends, good night."

Thanks were given to the Teacher for his care and attention to the improvement of the children entrusted to him. The house was crowded, and the stillness and attention of the spectators were proof positive that they were all delighted.[22]

From time to time District and County Councillors questioned the morality of the maintenance of two government-supported systems where the degree of support was so unequal. Thus, in June, 1851, when the Reverend E.M. Stewart, teacher of the grammar school, requested sufficient money to build a cow shed on the school property, a number of District Councillors objected strongly to such aid.[23] Doctor Henry Orton, whose two boys, Thomas and Harry, attended the school, came strongly to the school's defence. The grammar school was necessary, Doctor Orton argued, not because it provided a better education in scholastic subjects, but because it made gentlemen—it educated its students in habits, manners and tastes which would allow its graduates to join in the best society of England. Orton's comparison of the two systems of schooling is interesting in several respects:

I was told [that] Mr. Sparrow of Berlin [a County Councillor] had sent his son to the District School, but had taken him away and sent him to Mr. Wetherald's [common school], and that he preferred Wm. Wetherald's to the District School; he doubtless preferred utility to taste, and he was right in his choice; still the District School is the Grammar School, and should be, and Wm. Wetherald's never could be. If I am not too tedious I will make it plainer. I have myself two boys, and I wish to bring them up to common everyday trades, now I should rather, if the distance were equal, send them to Wm. Wetherald's or Wm. Cowan's [common school in Guelph] than to the District School: in the short time they will have for schooling, they might, perhaps, acquire more of the essential requisites of reading, writing, arithmetic, English grammar and geography than at the District School, for they are both picked schools of the kind,—yes and get a notion, too, of Latin if wished; enough to learn the connexion and derivation of many words in the English language; on the whole they would have a far better school than Farmers and Tradespeople usually send their children to with us. Again I have two boys I wished to be educated as for the medical profession, whether they ultimately adopt it or not. It is true that a little Latin or Greek will suffice to get admission into the medical school, and that little they might get at Wm. Wetherald's or Wm. Cowan's; but I want a little more,—I wish them to be recognized as having received a classical education in educated society. . . .For example—if they happened to visit the Old World and wished to fraternize or be received or visit amongst the learned Bodies, with the Latin from Wm. Wetherald's or Wm. Cowan's, they would be regarded as from the wilds of Canada or Towns of New England—Canadian boors or Yankee Adventurers. . . .[24]

To a group of people who still thought of Britain as "home," if the best British "public" schools were beyond their means and reach, they would do what they could to overcome that lack through the grammar school system.

In the case of the Guelph Grammar school, they would succeed very well indeed in duplicating the British "public" school system. As

The Rockwood Academy.
(Courtesy Public Archives of Canada)

Doctor Orton remarked, the quality of grammar school teachers hired in Guelph was very high:

The present masters of our District School would be deemed a credit to any Grammar School either here or at home; in fact, not many schools at home can boast of more elegant scholars and more efficient classical teachers, than we have in our District School. . . .both are so remarkable for that true delicacy, gentleness, and modesty in demeanor and character—the very characteristics of the gentleman and scholar.[25]

The ultimate prominence of so many students from Arthur Cole Verner's class of 1845 demonstrates the degree of success that the Guelph grammar school enjoyed. Greta M. Shutt gives this account of the pupils in attendance that year:

Tom Orton, who became senior surgeon of the Royal Navy; Tom Saunders, a lawyer, and Guelph's first police magistrate; Jimmy Thorp, a seedsman, who later held a position in the post-office; Jack and George Sandilands, one of whom was a bank manager; Jack Chipchase; Jack Lamprey, mayor of Guelph; Henry Lynch; John Hough. . . .was in the publishing business with J.W. Lyon. Alfred Howitt became a surveyor. . . .Joe and Josh Wright were sons of Samuel Wright, the baker. Then came four whose first names are forgotten and of whom nothing is known, Dawson, Lane, [John] Whitt and Sweetnam. Fred Verner was the son of the head-master and became a famous artist both in Canada and England. John Howitt became a doctor. . . .Then came Fred Whitt; Harry Orton [a brother of Tom, one of four of Doctor Orton's children who became doctors];[26] Charles and Mike Turner; Bill Chipchase; Sawney Macdonald; and last but by no means least, Bill Peterson. . .[27]

H.W. "Bill" Peterson would serve as the Crown Attorney of Wellington County, and a member and secretary of the Guelph Board of Education for many years.

The report of the Guelph Town Board of School Trustees of February, 1852, only nine months after Doctor Orton's letter appeared in the *Guelph Advertiser*, makes a dramatic contrast to the conditions and purposes that he described. According to the Trustees, of the 481 children in Guelph between the ages of five and sixteen,[28] an average of only 160 to 170 were in attendance at the three common schools with possibly 30 boys at the grammar school. In contrast to the Government grant of £100 to the grammar school, the total Town expenditure on all three common schools (including the payment of some bills that went back to 1849) was £133. 10s. 10d. As mentioned previously each parent paid fees to the teachers who taught their children. Finally, two of the common schools in 1852 were conducted in rented premises in private homes. The introduction to the 1852 Report gives some indication of the difficulties under which the common school teachers laboured:

The Board of Trustees for Common Schools of the Town of Guelph, in laying their Report before the public, beg to state—that the number of Schools under their charge are three, namely, two boys' and one girls' school; all kept separately, and in different parts of the Town. One of the boys' schools is kept by Mr. Hough, and contains sixty scholars: with the junior classes and female scholars he is greatly assisted by Mrs. Hough, who had had considerable experience in teaching, and is a great acquisition to the School,—which is, in fact, in a very efficient state. The other boys' school is kept by Mr. Oliver, and contains about forty scholars. He commenced under very disadvantageous circumstances about six months ago, the preceding teacher leaving it in a disreputable state. The girls' school is kept by Miss Kennedy, and is a large one, containing between sixty and seventy scholars, and is very satisfactorily conducted.[29]

Henry W. Peterson, Jr., Crown Attorney of Wellington County, Chairman of the Board of Education, and Mayor in 1863.

Salaries paid by the Town to these teachers (in addition to the fees collected from the students) were James Hough, £32. 5s. 3d. for twelve months, Henry Oliver, £20. 16s. 8d. for seven months, and Miss M.S. Kennedy, £25. for twelve months. Mrs. Hough apparently was not paid.

Many years would pass before the differences in quality and financial support between the grammar and common school systems would be overcome.

Two interesting organizations developed in Guelph in the eighteen-forties and early eighteen-fifties. The origins of these institutions, the Benevolent Association and the Mechanics' Institute, can be traced to specific needs. It was the flood of desperately poor Irish and Scottish immigrants who began to arrive at this time which would cause local residents to move towards a more organized form of welfare.

Due to the Scottish and Irish landlords having found that the raising of sheep and cash crops was more profitable than the rents paid by the tenants and crofters, the British Parliament passed more than four thousand Acts which drove the small farmers from the estates of the rich. These "enclosures" forced millions of men, women and children out of their homes, and the Irish famine of 1846 compounded an already desperate situation.

Facing an ever-increasing flood of immigrants whose desperate need for charity could not be denied, in 1845 Guelph's residents decided to create the Wellington District Benevolent Association.[30] The two main purposes of the Association were outlined clearly in the report of the Committee of Relief at the Annual Meeting, May 24, 1849. In part, that report said:

A great number of applicants have pleaded their claims to your charity, fifty-seven of whom have been considered proper objects for relief. According to the Journal, thirty-four cases of widows, and sixty-three of their children, besides many others, from various parts of the District, and of a truly distressing character, have shared in your benevolence; among whom have appeared persons whose manners gave ample proof of their having seen better days. . . .

The operations of your Association have established the fact that the lowest class of this community has changed its character; but a few years back it would have been a difficult task to have found a really needy person, but such is no longer the case, the late tide of emigration brought many whom various adversities have made very poor and helpless; these and the common misfortunes to which the labouring class is constantly exposed, will ever render a relief *fund* indispensible; and there are some few who would prefer sharing the profits of other men's industry rather than endure the fatigues of acquiring an honest living by their own, which enforces the necessity of guarding *that* fund, against the pretended claims of such worthless characters.

Your Committee have watched the rise and progress of a system of itinerant beggary practiced upon the neighbourhood. . .and they are fully persuaded that the principles of your Association are well adapted to this change of circumstances; and that an active and discriminating relief committee, whose business it may be to discountenance idleness, recommend industry, furnish as much labor as possible at a fair remuneration, and bestow your donations on proper objects, is the community's only defence against imposition and vagrancy, and that, if this or some other institution be not supported by voluntary contribution the neighbourhood will soon be over-run by mendicants; and poor rates will have to be levied for the relief of widows and orphans.[31]

The method of operation of the Wellington District Benevolent Association was simple but

TOWN HALL, GUELPH.

GRAND CONCERT!

Under the Auspices of the Ladies' Benevolent Society

ON EASTER MONDAY, APRIL 2nd, 1866

PROGRAMME.
PART FIRST.

1—Chorus—The Chough and Crow.............. ....
MRS. LEMON, MRS. CUTHBERT, MESSRS. TAYLOR, BREADON & SAVAGE.
2—Song—The Flag of Old England forever ....W. Bradbury
MR. T H. TAYLOR.
3—Duet—We come from Fairy Bowers..S. Glover
MRS. LEMON AND MISS WYLD.
4—Song—I'll not throw away the flower........................Alex. Lee
MRS. CLARKE.
5—Song—Dear Home, I'll come to thee ....
MR. T. BREADON.
6—Song—Come into the garden, Maud ....Balfe
MRS. LEMON.
7—Duet—We are Fairies of the Sea ....S. Glover
MRS. CUTHBERT AND MRS. HODGERT.
8—Song—Home they brought her Warrior, dead .. ..Miss Lindsay
MISS WYLD.
9—Song—Pat Malloy..
MR. R. DICKSON.

PART SECOND.

10—Duet—Rheine Wine..
MESSRS. R. AND G. DICKSON.
11—Song—Nightingale's Trill...William Gans
MRS. CUTHBERT.
12—Song..
MR. GEALE DICKSON.
13—Song—At Five O'clock in the Morning..........................Claribel
MISS WYLD.
14—Duet—In the Starlight...S. Glover
MRS. CUTHBERT AND MRS. HODGERT.
15 Song The Little Cot beside the Sea...........................G. Lindley
MRS. CLARKE.
16—Descriptive Song—The Ship on Fire..........................Henry Russell
MR. T. H. TAYLOR.
17—Song—The Moonbeam..
MRS. LEMON.

GOD SAVE THE QUEEN.

Mrs. Budd and Mr. C. Murton will preside at the Piano.

DOORS OPEN AT SEVEN. . . TO COMMENCE AT EIGHT.

TICKETS - - - - - TWENTY-FIVE CENTS.

Printed at the Herald Cheap Job Office, Guelph.

effective. Residents of the district who wished to do so became members through the subscription of five shillings per year to the Association's funds. Female members might join for half that sum. To encourage those who might be reluctant to join, membership lists and the amount of donation were printed regularly in the Guelph newspapers. The list for 1846-1847 reads like a roll-call of the Guelph area's leading families: James Bates, C.J. Mickle, Esq., C. Mickle, Wm. Jackson, David Stirton, James Stirton, George Wilson, Wm. Phin, John Cockburn, George W. Allen, James Hough, D. Benedict, Dr. Wm. Clarke, Wm. Dyson, A. Stephens, R. Armstrong, T. McCarter, T. Heffernan, James Collis, Wm. Smith, Henry Fry, James Wright, Esq., J. Fergusson, James Scott, Thomas Ainlay, John Rennie, James Cowan, Esq., Wm. Hyslop, T. Bosworth, A.J. Fergusson, Esq., Dr. Henry Orton, Samuel Wright, John Smith, James Phin, John Kirkland, John Petty, Robert Sunley, W. Nicholson, James Smith, David Darby, A.D. Ferrier, Robert Thompson and Rev. William Barrie. All gave five shillings except John Rennie who donated double that amount. The "ladies'" subscription list was headed by Mrs. Dr. Alling, Miss A. Stannard, Miss Aldous, and Mrs. Armstrong who gave five shillings, while Mrs. T. Ainlay, Mrs. R. Ainlay, Mrs. J. Smith, Mrs. Richardson, Mrs. McCarter, Mrs. W. Sunley, and Mrs. G. Wilson gave the standard six shillings, sixpence.[32]

At each annual meeting, a Relief Committee was elected whose duty it was to determine whether or not an applicant was worthy of charity. In 1847 that committee consisted of Drs. Alling and Clarke, A.D. Ferrier, Esq., Messrs. Wm. Dyson, John Cockburn, George Wilson, Anthony Stephens, David Stirton,

George W. Allen, John Rennie, Robert Sunley, Robert Armstrong, James Fergusson, Robert Thompson, William Hyslop, James Phin and Edward Carrol.[33]

Whenever a person applied for aid, a panel of any two of the committee would examine the applicant in detail, and decide whether or not, and to what degree, charity should be given. Having made that determination, an order was issued to John McLean, the Treasurer, and payment was made. At the same time, details of the case were entered into the Association's journal. The following entries, chosen by the Relief Committee for publication in the *Guelph & Galt Advertiser*, May 28, 1847, give some indication of the variety of cases to which aid was given:

June 27 [1846]—Dennis McNamara, an emigrant from Ireland, a poor but seemingly respectable man, and a very worthy object of charity. He stated that he was out of money, and was on his way to Sydenham [Owen Sound], where he expected to find a brother who had been in the country 5 years. His statements were very satisfactory. By an order signed by Messrs. Heffernan and Robert Armstrong he obtained 10s., for which he seemed very thankful.
Same day—from England, a stone-cutter. He observed that as a stranger he knew not where to go; did not want relief, but should be very glad to get work; found him employment with Messrs. Black and McNab, masons.
Nov. 27—George Clarke, blacksmith from Bridgeport. His leg was swollen to a prodigious size. On inquiring what was amiss with it, he stated, rather to my surprise, that it was a white swelling. This man's conduct was the only instance of abuse of the society's funds that we are aware of. The worthless fellow was intoxicated in the evening of the same day that he had received 5s. by an order signed by Messrs. Orton and Dyson. . .
Dec. 19—Widow Kennedy, a poor old woman who said she had nothing to eat, and nothing to depend on but her son-in-law, who was sick and unable to work for his wife and children. Order signed by Messrs. Smith and Heffernan—amount 10s.
Dec. 19—Mary Parish, a poor widow with 2 children—burned out. This case was recommended by Messrs. Webster and Fordyce. Order signed by Messrs. Smith and Heffernan—amount 10s.[34]

In all, the Wellington District Benevolent Association distributed £13. 12s. 6d. in 1846-1847, £17. 5s. 0d. in 1847-1848, and £32. 15s. 0d. in 1848-1849.[35]

During 1849-1850, in a period of severe economic depression, only £11. 5s. 7½d. was donated to the society. As the Report of the Relief Committee of the Association said:

The hearts and efforts of the association were straightened from want of funds; and whatever desires felt by the members to make the institution purely voluntary, they soon found that the income was so inadequate to meet, in a sufficient manner, the calls made upon the committee that, after mature deliberation, it was found absolutely necessary to apply to the Municipality of the Township, for that aid which was otherwise so scantily afforded.[36]

In response to this appeal, the Township Council voted twenty pounds to aid the Association's work.[37] In gratitude for this aid, the Benevolent Association was renamed the Guelph Township Benevolent Association at its Annual Meeting, May 24, 1850.[38] By the terms of the Township grant, all relief given by the Association after that date had to be restricted to residents of the Township.

Once the Town of Guelph had achieved its separate corporate status in 1851, a final change was made in the Benevolent Association's name and terms of reference. The Minutes of the Town Council of Guelph for February 11, 1851, outline the reasons for the changes:

Mr. Thorp moved, seconded by Mr. Hubbard:
That the Petition of the Guelph Township Benevo-

lent Association be received, and that the sum of *Twenty Pounds* be assessed upon the taxable inhabitants of the Town of Guelph, and collected for the purpose of relieving indigent persons and that the said sum be assessed and collected, after the same manner as other taxes, and that the said sum, when collected be paid by the Town Treasurer to the Treasurer of said *Benevolent Association*.

Provided that in case the Township Council refuse to grant a sum towards supporting the said association; that the funds of said Benevolent Association shall be appropriated to the relief of those persons residing within the limits of the *Town of Guelph*; and the other:

Providing also that the Committee of said Association substitute the *"Guelph Town Benevolent Association"* in place of its present designation.[39]

When the Guelph Township Council rejected the Benevolent Association's request for a grant, the Association made the changes requested by the Town Council.

The Annual Report of the Benevolent Association for 1852 made the following comments:

Your Committee beg leave to report, that your Association. . .has not only been in existence, but has for six years, according to its ability, been affording alike to all the deserving poor irrespective of nationality or sectarianism, that sympathy and relief which has often dried the widow's tear, and made the lonely stranger feel at home.

During that period the Association has disbursed for relief alone the sum of £154. 13s. 6d. of which. . .£70. 3s. 4½d. [was] the amount of donations and subscriptions, which have been paid by a comparatively charitable few of this neighbourhood.

Your Committee have only to refer to the above for proof that the voluntary principle of this locality is not adequate to the support of the aged and infirm, much less to the additional relief of those who through sickness, misfortune, and emigration, are constantly dependent upon charity; and they fear that professions of regard for the voluntary principle are too often substituted for the exercise of that benevolence which has for its object the welfare of a fellow creature.

Your Committee therefore recommend that the Town Council be requested to continue their assistance. . . .[40]

The retention of the appearance of being a voluntary association, while becoming more and more dependent upon municipal funds, would remain a constant factor in Guelph's social institutions from that time on.

The creation of the Guelph Mechanics' Institute in 1850, like the founding of the Benevolent Association, was a response to changing social conditions. The wealthier and well educated British families of Guelph had a strong desire to maintain a high level of culture among themselves, and had done their best to provide for their children as many of the cultural amenities as the community could support. When Thomas Sandilands came to Guelph in 1832, he opened a general store in a log building, and, at the rear, maintained a circulating library.[41] For more than fifteen years this circulating library remained the principal repository of information for the area, although poverty and lack of interest on the part of the general population severely retarded its growth.

In 1847, at the point when public feeling concerning the Oliver-Coghlin feud and hanging was at its highest, this letter, signed "A Mechanic of Guelph" appeared in both the *Advertiser* and *Herald*:

Sir,—The excitement which has for some time existed in this neighborhood in consequence of a number of untoward events, renders it highly probable that the newspapers will for a time, receive a considerable amount of attention. Taking advantage of this circumstance I would ask of your readers whether they would not contribute more to the happiness and welfare of the inhabitants of Guelph, and the district of which it is the chief town, by the establishment of a Mechanics' Institute, and thereby foster the growth of sound and useful knowledge, than by countenancing or acquiescing in the perpetuation of feuds and party demonstrations which have their origin in ignorance and are nursed by superstition and fanaticism.[42]

The second influence that would be melded into the development of the Mechanics' Institute, was the public educational programs of the various evangelical churches. An advertisement, which appeared in the *Guelph Herald* in the winter of 1848, illustrates the nature of these programs.

PUBLIC LECTURES

The inhabitants of Guelph and neighbourhood are respectfully informed that the following Clergymen will deliver a course of Lectures in the Court House, on the following subjects:

Rev. R. Torrance, 31st January.
The utility of Knowledge in general—The special importance of religious Knowledge.

Rev. Mr. Hunt, 14th February.
Authenticity and Genuineness of Scripture.

Rev. Mr. Grigor, 28th February.
An argument for Christianity, deduced from the Word and Works of God, especially consonance of Revelation and Providence.

Rev. Mr. Bredin, 13th March.
The moral influence of the Press.

Rev. Mr. Braine, 27th March.
Astronomy—the character and power of the Telescope, and the character and power of the mental machinery.

Lectures to commence at half-past seven.

ADMITTANCE FREE[43]

Although these ministers represented varied Protestant sects (Braine, Congregational; Bre-

Thomas Sandilands.

din, Methodist; Grigor, Presbyterian; and Torrance, United Presbyterian) they were fully agreed upon the general social value of providing a source of information for those who wished to augment their education. It was this purpose, impetus and energy which the Evangelical Protestant ministers and lay leaders brought to the formation of the local Mechanics' Institute.

Another factor contributing to the creation of the Mechanics' Institute was the need to "counteract some of the evil influences and attractions of bar rooms and other similar places" by the provision of "facilities for self-improvement after the hours of labour."[44]

Finally following passage of a bill by the Parliament of Canada providing for grants to Mechanics' Institutes, the stage was set and the *Guelph & Galt Advertiser* gave this account:

For some weeks past, a number of persons have convened, weekly, in a private house, for the purpose of instituting a Debating Club, to afford a source of intellectual enjoyment to all who may feel disposed to embrace the opportunity presented of becoming members of an Institution so eminently calculated to diffuse useful knowledge, and to mould and refine the character of its members. At one of the meetings of the Society the officers were empowered to act as a Committee to prepare a Constitution to be governed by in future; consequently, on Friday evening, 28th [December, 1849], at the usual place of meeting, the Vice-President submitted to the Society, for their approval, a code of laws, which were adopted. At the close of the meetings, the officers were instructed to solicit books and subscriptions from the inhabitants, and Lectures from professional gentlemen, and a collection to be taken up, at the close of each lecture to enable the Society to carry out its intentions. Mr. Hough has kindly given the use of his stone School House, in Nottingham Street, to the Society, until a more suitable place can be procured.[45]

The Society's committee, consisting of Alexander Campbell, President; William Crawford, Vice-President; Robert Whitelaw, Recording Secretary; Alfred H. St. Germain, Corresponding Secretary; and Henry Richards, Treasurer, all skilled craftsmen and store clerks, called a meeting for January 11, 1850, to gain public support for the new institution.

This meeting called by the Mechanics' Debating Society, was from an organizational point of view, a distinct success. With little delay a committee was struck to draw up rules and regulations to govern the proposed institution, and a meeting was called for the next week to actually start up operations. It was clear, however, that the original proponents of the Mechanics' Institute were quickly overshadowed by the emergence of the evangelical

churches' ministers and lay leaders as the predominant voices. Even the title of the new organization was changed at the initiative of one of these ministers, Reverend J.G. MacGregor (Free Church). Reverend MacGregor phrased his suggested title in this manner:

He hoped that all classes of the community would unite as one man to support the proposed institution; but he would suggest that the name be "The Farmers' and Mechanics' Institute of Guelph." He made this proposition because Mechanics were more or less connected with Farmers and Farmers more or less connected with the Mechanics of Guelph. It was very desirable they should all unite in this great and good work.[46]

The Institute bore this title for a long time.

Elected at the meeting called for January 18, 1850, to form the first executive of the new Farmers' and Mechanics' Institute, were C.J. Mickle, President; Dr. Liddell, First Vice-President; J. Harrison, Second Vice-President; A.H. St. Germain, Secretary; and T. Sandilands, Esq., Treasurer; of whom only one was a member of the original debating society. Also formed were a Finance Committee, a Lecture Committee, and a Library Committee, having the following members: Sheriff Grange, Col. Hewat, Rev. R. Torrance, Messrs. R. Scott, P. Gow, J. Ferguson, J. Watt, D. Savage, J. Armstrong, W. Crowe, R. Thompson and J. Jackson.[47] It was reported that there were nearly one hundred paid members,[48] with annual fees of 5 shillings for adults and 2 shillings six pence for junior members. The objectives of the Farmers' and Mechanics' Institute were:

1. The advancement of literature and the diffusion of knowledge amongst its members,
2. The formation of a library,
3. The delivery of lectures, which were to be illustrated as far as possible,

4. The organization of classes for instruction and reading.

At the first general meeting on February 1st, 1850, Mr. A.H. St. Germain, Secretary, the only member left of the Mechanics' Debating Society, resigned and was replaced by A. McDonald.[49] By March the "Institute" could report that it had subscribed to four quarterly journals, including Blackwood's and the Art Journal, and that it possessed a library of 250 volumes and a reading room open three evenings a week.[50] In April, Mr. Sandilands transferred the contents of his Circulating Library (some three hundred books) to the new "Institute", and fifty-six new volumes had been purchased.[51] By 1854 the book collection had reached 740 volumes.[52] One of the first acts of the Mechanics' Institute was to apply for a government grant to help with its operation. They received £50 a year until 1857, when the currency changed and the grant became $200 a year.[53]

Directors of the Mechanics' Institute were drawn from all levels of society, and over the years in addition to those already mentioned, included: Doctors—Parker, T. Keating, P. Bryce and Howitt; clergymen—Reverends H. Stewart and J. Spencer; lawyers—H.W. Peterson, Donald Guthrie and Robert Mitchell; publishers—George Pirie and James Innes; teachers—W. Tytler, J. Dunn and Charles Walker; Government employees—James Gow and C. Romain; mill operators—David McCrae, John Allen, David Allan, James Goldie and Robert Stewart; manufacturers—George Bruce, J.C. McLagan, Charles Raymond, John Inglis, and Robert Bell; merchant—John Horsman; druggist and chemist—N. Higinbotham; others included John McLean, banker; John Rogers, book-keeper; Peter Kerr, action maker (maker of assemblies for organs and pianos) and Edward Galloway, labourer.[54]

The financing of the Institute was always a problem, and money for its operation was raised in various ways through concerts, plays, exhibits, lectures and social functions. Thus by 1878, the ladies of the Town had been so active and successful in these projects that the Board of Directors permitted the formation of a Board of Lady Directors, and set aside one table in the reading room for their use.[55]

By 1881, the Mechanics' Institute could report that it had a collection of 2625 books "furnishing an amount of reading in all departments of literature which can rarely be met in a library of the same character." During the year, 7433 books had been borrowed by 340 members, and the expenditures were $976.80.[56]

In 1882, an Act was passed by the Province of Ontario providing for the setting up of "Free Libraries." Thus on December fourth, on receipt of a petition signed by "upwards of four hundred electors. . . .praying for the establishment of a Free Library under the Free Libraries Act 1882,"[57] City Council arranged that a referendum take place on January 1, 1883. On January fifteenth, having been approved by the electors, the by-law was read a third time and passed into law.[58] On April 16, 1883, a further by-law was approved covering an agreement between the Mechanics' Institute and the Board of Management of the Free Library, and the new Free Library came into being.[59]

Guelph was the first place in Ontario to take advantage of the provisions of the Public Libraries Act, and the first Board of Management consisted of Caleb Chase, Mayor of

Guelph; James Goldie, George Bruce and James Cormack appointed by City Council; David McCrae, James Innes and William Tytler, appointed by the Public School Board; and Maurice O'Connor and Joseph Harris, appointed by the Separate School Board.[60]

The Free Library occupied leased premises for a number of years, but realizing that a library building was required, in 1901, Mr. James Watt (Chairman of the Library Board) brought the library to the attention of Mr. Andrew Carnegie. Mr. Carnegie, a wealthy American industrialist who devoted immense sums of money to various purposes, chiefly the erection and extensions of libraries, offered the Board the sum of $20,000 for the erection of a library building, stipulating that a free site be provided and that $2,000 per year be spent in maintenance. Thus on April 23, 1903, a ceremony was held laying the corner stone of the new library on Nelson Crescent. The architect was W. Frye Colwill, and the corner stone was laid by Mr. James Watt.[61] The building was completed and occupied by 1905, and was in continuous use for many years.

Although neither the Benevolent Association nor the Mechanics' Institute could have been said to be outstanding successes in their early years, they did reflect significant advances in Guelph's social life.

Carnegie Public Library, Guelph.

Guelph Railway Viaduct, 1861.

VII

The Coming of the Railrods

For the residents of Canada West, the decision in the 1850's to build a vast network of railways throughout the province meant something far more important than the mere cost accounting of investments, stocks, bonds and rates of return. It meant a commitment to a belief in the virtues and possibilities of eternal growth, and the equation of progress with economic expansion.

Of the images created by the skilled publicists of the time, that of Thomas C. Keefer would be particularly important to the history of Guelph. In 1850 T.C. Keefer published a pamphlet entitled *Philosophy of Railroads*[1] which was eagerly seized upon by John Smith, the editor of the *Guelph Advertiser*.[2] When Keefer drew his portrait of "Sleepy Hollow", the similarity to Guelph's position was indeed striking:

Let us take a case of which Canada (we are proud and sad to say) presents more than one instance. A well cultivated district, in which all the lands are occupied (perhaps by the second generation) with or without water power, but situated twenty to fifty miles from the chief towns upon our great highway, the St. Lawrence, and without navigable water communication with it. The occupants are all thriving and independent farmers, the water power is employed only to an extent to meet their local

From an original copperplate used prior to 1861 during the early years of the Grand Trunk Railway.

wants, and the village is limited to a few mechanics and the one store required for this rural district. The barter of the shopkeeper is restricted by the consumption of his customers and he becomes the sole forwarder of the surplus produce of the district. . .Each farmer has his comfortable house, his well stored barn, variety of stock, his meadows and his woodland; he cultivates only as much as he finds convenient and his slight surplus is exchanged for his modest wants. Distance, the expense of transportation, and the absence of that energy which debt or contact with busier men should produce, have prevented any efforts to supply the commercial towns on the part of the contented denizens of our 'Sleepy Hollow'. . .If they have no water power, or one limited to the supply of the needful grist or saw mill, it is clear to their minds that they were never destined for manufacturing people; and if they have abundant water power, their local market would not support one manufactory, while land carriage, want of people, money, and more than all, *information*, precludes the idea of their manufacturing for a distant market. . .[3]

It was, however, the changes that the railroad might bring that most fascinated Smith. The conversion of subsistance agriculture to commodity production, the expansion of the market area and the development of local manufacturing were all promised by Keefer to be the result of railroads, and all of these were certain to expand economic opportunities. For the merchants and millers of a small commercial centre like Guelph who were constantly faced with the threat of neighbouring rivals, such enormous opportunities and security were attractive indeed.

Armed with these arguments, hopes and expectations, the proponents of railroads would, in the 1850's, once again take up the battle for a rail line to Guelph. Although both the Toronto and Goderich and the Toronto and Lake Huron railway promotions had collapsed in 1847, several attempts to revive these companies had been made between that date and 1851. In April, 1848, a deputation from Toronto led by Thomas Galt (John Galt's son) arrived in Guelph in an attempt to revive the Toronto and Goderich scheme. A public meeting chaired by Sheriff George J. Grange was held in an attempt to persuade local residents to donate money to defray the costs of a survey, and although a considerable excitement resulted, the attempt soon failed for a lack of investor interest.[4]

During the fall of 1850 and Spring of 1851, the leading businessmen of Galt, the self-styled "Manchester of Canada", believing that in railways lay the key to commercial success, guaranteed the Great Western Railway Company that they would invest £25,000 in railway stock, if that Company would charter, build and operate a branch line to Galt. As soon as the news reached Guelph that an agreement had been made, Guelph's business community, led by John Thorp, hotel keeper and stage coach operator; Edwin Hubbard, nurseryman; Doctor William Clarke, mill owner and Guelph's largest property owner; and John Smith, proprietor of the *Guelph Advertiser*, owner of a book and stationery shop, and a real estate dealer, immediately undertook to promote a railway from Guelph to Toronto.

The initial step in the creation of the Toronto and Guelph Railway Company was the introduction of a motion at a meeting of the Guelph Town Council proposing that the Council would purchase £20,000 worth of stock in any railway that would be built between Toronto and Guelph. Hubbard and Thorp, members of the Council, were made responsible for this part of the campaign.[5] Two days later on June 26, 1851, the *Guelph Advertiser* published a long letter by John Smith justifying this controversial proposal:

Many will be startled at such a proposition—many will disclaim against such extravagance and responsibility; but Guelph has been too long inactive or asleep, whilst all around is alive. . .

I once viewed the investment of £25,000 by the people of Galt in a similar enterprise as venturesome, yea—foolhardy, in its character; but on mature reflection, I am convinced that the foresight and energy of the people of that place will be amply rewarded by the extending of the "Great Western" to Galt. Whatever may be the annual calls upon them in the shape of interest, will scarcely be felt, in consequence of the very large additional business and profits accruing to the population in and around that village. . .

I have long been under the impression that it required some public and simultaneous move on the part of the inhabitants of this Town, to keep it in its proper position, and advance its interests at the same ratio as other places. But want of unanimity has been the great drawback; want of energy and enterprise not less so. . .and if the inhabitants do not join heart and hand in favor of the proposition of Messrs. Hubbard and Thorp, may shame rest upon them. There is one hope yet for Guelph, and only one—it rests on the construction of a RAILROAD.[6]

The editor of Smith's newspaper, G.M. Keeling, supported Smith's letter with a strong editorial. Keeling's main point was:

If this railroad, or some other line leading to Toronto or Hamilton, be not proceeded with, the branch of the Great Western, terminating at Galt will cause the almost total annihilation of Guelph as a place of business: its carrying trade will be ruined, by the cheaper rates at which flour will be carried to the lake, by way of Galt; and the higher price which can then be given at Galt for farm produce, will divert almost the entire current of business from the locality of Guelph. Whilst Galt remains without a railroad, Guelph may get on comparatively well without one also; but as the construction of a railroad to Galt is now a matter of certainty, there is no choice for Guelph other than

to get a railroad also; or to sink as a place of business, into utter insignificance.[7]

Keeling made it clear, however, that he expected vigorous opposition to such a costly venture.

In bringing forward the railway motion at the next Council meeting (June 28, 1851) Hubbard and Thorp abandoned entirely the negative aspects of Smith's and Keeling's arguments. In moving the resolution to take stock in a railway (the figure mentioned now was £25,000) Hubbard said:

Questions had occasionally been brought before the Council, upon which strong differences of opinion existed; but he trusted there would be more unanimity on the subject he was about to introduce, as it was a matter which was eminently calculated to benefit the whole of the inhabitants of the Town. . .He believed that of all enterprises which would be conducive to our prosperity, the construction of a railroad from Toronto to Guelph would be the greatest and best. . .and he hoped, and believed, that the resolution he was about to propose, would be approved and supported by every influential inhabitant of Guelph. . .[8]

John Thorp, too, evoked a "Higher Power" in his espousal of railways and progress:

. . .He hoped the higher Power which had led us on to our present prosperity, would lead us on to still greater—a result which must follow the construction of the proposed railroad.[9]

The motion passed unanimously.

At that time the Municipal Act stipulated that all money by-laws requiring the issuance of debentures must be put to a general vote of all municipal ratepayers. Although the Guelph Town Council had voted unanimously to purchase shares in the railway to Toronto, it was necessary to persuade a majority of the electorate to vote for the expenditure, before it could become law. On July 3, 1851, a public meeting was called at the Court House to rally support. The *Guelph Advertiser* gives this description of the event:

The meeting was attended by most of the property holders and largest ratepayers in Town, and after some discussion of the merits of the question, the following resolutions were proposed, and passed unanimously. . .

The Rev. Arthur Palmer was called to the Chair; and John Smith, Esq., was appointed Secretary.

Dr. Clarke then moved, and John Smith, Esq., seconded—

"That this meeting highly approves of the action of the Municipal Council for this Town proposing to take Stock to the amount of £25,000 in the Toronto and Guelph Railroad; and pledges itself to sustain that body to the utmost of its power in relation to the vote in question."

Moved by Rev. J.J. Braine, seconded by Judge Powell,—

"That a Committee be appointed on behalf of the ratepayers of the Town, to co-operate and confer with the Council in reference to the subject; with power to appoint a joint Deputation to proceed to Toronto in order to effect the necessary arrangements with the Directors of the Road: and that such committee be composed of Messrs. Hodgert, Day, White, Baker, and Smith, and Drs. Clarke and Liddell."[10]

In addition, the meeting requested the "co-operation and services" of Adam J. Fergusson, the local member of the Legislative Assembly, to watch over legislative proposals regarding the new railway.

On July fifth, the delegation from Guelph travelled to Toronto to meet the major figures of Toronto's business community. The *Toronto Patriot* gave this account of the meeting:

On Saturday, a deputation of gentlemen from Guelph, including S. Smith, Esquire (Reeve); Dr. Clarke, James Hodgert and John Smith, Esquires,

was met by appointment, at the Mayor's office, by a number of our leading citizens, including the Mayor [Bowes] and other members of the Corporation, the members for the city, and other gentlemen interested in Railroad enterprise, whose names will be found below. . .

We understand that the interview was extremely satisfactory to both parties; and that with a view to facilitate the speedy commencement of operations, it was proposed to fuse into one line the Toronto and Goderich and the Toronto and Lake Huron Companies. This object, as will be seen by the accompanying resolutions, which were adopted unanimously, was completely attained. . .[11]

From Guelph's point of view, the most important motion passed by the meeting was:

Moved by Mr. J.W. Gwynne, seconded by Hon. H. Sherwood and:
Resolved—That this meeting have received with great pleasure the deputation from Guelph, testifying the interest which that portion of the country takes in this project; and that this meeting will use

From a water colour by David J. Kennedy. (Courtesy University of Guelph Art Collection)

all its influence, individually and collectively, to have that spirit met with corresponding vigor by the Corporation of Toronto and the citizens individually.

J.G. Bowes, Chairman, F. Widder, W.N. Boulton, H. Sherwood, John Fiskin, J. Beverley Robinson, jr., E.F. Whittemore, J.C. Morrison, W.J. Fitzgerald, W. Cayley, Thos. Galt, J.W. Gwynne, John A. Macdonald, Wm. Gwynne,E.G. O'Brien, H.J. Boulton, Wm. Herrick.[12]

Two nights later, the Guelph delegation appeared before the Toronto City Council to initiate a campaign to obtain their financial support for the railway. So successful was this meeting that on August 30, 1851, the first of the necessary arrangements was completed when the Act incorporating the Toronto and Guelph Railway Company was passed by Parliament and signed into law. Named as Incorporators and Provisional Directors were John Arnold, John G. Bowes, A.M. Clark, William Clarke, James Colton, John Fiskin, William C. Gwynne, George Herrick, James Hodgert, John Holmes, William P. Howland, Samuel Jarvis, John McDonald, Samuel Smith, John Smith, James McGill Strachan, James Webster, Ezekial F. Whittemore, Frederick Widder and George Wright.[13]

Even before the Act incorporating the Toronto and Guelph Railway Company had been declared law, the promoters were holding public meetings in the towns and townships involved to convince local councils to vote money for the project. The first of these held locally was at Blyth's Tavern in Guelph Township on July 28th. The *Guelph Advertiser* reported:

In compliance with a requisition signed by Mr. Sheriff Grange, Jas. Wright, Esq., John McCrea, Esq., and a number of other gentlemen, the Reeve of the Township of Guelph has called a Public

Meeting of Township Freeholders to be held at Blyth's Tavern, Scotch Block Road, on Monday next, at 2 o'clock, p.m., for the purpose of taking into consideration the propriety of the Township taking stock in the proposed Railroad. As the general feeling of the great majority of the inhabitants of the Township is in favor of the undertaking, probably there will be an almost unanimous vote to give a helping hand to the enterprise. It is asserted by the "knowing ones" of Toronto, that the proposed Line to Guelph will *pay* better than any Line now contemplated—the Great Western excepted. But supposing that this should not be the case, at first, the farmers along the line, and of this locality in particular, could well afford to pay a small quota towards the enterprise, on account of the increased price they would obtain for all sorts of produce. The matter, however, is highly important, and a full attendance at Blyth's, next Monday, is desirable.[14]

Although from the point of view of numbers the Guelph Township meeting was a disappointment, (only 50 or 60 were present) in every other aspect it was a success. The meeting was attended by the wealthiest landowners and farmers, many of whom owned businesses or property in the Town, and there was unanimous support for the proposal that the Township should invest £10,000 in shares of the Toronto and Guelph railway.

The arguments used[15] were based upon three basic premises: the railway would greatly reduce the cost of transporting wheat to an export point; the railway could be built for £210,000; and the market area served by the railway would ship more than 1,000,000 bushels of grain to Toronto each year. In the development of these arguments, Doctor William Clarke took the leading role.

On August twenty-fourth, a joint session of the Town and Township Councils and the Railway Committee was held at the Court House, at which Mr. Sheriff Grange was elected Chairman and Mr. John Smith, Secretary. Following the reading of a letter from James Webster concerning the actions of the Toronto group, it was:

. . .*Resolved*—That Messrs. Hodgert, Clarke, J. Smith, Hubbard, Thurtell, Harland, Wright, McCrea, and Grange, be a deputation to meet one from Toronto, at Georgetown, on such day as may be hereafter arranged. . .[16]

In the meantime, the Toronto promoters had not been idle. On the day previous to the Guelph joint meeting, they had been in Weston attempting to persuade the farmers of York Township to support the road. This meeting was noteworthy for an argument made by Mayor Bowes of Toronto concerning the harmony of interest between merchants and farmers in the development of such enterprises.[17] The York Township farmers, perhaps a little too familiar with the consequences of the attentions of the Toronto merchants, would remain immune to the pleas for co-operation. No money would come from that source.

The long-awaited Georgetown meeting, held on September tenth, provided the first critical test for the railway promoters. Without a major success in Esquesing Township, it would be most difficult to convince future investors of the necessity of the proposed line. Every major supporter of the railway's construction was in attendance. From Toronto came Mayor Bowes, John Beverly Robinson, James Duggan, J.W. Gwynne and A.M. Clarke; from Guelph, the Reeve, Samuel Smith; Councillors Edwin Hubbard, John Thorp and William Stevenson; Sheriff George Grange, A.J. Fergusson, M.P.P., and Doctor William Clarke, Colonel Hewat, J. McCrea, J. Wright, J. Smith, B. Thurtell, F. Kerr, F.

Smith, J. Hodgert and J. Harland; from Esquesing, Reeve William Young; and from Erin Township, William Barber, W. Clarke, D. McBain and W. Taylor; as well as "a large number of other gentlemen."[18] The leading speakers were Sheriff Grange and Doctor Clarke of Guelph. Part of Grange's argument follows:

. . . .He had collected some statistics on the subject, which he thought would prove that the line would not only *pay*, but would bring a return of 9 per cent upon the capital expended. . .[19]

It was a rosy picture, but one which was almost entirely false. Again as at the previous meetings, motions supporting the railway passed unanimously. The difficulty was, that most of these motions were moved and seconded by outsiders—men like Sheriff Grange, John McCrea, Mayor Bowes and Doctor Clarke. Esquesing's residents were ominously silent. A similar situation arose when a meeting was held the next day at James Wellwood's home in Eramosa.[20]

Having obtained uncontested resolutions from the meetings in Georgetown and Eramosa, the promoters moved on to Toronto. Again Sheriff Grange presented his figures on agricultural production and expected traffic. Doctor Clarke's statements are especially interesting:

Dr. Clarke, of Guelph, in seconding the resolution urged very forcibly the advantages which the citizens of Toronto generally, would derive from the construction of this line of railroad. He was convinced that it was no use in the present state of the country to expect that such a work could be constructed by private enterprise, and therefore he looked to Municipalities as the source of necessary power. . .The Doctor then detailed the incidents of his mission to Toronto in 1846, to request the Corporation to assist them in making a macadamized road from Toronto to Guelph.—That mission failed; but they were subsequently taken by hand by the City of Hamilton which cheerfully voted £12,000 to construct a road from Guelph to Dundas. Hamilton was so far benefitted by that, inasmuch as the merchants of Guelph purchased at an average, goods to the amount of £50,000 a year from the stores in Hamilton.[21]

The meeting unanimously supported a resolution in favour of the project,[22] and voted that Toronto should subscribe to stock in the Toronto and Guelph Railroad Company to the amount of £100,000.

There were, of course, strong objections, for if the railway was such a sure proposition in its expectations, why were not private investors ready and willing to buy shares? The Toronto Railway Committee answered with this unique bit of economic philosophy:

. . . .If our capitalists and merchants would unadvisably subscribe such a large amount of stock, the sudden abstraction of such a large amount from the active capital of the country, would inevitably produce a most injurious effect in our financial position, and probably terminate in a panic bankruptcy and general distress.[23]

Upon receipt of the report of this meeting, the Toronto City Council agreed to purchase £100,000 of stock in the railroad company.[24]

Proceeding on the general principle that the best way to convince the more reluctant municipalities to support the railway investment was to hold referendums in the sure areas first, the initial vote was held in Toronto. It was a major disappointment. Although an overwhelming majority of those who voted favoured the £100,000 investment, only a small number of ratepayers cast ballots.[25]

No sooner had the publicity campaign begun, than a new element was added. Hamilton's merchants and the promoters of the Great Western Railway Company decided to intervene. In its support for building the Guelph and Dundas road and the Great Western branch from Hamilton to Galt, Hamilton's merchants and shippers had been intent upon enhancing their economic dominance in the vast pie-shaped area north and west of Guelph and Berlin, which reached almost to Owen Sound. The local rivalry between Galt and Guelph to become the main sub-centre of this trade was, of course, unimportant from Hamilton's point of view, as long as both were dependent upon Hamilton and Dundas for trade and transportation. With Toronto's vote of £100,000 to build a railway to Guelph, Hamilton was faced with the threat of a serious loss. It was time to act. A group of Hamilton's leading businessmen called a public meeting which passed the following resolution:

The consideration of the undersigned having been drawn to the importance of extending the branch of the Great Western Railroad from Galt to Guelph, in order to provide at the least expense, an outlet for the surplus produce of the Northern Peninsula, it has been resolved to cause a preliminary survey to be immediately made of the country between Galt and Guelph, with the intention of taking steps to provide the means to build a Railroad between these points without delay, so that it may be ready to work in connection with the Galt Branch of the Great Western Railroad. Hamilton, November 22, 1851.[26]

This motion was signed by Sir Allan MacNab, D. McInnes and Company, Isaac Buchanan, Edward Jackson, Dennis Moore, John R. Holden, George S. Tiffany, H. McKenstry, Neil Campbell, John Young, William P. MacLaren, Richard Juson, Archibald Kerr, Hugh C. Baker, Daniel MacNab, Colin C. Ferrie, Charles A. Saddler, Daniel Kelly and John

Fisher. Two days after the Hamilton meeting, a delegation composed of Isaac Buchanan, Archibald Kerr and Richard Juson journeyed to Guelph to open their campaign. The Hamilton strategy was simple: for their interests to be served it was not actually necessary to build a railway, but only to prevent the Toronto and Guelph line from being built.[27]

The response of the Guelph residents to the Hamilton proposal was cool. Its strongest opponent was Edwin Hubbard, who feared that the Toronto interests would feel betrayed if Guelph made any statement supporting the Hamilton proposal. He withdrew his objection, however, when he was reassured that the Town Council had no intention of "interfering in the matter."[28] In the end, the meeting supported this ironic resolution moved by Doctor Clarke and seconded by John Smith, that:

This Meeting, having heard the explanations of a number of gentlemen from Hamilton relative to the construction of a Railroad from Guelph to Galt in connection with the Great Western Railway, believe that it would be exceedingly beneficial to Guelph and the neighboring townships, and also be the means of bringing an immense income of traffic upon the Guelph and Toronto Railroad.[29]

Needless to say, the last thing the Hamilton delegation had in mind was to make Galt a feeder to Toronto by means of the proposed Galt and Guelph line. Smarting not a little at this rebuke, the Hamilton delegation retreated, and the matter of a railroad between Galt and Guelph was dropped for some time.

The question which remained to be answered was whether the Hamilton delegation had managed to shake the resolve of the Guelph ratepayers' support of the Toronto line. To prevent this possibility the editor of the *Guelph Advertiser* wrote the following:

We understand that some of the inhabitants, who are amongst the largest ratepayers, intend to vote against the By-law, believing that the sum of £25,000 will involve a greater amount of taxation than the Town will be able to bear. . . .

This is a very serious consideration; but it must be borne in mind that if the By-law, as it now stands, be not passed, its rejection will influence other Municipalities, and may possibly cause the loss of the Road, at least for some years. The question is—RAILROAD OR NO RAILROAD; RUIN OR PROSPERITY. The Road, for a year or two, will involve heavy taxation, but the ratepayers had far better meet such taxation than allow the business of the Town to droop and die; and Galt to rise into eminence on the ruins of their prosperity. . . .[30]

Although the Great Western Directors scheduled the sod-turning of the Galt branch for December twelfth, the date of the Guelph vote, their manoeuverings apparently had little impact. On that date, Guelph's ratepayers voted 112 to 6 (with 72 abstentions) to purchase £25,000 stock in the Toronto and Guelph Railway Company. Four days later, Guelph Township followed suit by 130 to 4 margin. The drawback in the latter vote was that 416 ratepayers abstained, thereby casting some doubt on the validity of the by-law.[31] Nevertheless, the Toronto and Guelph Railway's backers declared the votes an overwhelming triumph.

From the point of view of the Railway's promoters, the critical stage to be reached was to acquire £150,000 in stock subscriptions. In the Act which chartered the Toronto and Guelph Railway, the total capitalization was £225,000, but the Act came into effect only when £150,000 had been subscribed and ten percent of that amount had been paid into the treasury. With £135,000 already guaranteed by the Toronto, Guelph and Guelph Township votes,

only £15,000 more was required to make the Company a legal entity. To attain this amount, the campaign now turned to Eramosa Township.

In spite of an aggressive campaign, the Eramosa voters in January, 1852, soundly defeated a vote to purchase £10,000 worth of stock in the Railway.[32] The main objection, apparently, was that there was no guarantee that the rail line would pass through the Township, thus residents would not enjoy the rise in land values associated with the building of local stations and the creation of a local market, mills, etc.[33] A second by-law, to take £5,000 worth of stock, was brought in immediately after the defeat of the £10,000 by-law, but because of the refusal of the Railway promoters to promise them a station, Eramosa Township Council did not give the £5,000 by-law a third reading, and there the matter died.[34]

Simultaneously, the railwaymen received a second major setback, when the Wellington County Council refused to endorse the Town and Township debentures. In January, 1852, John Smith had moved, in the Town Council, that:

The Reeve be requested to urge upon the County Council the propriety of endorsing all Debentures issued by Municipal Councils within the United Counties for taking stock in the Toronto and Guelph Railroad, and that he bring in a By-law to that effect, in which each County, at any separation, shall be responsible only for the Debentures issued within their respective bounds.[35]

Seconded by W.S.G. Knowles, the motion carried without debate. This motion was necessitated by the fact that town and township debentures sold badly on the British market, and at huge discounts, while an endorsement by the county would improve the amount received by the Railway Company for their sale. Of course, such an endorsement would make the County liable if, for some reason, the Town or Township of Guelph were unable to pay off their debentures when they came due. To the consternation of the Guelph Town Council, the County refused to endorse the debentures.[36] In the long run, only Chinguacousy Township, in an effort to acquire a station at Brampton, voted additional municipal debentures to support the Railway. That vote, for £10,000, was carried only after the Railway promoters threatened to take a southern route through Milton, bypassing Brampton completely.[37] Thus, with £145,000 secured and the hopes of £5,000 more from Eramosa, the local Railway promoters set out to find someone to undertake the building of the Toronto and Guelph Railway.

Once it became clear that no substantial new municipal funds were likely, the Railway promoters began the search for private funds to complete the Railway's initial financing. In a vigorous Toronto campaign sufficient shares were subscribed to allow the Railway Company to elect its first Board of Directors. Early in April, 1852, the Toronto *Patriot* reported that the following amounts had been subscribed:

The City of Toronto	£100,000
The Town of Guelph	25,000
The Township of Guelph	10,000
Private Stock	21,085
	£156,085[38]

Of this amount £15,110, or £110 more than enough to bring the charter into effect, had actually been paid into the treasury.

The first major controversy was an attempt by the private shareholders to acquire complete control over the Railway's Board of Directors and thereby over the municipal funds. On March 26, 1852, a meeting of the private shareholders was held at Toronto's St. Lawrence Hall. The *Guelph Advertiser* gave this report of the meeting:

The meeting was attended by many highly influential gentlemen of the city; and the following business was transacted:

W. Gooderham, Esq., having been requested to take the Chair, and S. Thompson, Esq., to act as Secretary, it was

Resolved,—That as the private Stockholders in Toronto, to the Toronto and Guelph Railway, represent stock to upwards of £20,000, and are besides the largest ratepayers in the city, they are entitled to a voice in the Board of Directors of the Railway, and trust that this matter will receive the due consideration from the Mayor and City Council, in the election of Directors for the ensuing year.

Resolved,—That the following names be submitted to his worship the Mayor and the Council for their consideration, for Directors in the Board of the Toronto and Guelph Railway; and that the Mayor and Council be respectfully requested to select the names of Directors therefrom:—

J. McMurrich, S. Thompson, T.D. Harris, F. Widder, J. Fiskin, E.F. Whittemore, W. Gooderham, W.P. Howland, L. Moffatt, W.C. Gwynne, Sheriff Grange, D. Patterson, J.H. Cameron, J. Arnold, A.M. Clarke, J. Beatty, and J.G. Beard.[39]

As Mayor Bowes had been delegated by Toronto City Council to vote that municipality's stock, the choice of Directors was in his hands. To no one's surprise, nine of the thirteen Directors elected came from the private shareholders' list, while the four other successful candidates were all close associates of Mayor Bowes. Of the thirteen, only Sheriff George J. Grange was from Guelph.[40] In addition, J.G. Bowes and Doctor William Clarke were members of the Board by virtue of their positions as Mayor of Toronto and Reeve of Guelph. With this Board of Directors in control, Guelph would no longer have a significant voice in the management of the Railway's affairs.

Even before the new Board had formally been elected, significant and disturbing news began to filter back to Guelph. The same day that the *Guelph Advertiser* carried the news of the election of Directors, it also carried a notice that the Toronto and Guelph Railway Company intended to apply to the Government for the power to increase its capital and to extend the line to points on Lake Huron and the St. Clair River, with a branch line to Woodstock and London.[41]

From the point of view of Doctor Clarke and the Guelph businessmen, this decision was a betrayal of their interests. With Guelph as the terminus, much of the trade of Berlin and the area west and north of Waterloo Township would flow to the Guelph merchants and grain buyers. With the Toronto and Guelph Railway running to Berlin and west, the towns along the track would capture the local grain trade, leaving Guelph only that which was generated locally or flowed down the Guelph and Arthur Road. Doctor Clarke, however, did manage to win one concession. In order to prevent the Guelph interests from opposing the amendments to the charter of the Railway at the Legislature, the Directors of the Railway agreed to let the Town of Guelph reduce its purchase of shares from £25,000 to £10,000.[42] Mayor Bowes of Toronto explained the matter this way:

The Council of the Town of Guelph took £25,000 stock before the extension to Sarnia was settled. . . .The people of Guelph since said, when it

was proposed to extend the road to Sarnia, that they should be allowed to change the amount of their stock from £25,000 to £10,000, and this was agreed to by the Board, and Dr. Clarke, of Guelph, refused to support the extension till he had a pledge that the amount should be reduced. The city of Toronto wished to continue the road to Sarnia, for when they got there they are in a direct line to obtain the whole business of the north part of the State of Michigan, of Chicago, and of the State of Iowa. Are the people of Toronto prepared to expend £100,000, and then stop at Guelph, and lose the whole of this immense business, and allow the Great Western to obtain it?[43]

Hardly had the excitement about the Sarnia extension died down, than a second piece of news began to circulate. The actual cost of building the Toronto and Guelph line was not £210,000, as Sheriff Grange had earlier claimed, but a much larger figure—perhaps as much as £400,000. The *Guelph Advertiser's* response was a combination of shock and despondency:

Last year it was stated by the parties who took the lead in placing this railroad project prominently before the public, that the road would certainly not cost more than £250,000, including rolling stock, and every contingent expense. *Now* it is estimated the road will cost £350,000; and probably will really exceed even that sum. . .If the road is commenced on the plan of estimates making it cost £400,000, it will not be built for years. The money cannot be raised; and even if it could, the road. . .would be a dead weight upon the unfortunate stockholders.[44]

The *Advertiser's* predictions would prove to be only too correct. Although numerous reports circulated through the summer and fall of 1852 that the Canada Company had bought sufficient of the Railway Company's bonds to complete the line to Guelph, or alternately, had managed to sell the bonds at a good price on the London market, neither report was true.

It was to the Grand Trunk Railway scheme that the Toronto and Guelph promoters now turned.

Little needs to be said here about the conception, creation and building of the Grand Trunk Railway. Historians have long since agreed upon both its importance to the economic development of Canada, and that it was one of the most corrupt, mismanaged and inefficient projects ever undertaken. Put together by a combination of British and Montreal entrepreneurs, and chartered on November 10, 1852, the Grand Trunk was surrounded by controversy from the beginning. Two weeks after Parliament passed its Act of Incorporation,[45] the *Guelph Advertiser* gave this account of its beginnings:

RAILWAY CHISELLING

The Main Trunk Railway bill has become law in spite of the vigorous opposition of Messrs. [George] Brown and [John] Young. . .It is impossible to avoid coming to the conclusion that there is something fearfully wrong in agreeing to give the railway to Messrs. Jackson & Co. [Peto, Brassey, Jackson and Betts] at £10,130 per mile. Messrs. Chamberlain & Co., a very able firm, offered to build that part of the road between Montreal and Kingston for £6,250 per mile. Ira Gould, a wealthy Montreal merchant, offered, on behalf of himself and others, to build it for £6,000. . .In the face of such facts, it is impossible to understand why Mr. Hincks should think of paying such an enormous sum as £10,130 per mile to this English Company; and equally incomprehensible how such a proposition could be entertained by the House. Yet it is done, 386 miles from Hamilton to Montreal, at £4,000 per mile (this is about the overcharge in round numbers) amounts to £1,544,000. . .We cannot help thinking, that there must be some unknown reasons for such an extraordinary proposition.[46]

As time would reveal, such "extraordinary

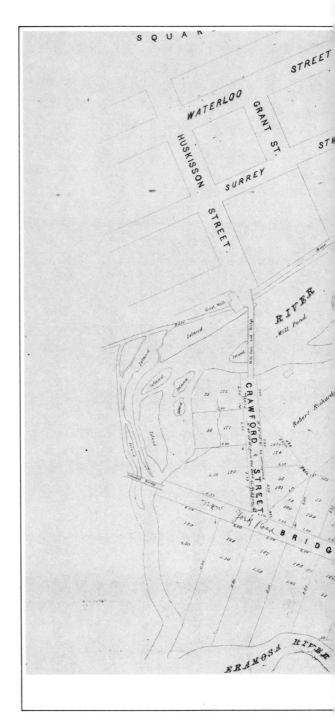

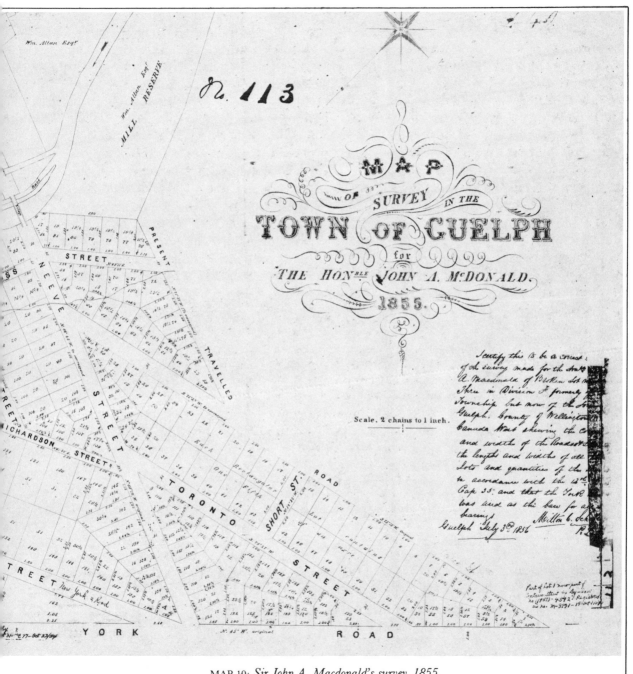

MAP 10: *Sir John A. Macdonald's survey, 1855.*

reasons" abounded. Cabinet members were secret partners with contractors, bribes were lavishly given, and the notoriety of the whole scheme would snowball as the years passed.

In chartering the Grand Trunk, the Canadian Parliament had given it the power to amalgamate with any other company whose route would form part of the "main trunk" across the Canadas.[47] When the Toronto and Guelph was, at the same time, given permission to extend its line to Sarnia,[48] that line could now be amalgamated with the Grand Trunk, and thus receive the £3,000 per mile subsidy which the Provincial Government guaranteed to builders of the "main trunk" line. By these manoeuvres, it became possible to finance the Toronto and Guelph line until the British investors could be persuaded to invest.

Key figures in the negotiations between the Toronto and Guelph Company and the Grand Trunk were Alexander Tilloch Galt, son of John Galt, John A. Macdonald, C.S. Gzowski, A.J. Fergusson, M.P.P., Sheriff Grange and Mayor J.G. Bowes, of Toronto. George J. Grange's role was particularly interesting. As a family connection of Thomas Baring, the British banker and Director of the Grand Trunk,[49] Grange had a unique position as a go-between and would, with A.J. Fergusson, be the only Guelph businessmen to profit personally by the amalgamation.

As soon as it was certain that the Grand Trunk and Toronto and Guelph Amendment Acts were certain to pass (and perhaps as the price of their passage) a contract to build the Toronto and Guelph Railway was signed with C.S. Gzowski and Company for £7,408 per mile, not including right of way or stations, for a total cost of £354,764.[50] Silent partners with

Gzowski in the firm or subsequent land deals were leading politicians, including Alexander Tilloch Galt.[51] In addition, John A. Macdonald,[52] John Ross and other cabinet ministers were either involved in land deals with Gzowski[53] or were employed by the Grand Trunk Railway Company at the same time they were members of the Cabinet.[54]

The means by which Sheriff Grange and A.J. Fergusson profited was more indirect. By receiving advance information concerning the route of the rail line and the location of stations, they could buy up land around the site, subdivide it, and sell it at a large profit. Thus Fergusson successfully speculated at Stratford and Guelph, and Grange at Berlin and Guelph.

Work on the Toronto and Guelph line began in February, 1853, when a gang of men arrived in Guelph to build shanties, workshops and storehouses for the future construction,[55] and by April it was reported that 400 workmen were soon to be employed at Brampton.[56] At last the project was under way.

It was at this point that the efforts of the British promoters of the Grand Trunk began to pay off in England. Overnight prices skyrocketed, and the Grand Trunk promoters, attempting to enlarge their project, were now ready to complete the acquisition of the Toronto and Guelph line. In May, 1853, the Town and Township of Guelph received identical letters offering to take over their shares in the Toronto and Guelph Railway:

Office of the Toronto & Guelph Railway
Company, Toronto, May 5, 1853
Sir,
    I am directed to inform you, that the Board of Directors of this Company have received advices

from their agents in London, Alex. Gillespie and A.T. Galt, Esquires, informing them of the completion of an arrangement for the amalgamation of the Toronto and Guelph Railway with the Grand Trunk Railway of Canada, subject to the approval of the Stockholders of this Company, at a General Meeting to be summoned for that purpose, of which you will be duly notified, in accordance with the provisions of the Act authorizing such amalgamation.

I am further directed to state, that the Contractor, Messrs. C.S. Gzowski & Co. have authorized the Board to inform you, that so soon as the amalgamation is duly sanctioned by the Toronto and Guelph Railway Company, they are prepared to assume the whole of the Stock held by Municipal Bodies in Canada, including that subscribed by the Municipal Council of the Township of Guelph, to the amount of £10,000 at par, paying interest on all paid up instalments. . . .

S. Thompson
Secretary & Treasurer T. & G. R.R. Co.[57]

The municipalities were given until May twenty-first to make up their minds.

At the Town Council meeting called to discuss the Gzowski stock proposal, Doctor Clarke, the Reeve, felt strongly that the shares should be retained in hopes that the Town might have some voice in the Railway's management. Several Councillors, however, were doubtful of the desirability or effectiveness of such a move. Finally it was decided by both the Town and Township Councils to call public meetings to discuss the question. In these deliberations, a long editorial by John Smith in the *Guelph Advertiser* was probably the decisive factor.[58]

At the public meeting in Guelph, the following resolution, moved and seconded by William Stevenson and William Day, was passed unanimously:

That though it would be highly advantageous to the Town of Guelph to retain the stock in the To-ronto and Guelph Railroad (believing as we do that it will amply repay the capital invested in it) nevertheless, for the various conflicting interests which must arise between the Municipalities and the private stockholders, this meeting is of opinion that it would be advisable to resign the stock held by the Town of Guelph on the terms proposed by Messrs. Gzowski & Co.[59]

It was a wiser decision than they knew. Within three years the Grand Trunk was not only bankrupt, it was rapidly dragging the credit of the country down with it. Guelph and Guelph Township could both congratulate themselves for having escaped a similar fate.

In spite of early reports of rapid progress on the line, during 1853 very little actual construction was carried out beyond surveying and engineering studies. With progress lagging, rumours swept the Town that the Grand Trunk and Great Western Companies would be amalgamated, and that the Toronto and Guelph line would be abandoned.[60] Fortunately Guelph's fears were unfounded. The discussions concerning amalgamation between the Grand Trunk and the Great Western were eventually broken off, and the Toronto, Guelph and Sarnia line once again figured largely in the Grand Trunk plans.

During the dismal summer of 1853, two bright notes appeared. In July, the *Advertiser* reprinted this note from the *Montreal Herald*:

Demand for Laborers.—The walls of our city are this day placarded with bills, calling for five thousand men for that portion of the Main Trunk Line between Toronto and Sarnia. This furnishes a sample of the probable demand which is likely to be created in this country for thews and sinues.

Montreal Herald of the 27th[61]

A week after the Montreal item, this notice appeared:

The parties interested in the road visited Guelph

this week, and decided upon adopting the route originally surveyed, crossing the bridge at the Guelph Mills lengthwise, arches being thrown over it at each end and at some distance therefrom, to support metal tubes, somewhat on the principle of the tubular bridges on English railways. On approaching the lot occupied by the Rev. A. Palmer, the line separates and passes on each side of the residence of that gentleman, the principal building being taken for a passenger station and offices. A junction will take place again on the Market Square. . . .A course is then taken in the opening between the stores of Messrs. Richardson and Murphy, thence down Kent Street, across the farm of Mr. Fergusson, M.P.P., and thence towards Stratford.[62]

In August, Guelph's businessmen could finally breathe easily. On the fourth of the month, this notice appeared:

Sarnia Road.—Mr. Rowland, a contractor on the Lower Canada Railroads, has taken thirteen miles of grading, hence towards Berlin; and on Saturday last about 150 of his workmen arrived at Guelph, with a vast number of barrows, horses, carts, etc., to commence operations.[63]

At last the commercial future of the town was secure.

With the Toronto and Guelph Railway project having been taken over first by the Toronto private shareholders, and later by the Grand Trunk, Guelph's leading businessmen, A.J. Fergusson, Sheriff George Grange and Doctor William Clarke, turned their minds to another project, this one a little closer to home. Having learned of the close association between railway promotion, land speculation and municipal politics, they decided to undertake the construction of a railway from Galt to Guelph. Although they had publicly rejected

the Hamilton proposals in November, 1851, no sooner had Guelph and Guelph Township voted £35,000 in municipal funds to purchase Toronto and Guelph Railway shares, than Fergusson, Grange and Clarke secretly began to negotiate a deal with the Hamilton businessmen to build the Galt and Guelph line. Prominent in these discussions were Absalom Shade of Galt and Jacob Hespeler of Preston and New Hope (Hespeler).

On the same day that the Guelph to Sarnia extension of the Toronto and Guelph Railway was signed into law (November 10, 1852), the Act incorporating the Galt and Guelph Railway Company[64] was signed into law as well. Its incorporators represented the wealthiest businessmen in the region: Isaac Buchanan, William P. McLaren, H. McKinstry, Richard Juson, Edward Ritchie, Alexander Campbell, William L. Distin, John Young, George S. Tiffany, John Fisher, Hector Munro and Andrew Stewart of Hamilton; Doctor James Hamilton of West Flamborough; Absalom Shade, Andrew Elliott and William Dickson of Galt; Jacob Hespeler of Preston; and George J. Grange of Guelph.[65] Capitalized at £140,000, it was to run from the Great Western branch line terminus in Galt to Guelph.

Little more of the project was heard until June, 1853, when a notice appeared in the local newspapers stating that the stock books for the Galt and Guelph Railway would be opened to subscribers at the Bank of Upper Canada, Hamilton; Gore Bank offices in Galt and Guelph; and the post office in Preston.[66] The key to the promotion was a proposal that the Great Western should lease the line, thereby guaranteeing that it would be profitable.

With the Toronto and Guelph line shares

Allan's Mill and G.T.R. Bridge, Guelph.
From a pencil sketch drawn by Charles Lemon in 1861, who later joined the firm of Lemon and Peterson,
attorneys at law, with Andrew Lemon and H.W. Peterson, Jr. as partners.

now taken over by C.S. Gzowski, and the Grand Trunk amalgamation secure, the *Guelph Advertiser's* attitude to the Galt and Guelph project changed remarkably. Concerning the opening of the stock books, the *Advertiser* said:

Guelph and Galt Railway.—By advertisement it will be seen that the subscription books will be opened in a few days, and it is equally the duty as it is the interest of our Municipality to make a move in the matter. A few thousand pounds of stock would not hurt us, especially as the Great Western offers to lease the road at 6 per cent. and keep it in repair for a term of 20 years. We believe a move is now making to present to Council the propriety of at once taking action in the matter.[67]

To no one's surprise, there was the usual reluctance on the part of the general public to buy shares. With dozens of such projects in every conceivable direction being promoted around the country, even more than the usual cynicism was being displayed by potential investors. The *Son of Temperance*, for example, after giving a long list of Canadian railways contemplated or under contract, concluded by describing "another from the middle of Lake Ontario direct to the *Moon*, on *Electrical Wires*, suspended by counterbalancing magnetic powers, existing between the volcanoes of the moon and mother earth."[68] Another writer waxed poetic in the same journal:

Railroad Mad! Railroad Mad!!

Railroad mad! say what is all this clatter about,
  Speculation's the cry of us all;
Ho for a railroad on this splendid route,
  Another, for that, keep rolling the ball!

Did you know we were off to the moon?
  Who'll go for this grand speculation,
The road will be made pretty soon,
  To-morrow's the grand elevation.

Did you hear of our glorious projects?
  A railway to Guelph is now making,
And another by *Owen Sound* logics,
  Is started by noodles, and taking. . . .

There's a bother and fuss in the west,
  The east's not along in this matter,
For Hamilton thinks she's opprest,
  And is making a terrible clatter.

There's Buffalo's Brantford Projection,
  The Woodstock and Simcoe design;
Guelph's looking in Sarnia's direction,
  And St. Thomas says Bertie's divine. . . .[69]

During July and August, A.J. Fergusson, Sheriff George J. Grange and Doctor William Clarke conducted a whirlwind campaign to gather support for municipal purchases of stock in the line. On August nineteenth, Doctor Clarke, the Reeve, introduced a motion in the Guelph Town Council to have that municipality take £10,000 stock in the Galt and Guelph line.[70] At the same time, a similar motion to take £5,000 worth of shares, was made in the Township Council, and public meetings were scheduled for both municipalities:

On Monday last [August 19, 1853] a meeting of the Ratepayers of the Township of Guelph was held at Blyth's tavern to consider the propriety of recommending the Council to take stock in the Galt and Guelph Railway. About one hundred attended, including a goodly portion from Guelph, the Reeve, B. Thurtell, Esquire, was called to the chair, and Mr. Davidson, acted as Secretary.

Some conversation took place in reference to a very general understanding, that in the event of the municipalities taking stock and the road being built, that the Great Western Company would lease the same for 20 years and meet the interest on the amount of cost.

Mr. Fergusson [M.P.P. and a Director of the Galt and Guelph] having assured the company that the resolutions produced bound the Great Western, two resolutions were passed with scarcely any opposition, one in commendation of the work, and the other in favor of the Council taking stock to the amount of £5,000.[71]

Fergusson's assurances would become a critical element in the future of the line. Although the Guelph Township meeting had gone according to plan, other matters had not. It was at this point that the public became aware of that remarkable series of events which became known as the "McCracken affair."

In the discussions concerning the building of the Galt and Guelph Railway, a difference quickly arose between the merchants and millers of Galt and Preston concerning the route of the line. From Galt's point of view, it was desirable that the line should run directly from Galt to New Hope (Hespeler) and Guelph. Of course, Preston's businessmen wanted the slightly longer route through Preston to be chosen. With Jacob Hespeler pushing hard for the Preston line, Galt's businessmen recognized that they were in serious trouble.

On the other hand, Guelph's businessmen found that either plan had advantages. On the one hand, the Galt-New Hope-Guelph line was cheaper, but on the other hand, the Preston route offered the possibility of making both that town and New Hope trading subsidiaries of Guelph. For the latter reasons, the Guelph promoters tended to favour the Preston route.

The initial response of Galt's businessmen was to refuse to purchase shares or to vote a municipal subsidy to the Galt and Guelph line. If they subscribed for stock and the Railway went by Preston, they were likely to become the authors of their own undoing. On the other hand, if they abstained from subscribing, and sufficient private shares were purchased to allow the Galt and Guelph charter to come into legal effect, then the line would certainly be built by the Preston route. Faced with this dilemma, Galt's businessmen determined upon a coup.

According to the Act of Incorporation of the Galt and Guelph Railway, only £4,500 worth of shares had to be subscribed for the charter to come into effect. By early August this amount had been reached and the Provisional Directors called a meeting of shareholders for August eighteenth to elect a Board of Directors. On August seventeenth, the day before the proposed meeting, a number of Galt businessmen learned the amount of shares which had been subscribed for in Guelph, Preston and Hamilton, and put their names down for double the total that had previously been subscribed. At twelve noon, on the eighteenth, the amount subscribed stood as follows:

Stock Book at	Approximate Amount Subscribed	Approximate Number Shares
Guelph[72]	£2,500	100
Hamilton	£2,500	100
Preston	£3,000	120
Galt	£15,750	630

The purpose of the Galt coup was not to see the Galt and Guelph line built, but rather to seize control of the Board of Directors in order to scuttle the whole project.[73]

In light of Galt's large, if late, subscription for shares, the railway promoters first attempted to make a deal regarding the election of Directors. The Galt shareholders, however, fearing ruin, were in no mood to compromise.

The *Advertiser* described the scene:

A proposal was made to give Guelph three Directors, and Preston, Galt and Hamilton two each, but this was spurned by the Galt agents, and a determination exhibited to carry the day. But this time they found others as keen as themselves, and it is a fact that "Henry McCracken, Bar-Keeper, City Hotel [Hamilton], subscribed to the Preston Stock Book for £25,000,—a thousand shares."[74]

Jacob Hespeler, holding McCracken's proxy, now proceeded to exercise the votes derived from McCracken's shares, and swept all nine Directorships from the Galt candidates. The results of voting were: Sir A.N. MacNab, 1920; Sheriff Grange, 1920; G.S. Tiffany, 1920; Dr. Clarke, 1310; George Sunley, 1310; Col. Hewat, 1310; Jacob Hespeler, 1310; Abraham Erb, 1310; R. Juson, 1310; John Davidson, 634; James Crombie, 634; M.C. Lutz, 634; Wm. Robinson, 634; D. Ramore, 634; E. Irving, 634; and a Mr. Morton, 20.[75] Thus of those elected, four (Grange, Clarke, Sunley and Hewat) were from Guelph, three (MacNab, Tiffany and Juson) were from Hamilton, and two (Hespeler and Erb) were from Preston.

Having lost the struggle to control the Galt and Guelph line, the Galt subscribers were in a serious dilemma. The Directors of the Railway had the right, under the law, to sue them for the full £15,750 for which they had signed, and exhibited every intention of so doing. The *Guelph Advertiser* showed little sympathy for their plight:

However amazed then, or indignant now, the Galt people have no just grounds of complaint. They subscribed for stock for which they never intended to pay, for a road they never intended should be built, and by this dodge they hoped to effect their purpose; but they appeared to forget that amongst adepts at dodging, *chiselling*, if you like, it was a dangerous game to play at; and if Mr. Hespeler understands these things well now, it is not long since he and the Dutchmen of Waterloo were the pupils of Galt in the County Town business. . . .And when taught the art of railway manoeuvring how quickly they went to the root of the matter, with the assistance of *Mr. Henry McCracken.*[76]

From the point of view of the Guelph promoters and Jacob Hespeler, the choice of Henry McCracken, "bar-keeper", was the key to the affair. Whereas the Galt signers such as John Davidson, James Crombie, M.C. Lutz, William Robinson, D. Ramore and E. Irving were men with considerable property, and thus could be sued for their stock subscriptions (indeed, they had paid into the treasury of the Galt and Guelph Railway Company five percent of the face value of their shares), Henry McCracken was penniless and, as Hespeler's nominee, was perfectly safe in so doing. By using McCracken in this way, Hespeler, Fergusson, Grange and Clarke were secure from reprisals had the Galt forces triumphed.

Henry McCracken was well rewarded for his efforts. A year after the "affair" this notice appeared in a Hamilton newspaper:

We perceive that Mr. Henry McCracken, an old resident of this city, and bar-tender at the City Hotel for some four years, has opened the Burlington Hotel, and furnished it throughout with entirely new furniture, etc. We have no doubt that this hotel will, under Mr. McCracken's management, be well patronised by the travelling community, as he has had many years experience in the business.[77]

The *Guelph Advertiser*, noticing McCracken's new venture, commented with more than its usual irony:

Mr. McCracken.—Some names become household words, some people rise to immense importance, and some perform acts of merit or of demerit, that make their names immortal. . . .Who will not support Mr. McCracken, after the benefit he has conferred upon Guelph? We shall certainly visit him if only to see the man who, as an act of patriotism or charity, took £25,000 in the Galt and Guelph Railway.[78]

Having defeated their Galt opponents, the promoters of the Galt and Guelph line were ready to swing into full activity in the process of persuading municipalities to purchase shares in the line. In quick order, notices were published in Hamilton (£10,000), Preston (£10,000) and Guelph (£10,000) that public meetings were to be held to discuss the appropriate by-laws. No doubt to their surprise, the promoters encountered stiff resistance from both the *Guelph Herald* and *Advertiser*. In the latter paper, John Smith, using his old pen name "Aliquis", opened the anti-railway campaign with this letter to the editor:

Sir,—Has it not occurred to you that the rail chiselling so rife elsewhere is now being enacted very near home?

Don't you believe that the Great Western would build the route from Galt to Guelph without the cost to us of a single sixpence, if some of our meddling friends would not interfere; or perhaps, even build on a route by which we could get to Hamilton in 28 miles, instead of 46—the length of the Galt route?

Shouldn't we be grateful that our local position and commercial importance are sufficient stock for us to subscribe to ensure the completion of the road, without adding to our debt—now becoming burdensome?[79]

With both the *Guelph Herald* and *Advertiser* convinced that the Galt and Guelph Railway Company was at best a bungled job and at worst an outright fraud upon the municipalities,[80] the line's Directors found themselves facing a barrage of complaints and criticism. In order to counteract this attack, the Directors decided to fight fire with fire by founding their own newspaper, the *Mercury*, under the direction of George M. Keeling, ex-editor of the *Advertiser*.[81] The first edition of this newspaper appeared on September 17, 1853, just in time to lead the fight for municipal backing for the line.[82]

At a second meeting in Guelph Township, held on September twenty-second, Doctor Clarke mounted a strong counter-attack to the charges made by the *Herald* and *Advertiser*.[83] The meeting was a noisy, tumultuous gathering, with Doctor Clarke, in particular, involved in angry charges and name calling. Nonetheless, the Township ratepayers were strongly in favour of the investment, while the Guelph Town vote was unanimous in its support.[84] Within a couple of weeks the Preston and Hamilton ratepayers also demonstrated their willingness to invest in the line.[85] The Galt and Guelph Directors with these votes had the assurance of £35,000 in municipal funds with which to begin.

In the meantime, the Galt subscribers had not been idle. Facing both personal and municipal ruin if the result of the shareholders' meeting stood, they took the matter to the Court of Queen's Bench in an attempt to have the election of the Guelph, Hamilton and Preston Directors declared invalid. This Court, however, ruled that it had no jurisdiction in the case.[86] In order to give the municipal campaigns in Guelph and Guelph Township an impetus at a crucial moment, A.J. Fergusson's law firm published this advertisement on September 22, 1853:

GALT AND GUELPH RAILWAY COMP'Y
Understanding that various exaggerated and unfounded reports have been circulated relative to the legal proceedings arising out of the late election of Directors of the above Company, and having been engaged professionally in the matter in question, we think it right to inform the public that there are not, never have been, nor can be any proceedings in regard to the said election in the Court of Chancery, and that the only proceeding which has been instituted was an application to the Court of Queen's Bench on the part of certain gentlemen resident in Galt and claiming a right to seats as Directors, in the place of certain of the existing Directors and further that we have learned by letter from Toronto that the said application was on Tuesday last, refused by the Court of Queen's Bench, which finally disposes of the question.

Fergusson & Kingsmill[87]

Despite Fergusson's assurances that the Galt shareholders had no recourse to the Court of Chancery, they promptly took their case to that Court and received a favourable hearing. The Galt and Guelph Directors, facing a possible loss of the suit were forced to offer a negotiated settlement: if the Galt shareholders would withdraw their suit, they would be allowed to return their shares to the Company without liability, and, as well, have their deposits returned. Each party was to pay their own legal costs.[88] The Galt shareholders agreed.

The loss of the Galt shares was a severe blow to the finances of the Railway Company. Although the £35,000 of municipal stock was still intact, the private shares had, at a stroke, been reduced by almost two-thirds from £23,750 to £8,000—and a good deal of the remainder was rapidly proving to be uncollectable.

In the face of this crisis, the Galt and Guelph Directors, apparently believing that a bold face and a strong offence was the best strategy, pushed ahead as though the future of the Railway was never in doubt. In October, 1853, they placed a notice in the Guelph newspapers stating that they intended to apply to

Parliament for a charter to build a railway from Guelph to Owen Sound.[89] At the same time, the Directors of the Buffalo and Brantford Railway gave notice that they were applying for a charter to build the "Brantford, Guelph and Owen Sound Direct Railway Company."[90] Commenting on Sheriff Grange's involvement in the promotion of the "Brantford, Guelph and Owen Sound Direct Railway Company," the *Advertiser* said:

TAKING CARE OF FOREIGN INTERESTS.—

We understand that Mr. Sheriff Grange, has gone to Quebec, under the sanction of Mr. Carney, [Reeve] of Owen Sound, to look after the interests of Buffalo and Guelph by endeavoring to get the sanction of Parliament to a line of Road from Owen Sound *via* Guelph to Buffalo. He will have his trouble for his pains. We are confident that Parliament will sanction no line so injurious to the Grand Trunk Railway as this would be.[91]

The *Advertiser* was correct in its estimation of the chances of the Brantford, Guelph and Owen Sound receiving a charter. In spite of this setback, Grange and his associates would continue to push for a charter for a railway to Owen Sound. Although neither of the Owen Sound railway projects had a chance of being financed or built in 1853, they were both invaluable to their promoters in maintaining public confidence in the faltering lines of which they were extensions.

In January, 1854, the *Mercury* announced the details of the contract to build the Galt and Guelph rail line:

The contract for this line of Railway was given to General Orville Clarke by the Board of Directors. . . .The amount of General Clarke's tender was £112,000; it was neither the highest nor the lowest, but deemed the most advantageous. The General is bound to make the road ready for the Cars by the 1st of January, 1855, to purchase the

right of way, and to build the line and all the Stations on it, for the sum named. He will require no cash down, but will take Municipal Debentures, £50,000 in Road Bonds and the balance in Road Stock.[92]

This deal would have made General Clarke by far the largest individual shareholder, owning some £17,000 in stock.

In commenting on the Galt and Guelph contract, the *Mercury* once again reaffirmed that:

The Great Western Company will lease the road at 6 per cent. for 20 years. They have guaranteed 6 per cent., but are also bound to give half of what additional profits may accrue. Thus, if the line pay 10 per cent., they will give 8 per cent.; but are bound to give 6 per cent., under any circumstances.[93]

Unfortunately for the peace of mind of the municipal councils, the contract was by no means settled. At a meeting of Directors held on March 22, 1854, it was announced that a second contract had been signed. Upon this news the *Advertiser* commented:

It must be a satisfaction to think that the road will be finished in a year or eighteen months, and that the Great Western will *eventually* take the whole affair. But that satisfaction is not without alloy when it is known that the work was not freely offered to public competition, the route not selected with a single eye to the benefit of the stockholders, and that after humbugging General Clarke out of the contract it has fallen into the hands of two of the Directors in conjunction with Messrs. Cotton and McDonald.[94]

At long last, the Galt and Guelph Railway appeared ready to get under way.

On May 12, 1854, the formal sod turning of the Railway was held at Preston. The *Galt Reformer* displayed the pique felt by that Town's business community at the "McCracken affair" and subsequent events:

This *splendid* affair came off last Friday at Preston. . . .*Honest* Dr. Clarke made an oration behind the Catholic Church, "in his usual style." Mr. Tiffany and Mr. Hespeler also did their first-best to heighten the effect of the glorious occasion of breaking the first clod on the *honourable* line of railway projected from Guelph hitherward. . . . A cold luncheon at Mr. Klotz's constituted the whole fodder supplied at the 'great celebration'. . . .By three o'clock, with the exception of about one hundred people standing near Mr. Hespeler's store, the long single street of the ambitious railroad village of Preston, was as deserted and dismal as it is upon any ordinary day.[95]

In spite of the official sod turning, the turmoil surrounding the contract to build the Galt and Guelph was not yet over. A month after that event the newspapers carried the news that yet another contractor had been found:

Galt and Guelph Railway. After much shuffling and cutting, the transfer of the contract from General Clarke, the Great Western pet, to Messrs. Cotton & Co., and various hitchings backward and forward, we are glad to learn that it at last devolves upon Mr. Rowland the preparation of the road for the iron. Mr. Rowland has obtained for himself a good name in this neighborhood for promptness and efficiency in the performance of his contracts on the Grand Trunk hence [from Guelph] to Berlin, and he will doubtless push on this contract in a manner equally satisfactory.—We learn that the road will be opened in less than twelve months from this date.[96]

At the same time, Rowland began advertising for tenders to chop, clear and grub the stumps and roots along the right-of-way, and for passenger depots, freight and engine houses, and other out-buildings at Preston, New Hope and Guelph.[97] On July fourteenth, additional tenders were called for masonry work on the bridges and culverts. By August seventh, the usually sceptical *Guelph Advertiser* reported

two most encouraging pieces of news: the long delayed Galt branch of the Great Western would be open to traffic on August fourteenth, and that the Galt and Guelph Railway was scheduled to be completed and open to travel as far as Preston in short order.[98]

With construction on the Grand Trunk slowed to a crawl by continuing financial difficulties, here was good news indeed. For a time, local hostility to the Galt and Guelph Company's Directors was submerged in the expectations of increased trade and prosperity.

In spite of the optimistic assurances of summer, the cold winds of November soon uncovered the truth about the finances of the Galt and Guelph line. Far from having completed the financing of the project, the Directors had merely been using the municipal investment to put on a show of activity while they sold off their land around the prospective railway stations.[99] With the municipal money exhausted, construction stopped. On November twenty-fifth, this report startled local readers:

The works on the Galt and Guelph Railway, which lately have been carried on with considerable vigor, were brought to a stand still at the commencement of this week, in consequence of the wages of the workmen not being forthcoming. We learn, however, that this will be soon remedied, and that the work will shortly be recommenced. A considerable part of the line between Galt and Preston is now ready for the rails, and a few weeks' active work will see it completed, although we doubt much if it will be in operation for *some time to come.*[100]

With the affairs of the Galt and Guelph Railway in complete disarray, the truth about its promotion began to come out. There was no contract with the Great Western to lease the completed line and to guarantee the payment of interest on the municipal bonds; there was no obligation by the contractor to pay the interest on the municipal bonds during the line's construction; there was no commitment by the contractor to take the Railway Company's stock or bonds as payment to complete the works. In a word, the municipal money had been spent; the treasury of the Railway Company was empty; and, unless matters changed drastically, Guelph's investment was gone. In January, 1855, in reviewing the whole affair, the *Advertiser* gave this bitter summation:

. . . .The assurance was given by our leading men, the men of honor and integrity in the place, that the advantage of the road to the Town would be immense, whilst neither principal nor interest would be required from Municipalities for twenty years. On such representation scarcely a word was uttered against an investment of £10,000. In the Township a different feeling prevailed, and it required great efforts on the part of Mr. Sheriff Grange, Dr. Clarke, and Mr. Fergusson, to induce the taxpayers to sanction the stock taking by their votes. Again and again were the ratepayers told that no interest on the Debentures would be demanded of the Township for twenty years, that the Great Western Company had agreed to lease the road, at the interest on the investment, and that the Contractor would pay the interest until they had finished the contract.

But, instead of that being the case. . . .the very men who thus represented the matter aided in letting out the Contract for the road at a very brief space of time afterwards, without any stipulations whatever as to interest being paid during construction of the road and without any guarantee that the Great Western would lease it.

The Town of Guelph has a deep interest in this road, and are liable to pay £600 a year of interest on their Stock which will amount to 10d. or 11d. in the £ [equivalent to 42 to 46 mills on the dollar] over and above the present rates. Is it not then, right and proper that some knowledge of the transactions of the Board should be made public, and that the interests of the Municipality should be more fully represented and protected than heretofore?[101]

The release of the Annual Report of the Galt and Guelph Railway Company for 1854 provided yet another shock. Although it required at least £6,000 of shares to be held by the Directors so they could qualify to become members of the Board of Directors, the balance sheet revealed that only £2,453 had actually been received from all private shareholders.[102] In commenting on the Annual Report, John Smith, editor of the *Advertiser* said:

The Galt and Guelph Railway will form a connecting link between this Town and Hamilton, whilst it will unite the Grand Trunk with the Great Western, making Guelph an important station on the former line. The completion of the road will thus prove of consequence to Guelph, in addition to the instalment which she has of £10,000 stock in the Company. But the Galt and Guelph Railway *un*-finished will stand forth as a memento of the rashness and folly of those who commenced the work without the prospect of means to complete it. . . .[103]

Clearly, if Guelph's good name and investment were to be protected, something had to be done.

As the spring of 1855 approached and the construction season opened, the Great Western decided to take a hand. With the Grand Trunk crossing the traditional flow of grain from the north-west, Hamilton businessmen were anxious to see a second branch of the Great Western reach Berlin. Unless the Galt to Preston section of the Galt and Guelph were finished, this would be impossible. Thus the Great Western offered the Galt and Guelph line a deal: it would sell the Galt and Guelph sufficient rails to finish that line for £32,000. To pay for these rails the Galt and Guelph would give the Great Western £50,000 of six percent first mortgage bonds, payable in seven years.[104] Early in June work began again on the Galt to Preston section of the line.

It was at this point that the Guelph Town Council under the leadership of John Smith, the Reeve, decided to intervene to save the Town's interest in the Galt and Guelph line. On June 4, 1855, Doctor Clarke appeared before a special meeting of the Town Council with yet another proposition. Because of the Great Western mortgage and the depressed money market, Galt and Guelph Railway Company bonds were virtually worthless on the open market, while municipal debentures were selling at a large discount. Doctor Clarke proposed that the Town of Guelph should borrow £20,000 from the Municipal Loan Fund and lend it to the Railway. In return, Guelph would receive a combination of municipal debentures and railway second mortgage bonds with an equivalent face value.[105] Taking market values into consideration, Doctor Clarke was in effect asking the Town for an indirect subsidy of something over £10,000. The proposition had the advantage, however, that for the ordinary taxpayer it appeared to cost the Town nothing.

After a lengthy discussion during which Doctor Clarke once again made the oft-repeated assertion that the proposition would never cost the Town a penny, John Watt moved and Peter Gow seconded this motion:

That this Council view with favor the proposition to raise £20,000 under the Municipal Loan Fund Act, for the purpose of completing the Guelph and Galt Railway, and on the undertaking of the Directors of that Company, that the debentures not yet issued of the Municipalities holding Stock in that road be transferred to the Town of Guelph, this Council pledge themselves to endeavor (subject to the opinion of the ratepayers) to obtain such loan, with the understanding that £15,000 of the sum so

to be raised be expended on the line of Road between New Hope and Guelph, commencing at said Town of Guelph. . . .[106]

After several bitter meetings in which Doctor Clarke strongly objected to any examination of the Railway's books or any conditions being placed upon the loan, the Railway's Directors ultimately accepted the Town's terms.[107] On August 1, 1855, the Town Council finally passed the by-law to lend the Railway £20,000.[108] With this incentive, the Great Western agreed to undertake the construction of the line from New Hope to Guelph.[109] With the Great Western in charge of construction work progressed slowly but steadily, the line to Preston being opened in December, 1856, and to Guelph on September 26, 1857.

There was as yet, however, one more act to be played out in the chequered drama of the Galt and Guelph Railway. One of the steps taken by the municipalities to protect their interests in the Galt and Guelph Railway's troubled affairs, was to ask the Legislature for an amendment to that Company's charter which would allow any municipalities owning at least £5,000 worth of shares to elect one Director to the line's Board of Directors. This amendment became effective in October, 1855. No sooner

had the new Directors taken office than they were met by a demand from Sheriff Grange and Jacob Hespeler for £1,500 each as payment for the land upon which the stations in New Hope and Guelph were built.

When the contracts to build the Galt and Guelph Railway had first been let, Sheriff Grange and Jacob Hespeler, in addition to performing their duties as President and Director of the line, were appointed by the Board of Directors to purchase the land necessary for the stations and right-of-way. As was usually the case in such railway promotions, Grange and Hespeler had placed the stations in the middle of property which they either owned previously, or had purchased before announcing where the railway was to run. Thus the station at Preston was placed well away from the business district in order to benefit two of the Directors, George S. Tiffany, of Hamilton, and Jacob Hespeler. Concerning the Preston station, the Galt *Reporter* said:

At Preston, the road runs on the north side of the Town, till it reaches the farm of Mr. Henry Hagey, situated north of the Roman Catholic Church, where the terminus buildings are to be erected, and the business of the road concentrated. It will thus be seen that New Cambridge, the most thriving part of the Village of Preston, is to be sacrificed to building up the eastern and ruinous part of the aforesaid Village, in which Mr. Hespeler has some property. And it will also be seen that the north side of the Village has been chosen for the site of the Railway buildings, instead of the south side, which is their natural and most generally beneficial location, because Messrs. Tiffany and Hespeler had purchased some land there for a terminus, which they sold to the Company at an enormous advance, and made themselves rich at the expense of the people of Preston.[110]

Similarly, the station in New Hope was erected on property owned by Jacob Hespeler,

and the Guelph Station was scheduled to be built on a farm west of Guelph which Sheriff Grange had purchased from William Day.[111] Having located the stations on their properties, Hespeler and Grange had proceeded to subdivide the remainder of their land and to sell it off at high prices.[112]

It was usually the case that when railway directors set up such "insider" land transactions, they justified their actions by "donating" the station site to the railway. As an encouragement to landowners to sell rights-of-way cheaply to the Galt and Guelph Railway both Hespeler and Grange had announced to the public that they had made just such donations.[113] In fact, although they had been paid by the Galt and Guelph Railway Company to purchase rights-of-way, and in every other case had done so, neither Hespeler nor Grange had transferred title of the station sites to the Railway Company. As soon as they lost control of the Railway's Board of Directors to the newly-appointed municipal representatives, both demanded payment for the station sites.

The Guelph Town Council, led by Mayor John Smith, was furious. Their initial reaction was simply to reject the demands for £1,500 each from Hespeler and Grange, but were persuaded to accept arbitration in order to save the costs of litigation. To the Town's astonishment, the arbitrators awarded Grange £3,500 and Hespeler £1,000.[114] Although the Town Council sought alternate remedies, such as proposing to the Great Western that the stations should be moved to other sites,[115] in the end, Hespeler and Grange had to be paid.

When the Galt and Guelph Railway was finally opened on September 28, 1857, everyone involved heaved a sigh of relief. For a mere fifteen miles of track, more promises had been broken, more harsh words uttered, and more hopes shattered, than for any equivalent line in the country. In this case, Guelph had paid dearly for its economic development.

In spite of almost endless schemes, scandals and rumours, construction on the Toronto and Guelph section of the Grand Trunk made steady progress through 1854 and 1855. Al-though shortage of funds had caused the Strat-ford to Sarnia section to be allowed to lapse for several years, and delayed the completion of the Toronto and Guelph section well past its initially predicted opening date, on January 30, 1856, a train carrying the Governor-Gen-eral, Sir Edmund Head, and various Railway and Government officials managed to reach Guelph over the still unballasted track.

While the Grand Trunk officials had in-tended that the visit to Guelph should be

*Scene of Guelph circa 1855. Note that the Railway is incomplete
and that the Town Hall has not been constructed.*

unofficial—no more than an inspection tour of the route—the last minute decision by the Governor-General to join the party changed the situation considerably. Rumours had circulated in Guelph for a week previous to the occasion that Guelph's first train was about to arrive. It was only by accident, however, on January twenty-ninth that James Webster, in a telegraphic communication on another subject, received the news that the Governor-General would be included in the Railway party.

The Grand Trunk party included twenty-three members led by the Governor-General, the Attorney-General, Postmaster-General, three High Court Justices (Richards, Burns and Chancellor Blake), and the Mayor and ex-Mayor of Toronto. They were met by A.J. Fergusson, M.P.P., Sheriff Grange, and a bevy of County and Town officers and officials. After addresses read by the Warden, the Mayor, and the President of the Mechanics' Institute, both delegations lunched at Thorp's British Hotel. The whole event, in spite of the hurried preparations,[116] was a smashing success, and left the Town looking forward eagerly to the official opening of the line, and the commencement of regular freight and passenger service to Toronto.

As the spring of 1856 passed and the final stages of work on the Toronto and Guelph line were completed, excitement mounted in Guelph. Throughout May and early June rumours circulated, speeches were prepared, and finery readied in anticipation of the celebration of the historic event. On Tuesday, June tenth, a train carrying some of the Grand Trunk Directors and contractors passed over the railroad from Toronto to Guelph, and they informed newspaper reporters that they "were generally much gratified with what they had

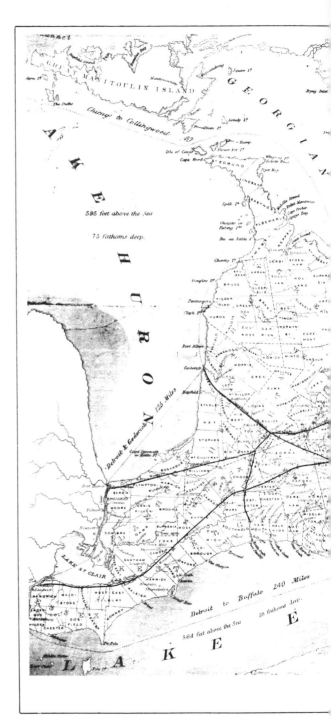

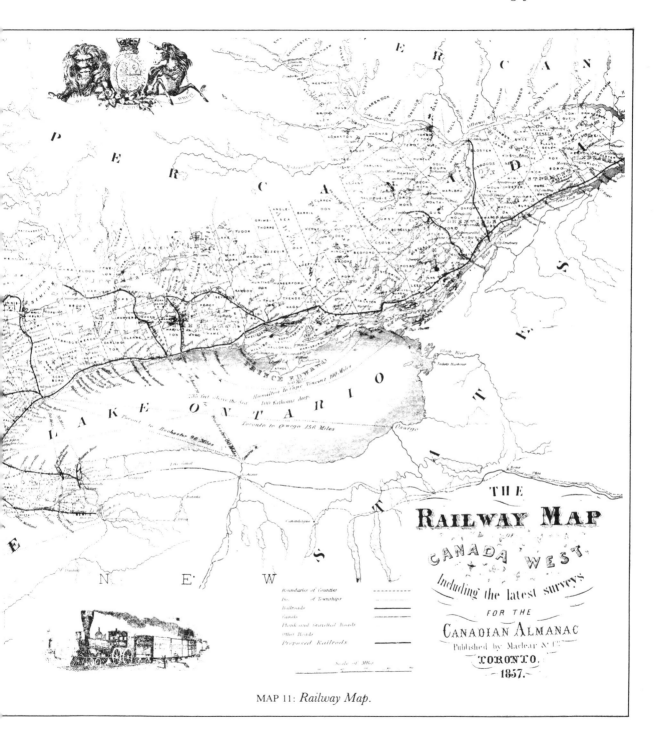

MAP 11: *Railway Map.*

seen."[117] On Thursday evening, the twelfth, the Mayor of Guelph, John Smith, received a telegram from the President of the Grand Trunk Railway Company, informing him that the President had invited the members of both Houses of the Legislature to visit Guelph on Saturday, June fourteenth, to take part in the official opening ceremonies.[118] The *Advertiser* commented:

We fully anticipate that during this [Saturday] afternoon the Governor-General, the members of the Executive Council, and of the House of Assembly, will visit Guelph.[119]

Immediately plans went ahead to decorate the Town and to put on a display that would live long in the memories of all those present.

In the meantime, matters had become complicated in Toronto where the Assembly was sitting. The Toronto *Leader* gave this report:

Yesterday [Friday the thirteenth of June] the Ministry opposed the acceptance of the Grand Trunk Railway Directors to take a trip by special train to *Guelph* to-day, at one o'clock. After the invitation had been read by the Speaker, Mr. Solicitor-General Smith, who had a notice on the paper that the House meet to-day [Saturday the fourteenth] at one and sit till six, professed to be sorry at this clashing between his motion and the invitation. Mr. Drummond, however, moved an amendment that would have rendered it possible for the House to accept the invitation without interfering with the progress of the public business: that the hour of meeting to-day should be ten instead of one, and that it rise in time to go by the train.[120]

This amendment was defeated. As a result of the Government's decision to continue the sitting on Saturday, only a few of the members of Parliament could get away to join the celebrations. Unfortunately, the residents of Guelph were apparently not informed of this change of plan.

The Grand Trunk Railway station as it appeared circa 1908.

On Saturday, June fourteenth, a party of about two hundred persons, comprised of "some of the members of the Legislative Assembly, a few of the Legislative Council, quite a number of the Clerks of the two Houses, and a few of the citizens of Toronto, the Directors, Contractors, etc.,"[121] set out by train to see the line and to take part in the Guelph ceremonies.

Meanwhile, in Guelph, a large crowd had gathered in anticipation of the arrival of Governor-General Sir Edmund Head, who, it was supposed, was on the train. As the train approached, a number of members of Parliament, apparently a little the worse for a champagne luncheon,[122] prepared a surprise for the welcoming crowd in Guelph. The *Leader* offered this description:

Some of the worthy M.P.P.'s it is said concocted a

scheme to introduce Mr. Shaw, the M.P.P. for La-
nark, to the inhabitants of Guelph as the Governor-General. Accordingly when the hon. gentlemen
stepped out of the cars, they took off their hats and
gave him a hearty cheer as the Governor-General.
Mr. Rankin, the hon. member for Essex, then took
Mr. Shaw's arm and they walked along to the new
hotel [Horwood's, now the Royal] followed by
nearly all the excursionists, with a large turnout of
townspeople. Upstairs the gentlemen marched and
made their appearance on the balcony in front of
the hotel, which was speedily surrounded by a large
crowd of persons eager to get a glimpse of His Excellency. The hon. member for Essex, without paus-
ing for a moment to define his new position, introduced Mr. Shaw to the audience as Sir Edmund
Head, the Governor-General of Canada. His Excellency then came forward, and stated that he had
come to Guelph along with a number of their representatives, both from Upper Canada and Lower
Canada. . . .He was happy to see so large and thriving a town as Guelph, and he was sure that the representatives of the people now that they had
witnessed the beautiful country through which they
had passed—and the magnificent road over which
they had travelled, would go back to their places in
the Legislature, determined to meet in a more liberal spirit the demands which the Grand Trunk
had made upon them.

Mr. Turcotte then came forward and spoke at
some length, referring to the necessity of maintaining the Union intact, and the fact that if they did
so, the two provinces, each representing the most
civilized nations on the earth, would, by the combination of French vivacity with English reserve,
make the most noble people in the world.[123]

At this point in the charade, Foley, the M.P.P.
for Waterloo, attempted to address the audience to expose the fraud which had been
perpetrated on the citizens of Guelph. The
Leader continued:

Mr. Foley, the hon. member for Waterloo, came
forward—seemingly in a state of great excitement.
He said that a fraud had been practiced upon
them. . . . Gentlemen, you have been imposed
upon—most foully imposed upon. You have been
led to believe that the Governor-General is here to-
day, while he is not here. (Here the hon. gentleman
was forcibly dragged from the front of the balcony,
perhaps in mercy to himself, for he was speaking
above his strength.)[124]

At this point the scene broke down in a general tumult of shouting, pushing, booing and
uproar which ended only with the train returning to Toronto.

The shock and anger felt across the Province at this display of drunken boorishness by
members of the Assembly was exceeded only
by Guelph's chagrin that their great day had
been so utterly spoiled.

If the unpleasant surprises and disappoint-
ments that had accompanied the building of
the first main roads and railways to Guelph
never seemed to end, there were compensa-
tions. The economic boom created by railway
building, land speculation and high prices for
farm produce created by the Crimean War,
changed Guelph's face forever. By 1857,
Guelph's economy had so grown and developed that the fears and insecurities felt in 1851
were remembered only as a bad dream.
Keefer's vision of the transformation of Sleepy
Hollow had taken on material reality in the
transformation of Guelph. For Guelph's residents, the future seemed to be unlimited.

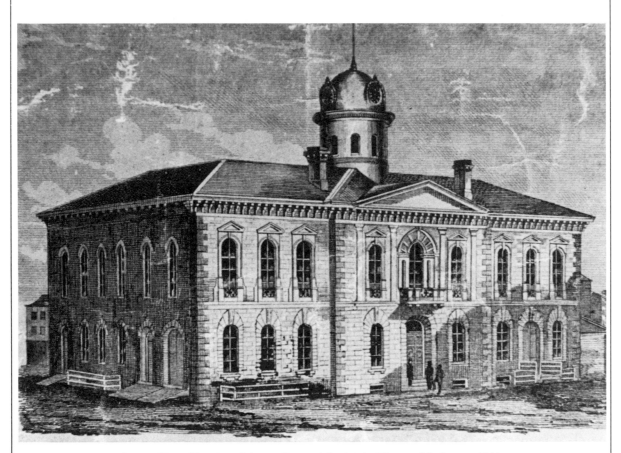

Guelph Town Hall from Map of Town of Guelph by Thomas W. Cooper, 1862.

VIII

Guelph achieves Town Status

No sooner had the residents of the Town of Guelph voted to take shares in the Toronto and Guelph Railway Company, than local shopkeepers, tradesmen, and innkeepers jumped on the railroad band wagon. Swallows and Irons, proprietors of the "Manchester House", selling dry goods, clothing, groceries, boots and shoes, renamed their business "The Railroad Depot" cash store, while D. Byrns, shoemaker, advertised the "Railroad Boot and Shoe Store", and the "Railroad Inn", lot 15 Market Square, was offered for sale.[1]

In June of 1852 the *Guelph Advertiser* reported:

During the coming summer, a considerable number of buildings, of "various sorts and sizes," will be erected in this locality. Sundry valuable Town Lots have been purchased by gentlemen from Toronto and other places for building purposes; and there is every sign of there being more than ordinary activity and prosperity in the Town during the present season.[2]

Once actual construction of the Toronto and Guelph line was under way, and the Galt and Guelph line negotiations started, the image of Guelph as a place filled with opportunity was greatly enhanced. In April, 1853,

John Smith,
Reeve, 1855, Mayor 1856.

the *Advertiser* made this estimation of the situation:

Town Assessment.—Although circumstances have occurred to reduce in some instances the assessed value of property in the Town, we are happy in being able to state that on the whole there will be an advance over last year of upwards of £1,000 or about 11 per cent. This is gratifying, but we fully anticipate that the railroad will next year increase the present assessment fully 20 per cent. Up to this time the Town has scarcely felt that the works are progressing, but the cutting of stone, building of the Station House, and laying the rails, will not only make the place appear busy, but will make it so.[3]

As work on the Grand Trunk Railway began in earnest in the summer of 1853, the tempo of economic life throughout the Province began to increase. Millions of pounds sterling of British capital flowed into the country to finance the Grand Trunk, and tens of thousands of labourers were hired to carry out the construction projects. With wages rising due to strikes and competition for labour, money flowed to commercial outlets creating a sense of boundless optimism. As the *Guelph Advertiser* reported in September, 1853:

Progress of Guelph.— The material progress of the country was never more fully evidenced than at the present time, whilst the increase of agricultural produce, the facilities for conveying it to market, the spread of manufactures, and the increase of population in Town and country, all mark the onward progress of the Province. The building everywhere going on has increased the wages of the mechanic, the railroads are paying 5s. to 6s. 3d. to the labourer, whilst Town Lots are rising in value and money is everywhere plentiful. The reference from time to time in our contemporaries of the erection of a block of buildings here, the opening of new streets there, and the founding of villages in other places, all tend to encourage and elevate our expectations of Canada's future. . . .

All who take into consideration what has been done during the past ten years, and the prospects now opening for the future will admit that in three years or less from this date few inland towns in the Province, without manufactures, will compare with Guelph for a moment. Enjoying the freest communication with the western capital [Toronto] and its harbor, by the Grand Trunk Railway, a probable communication with the States by way of Buffalo, a splendid gravelled road to Hamilton, others spreading into the country north, and north west, this Town, by good management, may become the centre point of transactions between the cultivator of the soil and the wholesale businessmen of the Province. But position is not all—good management is requisite to avail ourselves of all the advantages which are within reach, to enable us to turn to best account the opportunities presented by the situation and circumstances. Due caution must be exercised in the management of the Town funds, responsibilities must not be recklessly entered into, [and] our business men must advance with the spirit of the times. . . .[4]

At a dinner given for Adam J. Fergusson, M.P.P. for Wellington, in September, 1853, the "Idea of Progress" was expounded further:

Year has succeeded year in engendering a spirit of public enterprise; first the Government commenced with a gigantic scale of canals to connect our lakes with the ocean, and almost no sooner were these in operation than the contagion—if I may be allowed the expression—took hold of the minds of the people. Plank, gravel and macadamized roads were constructed to a considerable extent; still the spirit of improvement marched onward until the railroad mania got hold of the minds of both Government and people—until railroads of an unprecedented extent have been and are on the way of being constructed,—and still onward the spirit of improvement until the whole Province has been wrought up like a net-work with telegraph wires where thought may be communicated with thought and action with action from one end of Canada to another.[5]

In February, 1854, the *Toronto Leader*, concerned at the rapid increase in speculation both in shares of railways and town lots, offered this caution:

The railway mania never assumed that aggravated form of recklessness in the United States that it wears in Upper Canada at this moment. Every man has a scheme for increasing the value of his property, by making a railroad to his own door. Every one is looking for sudden riches by land speculations connected with imaginary railroads. It is not enquired whether the schemes that look so well on paper are required by the necessities of commerce and travel; or whether they will yield a return to the shareholders.[6]

In the enthusiasm of the moment, few if any of Guelph's residents paid heed. In May, 1854, the *Guelph Advertiser* commented as follows:

Land Speculation is the order of the day, and just now the most certain mode of making money. The natural progress of the country, the dense population of the larger towns compelling settlements in the neighborhood, the rapidity with which new places fill up, and last, the laying out of railway lines in different directions through the country, all tend to induce speculation in town and village lots. . . .

Last year Mr. Sheriff Grange made several fortunate speculations, amongst others a large block of land at Berlin, from which he realized two-thirds of the purchase money last fall; and his sale advertised for next month will probably leave him a large quantity of land and some thousands of dollars an overplus.

The property in this Town is also rising rapidly, and every sale shows an advance on the preceding one. In Fergus, Elora, Durham and Sydenham, the result is the same, and no matter how high the price of lots may appear when bought, there is always some one ready to pay an advance on them. Indeed, the safest speculation we know of in a small way, is to attend these land sales, and immediately re-sell.[7]

In 1854 a number of large subdivisions were laid out around Guelph, the most important being that of Robert Thompson on the south side of the Speed River. The *Advertiser* described Thompson's subdivision:

The Land [recently purchased from Mrs. Lamprey] is situated partly on the River Speed, which forms the boundary of the Town of Guelph on the southern and eastern sides, is in the neighborhood of the business places, and within less than ten minutes walk of the Market Square. The Building Lots comprise one-fifth of an acre each, and are well adapted for Cottage Residences and the carrying on of various mechanical occupations: whilst the Park Lots present some of the most commanding and prettiest sites for residences to be found in the Town or neighborhood.[8]

In describing Thompson's subdivision, the *Advertiser* remarked that small lots would sell well, as speculation had driven the price of similar lots in the Town to between £100 to £200 each.[13] After the sale the newspaper reported:

The Land Sale of Mr. Thompson on Wednesday last, went off well, quite a number of lots being disposed of at remunerating prices. The building lots of one-fifth of an acre fetched from £20 to £55 each, and the Park Lots averaged about £70 per acre. The sales amounted to about £1,200. The remaining lots are at private sale.[9]

With so much new growth occurring outside the Town limits, the Town Council decided to ask the Provincial Government to allow them to expand the Town's boundaries, thus taking in the new subdivisions. On September 30, 1854, the *Canada Gazette* printed a description of the Town's new limits which came into effect on January 1, 1855.[10]

The newly enlarged Town was to be bounded by Speedvale Avenue on the north and Victoria Road on the east. On the south the limits were a little more complicated, following the Eramosa River between Victoria Road and Dundas Road (now Gordon Street), down the Dundas Road to Forest Street, then west along Forest Street to a line extended south from Silvercreek Road which was the western boundary. When one considers that the original Town plot as laid out by John Galt was less than one-sixth this size—that is, a rough square bounded on the north by London Road, on the east and south by the Speed River, and on the west by Edinburgh Road—this expansion was enormous indeed.

Following this extension, a new subdivision was announced by A.J. Fergusson and Sheriff George J. Grange:

TOWN LOTS

The undersigned having completed their Survey of Town Lots on their respective Properties adjoining the Depots of the Grand Trunk and Galt and Guelph Railways at Guelph, are now prepared to dispose of a limited number of Lots at stated prices, by private contract. Full particulars to be obtained at the Office of Messrs. Fergusson and Kingsmill, Quebec Street, Guelph, who are authorized to conduct the sales.

Signed: George J. Grange
January 6, 1855.   A.J. Fergusson.[11]

The area offered for sale by Fergusson and Grange was made more attractive by the proposal to extend the Galt and Guelph Railway to Owen Sound. This subdivision was opened during the Crimean War, and the streets were named for British heroes and victories. Thus, Alma, St. Arnaud, Crimea, Raglan, Inkerman, Omar, etc., were added to the catalogue of Guelph's street names.[12]

In spite of increasing signs of economic problems in the general economy, runaway inflation and a sharp decline in retail trade,[13] land speculation continued to accelerate. In May, 1855, the *Advertiser* printed this description of new subdivision sales in Guelph:

At no previous time has there been such a demand for Town Lots, or such a very general desire to meet the demand. Prices have risen enormously, and the more cautious bystander who looks on with a shake of the head and a grave calculation that things must take a change and that property must go down, is surprised to find that at every successive sale, prices advance, money is plentiful and purchases do not diminish. But a few months since Mr. Tiffany advertised a number of lots for sale on the Woolwich road, and was well pleased to make £800 off them on the day preceding the sale. The same lots on the following day produced double the amount. Since then the McCartney property realized about £1200 being at the rate of £225 per acre. Next we hear of Mr. Pipe's eight acres, occupying a situation far inferior to either of the others, though in the same neighborhood, and nearly £200 per acre was the result. About eighteen months since the same property was sold for £350. Her Majesty's Birthday was fixed on by Mr. Thorp to celebrate his land sale, and we learn that very large prices were realized for his property in Guelph, Berlin and Fergus.

To furnish a continued supply for the apparently increasing demand, we announce a sale of Park Lots on the York Road immediately adjoining the Guelph Mills property, which offers great inducements to all desirous of owning a Park Lot or grazing field conveniently at hand.[14]

The peak of the Guelph land boom was reached in November, 1855, when John A. Macdonald visited the Town to sell his property. Macdonald, because of his close connection with the development of the Grand Trunk Railway and with C.S. Gzowski and Company, had been involved in several land sales in towns served by the Grand Trunk. In Guelph he had purchased some acreage near the Market Square before the choice of that location for the station was officially announced. The *Guelph Advertiser* gives this account of Macdonald's sale:

St. Andrew's Day.—On Friday last, a large concourse

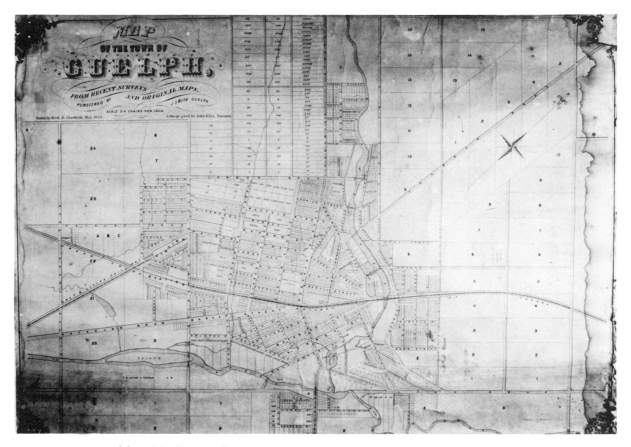

MAP 12: *Map of the Town of Guelph, published by J. Smith, drawn by F.J. Chadwick, May 1855, Lithographed by John Ellis, Toronto, showing the new Town limits.*

of people honored Guelph with their presence, brought together partly by the land sale advertised by Mr. Webster, and not less by the annual festival of the Scotsmen, St. Andrew's Day.

At noon a numerous company partook of lunch at the British Hotel, which was got up in the best style, and reflected equal credit on "Mine Host," Mr. Moran, and the gentlemen through whose instrumentality it was provided. The Hon. J.A. McDonald [*sic*], with a number of other strangers, was present, and everything betokened a grand field day. The preliminaries of the sale having been discussed, an adjournment took place to the Macdonald property when the first lot composing a trian-

gle of about one-fifteenth of an acre, was sold for £48, and after a spirited bidding for about an hour, the lots of the Hon. J.A. Macdonald, so far as sold, realized about £2000.[15]

The highlight of the sale, however, were several lots on the Market Square itself:

Coming nearer the Grand Trunk Station, the property of Mr. John Neeve, sold for upwards of £2000, whilst the corner lots in the Market Square, nearly balanced £2000. Some of Mr. Neeve's lots sold at the rate of £10,000 an acre, whilst the Square lots fetched £20 per foot frontage, exclusive of the buildings.[16]

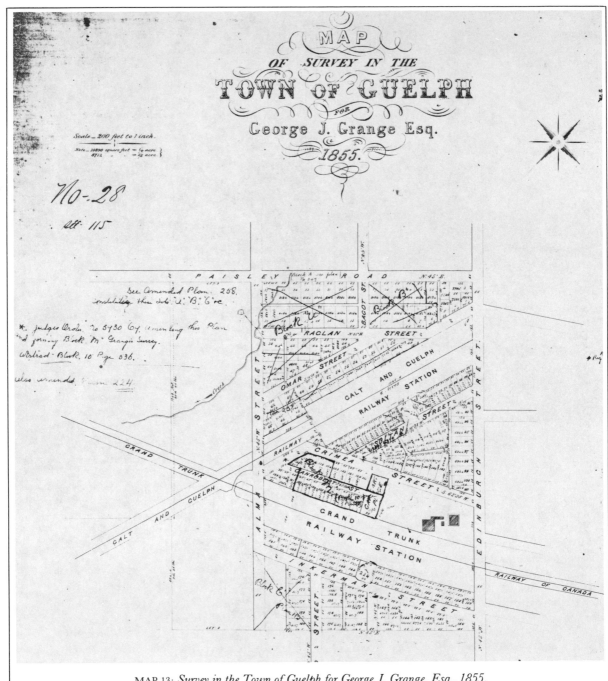

MAP 13: *Survey in the Town of Guelph for George J. Grange, Esq., 1855.*

On May tenth, 1856, A.J. Fergusson auctioned off the balance of his acreage at Guelph Junction (near Edinburgh Road). The *Advertiser* noted:

Mr. Fergusson's land sale on Saturday last was all that could be desired, realizing about £4000 in a couple of hours. The size of the lots was from the tenth to the fifth of an acre, and ranged from £25 to £205 each, depending upon their proximity or distance from the railway stations. These prices were from 25 to 50 per cent in advance of the sale last fall![17]

Fergusson's sale was the last reported that brought high prices. When Frederick George attempted to sell off the excess of his property around the Wellington Mills, the *Advertiser* noted that:

Yesterday, the 15th [May, 1856], the sale of Mr. George's Town and Water Lots took place on the ground adjoining the People's Mills and on both banks of the Speed. The great majority of the lots were small and realized from £50 to £150 each. There was not much desire manifested for the Water Lots, and we are not aware what proportion of them sold.[18]

Although further sales were advertised by W.D.P. Jarvis, Robert Scott, John Pipe and John Thorp (who advertised that he had established a new village named "Thorpville" half way between Guelph and Elora),[19] results were sufficiently disappointing that no prices were reported and no further subdivisions were laid out. For Guelph, the great Canadian land boom was over.

Throughout the spring and summer of 1856, signs of economic depression in Guelph multiplied. Money was short, bills went unpaid, and thinly capitalized firms began to fail. On May eighth, the editor of the *Advertiser* commented on this new state of affairs:

Elopements appear to be getting into fashion in Guelph, if we may take the present week as an illustration.... Failures have occurred more frequently and this week has added to the number. A few months ago the new stores on Wyndham Street [built by Robert Corbet, the postmaster] were occupied by quite a number of new business men, amongst whom *Steenbock, Bros.* cut quite a figure.... Although they only opened in November or December, when the "birds were discovered to be flown" on Monday morning last, debts to the amount of £300 quickly made their appearance. In addition to legitimate business debts, those for horses, wine, with which was mixed no small quantum of music and dancing, figured largely....

Thursday last found us deficient another business man, Mr. Johns, a Cabinet-maker, who opened here about the same time as the above firm, and quickly followed their example. His favors were as generally scattered as those of Steenbock's, but not to so large an amount whilst he has left even less to pay with.[20]

Given the troubled history of the Grand Trunk Railway, it was perhaps appropriate that in Guelph, the railway boom collapsed in the month that the railway was opened. It would be twenty years before another period of such rapid growth occurred.

Ten years later in May, 1866, hundreds of lots in Guelph's new subdivisions were sold for delinquent taxes. The inevitable "bust" that followed Guelph's speculative boom had swept away the golden dreams of hundreds of unwary small speculators. In contrast, the graceful mansions of those who laid out the surveys would, for some time, remain the homes of Guelph's business and civic leaders.

Not only had the railway boom of 1853-1856 greatly changed Guelph's size and appearance, it made some drastic changes in Guelph's commercial life as well.

Prior to this time, despite the poor transportation then existing, Guelph had several large general stores which sold a wide variety of groceries, hardware, dry goods, clothing, wines and confectionery. The advertisements of John Ross,[21] W. MacKay,[22] and Jackson and Davidson[23] in 1847 give some idea of the enormous selection, both in quality and in quantity, of the merchandise available. These stores catered to both town and country trade, and all merchants expressed their willingness to accept farm produce in exchange for store goods.

Guelph also had a number of shopkeepers who created their commodities in their own shops. Among these was Joseph Hayton who manufactured a wide range of household furnishings in his cabinet and upholstery warehouse in 1847.

The bookseller, John Smith, owner of the *Guelph Advertiser*, was both a bookbinder and a printer, as was George Pirie, owner of the *Guelph Herald*.[24] John Godfrey[25] and T. Elliott[26] were makers and sellers of boots and shoes.

By the year 1851 the Canada Directory lists no less than twelve general merchants, ten boot and shoemaking establishments, whose products were made on the premises, two "compounding chemists," two watchmakers and jewellers, two dry goods stores, two grocers, two confectioners (one who also sold groceries) and one bookseller and stationer.[27]

By 1853 Guelph had fifteen general merchants, four dry goods, three grocery stores, thirteen shoe stores, six bakers and confectioners, five tailor shops, three saddlers and harness-makers, three dressmakers, two chemists' shops, two butchers, two milliners, and one each of the following: eating house, barber, writing master, brewer, stationer and printer, wagon maker, sleigh maker, fanning mill maker, pump maker, watch maker and carriage maker.[28]

(Guelph Herald)

(Guelph Herald)

The addition of so many small businessmen to Guelph's commercial community would have an important long range effect upon Guelph's economic and social life. They were the backbone of "respectable" society in the Town,[29] and were the strongest backers of every cause for the betterment of Guelph from improved educational facilities to the building of the Guelph Market House.

Ultimately a significant number of them would become important industrialists, and civic leaders, such as Peter Gow, shoemaker and George Sleeman, brewer, both of whom would become Mayors of Guelph.

As the business community in Guelph developed, the need for a lending institution became apparent. Although the Gore Bank had appointed Thomas Sandilands as its agent in 1845, and the same year the Bank of Montreal gave a similar appointment to Doctor Alling,[30] neither of these men acted as loan officers, but rather handled commercial notes and made loan recommendations to the main offices in Hamilton and Toronto respectively. Finally, citizens who wanted a safe investment found that municipal, provincial and railroad bonds offered relatively low rates of return and at times were a high risk venture. To local investors, the creation of a building society appeared to solve many of these problems.

In the fall of 1848, the question of whether or not a building society could (or should) be undertaken in Wellington District began to be discussed in Guelph newspapers,[31] but it would require another eighteen months before concrete steps were taken.

In April, 1850, this notice appeared in the *Guelph Advertiser*:

Building Society,—At length there is a prospect of an

institution of this kind being established at Guelph, for the County of Waterloo. About 100 shares were subscribed on the first day, and many more are now taken. . .[32]

Within the next few weeks, some 413 shares having a face value of fifty pounds each—a total of £20,650—were subscribed.[33] For such low risk, high return enterprises, there was ample money available in Guelph.

Until the eighteen-fifties, society generally viewed high rates of interest as being immoral. Under the laws of the time, "usury"—charging more than six per cent per annum on the face value of a loan—was illegal. Although financiers waged constant battles to have the six per cent limit removed, they were unsuccessful. The "Building Society" was a useful stratagem to evade such "usury" laws, and the proponents of these societies justified them on the ground that they were nothing more than mutual savings associations designed to allow people to accumulate sufficient capital to buy their own homes.

Rule No. I of the "County of Waterloo Building Society" as the Guelph society was called, read as follows:

That this Society is established for the purpose of enabling its members, by advancing their shares, to acquire freehold or leasehold estate, or to remove encumbrances upon property held by them, and also to afford such as do not desire their shares in advance a safe and profitable mode of investing small savings.[34]

The Directorate of the Building Society elected April 29, 1850, was composed of A.J. Fergusson, George J. Grange, Thomas Sandilands, Alfred A. Baker, John Smith, Dr. Liddell and H.W. Peterson of Guelph, Charles Allan of Elora, and John Watt and George Jardine of Fergus, Thomas R. Brock and Colonel Hewat.[35]

The Society operated as follows: when an individual subscribed to a share, he was required to pay into the Society five shillings a month, plus three pence halfpenny operating expenses, until such time as the Society was "closed." In other words, if the Society made nothing from the investment of the accumulated funds, such a person would continue to pay in his five shillings for 200 months, until his share was paid up, at which time he would receive the £50 face value of his share, and the Society ceased to exist. Rule VI of the Waterloo Society covers the closing out procedure:

When the funds of the Society shall be equal to the amount of Fifty Pounds currency for every share held by members who have not already been paid in advance, the Directors shall announce the same and cease to receive the monthly payments of instalments and interest, and proceed to close the Society as speedily as possible, paying Fifty Pounds currency to the holder of each unreceived share; and, should any surplus remain, dividing it amongst all the members according to the number of shares held.[36]

So successful had the Waterloo Building Society been, that in February, 1854, it was decided to take advantage of new legislation to establish a permanent building society. The primary difference between the two types of building societies was that the permanent society issued a new class of accumulative and closed out shares each year. In this manner, the society had a continuous existence or, in other words, was "permanent."

In February, 1854, the *Guelph Advertiser* carried this item:

Permanent Building Society,—A meeting of the subscribers to this Society was held yesterday [the eighth] at Mr. Newton's office, when the following gentlemen were appointed to draw up rules and submit them at an early day to the consideration of the subscribers: Messrs. Liddell, Kingsmill, Newton, Smith, Allan, Jackson, Pirie, Thompson. Upwards of 200 shares are already taken, and by the time the rules are ready the number will probably be doubled. The facilities for investment are much more favorable than by the old system.[37]

At the first general meeting of shareholders on March thirteenth, J.J. Kingsmill, G.J. Grange, T. Sandilands, W. Alexander, G. Pirie, D. Allan, J. McLean, John Smith and R. Thompson were elected Directors. Subsequently, Thomas Sandilands was elected President; George Pirie, Vice-President; Edward Newton, Secretary and Treasurer; and J.J. Kingsmill and A.J. Fergusson, solicitors.[38] When Sandilands could not accept the office of president, A.J. Fergusson was elected in his place.[39]

The Wellington Permanent Building Society, as the new institution was officially named, was an immediate success. By the first of April, 1854, 468 shares had been taken, giving the Society an initial capitalization of £23,400.[40] The first annual report issued April 2, 1855, showed excellent results. In part, the report read:

The Directors have much pleasure in submitting for the information of the Stockholders the audited statement of the financial transactions of the Society during the first year of its operations, and in congratulating them on the result, which shows an amount of profit exceeding their anticipations. The paid-up capital stock of the Society received on 468 shares during the past year, including the payments on account of expenses, amounts to £2002. 2s. ½d., and the net profit derived from 45 shares paid up and 7 shares forfeited amounts to £403. 9s. 1½d.

Acting in the belief that the Society is intended

Guelph and Ontario Investment and Savings Society.

to promote the mutual benefit of both classes of Shareholders, of the borrower as well as the lender, the Directors have not sought to exact a usurious rate of bonus, but have been content to obtain a more moderate premium on the shares advanced than has been customary in similar institutions; they have consequently experienced no difficulty in investing the income of the Society as it was acquired, securing, by the rapid investment of the funds, the well-understood advantages of compound interest. A uniform rate of 20 per cent bonus has been received on the whole amount of shares advanced, and the Directors have every reason to be satisfied with the sufficiency of the real estate pledged in security.[41]

Eventually, in 1876, the Wellington Permanent Building Society would be converted into the Guelph and Ontario Investment and Savings Society.

Not only did the rapid expansion of population and trade bring about fundamental changes in its economic life, it allowed Guelph, finally, to acquire the powers as well as the title of Town status. By 1855 Guelph had acquired the 3000 residents necessary to be moved from Schedule D of the Municipal Act to Schedule B. The wider powers of action available under Schedule B were of particular interest to the Town's commercial elements, who were anxious to use such powers to improve the commercial district's appearance, and to establish a market down town.

Acton Burrows summarizes the vigorous debate that stirred local politics during November and December, 1855:

It was proposed to place it [the Town] in schedule B., and to divide it into wards, with an increased number of Councillors and with a Mayor as the presiding officer. The *Herald* and *Advertiser* both advocated this measure, but the *Mercury* opposed it, Mr. G. Keeling, the editor of that paper making some most absurd and extravagant statements with respect to the proposed change, with a view to influence persons to sign a petition against the proposed incorporation. Among the other bugbears conjured up by this gentleman to frighten the people, was the statement that the incorporation would entail upon the Town an additional expenditure of about £1200, £400 as salary for the Mayor, £250 or £300 for a Chamberlain, besides payment of Councillors and an endless array of officers of various grades. This was represented as necessary under the Act, although in fact the Act provided that the payment of the Mayor and Councillors should be altogether optional. The other two papers in harmony with the great body of the ratepayers, urged that the Town having reached the requisite status as to population—3000,—was in duty to itself, and in defence of the business interests of the inhabitants, bound to take the necessary steps for incorporation, and so maintain its position among the neighboring municipalities, some of which were petitioning for such incorporation even before they had acquired the population specified in the Act. The majority of the Council took the same view, and accordingly ordered a census to be taken, with a view to the division of the town into wards, some of them favoring three wards, and others four.[42]

On November fifteenth the Town Council decided upon a three-ward system, and delegated the Reeve, John Smith, and a Councillor, Peter Gow, to travel to Toronto to petition for an Order-in-Council to make the necessary changes. Immediately their opposition led by Frederick George, G. Keeling, James Watt, R. Scott, Samuel Smith, and Mr. Kelly left for Toronto with a counter petition. Finally, another group of ratepayers got up a second petition signed by 260 persons, and Thomas Sandilands, John Harris, George Sunley, William Day and a Mr. Fisher also went to Toronto to support Smith and Gow. To broaden their appeal, the latter group advocated a four-ward system of representation.[43] Faced with these conflicting petitions and claims, the Government deferred their decision. On December seventh, the Town Council, concerned lest the opportunity be missed to make the change in municipal status, adopted a long memorial to the Governor-General which recounted the events leading up to that point, this time asking for the division of the Town into four wards.[44] This petition was granted, and on January 1, 1856, Guelph, in reality as well as in name, became a Town.

The election of Councillors in January, 1856, was noteworthy for a concerted attempt to defeat John Smith, the leader of the municipal progressives. It had been Smith who had taken the strongest stand in favour of the acquisition of Town status, and it was Smith who now proposed the immediate construction of the new Market House.

The municipal elections, held on Monday and Tuesday, January fourteenth and fifteenth, were the first held under Guelph's new ward system. By the proclamation making Guelph a Town, the four wards had been created by drawing the following bisecting lines:

the east-west line followed the Grand Trunk railway tracks; while the north-south line followed Dundas Road, Gordon Street, Wyndham Street and Woolwich Road. Three Councillors were to be elected from each ward. Acton Burrows describes the exciting events in the West Ward, where John Smith was a candidate:

The West Ward appeared from the first to attract most attention, from the strenuous efforts made to prevent the return of Mr. John Smith, his nomination being very unpalatable to a certain portion of the ratepayers. After some delay, arising out of the difficulty in settling the tickets to suit some malcontents on both sides, Mr. Fraser moved, and Mr. Barber seconded the nomination of Messrs. Samuel Smith, G. Elliott and Robert Scott as Councillors, and Mr. Joseph Higginson as Inspector [of taverns]. Mr. J.T. Tracey moved, and Mr. Ainlay seconded, that Messrs. G. Elliott, George Sunley and John Smith be Councillors, and Mr. William Wilson be Inspector. The show of hands was in favor of the second ticket. . .it was not until 3 p.m. [on the second day] that the poll closed, when the numbers stood,—Elliott 89, John Smith 65, Sunley 60, Samuel Smith 47, Scott 43—Wilson 53, Higginson 29.[45]

The proposal to build a substantial Market House in Guelph had first been made in a serious way in February, 1851. The old Market House built by John Galt had never been a satisfactory place to hold a market, being open on all sides, and had long since fallen into ruin. Now, the merchants and tradesmen around the Market Square, hoped to increase down town business and draw both farmers and customers into this area by constructing a handsome stone building in which farmers could sell their produce.

As was usual with such large scale undertakings, the plan was to incorporate a company which would erect the building, and receive a large municipal subsidy in the form of share purchases by the Town of Guelph. The subscription list for shares circulated early in February, was headed up as follows:

PROSPERITY TO GUELPH!

Proposal to raise *One Thousand Pounds*, to build a *New Market House*!!

The Agriculturalists of Guelph and adjoining Townships have long felt the want of some Public Mart, to which they might resort for the purpose of turning their Produce into *Cash*; and the Inhabitants of this Town having also long felt the want of such a place of general accommodation, the Undersigned hereby agree to take the number of Shares opposite their respective names, in the above important undertaking; such shares to be £5 each, and to be called up in instalments of 20s. each, at intervals of three months. A Committee of Management to be appointed when half the amount shall have been subscribed.[46]

So successful was the subscription campaign, that the sponsors of the Market House called a meeting for February 10, 1851, to put the idea to the general public.

At this meeting, John Smith read the keynote address prepared by John Thorp,[47] and reported that some 121 shares worth £605 had already been subscribed. After Smith's speech, the meeting elected a Committee of Management consisting of A.J. Fergusson, David Allan, George Sunley, Robert Corbet, John Smith, Alfred A. Baker, James Hodgert, Frederick George and John Thorp to meet the Town Council and to get the project under way.

When the Committee of Management appeared before the Town Council not only did they outline plans for a market building, but also facilities for a fire hall, meeting rooms, Town lock-up, council chamber, etc. These sections of the petition were phrased as follows:

3. That your Memorialists are of opinion that the erection of a Market House would tend materially to increase the business and importance of the place.
4. That your Memorialists have been elected by a large number of the rate-payers of the Town for the purpose of obtaining funds and otherwise making arrangements to lay before your Hon. Body, a scheme by which your Municipality may be supplied with those public buildings; which, whilst they are necessary for the order, convenience, and safety of the Town, will add to its beauty, facilitate business, and ultimately contribute to the revenue of the corporation.
5. After mature consideration, your Memorialists have devised a plan which they consider would be most advisable, for the purpose of carrying out the views of the inhabitants: meeting the wants of the Town, and relieving the rate-payers from any undue oppressive burden. . . .
9. That your Memorialists would respectfully suggest the propriety of erecting a public building in which would be included a Lock-up, Engine House, Fire Company's Room, Market House and Shambles, Council Chamber, and General Assembly Room, with such accommodation as may be deemed advisable.[48]

All of this, it was claimed, could be accomplished for £1500, of which £750 had already been guaranteed by subscription.

The ensuing debate in the Town Council revealed two additional troubling facts. First, the £750 already subscribed for the Market House was not to be used to buy shares, but to purchase Town Debentures to be issued for the building's construction. Second, although the proposers of the larger project claimed that it would cost only £1500, other spokesmen argued that such an elaborate structure would cost a minimum of £2000 and perhaps much more.[49]

The most eloquent plea for the new build-

ing came from a Town Councillor, John Thorp, who owned a hotel, "The British," on the Market Square:

When he came to the Town of Guelph [in 1828], he came like many another man came—with little in his pocket,—but a determination and a will to work. . .No one could tell the difficulties which the first settlers had to contend with, nor the privations they had to suffer. . .and if they, by their enterprise and exertions, had succeeded in getting some property together, and now paid by far the largest proportion of taxation, their wishes in regard to a Market House—a matter of pounds, shillings, and pence—ought to be considered of weight, in proportion to the amount of taxes they paid. . . .There were many men whose interests were inseparably bound up with the Town of Guelph; and who were anxious to push the Town forward by every means in their power. These men would not mind being taxed a little for the improvement and benefit of the Town. . . .[50]

After hearing Thorp's stirring appeal, the Town Council decided to call a public meeting for March twenty-second, where the project would be discussed and a vote taken. As the newspaper account of the meeting made clear, the opponents of the Market House project, led by Dr. William Clarke, were in no mood to be swayed by the rhetoric of John Thorp or John Smith. As the *Guelph Advertiser* said:

Soon after 10 o'clock the Court Room began to fill, chiefly by persons "from the suburbs," and from the Township. There were comparatively few of the large rate payers of the Town present; and, during the proceedings there were sufficient proofs given that many persons attended, not to hear "facts and argument," and to decide accordingly; but to shout down the enterprise altogether.[51]

At the meeting Doctor Clarke was apparently at his spectacular best—shouting, bullying, and generally creating a shambles of the proceedings. This performance drew from

"Will Watch," an anonymous letter writer to John Smith's *Advertiser*, one of the best pieces of editorial writing to appear on the pages of that normally staid newspaper. In part, here is "Will Watch's" report of the affair:

I was very much elevated with the speechifying of Mr. Smith on the occasion. He showed the folks that he had a trifle more wheat than chaff about him—and that he didn't deal in soft soap and blarney. But while he was pouring out important facts and sound sense in a clear and fertilizing stream, I was sorry to see mischief brewing. There was little Doctor Firebrand a watching all the while like a jealous Tom Cat watching a favored rival, with eyes glaring as if they had the scarlet fever, and lips quivering as if they were just going to commit some awful sin they wasn't used to. Well, when Mr. Smith had done speaking, up sprung Hescalapius; and out came fire, and smoke, and thunder, and lightning, and gall, and vinegar, and brimstone, and melted physic bottle, in one terrible, scorching, withering, raging stream, fizzing, whizzing, blizzing, about the devoted heads of Mr. Smith and the Building Committee; and ending in a whirlwind of applause from the "pet lambs" of the suburbs. This having become partially spent, and Firebrand almost "done up," I was happy to see a fresh demonstration of spirit on the part of "the lambs." NO MARKET HOUSE!! bellowed the gentleman what went round the suburbs! NO MARKET HOUSE! responded the coons, who, of all the others the Market House would most benefit. No Market House! No Market House! No Market House! No Taxes! No Progress! No Nothing! Hooray! Hooray! burst forth in one sublime chorus of solemn grandeur from "the Suburbs."[52]

Faced with such an outcry and concerted opposition, the Market House project appeared to be doomed.

Smith, Thorp, and the other "progressive" businessmen did not accept their defeat gracefully, but continued to complain of the economic quality of those who had voted. As the *Advertiser* put it:

When the division upon the question was taken, at least three fourths of the meeting voted against it: but such a decision cannot justly be taken as the decision of the majority of householders,—many of those who voted, not being on the Assessment role for any house whatever; and a large number of respectable householders being absent from the meeting. As far as we can learn, a majority of the householders of the Town are in favor of a Market House; and a Market House will assuredly be put up, ere long. The matter is a question of time.[53]

Although John Thorp introduced a motion into the Town Council to issue a £1500 debenture to construct the Market House, it was rejected on the grounds that it would never be approved in a referendum. Instead, the Council voted £200 to erect a suitable building for the fire engine.[54] The Town Council Minutes for May 10, 1851, records their next step:

The following petition, signed by the Rev. A. Palmer, and 63 other parties, was read:

To the Municipal Council of the Town of Guelph.
The Petition of the undersigned inhabitants of the said Town, humbly sheweth:
That the Market Square has long been, and still remains, in a state at once disgraceful to the Town, and dangerous to the inhabitants and persons in it.
That the feelings with which strangers arriving in Guelph are consequently impressed, is most unfavorable to the place, beholding, as they do, on their very entrance into the Town, so large a piece of ground in so unsightly a condition,—full of sandholes and gravel pits, and bearing the general appearance of neglect and desolation. That if steps were taken to level the said Square, and to plant trees at regular intervals along the outer limit of the street by which it is bounded, the improvement of the Town would be greatly promoted, and the interests of the inhabitants in general would be advanced.[55]

Although the Town Council voted only £30 for the Square's improvement,[56] it was, nevertheless, an important precedent.

From all reports, the rather minor improvements to the Market Square made in the summer of 1851 had a considerable influence upon the outlook of local merchants and residents. In December, 1851, a group of these united to create the Guelph Horticultural Society, to promote the beautification of the Town in general and the Market Square in particular. The first officers—A.A. Baker, President; W.S.G. Knowles, J.T. Tracy and W. Benham, Vice-Presidents; and Robert Sunley, Secretary-Treasurer[57]—would labour to good effect. Within ten years Guelph would be widely known as one of Canada's most beautiful cities.

In spite of their resounding defeat in 1851, Guelph's down town businessmen did not stop their agitation for a large scale combined Market House, Police and Fire quarters and Town hall. Their plans were complicated, however, by a sudden decision by the Canada Company to claim ownership of the entire Market Square, and to offer the lower part for immediate sale. The resulting court cases which dragged on from March, 1852, to October, 1854, added greatly to the Canada Company's reputation for rapaciousness. Acton Burrows gives this summary of the controversy:

About this time an advertisement was published by the Canada Company, offering for sale the lower portion of the Market Square. This, as may be imagined, created no small consternation in the Town, especially among those who owned property in that neighborhood, and a public meeting was called, at which a resolution was unanimously passed calling upon the Council to take such steps as might be necessary to prevent such an encroachment on the rights of property owners, and such a high-handed confiscation of what had always been looked upon as Town property. The Council subsequently obtained the advice of Mr. [A.J.] Fergusson, and the opinion of eminent counsel in Toronto, the result being that the case was thrown into Chancery, where it continued pending for a long time. At length the trial took place, when some score or more of witnesses were subpoenaed from Guelph, and in course of evidence it was clearly shown that on all the maps published by the Company the land in question was distinctly marked "Market Square," and, also, that in all sales of land in that vicinity, it had been clearly stated by the agents of the Company that it had been reserved as an open space for market purposes in perpetuity, upon which representations the adjacent lots had been considered more valuable than those more remote. In reply to this the Company asserted that their agents had never been authorized to make such statements, but the Court held that the fact that all the agents had made the same representations, together with the evidence afforded by the maps, if not conclusive proof that it had been the intention of the Company so to reserve the land for a market as contended by the Town, was sufficient to entitle the Town to retain the land, and judgment was given accordingly, thus securing the land in question as a market place or for such municipal purposes as might be lawful, for ever.[58]

In March 1854, John Smith reopened the Market House controversy by printing this article:

Market House.—We have long felt the inconvenience resulting from want of a Market House, though the peculiar circumstances of Guelph render it inexpedient to erect one this year. A correspondent of the [*Galt*] *Reporter* urges the erection of a building of this description in Galt, and furnishes a very plausible Dr. and Cr. account to show that the revenue would more than meet the expenditure. He further says,—

"A Market House would regulate prices, increase supply, and do away with a useless monopoly. You would live cheaper and would live better. Poultry of all sorts would pour in, while now you can perhaps hunt up a diminutive fowl or two in some merchant's cellar, where they have possibly been sweetening these six weeks. In fact, my worthy friends, by buying direct from the producer, you would benefit on every article of Farm Produce that you consume."[59]

With the election of John Smith as Mayor in 1856, the Market House took a giant step towards completion. In spite of the opposition campaign led by the *Mercury*, the Town Council went ahead in their plans to place the building on the Market Square. Of particular interest to the Council was the site then occupied by St. Andrew's Presbyterian Church. With the rapid increase in population, their congregation had outgrown their original building, and moreover, its site at the head of the "upper square" was convenient to both the Grand Trunk station and down town merchants. On April 9, 1856, at the Town Council meeting:

Mr. Gow moved, seconded by Mr. Thorp, That the Market House Committee [headed, incidently, by Frederick George] be requested to procure plans for a Market House and estimate of the probable expense of erecting the same, and report at next meeting of Council; and if deemed necessary, that they be authorized to visit and examine the market houses in other towns.[60]

At the same time, advertisements were inserted in newspapers around the country asking for plans for such a building to be submitted by May twenty-sixth.

On May seventh, a special meeting of the Town Council was called to discuss the Market House, and to pass a by-law for its financing. The report of the meeting was short and to the point:

A special meeting of the Council was held on Wednesday—all the members present—to take into consideration, a by-law to authorize an issue of Debentures, to the amount of £6000, for the purpose of building a Market House, and if necessary, of purchasing a site for the same.

The by-law which provides for the liquidation of the debt within ten years. . .was read a first and second time. . .The meeting of electors for approval, or disapproval is appointed to be held on the 23rd. inst., at 11 a.m.[61]

For the next two weeks, the residents of Guelph remained in a state of constant excitement. Charges and counter-charges, rumours, hand-bills and advocates—pro and con—circulated through the Town in a steady stream. On May twenty second, the day prior to the vote, the *Guelph Advertiser* made this analysis of the issues:

The Market House Vote.—For years past the question of a Market House has been discussed in this Town, and for years there has been a strong desire on the part of inhabitants, and an earnest wish existing in the minds of the agricultural population around, to possess such a building as would form a common ground, on which to meet and transact the business so mutually beneficial to both parties. . . .There is little doubt but that the facilities offered in the erection of a Market House will be felt and appreciated in a business point of view to a much greater extent, in proportion to the outlay, than the Galt and Guelph Railway. To be sure, it holds out no chance for personal benefit to the extent of thousands of pounds, it presents no opportunities for personal advancement or popularity, but it offers facilities for the man of business, for the buyer of produce, for the housewife, and will add to the convenience of all who depend upon purchases being made for the daily supply of the table. It will also be a means of bringing into Town quite a number of farmers who have produce to dispose of, that at present seek other places where markets exist.[62]

After arguing the financial credits and debits of such a building at considerable length, the *Advertiser's* editor concluded by an appeal to the civic pride of the Town's residents:

It is a notorious fact, and by no means creditable to the place, that there is not a public building of any kind owned by the corporation. A Town hall, a

Market House, a fireman's hall, an engine house, or anything of that kind does not adorn the municipality, whilst we pride ourselves in having *almost* two railways, half-a-dozen more in embryo, and anticipate soon being "the centre of creation." Let Friday present the dawn of a better state of things. . . .[63]

As everyone expected, the public meeting and vote held on Friday, May twenty-third, was hotly contested. According to the newspaper reports, about 150 ratepayers were assembled when the Mayor, John Smith, took the chair. To open the meeting John Harris and W. R. Fisken moved the following resolution:

That the By-law for raising £6000 for the erection of a Market House, submitted to the ratepayers, be approved.[64]

To this motion, John Harrison and A.A. Baker moved an amendment which would have had the effect of delaying the vote for a year. To the dismay of the supporters of the Market House by-law, after a long afternoon of speeches, when the Mayor asked for a show of hands, those who favoured a delay were clearly in a majority. At this point John Harris, Jr., Thomas Sandilands, John J. Braine, H.W. Peterson, W.R. Fisken and J.T. Tracy, demanded a formal vote on the original motion as was their right according to the municipal act. The *Advertiser* recorded the result:

In a few minutes polling commenced, and so earnestly was it carried on that in less than half an hour upwards of 100 votes were recorded, and the majority stood at one time as high as 23 against the By-law. The opponents of the Market House had their votes ready, whilst teams were flying about for voters, the large omnibus with four horses was round the Town from 9 o'clock in the morning beating up for recruits, large bills thereon urging the ratepayers to veto the By-law, whilst various handbills were in circulation representing all kinds

of dire consequences should it be allowed to pass. But the strength of the opposition soon closed, and before 4 o'clock the majority was reversed, and voters became so infrequent that a note of each voting was taken. At one time 28 minutes had elapsed without a vote, and as the Chairman of the Market House Committee [Frederick George] could not induce any one else to vote against the By-law, he had to do it himself. Eventually, at a few minutes past 6 the full length of time had elapsed without a vote, which the law prescribed for closing the poll, and the chairman announced the same concluded, the numbers being 128 for the By-law, and 115 against it.[65]

Guelph was to have its Market House-Town Hall.

From the Market House vote on, the Council were busy viewing plans, purchasing the site and preparing for the grand celebration commemorating the laying of the edifice's corner stone. When tenders were called for plans, no less than eighteen complete sets were entered. Competing were six firms from Toronto, five firms from Guelph (George Bruce, D. Murray, Pasmore and Hopkins, S. Boult, and W. Robinson), two from London and one each from Richmond Hill, Hamilton, Brantford and Dundas. One firm, D. Murray of Guelph submitted two different sets of plans.[66] After long deliberation the design submitted by William Thomas of Toronto (architect of St. Lawrence Hall, Toronto) was selected. Almost simultaneously, an agreement was concluded with the Trustees of St. Andrew's Church to purchase that site for £1750. With the last major difficulty out of the way, the formal ceremonies launching the project could now be held.

On September 18, 1856, the corner stone of Guelph's Market House-Town Hall was laid. It was a joyous occasion—one when speakers

Guelph Town Hall circa 1867. Hose drying tower for the Fire Department can be seen above the building at the rear.

"looked back with pride" and "looked forward with hope." Acton Burrows gives this account of the festivities:

The Town Council, contractors, etc., assembled at the Court House, and preceded by the band of the Rifle Corps, marched to the site of the new building, where a large number of the inhabitants had assembled. A platform had been erected, and from this the Mayor addressed the people, explaining the object for which the meeting had been called. . . .[67]

After James Hough, the Town Clerk, had read to the audience a list of the articles to be

placed in a bottle in the corner stone[68], including local newspapers, specimens of current coinage, a lithographed map of the Town dated 1855, the names of the members of the Corporation, the building committee, and the architect and contractors, the ceremony proceeded:

The stone being suspended by a windlass, Mr. Elliott proceeded to deposit the bottle in the cavity prepared, and the Mayor performed the usual ceremony of laying the corner stone, the Rifles firing a *feu de joie*, and the band playing appropriate music.

The Mayor then addressed the audience from the stand...Mr. Fergusson then delivered a brief address, and in pointing to the past looked upon it as an index of the future, and fully anticipated that in a few years the population of the Town would be tenfold what it was then. The band then played "God Save the Queen," and the company dispersed.[69]

The day's festivities concluded with a dinner for sixty guests at Horwood's Hotel. For those who, with A.J. Fergusson, looked forward to even more rapid growth in the future, it had been a satisfying day.

Although generally retaining its exterior design for over a century (the exception being the dome and clock tower) the original interior of the Market House was different both in layout and function than it would be when it served exclusively as Guelph's City Hall. In November, 1856, the *Guelph Advertiser* gave an interesting description of the building as its exterior neared completion:

The casual visitor...will be attracted by the handsome Market House, the walls of which are on the point of completion, and present a front which shows what can be done with Guelph stone when operated on by Guelph workmen. This building yet

Guelph Fire Brigade at Town Hall.

requires a massive stone cornice to complete its imposing appearance, which will be added to when the lofty dome holds its head about 40 feet above the present walls. As much discussion has arisen in regard to this building, and but few are aware of the accommodation it will afford, we shall give a few particulars. Composed of two wings joined by a centre piece of some extent, the building forms an oblong and irregular square, having a frontage of 108 feet, the depth of each wing being 70 feet. The basement of the western wing will be appropriated for Market purposes generally, with stalls for market gardeners; the ground floor is divided into twelve butchers' stalls, and the upper floor will form one large hall and court room measuring 64 feet by 30 feet inside, and calculated to seat 500 persons. The eastern wing will afford considerable storage in the basement for bonded or other goods; on the ground floor will be an engine house, police office, committee room, and two lockups; and the upper floor will be appropriated for Council meetings, committee rooms, etc. The centre will have a hot-air apparatus in the basement; clerk's office with fireproof safe, library and reading room for the Mechanics' Institute, staircase, etc., etc., on the ground floor; a treasurer's office with safe, Mayor's office, and two committee rooms on the upper floor. The police office may be used by the fire and rifle companies for their meetings; and when the court room is used for performances, the committee rooms can be appropriated for ladies' and gentlemen's dressing rooms. The council room will also be large enough for a supper room in connection with public affairs which might be conducted in the main hall.[70]

When completed the Market House was a handsome, well-designed building, admirably suited for the purposes for which it was built. The ultimate cost, nearly £11,000,[71] with land, was far beyond anyone's prediction. In the depression which followed, many bitter words would be exchanged about the tax burden required to carry the debt.[72]

Guelph, however, had progressed greatly, and in 1856 and 1857 a number of observers left accounts of the substantial Town that Guelph had become in just three years of extensive building and expansion. Between 1853 and 1857, the population of the Town had increased from about 2,000 to 4,500.[73] Viewing this rapid growth the Toronto *Globe* commented:

There is no Town of its size in Upper Canada, which has a more "rising" air than Guelph. The erection of substantial stone buildings is being carried on in all directions, and yet the supply does not equal the demand. The inhabitants of the Town are, as a class, all well off in the world, whilst they number amongst them some self-made men who have built up very large fortunes for themselves by their own industry and tact. . . .The River Speed on which Guelph is situated affords great facilities for turning its water power to advantage. There are several mills in the vicinity of the Town already. The neighborhood and district, of which Guelph is the centre, is peopled by a substantial and enterprising class of farmers, and we may add that there is no more healthy locality in the Province.[74]

The Toronto *Colonist* was particularly impressed by Guelph's appearance of health and prosperity:

Guelph is particularly fortunate in possessing a building stone easily worked, and very pleasing in appearance, closely resembling in color the white brick so much used in Toronto. This is well displayed in a street newly built, called Wyndham street, leading north from the Market Square, and branching off to the right and left on either side of the Wellington Hotel. This is now the chief business street, many shopkeepers and others recently moved into it from the Market Square. St. George's Church, which, when finished, will be a handsome building, is in this street. . . .The trade and manufactures of Guelph are rapidly increasing. Ten years ago the quantity of flour sent to market by the principal miller was considered too highly estimated at eight hundred barrels. This season the ex-

Wyndham Street showing the second St. George's Church in the Square, circa 1866-1867.

ports of wheat and flour are set down at fifty thousand bushels of the former, and fifty thousand barrels of flour. One mill alone is estimated to manufacture twenty-five thousand barrels. The manufacture of whiskey is also large, the quantity sold amounting this year to about twelve thousand five hundred barrels. The opening of the Grand Trunk has given the means of turning the stone quarries of Guelph to valuable account. There are now four in full operation, and arrangements are being made for the delivery and sale of the stone all along the railway. There are also several foundries and breweries, some of them doing a large business.

The water power afforded by the River Speed is quite sufficient to supply much more than what is required by the factories now on its banks; but now one mill owner has let power for ten additional factories to be erected next year. The local trade of Guelph is very considerable, the country about it in all directions being of the most fertile description and well settled. The Guelph storekeepers have hitherto done a large business with Hamilton, but the competition of the Grand Trunk renders their communication with Toronto and Montreal so much more direct, their trade will be chiefly with those places, especially Toronto.[75]

In a second article on Guelph, the *Colonist* said:

Amongst the many healthful summer resorts, brought so easily within reach of the citizens of Toronto by increasing railway facilities, the pleasantly situated and salubrious Town of Guelph has attractions inferior to none. The site is healthy and picturesque—the distance from Toronto convenient, over as smooth-running a section of the Grand Trunk as there can be on the whole line from St. Mary's to Riviere du Loup—abundance of sporting in the vicinity—and surrounded by neighboring villages, which are peculiarly inviting to the visitor, who longs for a cool afternoon drive. It altogether forms as pleasant a retreat from city life as could be desired. There are several good hotels in the Town: but Toronto readers, only need be told that Mr. G.C. Horwood, formerly of the North American, on Front Street [in Toronto], keeps a fine roomy house, well ventilated and comfortably furnished. Besides the advantage of Mr. H.'s experienced proprietorship, this house combines the advantages of an airy location close to the railroad depot, and has in the cellar a never-failing spring of excellent water—rivalled, however, by the choice wines ranged in cool atmosphere on the dripping rocks which surrounded it.[76]

In all, the years 1851 to 1856 had been troubling and tumultuous, but exciting for Guelph's residents. In the euphoria of expansion and prosperity, few people doubted A.J. Fergusson's predictions that Guelph's explosive growth would continue indefinitely, or that Guelph's population would reach 50,000 within a few years. However, with the collapse of the international economy and the end of the Canadian railway boom in 1857, Guelph was made acutely aware that its economic base had not grown as rapidly as its population. Until that base was expanded, Guelph's commercial community would, as it had done in 1828, 1833, 1843 and 1852, find itself searching for ways to increase its market opportunities. They now turned their attention to the development of manufacturing.

Speedvale Mills, from a drawing by Alfred Smith, circa 1866.

IX

Industrial
Expansion, 1847-1870

Taken as a whole, the years 1856 to 1871 were a period of slow but solid economic and commercial growth. The foundation for Guelph's continuous development was the steady expansion of the agricultural economy of the older southern townships in Wellington County, combined with the rapidly increasing settlement and development of the newer areas to the north. By 1871, population there exceeded that of the southern, longer settled, area. Although farmers in the new townships were not yet as productive or generally as wealthy as those resident in the south, the fact that the number of people there was expanding at a much faster rate, made the area an attractive market.

The desirability, indeed the necessity, of encouraging manufacturing in Canada and in Guelph was a theme to which every local newspaper turned time and again. For example, in November, 1847, this editorial appeared:

HOME MANUFACTURES

Perhaps there is nothing in a secular point of view so conducive to human happiness and prosperity, as industry and economy.... To attain true greatness, and develop and increase its resources is the

Adam Robertson, Sr.

imperative duty of a nation. It is for its prosperity and independence to encourage every kind of useful home manufacture. The nation which neglects that, and bestows its encouragement on the manufactures and mechanics of a foreign country in preference to its own is unwise. It discourages and enfeebles itself, and ultimately must work its own ruin. There is not a country under the sun which neglects more its own manufactures and mechanics, and bestows its patronage on foreigners than Canada... The Canadians expend more money on articles manufactured in the United States—articles which could be as well made in Canada and the money kept among ourselves—than what is received by our own mechanics all put together. It is an incontrovertible fact that Canada supports the American manufacturer and mechanics better than her own....

Our hay is cut, made and raked, with scythes, forks and rakes, of American manufacture. Scythe-snaiths, hoes and almost every implement of husbandry used by our farmers, come from the States. . . . For all which we pay *hundreds of thousands* of dollars. Canada look to yourself,—encourage your manufacturers and mechanics—elicit the genius of your sons, and strengthen and enrich your territories.[1]

As the newspapers saw the problem, two major difficulties had to be surmounted before manufacturing could flourish in Canada: first, some method had to be devised to overcome the shortage and high cost of risk capital, and second, a stable market for domestic production had to be developed among Canadian

Sallows' Blacksmith Shop on Wellington Street at the corner of Dundas Road.

farmers. Moreover, it was well recognized that in periods of severe economic depression when inventories built up in the major manufacturing countries, industrialists in those countries would dump their surpluses in the colonies, thereby undercutting local enterprises which in ordinary times had been able to prosper.

There was a general recognition that reliance upon borrowed capital and imported manufactured goods created an unhealthy situation for debtor nations. They drained the national economy of its gold, made money scarce, raised interest rates, and made investment in manufacturing less profitable, which in turn increased the cost of borrowing abroad and consolidated the dependence upon foreign goods. So important was the question of "home manufacturing" that whenever a businessman put money into a local enterprise, he was hailed as a hero. When Adam Robertson took over the Guelph Foundry in 1847, he received the full support of the *Advertiser*:

GUELPH FOUNDRY

We would direct the attention of our readers to the Advertisement in another column, headed "Guelph Foundry." Every year brings evidence more and more conclusive, that to prosper, Canada must become a manufacturing country so far as her domestic wants are concerned, and to encourage our manufacturers in a duty each one owes to himself. The principle applicable to a country is equally applicable to a community; and as we have opportunities of knowing that Mr. Robertson well understands his business, and will turn out a fair article at a moderate price, we confidently recommend him to the favorable notice of all.[2]

Robertson's first advertisement read:

GUELPH FOUNDRY

The undersigned having purchased this Establishment, which is fitted up with a general assortment

of Patterns and Models of various descriptions, begs to state that he is now prepared to furnish
Ploughs, Stoves
and various *Castings* in general use. He will also be able, immediately, to Contract for the erection of Saw and other *Mills*. He also anticipates being able to turn out a few superior
THRASHING MACHINES
Of from 1 to 8 horse power.
Orders for *Casting* executed with promptness.
Boring & Turning In Iron, Brass, etc.
The Public are invited to call and inspect the Foundry, where they will find everything necessary for carrying on the business, the Proprietor being determined to conduct the Establishment with that spirit which, whilst it gives him a return, will at the same time accommodate his customers at *very moderate prices*.

Adam Robertson.[3]

The Guelph Foundry was typical of both the strengths and weaknesses of local manufacturing. Adam Robertson came to Guelph from Paris, C. W., in 1847 to operate the moulding and machine shop previously described. By 1848, Adam Robertson, Sr., his son, Adam, Jr., and John Watt had formed a partnership under the title of Messrs. Robertson & Co., and had rented the new foundry built by Doctor William Clarke. On November 3, 1848, the new premises were opened:

New Foundry—Some time since we stated that Dr. Clarke was erecting a Foundry on an extensive scale, near the Wellington Mills. We have now the pleasure of announcing its completion, and that business will be carried on by the firm of Messrs. Robertson & Co. We are informed that unusual facilities will be provided for carrying on the business on the most extensive scale, and the character of the managing partners, Robertson and Watt, is such as will present every guarantee that satisfaction will be given. On Friday night last the first metal was run in the presence of the proprietors and a number of gentlemen of the Town, after which an adjournment took place to Dr. Clarke's,

who furnished an elegant entertainment to celebrate the event—Success to the undertaking say
we.[4]

In 1852, the firm was dissolved with John
Watt carrying on the larger establishment,
while the Adam Robertsons, father and son,
occupied a foundry and machine shop at the
corner of Eramosa Road and Mitchell Street.
There the Robertsons conducted a small but
prosperous business for several decades.[5]

In contrast to the more limited business carried on by the Robertson's, John Watt expanded his business rapidly. In September,
1854, the *International Journal* in describing
Guelph's manufacturing enterprises paid special attention to Watt's foundry:

There are three foundries in Guelph. The establishment of Mr. John Watt gives employment to over
60 men. The machine shop is in a large three-story
stone building, the first and second stories of which
are used for manufacturing and general machine
work, the third for preparing patterns, etc., and the
attic or half story, is used as a pattern loft. In an L,
or wing of the main building, is the moulding and
casting room; the blacksmith work being done in
an adjoining building. Steam engines and boilers,
mill work, stoves and agricultural implements, are
manufactured in this establishment.

The foundry and Tin-ware Manufactory of
Smith, Mathewson & Co., is devoted to stoves, agricultural implements, etc., and is a neat and well arranged establishment. The other Foundry is that of
Mr. A. Robertson, devoted to general castings and
machinery.[6]

Watt, however, appears to have suffered
from too-rapid expansion. When the post-1856
depression struck, Watt's firm failed, while the
smaller foundries survived.

In addition to the foundries, other enterprises enjoyed considerable success. The
International Journal described the following:

The Tannery of Mr. John Harvey is very extensive,

*The stone residence of Adam Robertson
on Mitchell Street behind the Foundry.*

and turns out annually about 5000 sides of sole
leather, besides upper leather and kipskins. Mr.
Gow has a large tannery in operation, and there
are three others in the suburbs of the Town, owned
by Mr. Jackson, Mr. Clarke and Mr. Horning.

A Fanning-mill manufactory is carried on by
Mr. James Mays, where fanners capable of cleaning a bushel of wheat per minute, are made and
sold for $25 each.

There is a Chair Factory in the town, carried on
by Mr. Allen, and a number of Furniture Manufactories, some of which are aided by steam or
water power, and use the most approved machinery
for expeditious work. . .

In the suburbs of the Town, there is a Woollen
Factory in operation, by Messrs. Campbell & Co.[7]

In contrast to those firms which grew out of
one or two-man operations, others had quite
different beginnings. The most important of
these were the two large flour-and-grist mills
owned and operated by William Allan and
Frederick George. Both the Guelph Mills (Allan) and the Wellington or "People's Mill"
(George) had begun as large-scale operations
with extensive use of labor-saving devices. In

addition, both had been considerably enlarged by the addition of ancillary enterprises such as distilleries, cooperage shops, livestock feeding, cloth finishing and custom milling. Fortunately excellent descriptions of both mills were left by contemporary observers. In June, 1853, William Allan's Guelph Mills were described as follows:

Situated on the Speed, which here forms the boundary of the Town, the water power is considerable, and during the greater part of the year scarcely can be exhausted. Turning to the right we entered the mill-yard through a tastefully constructed gateway, and at once proceeded to inspect the mill and granary. This building is 100 feet long and 40 feet wide, 3½ stories high, and having 4 run of stones, driven by a water wheel measuring 16 feet in diameter and 13 feet wide. For many years this was the only milling establishment in the Town, being erected by the Canada Company, and owned for the past 20 years by the present proprietor. Adjoining the mill, and to form part of it, is a new stone building, neatly finished, 50 feet by 38, of 5½ stories high, and intended to have separate power, to run two pairs of stones and a barley mill, the machinery for which is in a forward state of preparation. Leaving the mill, we passed over the river on an elevated scaffolding or piece of frame work, supported by buttresses placed in the bed of the stream, and as a means of communication between the two sides of the river, whilst a run of railway along the same facilitates the conveyance of grain and other material from the mill to the distillery opposite. Whilst crossing, Mr. D.[avid] Allan remarked with a smile, that we were passing over the first *Guelph* railway, and although only 190 feet long, it has proved a railway of no mean importance to its proprietor, and contributed materially to the prosperity of the establishments on each side of the river. Arrived at the distillery, we were struck with the extent to which operations were carried on, and the great facilities afforded for enlarging the business.

But a few years since a low, dirty and mean looking building occupied the site of the present

David Allan, son of William, owner of The Guelph Mills.

William Allan's "Guelph Mills",
from a lithograph on an old invoice.

handsome structure, which extends 140 feet in length, 50 in width, and some part of it 56 feet high. We also observe that the old tubs and other utensils are making way for new and much larger ones, the old furnace and boiler look quite pigmies beside the new ones just fitted up at an expense of $1,000., and the fact that the present power of mashing 50 bushels of grain daily will in a few weeks be increased to 100 bushels. . . .£4000 would not compensate Mr. Allan for closing this part of the business.—As in the mill, the machinery here, which is considerable, is driven by water-power. Having thoroughly explored this building, we turned to the malt kiln, measuring 20 feet square inside, with upper and lower floors 70 feet long, and pipes, spouts and conveniences for conveying the grain with the least possible expenditure of labor. The yards adjoining the distillery next command our attention, and however pleasing it may be to see beautiful machines and well ordered manufacturing establishments, the majority of our readers would be pleased to see the accommodation afforded to the hogs and cattle, the latter especially. Entering the pig-yard we walked through a building 120 feet long intended to house 50 head of cattle, for stall feeding during the winter, lined inside and out with inch boards and the space between filled up with tanbark to keep the house warm, whilst the loft overhead is filled with straw. Here are fixed two sets of feeding troughs, one for dry food and the other for slops, both being supplied from the distillery by spouts entering the top of the building. Besides this place were yards with open sheds, accommodation for 250 pigs, and other conveniences. The Carding and Fulling establishment deserves a passing notice, although on a small scale compared with many others,—whilst the place was furnished with fulling, napping and other apparatus, dye-house, etc. The whole building was crowded with bundles of wool, some carded and others waiting their turn.

On every part of the premises, in addition to the wheat, rye, etc., we observed heaps of barley, amounting to some 13 or 14,000 bushels, thus presenting a guarantee of a continued supply of the "dear cratur," although it not infrequently happens that the distillery is run to its last barrel.

About thirty hands are constantly employed on

Allan's Distillery across the Speed River.

the premises, and several teams are daily engaged in carrying whiskey, flour and mill stuff to their Hamilton warehouse and general customers.[8]

Nor was Frederick George's "Wellington Mills" overshadowed by Allan's establishment. In September, 1854, the *International Journal*, an American monthly, described it as follows:

One gentleman, Frederick George, Esq., who came to this country a few years ago, as a farmer, has now upon the Speed, a flour mill with four run of stones, to which workmen are preparing to put in an addition of four pairs more. On the opposite side of the Speed, and connected with this mill by a platform and railway, there is a distillery, capable of using nearly 200 bushels of grain per day, and adjoining this there is a piggery containing 200 sleek-looking "porkers." The same proprietor has on his premises a sawmill, a tannery, and a building used as a foundry which are leased to tenants.

Besides this he has about 1200 feet of land fronting on either side of the Speed, with sufficient water power to drive the machinery in any building that may be erected on the premises for manufacturing purposes. The dam across the river is built of stone, and is amply secured from accident.[9]

Despite the fact that both William Allan and Frederick George shipped considerable amounts of grain, flour and whiskey and live-stock to Hamilton, the principal market for flour manufactured by their mills was the Town of Guelph and the area to the north.

In addition to the flour mills, a second type of manufacturing enterprise appeared in Guelph. That was the stove foundry that grew out of the stove retailing business owned by George Sunley. The relationship between Sunley's mercantile and manufacturing inter-ests is particularly interesting:

[In 1845], Mr. Sunley occupied but one building for his dwelling, workshop, and show and business establishment; now we find him the owner of a splendid stone store of three stories, his former es-tablishment turned into a handsome stove shop, and his workshop thrust into a building in the rear. On looking over his stock a few days since, we learned that he and his partner, Mr. Melvin, have

for sale about 70 different patterns and styles of stoves, to obtain which they have visited the best markets, and laid under contribution the foundries not only of Canada, but Buffalo, Albany, and other American cities, thus presenting to the purchaser as great a variety, and equal facilities for a choice, as are offered in any part of the Province: whilst the well-known liberality which they always manifest in business will secure them the bulk of the patron-age in their department. And, not satisfied with what others may manufacture, Mr. Sunley has a share in the foundry business of Smith, Sunley & Co., by which means he presents to the buyer the additional choice, and the lovers of "domestic manufactures" can have, of Guelph make, as good a stove as may be found on the continent. Messrs. Sunley & Melvin's shops have a glass frontage of 50 feet, and are quite an ornament to the neighborhood.[10]

In spite of a continued campaign to per-suade local financiers and investors to build up Guelph's manufacturing capacity, the depres-sion of 1857-60 meant that little could be done. Guelph remained dependent upon its retail trade and agricultural customers for its pros-perity.

During the 1860's a number of new manu-facturing enterprises were started which would have a long-term effect upon Guelph's growth. The most important of these were the James Goldie Company Limited, McCrae & Co., The Raymond Sewing Machine Company, and the Bell Organ Company.

On November 14, 1859, John Goldie, bought a mill seat on the Speed River from its owner, William Hood, (now the site of the John Galt Gardens on Speedvale Avenue.) In this transaction, Goldie was acting for his sons James, and William. Previous to this purchase, this site had been used by Samuel Smith to power a saw mill and stave factory.

James Goldie, was born in Ayrshire, Scot-

G. SUNLEY,
TIN, COPPER & SHEET IRON
WORKER,
MARKET SQUARE GUELPH.

Box, Parlor, & Cooking Stoves
IN GREAT VARIETY.
Call and see before buying of Pedlars.

OLD COPPER, BRASS, RAGS, &c. TAKEN IN EXCHANGE

(Guelph Advertiser Almanac, 1853)

land, on Nov. 6, 1824, and in 1860, with his wife and three sons, Thomas, John and James, moved into the old stave factory while the new flour mill and house were built.[11] David Allan described the building of the "Speedvale Mill," as follows:

When Mrs. Goldie arrived with her three children, Thomas, John, and James, there was only a pathway leading from the Elora Road through the woods to the river, over which there was no bridge. At first sight of the place, Mrs. Goldie was filled with dismay, it looked like a bit of the back woods, after having lived for a few years in New York. . .She often told of the construction of the mill, when she cooked for sixteen men, looked after her family, and did all the housework with little assistance. Work at the mill continued on through 1860-61. The building was in two sections, one of stone, containing four run of stone, water wheels, and all the cleaning machinery required for the making of flour. The other section was for grain storage. The dam, as left by Mr. Smith, was situated about two hundred yards below the present cement bridge above the Country Club, a long raceway leading from it to the stave factory. . . .All this was discarded and a new dam made lower down, with a larger raceway connecting with the power house. Toward the end of 1861 the work was finished and the mill ready to operate. In those days, an ample supply of wheat was delivered at the mill by farmers, who came from every direction, sometimes from distant sections as there were no railways to the north. Usually the mill yard was crowded with teams awaiting their turn to unload, and there were days when the line extended up to the Elora Road, and beyond. The first head miller was James Hitchcox of Paris, [C.W.]. Most of the flour in those days was packed in barrels, and the cooper trade was in a flourishing condition, there being about seventy-five or more coopers employed in Guelph, making barrels for the several mills.[12]

In the fall of 1860 J.C. Presant's "Victoria Mill" at the corner of Huskisson and Wellington Streets was destroyed by fire, and this com-

James Goldie.
(Historical Atlas of Wellington County, 1906)

The People's Mills owned by James Goldie.

bined with the rise in prices for flour caused by the American Civil War, helped the new Goldie Mill to prosper greatly.

The second stage in the development of the Goldie concern came about as the result of another serious fire. On the night of Wednesday, June 8, 1864, the People's or Wellington Mill, now owned by W.P. McLaren of Hamilton and leased by Charles Whitelaw of Paris, was burned, apparently by an arsonist. The total loss exceeded $30,000, and as there was little insurance, the mill was not immediately rebuilt.[13] Upon McLaren's death, James Goldie, bought the premises in 1866, and immediately set about repairing and expanding it, the result being a "fine substantial stone structure 90 by 40 feet in size and five storeys high, with two storehouses in connection 60 by 50 and 35 by 40 feet, and an elevator 70 x 50."[14] Once the People's Mill was rebuilt, Goldie sold the smaller Speedvale Mill to John Pipe who operated it for the next fifteen years. Goldie's new mill prospered, and he soon became prominent in local business and politics.

Another manufacturing enterprise, which would later grow to a substantial size, was the knitting and weaving establishment of Armstrong, McCrae & Co. Started in 1860 in a small way, it grew rapidly during the American Civil War years. By 1867 they were able to erect a large building and import considerable new machinery. A description of the business as it appeared in October, 1867, follows:

Some months ago when the building of this Hosiery and Yarn Factory was first spoken of, we hailed the project as a most hopeful one, and as an indication that ere long the woollen manufactures of Guelph would become not only profitable but much more widely extended. Messrs. Armstrong, McCrae & Co. have set a good example, in the enterprise which they have displayed in starting such an ex-

tensive factory, and the energy and spirit which they manifested in pushing on the work connected with the building and fitting up the machinery. Operations began in the month of April, and by the middle of August the factory was in running order. . . .

The building stands on the corner of Huskisson and Surrey Streets, with the main front looking towards the Market. It is, including the scouring and engine house, 83 feet long by 34 deep, and is two storeys and a-half high. It is built entirely of stone, and is a fine specimen of tape-pointed rubble work. . . . The factory when in full operation can turn out one hundred pairs of shirts and drawers a month, besides a considerable quantity of sale yarn, to say nothing of many dozen pairs of socks. The proprietors have lately been giving their attention more to the manufacture of the finer kinds of goods, in men's and women's underclothing, and the quality and finish of some of the samples that we saw on our visit cannot be matched in Canada. Indeed, it would be superfluous praise from us to commend these goods, after they were awarded all the first prizes at the late Provincial Exhibition. . . .[15]

It is significant that the firm, considered large by contemporary standards, was expected to employ no more than thirty hands "including those engaged in mounting and finishing. . .to work the factory to it full power".[16]

Unlike the James Goldie Company and Armstrong, McCrae & Company, the Raymond Sewing Machine Company appears to have developed upon the basis of technological innovation. Charles Raymond was born in Ashburnham, Massachusetts, January 6, 1826, and at the age of seventeen apprenticed himself to the Massachusetts Cotton Mills Company at Lowell, to learn a machinist's trade. After completing his apprenticeship and working three years as a journeyman for that company, Raymond moved to Bristol, Connecticut, where, after a few years, he went into business for himself. Observing the current interest in the invention of a practical mechanical sewing machine, Raymond constructed one in the spring of 1852, and, although he had made considerable progress in its perfection, when Singer was issued a patent for their sewing machine, Raymond temporarily discontinued his project and concentrated upon perfecting clock-making machinery. In 1856, however, Raymond turned his attention once again to sewing machines, and in 1857 he received his first patent. In 1858 he began to manufacture sewing machines on a full time basis.

Unfortunately for Raymond, the sewing machine business in the United States was already well established, and he soon found himself facing lawsuits regarding patent infringements, while his own innovations were appropriated by his competitors. In the face of these difficulties, he decided to move to Canada, and in 1860 set up a small factory in Montreal. This business proved unsatisfactory and Raymond withdrew, losing one-third of his capital in the process.[17]

Determined to try again elsewhere in Canada, Raymond came to Guelph, and on October 29, 1861, opened a small manufacturing establishment in an old carriage works at the corner of Yarmouth and Suffolk Streets. Here the business prospered, and during the Civil War when American competition was eliminated, the firm grew rapidly. Always an innovator, Raymond's machines began to attract an international reputation. By 1873 he could confidently advertise that "Hundreds of Thousands of these Machines have been made and are now in use. They are sold all over the world."[18]

The fourth important firm started in the

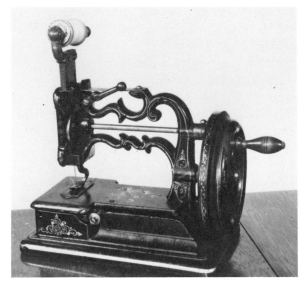

Early Raymond chain-stitch sewing machine.

early eighteen-sixties was the Bell Organ Company. William Bell, the future head of the Bell Organ Company was born in Dumfries, Scotland, on September 5, 1833. In 1853 he moved to Toronto, then lived for a time in the United States. Returning to Canada in 1860 just before the outbreak of the American Civil War, he married Isabella Christie, daughter of Thomas Christie, a miller in Edwardsburg, C.W. They returned to the United States, and remained there until 1864:

during which year he paid a visit to his brother, who had begun the manufacture of organs and melodeons at Guelph, Canada. So allured was he with the prospect which the enterprize held out, that he took a partnership in the business, and remained in Guelph. After a little, his was the head that planned and the hand that directed the business.[19]

Initially the business was a small one, employing only two workmen, turning out "one complete organ each week," in the upper room of a building on Wyndham Street. Shortly thereafter they moved to a stately three-storey building on Carden Street:

Equipped with every convenience for the trade to be carried on within its walls. In the newly equipped establishment there were turned out each month 100 organs; and there were about 100 hands employed. In a little, Mr. Bell's instincts taught him to look to England for a market, and the result of the effort was splendid success.[20]

The American Civil War not only produced a period in which Guelph's new manufacturing firms could prosper, it also directly involved one of Guelph's oldest and most respected establishments, the foundry and machine shop of Adam Robertson and Son. When the American Civil War broke out, Bennet Burleigh, a Scotsman related to the Robertsons, was living in the southern States. Burleigh joined the Confederate army as a lieutenant and served in that capacity for some time. In 1862, Burleigh concocted a plan to aid the south, and came to Guelph to seek the help of the Robertsons who were sympathetic to the Rebel cause.

There was a large prison camp on Johnson's Island in Lake Erie, just off Cleveland, Ohio, where thousands of Confederate prisoners of War were interned. Burleigh persuaded the Robertsons to manufacture cannons, cannon balls and hand grenades, which a group of Confederate sympathizers would use to attack the camp and liberate the prisoners. The war material made by the Robertsons was shipped to Sarnia—some by train and some via Georgian Bay marked "potatoes"—but the plot failed and Burleigh was taken prisoner. He was held in Port Comfort, but escaped and returned to Guelph. Later Burleigh became an internationally known war correspondent and

DIPLOMA

TO

W. BELL & CO

ORGAN

—AND—

Melodeon Manufacturers

GUELPH, ONT.,

OVERWHELMINGLY ahead of all competitors at the Quebec and Ontario Provincial Exhibitions held at Montreal and Toronto for 1870—all the prizes at Montreal—and at Toronto we received the first prize and diploma for the best Harmonium or Large Cabinet Organ, and the first prize for the best Melodeon.

All Instruments Warranted for Five Years,

And entire satisfaction guaranteed. ☞ Illustrated Catalogue sent free on application,
W. BELL & CO.
Guelph, Oct 13, 1870.   d1mwtf

Advertisement, Bell Organ Company from the Guelph Mercury, Oct. 13, 1870.

reported on campaigns in Egypt, Madagascar, Ashanti, South Africa and the Balkans. One of the cannons, not shipped because of a fault, stood in front of the Robertson residence on Mitchell Street for years. Later it was moved and placed in front of the residence of Dr. Norman Wallace at 5 Queen Street.[21]

Although all of these manufacturing firms contributed significantly to Guelph's prosperity during the eighteen-sixties, their real importance lay in two areas. First, they concentrated skilled labour in Guelph, and second, they formed the basis for Guelph's rapid industrial expansion during the Franco-Prussian war years (1870-1874) and the National Policy period (1879-1883). This concentration of skilled labour and the accumulation of capital by financial and mercantile enterprises would prove of particular importance. Older firms expanded rapidly and from 1869 on, a large number of new enterprises were created around skilled employees from such established firms as Robertson & Son, Raymond Sewing Machine Company, The Bell Organ Company, and Armstrong and McCrae. Although not all of these new firms would survive, many did, and were significant in the transformation of Guelph from a mercantile to an industrial centre.

In spite of considerable progress made in developing an economic base, events between 1866 and 1871 showed how vulnerable Guelph's economy was to outside interference. In particular the building of the Toronto, Grey and Bruce and Wellington, Grey and Bruce railways would cause difficult local problems.

For more than a decade, merchants in both Toronto and Hamilton had investigated the

The residence of Dr. Norman Wallace at 5 Queen Street with cannon in front of steps.

feasibility of building a railway into the rapidly growing areas of North Wellington, Grey and Bruce. From time to time charters had been granted to groups proposing to build a railway from either Guelph or Toronto to Owen Sound, and the residents of such towns as Fergus, Arthur, Mount Forest and Orangeville had proclaimed their enthusiasm for any project which promised to bring rail transportation to their town.

The report of the Railway Committee of Wellington County Council made June 4, 1858,[22] supported the building of a railway from Guelph to Owen Sound. Similar support was given by a Committee established by the Provisional Council of Bruce County in their report of January 3, 1862, in which they suggested that a bonus of $400,000 in debentures be given upon completion of such a railway.[23]

In 1864, a group of promoters led by the Hon. John McMurrich and Francis Shanley of Toronto, acquired a charter to build a railway from Guelph to Owen Sound.[24] By its charter, the Wellington, Grey and Bruce Railway Company was to have a capital of $1,500,000 divided into 15,000 shares of $100.00 each. In spite of a short flurry of excitement, the obvious fact that the railway could not pay its way soon cooled investor interest.

In 1866, two Toronto-based railway projects were under discussion, which had the potential of cutting off much of the grain that flowed to Guelph and diverting it directly to Toronto. The first, being pushed by William Gooderham and his associates, proposed to extend the Northern Railway from Collingwood to Owen Sound, and to build a branch line (the Grey and Simcoe) from Durham to Angus. The second Toronto project, promoted by John Fowler, (an itinerant railway contractor from Port Hope) was to run from the Grand Trunk line somewhere near Weston or Brampton, then north-west to the Arthur, Mount Forest area, through whichever town would give it the best bonus, and thence to Owen Sound. With this indication that Toronto interests were looking seriously at their area, merchants and millers in Wellington, Grey and Bruce began, once again, to agitate for a bonus or stock subscription to encourage such a project.

For the merchants of Hamilton, the Toronto railway projects and the eagerness of the businessmen in the Counties of Wellington, Grey and Bruce for a railway into that area, spelled a serious threat. Should the trade of Waterloo, Wellington, Grey and Bruce be diverted exclusively to Toronto, a severe blow would be dealt to the "ambitious city." The *Hamilton Evening Times* of April 30, 1866, offered this analysis of the situation:

Our exchanges from the Counties of Grey, Bruce and Wellington, come to us laden with accounts of meetings held for the purpose of devising some

scheme for the improvement of that district by bringing it into connection with the main lines of Railway in the Province... Various schemes are being proposed for the opening up of this extensive country, and not less than four or five different routes have been suggested. . . .

To the Great Western, the construction of the Branch in question [the Wellington, Grey and Bruce] would be of the utmost value. It would give it the almost sole control of the great local traffic which before long this district of the country must supply. . . .The proposed line recommends itself to the serious attention of the people of Hamilton, and more especially to its wholesale merchants. That some line for the opening up of this district will shortly be built is a matter which does not admit of doubt; the only question is as to the route which shall be decided on. If it be built from Owen Sound to Weston, or to Stratford, then the whole trade of the district through which it runs will be diverted from Hamilton to rival cities. If the line proposed by Mr. Watkins is constructed, Hamilton will not only have an equal chance with Toronto but will have the advantage over it inasmuch as its connection with the Great Western will tend to draw its traffic and travel in our direction. . .An opportunity is now presented to Hamilton which, if not improved, may never present itself again. It is for our merchants to say whether they will take advantage of it, or turn it from their doors.[25]

For Guelph's business community, the possibility that some rival centre would build a line into Guelph's market area was a serious situation. However, in late May a little of the pressure was relieved when, in a face to face confrontation at a meeting in Toronto, the supporters of John Fowler's "Central Railway" from Brampton to Owen Sound were soundly defeated by the promoters backing the Northern Railway's extension from Collingwood to Owen Sound and from Angus to Durham. The editor of the *Guelph Herald* was overjoyed,[26] but if the defeat of the Central Railway was seen as a triumph in Guelph, the approval of the Northern Railway extension was still a threat to Hamilton's larger interests. As the *Hamilton Evening Times* put it, whichever railway the Toronto interests chose, "The efforts of the latter city are to monopolize the whole trade of the district to be served by the proposed line."[27] Thus Hamilton's businessmen had no choice but to push ahead with the Wellington, Grey and Bruce line from Guelph to Owen Sound.

From Guelph's point of view, however, there was an important tactical consideration to be kept in mind. If either Toronto or Hamilton interests were to build a railway into Guelph's market area, against the wishes of Guelph's business community, it was desirable that such a railroad should have its terminus in Guelph. That way, at least something would be salvaged.[28] Moreover, too vigorous opposition on the part of Guelph's businessmen might drive a considerable amount of the northern trade away in retaliation.

During May, June and July of 1867, it appeared that the Hamilton based Wellington, Grey and Bruce promoters would sweep the field before them. After a series of large public meetings and demonstrations in Fergus, Elora, Drayton, Harriston, Mount Forest, Clifford, Ayton, Holstein and Walkerton, the first Board of Directors was elected in Hamilton, and on June twenty-eight, the sod-turning ceremonies were held at Fergus. These ceremonies were immediately followed by a vigorous campaign to persuade local municipalities to grant large subsidies to aid in the construction of the line.

At first, the bonus campaigns appeared to be going very well.[29] By December, the following bonus by-laws had been passed: Nichol, $10,000; Fergus, $10,000; Elora, $10,000; Peel, $40,000; Maryborough, $40,000; Minto,

$70,000; Wallace, $25,000; and Howick, $20,000; for a total of $225,000.[30] There the campaign halted, far short of its objective. By this time it was clear that the cost of the Wellington, Grey and Bruce was likely to exceed $30,000 per mile or more than $2,500,000 total. Thus, without an enormous increase in municipal subsidization or a much greater threat by Toronto interests, the project was not a viable proposition. In recognition of this fact, as winter approached, the whole enterprise ground to a halt, and Guelph's businessmen once again heaved a sigh of relief.

In the meantime, the Toronto Board of Trade, having been persuaded that wide gauge railways were too expensive to build and operate, had decided to back the narrow gauge proposals being promoted by George Laidlaw. According to Laidlaw and his backers, the total cost of construction of their railway would not exceed $15,000. per mile. Based upon this, the Toronto businessmen argued strongly for the construction of two narrow gauge lines: the Toronto, Grey and Bruce and the Toronto and Nipissing. According to the Toronto spokesmen (led by William Gooderham and J.G. Worts) the benefits of building these two lines would be enormous. The *Monetary Times* made this report of a meeting held in Toronto on November 23, 1867:

Narrow Gauge Railway.—A meeting was held in Toronto, on the 23rd inst., of those interested in the construction of two lines of railway on the light narrow gauge principle, known as the Toronto, Grey and Bruce Railway, and the Toronto and Nipissing Railway. The Chairman (Mr. J.G. Worts) stated the projected roads would increase the imports of Toronto by 1,000,000 bushels of grain, and 40,000,-000 feet of lumber the first year, and would open up sections of country at present not served by any railway. . . .[31]

As a result of this meeting it was decided to

apply for charters for the two narrow gauge lines, and to ask the Toronto City Council for a large subsidy.

On March 4, 1868, the Act incorporating the Toronto, Grey and Bruce was signed into law. According to its terms the capital was set at $3,000,000; the gauge established at 3'6", and the route was to run from Toronto, through Orangeville to Southampton.[32] Viewing the great energy being put into the Toronto line by its backers, the *Hamilton Evening Times*, on March 26, 1868, remarked plaintively:

The friends and advocates of the Toronto, Bruce, and Grey narrow-gauge Railway held a meeting in the drill shed at Owen Sound, on Thursday last. Mr. Medcalf, ex-Mayor of Toronto, Adam Crooks, Esq., and Mr. Laidlaw were present and addressed the crowd. The estimated cost of the road is $15,000 per mile. Of this amount it is expected that the municipalities through which the road is to be built will pay one-third of this amount, and that the balance will be raised by private subscription. What are the friends of the Guelph, Wellington, Bruce and Grey doing at the present moment? They should be hard at work, or the Torontonians will steal a march on them.[33]

The *Times* had every reason to be concerned. In township after township, in spite of the stiff opposition of the Hamilton interests, the Toronto, Grey and Bruce narrow gauge won municipal backing. When the City of Toronto voted a bonus of $250,000 in the fall of 1868, the construction of the line, at least to Mount Forest, was assured. Hamilton, already bankrupt from previous railway ventures, could give only $86,000, raised from the sale of its shares in the Great Western, to the subsidies for the Wellington, Grey and Bruce.

In terms of construction, the Wellington, Grey and Bruce actually got under way first, in an attempt to steal a march on the Toronto line. Work began on the Guelph to Alma section at the end of March, 1869, but proceeded so slowly that it was not completed to Fergus until September, 1870,[34] and to Alma (making a total distance of 21 miles) by December of the same year.[35] In contrast, the sod-turning ceremonies of the Toronto, Grey and Bruce were held on October 3, 1869, (with Prince Arthur wielding the spade), and by May 1, 1871, the line opened to Orangeville (48 miles), and the work of grading and bridging was almost complete to Arthur village, a further 24 miles.[36]

Although Guelph's businessmen had remained cool to both railway projects in their early stages, once the Toronto line began showing signs of success they immediately took an active part in support of the Wellington, Grey and Bruce. If railways must come into Guelph's market area, it was more advantageous that they lead directly to Guelph.

In the end, of course, Guelph's business community could salvage little from the whole affair. The Town's whole strategy up to 1871, had been to make itself the "great centre of attraction and radiation"[37] to all the adjoining townships, and to do so the Town's ratepayers had taxed themselves to build roads, railways and a Market House, and had, again and again, fought off challenges by the businessmen of other centres for control of its market area. Now it had lost the main battle for that area, and the Town, by that loss, was made even more dependent upon the rapid development of manufacturing for its future prosperity and growth.

St. Bartholomew's Church circa 1877.

X

Religion and Education

From the standpoint of social and institutional development, the years 1851 to 1881 were a period of considerable growth. During this time the construction of churches, schools and hospitals was an important part of this progress, and municipal government would play an expanded role in social affairs. The large influx of settlers during these years came primarily from the British Isles, as shown in Table XXIV, but by far the most important change to occur was the growing predominence of Canadian-born second and third generation residents.

With the Town's rapid increase in population and wealth in the 1853-1856 period, many of the well established churches found their buildings too small for the needs of their congregations. At the same time, many of the smaller religious groups were able to finance their first permanent homes. As a result, a great many new and substantial churches were erected.

The first new church to be built was the Roman Catholic. When their original wooden church was burned by arsonists in October, 1844, the Reverend Thomas Gibney immediately undertook to erect a larger and more im-

Captain Walter Clark, physical education instructor and drill sergeant at the Guelph Collegiate Institute. He founded his famous Highland Cadet Corps and the Daughters of the Empire in the 1880's.

Table XXIV
Population of Guelph by Country of Birth, 1851-1881[1]

Country	1851 No.	1851 %	1861 No.	1861 %	1871 No.	1871 %	1881 No.	1881 %
England and Wales	507	27.3	958	18.8	1203	17.5	1258	12.7
Ireland	392	21.1	901	17.8	695	10.1	698	7.1
Scotland	200	10.8	578	11.4	615	8.9	686	6.9
Canada	722	38.8	2422	47.7	4062	59.1	6857	69.3
United States	34	1.8	142	2.8	236	3.4	276	2.8
Other	5	.3	80	1.6	67	1.0	115	1.2

posing structure. "The good parishioners toiled for two years. . . . The church, this time of stone, was placed under the patronage of St. Bartholomew. In the same year. . .Father Gibney suffered a broken leg when thrown from his horse, and died a few days later".[2]

In 1852, the Guelph Catholic Church and missions had been placed in the charge of the Jesuit Order led locally by Father John Holzer, who was assisted by the Reverends J. Frazerini and Gaspanns Matoga.[3] Together the three priests set out to create in Guelph a full range of educational, welfare and social institutions. In 1852, Holzer obtained a charter for "St. Ignatius College" which he intended to found in Guelph. In 1853, an orphanage was established and a large school building begun.[4] The passing of the Separate School Act, however, appears to have changed Father Holzer's plans for the college. With taxes available for the education of Catholic children, a separate school was opened under the direction of Patrick Downey, formerly a teacher in the Guelph common schools. With Downey in charge, St. Stanislaus Separate school was opened on January 14, 1854.

Having erected a stone church and school, a third important step in the building program was taken in 1855 with the building of a convent. At the same time, Bishop Farrel of Hamilton invited the Sisters of the Blessed Virgin Mary to take up residence and to establish a private girls' school in Guelph. Thus, on June

Father John Holzer.

10, 1856, four Sisters of that Order, designated by the driver of the Hamilton stage coach as "Mrs. Lynn and daughters", travelled from London to Guelph to take up residence there. Although the convent was not yet complete, the Sisters began the school, "Loretto Academy", by teaching in the private homes of John Harris and Mrs. M.J. Doran.[5]

In 1857, Loretto Academy, a residential and day school for female pupils of all denominations, was completed. The *Guelph Directory* for 1875-1876 gives this description of Loretto Academy:

The Loretto Convent of the Immaculate Conception, in affiliation with Loretto Abbey, Toronto, is beautifully situated on the Catholic Hill, and with the Church and College is one of the first objects that attracts the eye when approaching the Town. It consists of a large and spacious building particularly convenient to the Town and yet remote enough to secure the quiet and seclusion so necessary to an institution of its kind. It is conducted by the Ladies of the Loretto, is open to young ladies of all denominations, and is carried on in precisely the same system and equally as well as the Loretto Abbey of Toronto, both as regards the efficiency of teachers and comfort of pupils.

Rev. Mother Regis Harris, Superioress.[6]

After a successful campaign to build a rectory in 1857, Father Holzer took a fourth major step in the creation of Catholic institutions. In 1861, he and the Jesuit Order invited the Sisters of Saint Joseph, who had a convent at Hamilton, to undertake the care and supervision of a hospital and House of Providence in Guelph. The latter institution was charged specifically with the care of the aged, invalid and infirm of the area. During the first year, St. Joseph's Hospital and House of Providence, under the care of five Sisters, was housed in a small stone building called the "Gate House",

which contained only sixteen beds for both hospital and residence purposes. In 1862, however, a stone building was completed and the hospital moved into the new premises. In the *City of Guelph Directory* for 1882-1883, this description of these institutions is given:

St. Joseph's Hospital and House of Providence under the superintendence of the Sisters of St. Joseph,

The First St. Joseph's Hospital, 1861.

The Second St. Joseph's Hospital, 1862.

is located on Hospital street north of the London road, and is a fine three-story stone building, fitted up with all necessary appointments for the care of the sick. In connection with the Hospital is a farm of 30 acres, from which is procured the vegetables and fruit used in the institution. The Hospital was chartered in 1862, and additions made from time to time, as necessity required. The House of Providence, in connection, is designed for aged people, and those requiring a temporary home. The Hospital is supported by the usual Government and Municipal grants, and voluntary aid. At the time of our visit it contained 12 patients in the Hospital, and 41 in the House of Providence.[7]

The final stage of the building program instituted by Father Holzer, however, was somewhat less successful. In 1862 or 1863, a large, new church was begun. On October 4, 1863, the ceremony of laying the corner stone was held with dignitaries from all over the Province in attendance. Acton Burrows gives this description of the event:

On Sunday, October 4th, the ceremony of laying the corner stone of the Roman Catholic Church of St. Bartholomew was performed. The work had been in progress for some time, and the stone work had been raised to a considerable height, and the south side of the partially-built walls was tastefully decorated with evergreens and streamers. The procession, headed by the Bishop, passed from the old church to the west end of the new buildings, where the sanctuary was to be, at which place the Bishop blessed a large wooden cross, placed on the site to be occupied by the altar. The procession then passed to the front of the church, where the corner stone was placed.[8]

Unfortunately, the work of building, begun with such hope, was not completed.

Father P. Hamel, who succeeded Father Holzer in 1863, had travelled extensively in Europe during his student days and had been fascinated with the grace and beauty of the Cathedral in Cologne, Germany. When he came to Guelph, he decided to create a miniature replica of the Cologne Cathedral, and hired Joseph Connelly, a pupil of Pugin, the renowned English architect, to draw up the plans.[9] The foundations laid by Father Holzer were abandoned, and on July 10, 1876, a ceremony was held planting the cross and turning the sod for the new church.[10] The following year, the corner stone was laid and construction begun adjacent to St. Bartholomew's Church. In a project lasting many months, the apse with its crown of chapels, the chancel and transepts were roofed over, and a spire was erected. Then the wall between St. Bartholomew's and the new church was removed and the two areas joined. The *City of Guelph Directory* for 1885-1886 gives this excellent description of the building:

The Church of Our Lady of the Immaculate Conception is a magnificent stone building, on the most elevated site in the City, at the west end of Macdonald [*sic*] street. It was begun in 1876. One half of the edifice is completed at a cost of $50,000. The remaining portion it is expected will soon be erected. A crypt extends under the part completed, and a spacious hall will be provided under the naive [*sic*] and aisles. The Church will have a seating capacity of 1800. The following is a condensed description of the principal features of the Church: The style of the building is of the early 14th century French Gothic, and will be carried out in its purity in all the details, carving, frescoing, decorations, etc. The exterior views on all sides are bold, varied and picturesque, while those of the interior, with its forests of pillars and pointed arches, its great traceried windows of different designs, its numerous chapels, seen in the distance through the opens of the great chancel, give ever changing perspectives at each step. The beautifully designed traceried windows will be filled with stained glass of gorgeous hues, speaking in silent language the grand lessons and sublime legends of Holy Scripture, while the walls, pillars and ceiling will continue the glorious narra-

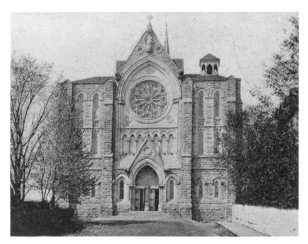

A view of the Church of our Lady about 1905.

The Church of our Lady, rear view with spires completed.

tive in magnificent frescoes, rich carvings and costly mosaics. . . .

Rev. Wm. J. Doherty, S.J., pastor. Assistant Priests, Rev. David Plante, S.J.; Francis Dumortier, S.J.; Theodore Fleck, S.J.; John A.S. Macdonald, S.J.[11]

In 1888, under Father Doherty's supervision, the body of the church was completed, and the towers built to the level of the nave. In 1907, Father J.J. Connolly undertook the decoration of the interior, adding the marble sanctuary, stained glass windows, and mural decoration. The final step, the completion of the towers, was taken in 1925 and by the fall of 1926, fifty years after its initiation, the Church of Our Lady, was completed.[12] For a relatively small parish it was a remarkable achievement.

The second congregation to build a new church was St. George's Anglican in 1851. Acton Burrows describes the circumstances:

The church of St. George. . . was now found to be quite inadequate to the accommodation of the rapidly increasing congregation, and it was therefore determined to build a larger edifice, of stone, the corner stone of which was laid July 17th, 1851, by Rev. Arthur Palmer, assisted by Rev. E.M. Stewart, Assistant Minister; Rev. J.G. Geddes, Hamilton; Rev. M. Boomer, Galt; Mr. Sheriff Grange, Mr. R. Jackson, Col. W. Hewat, churchwardens, and others. . . . The Building Committee consisted of Messrs. F.W. Stone, James Wilson, G.J. Grange, A.A. Baker, W.H. Parker and Frederick Marcon, together with the Rector. The architect was Mr. William Thomas, and Messrs. John Worthington, John Harrison and James Thompson were the contractors. . . . The estimated cost of the new building was £2,500, and the work was at once commenced, but the original design was never fully carried out, only a part of the contemplated stone building being erected, as an addition to the original wooden structure. The work was completed in the course of a few months.[13]

With the rapid expansion of the Town's population between 1853 and 1856, this enlarged church was quickly outgrown.

In 1859, a movement led by Dr. William Clarke and J.W. Brown was begun to erect a new Anglican church away from the developing commercial centre of Town. In November, Clarke and Brown offered to purchase the St.

The Second St. George's Church in the Square, 1851-1873.

George's Square site for £2,150, on the condition that if the Town did not buy it from them within two years, the property would revert to them. Reverend Arthur Palmer, the minister, countered with a proposal "that if the congregation would donate £1,500", he would "provide the balance of what would be required to finish the church" begun in 1851 with money obtained "from other sources". With the congregation split on the subject, nothing was done at that time.[14]

In April, 1863, Doctor Clarke once again renewed his offer to the vestry of St. George's Church, this time offering $10,000. By that time, traffic had become so heavy, and the general area so unsuitable for expansion, that the congregation was now anxious to sell and accepted his offer in order to build a new church on Woolwich Street. "In July, Doctor Clarke offered to transfer the site to the Town at the same price, an offer which was not then accepted".[15]

As a result of these setbacks and the commercial depression of 1866-1870, the new An-glican church did not get under way until 1871, with Archdeacon Arthur Palmer, William Reynolds, T.W. Saunders, George Elliott and Judge A. Macdonald acting as the building committee. Acton Burrows gave this description of the laying of the corner stone:

On Tuesday, May 23rd, the event so long hoped for by the congregation of St. George's Church, the laying of the corner stone of the new church, took place. A special and largely attended service was held in the old church, after which the children of the Sunday School, followed by the members of the congregation, the building committee and the clergy present, including Revs. Messrs. Geddes, Hamilton; Boomer, Galt; Cooper, Fergus, and others, formed a procession and proceeded to the site of the new building. . . . The cost of this building. . .was to be $29,998.60.[16]

St. George's Church was opened for religious services on April 20, 1873.[17]

In the meantime, negotiations had gone on between Doctor William Clarke and the Town Council for the acquisition of St. George's Square. By February, 1873, an agreement had been reached whereby the Town would lease the Square and turn it into a park. After the by-law had been read a second time, and was ready for ratification, further negotiations took place. Instead of a lease, Doctor Clarke now agreed to sell the Square to the Town for $6,250, and on March 18, 1873, a by-law embodying these new terms was passed.[18] In effect, Dr. Clarke had made a gift to St. George's Church of $3,750.

The *Town of Guelph Directory* for 1873 gives this information regarding St. George's Church:

St. George's Episcopal Church. . . .The site was recently purchased by the Town, and the building removed. The magnificent Church recently erected near the river-edge and almost opposite the Court House, was formally opened on the 20th of April, 1873. The Rev. Archdeacon Palmer officiates, assisted by his curate, the Rev. F. Alexander. The Churchwardens are T.W. Saunders and Judge Macdonald.[19]

Soon after the completion of St. George's Church, the career of one of Guelph's most remarkable clergymen drew to a close. In 1875, Archdeacon Arthur Palmer, after more than forty years in Guelph's most influential pulpit, resigned. In failing health, he had travelled to Europe, but in midsummer returned to Guelph to wind up his affairs. On August 25th, he and his family sailed to England, never to return. He was succeeded by the Reverend Alexander Dixon.[20]

In 1886, the *City of Guelph Directory* described St. George's as follows:

St. George's Church. . . .It has a seating capacity of 900. . .The Sunday School has an attendance of between 300 and 400 pupils and 32 teachers; E. Morris, Supt.; Robert Mackenzie, Sec., Mr. Grub, Librarian. A Sunday School is also sustained at the Schoolhouse on Waterloo avenue. . . .Ven. Arch-

St. Andrew's Presbyterian Church, Norfolk Street, completed in 1858.

deacon Dixon, rector; Rev. E.A. Irving, curate; Edmund Morris and Geo. Murton, wardens; Mrs. Harvey, organist. The Rectory, adjoining the Church, was erected at a cost of $8,000. The Church and Rectory are considered the finest specimens of early English architecture in Canada. The Church is entirely free from debt.[21]

The third of Guelph's congregations to undertake a major building program was St. Andrew's. When the Municipal Council bought St. Andrew's Church in 1855, (for the site of the Market House-Town Hall) the congregation decided to erect a handsome stone structure on the south-east corner of Norfolk and Suffolk Streets:

David Allan, in collaboration with Mr. Hay, of Toronto, was the architect, and superintended the erection of the building. Work began in 1857, but was not completed until the fall of 1858. Services in the meantime were held in the Court House. The

The third St. George's Church, erected on Woolwich Street, showing footbridge across the Speed River.

building, which is pure pointed Gothic style, was built in a most substantial manner. The spire being well proportioned, stands one hundred and fifty feet high, and is surmounted by the Gallic cock as a weather vane. Eight bells were added, suspended by strong springs, giving a handsome finish to the spire. The money available for the building was not sufficient to include a spire, and Mr. David Allan, personally, subscribed the one thousand dollars necessary for its erection, so that the church would be complete.

The church was completed in 1858 at a total cost of £6,089. 13s. 2d. The contractors were Messrs. Morrison and Emslie for the stone work, and Messrs. Bonet and Ryan for the carpenter work.[22]

On July 1, 1859, the Rev. John Hogg was formally inducted as pastor.[23]

In 1868, a fourth Presbyterian congregation was established in Guelph. Acton Burrows gives this description of the event:

For some months past an unhappy division had existed among the members and congregation of Knox's Church, and the Presbytery had to be called upon to adjudicate on the matter but as some of the adherents were stilll disaffected, it finally became evident that the breach was such as to be almost beyond the hope of healing, and a committee of the Presbytery was therefore appointed to organize those who wished to secede into a separate congregation. On July 27th, therefore, the committee met at the Court House, Rev. Mr. Middlemiss, of Elora, convener, and a large deputation of church members being present. Certificates from Rev. W.S. Ball in favor of 114 members in good standing withdrawing from Knox Church were presented, and being found sufficient, a communion roll was made up, and the congregation of Chalmers Church was declared to be constituted.[24]

On December 19, 1868, Reverend Dr. Wardrope was called from Ottawa to serve as pastor of the new congregation, and on June 22, 1870, the corner stone of Chalmers Church was laid. It was officially opened on December

17, 1871. In 1873, the *Town of Guelph Directory* gave this description:

Chalmer's Church was built in 1870-71 and is one of the handsomest churches in the Town. Pastor, the Rev. Thomas Wardrope. Elders—D. McIntosh, Jas. McIntosh, Wm. Watson, John McCorkindale, Geo. Hadden, Wm. McPhail, David Kennedy, Wm. Stewart. Managers—Donald Guthrie, Chairman, R. Melvin, Sec. and Treas'r, John Inglis, Wm. Stewart, Hon. Peter Gow, David Stirton, M.P., Geo. Hadden, Gideon Hood, John Thomson, Evan Macdonald, John Macdonald, John McCorkindale, Geo. Shortreed. Sabbath School—Donald Guthrie, Superintendent; Wm. Russell, Secretary and Treasurer; Wm. J. Watson, Librarian.[25]

In spite of the loss of so many of its members to the new Chalmers congregation, the remaining members of Knox Presbyterian went forward with their plans to build a church. On Monday, October 19, 1868, the corner stone of the new Knox Church on Quebec street was laid by Reverend Dr. Ormiston and the church's pastor, Reverend W.S. Ball.[26] The following spring, the old Knox Church was sold

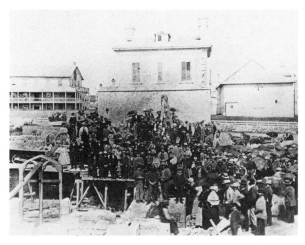

Laying corner stone of Chalmers Church.
The Wellington Hotel, the Bank of Montreal and
St. George's Church on the Square are in the background.

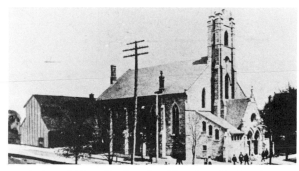

A view of Knox Presbyterian Church on Quebec Street, showing the Roller Rink in the background. Circa. 1906.

to Charles Raymond who converted it into part of his sewing machine factory.[27] In 1873, the *Town of Guelph Directory* gave this description of the new Knox Church:

Knox's Church. This fine building, situated on Quebec street, is of comparative recent date, having been erected in 1869, at a cost of $18,000....Pastor—Rev. Wm. S. Ball. Dr. McGuire, Ruling Elder; Wm. Wilkie, Chairman, J.C. McLagan, Treasurer. Managers—J.D. Williamson, Thos. Manderson, Jas. Miller, John Carter, Jos. Hobson, J.C. McLagan, Chas. Mickle, Jas. Cleghorn, Robert Bell, Wm. Whitlaw, Wm. Wilkie, P. Hunter. Dr. McGuire, Superintendent of S. School; Wm. M. Mann, Church officer.[28]

In spite of the divisions in the Presbyterian Church, in reality there were no deep doctrinal differences. During the eighteen-seventies a number of meetings were held in an attempt to reconcile the various branches, and in 1875, negotiations were successful in a country-wide amalgamation. Locally, the immediate effect of the union was that St. Andrew's, First Presbyterian, Knox and Chalmers congregations now found themselves within one denomination.[29] On July 14, 1875, Reverend Dr. John Hogg of St. Andrew's Church, was appointed moderator of the first union presbytery in Guelph and Reverend Dr. Torrance of First Presbyterian, secretary.[30]

During the period under discussion, three denominations of Methodists had significant congregations in Guelph. In 1846, the Primitive Methodists had built a chapel on Waterloo Street, but with the rapid growth of the Town, by 1863 they required new quarters. An early historian gives this short summary of the congregation's history:

Their second church building was on Paisley Street, and was known as the Paisley Street Primitive Methodist Church. The land was purchased during the pastorate of Reverend Thomas Adams, on the 6th of November, 1863, and the contract for the new church awarded to Joseph Ryan.... The original trustees were: Wm. Welsh, John Hockin, Joseph Ryan, Wm. Brown and Chas. Cousins.[31]

The *Town of Guelph Directory* of 1873 gives this information:

The church [Paisley St. Primitive Methodist] was built in 1864.... Mr. Rickaby is leader of the choir; Organist—Miss Jane Hockin; Pastor—Rev. Geo. Wood. Trustees—Wm. Welsh, Jno. Hockin, Wm. Brown, Wm. Graham, Jos. Ryan. Sunday School teacher, Robt. Easton and staff of twelve. Congregation about 200. Until the erection of the new building, the congregation met in the old brick church, east of the G.T. railway track, afterwards converted into a melodeon factory.[32]

In 1883, the church entered the union of the Methodist bodies in Canada.[33]

The oldest and most numerous of Guelph's Methodist congregations, the Wesleyans, decided to build their second church in 1854. Acton Burrows says:

During the winter of 1854-5, an energetic effort had been made to raise subscriptions for the erection of a commodious stone church, on the corner of Norfolk and Cork Streets. These efforts had been so far successful, that in April of this year [1855] a sufficient sum had been raised to warrant the commencement of the building, and on the 23rd of April the foundation stone was laid. A short service was held in the church then in use, immediately adjoining the site of the new building, after which the congregation adjourned to where the corner stone was to be laid. . . .by Mr. John McLean. . . . Addresses were then delivered by Mr. John McLean, Mr. Wm. Day, Rev. Lewis Warner, pastor, and Rev. G. Goodson, of St. Catharines, former pastor. . . .The estimated cost of the building was £2,400, the contractors being, for the stone work, Mr. Freeman, and for the wood work, Messrs. Hatt & Robinson.[34]

This church was finished on March 2, 1856. The *Town of Guelph Directory* of 1873 gives this description:

Wesleyan Methodist Church. This substantial edifice was built. . . at a cost of $15,348. . . the number of seats being 960. . . . The interior of the building is handsomely frescoed. . . . It numbers 350 members, and the congregation has been increasing in such proportion, that it is intended to erect a second edifice in another part of Town. The pastor is the Rev. J.B. Howard. The Sabbath School in connection with the church numbers 350 pupils, of which M.A. Keables is superintendent; J.D. Hutton, Secretary, and E. Stannard, Treasurer. It has 29 teachers and a library of 600 volumes.

The official members of the church are: James Hough, Wm. Stevenson, J.W.B. Kelly, George Smith, W. Heather, Henry Kirkland, Luke Millington, J.D. Hutton, Henry Metcalf, M.A. Keables, Jas. Schofield, Wm. Galloway, T. Wilcocks, A.O. Bucham, C. Campbell, A.M. Lafferty, J.H. Osborn, John Jackson and Hugh Harley.[35]

As the *Directory's* author had predicted, the Wesleyan Methodists soon found it necessary to erect a second church to accommodate their numbers. Guelph's manufacturing prosperity was at its height, and the congregation gave generously to aid the building program. In July, 1874, the foundation stone of Dublin Street Methodist Church was laid by James

Norfolk Street Church.

Hough. Present at the ceremony were the Reverend J.B. Howard and Reverend J.E. Lanceley, pastors of the church. The trustees of the new pastorate were: John B. Kelly, W.T. Chipchase, W.B. Clarke, J.H. Osborn, M.A. Keables, J.A. Davidson, R.S. King, John Jackson, Jr., Hugh Hurley, G.O. Maddock, John McConnell, Alfred Smith, Wm. Wheatley, J.H. Bishop and W.H. Husband.[36] On January 19, 1876, this church was officially opened.

Immediately after the decision was made to build the Dublin Street church, the Wesleyans undertook the renovation and expansion of the

Norfolk Street church as well. The *Guelph Herald* in November, 1876, gave this description of the changes:

The architect who designed these improvements was Mr. John Hall, Jr., and the highest credit is deservedly due him. The alterations embrace a wide area, extending from the basement to the topmost point of the tower. The tower has been built 24 feet higher, of cut stone laid in cement, and the windows in it are finished with Gothic tracings. . . .The whole is covered with galvanized iron, and the battlement adds much to the appearance of the church. . . .On the side facing Cork-st. a new entrance has been made. . . . A rear addition has also been erected, 18 x 46, and built in stone in accordance with the general style of architecture of the church.[37]

Although seldom mentioned in the press, the British Methodist Episcopal congregation (or "Colored Methodists" as they were usually called) had an interesting history. The original congregation had been made up of escaped slaves, but after the American Civil War, a considerable number of immigrants from other areas appear to have joined the original group. The *Town of Guelph Directory* for 1873 shows their "place of worship on Market Street and entered from Essex Street. Pastor—Rev. —Johnson. Trustees—Louis Bolden, Wm. Thomas, Eli Buckner".[38]

The census of 1881 gives a total coloured population of 107. An historian, writing in 1927, gave this summary of the congregation's development:

The [British Methodist Episcopal] congregation erected their present stone edifice, situated on Essex Street, in 1880. . . .Pastors—Rev. E. Roberts. . . . Revs. Moore, Collins, Miller, Townsend, Minter, Oliver, Davis, Drake, Ly-Bertus, Lucas, Brooks, Snowden, Washington, Jones, Slater, Wright, King, Lucas (second term), and Rev. S.D. Smith. During the pastorate of Rev. Dr. Oliver, the parso-

nage was built and occupied. Rev. Minter, when he took charge, reorganized the church. He also had the church renovated, and the present organ installed. Rev. Drake held the first conference of the B.M.E. Church ever held in Ontario, in 1895. Rev. King held the second conference in 1903. . . .

Throughout the following years this church has made steady progress from 1917 to 1927, although that progress and growth has been retarded by several families removing to other cities.[39]

Of the other religious groups in Guelph, only the Congregationalists and Baptists had sizable congregations. By 1866, the stone chapel erected by the Congregationalists in 1840 had long since outlived its usefulness. By 1867, a new church had been erected and Acton Burrows comments:

On the 16th May, the corner stone of the new structure was laid by Rev. Adam Lillie, D.D., Professor of Theology in the Congregational College of British North America, among the ministers present, being Revs. R. Torrance, W.S. Ball, John Hogg, J. Carroll, Geo. Graftey and G. Wood, of Guelph, W. Barrie, of Eramosa, T. Pullard, of Hamilton, H.W. Allworth, of Paris and J. Wood, of Brantford. The Rev. W.F. Clarke, pastor of the church, in the course of an address in which he explained the progress of the work and the design of the new building, said the estimated cost was $7000, towards which upwards of $3000 had been subscribed, in addition to which they expected to realize about $2000 from the sale of the old church property. . . .He acknowledged the obligations the committee were under to Mr. S. Boult and Mr. John Davidson, for generous contributions and practical suggestions, and to Mr. James Goldie, who in addition to large subscriptions, had presented the stone, from his quarry near the People's Mills, thus cheapening the cost of the masonry to the extent of at least $500; and to Mr. Chas. Raymond, for liberal contributions towards the purchase of the site. . . .At this date the membership of the church numbers 86. Its officers are: William Fletcher Clarke, Pastor; Richard Baker, Robt. Thompson, Edwin Newton, Samuel Hodgskin,

Robert J. Jeanneret, and Chas. Raymond, Deacons.[40]

The church was opened on January 15, 1868. In 1886, the Congregationalists were described as follows:

The Congregational Church is a stone building, on the corner of Norfolk and Liverpool streets. It was erected in 1867, at a cost of $13,000, the present valuation being about $20,000. The seating capacity is 500. . . .There are 190 members. Rev. Duncan McGregor, M.A., Pastor; John Crowe, Chorister; Mrs. Crowe, Organist; David Spragge, Sunday

The Second Congregational Church, Norfolk Street.

School Superintendent; Samuel Bailey, Church Secretary. The Church is free from debt.[41]

Although there is evidence that Baptist religious services were held from time to time in Guelph before 1850, the actual organization of the local Baptists into a congregation did not occur until May 9, 1853. On that date nine men and eight women met together under the leadership of David Savage to establish the Baptist church in Guelph. Savage would continue to act as pastor until a regular appointment could be made.[42] In 1855, a lot was purchased on Norfolk Street, and a frame building was erected that year. Reverend John Clarke was named the first minister.[43]

By 1871, the congregation had grown sufficiently that a new church was required. In September of that year, Charles Raymond deeded over two lots on Elora Road to the congregation, and, as well, agreed to purchase the old church. For several years, while the new building was being erected, services were held in the basement.[44] It was finally completed in October 1875.

In 1873 the *Town of Guelph Directory* says this of the Baptist Church:

Baptist Church. The members of this growing congregation finding their church too small, have, within the past year, built a new edifice on Woolwich street. The old building has been converted into a Ward School for girls. . . .The new place of worship when completed is calculated to seat about 500.[45]

In 1886, this further description is given:

The Baptist Church is a stone building on Woolwich Street, with a seating capacity of 750. It was erected. . .at a cost of $25,000. . . .There are 298 members, Rev. W.W. Dawley, pastor, Robert Evans, clerk.

A branch Sunday School is held. . .in a frame building recently erected for the purpose, at the

First Baptist Church.

corner of Berlin and Yorkshire Streets. There are 60 scholars.[46]

Among the very small religious groups which existed in Guelph before 1891, the Evangelical Union of Scotland, the Christian Brethren or "Quakers", Christadelphians, and Disciples of Christ were the best organized. The Evangelical Union built a chapel in Guelph in 1856 on land given to them by John Mitchell. Acton Burrows describes the opening ceremonies as follows:

On Sunday, May 10th [1857], a chapel intended for the Evangelical Union congregation, was opened, sermons being preached by Rev. R. Peden of Hamilton, who was assisted in the devotional exercises by Rev. E. Barker of Eramosa, and Rev. John McDougall, pastor of the church. The chapel, capable of holding between two and three hundred persons, was well filled at all the services. . . .[47]

In 1873, the *Town of Guelph Directory* gives this description:

Zion Church. Evangelical Union of Scotland. This building stands upon a plot of land, known as 'Mitchell's Survey', over the Eramosa bridge; was erected in 1856. Pastor, the Rev. James Howie. Elders—William Simpson, James Anderson, James Dowrie and Jas. Tindal.[48]

By the 1880's, however, the group had lost its vitality, and the chapel was sold to the Disciples of Christ.[49]

The history of the Brethren in Guelph goes back to the middle eighteen fifties. Commonly called "Quakers", they had a meeting house on Waterloo Avenue and held yearly general conferences outdoors on the grounds of Mr. Wells across the river from their place of worship.[50] Never a large group, the census of 1881 gives their number as 16. The 1883 *Directory* gives this information:

Plymouth Brethren. Meet on upper floor, Brownlow's block, near the post office. Breaking bread at 11 a.m.; preaching at 6.30 p.m. Prayer meeting on Wednesday at 7.30 p.m. Scriptural reading Friday evening.[51]

The Christadelphians received their first notice in Guelph's directories in 1873. It said simply "Christadelphians. Meet in a Hall on Wyndham street every Sunday afternoon, at 2 o'clock. Jas. Lamson, Secretary.".[52] In 1886, the notice was only a little more informative:

The Christadelphians meet over the store of Geo. Williams, Upper Wyndham street, every Sunday at 11 a.m. and 7 p.m., and on Wednesday evening at 7.-30. There are about 50 members.[53]

The Disciples of Christ, the congregation which purchased Zion Chapel from the Evangelical Union, were organized about 1878 or 1879. In 1881 they numbered 53.[54] In 1886 this description was given of them:

Zion Chapel is a stone building, seating 250.

...There are 40 members. James Kilgour, Pastor.[55]

The religious event which caused the greatest local excitement in the 1880's was the arrival of the Salvation Army in Guelph. Some idea of the impact of their first meeting on Sunday morning, March 9, 1884, can be gathered from the news story covering the arrival of this new force in Guelph's religious life. Snow lay deep on the ground and was still falling as:

The first gun of the Salvation Army belched forth its thunder on St. George's Square at a quarter past ten o'clock precisely on Sunday morning, a convenient time to excite the interest of church-goers on their way to their respective places of worship. The crowd that lined Wyndham Street was immense. Nothing short of a circus would have been sufficient to draw out such a number of people, conspicuous among whom were a large number of young men and boys, drawn no doubt by curiosity....The army consisting of Capt. Glover, Drum Sergt. Colman, and Capt. Churchill and her Lieut. Miss Russell marched from the Drill Shed on the sidewalk, followed by a large crowd. When opposite the Lion they were requested by the police authorities to take to the street which was done. They took up their position in the centre of St. George's Square, an audience of fully a thousand people surrounding them....This lasted for about twenty minutes, when they marched back to the [old] Drill Shed [which had been rented for the indoor meetings] where services of a similar nature took place. The Drill Shed was crowded to the door, and several were unable to get admission....The officers state that two recruits joined the army in the morning, four in the afternoon, and six at night, making twelve in all.[56]

Amongst those converted in the next few weeks were Alex. Cormie, Walter Scott, "Dad" Pike, Bob Smith, Charles Dawson, Alex. Cross, Arthur Dennis, Mrs. Smith and Mrs. R. Dunbar.[57] With this early success, the Guelph members of the Salvation Army decided to build a large hall at the corner of Dublin and Paisley Streets. The corner stone was laid on November 6, 1884, and the opening ceremonies held on January 1, 1885. The *Guelph Daily Herald* of January 2, 1885, gives this description of the event:

New Year's Day, 1885, will ever be remembered as a red letter day in the history of the Salvation Army in Guelph. The opening of the splendid new barracks was an event important and interesting to everyone in sympathy with the great religious movement so recently established in our City. The work of erecting the new structure has progressed rapidly. It is only about two months since building operations commenced, and now all that is required to make it complete is the plastering and painting. New Year's Day, it was thought by the officers, should not be allowed to pass without holding a celebration in the new barracks, even though the finishing touches had not been performed.

The cost of the building was $5,000, raised largely by voluntary subscriptions.[58]

Typical of the movements which gained strength from the growth in organized religion was the Guelph Branch of the Upper Canada Bible Society. Founded in Guelph in 1836,[59] the Bible Society was made up of the ministers and leading laymen of the Town's Protestant churches. Elected to office in 1848 were: President C.J. Mickle; Vice-Presidents, the Reverends Colin Grigor (Church of Scotland), J.G. MacGregor (Free Church Presbyterian), R. Torrance (United Presbyterian), John Bredin (Methodist), J.J. Braine (Congregationalist) and three leading Anglican laymen, A.J. Fergusson, Doctor Alling and Doctor Henry Orton.[60]

The Society's purposes were explained in a resolution passed at the Annual Meeting in 1851:

Moved by the Rev. J.G. MacGregor, seconded by the Rev. C. Grigor,

That this Branch Auxiliary Bible Society....

recognize it as their bounden duty as believers in divine revelation [*sic*] to endeavor to promote every scriptural scheme which has in view the spread of the pure Word of God.[61]

In 1857, the local Bible Society's efforts were augmented by the creation of a local branch of the Upper Canadian Tract Society. In 1873, this description was given of the latter group's work:

Since its establishment, the Guelph Branch has distributed about 50,000 tracts annually. The Young Men's Christian Association has interested itself in the work, and has been instrumental in enlarging its sphere of usefulness. Its affairs are in a prosperous condition. The officers are: President, Thos. McCrae; Vice-Presidents, C. Raymond, D. Savage, and all the ministers of the Town. . . .[62]

In no sphere was the presence of ministerial leadership more prominent than in the promotion of the cause of temperance. A temperance society had been founded in Guelph as early as 1833, but does not appear to have been active until the late eighteen forites. In March, 1848, this item apppeared in the *Advertiser*:

Temperance Meeting.—We have received a communication giving an account of a meeting in the School-house, Upper Woolwich [street], for the organization of a society for the promotion of tee-totalism. We are glad to hear of any thing being done which is calculated to elevate the standard of morality, and give a greater degree of respectability to our countrymen.[63]

The Cadets of Temperance (the junior branch of the Sons of Temperance) was organized in January, 1851, and the preface to their constitution read in part:

Now. . .it is desirable to organize the Youth of the Province between the ages of twelve and eighteen years into a Juvenile Order. . .having for its primary and chief object the formation of temperance habits, and the protection of this interesting portion of society. . . .[64]

The various temperance groups were not content, however, merely to use their influence on the individual. As well, they brought pressure to bear upon both municipal and provincial governments to legislate against the "evils" to which they were opposed. Thus from 1850 on, the temperance issue figured largely in almost every municipal election in Guelph.

Intemperance and drunkenness, however, were not the only forms of immorality that the church leaders campaigned to eradicate by legislation.

Initially, laws dealing with moral behaviour were few and simple. For example, by-law number four, the first omnibus by-law, dealt with only four moral issues. These clauses read as follows:

8. That no person or persons shall bathe within the distance of 80 rods from any inhabited house, bridge, or thoroughfare, except before sunrise, in any river or other public water in the Town of Guelph, or in any way indecently expose his or their persons.
9. That no person or persons shall engage in Charivaries, or aid or assist others so engaged, or blow horns, ring bells, shout, or make any other disturbance by firing guns, crackers, squibs, or any other fireworks, or in any way among peaceful persons, by swearing or obscene language, within the municipality.
10. That no person shall abuse any horse, ox, cow, or any other animal whatever. . . .
12. That no person shall. . .write any indecent or immoral language, or make any indecent figure, on any fence, wall or building or in any manner mark, daub or deface any fence, wall, or building, whatever.[65]

Between 1851 and 1866, only five more "victimless" crimes were added, as per Table XXV.

In 1867, however, a vastly more comprehensive and complex law was passed (by-law no. 164). Containing eighty-eight clauses, it would

Table XXV
"Morals Legislation" in Guelph, 1851-1871[66]

By-law No.	Date Passed	Description
4	27- 2-51	For the good government of the Town.
48	5-10-55	To prohibit the use of bowling alleys.
70	3- 8-57	For the better government of the Town.
99	5-11-60	For suppressing houses of ill fame.
100	5-11-60	For suppressing gambling.
101	5-11-60	For restraining and punishing vagrants.
164	9- 7-67	For revising, consolidating and repealing certain by-laws.
191	26- 9-69	Amending by-law 164.
207	17- 4-71	Amending by-law 164.

form the basis of Guelph's "criminal code" for years to come.[67] Omitting those items which deal with administrative matters, the following additional items relating to individual morality were prohibited: blasphemous language, billiard playing on Sunday, disorderly house, drunk or disorderly person, exhibitions, firing of guns, horse race, sale of liquor to child, servants and apprentices and in billiard rooms, improper language, mendicants, obscene language and swearing. Henceforth, these laws would be amended or added to almost every year. No longer could morality be described as being a matter of individual conscience and individual responsibility. It was now to be imposed upon pain of fine or imprisonment.

In addition to the rapid proliferation of religious and moral organizations, the increased population and wealth of the Town allowed the development of innumerable fraternal, mutual and friendly associations—so many that no attempt can be made here to examine their rise and development. The list of those given in the 1886 Directory gives an indication of the rich social life available in Guelph at that period:

SOCIETIES.
AGAZZIZ ASSOCIATION.
GUELPH CHAPTER A, No. 602, was organized in March, 1884. Miss Alice M. Petrie, Prest.; Miss Daisy M. Dill, Sec. Meets weekly. There are 25 members.

FORESTERS.
COURT PERSEVERANCE, No. 5866, ANCIENT ORDER OF FORESTERS was organized in Feb. 1872 Herbert Nicholson, C.R.; Robert Howie, Sec. Meets each alternate Thursday, over Old Bank of Commerce. There are 80 members.

COURT GROVE, No. 69, CANADIAN ORDER OF FORESTERS, was organized April 28, 1880, and incorporated the first of December the same year. H. Gummer, P.C.R.; George Selwood, C.R.; David Tripp, V.C.R.; Geo. Wilkinson, F.S.; W.B. Sparkman, R.S.; Archibald Campbell, Treas. Meets the second and fourth Wednesdays in Foresters' Hall, Lower Wyndham Street. There are 40 members.

KNIGHTS OF LABOR.
LOCAL ASSEMBLY No. 2980, KNIGHTS OF LABOR. Organized in 1884. Meets at Foresters' Hall.

MASONIC.
WELLINGTON COUNCIL, No. 15, R. & S.M., was organized six years ago. S.R. Moffat, Thrice Ill. Master; Robert Hunter, Recorder. Meets the third Thursday in each month. There are 25 or 30 members.

GUELPH CHAPTER, No. 40, R.A.M., has been organized 16 years. H. Lockwood, Z.; A. Bruce, H.; W. Clarke, J.; R. Gemmell, Scribe E. Meets second Friday in each month. There are 70 members.

HURONTARIO PRECEPTORY, KNIGHTS TEMPLAR, No. 10 G.R.G., was organized in December, 1883. V.E. Sir Kt. H. Lockwood, Presiding Preceptor; Sir Kt. J.A. Nelles, Registrar. Regular Assembly, third Monday in each month. There are 20 members.

ROYAL CITY LODGE OF PERFECTION, A. & A.S. RITE, was organized January 25, 1884. A.B. Petrie, T.P.G.M., T.S. Petrie, Sec. Meets the first Wednesday in each month. There are 15 members.

GUELPH LODGE, No. 258, A.F. & A.M., was organized in 1872. John Angell, W.M.; J. Mahoney, S.W.; W. Marcroft, J.W.; C. Banting, Sec. Meets the second Tuesday in each month. There are 95 members.

SPEED LODGE, No. 180, A.F. & A.M., was organized in 1864. Wm. Parker, W.M.; Wm. Gibson, Sec. Meets the first Tuesday in each month at Masonic Hall, Upper Wyndham street. There are over 100 members.

WAVERLY LODGE, No. 361, A.F. & A.M. Geo. A. Somerville, W.M.; H.E. Richardson, Sec. Meets the fourth Tuesday in each month, at Masonic Hall, Upper Wyndham Street. There are 60 members.

ODD FELLOWS.

WELLINGTON ENCAMPMENT, No. 31, I.O.O.F., was organized Feb. 9, 1876. Jacob Werlich, C.P.; T.D. Fenwick, H.P.; Wm. Bourne, Scribe; Chas. Cottis, Treas. Meets second and fourth Fridays, in Odd Fellows' Hall, Upper Wyndham Street. There are 70 members.

EXCELSIOR DEGREE LODGE, No. 14, I.O.O.F., was organized in 1881. W. Bourne, D.M.; R. Mackenzie, Sec. Meets the third Friday in each month.

PROGRESS LODGE, No. 158, I.O.O.F., was organized March 7th, 1875. J.H. Hamilton, N.G.; Wm. Walker, V.G.; Chas. Cottis, R.S.; G.J. Brill, P.S., Geo. Sleeman, Treas. Meets Thursday, in Odd Fellows' Hall, Upper Wyndham Street. There are 115 members.

RELIANCE LODGE, No. 89, I.O.O.F., was organized March 15th, 1872. Geo. Wheeler N.G.; John Colson, R.S. Meets Monday, in Odd Fellows' Hall, Upper Wyndham Street. There are 150 members.

ORANGEMEN.

PRINCE ARTHUR LODGE, No. 1331, L.O.L., was organized 15 years ago, A. Sweetman, W.M.; John Smith, Sec. Meets first and third Thursdays, in Orange Hall, Day's Block. There are 40 members. In connection with the Lodge is a Life Insurance Association for the benefit of members of the Order.

ROYAL ARCANUM.

WYNDHAM COUNCIL, No. 810, was organized Aug. 20th 1884, John Day, Regent; Chas. Cottis, Vice Regent; R. Scott, Sec., R. Lund, M.D., Tres. Meets first and third Wednesdays. There are 30 members.

TEMPERANCE SOCIETIES.

BEAVER LODGE, No. 56, I.O.G.T. was organized in 1868. Harry Moulden, W.C.T.; Harry Heather, Sec., J.J. Mahoney, Lodge Deputy. Meets Mondays in Good Templars' Hall, over old Bank of Commerce. There are 200 members.

GUELPH COUNCIL, No. 127, ROYAL TEMPLARS OF TEMPERANCE, was organized in February, 1884. R.B. Hare, Ph.D., S.C.; E.L. Hunt, R.S. Meet each alternate Thursday, over old Bank of Commerce. There are 35 members.

GUELPH CHRISTIAN TEMPERANCE CLUB. E.H. Maddock, Prest.; Joseph Ryan, Sec. Meets every Sunday, at 8 p.m., in Caledonian Hall, Upper Wyndham Street.

THE LEAGUE OF THE CROSS (Catholic Temperance) was organized in June, 1883. Edward J. O'Brien, President; Francis Nunan, Secretary. Meets the fourth Sunday in each month, after High Mass; also each alternate Tuesday, at 8 p.m., in Hazelton Block, Upper Wyndham street. There are 200 members.

UNITED WORKMEN.

WELLINGTON LEGION, No. 18, SELECT KNIGHTS, A.O.U. W. William N. Husband, S.C.; George Lamond, R.S. Meets second and fourth Tuesdays, over old Bank of Commerce. There are 35 members.

GUELPH LODGE, No. 163, A.O.U.W., was organized in January, 1882. J.C. Walker, P.M.W.; H. Macdonald, M.W.; Albert Snyder, Rdr. Meets first and third Tuesdays. There are 80 members.

Royal Lodge, No. 60, A.O.U.W., was organized five years ago. Robert W. Stewart, M.W.; W. Suddaby, F.; F. Lawrence, Rdr. Meets first and third Fridays, over old Bank of Commerce. There are 140 members.

MISCELLANEOUS SOCIETIES.

St. Andrew's Society was organized in 1849. H.K. Maitland, President; A. Bruce, 1st Vice-President; Duncan Stewart, Secretary-Treasurer. Meets monthly. There are 150 members.

St. George's Society. Wm. Jenkinson, Prest.; Wm. Clark, 1st Vice-Prest.; W. Marcroft, 2d Vice-Prest.; John Thompson, Sec.; Geo. Elliot, Treas.; Meets the first Thursday in each month, over old Bank of Commerce. There are 120 members.

St. Patrick's Benevolent Society. John C. Coffee, Prest.; James Mills, M.A.: 1st. Vice-Prest.; Thos. P. Coffee, 2d Vice-Prest.; J.L. Murphy, Sec.; J.C. Chadwick, Treas.

Guelph Branch Bible Society. James Hough, Prest.; Geo. Elliott, Chas. Raymond, and all ministers who are members of the Society, Vice-Prests.; D. McCrae, Sec.; E. Newton, Treas.; B. Savage.; Depositary.

The Young Men's Christian Association, Alma block; Upper Wyndham street. J.D. Williamson, Prest.; E.L. Hunt, Vice-Prest.; Chas. B. Tweedale, General Secretary; Wm. Anderson, Treas. Young Men's prayer and praise service every Sunday, from 9.30 to 10.30 a.m. Bible class on Tuesday evening. Gospel meeting on Saturday evening. Monthly socials and entertainments are held, and, during the winter months, a free course of lectures and practical talk to young men. Reading and recreation rooms, supplied with leading dailies and periodicals, and social games. There is also a small circulating library, for the use of members. Rooms open daily, from 9 a.m. to 9.30 p.m. There are 40 active members and 10 associate members.

The Church of England Parochial Association, containing Temperance, Literary and Visiting Branches. Ven. Archdeacon Dixon, Chairman; James Clark, Sec.-Trea. General meeting the first Tuesday of each month. Weekly meetings of the Branches. R. Lund, M.D., Chairman Temperance Branch; J.B. Powell. Chairman of Literary Branch; Geo. Murton, Chairman Visiting Branch.

The Catholic Mutual Benevolent Society, was organized in the summer of 1884. Edward J.O. Brien, Prest.; James Duffy, Sec. Meets each alternate Tuesday evening, in Boys' Separate School. There are 25 or 30 members.

St. Vincent de Paul Society was organized 18 years ago. Rev. Wm. J. Doherty, S.J., Director; J.E. McElderry, Prest.; Francis Nunan, Sec., Patrick Purcell, Librarian. Meets every Monday evening in Boys' Separate School. There are 80 members. The library contains 600 volumes.

Guelph Agricultural Exhibition Building and Curling Rink was incorporated 15 or 16 years ago. D. Stirton, Prest.; A. Robertson. Jr., Vice-Prest.; John Davidson, Sec-Trea.

South Wellington and Guelph Township Aricultural Society.—Thos. Waters, Prest.; James Millar, 1st Vice-Prest.; M. Kirby, 2nd Vice-Prest.; R. Mackenzie, Sec-Trea. Annual fairs are held.

The Guelph Choral Union was organized in 1883. James Mills, M.A., Prest.; W.J.H. Emory, M.D., Sec.; Edward Fisher, Conductor. Meets Fridays in St. George's Hall. There are 140 members.

Guelph Bicycle Club was organized in 1882. Geo. Sleeman, Prest.; Wm. Allan, Sec.-Treas. There are 18 wheels.

Guelph Caledonian Society was organized in 1875. H.K. Maitland, Chief; Chieftains, Geo. Anderson, John Clark, Wm. Gibson, G. Bruce; Wm. Stewart, Sec. Treas. Rev. Thos. Wardrope, D.D., and Rev. James C. Smith, M.A., B.D., Chaplains; Drs. Cowan, Mackinnon and McPhatter, Physicians. Meets Thursdays, in Caledonian Hall, Upper Wyndham street. Average yearly membership, 200.

Guelph Cricket Club was organized in 1846. F.J. Chadwick, J.H. Finlay, and Geo. Sleeman, Patrons. E. Morris, Prest.; J.L. Hardman, Sec. There are 150 members and one of the strongest clubs in Canada.

Guelph Rifle Association was organized in 1854. Geo. Sleeman, Prest.; R. Stewart, Vice-Prest.; Chas. Cottis, Sec.-Treas. Weekly practice from May 1st to October 1st. Range on Waterloo Avenue. There are 120 members.

GUELPH TURF CLUB was organized in 1871. Geo. Sleeman, Prest.; Thos. Watt, Sec.-Treas. There are 13 members.

GUELPH UNION CURLING CLUB was organized in 1838. C. Davidson, Patron; Mrs. Davidson and Mrs. Robertson, Patronesses; Thomas Gowdy, Prest.; A. McBean, Vice-Prest.; D. Stirton and Geo. Murton, Representative Members; Geo. Murton, Sec., Rev. J..C. Smith, Chaplain. There are 50 members.

MAPLE LEAF BASE BALL CLUB was organized about 1860. Geo. Sleeman, Prest.; John Henderson, Sec-Treas. The Club has a very fine practice ground, located west of Edinburgh road, near the G.W.R., station. The grounds are well fitted up and have two extensive.stands for spectators, with other necessary conveniences. This Club enjoys the honor of being the champion nine of Canada.

THE SPEED SKATING RINK CO. was incorporated in Dec. 1881. The Rink is located on the bank of the river, with entrances from Woolwich and Thorp Streets, and is one of the handsomest rink buildings in Ontario. It is built of stone and was erected at a cost of [$]15,000. It is fitted up with all the necessary accessories, including commodious waiting rooms, parlors, &c. Adjoining is a bowling alley, also croquet and tennis lawn. D. Stirton, Prest.; James Innes, M.P., Vice-Prest.; Alfred Burrows, Sec.

WOLSELEY LACROSSE CLUB was organized in April, 1884, N.L. McPhatter, M.D., Prest.; Geo. M. Gibbs, Sec., C. Hetherington, Captain. Practice on Mondays, Wednesdays and Fridays, at Exhibition Grounds. There are 40 members.[68]

Nor were these by any means the only organized social activities. In all, it was a period when social initiative shifted from the individual to the organization, and from spontaneous to planned action. Whereas before 1850 a few such organized activities had existed, by 1890 they encompassed almost every aspect of social life.

Not only did Guelph's increased population and wealth allow an enormous increase in number and importance of organized religious and social institutions, it also brought about the need for better health and educational facilities. Thus both the Guelph General Hospital and numerous new schools were built.

The initiative to construct the Guelph General Hospital was taken in 1861. In that year a hospital association was formed, and an Act of Incorporation was passed on May 18th. The Act, however, contained two limiting provisions: first, that hospital revenue should not exceed $20,000, and that membership should consist of at least 100 annual subscribers before the charter could come into effect. The first was, apparently, intended to make sure that it remained a non-profit, charitable organization, the second to ensure that it had both public support and a considerable sum of funds from private sources. It was the latter provision that created a major stumbling block. It was not until 1872 that the hospital's organizers managed to acquire a hundred subscribers.[69]

The Guelph General Hospital opened August, 1875.

A public meeting was then called in the Town Hall to elect officers and directors. At that meeting the following appointments were made: Chairman, George Elliott; Vice-Chairman, John Horsman; Treasurer, Charles Raymond; Secretary, Andrew Lemon; Directors, D. Stirton, Dr. Clarke, N. Higinbotham, F.W. Stone, James Massey, Peter Gow, Robert Bell and John McCrea. Immediately various committees were established to carry out the work, and on January 11, 1873, four acres of land on Delhi Street were purchased from Dr. Clarke for the sum of $1,000. The early history of the hospital was as follows:

The original plan was that the building was not to cost more than $6,000 at its completion, the County Council having granted $1,500 of this amount. The amount allowed was later changed to $8,000, and the plans of Mr. Victor Stewart, architect, accepted, and work began at once on the erection.

When the hospital was opened on the 16th of August, 1875, with Miss Law as Matron, there were twelve beds. Mr. Gerald O'Reilly was hospital assistant, and two nurses were in attendance. There was no operating room proper, but a small infectious ward, a dispensary, a public ward for men and women, and two or three private wards, plainly and comfortably furnished by money raised by subscriptions collected by ladies of the Town who formed a committee for the purpose.

The first public grants, apart from the building fund, were received in 1875, namely, $500 from the County of Wellington, and a similar amount from the Town. A year later the County gave another grant of $600, and the Ontario Government, $800.[70]

Although the hospital's founders had difficulty getting public support before 1872, once it was in operation, its necessity and utility became obvious. In 1886 an enlargement was proposed and received widespread support. Thus in 1888 the "Victoria Jubilee Wing" was opened[71] which contained the hospital's first regular operating room, nurses' rooms and a diphtheria patients' room, these rooms being completed in 1891.

Parallelling the rapid growth of institutional life in Guelph, the period 1850-1880 saw a great expansion of educational facilities as well. This development arose from the increased legal requirements of the Provincial educational authorities, combined with the huge increase in the numbers of school aged children. When Egerton Ryerson, the Provincial Superintendent of Education, introduced legislation in 1850 calling for the establishment of local "free" public schools, supported by real estate taxation, he did so with full knowledge of the strong hostility that such a proposal would create.[72] By the Act, the Boards of Trustees of common schools in towns and cities were permitted to decide whether or not to establish free schools.

In Guelph, the battle to bring into effect the tax-supported free school system was led by the local Superintendent of Common Schools, John Kirkland. Kirkland's arguments[73] in favour of free schools were similar to those used by Egerton Ryerson.[74] In spite of Kirkland's pleas, free schools would not come to Guelph until legislated by the Province in 1871.

In 1852, as previously mentioned, Guelph had three common schools, but only that kept by Oliver, John Galt's stone "seminary" was owned by the Town. Hough's school was conducted in his residence, and Miss Kennedy's girls' school in a residence owned by T. Sayers. These already overcrowded premises were stretched beyond capacity by the large increase in school population of 1853 to 1856.

Nor were inadequate premises the only problem. The lack of materials with which to conduct classes was keenly felt. In November, 1852, in an effort to force the Guelph Board of Trustees to provide the necessary equipment, the local Superintendent, John Kirkland, wrote a letter to the *Guelph Advertiser* complaining of the lack of "maps and apparatus", and stating that many rural schoolhouses are better furnished with apparatus than the Town schools.[75] As a result of Kirkland's public pressure, the Trustees reluctantly spent £10 for maps.[76]

The only important change in Guelph's school system between 1852 and 1856 (beyond the establishment of the Catholic schools) was the building of a new grammar school. In 1854, recognizing that the Grand Trunk Railway would make it impossible to hold classes in the old school because of noise and danger to the students, the Grammar School Board contracted for the erection of a new building on Arnold Street near Paisley. In 1855 the new school was described as follows:

The house is built of stone, two stories, in the form of the letter T. The front part was occupied by the master as a dwelling place, to accommodate boarders. Good playground. The schoolroom consists of one very large room, a number of desks with alleys between, and benches without backs. A small blackboard, few small maps, and a clock, not keeping good time. Both masters teach in the same room, some confusion, discipline is tolerably good, enforced by rod by second master (Rev. Mr. Fisher). School is opened by head-master reading and expounding of the Scripture. Names on roll, 25; present, 20. Prizes are offered. Pupils change place in class.

The present teacher (Rev. Edward Michael Stewart) is a clergyman of the Church of England, somewhat advanced in life and in feeble health, timid, affectionate and winning, and on that account is loved and obeyed, but not active or energetic.[77]

In spite of the fact that the opening of the Catholic separate school had helped alleviate the crowding in Guelph's common schools, by 1855 it was clear that something had to be done. In 1854 the Board had struck a committee to investigate the situation, and in February, 1855, it made its report. That report read as follows:

The Committee appointed by the Board of School Trustees to obtain information respecting the necessity of erecting a Central School House for the Town of Guelph, beg leave to report:

1st. That there are within the Corporation upwards of eight hundred children between the ages of five and sixteen years.

2nd. That the two School Houses belonging to the Town will not accommodate more than one-fourth of that number; also, that one building is in a bad state of repair, and situated so near the Railway that it would be advisable to remove from it altogether.

3rd. That the Trustees have been under the necessity of hiring School accommodation at the cost of about thirty-five pounds per annum; they have also received notice from the landlord of the Female School Room that he will require it for other purposes at Midsummer, and that the School House at present in charge of Mr. Hough may be required in like manner, as the term for which it was rented expires at that time.

4th. That under the present management the Trustees employ four Teachers [one grammar school and three common schools], at an aggregate salary of three hundred and twenty pounds a year.

Your Committee would therefore recommend the selection of a suitable site of not less than one acre in a central part of the Town; and the building of a School House of sufficient dimensions to accommodate the present and fast increasing School population, and place the same under the management of one efficient Head Teacher, where all the advantages derived from centralization will be acquired without a large additional outlay to the ratepayers.[78]

In April it was announced that lots 1046, 1047, 1051 and 1052, which comprised "about an acre of ground, on the crown of the hill, adjoining the Catholic Church property", could be purchased as a Central School site for the sum of £445.[79] While the Board authorized the purchase of the site, the public meeting held to discuss this question voted against building the school,[80] and the lots were not acquired at that time. However, in 1856 the School Board decided to attempt to achieve at least some of their goals by a complete reorganization of the school system. The Common School and Grammar School Boards were united. There was to be a junior school in each ward to be attended by young children of both sexes, junior and senior girls' schools, a senior boys' school and the Grammar School which would provide a classical education for those desiring to enter the professions. In order to meet the needs of expanded enrolment, the old Grammar School was taken over for common school purposes, and the old Methodist Chapel rented and divided into two classrooms by a temporary partition. Fees were struck at one shilling three pence per student per month, payable in advance.[81]

Although these changes were an improvement over the previous year, the report makes it clear that even after the acquisition of the Methodist Chapel, the students faced serious overcrowding. The Grammar School was attended by only 34 students, but other children were far less fortunate. During 1856, some 207 children attended Mr. Walker's one room Senior Boys' school; 235—Mr. Masters' Junior Boys' School; 163—Mr. R. Smith's Junior Boys' School; 56—the Senior Girls' School taught by Miss Kennedy for part of the year, and by Miss Gillespie for the balance; and 106 children—the Junior Girls' School taught by Miss Clarke.[82] It should be noted that al-

though the schools were designated as "Girls" or "Boys", in actual fact, they were attended by students of both sexes.

School attendance, however, was still very low, as shown in Table XXVI.

In 1871, Egerton Ryerson, now confident that there was sufficient support across the Province to back him, had an amendment passed to the Education Act which once and for all ended fees for the common or "public" school system, and made attendance compulsory for all children between the ages of 7 and

Table XXVI
School Attendance in Guelph, 1859-1879[83]

	1859	1865	1870	1879
Total children 5-16 years	1,020	1,220	1,600	2,431
Total pupils 5-16 years	785	1,172	1,523	2,073
Pupils- other ages	45	27	22	16
Pupils-boys	475	697	799	1,065
Pupils-girls	355	502	746	1,024
Attendance:				
- less than 20 days	45	75	153	81
- 20-50 days	57	231	266	253
- 50-100 days	173	396	413	500
- 100-150 days	219	306	376	513
- 150-200 days	163	163	234	701
-200 or more days	125	28	103	41
Pupils- not reported	93	—	—	—
Average daily attendance	354	481	667	1,124
Percent daily attendance	33.2	38.6	41.1	45.9

12.[84] This move was widely denounced as being dictatorial and as interfering with the rights of parents over their children.

Before the 1871 Act, children of all ages attended school at their parents' convenience, until they acquired a socially acceptable level of competence in reading, writing, etc. Because their attendance was sporadic, they tended to continue in school until sixteen or even older. After Ryerson's Act, children were required to be in attendance until they passed their twelfth birthday, whether or not their parents found their absence from the store, workshop or farm convenient. By such regular attendance, they acquired the rudiments of education at an earlier age than formerly, but having done so, once having reached the age of twelve, many left school altogether.

From 1856 to 1874, only one or two small one-room schools were erected to take care of the burgeoning school population. Such expenditures were made reluctantly and Acton Burrows describes the events leading to the building of a new girls' school on the Dublin Street hill in 1865:

The school accommodation having for some time been very inadequate for the accommodation of the large number of children in attendance, it was resolved, at a meeting of the School Trustees held in May, to call upon the Council to assess the Town

Central School at the head of Commercial Street, with the Senior Girls' School at the right.

for the purpose of building a new girls' school, the attendance of the female pupils having largely fallen off recently on account of the health of many of the children having been affected by insufficient accommodation. A public meeting was called a few days afterwards, when resolutions were passed to the effect that it was inexpedient to build another school house as it was not then required by the inhabitants, especially while business was in such a depressed state as at that time. . . .At the next meeting of the Trustees a committee was appointed to confer with a committee of the Town Council as to the best means of raising the required money for building the school house, but the Council declined the conference.[85]

For once the Board of Trustees was not to be put off. Exercising their legal right to require the Town Council to levy taxes for school purposes, they let tenders for its immediate erection, and the Town Council had no choice but to comply. A new era was beginning in the management of Guelph's school affairs.

The key to the changing attitude towards the provision of adequate school facilities in Guelph was the growing importance of industrialists amongst Guelph's civic leaders. In particular, Charles Raymond, owner of the Raymond Sewing Machine Company, would play a crucial role. These industrialists, as large employers, recognized the validity of Ryerson's arguments that education provided them with more disciplined, and more productive employees, and that, indeed, "Public money employed in education is a most profitable investment".[86] Indeed, in the 1850's, the main criticism levelled by John Kirkland against Guelph's teachers was that they were failing to instil a proper attitude towards duty and discipline in their students:

The children are not taught to feel sufficiently *vexed* when they fail to answer a question, or are cor-

rected by their fellow-pupils. Each scholar should be made to feel the desirableness of excelling his classmates; the fires of ambition should be enkindled in his breast, and it should strike him as a dishonor when he has not made such an appearance in his class as should be expected from a diligent and attentive student. Farther, students ought to know that their teacher is their *master*. He who expects to succeed in teaching must maintain authority over his scholars. It is not necessary for this purpose that he should be harsh with them; kindness and firmness, an equal temper and treatment, with a manifest determination to be obeyed, will render his government easy and effective.[87]

If these attitudes were to be instilled in children, not only must teachers be kept aware of their duties, but facilities had to be provided so that their duties could be effectively carried out.

In 1870, under the leadership of William Stevenson, George Pirie (editor of the *Guelph Herald*) and Charles Raymond, the Central School project was once again brought forward. Premises were rented at the corner of Essex and Gordon Streets and five classrooms fitted up. In 1870 these classes were taught by Mr. Hutton, Mr. Hunter, Mr. Ferguson, Mr. Anderson and Miss Goodeve. In addition, the Grammar School, Senior and Junior Girls' Schools, and the North Ward School were continued in operation.[88] Immediate steps were taken to acquire a suitable site for a new Central School and eventually lots 1046 and 1047 on Dublin St. were purchased from the Rev. Hector Glackmeyer. Lots 1051 and 1052 were not acquired at that time, and were subsequently sold to the Catholic Church in 1875. In 1871, tenders were called for plans for a building to be constructed of Guelph stone, and whose cost would not exceed $20,000. The plans of W.R. Stickland of Toronto were accepted and construction began in September,

Guelph Collegiate Institute.

1873, with the building being completed in 1876. In total, it cost about $50,000.[89] The *Guelph Herald* of November 1, 1876, carried this description of the building:

It is built of Guelph stone, the dimensions being 120 ft. in length and 86 ft. in width, four storeys in height, consisting of basement, ground and 1st floors and mansard storey; 9 ft. 14 ft. 13 ft. and 12 ft. in height respectively. The centre portion of the building breaks out from the line of building 4 ft. and is carried up 10 feet higher in the centre than the surrounding parts, which gives relief to the structure and from the additional height affords space for a large assembly hall. The roof is of the French or Mansard style, covered with purple and green slate arranged in appropriate patterns, and the deck or flat portion of the roof is covered with tin, surrounded by a handsome railing. The slopes of the roof are pierced by dormer windows, by which the upper rooms are lighted, and by which the plain surface is relieved. . . .The basement contains the caretaker's apartments, lunch rooms, fuel rooms and heating apparatus. Upon the ground and first floors are situated the class rooms, 16 in number, 8 on each flat, also the teachers' and apparatus rooms. The upper or Mansard storey contains the assembly hall and 4 ante rooms two on either side. . . . The dimensions of each class room is 25 x 35 ft., arranged for 30 double desks, to accommodate 60 pupils, or a total of 960 for the whole building. In addition to the class rooms, on the first floor, there is the library 35 x 12 ft. . . .[90]

Daughters of the Regiment under Captain Clark, 1888.

Capt. Clark's Famous Highland Cadet Corps of Guelph.

When Guelph achieved the status of a City on April 23, 1879, and became a corporation separate from the County of Wellington, the old Wellington District Grammar School became the exclusive property of the City of Guelph. Immediately the Board of Education began the building of the Guelph High School, retaining only the rear part of the old Grammar School. The headmaster's dwelling and dormitories were torn down and replaced by a stone structure with a bell tower. The two original classrooms were retained, while two more rooms were added on the west side, and a large assembly hall was built on the second floor.

In the year 1887, after Captain Clark had arranged for the building of a gymnasium at the rear, the Guelph High School was raised to the standard of a Collegiate Institute, and from that time on the Board of Education erected a number of new schools to accommodate the growing school population.

Of all the educational institutions established in Guelph, none would become better known nor more widely respected than the School of Agriculture and the Experimental Farm situated just south of the Town. Originally the school had been scheduled to be built on land purchased at Mimico. However, when the proposed site proved to be unsuitable, the Provincial Government in 1873 purchased the F.W. Stone farm on the Dundas Road.[91]

In July of that year the Government appointed as Principal of the School of Agriculture, Mr. Henry McCandless, a Scotchman, trained in Ireland, who for two years had been Professor of Agriculture at Cornell University—"Mr. McCandless, however,

proved to be wholly unfit for the position and after a few months he was forced to resign."[92]

Following his resignation, a young man named William Johnston, a recent graduate of the University of Toronto, was invited to Guelph as Resident Master of the School of Agriculture until a successor to Mr. McCandless could be named. The following year a Mr. Charles Roberts was appointed Principal, but owing to illness was unable to take the position, and Mr. Johnston was appointed as Principal.[93] He held the position for five years, the most trying years in the history of the College.

The purpose of this institution was to improve agricultural production and standards, but needless to say, many of Ontario's farmers were more than a little affronted by the pretentiousness of a group of urbanites proposing to change the farmers' accustomed economic and social behaviour. From the farmers' point of view, the proposal to send farm boys to such a school would have the consequence of filling their heads with impractical ideas and ambitions, thereby rendering them unfit for farming. Although the Agricultural School's curriculum stressed "practical" experience on the farm at the expense of "book learning," this did little to reduce farmer hostility. As a result, enrolment grew slowly before 1900, and concern was expressed frequently about the institution's future.

In spite of the seriousness of these problems, the Agricultural School made important progress before the turn of the century. Although the original academic curriculum was designed to be suitable for boys just leaving public school, the possibility of expanding the course of study to the college level was a continuing interest of the first permanent Princi-

An artist's impression of the College and Experimental Farm in 1889. (Courtesy The College on the Hill)

Ontario Agricultural College, Guelph.

pal, William Johnston (1874-1879). His successor, James Mills (Principal 1879-1880, President 1880-1904) was equally enthusiastic, and in 1880 the charter was amended by an Act of the Ontario Legislature affiliating the school with the University of Toronto, and thereby allowing the degree of Bachelor of Science of Agriculture to be conferred. At the same time the school was renamed The Ontario Agricultural College and Experimental Farm. In 1888 it graduated the first of its degree students.

Under the leadership of William Johnston and James Mills, the College established Farmers' Institutes, sent out travelling lecturers and model dairies, and numerous short course programs were developed to serve the special needs of rural Ontario. All of these worked to improve farmer-College relations, and after 1900 attendance improved.

Of particular significance to the future of the College was the establishment of the Macdonald Institute in 1903. Designed particularly for the training of public school teachers, the Institute offered for teachers, male and female, courses in Nature Study, Home Economics and Manual Training. Before the establishment of Macdonald Institute, few female students could attend the College, the exception being those taking the short course in dairying. With the opening of the Macdonald Institute, new opportunities for education were seized upon eagerly by female students, and the reputation of the College was greatly enhanced.

During the years prior to 1927, many new buildings were added and additional land purchased to provide a total of 717 acres.[94] In 1922 the Ontario Veterinary College was moved from Toronto to Guelph, and was an important addition to the Campus.[95] In 1924, War Memorial Hall was erected and formally dedicated by General Sir Arthur Currie.[96]

By 1927, the three Colleges were firmly established, and making an important contribution to life in the Guelph area.

Upper Wyndham Street and St. George's Square circa 1880,
from an oil painting by Evan Macdonald.

XI

Guelph becomes a City

In order to encourage Guelph's economic growth, a Board of Trade was established in 1866 representing all of the main financial interests of the Town. A conscientious effort was made by the general membership to have the executive reflect these interests, and in 1873 the following made up the Council of the Board: Robert Melvin (foundry), President; David Allan (flour mill, distillery, etc.), Vice-President; James Goldie (flour mill); George Murton (malt house); W.S.G. Knowles (auctioneer); J. Stewart (planing mill and lumber dealer); John McCrea (coal oil refinery); H.W. Peterson (lawyer); David McCrae (woolen mill); Charles Raymond (sewing machine factory); J.T. Brill (butter and pork merchant); James Massie (wholesale grocers, &c.); Chas. Davidson (agent, Canada Permanent Building and Loan Society) and John Hogg (dry goods and clothing store).[1] The Board of Trade concerned itself with everything from the establishment of new manufacturing enterprises (to the extent of helping to raise the necessary capital), the erection of a station downtown by the Galt and Guelph Railway, Town Council taxation policy, Town beautification, etc., etc. They worked constantly to make

those changes which its members felt were for the betterment of the Town. Internally, its meetings and discussions tried hard to overcome and to reconcile differences among its members and to democratically arrive at a suitable solution. Externally, it tended to work behind the scenes of Town and City government, through its close relationship with the Town's newspapers, and the fact that some of their members were also elected members of the Town and City Council.

When the Guelph Board of Trade found consensus among its members, the results could be impressive. Two major undertakings in 1870, Levi Cossitt's "Guelph Agricultural Works" and the Guelph Gas Company show how the Board of Trade functioned when it

found a common interest. In 1870, with the two rail lines north of Guelph nearing completion, Guelph's business community recognized that a united effort was necessary to spur manufacturing in Guelph. In mid-summer, the Board of Trade struck a committee to undertake an investigation of the problem, and by the end of November, it was ready to report. A public meeting was then called to hear the committee's recommendations and to take action upon them. The *Guelph Mercury* report of that meeting is particularly interesting:

PROPOSED NEW ENTERPRISE IN GUELPH.
An Agricultural Implement Association Formed.

A meeting of our merchants, manufacturers and businessmen was held in the Royal Hotel on Monday night [November 28, 1870] to consider the de-

The Galt and Guelph Railway station near Goldie's Mill. Later used as office by the James Goldie Milling Company.

sirability of forming in this Town an Association for the manufacture of Agricultural Implements, and to receive the report of the committee who had undertaken the duty of getting all needful information on the subject. The meeting was well attended, and an evident interest was manifested in the proceedings. Mr. John Hogg was appointed chairman, and Dr. Bessey, secretary.

The chairman, after stating the object of the meeting, called upon Mr. Higinbotham, one of the committee, who explained how the project had first taken shape, and pointed out the many advantages in doing business at an important and commanding point like Guelph. . . .

Mr. Massie, another member of the committee, also made a few remarks, in which he pointed out the importance of initiating such an enterprise in Guelph, and the benefits that would accrue to the Town by its establishment. It was estimated that a paid up capital of thirty thousand dollars would be sufficient to start with, and as the business enlarged the amount could be increased.

Mr. Charles Davidson spoke strongly in favor of the enterprise, and in order to test the feeling of the meeting, and put the matter fairly before them, he would move, That this meeting deem it desirable to form a Joint Stock Company in Guelph, for the manufacture of Agricultural Implements.

The motion was seconded by Mr. Massie and carried unanimously.

Mr. Higinbotham moved, seconded by Mr. Chadwick, that a stock list be opened for the purpose of ascertaining what amount of stock can be secured towards the furtherance of this enterprise. Carried.

Moved by Mr. Davidson, seconded by Dr. Bessey, that. . . a committee [be appointed] for the purpose of initiating and carrying on such measures as may be necessary to advance the Agricultural Implement Association. Carried.

A stock list was at once opened and stock to the amount of $11,500 subscribed among those present.[2]

The committee appointed to raise capital for the proposed implement factory was composed of: Adam Robertson, Levi Cossitt, John Inglis and W.H. Mills, manufacturers; John Hogg and James Massie, merchants; William Collins, carpenter; John Mitchell, undertaker; Stephen Boult, architect and builder; James Hazelton, cabinet maker; N. Higinbotham, M.P. North Wellington and insurance; and Charles Davidson, agent for a major source of mortgage funds, the Canada Permanent Building and Loan Society. By 1873, James Hazelton, the cabinet maker, had discontinued the manufacture of furniture to operate his own retail furniture store.[3]

In supporting the proposed Agricultural Implement Company, the *Guelph Mercury* explained its importance to the economic future of the Town:

We are glad to be able to lay before our readers so satisfactory a report of the doings of the meeting held to form an Implement Manufacturing Company as the one to be found in another column. We need not urge at any length the reasons which exist for the formation of such a Company. At no time in the history of our Town has it been more necessary for its citizens to look well to its standing than at the present moment. We are, as it were, in a state of commercial chrysalis, in a condition of transition from old to new that may prove either injurious or beneficial to our entire hereafter, according to the manner in which we mould and shape the opportunities of the moment. It cannot be denied that the railway extension so rapidly progressing to the northwest of us, while producing many beneficial results, will also bring with it accompanying changes and diversions, opening up new channels of trade and closing old ones, therefore it behooves us to prepare ourselves for the change that we may lead as many of these new channels as possible to flow hither. No step could be taken better calculated to secure this result than the establishment of manufactories upon, at least, a respectable scale, and there is no branch of industry which, at the present moment, promises so large a return as the production of agricultural implements. Possessing unrivalled and increasing methods of communication in all directions, with a rich and occupied tributary district, it will be our own fault if we do not secure for ourselves a monopoly of this trade for an area of scores of miles. Manufactories beget manufactories. Once firmly established they branch off and spring up side by side in a marvellous manner.[4]

The committee's campaign was apparently successful, as soon thereafter the Guelph Agricultural Works, Levi Cossitt, proprietor, announced its existence. Although its advertisements for "The Farmers' Friend Gang Plough—The most successful *Plow* wherever exhibited, unsurpassed for simplicity and durability, and stands without a rival"[5], appear regularly, it remained a small concern throughout its existence. Its plant on Nelson Crescent (opposite the site of the present Public Library) burned on July 10, 1877.[6] Cossitt rebuilt and continued there for a few years.[7] By 1882, the business had been taken over by Thos. Gowdy, whose agricultural works were at the corner of Suffolk and Yorkshire Streets. While the Guelph Agricultural Works did not live up to expectations, several similar campaigns to raise local funds for other enterprises were undertaken by the Board of Trade.

The Guelph Gas Company was started in exactly the same manner as the Guelph Agricultural Works. In early 1870, a committee was organized to investigate the profitability and utility of a company to produce and distribute coal gas in Guelph. On July twenty-seventh, a public meeting was called to discuss the committee's report and to undertake the formation of a Gas Company. The *Guelph Mercury* carried this description of the meeting:

GUELPH GAS COMPANY

At a meeting of influential merchants and others held on Wednesday night at the Great Western Hotel, a company was organized under the above

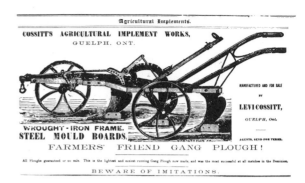

Advertisement for Cossitt's Agricultural Implement Works.
(Weekly Globe, Jan. 26, 1877)

title, and Messrs. Richard Mitchell, F.J. Chadwick and Higinbotham appointed a committee to canvass the town in order to obtain the subscriptions of citizens and capitalists to the Company's Stock List, then opened at the meeting. The sum of $4000 was at once subscribed which, with the sum taken by Mr. Perry (the projector of the Company), amounts already to $10,000. For $16,000, Mr. Perry offers to purchase a site and erect stone building 80ft. by 40 and 16 feet high, and to provide all that is necessary to register 20,000 ft. of gas in 24 hours, also to buy the necessary pipes, metres, &c., for 100 consumers and main pipes running from the gas works up Wyndham-st. as far as Suffolk-st., thence across to St. Andrew's Church, up Quebec-st. and Paisley-st. to Dublin-st., along Macdonnell-st. to Allan's Bridge, up Woolwich-st. to the Court House, around the Market Square from Wyndham-st., up Church-st. to Norfolk-street.[8]

As the result of energetic canvassing sufficient capital was raised to get the enterprise under way and by August twenty-third, the company was ready to go ahead. The *Guelph Mercury* gave this report:

Guelph Gas Company.—This Company was fully organized on Tuesday evening, at a meeting of the stockholders and others in the Town Hall, when the Committee appointed to canvass the Town and complete the stock list reported that the required amount had been subscribed. Accordingly the necessary legal documents were drawn up by Mr. Thomas W. Saunders, acting Solicitor to the Company, and presented to the Mayor, who was asked to call a special meeting of the Council to pass a By-law authorizing the construction of the works. . . .

The Company is to be called "The Guelph Gas Company." The capital of the Company $30,000 in 1,500 shares of $20 each "the amount so raised to be appropriated to the purpose of constructing, completing, acquiring and maintaining the gas works of said Company, and for no other purpose whatsoever." The term of the Company's existence to be fifty years. The Directors, for the first year, chosen at the meeting, are Messrs. N. Higinbotham, James Massie, Richard Mitchell, Frederick J. Chadwick, Donald Guthrie, John McLagan and John Hogg.

Mr. Perry, the proprietor of the undertaking, has been engaged as manager of the works for twelve months. He will commence the work of construction immediately on the passage of the By-law, and expects to be able to have gas burning in the Town by the 1st of November next.[9]

By-law number two hundred, passed by the Town Council on October 21, 1870, granted the Gas Company the right to lay its mains under city streets and through public property. In return, the Council made only one restriction:

3. That the said Company shall supply the said Corporation with such quantity of gas as they may require for the lighting of the Streets and Town Hall and other public buildings of the Town of Guelph, and to the inhabitants thereof at such rate as shall be charged from time to time by the Company to the shareholders thereof being consumers.[10]

At the adjourned special meeting of Town Council on Friday evening, August 26, 1870, "the Mayor read a communication from Mr. D. Guthrie, Town Solicitor, communicating that he had examined the By-law proposed to be passed for granting certain powers to the proposed Gas Company to lay down pipes in the streets, etc, of Guelph, and was of opinion that it would be legal for the Council to grant the powers sought and that the restrictions specified in the By-law were legal and proper. . . ."[11].

The first gas was delivered for use on January 18, 1871[12], and on January thirty-first, the Town Hall was lit by gas in a gala display.[13]

Although not all new manufacturing firms established after 1866 could be attributed to the activities of the Board of Trade, the increase was significant. Whereas between 1861 and 1866 only seven new manufacturing enterprises had been started: 1861, none; 1862, Charles Raymond, sewing machines; Robert Parker, carriages; Charles Thain, implement manufacturer; and Thomas Gowdy, agricultural implements; 1863, T.F. Grant, pumps; 1864, Bell Organ Company; 1865, none; 1866, Tolton Brothers, ploughs; in 1867 alone, eleven new manufacturing businesses were set up: McLeod, Wood & Co., organs; Solomon Myers, cigars; George A. Bruce, carriages; McNally, Clemens & Co., woollen goods; Alex. Ferguson, grist mill; O. Pooley, pork packing; Prest & Hepburn, shoe making; George Murray, woollen goods; Nathan Tovell, planing mill; McCrae, Hogg & Hockin, coal oil refiners; and Hockin & Son, cooperage and coal oil distillery.[14]

Originally, Hockin & Son had been coopers —barrel makers—but in 1867, with the opening of the oil fields at Petrolia, they had raised additional capital to start a large coal oil distillery, which in turn enabled them to greatly enlarge the cooperage side of their business. The Wellington County Directory for 1867 gives this description of the firm:

Guelph Coal Oil Refinery and Stave and Barrel Factory.—Hockin & Son, steam power, (twenty-horse), employing about 100 hands; united by switch with the Grand Trunk freight depot. This extensive establishment consists of seven large buildings, besides sheds, shops, etc, in connection with the largest cooperage in Canada. The business is increasing, and the proprietors intend making several additions to their already large premises. This company manufactures about 200 barrels of refined oil per week, and average two and a half million of staves, fifty thousand flour, and fifteen thousand oil barrels per annum, besides several thousand of various other kinds.[15]

Unfortunately, about this time an oil cartel in the United States, led by John D. Rockefeller, had been established and this group soon spread its operations into the Canadian oil fields. By gaining control of almost all of the crude oil produced, prices were driven up, gradually forcing the independent refiners out of business. On September 6, 1869, the Petrolia correspondent of the *Monetary Times* reported:

Since my last, the crude market has been very much excited, and $2 per barrel have been freely offered. . . . The chief cause of the present demand is simply the fact, that the Combination have sold so much oil ahead, and that the producers are bound. There actually is not oil enough available for the small refineries to make for the home market; consequently, every lot, small or large, is snatched up with avidity. . . .[16]

With the "Combination" controlling supply as well as selling refined oil to retailers in Guelph, it was not long before both local oil refineries were bankrupt. The *Guelph Directory* for 1882-1883 summarizes their fate in a few simple words:

Coal Oil Manufs.
Standard Oil Co., Col. N. Higinbotham [manager], office Higinbotham block, McDonnell, refinery

junction of G.W.R. and G.T.R. [Crimea Street].[17]

By 1885, the business was closed and Guelph's needs were supplied by other Standard Oil Company refineries in Canada and the United States.

From 1868 to 1871 more than a dozen new manufacturing enterprises were established, several of which would grow to a large size. Of these Caleb Chase, carriages (later the Guelph Carriage Goods Company), 1868; Crowe's Iron Works, 1868; Guelph Sewing Machine Company (Wilkie and Osborn), 1869; Samuel Smith (later Beardmore) Tannery, 1869; Thomas Worswick, steam engines and machinery, 1871; and the Guelph Spring and Axle Company, 1871,[18] were the most important. It must be emphasized, however, that in spite of the large number of new businesses established, the depressed condition of the economy generally restricted industrial output and slowed population growth, as shown in table XXVII.

From 1871 to 1876, with the return of pros-

Table XXVII
Guelph Population, 1861-1911[19]

Year	Population	Year	Population
1861	5076	1875	8584
1867	5357	1876	9015
1868	5901	1878	9918
1869	5799	1879	10072
1870	6470	1881	9890
1871	6878	1891	10537
1872	7189	1901	11496
1873	7798	1911	15175
1874	7998		

Charles Raymond.

Raymond's Sewing Machine Co.

perity due to the Franco-Prussian War and the expenditures for the construction of the Wellington, Grey and Bruce Railway, industries expanded rapidly and several new manufacturies were started. In particular, the Bell Organ Company; Armstrong, McCrae & Co.; J.B. Armstrong & Co.; McLeod, Wood & Co.; Raymond Sewing Machine Company; Tolton Brothers and Osborn & Wilkie (Guelph Sewing Machine Company); and all the local flour mills enjoyed huge success. A description in the *Toronto Telegraph* in 1870, of the business carried on by the Raymond Sewing Machine Company, gives a good idea of why these enterprises succeeded:

One of the oldest established and most successful manufacturers of sewing machines in the Western Province is Chas. Raymond, of Guelph. This establishment was first started in 1862, since which it has at various times been enlarged to meet the requirements of a rapidly expanding business... About a year ago...to secure an increased manufacturing capacity, Mr. Raymond purchased the adjoining Knox Church, and upon the removal of the congregation to their new edifice, he, at an expense of several thousand dollars, added the old kirk to his former factory.... Mr. Raymond, in addition to the Raymond's improved chain stitch machine [his original patent], formerly the sole manufacture, now makes a much improved shuttle machine, and has lately produced still another, a heavier and stronger specimen, styled No. 2, of the same pattern, but more adapted in the requirements of heavy sewing and manufacturing purposes. Judging by the perfections of its workings we are inclined to believe that it will prove one of the most valuable saving assistants yet offered to tailors, and those who sew for a living. The factory provides constant employment to between 70 and 80 people, and the annual value of the sewing machines is over one hundred thousand dollars.[20]

Like the "Raymond" sewing machine, the "Osborn", made by the Guelph Sewing Machine Company, was a consistent winner at exhibitions across the Province. For example, in 1870 the "Osborn" machines won three firsts at the Western Fair, and two firsts and two seconds at the Provincial Exhibition.[21] The key to the "Osborn's" success, as with the "Raymond", was innovation and quality of workmanship. With a pardonable pride, the manufacturers advertised:

THE OSBORN
LOCK STITCH SEWING MACHINE—
COMPLETE $35.

"The Osborn" is assuredly the King of Sewing Machines. It is the most substantially built, has the fewest working parts, and the easiest accessible. Derangements and breakages are obviated in consequence of the excellent mechanism employed in its construction. It is beautiful in design and finish, incomparable in the simplicity of its construction, very rapid in its movements, and the most thoroughly perfected yet offered purchasers. It is built on the "cam" principle, the more lasting and only reliable one. Runs with the precision of a steam engine. Is capable of performing a range of work hitherto thought impossible for Sewing Machines. A trial will convince the most skeptical [*sic*] of its unquestionable superiority. At the late Provincial Exhibition, in the 25 entries in the Family Sewing Machines class, The OSBORN was awarded the second prize: at Berlin County Show, the first prize over Howe, Singer, Lockman and Raymond. . . .[22]

Nor were such advertisements by Raymond and the Guelph Sewing Machine Company idle boasts. In 1876 the American Consul in Guelph reported that, in spite of high U.S. tariffs, $158,180.80 worth of sewing machines was shipped to the American market. This figure is significant when it is remembered that only one other manufactured product, malt, having a value of $79,450.81, was even mentioned in the total Guelph exports of $710,183.39 to the United States for that year.[23]

GUELPH SEWING MACHINE COMPANY

Factory and Show Rooms—Nelson Crescent, road leading to the Great Western Station.

"THE OSBORN"

Family and Light Manufacturing Sewing Machine.

Perfect, Simple and Reliable—incomparably ahead of all Competitors

*Advertisement, The Osborn Sewing Machine.
(Guelph Evening Mercury, November 22, 1870)*

Similar evidence regarding quality can be found in Guelph's other major manufactured products. For example in 1870 Armstrong, McCrae & Co., won first prizes at the Provincial Exhibition for many items including woollen shirts, drawers, socks, stockings, shawls, mitts, etc.[24] At the same exhibition, a Toronto newspaper said of J.B. Armstrong's carriages:

In the department of carriages these veteran exhibitors are, as usual, the most fortunate prize winners. They exhibit four carriages, two cutters, a hearse and a set of wheels. Their record on the present occasion is six first prizes, and one extra prize, making a grand total of twenty-two first prizes gained by them at the different Provincial Exhibitions. One of their entries, a double seated sleigh, is a novel design, and judging from its merits likely to become a very popular vehicle. The foot-board of the back seat, when closed, converts it into a single sleigh. Another of its advantages is its roomy capacity, the space underneath the seats affording accommodation for a large amount of luggage.[25]

With the expansion of Guelph's manufacturing firms, population once again began to increase as workers flocked to take jobs. Commercial prosperity returned, and new buildings were erected in the downtown area. So strong was the Town's image as a growth centre, and so well established were its factories, that despite the general depression of 1875-1880, Guelph's population continued to grow, as per table XXVII.

In reviewing the Town's economic situation, the President of the Board of Trade commented in February, 1877, upon the contrast between the difficult and depressed business conditions on the one hand and the continued growth in population and building on the other. He said:

Your Council regret that the trade and commerce

of the Dominion for the past two years has been in a very depressed condition, and that so far there is no good ground for believing that commercial prosperity is about to return at once. . . . But whilst the trade and commerce of the Town has been very depressed, in some respects Guelph has progressed more within the past two years than it ever did before in the same space of time, as is evidenced by the magnificent blocks of buildings erected for commercial purposes, and the very great number of dwelling houses, from the humble cottage of the labourer to the mansion of the wealthy. We find that during the year 1875 there were erected 130 buildings at a cost of $200,000; and in 1876, 160 buildings at a cost of $275,000.[26]

In 1877, 1878 and 1879, the international depression affected Guelph severely. Not only did foreign manufacturers dump their surplus goods into Canadian markets at ruinous prices, but the American government increased tariffs drastically, thereby effectively closing their doors to Canadian manufactured products. For Guelph's sewing machine industry these changes amounted to near disaster. Whereas in 1876 they had shipped $158,180 worth of machines to the United States, in the first quarter of 1877 this figure had been reduced to $7,003.16.[27]

With the Town's manufacturing severely curtailed, the loss of the market area to the north began to have its full effect. Unemployment rose, and many of the Town's citizens experienced hardship and suffering. An article in the *Guelph Evening Mercury* in December, 1878, gives some idea of this situation:

Soup Kitchen.—Mrs. Edwards, the matron of the soup kitchen has received permission. . .to use the engine house for a soup kitchen. . . . There is much destitution in the Town at the present time, and the poor that are out of employment will hail the advent of the soup kitchen with joy. Ever since winter set in children and women have paid diurnal visits

Advertisement, J.B. Armstrong & Co., Cutters and Sleighs. (Guelph Evening Mercury, November 21, 1870)

to Mrs. Edwards to enquire at what time the kitchen would be open to relieve the destitute. No doubt now, that the kitchen has been opened, the ladies of the Town who have in previous years superintended the distribution of charity, will not be backwards in again stepping in the breach. It is pleasing to learn that room has been provided for the distribution of soup, even though the Town is somewhat cramped. Farmers and others who will leave turnips, carrots, peas, meat, and bread, will receive the thanks of the suffering for their generosity.[28]

As a result of the economic losses experienced at that time, John Horsman, a hardware merchant and local conservative, wrote to Sir John A. Macdonald concerning the political and economic climate in Guelph. It had been proposed that the Governor-General, the Marquis of Lorne, and his wife, Princess Louise, should visit Guelph to take part in the celebration of Guelph's elevation to City status. In recommending against their visit, Horsman's letter read as follows:

The Town Council have appointed a deputation consisting of the Mayor [George Howard] & F.J. Chadwick [proprietor of the *Guelph Herald* and ex-Mayor of Guelph] to invite his Excellency and Her Royal Highness to honor us with their presence on the 23rd [of April] (St. George's day) to celebrate the inauguration of this Town into a City.

When the proper time comes (*not now*) the whole population of the City and County will be delighted to see them and will turn out en masse and go for any reasonable expense for the occasion.

I know it would be an exceedingly unpopular move now, there is a strong feeling against it by leading men of all parties, and they even talk of getting up a public meeting to oppose it. I mean their coming so early as the 23rd April. . . .

Horsman's Hardware, Lower Wyndham Street, circa 1870.

The depressed times and consequent scarcity of money is of course the chief cause assigned to their objection.

Their Excellencies will in all probability visit Toronto and other places within the Summer and when the Country will appear at its best. Should they then honor us all, *all classes will turn out with a heartiness that would do credit to the Queen.*

The fact is, Sir John, you know better than I can tell you that the whole country has been left by Mackenzie's Government in such a deplorable condition that the people are depressed in spirit & no town I think feels this worse than Guelph. Should the Marquis and Her Royal Highness be advised to delay their visit till later in the Spring or Summer all classes will by that time understand the benefits likely to result from your National Policy and everything will be *buoyant*; speaking of this, allow me to congratulate you on your successful efforts to so rearrange the tariff that it pleases nearly every body excepting of course that dreadfully partisan sheet the [Toronto] Globe and the smaller fry its echo—the Grits round here never expected your Government could have accomplished so well what they had not brains to do—but to return, Guelph is now the dullest place in the province & quite uninviting—David Allan's Mills & Distillery have lately passed into other hands paying about 10 cts. in the $. The Wilkie & Osborn Sewing Machine Factory all Mortgaged to the Bank of Commerce & working on half time. The Raymond Factory but little better, Cossitt's Agricultural works under a cloud, McBean & Co. [wholesale] Hardware called another meeting of their Creditors, the Guelph Lumber Co., friend [Donald] Guthrie (opposite) could tell you how a lot of business men in Guelph have been soaped into that & how it is paying and that the Ontario Bank is worrying them about to death.[29]

Macdonald took Horsman's advice and the Governor-General delayed his visit to Guelph until the following September.[30] Of the firms mentioned by Horsman, Allan's Mills had been sold to David Spence of Brantford, and by 1884-1886 the Guelph Sewing Machine

Arch constructed for the visit of the Marquis of Lorne and Princess Louise in 1879.

Company was known as the Guelph Sewing Machine and Novelty Works with Russell & McCrae as owners; and the Guelph Agricultural Works (Levi Cossitt) had William O'Connor as proprietor. The Raymond Sewing Machine Company, however, retained its original owners. The economic situation was further complicated by the decision of the old Guelph firm of Inglis and Hunter to move to Toronto in 1881.

John Inglis was, in most respects, a typical Guelph manufacturer. A short biographical sketch, taken from *Mechanical and Milling News*, October, 1886, gives a good picture of the "mechanic" turned "manufacturer":

Mr. Inglis was born in the parish of Castleton, Roxboroughshire, Scotland (better known as Leddesdale), on the 12th January, 1823. At an early age he began an apprenticeship with Thomas Anderson, millwright, in Gallowshiels. When "out of his time" he left his native land and went to England, finding employment in the Vauxhall Foundry in Liverpool. From Liverpool, after a time, he removed to Manchester, and spent some years in the service of Sir William Fairburn, after which he worked three years in the Government steam dock yard at Portsmouth. When here he made up his mind to come to Canada, and arrived here in the year 1850. For seven years after coming to this country, he worked with Thomas Lowrie, of St. Catharines, the celebrated millwright, building such well known mills as J. & R. Lowrie's Mills, Port Dalhousie, Ont. [*sic*]; Coleman's Mills, Port Robinson, Ont.; Chisholm's Mills, Oakville, Ont.; the Campbell Mills, Cayuga, Ont.; Ford's Mills, Simcoe, Ont.; Brown, Band & Chamber's Mills, Dunnville, Ont.; and Webster's Mills, Dundas, Ont. He also worked for Jno. Gartshore & Co., Dundas, for three years, and was foreman pattern-maker at the time the Hamilton Waterworks were built. In 1860, he went to Guelph and formed a co-partnership with Thos. Mair and Francis Evatt, under the title of Mair, Inglis & Evatt, the firm doing business in the old Wellington Foundry, formerly carried on by John Watt. After six years, changes were made in the firm, which then became Evatt, Inglis & Co., and continued so for five years, or until 1871, when Mr. Evatt retired, and Mr. Hunter, Mr. Inglis' present partner became associated with him under the style of Inglis & Hunter. This firm carried on a large business in Guelph, both in mill building and engineering, until the fall of 1881, when they deemed it advisable to remove their business to Toronto, purchasing their present commodious workshops on Strachan Avenue from the defunct Canada Car Co.[31]

John Inglis' decision to move was, apparently, a wise one because five years after the move it was reported that:

The last five years has seen a wonderful increase in the volume and extent of their business, it is now double what it ever was in Guelph. The firm have the honor of making the first Corless engine built in Canada, having started the manufacture of this class of engines the year of the [American] Centennial [1876]. They also enjoy a reputation for marine boilers, etc., second to none on the continent. In the early part of this year [1886], they obtained the sole right to manufacture in Canada the Case patent mill machinery, and are going into the business with all their well-known push and energy.[32]

Guelph could ill afford such a loss, and although it was believed that Macdonald's National Policy[33] would aid manufacturing in general, it was recognized that something had to be done, some direct action taken, if Guelph's industries and commerce were to share fully in the benefits of the National Policy.

During the period of economic expansion from 1871 to 1875, the Guelph Board of Trade meetings became less frequent, and fewer projects appear to have been undertaken. Now, with the Town once again in the grip of a depression, businessmen turned to the Board of Trade as an important institution in the solution of their problems.

At the Annual Meeting in February, 1877, the President of the Board of Trade, Robert Melvin, gave this assessment of the Board's value, function and accomplishments:

In presenting to the Board what might be called their annual report, your Council regret that they are not in a position to give as full and accurate a statement of the trade and commerce of the Town as they would desire to do, in consequence of the Board and Council not having been as active and regular in their meetings as they should have been. But we would express the hope, that with a fresh organization, and a determination to impart a new life and vitality, the Board may go on and prosper and fulfil the laudable objects contemplated by its founders, namely the bringing together of the businessmen and manufacturers of the Town, to consider and talk over topics of mutual interest, not only as affecting the Town but likewise the country at large, on matters relating to trade, commerce and manufacturing. By such conferences your Council know that during the short time the Board was in active operation it was the direct means of giving to us increased railroad facilities, return tickets; suggested and inaugurated the Elmira road. . ., kept close watch over all legislation affecting trade and commerce and in a great many ways directly or indirectly aided and directed measures for the benefit of trade and commerce generally.[34]

The revitalized Board of Trade soon determined that two main objectives had to be achieved: civic improvement to attract more customers to the stores and shops; and subsidization—direct and indirect—to aid the manufacturers. An important step in both strategies was the acquisition of City status.

City government, although more costly, gave much wider powers to municipal councils, but required a population of 10,000. Therefore, in April, 1878, when it was announced that the assessment rolls showed the Town's population had reached 9,918, immediate steps were taken to request the Provincial Government to pass the necessary legislation to raise Guelph to the status of a City. In spite of some delay, April twenty-third, 1879, the fifty-second anniversary of Guelph's founding, was named as the day on which its new charter would take effect.[35]

In preparation for the festival, every effort was made to follow John Galt's example, and to make the event one which would linger long in the memories of all those who attended. First of all, the Town was decorated and beautified to a degree never before attempted. The *Guelph Weekly Herald* said:

Flags were displayed with great profusion throughout the City. The Royal Standard floated from the City Hall, and underneath, in the dome were transparencies representations of the arms of the national societies. The White Horse of Brunswick, the arms [new City crest] of the Royal City was particularly noticeable, and attracted very considerable attention. From this central point, flags and bunting were discernable on almost every public building, stores, and private residences. Everybody seemed to have vied with every other body in showing so far as decorations, bunting, flags, etc., were concerned, that they felt that the greatest day in Guelph's history had arrived. . . .

The Wyndham Street stores were actually the glory of Guelph. They are palatial and magnificent in appearance on ordinary occasions, but the effect of the decorations on their exteriors, and the freshly dressed windows with suitable goods made up a holiday display such as reminded one of the descriptions of Oriental streets. The street, had been scraped, cleaned and watered, which, besides adding much to the appearance of the business portion of the Town, added much to the comfort of those walking and driving. The other streets had been straightened up, and the whole appearance of the City was so cleanly, so happy-looking, and so holiday-like that visitors were not sparing in their need of praise. Commendations of the conduct of the City's inhabitants were as freely bestowed as deserved.[36]

The second major event of the day was a gala parade, the largest in Guelph's history. It required twenty-two minutes to pass one point, and followed the following route: from the City Hall, east, past the Royal Hotel and railway station then along Woolwich, Suffolk and Glasgow Streets, Waterloo Avenue, Norfolk, Woolwich and Wyndham Streets, and back to City Hall. The order of procession was as follows:

Grand Marshal—Charles Sharpe, Esq.
Thos. Lynch (first male child born in Guelph),
bearing
the Royal Standard.
Lieut.-Col. Armstrong commanding militia.
Artillery Brigade Band.
Wellington Field Battery and Ontario Field Battery, with

field pieces, under command of Major
Macdonald and Capt. McCrae.
30th Battalion Band.
Guelph Rifles, no. 2 company under command of
Capt. Speirs.
Eramosa Rifles, under command of Capt. Mutrie.
Goderich band.
His Worship Mayor Howard, ex-Mayors Chadwick
and Harvey, Mayor Beatty, Toronto; and Mayor
Carlyle, of St. Catharines, in a carriage.
City Council with guests in carriages.
Board of Education.
Chas. Knowles, Mounted Marshal St. George's
Society.
Preston band.
Banner of St. George's Society.
St. George's Society.
29th battalion band.
J.C. Chadwick Mounted President St. Patrick's
Society.
Banner of St. Patrick's Society.
St. Patrick's Benevolent Society.
Mounted Marshals G.S.Grange and J.McAstocker.
Banner of St. Patrick's Benefit Society.
P. Mahon, Marshal.
St. Patrick's Benefit Society.
Banner of St. Andrew's and Caledonian Societies,
borne by four, and David Massie, in Highland
costume, walking under the banner
Pipers Ross, Smith and Mathieson.
St. Andrew's and Caledonian Societies.
C. Chase, Chairman Fire and Water Committee,
with visiting fire brigade officials in carriage.
28th Battalion Band, Stratford.
Stratford fire brigade, with salvage wagon.
Preston fire brigade.
Berlin fire brigade with banner.
Mitchell fire brigade.
Guelph Silsby steam fire engine.
Guelph fire brigade.
Guelph hose carriage and reel.
Guelph hook and ladder company.
Hook and ladder truck.
Geo. Hood, Marshal of butcher's company,
mounted with white tunic and red hat band.
Oakville band and banner.
45 butchers, mounted, three abreast, with white

tunics and red hat bands.
John Bunyan, with old fashioned cart and ox team,
containing old V. harrow and plow, and
bearing the legend "Guelph Agri-
cultural works in 1826."
Mitchell band.
Herald and Mercury offices representation,
consisting of men setting type and a small
Gordon press in operation.
St. Marys band.
Sleeman's monster cask of lager beer, on which was
sitting Walter Cook, who weighs 350 pounds.
Sleeman's small cask representation.
Holliday's brewery.
G.D. Pringle's jewellery case.
J. Hewer, Jr., Flour and Feed.
Chas. Raymond's Sewing Machines.
Weir, Bryce & Co's Confectionery Wagon.
W. Kerr's Tin Wagon, with men at work on it.
Cossitt's Agricultural Works.
Four Wagons.
Hearn's Pure North River Ice Manufactory.
Tolton Bros. Agricultural Works.
Collins & O'Connor's Agricultural Works.
Gilchrist Bros. Floral Wagon.
Wellington Marble Works,
McQuillan & Hamilton.
J. & A. Armstrong's Carpet Loom in operation.
W. Bell & Co's Organ Manufacture.
Guelph Carriage Goods Company's representative
wagon.
McConnell & Thompson, Carriage Works.
E.D. Clark's Photographic Show.[37]

The parade had its desired purpose, as the
Herald commented in this amusing quote:

The unique and appropriate representation of the
agricultural works of Guelph in 1826, when the city
was founded by John Bunyan and others, excited
much favorable comment, and involuntarily all
eyes were directed to the great progress made in
this industry, and which was amply represented in
the procession.[38]

Nowhere was the attempt to rally the spirits

of Guelph's residents more apparent than in the proclamation naming Guelph a City, and in the addresses presented by the various public figures. Two speeches, one by Mayor Howard, of Guelph, the other by Mayor Beatty of Toronto, are worthy of note. In part, Mayor Howard said:

Like many present, I can remember when the ground upon which we are standing, and all the land south of the Catholic church was a dense forest, with only a chopped wagon road here and there through it, and I have seen every change municipally since 1851, when it formed part of the Township of Guelph, and had usually one representative in the Township Council. In 1851 it was incorporated as a village, and in 1856 as a Town, I attended the first meeting of the council at which my friend John Smith was elected the first mayor. While Guelph has always made steady progress since its survey made 52 years ago, its more rapid progress dates from its incorporation as a Town, the market being established the same year, and the railways being in operation since that time, it has enjoyed a continued prosperity, gratifying, not only to our citizens but equally so to the people of Wellington, of which it is the County Town.[39]

The official proclamation, read by Mayor

LEFT TO RIGHT: *John Harvey, City Clerk and Treasurer of Guelph. George Howard, Esq., Mayor of Guelph. Frederick Jasper Chadwick, Esq., Ex-Mayor of Guelph. (The Canadian Illustrated News, May 17, 1879)*

Howard as part of his speech, was as follows:

Whereas the corporation of the Town of Guelph have by their petition, represented that the said Town contains a population of upwards of ten thousand souls and that the said population is rapidly increasing, and that the said Town, by reason of its increased and extensive railway facilities, its large manufacturing and mercantile interests, and its situation in the midst of a rich agricultural district, is now, and will continue to be, an important commercial centre; and whereas the said corporation by their petition have prayed that the said Town might be erected into a City, to be called "The City of Guelph;" and whereas it is expedient to grant the prayer of the said petition;

Therefore Her Majesty, by and with the advice and consent of the Legislative Assembly of the Province of Ontario enacts as follows:

On and after the twenty-third day of April next after the passing of this Act, the said Town of Guelph shall be, and is hereby incorporated as a City, and shall be known hereafter as the Corporation of the City of Guelph, and as such shall enjoy and possess all the rights, powers and privileges which could have been exercised and enjoyed by the said City of Guelph if the same had been incorporated as a City under the provisions of "The Municipal Act" instead of under this Act.

By the authority of the Act of Parliament just read, I do now declare the municipality of Guelph to be incorporated as the City of Guelph, and I do further declare that the said City shall hereafter be known as the Royal City.[40]

Mayor Beatty of Toronto spoke glowingly of Guelph's future:

He said that on behalf of the Queen City of the west he was proud and happy to greet the Royal City of the interior. Toronto would never be jealous of Guelph, but rather rejoice over the rapid strides she was making in material prosperity and population. He glanced briefly at the history of the new City. It was a matter of rejoicing that the country was always advancing. True, there might be occasionally periods of exceptionally hard times, but notwithstanding, the march of Canadian enterprise

was never stopped. It never came to a standstill. The agricultural and manufacturing industries of Canada never stood still or went backward. As for the Royal City, with her prosperous manufacturing establishments and the splendid agricultural country in the midst of which she was situated, he would not be surprised to see her double her present population in a few years.[41]

This celebration did much to reduce tension and raise the spirits and expectations of the citizens.

Now that City status had been achieved, Guelph quickly proceeded to consider the question of subsidies to encourage manufacturers to locate within their municipality. Other cities were willing to subsidize industries in competition with Guelph; therefore, if Guelph wanted to grow, it would be necessary for its manufacturers to receive subsidies sufficiently large to overcome any disadvantages due to location and the cost of transportation. In discussing the merits of subsidies, the *Guelph Mercury* argued:

Let us once more scan our position as a city with respect to this question. We are at a disadvantage as compared with some other towns and cities in the matter of railway competition. Several places offer bonuses to well established industries to locate in their midst. We desire to flourish in trade. We must, therefore, offer some inducement to industries as an equivalent for that railway competition which we do not possess and which other places do, and we must offer these inducements also because other places are doing the same. Is that not a reasonable conclusion?

But there is more than justice on the side of the [subsidization] by-law. There is a powerful argument in the shape of what it means financially and industrially to Guelph. . . . It will immediately feel the benefit of money expended among masons, carpenters, laborers and others engaged in the erection of the new factory. Those who have houses to rent and land to sell will find an extra demand for the same in consequence of the additional number of men to be employed. Merchants will realize larger sales for the same reason. These are the classes who will be indirectly benefitted.[42]

Guelph did, however, set up requirements to define eligibility for industrial subsidization and how it was to be applied. First, it normally took the form of a remission of taxes and free water for a period of ten years after the new business was established. Secondly, subsidies were given to a new enterprise only when its products were not already manufactured in Guelph. This was true whether a new firm wished to move to Guelph or an old firm wished to expand into a new line of merchandise. Third, attempts were made to write into the subsidization by-law certain guarantees of performance on the part of the company. These requirements generally stipulated the minimum number of persons to be employed in order that the company might retain its subsidy. The first by-law of this type, No. 29, passed June 21, 1880, offering the firm of A. Murchy and Company a remission of taxes for ten years to establish a factory for the manufacture of malleable iron castings, contained these restrictions:

Provided, however, and the exemption herein contained is based upon the express conditions first that there shall be continuously employed in and about the said Manufacturing Establishment after the same shall have been put in operation and exclusive of the owners or Lessees thereof an average Number of not less than ten employees or Workmen.

And second that the said Establishment shall be operated Solely and exclusively in the production of Malleable Iron Castings.

The said Establishment shall nevertheless in each year be assessed in the usual way and rated and placed on the Collection Roll but on production to the Mayor of the said City on or before the first day of December in each year of satisfactory evidence of the preceding Conditions having been Complied with the taxes Assessed and rated against the said Establishment shall not be Collected and the Mayor's Certificate that such evidence has been produced shall be a Sufficient Authority to the Collector to and it shall be his duty to refrain from Collecting such taxes.[43]

Over the years, many Guelph industries received such subsidies.[44] It must be made clear, however, that the City Council's subsidization policy had the support of the property owners, who comprised at least half of the City's taxpayers. Although such policies would increase taxation, it was recognized that Guelph's prosperity depended upon the employment of the maximum number of workers.

For the first few years of the operation of Macdonald's National Policy and Guelph's program of industrial subsidization, the results appeared to be worth the cost. With the huge infusion of foreign capital to build the Canadian Pacific Railway and the creation of protected markets, several of Guelph's industries expanded rapidly. In a survey of selected industries conducted by the Canadian Government in 1885, it was reported that between 1878 and 1884 employment in Guelph had virtually doubled from 517 in 10 industries to 1,050 in 13.[45] The *Guelph City Directory* for 1885-1886 gives this description of the City's major employers:

Prominent among them may be mentioned Raymond's Sewing Machine Works, employing 200 hands; the Bell Organ Works, employing 200 hands; the Woollen Mills of McCrae and Co., employing 250 hands; the Piano Factories of Sweetnam and Hazelton, and of Rainer and Son, employing 25 hands each; Gowdy's Agricultural Works, employing from 50 to 60 hands; **Guelph**

Carpet Factory, employing 35 hands; Silver Creek Brewery, employing 30 to 35 hands; the Foundry of Thos. Worswick, employing 30 hands; Crowe's Iron Works, 30 hands; Stewart's Planing Mill, 30 hands; the Furniture Factory of Burr Bros., 85 hands; the Foundry of W.H. Mills, 21 hands; the Cigar Factory of Solomon Myers, 20 hands; the Guelph Sewing Machine and Novelty Works, 60 hands; the extensive Flouring Mills of James Goldie; the Guelph Carriage Goods Works, employing from 50 to 70 hands; the Ornamental Flower Goods Factory of W.H. Marcon, employing 25 to 30 hands; Brown's Boot and Shoe Factory, 22 hands; the Guelph Buggy Top Works; the Organ Factory of T. James & Co.; the Foundry of Robertson & Son; the Guelph Axle Works [T. Pepper & Co.]; the Oatmeal Mill of H. Murton; Tolton's Agricultural Works; the Union Foundry; Thain's Agricultural Implement Factory; the Knitting Factory of Francis Smith; Clark & Thompson's Carpet Works; Eureka Paint and Color Co., and others of lesser note.[46]

As time went on, subsidies were extended to many industries in an effort to maintain steady employment.

During the 1880's, Guelph's position was further aggravated by the monopolistic freight pricing policies of the Grand Trunk Railway. As far back as the 1850's, discussions had been held between the Grand Trunk and Great Western Railway Directors regarding either amalgamation or freight rate agreements. One such agreement, signed June 12, 1867, provided that:

Whereas, with a view to avoid undue competition and to facilitate and encourage the interchange of traffic between the systems of the two Companies to the extent of the circumstances of both will conveniently admit of, to establish uniform and remunerative rates and fares, and generally to place and continue the relations of the two Companies upon a perfectly friendly footing, the two said Companies

have agreed to co-operate as hereinafter mentioned, and to secure to each other such rights and facilities, and to enter into such arrangements as are hereinafter contained. Now, therefore, it is hereby mutually agreed between the two Companies' parties hereto as follows:

1. Equal fares, rates, and charges (to be from time to time agreed upon between the two Companies), shall be charged by the said Companies in respect of traffic between all competitive places, which the two Companies can respectively command, that is in respect of traffic to or from stations in Canada.[47]

Included in the list of points between which all competition would end were Guelph and Toronto, Guelph and Buffalo, Guelph and Suspension Bridge and Guelph and Detroit.[48] In effect, this agreement ended any benefits that Guelph might have derived from being at the junction of two rail lines.

In 1882, this agreement became permanent when the Grand Trunk and Great Western Companies amalgamated. The *Guelph Evening Mercury* put the situation clearly:

Guelph people had congratulated themselves that at any rate they had two competing railways, in the Grand Trunk and Great Western, this City being on the main line of the former and on the Wellington, Grey and Bruce branch of the latter, so that the situation was not considered too bad, but in August, 1882, this comfort was removed by the amalgamation of these two railways and Guelph became a one railway town. It was gradually realized also that Guelph was now on the main line of the Grand Trunk in name only, and that in reality the Great Western from Toronto to Hamilton, London and the western border, had become the main line of the Grank Trunk. With one railway it was felt that we were at a disadvantage in the matter of rates, of getting cars promptly and in other ways. We were out of direct touch with many parts of this Province and of our own district. . . .[49]

Once again Guelph felt the need to acquire a competing rail line.

No sooner had those energetic promoters, George Laidlaw, Francis Shanly and their Toronto associates in the Toronto, Grey and Bruce Railway succeeded in the launching of that line, than they began looking for other railway projects. One possibility that caught their eyes was the fact that a number of previously prosperous towns such as Streetsville, Milton, Galt, Elora, Fergus and Orangeville, were in economic decline and anxious for better railway accommodation. Laidlaw's answer was a sprawling, many-branched railway which called itself the Credit Valley. Built almost entirely with municipal bonuses and loans, its lines bracketed Guelph, with the main branch running through Milton, Morriston and Galt to the south, and another branch connecting Caledon, Hillsburgh, Fergus and Elora to the north.[50] The Credit Valley Railway was officially opened in 1879, and in 1883 it was amalgamated with the Ontario and Quebec Railway as part of the Canadian Pacific network. It was to this new line that Guelph now looked for relief. A connection with the Credit Valley would not only break the Grand Trunk monopoly but give Guelph's manufacturers direct connections with all points on the Canadian Pacific Railway and its subsidiary lines.

The seriousness with which Guelph's residents viewed the Grand Trunk's monopoly was expressed in a private letter written by James Goldie to Sir John A. Macdonald:

This City is at the mercy of the Grand Trunk Railway, our Millers are subjected to unjust, unfair and ruinously high rates when compared to what American millers pay. Our Importers and Exporters have all the same grievances and the G.T. Ry., in having the control, is not improving the trade in an otherwise energetic community.[51]

A news story in the *Guelph Mercury* pointed out that freight rates from Montreal to Guelph were 22 cents per hundred pounds while Galt, which had two railways in competition, paid only 16 cents per hundred pounds.[52] As one commentator argued in 1884:

These railway companies make fair promises to secure the monopoly of a paying business, but they never give one inch more than they have to, until competition compels them. There is enterprise, energy and capital enough in this City to guarantee the construction of a branch line [to tap the Credit Valley Railway] on short order. All that is wanted is united and concerted action.[53]

A charter for the Guelph Junction Railway, to run from the City to "some point between Campbellville and Galt" was obtained from the Federal Government in 1884.[54] As the list of incorporators shows, the project had wide support. The incorporators were: Caleb Chase, Edward O'Connor, James Innes, Frederick Jasper Chadwick, Thomas Gowdy, J.B. Armstrong, John Hogg, Frederick B. Skinner, Donald Guthrie, Nathaniel Higinbotham, William Bell, Charles Raymond, David Stirton, Charles Davidson, Thomas Auchmuty Keating, John A. Wood, John M. Bond, John Harris, David McCrae, William Nichol, Duncan McFarlane and Peter Gilchrist.[55] Chase, O'Connor, Armstrong, Bell, Davidson and McCrae were named Provisional Directors.[56] Although a number of meetings of the City Council, Board of Trade and Provisional Directors were held in 1884, the projected cost—approximately $200,000—proved to be more than the incorporators could raise at the time.

By the fall of 1885, however, the local situation had become more difficult and the necessity of acquiring a direct connection with the Credit Valley-Canadian Pacific network was once again raised. A letter appeared in the

Guelph Mercury dated December 11, 1885:

Dear Sir,—We are on the eve of a municipal election when matters of public interest are discussed. The general depression of business has been of long duration and the effect keenly felt. There are, however, some few places that have by well directed effort secured the best facilities for doing business, and have been abundantly rewarded with deserved success, notably; Galt, Woodstock and St. Thomas, all of which are on the line of the Canada [*sic*] Pacific Railway, from which they derive great advantage. With the same facilities for shipping and competitive rates, Guelph would be a successful rival to any of these places. Situated as we are distant only ten or a dozen miles from a point where the C.P.R. might be tapped, it is astonishing to think of the apathy and indifference that has prevented our securing before now, a connection with this road. Surely this is a matter of greater consequence than the petty subjects usually discussed at ward meetings and on nomination days.[57]

This letter evidently represented the feelings of many Guelph citizens, for by December twenty-first, C.E. Lumsden, Chief Engineer of the C.P.R. was in town to discuss the feasibility of the Guelph Junction line. The *Mercury* reported:

Mr. C.E. Lumsden, chief engineer of the Western Division of the C.P.R., arrived on Monday by the 11.30 train, and met the Mayor, the members of the City Council, the Railway Committee, Board of Trade, and a number of our business men, to have a talk on matters connected with the proposed Guelph Junction Railway. The meeting was convened in the parlor of the Royal Hotel, and Mr. James Innes appointed chairman. After some conversation Messrs. Brill, Hatch and Chase were deputed to accompany Mr. Lumsden on a tour of inspection with the view of looking up the best site of a terminus in Guelph. These gentlemen left on their errand, and after an hour's conversation on matters pertaining to the projected line, the meeting adjourned till half past three in the afternoon, to hear Mr. Lumsden's report.[58]

According to the committee and Lumsden, the best route was:

To follow the course of the river past the limekilns and quarries and mills, cross the Grand Trunk below the railway bridge at Spence's [Allan's] mill, and keep up the west bank of the river to Eramosa bridge, having the passenger station somewhere between these two bridges. Then to extend a track for freight across the Eramosa bridge to Goldie's mill with the same facilities for loading and unloading there as the G.T.R. at present possesses.[59]

The Board of Trade and City Council were in full agreement.   In February, 1886, it was decided that the Guelph Junction Railway should be built, and that the entire cost should be carried by the City. Accordingly, the Federal Government was petitioned to extend the time required to undertake and complete the line, and the capital structure of the enterprise was changed in several important aspects. First, the nominal share capital was reduced from $60,000 to $30,000, of which ten percent was to be paid up in order to bring the charter into effect. Second, the City was to appoint three Directors and the "private shareholders", five. Finally, the Provisional Directors were given all the necessary powers to enter into agreements, contracts, etc.[60]

While the amendments to the charter of the Guelph Junction Railway were proceeding through Parliament, a final agreement was being worked out between the Guelph City Council and the Provisional Directors of the Guelph Junction Railway Company. The terms were: first, the City Council agreed to buy and to pay in full $20,000 worth of shares, and to lend to the Railway Company $155,000, an amount, it was believed, which would be sufficient to complete the line from east of Schaw Station[61] (now Puslinch Station) to Guelph; second, $1,000 to cover the purchase of ten shares was to be subscribed by each of ten leading citizens, but initially only $100 each had to be paid. From their number would be elected the five private Directors who would hold voting control of the line. Immediately William Bell, Charles Raymond, John Hogg, Thomas Gowdy, Charles Davidson, J.B. Armstrong and David McCrae paid in their $100 each to become eligible for directorships,[62] and shortly after, John M. Bond, Christian Kloepfer and George Sleeman were added to their number. When the first regular Board of Directors was organized on April 5, 1887, Bell, Bond, Gowdy, Raymond and McCrae were elected to represent the private shareholders, while the Mayor (A.H. Macdonald) W. Husband and Henry Hatch represented the City.[63]

Needless to say, the peculiarity of an arrangement whereby an enterprise, in which the City was to invest $175,000, was to be directed by a group of citizens whose investment was only $1,000, brought considerable public comment. The newspapers pointed out, however, that when Parliament had amended the Railway's charter, it had specifically rejected control by the City Council:

Section seven of the Act. . .reads as follows:— "No person shall be a Director of the Company unless he be a holder of at least ten shares of the stock of the Company, and have paid up all the calls thereon." It was proposed to add to this the following:— "Or unless he is a member of a municipal council holding stock or bonds in the said Company". The Minister of Railways objected to this on the ground that it was without precedent, and that it might have the effect of throwing the whole directorate into the hands of a council whose members were elected for an entirely different purpose. The clause was accordingly struck out.[64]

The campaign to persuade the ratepayers to back the $175,000 debenture by-law (the vote was scheduled for December, 1886), was opened with a series of advertisements placed in the *Guelph Mercury* by J.D. Williamson and Company, proprietors of the "Golden Lion" dry goods stores, situated at 5 and 7 Wyndham Street, Guelph, and 84 Oswald St., Glasgow, Scotland. This advertisement from the *Mercury* of July 2, 1886, was typical:

Guelph Must Boom.—Times are on the mend. Let us rise equal to the occasion and improve our opportunities. . . If we allow our manufactures to close up and move away without any effort on our part to retain them; if we see manufactures starting up in other places, which we might have had for very little cost to the City; if we sit calmly by in indolent lassitude and allow the G.T.R. to have a monopoly of our trade and the C.P.R. to cut off a large section of country, with which we at one time did a large trade, without any effort on our part to construct a line of railroad which would break the monopoly of the G.T.R. on the one hand, and reconnect a large trade which we have lost on the other, which Line we have reason to believe would prove a paying speculation from the first; the result must prove disastrous. . . .

The advantages of such a line would be innumerable. Some of the immediate benefits would be the reopening of Mr. Spence's mill, enlarging the trade of all our manufacturers, especially in the iron and milling line, where the freights are heavy, the cultivation of a wholesale and the increase of the retail trade of our merchants, our markets would increase and Guelph would become more of a shipping port. Manufacturers would settle here without any further inducements than those offered by the natural advantages of Guelph. We have no doubt that this railway would make Guelph boom for years to come, and would give her such a start as would enable her soon to take rank among the first cities in the land. . . . If we could only recognize the value of our heritage there is no place like her in Ontario.[65]

In the meantime, negotiations with the C.P.R. were drawing to a conclusion. In exchange for an exclusive lease of the Guelph Junction track, the C.P.R. agreed to pay to that Company forty percent of the gross receipts before expenses.

As the time for the debenture by-law vote drew near, feelings in the City ran high. According to the *Mercury*:

The G.T.R. authorities have taken time by the forelock and are working tooth and nail for the defeat of the railway by-law on Thursday next. This morning they had every available office man in their employ in the City sworn in as scrutineers. Those who are in favor of the by-law are warned to be on their guard and work from the commencement of the voting till its close, and thus show the G.T.R. monopoly that they are not caught napping.[66]

In response to this opposition, large display advertisements were placed by the leading merchants in an attempt to ensure the passage of the by-law. E.R. Bollert's, for example, read:

ELECTORS!

Vote for the BY-LAW

Help the City's property in the present crisis!
Help the Manufacturers!
Help the Merchants!
Help the Employers and the Employees!
Help the Live, Active, Energetic Men of Guelph!
To place the City in the Position of being the
Leading Manufacturing and Commercial
Centre of this portion of our fair Province.
We have to deal with the Guelph of TO-DAY, who
unless she bestirs herself will be distanced
in the race by her enterprising and growing
sister towns.[67]

Ryan Berkinshaw & Co., "P.S.—Remember we still sell Dry Goods", made this plea:

WHAT ARE YOU GOING TO DO ABOUT IT?
Will you vote for the
C. P. R.
And by so doing Boom the City, Increase the value of your Property, Increase the population and by so doing decrease the Taxes,
OR WILL YOU PLAY
Penny wise and Pound Foolish by Voting against the By-Law, and by so doing, Decrease the value of your Property, Decrease the population of our City by driving many to other places of work and by so doing Increase the present rate of Taxes which must follow if the population is less.
WE THINK
The wise man must see that it will be to his interest to place Guelph on the same footing as other towns and cities, and by so doing, keep what manufactures we have here now and as well induce others to locate here.

We are to-day receiving as much trade from the country as we may reasonably expect for some time to come, as it is as thickly populated to-day as it will be in ten years, so how can we expect the place to grow, if we do not create trade within ourselves by increasing the number of our manufactures, and that cannot be done without placing Guelph on the same footing as our neighboring towns.[68]

Finally, one commentator chose to answer directly those who were complaining that with tax remissions, free water, money bonuses and now a railway, Guelph's manufacturers were receiving a disproportionate degree of favour:

There should be no false jealousy of the manufacturers, for it is in them that the chances of the future prosperity of Guelph chiefly lie, none of us should grudge them prosperity and think they are the only ones to be benefitted. They risk their capital, they employ men and pay them, and spend the money in the place, which they get by the sale of their products far and wide. If they get rich we should rejoice and be glad, for their prosperity is ours, and will increase the value of every man's property be he rich or poor, and to those who have no property it will give steady work and payment therefor.[69]

C.P.R. train in front of the Priory, circa 1900.

This powerful editorial and advertising campaign had the desired effect. In reporting the results of the vote, the *Mercury* said:

There was never a harder fought election in Guelph. The friends of the by-law had a thorough organization, and from the time the polls opened at nine o'clock in the morning until they closed at five in the evening they never ceased to work and bring in voters. The opponents of the by-law also worked hard, but it was not long before they found that the hope of defeating the by-law was a forlorn one indeed, and towards the close of the polls they gave up the contest. . . .[70]

The final vote was 745 for and 144 against.

With the passage of the by-law, construction went forward rapidly, and finally, at the instigation of local Conservatives, the Federal government gave a subsidy of $3,200 per mile—$46,000—to the line.[71] In all, the railroad cost a little over $240,000, and was completed and leased to the C.P.R. on Sep-

tember 8, 1888. To complete the financing of the cost of construction, the Guelph Junction Railway Company was forced to borrow an additional $18,000 from the City. A by-law[72] to provide for this was passed on April 1st, 1889, but as there was some irregularity in the voting by the electors, it was contested by a Mr. Slater. The case went to a single court sitting in Toronto before Chief Justice Galt (Sir Thomas Galt—a son of John Galt) and on May 9th word was received that the by-law had been "Quashed".[73] On the advice of Mr. Donald Guthrie, City Solicitor, a second by-law was passed by City Council, but was voted down by the electors on July 18, 1889.[74] After further discussion, the Board of Trade recommended that a third by-law be drafted, and on December 9th, 1889, Council gave it second reading and agreed to submit it once again to the voters in the January, 1890, elections.[75] On January 20th, 1890, at the last meeting of the old Council, and following approval by the electors, the $18,000 by-law was read a third time and finally passed.[76]

Initially the returns on the line were disappointing. From 1888 to 1901 a total of $69,241.80 was earned by the railway, an average of only $5,326.29 per year—far less than the annual total of $13,365 required by the City to meet interest payments on the Guelph Junction Railway debentures. After 1901, however, that situation was quickly reversed, and the line became a profitable investment.

The true worth of the Guelph Junction Railway could not be measured in the dollar value of its traffic. Its purpose was to force the Grand Trunk to lower its rates and to put Guelph's manufacturers in a better competitive position. There can be no doubt that it was successful on this account.

Guelph Streetcar Number I in front of George Sleeman's residence on the Waterloo Road.

XII

Public Utilities, a Municipal First

The years 1901 to 1921 saw Guelph's population continue to grow, but at a somewhat slower pace. The vast majority of new residents were of English origin or descent, and by 1921 comprised almost half the population, while those of Scottish origin increased by about fifty per cent, as shown in Table XXVIII. The number of Irish inhabitants during this period remained relatively constant, many having moved to the United States or western Canada seeking improved opportunities. As well, there was an influx of non-British immigrants particularly of Italian and French origin, many of whom settled in St. Patrick's Ward.

During this period industrial bonusing continued, and the City became involved to a greater degree in municipal investment and public ownership. In the nineteenth century as long as the general public was the main consumer, there was little need for municipal ownership of services such as water, sewers, electricity, gas, etc. It was the need for greater industrial development which brought about the widespread support necessary for the public acquisition of these services.

The first of these utilities to be developed was for the provision of coal gas for lighting by

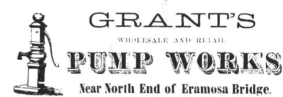
*Wooden pump advertised in
Guelph City Directory, 1882-83.*

the privately-owned gas company formed in 1870. The second, was the public water works established in 1878.

Until 1878, the needs of the Town for water were satisfied by private wells, cisterns and the Speed River. In addition, two or three public wells were maintained by the municipality for street watering and fire purposes, and for those persons who lived in the downtown area. One of these pumps stood at the corner of Wilson and Carden Streets and another at the old fire hall on Market Square.

In the municipal election of 1878, Mayor Howard campaigned for the creation of a public water works, pointing out that in the previous few years property worth more than $150,000 had been destroyed by fire because of an inadequate water supply. Although a num-

Table XXVIII
Population in Guelph by Country of Origin, 1881-1921[1]

	1881	*1901*	*1911*	*1921*
English	3866	4578	6383	9003
Irish	2810	3060	2874	2974
Scottish	2434	2550	3005	3720
Other British Isles	—	34	41	80
French	—	88	128	393
German	—	929	1267	774
Jewish	—	13	86	90
Italian	—	2	358	587
Polish	—	—	58	94
Chinese and Japanese	—	9	32	33
Black	—	94	91	44
Other	780	139	852	336
Total	9,890	11,496	15,175	18,128

ber of proposals were put forward to establish privately-owned water facilities, the fact that almost everyone had wells made such propositions of little interest. In the end, it was the great need for fire protection which persuaded the ratepayers that the creation of a waterworks and hydrant system was necessary.

As soon as he was elected, Mayor Howard established a committee to investigate the question.[2] In May, 1878, that committee proposed that the "Holly System" of waterworks be adopted, using a reservoir and standpipe to supply pressure for firefighting purposes. The Council accepted this proposal and immediately brought in a by-law to raise $75,000 to cover the cost of construction.[3] By the Guelph Waterworks Act of 1879, a three-man commission was established to manage the water works.

Because it was designed primarily for fire purposes, the initial proposal had been to use water from the Speed River for the system. In the course of construction, however, a spring was struck which had excellent drinking water and flowed at the rate of 250,000 gallons every twenty-four hours. This discovery opened the way for the water works to be used by industrial and domestic customers, and in 1880 an additional $25,000 was voted to put in the extra facilities.[4] As well, a catch basin was built at the river, and a line laid to the pumping station. Concerning this arrangement, one commentator in 1909 noted:

The old basin, which was never used, was made at the instance of the original Commissioners, viz.: Messrs. Morrison, Harris and Mitchell, for the purpose of keeping the river water and spring water entirely separate, and using the spring for all purposes so long as it would hold out. To provide for this contingency of shortage, or in case of fire, they built through the reservoir a tunnel to the river, so that the river water could be let into the pumping station direct. At such times the spring water was to be shut off.[5]

In 1883 the *City of Guelph Directory* gave this description of the system:

The City is supplied with pure spring water, obtained from living springs near the York road, and forced through the mains by means of the Holly system. About 13 miles of mains have thus far been laid, and 98 hydrants located at convenient points for emergencies of fire.[6]

Water rates were established which offered discounts to large users, and in numerous cases, free water was given to industries as part of the City's bonus system. Of course, both of these practices led to large scale, even wasteful use of water. On the other hand, although domestic users were few at first, they gradually became more numerous as surface drainage from hillsides and cesspools began to contaminate an increasing number of wells, and citizens began to appreciate the convenience of running water. As demand increased, the spring water reserves were more and more frequently exhausted, with the result that river water was introduced into the system on a regular basis. By 1887, the *Guelph Herald* made these observations in October of that year:

In the light of past events the admission made by Ald. [Thomas] Gowdy at the City Council meeting Monday evening is calculated to provoke a smile. "The water," he said, "at our end of the City is not fit to drink." Being twigged by several of the aldermen about his past declarations as to the crystal-like purity of the water, Ald. Gowdy replied that the water was all right, but there was mud in it,

"It was not the bonnet
But the head that was in it."

The *Herald* is prepared to agree with Ald. Gowdy on this point. Take the river water for instance. As it comes directly from the river, mixed with all the mud and filth gathered in its course, it is not fit to drink. But could the injurious foreign elements be removed by filtration or otherwise no one could object to the use of the water thus purified. Certainly no one objects to the water itself. . .The water is all right. It is the other stuff that comes mixed with it that the whole kick is about. . . .River water, unfiltered is not fit for domestic purposes.[7]

After a good deal of debate, the City Council in 1888 decided to borrow an additional $15,000 for extension and improvement of the system. The by-law vote was passed at the municipal elections in January, 1889, by a majority of only two, and was immediately challenged on the ground that many tenants (presumably down town residents with no wells of their own) had voted illegally.[8] In the end, the by-law was passed and the court challenge dropped.

During the 1890's, as more and more of the wells became contaminated and demand for water increased, mains were laid along most of the City streets. By 1894, seventeen miles of pipe costing $150,000 had been laid, and an average of 500,000 gallons per day was being pumped.[9] It was not long, however, before the ever-expanding demands of industrial and domestic customers, combined with a lack of proper maintenance, soon clogged the filter system, and water quality deteriorated rapidly. From the late 1890's on the number of cases of typhoid in Guelph increased, caused by contamination of its water supply.

In 1902, Doctor Howitt, the Medical Officer of Health reported that "There is no question about the advisability of having sewerage, not only as a matter of health, but as regards the future prosperity of the City. No doubt there are many who would have located in Guelph if we had had sewerage—people of means. They will not locate in the town, no matter whatever other advantages we may have, unless they have modern conveniences in the way of sewerage."[10]

Dr. H.O. Howitt, Medical Officer of Health.

At a special meeting of the Board of Trade held on April 25, 1902, the matter was debated at length with the Board finally passing a resolution to take a public stand in support of the sewer by-law.

In supporting this vote, the *Guelph Mercury* put forward these reasons:

On Monday the citizens will be called upon to vote on a by-law to provide for installing a system of sewerage in Guelph. The question has been discussed pro and con, letters have been published and all information that could be obtained concerning the system and the cost of its construction and maintenance has been freely given by the committee. . . .It now devolves upon the ratepayers to do their part in supporting the by-law. That sew-

erage is one of the great crying necessities of the City to-day, no reasonable person will dispute. Guelph, though a City, is years behind many of the smaller towns of the country in this respect. Sewerage is needed to insure the progress of the City, to increase its population, protect against disease, and to provide proper accommodation in factories, homes and stores.[11]

With Board of Trade backing, the sewerage vote passed by 573 to 303.[12]

It was decided to construct the sewage disposal works in Guelph Township along the Speed River west of Silvercreek Road, and an agreement with the Township was set forth in a by-law passed on August 18, 1902. As part of the arrangement the City was required to plant a grove of "Norway Spruce" to break the view along the Waterloo Road.[13]

On August 26, contracts were awarded by City Council for sewer pipe and construction,[14] and by September 11, Messrs. W.W. Read and Company, who had the largest part of the contract for digging the trunk sewers, were progressing favourably.[15] Sufficient construction had been completed by October, 1903, to allow the system to be put into use.[16]

As frequently happens, a controversy arose regarding sewerage rates and the City Council's position was summarized by the *Mercury* as follows:

The Sewerage Committee of Council met on March 22 [1907] with a Citizens' Committee to consider the assessment of sewerage rates.

The question hinged on the point of whether non-sewerage users should be expected to pay a share of the cost of installation. Ald. [J.W.] Lyon pointed out that from a municipal point of view the benefits of sewerage and the increase in property value more than compensated for the charges—and that it would be most unfair to tax those who received no such advantage for the benefit of those who did.[17]

In 1908 the municipal government finally settled the matter by having a special Act passed by the Ontario Government which legalized the sewerage by-law and enacted a method of determining the rates that property owners should pay. It was not quite what the Citizens' Committee wanted, but it settled the controversy.

In the meantime, in spite of the introduction of the sewerage system, the quality of City water continued to deteriorate. Time and again the question of filtration arose, but the

Laying sewer pipe on Woolwich Street near the Court House.

cost discouraged any action. Moreover, as the *Mercury* pointed out, it was pointless for the Council to consider a new filter for the old system, for with increased industrial and residential development the water storage basin would soon become contaminated. What was needed was a new source of supply.[18]

A new Water Commission was established in January, 1907,[19] and the *Mercury* reported:

In February of 1907, the appointment of the Commissioners took place, but it was not until July that the first real step was taken in this direction. Then commenced the excursions up the valley of the Speed, when the different springs were examined on the Love, the Cook, the Rudd and the Cameron properties, and the Stone and Blue springs. Each trip seemed to reveal new sources of water supply in the hillsides of the valley, until at length, the Commissioners [G.B. Ryan, R.L. Torrance and the Mayor, John Newstead] became of the opinion that there must be enough water for their purpose.[20]

Having satisfied themselves that the project was feasible, the Commissioners appointed an engineer, Mr. W.M. Davis of Berlin, to complete the survey. He concluded that the readily available springs could supply 4½ to 5 million gallons per day—enough for a city of 50,000 at the then current rates of usage. According to Davis, the whole project could be completed for $125,000. In January, 1908, the proposition was put before the public, and the result was a decisive vote in favour of bringing water from the springs.

During the summers of 1908 and 1909, the construction of the pipeline, reservoir, pumping station and stand pipe occupied the attention of Guelph's newspapers. The *Mercury* gave this description of the line:

The conduit is formed of huge tile pipe. . .The diameter inside is two feet, and the line is therefore capable of supplying a tremendous amount of water. . . . The total length of the line from the farm of Cameron Bros. [Arkell] to the new reservoir is 20,700 feet [3.9 miles]. This is all laid in tile pipe, except 1,200 feet, which has been laid in iron pipe. . . .

The conduit runs at a gradual scale down to the City. The point where the line starts near Arkell is 20 feet, 6 inches above the level of the reservoir at the pumping station. It will thus be seen that the water is brought from the springs into the City easily by force of gravity.

The springs from which the supply is being drawn are as follows:—

Cameron Bros.—Giving 1,250,000 gallons a day. . . .*Wm. Rudd*—Flow of 525,000 gallons per day. . . .*J. Rae*—Flow of 50,000 gallons. . . .*Cameron Bros.*—Giving 315,000. . . .*Cameron Bros.*—Giving 75,000 gallons. . . .*Wm. Rudd*—Giving 250,000. . . .

The reservoir is constructed of cement, reinforced with steel. It is 150 feet by 70 feet, and is 12 feet deep. . . .The capacity is 500,000 gallons of water. . . .

On the very brow of the hill, situated near Grove Street, the standpipe is located. It occupies by long odds the most prominent altitude in the City and it can be seen for long distances in all directions. . . . The standpipe is 100 feet in height measured from the base of the steel work. The diameter is 30 feet.

The steel was built on in circular sections, seventeen in all. The thickness and strength of these sections varied from 7/8 of an inch at the base to 1/4 inch at the topmost section.[21]

In undertaking the construction of the line, the Water Commissioners were also concerned with securing the greatest possible protection for the springs upon which the success of the whole project depended. Thus it was decided to reforest the Arkell Springs property. In 1908 some 275,000 Scotch Pine, White Pine, Spruce and Larch were planted. By 1927, some 212 acres were reserved around the springs. In all some 270,000 Scotch Pine, 80,000 White Pine, 38,000 White Spruce and 12,000 Larch were planted.[22]

The usc of this spring water had an immediate and important effect upon the health of the City's residents as well. In May, 1914, Doctor H.O. Howitt, the Medical Officer of Health, said:

The [water] supply comes direct from the springs to the consumer and I know of no better, or purer or cooler water in all Canada. . . .

Fifty per cent of our hospital bed space previous to the introduction of this water, was occupied in the fall of each year by typhoid cases, and to a lesser extent each spring. We averaged eight deaths

The standpipe as it appeared in later years.

per year from this disease. Since the introduction of this water supply, typhoid cases are almost unknown and the whole death rate from this cause has been wiped out.[23]

Unfortunately for Doctor Howitt's peace of mind, it would not be too long before Guelph's water supply would once again be the centre of a major controversy.

The development of Guelph's Gas and Electrical systems might be said to go back to 1866 when the first street lights were erected in the Town. In that year the Council gave a contract to Howard and Jones for 25 street lamps for $5.75 each including posts. The lamps used coal oil, and every evening Mr. Edwards, the Town Hall caretaker, made the rounds with a little ladder to light up the Town.[24] In commenting on the lights, the *Guelph Herald* said:

The Street Lamps.—The street lamps, recently erected under the direction of the Fire and Water Committee, were lighted for the first time on Saturday night, and appeared to fulfil the purpose of their erection as efficiently as, from their small number, could have been anticipated. The lamps look well, are judiciously arranged at street corners and crossings; they gave a brilliant light in their immediate vicinity and, where the rays are not intercepted by the verandahs or sign posts, the streets are lighted up to a considerable distance from each lamp post. There are still, however, considerable spaces where darkness is but made visible and where, "ample space and verge enough" is left for additional lamp posts so soon as the Council have the means and the mind to supply them.[25]

In 1870, with the formation of the Gas Company, the Town Council agreed to allow the company to instal gas pipes under the streets in exchange for free gas to light the streets, Town Hall and other public buildings.[26]

Old coal oil street lamp on Quebec Street, looking west towards Cossitt's Agricultural Works.

In 1887, a number of down town merchants and residents, anxious to keep Guelph abreast of the times, petitioned the City Council to replace the gas lamps with the new electric lights which were used in the big American cities. In response to their request, the Council entered into a contract with the Guelph Gas Company to supply the down town area with 22 arc lamps of 1000 candle power each at a cost of forty cents per lamp per night. On the strength of this contract, the Gas Company built a small water-powered generating station at Spence's Mill.[27] Four years later (1891) the system was converted to high tension alternating current generated by coal, and the City replaced all its gas lamps with electricity.[28]

By 1900, however, some public dissatisfaction had built up against the Gas Company's operations. It was claimed that the quality was poor (according to one City alderman "just within a fraction of being within the law")[29] and that prices were high. In 1902, having had the most successful year in its history financially (profits had increased by $1,500),[30] it was in the process of renegotiating its lighting contract with the City. Not content with its return, and claiming that it was expecting a coal shortage, the Company demanded a large increase in the price of gas.

At this time, the question of public ownership of hydro-electric power was starting to be discussed on a province wide basis. With improved technology, it was now becoming feasible to transmit cheap electrical power to Ontario's major industrial cities. This could have created a problem, however, for the smaller manufacturing centres. As one historian put the situation:

The public feared that these utilities and certain favoured industries in Toronto would obtain cheap power and that the small business man and the householder would be charged high rates. Urban centres outside Toronto feared that the provincial capital would receive favours at the expense of the small manufacturing centres.[31]

This attitude was openly expressed at the annual banquet of the Waterloo Board of Trade, held February 11, 1902, when E.W.B. Snider, a prominent miller and manufacturer from St. Jacob's, responded to the toast "The Manufacturing Interests," by proposing that the Boards of Trade of Berlin, Hespeler, Galt and Guelph join together to urge the development of an ample supply of cheap power. The obvious source of such power was Niagara Falls.

During the spring and summer of 1902, a series of meetings were held in the Grand Valley area at which engineering cost studies were presented and plans discussed. On June 9, 1902, a meeting was convened at Berlin which formulated a proposal for the use of Niagara power. The minutes of that meeting make it clear that Guelph's leading industrialists were

in the forefront of the movement. Christian Kloepfer made one of the speeches and both Kloepfer and Lincoln Goldie were appointed members of the management committee.[32] As the committee worked throughout the summer and fall to demonstrate the need for "public power" in Ontario, events were also developing in Guelph.

Negotiations between Guelph City Council and the Guelph Gas Company (now legally titled the Guelph Light and Power Company) had become deadlocked. In spite of arguments and pleas by Council members, the Company remained adamant. Because of the growing sentiment to bring all sources of energy under public control, this position proved to be an error. In June, 1902, the Fire and Light Committee of Council brought in a report on the negotiations. They recommended that in view of the price demanded for lighting, Council should consider purchasing the Gas Company. At the same time, W.E. Buckingham brought in a report which concluded that as provincial laws made it illegal for a municipality to generate its own power in competition with a local independent power company, the City must either pay the Gas Company the rates demanded or take it over. He pointed out that since the passing of the "Conmee Act" in 1899, municipalities had the right, under certain conditions, to acquire the assets of local utilities. In his report he outlined three possible methods of proceeding:

a) The council may make an offer for the plant to the company and the company may either accept the offer or elect to submit the price to arbitration. In any case when the price is ascertained, the assent of the ratepayers must be obtained.

b) A by-law may be passed with the assent of the ratepayers declaring that it is expedient to acquire the works and plant, and thereupon the corporation may take possession and the price shall be ascertained by arbitration.

c) The council may in the first instance, without making an offer and without submitting the question to the electors, submit the price to arbitration, but the by-law when the price is ascertained must be submitted to the ratepayers.[33]

According to the Conmee Act, the price for such a take over, should it go to arbitration, was the actual replacement cost of facilities, fully depreciated, plus ten per cent. Nothing whatsoever was to be allowed for franchise or for future profits.[34]

In presenting his report, Alderman Carter gave this summary of the economic advantages of taking over the Gas Company using the first method:

1. Your committee would recommend that we offer the Guelph Gas and Electric Light and Power Co., without prejudice, 70¢ per share on its $100,000 of capital stock, making $70,000, and also take over the debenture debt of $50,000, a total of $120,000. As far as your committee can find the amount paid on the stock is from 60 to 65¢, and it has been selling from 60 to 65¢ of late, and as far as your committee can learn it has not sold as high as 70¢.
2. Your committee think that at this price it would

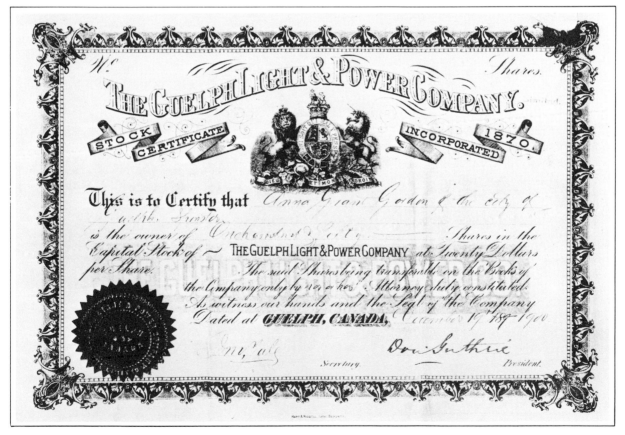

Stock Certificate, Guelph Light & Power Co.

pay the City to operate the plant, and it would be better than going into a costly arbitration, both for the company and the City. . . .[35]

Carter's report set off a long and complicated argument. The question of public ownership was not the issue. Instead, the controversy concerned the fact that the City Solicitor and several Council members were deeply involved in the affairs of the Gas Company, and as such, had a strong personal interest in the price set for the Company's assets.

In the draft by-law to acquire the Gas Company, the Fire and Light Committee of Council had included a clause which prohibited the City Solicitor and interested Council members from taking part in the takeover negotiations. In challenging this motion, Alderman James E. Day said:

He thought it verged pretty well on impertinence. It was unfair. The Directors of the Company were not enemies of the City and Council. They had risked their money when the success of the enterprise was doubtful, and the citizens should be grateful to them now. It was practically forcing these officials to defeat the measure or resign, and nothing would be gained by it.[36]

Alderman Carter, in support of the clause, replied:

[He] had always opposed the City Solicitor being interested in the greatest spending department the City had. . . . The Company's property was assessed for $8,700 on real estate and $12,500 on personal property, a total of $21,200. Yet they refused $120,000 for it. The taxes on $100,000 were thrown away. Real estate lately bought for $15,000 was assessed for $6,000. . . . He knew of houses assessed for $1,000 for which the sum would never be asked, and houses built for $1,100 that were assessed for $1,200. . . . They wanted the City officials who were Directors, out of the way if they went into arbitration, or entered into another contract on the same basis as the last.[37]

Alderman Carter's clause was challenged by several of the aldermen, and was finally defeated by a vote of 10 to 5.[38] The curious aspect of the whole debate was that Alderman Carter was by no means hostile to either business interests or the owners and Directors of the Guelph Gas Company. Indeed, when the Company rejected his proposal of $120,000 for the Company's shares and debentures, he immediately raised the offer to $155,000, and became a leading voice in the defense of the much larger offer. In addition, he strongly opposed going to arbitration. Carter's defense of the high purchase price was based entirely upon the profitability of the Company:

The City at present pays to the Light and Power Co. $6,000 in round figures annually for street lights. The interest on $155,000 at 3¾ per cent, the figure at which the City sold debentures, is $5,820 a year. So that, when the City owns the plant, the interest alone of the purchase money will not be greater than the amount the City at present pays the Company for the street lighting alone. And then we have besides the net income from all the private gas, lighting and heating and electric light sources, which is more profitable to the Company than the civic contract.[39]

The debenture referendum to buy the Gas Company passed easily in the municipal election in January, 1903 (the vote was 509 in favour and 413 opposed),[40] and the by-law taking over the gas and electric utilities was passed on February 9, 1903.[41] With the local electric service now in the hands of the Council, attention shifted once again to the acquisition of cheap Niagara power.

Although Berlin had been the centre of the original proposal with Adam Beck as the chief proponent, Guelph took an equally active part in its promotion. The *Guelph Mercury*, in particular took a strong stand in support of the proposition of "public power" for Ontario. This editorial was published in January 1903:

The Niagara Falls power question has reached a stage when the Government should appoint a commission, first, to place the people in possession of the facts; second, to estimate the prospects; and third, to suggest plans for dealing with the power situation in the interest of the people of Ontario. . . . No Niagara Falls power of any account is yet in use on this side; the original United States Co. is supplying Niagara Falls, N.Y., and Buffalo. St. Catharines gets its power principally from the Welland Canal, so that Hamilton is the first place on the Ontario side which is a large consumer of power, and it is supplied from Decew's Falls. . . . The transmission of power over long distances has now become a paying commercial service, and there is a strong demand from Toronto, Brantford, Guelph, Galt, Berlin, and other points within a radius of 100 miles from the Falls that they be allowed to share also in the benefits of the cheaper power. It is estimated, unless exorbitant figures are asked, that power could be laid down here at from $15 to $20 per horse power per annum, as compared with $40 per horse power per annum from steam. . . .[42]

Not only would there be large savings in the cost of power, but local industrialists and domestic consumers would be freed from the manipulations of the coal producing and distributing cartels.

From 1903 to 1906 leading members of the Guelph business community, the Guelph Board of Trade and Guelph City Council were in the forefront of the fight for what would become the Hydro Electric Power Commission of Ontario.[43] Thus when the Whitney Conservative Government passed "An Act to Provide for the Transmission of Electric Power to Municipalities" in May, 1906, Alderman J.W. Lyon, President of the Guelph Board of Trade, was appointed to the Executive Committee of the Western Ontario Municipal Niagara Power Union, the body charged with bringing the Act to realization. It was now the task of men like Lyon to persuade local ratepayers to undertake the financial responsibility of underwriting the bonds of the Power Commission, so that a generating plant and a power line grid from Niagara Falls could be built.[44]

On September 4, 1906, City Council decided to apply to the Power Commission for an allocation of 2000 horsepower,[45] and the City would be legally bound to pay for 1500 horsepower whether or not the electricity was actually used.[46] At a meeting of the City Railway and Manufacturing Committee held on November 27, 1906, Mr. E.W. Richards, a Hydro Commission engineer, and J.W. Lyon outlined the benefits that Guelph might expect:

Mr. Richards presented the figures for Niagara power for Guelph, which were from $18 to $24 per h.p. for 24-hour power, the latter figure being for 1500 h.p. and the former for 2000 to 3000 h.p. These figures allow a slight margin, so that if there should be a slight variation of the estimated rates, it would not be necessary to submit another by-law in the future, as might otherwise be the case.

Ald. Lyon submitted figures from prominent authorities on the estimated savings to the City by the use of Niagara power in connection with the waterworks, light and power plants and the street railway, which totalled approximately $10,000. It was suggested, though, that a standpipe be erected in connection with the waterworks, and that the capacity of the street railway storage battery be increased. If these suggestions were carried out, it would greatly facilitate the problem of averaging the amount of power used, because the power could be dispensed with in these departments when there was an unusual demand for power in other quarters. This is a very important consideration, as the rate of power would be charged according to the maximum amount used at any one time of the day—the peak load. For example, in the winter time, when the power was being used between the hours of five and six o'clock for both lighting and manufacturing purposes, it would prove a great advantage if the street railway power and waterworks power could be dispensed with, and thus maintain a favorable average.[47]

The Council passed the by-law unanimously, subject to a public referendum.

In his discussion of the merits of the Niagara power proposition, Alderman Lyon made it clear that he considered the acquisition of the Guelph Light and Power Company by the City to have been a crucial step in realizing the maximum savings. In one newspaper story, Lyon said:

Guelph was probably in the most favorable position of any city in Ontario. The rate of [local] distribution at Toronto was estimated at $4.50 to $5 per h.p., while at Guelph it was estimated at $3 or $3.50.[48]

Finally, in late December, a large public rally in support of Niagara power was held in Guelph, with Adam Beck the chief speaker. As Alderman Fryer of Galt said, it was "somewhat a useless errand to come to Guelph to preach cheap power; something like carrying coals to Newcastle."[49] Fryer was entirely correct in his estimation of sentiment in Guelph. The by-law referendum passed easily.[50] At the same election similar by-laws were passed in Berlin, Hespeler, Waterloo, Preston, New Hamburg, Toronto Junction, Toronto, Hamilton, Galt, London, Ingersoll, Woodstock, Stratford, St. Mary's, Weston, St. Thomas, Paris, and Brantford.[51]

The first contract entered into by the co-operating municipalities and the Provincial Hydro Commission was signed on May 4, 1908. By its terms the "Hydro" agreed to supply electricity to the fourteen co-signers (Hamilton, Paris and Brantford had dropped out due to the influence of the Cataract Power Com-

Table XXIX
H.E.P.C. Contract Prices and Capital Cost Liabilities [52]

Municipality	Quantity in h.p.	Price	Liability
Toronto	10,000	$18.10	$828,080
London	5,000	23.50	671,089
Guelph	2,500	24.00	347,420
Stratford	1,000	27.10	173,580
St. Thomas	1,500	26.50	244,140
Woodstock	1,200	23.00	155,350
Berlin	1,000	24.00	138,970
Galt	1,200	22.00	143,920
Hespeler	300	26.00	63,200
St. Mary's	500	29.50	95,677
Preston	600	23.50	80,530
Waterloo	685	24.50	98,460
New Hamburg	250	29.50	47,830
Ingersol	500	24.00	69,485

pany of which many Hamilton residents were shareholders) at a 25 cycle frequency at contract prices and capital cost liabilities as shown in Table XXIX.

Even before Niagara power was delivered, the benefits of public ownership of the gas and electric utilities were apparent to Guelph's consumers. In 1905 some $55,000 had been borrowed to improve the gas works,[53] and in 1908 another $50,000 was borrowed to improve electricity distribution in preparation for conversion to Niagara power.[54] The Annual Report of the Guelph Light and Heat Commission, issued March 1, 1909, demonstrated the rapid improvements made:

Over $34,000 profit from the Light and Heat Department for the past year was the outstanding figure of the annual report of the Light and Heat

Department as presented to Council last night by Chairman Samuel Carter.

The debenture indebtedness of $210,000 has been reduced to $192,054.61.

The citizens should bear in mind that the average price paid for gas when the City took over the plant was $1.35 2/5 per 1000 cu. ft. and the electric light 12 and 14¢ per kwhr. The gas price is now $1.00 net and electricity 10¢. Since the price was reduced in 1908 there have been savings to the customers of over $10,000 for gas and $5,000 for electricity.

The profits have been used to pay off the debentures and for extensions to the lines, and the commission now has $14,000 in the bank.[55]

In November, 1909, this report was made by the *Mercury*:

Steady progress is being made in the City in the preparatory work for the distribution of Niagara energy. At the power plant out on Edinboro Rd. the construction operations are going ahead rapidly. . . . The distribution lines are also being arranged for throughout the City by the erection of poles. The main line will come down the Edinboro Rd. from the power plant, and by the way of Waterloo, Bedford and Bristol Sts. will reach the present power plant. From the plant there will be a branch line through St. Patrick's ward to the manufacturing plants there, and also one by way of Arthur, Queen and Perth Sts. to the Goldie Mfg. Co. From these high tension lines there will be tributary branches constructed as required.[56]

The first Niagara power to flow through the system arrived on November 1, 1910.[57] Another landmark in public ownership in Guelph had been achieved.

The final major municipal acquisition was the Guelph Street Railway. It had been incorporated in 1894 by George Sleeman, a well known Guelph brewer and industrialist.[58] According to the agreement between Sleeman and the City, signed August 7, 1894, the Guelph Street Railway Company was to have an exclusive franchise to build and operate a street railway, carrying both passengers and freight anywhere in Guelph. In return for this privilege, Sleeman agreed to build a line commencing at the City boundary on the Dundas Road to follow Dundas Road, Gordon Street, across Market Square and Carden Street to Wyndham Street, thence north along Wyndham Street, Woolwich Street and the Elora Road to the City boundary. This line, to be known as Section I, was to be completed and in operation by April 1, 1897. After that date and for the next four years, the Street Railway Company was required to complete at least one additional mile of track each year upon

George Sleeman,
Mayor, 1880, 1881, 1882, 1905, 1906.

George Sleeman with his wife and family in front of their first stone home on Waterloo Road.

streets to be named by Sleeman. The contract also stipulated that:

21. Cars are to be of the most improved design for service and comfort, including heating, lighting, signal appliance, numbers and route boards. They must be kept clean inside and out, and shall not exhibit advertisements outside which shall be unsightly or disfigure the cars. The platform must be provided with gates. Smoking will only be allowed on the front platform of closed cars and the rear seat and platform of open cars.
22. Each car is to be in charge of a uniformed conductor, who shall clearly announce the names of cross-streets as the cars reach them. Conductors shall not permit ladies or children to enter or leave the cars while the cars are in motion. . . . On branch or light suburban lines where horse power is permitted single horse cars may be run in charge of a uniformed driver.[59]

In addition, the Street Railway was strictly limited to fixed rates of fare:

19. The said Sleeman shall not be entitled to charge fares upon the said railway higher than the following:—
Single cash fares are to be five cents each.

Fares after eleven o'clock at night and before five o'clock in the morning, to be double the ordinary maximum single fares.

A class of tickets [rush hour fares] must be sold at the rate of eight for twenty-five cents, the same to be used only by passengers entering the cars between the time the cars commence running after five o'clock a.m. and eight o'clock a.m., and between five o'clock p.m. and half past six o'clock p.m.

A class of tickets must be sold at the rate of twenty-five for One Dollar ($1.00); and

The Sleeman Brewery and home on Waterloo Road.

Another class at the rate of six for twenty-five cents.

Children under nine years of age, and not in arms are to be carried at half fare rates, and infants in arms are to be carried free; School children are to have school tickets at the rate of ten for twenty-five cents, only to be used between eight a.m. and five p.m., and not on Saturdays.[60]

Finally, the franchise was to be for twenty years, with the right to have it extended for another ten years, provided legislation could be obtained.[61] The first spike of the Street Railway was driven near Sleeman's residence on the Waterloo Road on June 20, 1895, and it was officially opened on September 18th of the same year.[62] In 1901, Sleeman secured an additional charter to construct extensions to Ber-

lin, Hespeler and Puslinch Lake where he owned extensive property, including the Island, a hotel and forty-eight acres of land.[63]

The Street Railway, however, consistently lost money, and by 1903 it was in receivership and its shares had been seized by the banks for debts. Although it continued to operate during the receivership period, the banks were anxious to dispose of the Railway. The minutes of the Board of Trade for April 28, 1903, reported:

A special meeting of the Board of Trade was held in the Council chamber last night to consider street railway matters. President Duff in the chair. . . . Messrs. Lyon and Ryan reported verbally that the committee appointed at last meeting had met the Guelph Railway Company, and that the Company had refused to give an option. They stated that their price was $100,000. To this the committee had intimated that if this was their price there was no use discussing it. The Company stated that, while this was their price, they were prepared to receive an offer for the road. They said that if the Board chose to appoint a committee the books of the Company would be open to them, to see what the road was doing at the present time, and then, if the Board was prepared to set a price, they were ready to consider it. . . .

Moved by J.W. Lyon, seconded by H.C. Scholfield:

That a committee be appointed consisting of Messrs. Lyon, Ryan and [J.E.] Day, to act in conjunction with a committee of three from the City Council, to ascertain what the City can purchase the street railway for, and to get as full information as possible as to the earnings of the road, and then report back to this Board.[64]

The banks' demand for $100,000 for the Street Railway Company's shares was clearly excessive. When George Sleeman had built the line, he had done so primarily by selling bonds (about $50,000 worth), and borrowing short term funds from the banks. Negotiations were necessary to bring the price down to a point where it reflected the line's actual value.

The City Council, Board of Trade and the banks co-operated in having the Ontario Legislature pass an amendment to the line's charter which gave it much broader powers. The Company's name was changed to the Guelph Radial Railway Company, and by the second clause, it was given the following rights:

The Company is hereby authorized and empowered to further extend, construct and operate the said railway by electric or other power, other than steam, from a point in the City of Guelph at the present terminus of the railway on the Elora Road to, near or through Elora, Fergus, Arthur and Mount Forest in the County of Wellington, with power to construct a branch from Arthur on the line between Arthur and Mount Forest to Conn or

Street car on Elora Road.

some other point near West Luther or a point therein, and also to construct an extension of its railway from some point on the said railway in the City of Guelph to Erin Village passing through the Township of Guelph, Eramosa and Erin and also to construct the extensions from Puslinch Lake to, or near Galt in the County of Waterloo passing through the Townships of Puslinch and Waterloo, and from Puslinch Lake or Hespeler to or near Preston in the County of Waterloo, passing through the Township of Waterloo; the extension first named may be known as the northwestern extension, and the extension secondly named to be known as the Erin extension, and the extensions thirdly and fourthly named to be known as the Galt and Preston extensions respectively.[65]

In addition the new Radial Railway Company acquired the power to borrow up to $20,000 per mile of line, and the right to sell electricity in any of the municipalities it served. On May 21, 1903, the *Mercury* reported:

The banks and the City Council and Board of Trade committees will probably come to some arrangement whereby the ratepayers will have an opportunity of purchasing the street railway interests for $78,000. . . . If the City comes into possession of its street railways, it will have more municipal services in its hands than any other place in the Dominion. We have the Guelph Junction Railway, the waterworks and sewer systems, we were taking over the civic lighting system, and the street railway would complete the group. . . .[66]

A week later, the *Mercury* pointed out that the figure of $78,000 consisted of $30,000 to the banks for the railroad's shares, and $48,000 to pay off the bonds held by the public.[67] On September 28, 1903, the ratepayers voted 787 to 532 to purchase the line.[68] The last piece of Guelph's "grand design" for municipal ownership was now in place.

In addition to the takeover of the electric railway system, the Board of Trade had one other involvement in railway promotion in 1903. Until that date, the performance of the Guelph Junction Railway had been, to say the least, disappointing. Not only had it not paid sufficient profits to carry the cost of its debt interest, but immediately after it had been leased by the Canadian Pacific, freight rates had been increased drastically.[69] In 1903, however, an opportunity was presented which made it possible for the line to make a profit.

In 1899, at the urging of the Goderich municipal council, a convention of municipal officials had been held in Guelph to consider the possibility of building a railway between the two centres. At the meeting, Donald Guthrie gave a history of the Guelph Junction-C.P.R. negotiations which culminated with the building of the line to Campbellville:

The basis of their proceedings was a promise by the C.P.R. to extend the Guelph Junction road to Lake Huron. He dare say they had all heard of the position of the City of Guelph with reference to the Guelph Junction Railway. The City practically owned that line. . . .At the time we first entered upon the matter the proposal was to construct the road to Schaw Station, which was only ten or eleven miles from Guelph. We were asked by the C.P.R. to change the road to Campbellville, which lengthened it to sixteen miles and materially increased the cost. That was done on the understanding that the Company would extend the line to Goderich, but subject to bonuses and other conditions. The City of Guelph had always regarded that promise as one that was given and accepted in good faith, and one that should be carried out.[70]

It was now time, Guthrie argued, for the C.P.R. to keep its promise. Committees were established to begin the agitation for bonuses from the various municipalities, and much local publicity resulted.

Although little immediate success was achieved by the 1899 committees, by February 1903, the first concrete suggestions were being made. A delegation of Guelph Junction Railway Directors went to Montreal to meet the C.P.R. officials and to lay several proposals before them.[71] In June, deputations from Goderich and Clinton met with Guelph's business leaders to discuss plans for persuading the C.P.R. to take action. The decision arrived at was that all municipalities along the route would offer to acquire the right of way if the C.P.R. would pay for construction.[72] This decision was communicated to the C.P.R. as well. By September, it appeared the C.P.R. was beginning to take the Guelph Junction extension seriously. A group of surveyors were sent from Montreal to look at the route and to report on its economic feasibility.[73]

It was not until early in 1904 that Guelph was informed that the C.P.R. had definitely decided to go ahead with the construction of the Guelph to Goderich line. By the fall the work was well under way. On November 24, 1904, the *Mercury* reported that:

Mr. D.R. Campbell, of Strathroy, has got his men working at last on section No. 1, the first ten miles of the Guelph and Goderich railway. They have got the section at Milverton nearly through and are now waiting at Guelph for the wheeled scrapers and gravel cars to get a full force working on this section.
The steam shovel is located in the field on the Pipe farm adjoining the cemetery where it has before it 1900 feet of a 9 to 12 foot cutting through the cemetery almost to the road leading from the far side of the cemetery to the Paisley Block. It is now waiting for gravel cars. The earth from this cutting will be used to fill in the line nearer the city and further on. Across the Paisley Block road beyond the cemetery the contractor has some forty or fifty men working under foremen Watson and McDon-

ald, and walking boss Montgomery. A gang of Italians are digging a ditch in a swamp to carry the water there into an adjoining drain. . . .[74]

These Italian workers would eventually settle in Guelph, and their descendents would ultimately contribute much to the flavour and colour of local social life.[75] The first regular trains to Elmira were begun on July 11, 1906, and the official opening of the Guelph and Goderich line was held on September 13th of the same year.

The extension of the Guelph Junction Railway to Goderich proved to be a bonanza for the residents of Guelph. Because the C.P.R. agreement had provided for a fixed proportion of freight charges to be allocated to the line rather than an outright rent, the new traffic from Goderich generated a handsome surplus. Thus, from being somewhat of a financial liability, the extension turned it into a handsome asset for the City's taxpayers. For the years

Canadian Pacific Railway engine No. 488 at Goldie's Mill.

1921 and 1922 the Railway achieved net earnings of $85,150 and $81,600 respectively.[76]

Guelph's vigorous program of municipal ownership and operation of its utilities and services quickly made it famous throughout Canada. Guelph businessmen were invited to speak on the subject by other Boards of Trade and Chambers of Commerce, and newspaper editors wrote praising the Guelph experiment. In September, 1909, J.W. Lyon gave this interview to the *Winnipeg Free Press*:

In Guelph. . .the City owns the public utilities with the exception of the telephone. It owns the city railway, the electric light plant, the gas plant, the waterworks, and sixteen miles of steam railway. . . .We got the gas plant five years ago. Since that time we have reduced the price of gas three times. We have put $100,000 into the plant, which is now complete. In future we will have a surplus of $20,000 per year from the plant, which may be used either in reducing the price of gas or in reducing the general tax.

Some years ago we had only one railway. We approached the C.P.R. with the object of securing the construction of that line into Guelph. The road was sixteen miles away. The manager of the C.P.R. stated that they had no money to build the line. The Company was poor then and could not get the money. The City got the money and built the line. A contract was made with the Canadian Pacific to operate under a lease for one hundred years. The line was then but a stub into Guelph. It was operated at a loss. Finally the Company built the line through to Goderich and instead of being a stub our portion became a part of one of the main lines. The earnings increased, and now all the deficit has been paid. There is a surplus to the City, and the returns to the City from the investment in the future will be very large. . . .

Our new waterworks will be opened on Thursday of next week. . . .The plant is operated by gravity and cost but $125,000. . . .

On the entire investment in municipal undertakings in Guelph, there is being realized 12 per cent. net. Gas is now furnished for all purposes to our citizens for $1 per thousand feet. Power is furnished from Niagara to Guelph at one half price at which it is furnished to Buffalo, although we are more than three times as far from the source. . . .[77]

As the *Toronto Telegram* commented:

Guelph may become a centre of influence in favor of public ownership just as Hamilton has become a centre of influence in favor of corporate privilege. . . .Guelph must incidentally reap great advantage from an absolute control of every public franchise. Gas, electric light and power and street railway services are all under the control of the municipality and Guelph must grow by reason of its ability to offer immunity from the exactions of private ownership.[78]

The *Mercury* was in entire agreement with the *Telegram*'s views. In September, 1910, in the midst of the campaign to expand the radial railway system to the north, the editor made this prediction:

Brantford has over 21,000 population. We'll be right on your heels soon, Brantford. We're striking our stride now, here in Guelph.[79]

In municipal ownership, Guelph believed that it had at last found the key to rapid economic growth.

Parade along Wyndham Street during Old Home Week in 1908.

XIII

Economic and Social Problems

Despite Guelph's energetic pursuit of industrial development and its leading role in municipal ownership, after 1908 events beyond the City's control began to place severe obstacles in the path of economic growth. When the extraordinary pressures of World War I were added to these problems, long-buried prejudices were revived, and it required the concerted effort of all of Guelph's residents to re-establish the harmony and good-will which was, they proudly asserted, the hallmark of the Royal City.

By being first in the area to introduce industrial bonuses, taxation rebates and free or low cost utilities to attract industry, Guelph had stolen a march on its municipal rivals. However, the type of industry which could be attracted by subsidies was equally ready to move elsewhere on receipt of a more attractive offer. With all cities forced to offer subsidies, the manufacturer's decision to locate was made on the basis of good transportation, cheap labour, or availability of supplies and markets.

In 1902, when a bonus by-law was passed to grant $42,500 and other considerations to the Page-Hersey Company for a tube mill, the *Mercury* enthusiastically announced:

Hitching or Tie Post manufactured in Guelph by the Taylor-Forbes Company Limited.

The Mayor, President Torrance and members of the Board of Trade and other supporters of the tube mill by-law are to be warmly congratulated on the success of their work yesterday. In view of the opposition to the by-law, it was hardly expected that the necessary three-fifths vote could be got out. . . .

The Mayor and other gentlemen [who] have been working hard for the by-law are receiving congratulations on every side today from merchants, manufacturers and workingmen for the success which their efforts have met with.[1]

Similarly in 1906, the *Mercury* proudly announced:

That yet another large and important industry will locate in Guelph is practically assured. The new concern is the Gilson Manufacturing Company of Port Washington, Wisconsin, manufacturers of gasoline engines, office chair irons, and other foundry and machine shop products. The firm have the largest trade in office chair fittings of any establishment in the United States, and their trade with Canada, in this line alone, is sufficient at the present time to employ at least 25 hands. . . . The latest place they entered into negotiations with was Berlin. . . . But, Ald. Lyon, Chairman of the Manufacturers Committee of the City Council, got wind of the Berlin proposition, and as a result of the negotiations into which he immediately entered with the Company, the latter have signed a contract which will be submitted to the City Council.

The Gilson Co. propose that in consideration of locating their plant here the City shall grant a fixed assessment upon their establishment and land of $5,000, and provide a water connection 99 feet in length, and a hydrant.[2]

There were, however, some very unhappy announcements to be made as well.

The failure of the Morlock Furniture Company in 1909, pointed out the weakness in the subsidy program. The Morlock firm had been established in 1889 to build sofas and other upholstered goods. By 1907, although it employed between 90 and 100 men, it was in serious financial difficulty. In January of that

year, the Board of Trade and City Council supported a referendum covering a loan of $25,000 to keep the Morlock plant in operation. Following a judicial recount by Judge A.C. Chadwick, the by-law was finally passed.[3] On December 20, 1909, however, the *Mercury* contained this short note:

A sale is to be held to-morrow by public auction at the Morlock factory on Suffolk St. of the tools, utensils, etc. of the Morlock firm, in the interest of the employees who have not as yet received the wages due them. But although everything available is being disposed of to meet their claim, there is not very much hope for the men. . . . The claims of the men total something like $1,600 and against this there is only a small number of articles which can be sold which do not come under the mortgages held by the City and the bank. Sheriff Allan, the assignee, speaking of the matter this morning stated that he did not see where the men were going to get very much on their wage claims.[4]

The weakness of many of these subsidized firms was illustrated in the reports of the Industrial Department which was created by City Council in 1910. According to a statement issued on January 29, 1914, since 1910 that body had been instrumental in attracting some sixteen industries to Guelph.[5] By 1919, no less than ten of the sixteen were either no longer in business or had moved elsewhere.[6]

From 1908 on, vast numbers of industries throughout Canada and the industrial world were amalgamated into giant concerns which monopolized significant sectors of industrial production.[7] As part of this process, many factories were closed and their operations consolidated into the major industrial centres, either in Canada, the United States or Great Britain. It was as a result of this process that two of Guelph's largest and oldest industries, both of which had been heavily subsidized by the City, were closed and their operations moved elsewhere.

The Raymond Sewing Machine Company, which had been founded in 1861, was sold in 1897 by Charles Raymond (then 71 years of age) to a local consortium headed by J.G. Sully who had been Superintendent of the firm under Mr. Raymond. In 1916, the Raymond Manufacturing Company, as the firm had been renamed, was sold to the White Sewing Machine Company of Cleveland, Ohio, to be operated as that firm's Canadian branch. The *Mercury* welcomed the sale enthusiastically:

One of the most important industrial transactions that has taken place in the history of Guelph was closed yesterday when the White Sewing Machine Co., of Canada, took possession of the business of the Raymond Manufacturing Co. of Guelph.... The coming of the White Company to the Royal City is a big win for Guelph....

"I have always liked Guelph", said Mr. Chase, secretary of the White Co., of Cleveland, to the *Mercury*.... "We intend to manufacture here not only for Canadian business, but for Great Britain and the British possessions. Our Russian business may also be done here, also our business with France. Our sales in Australia are increasingly large, and it may be that we will manufacture for Australia in Guelph."[8]

In conclusion, Chase stated that production of sewing machines would be increased from thirty to three hundred per day, and that more than $200,000 would be invested to build a new plant.[9] In 1922, however, the business and equipment were transferred to the main plant in Cleveland,[10] and the Raymond distribution system was used to sell American-made White machines in Canada.

The Bell Organ Company, established in 1864, suffered a similar fate. In 1883, a British branch was established and by 1888 about 450 workmen were employed in Guelph serving

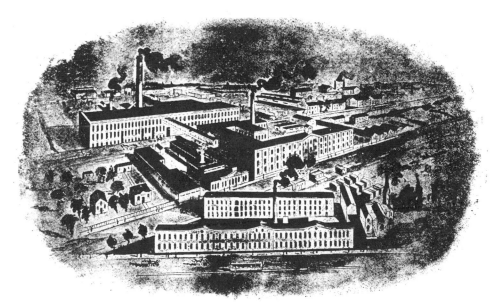

*The buildings comprising the plant of
the Raymond Manufacturing Company Limited.*

Factories of the Bell Organ and Piano Co., Guelph.

both markets. In that year the firm was sold to a British syndicate under the title of The Bell Piano and Organ Co. Ltd.[11] The British purchasers of the Bell Company continued to operate the Guelph factories, but at a reduced rate of production. During the depression of the 1930's, it was finally closed and operations were consolidated for the sake of efficiency into the British plants. The consequence of the merger movement was felt keenly in Guelph where so many smaller industries had been forced out of business, yet as this article printed in 1916 shows, a considerable list of enterprises had managed to survive and grow:

Bell Organ & Piano Co. Certificate, Dec. 29th, 1897.

Guelph has nearly 100 prosperous manufacturing enterprises. They comprise hardware, lawn mowers, agricultural implements, malleable iron mills, iron foundries and machine shops, cream separators, pianos and organs, sewing machines, iron tubing mills, flexible conduit, lamps, stoves and furnaces, axle works, marble and granite monuments, gasoline engines, carriage and wagon works, ingot iron products, wire works, flour and planing mills, lumber yards, soap, biscuits, furniture, paper boxes, carpet, hosiery, whitewear and ladies knit factories, spinning, weaving, cotton, knitting, textile and linen mills, store fronts, fence and metal products, caskets, pickles, breweries, mineral water works, farm specialities, waterproof clothing, furs, elastic stockings, etc., etc., etc.[12]

However, it would not be until after World War II that rapid growth returned again.

The desire to encourage industry would create severe problems in water supply and sewage disposal by 1914. In this case, it was the major subdivision in St. Patrick's Ward, initiated by J.W. Lyon, which precipitated the problem.

J.W. Lyon was one of the most remarkable men to take an interest in Guelph's business prospects. Born in Pennsylvania in 1848, he came to Canada in 1872 as a book salesman for the American Publishing Company of Hartford, Connecticut.[13] By employing a large force of American salesmen, he cleared more than $11,000 for the firm during that summer—an enormous sum for the time. In 1874, he returned to Canada to enter the book sales business on his own in Guelph. In 1878, he took a large group of salesmen with him to Australia to sell books, and by 1880 had cleared $70,000 to $80,000. Having established The World Publishing Company at Guelph, he published such books as *The Practical Home Physician, Foster's Story of the Bible* and *The Royal Path of Life*. The books were manufactured for Lyon by printers in Toronto and, according to him, in the year 1884 his books made up forty percent of all manufactured exports from To-

ronto. These books he sold through commission agents in Australia, Africa, The West Indies, China, Hindustan, Ceylon and elsewhere.

In the meantime, he and two other Guelph men, J.B. Armstrong and Robert Bathgate, purchased and rebuilt the gas works in Winnipeg and resold it at a $57,000 profit. After that, Lyon entered the real estate business in Winnipeg, Brandon, Fort William, and Port Arthur; several other locations in Manitoba, Saskatchewan and British Columbia; Gary, Indiana; Buffalo, New York; and Toronto.

In his Guelph land dealings, Lyon followed the method which had been pioneered in Guelph by John Galt—he gave acreages to large manufacturers, persuaded the City Council to grant them further concessions, and sold the land surrounding the factories to the workmen for residences. As Lyon said, the plan was a success.

About the year 1906 I...purchased four hundred acres of land partly inside and partly outside the City. From this land I presented sites and gave other inducements to secure factories. By so doing I secured eight factories for Guelph, giving them in all 120 acres of land without asking for payment of any kind.[14]

According to Lyon, these factories at their peak employed upwards of 2,000 men. The *Mercury* of May 4, 1914, commented on the water and sewage problems which arose in St. Partrick's Ward:

The Medical Officer of Health and the Board of Health have frequently drawn attention to conditions in St. Patrick's Ward, particularly since the population there began to increase with the coming of the factories. . . .

When the St. Patrick's Ward boom commenced the Board of Health reported on possible future danger. That danger is now on the verge of reality. At the time of the laying of the conduit scarcely any people lived in that area—is now settled and daily growing—which is in the vicinity of the Stove Works, Malleable Iron Works and Linen Mills, in fact between the river and the C.P.R. track west of Victoria Road. . . .[15]

The problem, of course, had not arisen overnight. An article in the *Mercury* described the situation:

The residents of St. Patrick's Ward want sewerage connection. According to many of them there is a crying need for it. . . . The factory owners in that section are beginning to lose their patience. . . . Now they *demand* sewerage service.[16]

The results of the factory owners' demands resulted in the building of a mile and a quarter of eighteen inch pipe to take care of the needs of the factories.[17] The residential needs, however, were not taken care of.

In July, 1915, Doctor Howitt, the Medical Officer of Health, gave this report to a citizens' group, "The Property Owners' Protective Association", which had been organized to fight for improved sanitation:

In my annual report of 3 years ago will be found a paragraph which laid stress in the fact that sooner or later the main conduit of the [waterworks] system would become infected due to the increased building of houses & factories in St. Patrick's Ward, which are in close proximity to the main conduit. . . . The tests have repeatedly shown that leaks existed in the pipe line. The epidemic of last winter was of an intestinal origin (probably animal) and the epidemic, although very many people were affected, was not serious, as far as loss of life went. . . . Had typhoid been the infection, we would have had a terrible epidemic & considerable loss of life.[18]

A careful survey of the water pipe line showed that Howitt was correct, that the heavily contaminated water from St. Patrick's Ward was entering the line, and that the

J.W. Lyon, owner of the World Publishing Company.

"Wyoming", the residence of J.W. Lyon.

Douglas Street circa 1875 looking towards St. George's Church.
The World Publishing Company occupied the small building at extreme left.

Water Commission had failed to carry out the recommendations of the Provincial Health Officers.[19] In an emotional defence of his actions, G.B. Ryan, Chairman of the Water Commission, resigned. The problem, however, did not originate from Ryan's supposed negligence, but rather from the Commission's great reluctance to spend money to replace porous pipe with iron pipe as recommended by the health officials. It was the desire to keep water costs at the lowest possible level that had created a potentially dangerous situation.[20]

Ryan's resignation, however, was not a solution to the problem of water contamination. Under the Commission form of management,

subsidization of water costs by taxation was illegal, thus improvement depended upon higher water charges. In 1919, City Council took over control of the water works, and in December of that year, $105,000 was voted to renew the pipe line, while an additional $35,000 was voted to renew and improve equipment and facilities.[21]

In an introduction to Guelph's military history, the *Mercury* in 1927 wrote:

It is a far cry from the time of the first military activity in Guelph down to the present time, and it is regrettable that the early records of the several military organizations are not available for the compilation of a comprehensive review in regard to military matters. For at least 90 years the citizens of Guelph have contributed their fair share in fighting the battles of the Empire and in upholding the Union Jack, and many thousands have passed through the ranks of the Artillery and Rifles Regiment, and numerous officers have been very prominent in the militia affairs of the Dominion of Canada.[22]

From the Upper Canadian Rebellion on, there was an active militia battalion in Guelph Township. The officers of the Guelph battalion as reported by the *Galt and Guelph Advertiser* in 1847 were:

COUNTY OF WATERLOO
First Battalion, comprising the Township of Guelph
Lieutenant Colonel-William Hewat, Esq.,
Major-Captains—Geoffrey Lynch, William Alexander, William Thompson, Edward F. Heming, Edward Murton, George J. Grange, Esquires.
Lieutenants—George Harvey, John C. Wilson, Thomas R. Brock, Rutherford Muttlebury, John Ross, Walter King, Robert Richardson, Edward Thompson, William Henry Parker, Gentlemen.
Ensigns—Alfred Baker, Richard Greet, James Grace Husband, James Davie, Arthur Hogg, John Thomas Tracy, William Porter, James Cain, David Allan, Gentlemen.
Adjutant-Ensign James Cain.
Quarter-Master—John Thorp, Gentleman.
Surgeon—William Clarke, Esquire, M.D.
Assistant Surgeon—Charles Jones, Gentleman.[23]

Although Guelph's officer corps appears to have been well organized, by 1848 the general public were opposed to the inconvenience of the annual militia training day. In November, 1848, the officers of the whole County of Waterloo militia met to talk over the situation. After considerable discussion this motion was adopted:

Moved by Lieutenant Col. Saunders, seconded by Lieut. Col. Webster: That the general muster of the different Battalions of Militia on the 29th day of June annually, is exceedingly inconvenient, and might be dispensed with; the *officers only* being required to meet and make their returns to Head Quarters.[24]

When the Government did not immediately take action on this and similar petitions from all over the Province, the *Advertiser* responded to the annual muster of 1849 as follows:

Training Day.—This is the day appointed for the annual training of the Militia of the Province. On these occasions some muster and some do not; some lose a whole day's work, and in the less settled parts two or even three days' work, whilst others never leave their occupations; but none derive one farthing of benefit from this farce called drilling, whilst the loss of time to the country is immense. In this Town there will probably be 600 persons assembled, on the Market Square, and if we value the loss of their time and the expenditure of money at 2s. 6d. each, it will be below the mark,—presenting a loss of £75 to this Township alone . . . .[25]

In 1855, the Guelph Rifles were organized with Captain Kingsmill, Lieutenant Higinbotham and Ensign Armstrong as officers. It was this unit that was called out on the twelfth of July, 1856, to protect the Roman Catholic church in the Orange Parade riots of that year.[26]

In 1857, the Canadian Government made fundamental changes in its military organization. The militia was put on a volunteer basis, the 1st Waterloo Battalion became extinct, and the Wellington County units were reorganized as the 1st Wellington Battalion, with the Guelph Rifles designated as No. 1 Company. On February fourteenth of that year, the *Canada Gazette* announced the names of the officer corps for the new battalion:

Majors, G. Harvey, John C. Wilson; Captains, Edward Thompson, Wm. Henry Parker, Walter King, Robt. Richardson, Alfred A. Baker, Richard

Greet, James G. Husband, Arthur Hogg and John Thomas Tracey; Lieutenants, W. Porter, James Cain, Charles Davidson, Henry Watson, Robert White, Thomas Watson, George Murton, Henry W. Peterson, John C. Allan and Nicol Kingsmill; Ensigns, George Tolton, Edmund Harland, James Webster, Jr., Colin Blyth, John C. Chadwick, Jr., Frederick J. Chadwick, Walter Murton, Thomas Heffernan and Leonard Harland; Surgeon, William Clarke; Assistant Surgeon, William S. Hewat; Adjutant, James Cain.[27]

Amid the growing tension between the British Empire and the United States, Guelph's military men were anxious to prepare for any situation that might arise. In December, 1861,

"as a consequence of the outrage committed by American cruisers on the British steamer Trent",[28] meetings were held all over Wellington County in order to make arrangements for a possible military confrontation with the Americans. Acton Burrows described the Guelph meeting as follows:

The men of Guelph were anxious to evince their loyalty by being prepared in case of an emergency, and, as had been the case on previous occasions, be the first to place themselves in readiness for any contingency, and take the van in any movement for the defence of the country and the British Government. A numerously signed requisition having been presented to the Mayor, a public meeting was

First Volunteer Rifle Company of Guelph, C.W., as they appeared after the inspection by the Baron de Rottenburg, Adjutant General of Militia, on Thursday, the 15th of October, 1857. Officers standing in front from left to right are Adjutant Armstrong, Lieut. Higinbotham, Captain Kingsmill, and Ensign Bruce.

called on December 17th, when the Town Hall was, within a few minutes of the doors being opened, filled to repletion, and the meeting was accordingly adjourned to the Market Square, the Mayor and the speakers addressing the crowd, the largest ever seen at any meeting in the Town before, from the balcony in front of the hall. The Mayor, in opening the proceedings said the situation in which the two countries was placed was a very grave one, and the result of the dispute might prove very serious, but he was sure the men of Guelph would be ready to do their duty. If war did come, it was the duty of Canadian citizens to show that they were in a position to meet their foes with resolution and decision. . .[29]

Other addresses were delivered by Colonel Webster, Honourable A.J. Fergusson, Lieutenant-Colonel George J. Grange, C.E. Romaine, Lieutenant-Colonel Saunders, George Elliott, John Harris and several others. The meeting decided to take whatever steps were necessary to prepare for a defence of the Town, to begin militia drilling throughout the County immediately, and to prepare munitions as quickly as possible. When the Americans released the *Trent* prisoners, Mason and Slidell, Guelph's residents returned to their customary affairs, but the organizations created to handle the expected American invasion were not immediately abandoned.[30]

So strongly did the Guelph's officer corps aspire to see active duty that in 1864 David Stirton wrote to John A. Macdonald to complain about the Government's "neglect":

My Dear Macdonald,
There seems to be a great deal of disappointment and ill feeling entertained by our Rifle Company (of this Town) on account of their not being among those selected for active service by the Gov't.

It is thought somewhat strange that not a *single* one is selected from the whole Military District—the largest I believe in the Province.

The Guelph Co. of Rifles is one of the oldest in the Province being the fifth or sixth in seniority. They have tendered their services on several occasions and are admitted to be in efficiency equal to if not superior to many of those selected.

Of course I am well aware of the difficulty which the Gov't have to contend with in giving satisfaction where so many are anxious to be employed—but I would respectfully submit that the claims to which I have alluded to above deserve some consideration. . . .[31]

Early in March, 1866, word reached Ottawa from secret agents in the United States that the Fenian Brotherhood—an organization of expatriate Irish rebels—was mobilizing with the intention of invading Canada as a means of striking at England. Immediately the Government ordered a military alert and the Guelph Rifles were directed to report for duty. On March ninth they were bound for Sarnia to protect the border, and later moved to St. Mary's and Windsor, returning home on July eleventh without having seen action.[32] During August, a second alarm caused the Guelph Rifles to be called out, this time to Thorold. Again they served without incident and after a short time returned home.[33]

In the midst of the Fenian alarms, it was decided to establish a second militia unit in Guelph, and on July 20, 1866, an artillery unit named the Guelph Garrison Battery was organized with James Barclay as Captain in command. In September, 1871, this unit was designated as a field unit under the title of the Wellington Field Battery.[34] At a later date, authority was issued to enroll an extra section at the Ontario Agricultural College, and on the twenty-second of March, 1878, this section was increased and converted into the Ontario Field Battery with Captain David McCrae in command. On March 24, 1880, the Wellington

Captain David McCrae, later Lieutenant Colonel,
father of the poet John McCrae.

and Ontario Field Batteries were combined to form the First Provisional Brigade, with Major A.H. Macdonald in command. Later on the brigade became the 1st Brigade, C.F.A., and the batteries were designated as the 11th Battery, dating from July 20th, 1866, and the 16th Battery, dating from March 22nd, 1878.[35]

In 1867, the Guelph Town Council undertook the building of a drill shed for the use of the Rifle Company. Initially a grandiose building was planned measuring some 300 by 80 feet, but ultimately this was rejected and a simpler building costing $2,000 was erected.[36] In 1873, the *Town of Guelph Directory* gave this description of the local militia units:

30th Wellington Battalion
Headquarters at Guelph. Staff officers—Colonel Clarke; Sen. Major, John A. McMillan; Jun. Major, James Armstrong; Adjutant, A. McBride; Paymaster,—McGregor; Quartermaster, E. Harvey; Surgeon, Dr. Orton, Fergus; Chaplain, Rev. Wm. S. Ball.

No. I Company Infantry
This Company of Rifles is the oldest in Ontario, having been organized in March of 1856. It has a complement of 53 men, and is one of the best companies in the Province. The commissioned officers are: Captain, Geo. Bruce, V.B.; 1st Lieutenant, John Hooper; Ensign, John Cleghorn. The non-commissioned officers are: Sergt.-Major, G.W. Porter; Color-Sergt. Keith; Sergt. Thrap; Sergt. Colson; Corporals Pearce, Clay and Keeling; Lance-Corpl. Porter.
Meet for drill on Thursday evening, at 8 o'clock.

Wellington Field Battery of Artillery
Headquarters at Guelph. The Company was gazetted as a Garrison Battery 20th July, 1866, and was changed to a Field Battery 13th Sept., 1871. Establishment—4 officers, 1 assistant-surgeon, 17 non-commissioned officers, 56 gunners and drivers and 55 horses. There is a detachment of two guns at Morriston, 9 miles from Guelph. The commissioned officers are: Captain A.H. Macdonald, M.S., G.S.; 1st Lieutenant D. McCrae, M.S.; 1st Lieutenant William Nicoll, M.S., G.S.; Assistant-Surgeon A.A. Macdonald, M.S., G.S., M.B., M.R.C.P. & S. Ed'g. The non-commissioned officers are: Sergeant-Major C. Knowles, G.S.; Sergeants, Sully, G.S.; McNaughton, G.S.; Murchison, G.S.; J. McNaughton, G.S.; Corporals, H. Sorby, G.S.; W. Young, G.S.; H. Thatcher, G.S.; Elliott; D.H. McNaughton; Bombardiers, Marsh, G.S.; Fraser; Vincent; H. McDermid; Quarter-Master, Sergeant Marshall; Farrier, Sergeant Spiers, V.S.; Orderly Room Clerk, Sergeant H. Vincent; Hospital Sergeant, C. Carthew; Trumpeter, Walter Macdonald.[37]

In 1894, this description of the Wellington County Militia was given by the *Guelph Mercury*:

The First Brigade of Field Artillery, Guelph, Lt.-Col. Macdonald commanding, contains two batteries, A and B, the latter composed largely of O.A.C. students. These are the most efficient batteries in the Dominion, having won the general efficiency cup eight times within the past ten years, and possessing an extensive collection of beautiful trophies. The brigade has always a representative on the Bisley team. The 30th Wellington Battalion of Rifles, with band and headquarters at Guelph, is the largest rural battalion in the Province, having ten companies.[38]

The militia also enjoyed an active social life and the local newspapers reported details of

these events and the patriotic speeches which accompanied them:

"Shout, shout, shout, ye loyal Britons!
Cheer up, let the rabble come,
For beneath the Union Jack
We will drive the Fenians back,
And we'll fight for our beloved Canadian home."

Quoting these words, The *Guelph Daily Herald* on March 10, 1891, carried the story of a complimentary dinner tendered the veterans who fought against the Fenian Raiders in 1866, by Col. Higinbotham and Capt. Bruce, on the evening of Monday, March 9. . . .

1st Brigade Field Artillery, 1880

Speeches were delivered by the chairman and by Col. Macdonald, Major Hood, Capt. Thompson, Quarter Master Mann and Bugler Dyson. Nearly all present had a few words to say, and joined in several lively songs. . . . The editor of the *Herald* had even written a poem, "The Volunteers of Canada", and this was read during the evening. All pronounced the dinner a great success.[39]

When England issued the call for volunteers for the South African War in October, 1899, five local residents, Lorne Walker, W. Wiggan, Joseph Bruce, J. Fitzpatrick and Samuel Bar-

ber volunteered. Walker and Wiggan were accepted among the 1000-man Canadian quota,[40] and later Barber went to South Africa as well. In all, some 28 Guelph residents would ultimately see service in the Boer War.[41]

Between the Boer War and World War I, several important changes were made in Guelph's militia arrangements. Acting at the request of Colonel Biggar, the Quartermaster General of Canada, Colonel White undertook the formation of a local Army Service Corps. By 1903, some 200 men had joined to form

The Guelph Armoury.

Company No. I, A.S.C. Colonel White commanded the Company for five years, when Major E.C. O'Brien took over.[42]

The most noticeable change in Guelph, however, was the construction of an imposing new armoury. The Federal estimates of 1903 allocated $10,000 for preliminary work, and actual construction began in 1906. It was not until 1909, however, that the new building was complete. With its castellated facade, it was one of the most imposing armouries in the Dominion. In December of that year, the *Mercury* repeated proudly the words of one important observer:

"You have not an Armoury here, you have a palace." This was the expression made this morning to the military officers by the New District Officer Commanding, Col. Hodgins of London, after he had gone through the handsome and elaborate military building. . . . Col. Hodgins coincides with the opinion that the building, which is now all but completed, compares very favorably with any armoury in the country.[43]

The total cost was almost $150,000, an enormous sum for the time.

The declaration of war by Great Britain in August, 1914, elicited in Guelph as always an enthusiastic response to the call to arms and members of Guelph's militia immediately enlisted in the regular army. On the first day of the call, August eighth, nearly 115 volunteers signed up, and on the twentieth, the first squad left Guelph for Camp Valcartier.[44] In Septem-

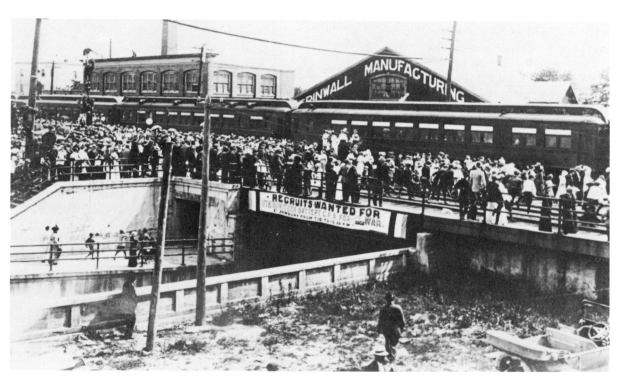

The 11th Field Artillery leaving Guelph in 1915 for overseas duty under the command of Lieutenant George Drew during the First World War, 1914-1918.

ber the local Army and Navy veterans of
Guelph formed a home guard unit, and forty-
five names were immediately placed on the
roll.[45]

Shortly after war was declared, the whole
tone of local social life appeared to change and
the streets filled with uniforms. Acting under
orders from the Canadian War Department,
the Guelph police seized all amateur radio
broadcasting sets in the area. The following
story was reported by the *Mercury*:

Puslinch Man is Owner of a Good Wireless Plant.
Chief Randall has Seized Three of Them to Date.
In Good Shape. Capable of Receiving Messages
Over Long Distance.
Chief Randall motored out to Mr. R.F. Howitt's
farm in Puslinch Tp. on Wednesday afternoon and
seized a wireless apparatus which had been installed on his farm. He is a wireless enthusiast. The
apparatus seized was most complete, and was one
of the finest in this section of the country. Mr. Howitt who operated this machine is an amateur. The
Chief also took charge of a machine in the possession of Mr. Hutcheon of the Bank of Montreal. It
was a small one, not fully equipped, which had
been placed in Mr. Hutcheon's hands by Scout
Master Street, when he left the City, and had formerly been used for boy scout purposes.[46]

In actual fact, the radio sets had been
turned over voluntarily, and in one case the
owner had offered to accompany the set overseas as its operator.[47]

In addition to Wellington County's two
original battalions, the Government, in 1915,
asked the County to raise a third, the 153rd.
This work was begun on December first, 1915,
under the leadership of Judge Hayes, honorary
president; James Beattie, Fergus, president,
and Alderman H. Westoby, of Guelph, secretary. The commander of the new battalion was
Lieutenant-Colonel J.J. Craig.[48] On April 25,
1917, the 153rd left for overseas.[49] By the time

the local recruiting office was closed on March
15, 1918, some 5,610 men had been examined,
and 3,328 were accepted for service.[50]

Guelph's residents also contributed generously to campaign fund drives. The most important of these was conducted on behalf of the
Canadian Patriotic Fund, which was designed
to:

Provide a fund for the assistance, in case of need, of
the wives, children and dependent relatives of
officers and men, residents of Canada, who, during
the present war, may be on active service with the
naval and military forces of the British Empire and
Great Britain's allies.[51]

The official history of the Canadian Patriotic Fund Association gives this account of
their success in Guelph:

Organized early in the month of September, 1914,
the Patriotic Association at Guelph was from the
first affiliated with the national body, and, in the
course of its existence, has both raised and administered large sums of money. It is one of the few
branches of which the officials have remained unchanged until the present time [1919], J.M. Taylor,
L. Goldie and C.L. Dunbar having held the respective offices of president, treasurer and secretary continuously. The success of the Fund at Guelph may
be said to be due almost entirely to the efforts and
ability of these three gentlemen.

The citizens of Guelph responded most heartily
to the several appeals of the committee and the national treasury was enriched to the extent of
$252,223.06 up to March 31, 1919. Against this, the
sum of $160,324.47 was advanced for the needs of
soldiers' dependents in that city, 465 families receiving assistance for shorter or longer periods. Despite the amount of work entailed every month in
administering money among so many families it
was all done gratuitously, the bulk of the clerical
work being faithfully discharged by the Misses
McTague and Clark.

The committee at Guelph early perceived the
value of a Ladies' Auxiliary for visiting families, in-
vestigating applications and giving to the benefici-

aries the advice that was so often needed, and a large number of ladies were organized for that work under the presidency of Mrs. P. Savage. The committee also adopted the suggestion of the national executive committee that arrangements should be made whereby soldiers' dependents should be assured of a supply of coal during the winters of 1916-17 and 1917-18.[52]

Although a steady stream of wounded and discharged soldiers began to return to Guelph from 1917 on, it was not until August, 1919, that the City held its official salute to the returned soldiers. The *Mercury* described that day's festivities as follows:

Returned men held a gala day and all Guelph made merry on August 20, 1919, when thousands of citizens turned out to witness the great homecoming parade of the veterans of the Great War. Fully fifteen thousand people lined the route of parade, from the City Hall to Exhibition Park, and as the veterans marched past with military precision, they were greeted with wild enthusiasm by the cheering multitudes. Arrived at the Exhibition Park the six companies of men marched past the reviewing station with perfect step. . . It was the greatest day of reunion ever held in the City. After the review the men gathered around the band stand, where Major General Macdonnell spoke briefly to them, complimenting them and complimenting Guelph for the fine parade and for the magnificent turnout. There was a great representation of industrial floats in the parade, and a hundred decorated automobiles that won admiration from the spectators. . . .[53]

In addition to the parade, there were ball games, Highland dancing and music by several bands. To top off the day, some fifteen hundred men were served a banquet in the armoury.

In 1921 the Guelph War Memorial Association was formed for the purpose of considering ways and means of erecting a memorial in the City of Guelph in honour of those who fell dur-

The Guelph War Memorial in Trafalgar Square.

ing the War of 1914-1918. The following officers were elected: President, H. Westoby; Vice-President, Mr. Dobson; Secretary, George A. Drew.[54]

A competition for the design of the memorial was held in 1923, and thirty-one designs were entered. First prize, the commission to do the work, was awarded to Mr. Alfred Howell, Principal of Central Technical School of Toronto.[55]

In 1926 a grant of $7,000 was received towards the proposed memorial, and a contract concluded with Mr. Howell.[56] The cenotaph was erected in Trafalgar Square in time for Guelph's 100th Anniversary Celebrations in 1927.

Although trade unions, as such, did not appear in Guelph until the late 1860's, there were occasional examples of labour organization before that date. Labourers on the Grand Trunk had struck several times between 1853

and 1856 for higher wages. In reporting the first of these events, the editor of the *Guelph Advertiser* commented:

During the present week there has been a general turn-out amongst the men working on the railway in the neighborhood of this Town, and after the contractor had agreed to pay a dollar a day the men then claimed to work only ten hours for a day's work. What will be the result we cannot say.

The Contractors of the Grand Trunk Railway have taken the only course open to them, in bringing over several thousand laborers, masons and engineers.[57]

As the Grand Trunk's labourers were only in the area for a short time, these strikes had little lasting effect on the labour situation in Guelph.

The first labour agitation to occur in Guelph was due to a group of retail clerks attempting to reduce the number of hours they were required to work. In January, 1855, the following letter appeared in the *Guelph Advertiser* announcing the new association:

EARLY CLOSING ASSOCIATION

Sir,—Last Monday evening, the clerks of the different establishments in Guelph, met at the British Hotel, to determine upon the best way of bringing about an early closing movement. As there is little or no business done in any store after the hour of seven o'clock, they thought it advisable to endeavour to induce the Merchants to close their different places of business at seven instead of eight o'clock, as has been hitherto done. A deputation of three of their number was therefore sent to call upon the merchants, to try to persuade them to combine with their young men in carrying out a movement as beneficial to themselves as to those in their employment. Without hesitation, all the storekeepers agreed, with the exception of three, from whom no definite answer could be obtained. The clerks assembled a second time on Wednesday evening, to hear the report of the deputation; and as it was so very satisfactory, they formed themselves into a so-

ciety called the Guelph Young Men's Early Closing Association, in order that their measures might be carried out more successfully.[58]

The three holdout merchants, however, proved to be a severe stumbling block. As long as any merchant remained open, all his competitors were forced to do so as well. In the end, the movement for shorter hours failed because all the merchants would not agree, and the Guelph Young Men's Early Closing Association soon disbanded. The issue of shorter hours was taken up once more in 1872, but again failed to gain general acceptance.[59]

The first body of workmen to establish a union in Guelph were the shoemakers. Their organization, the Knights of St. Crispin, Guelph Lodge, No. 202, was organized in 1869. It was, however, far different in principle than later

"Sam Tawse", a pine leprechaun carved in 1858 by Douglas Bruce, and used as a shoe display figure in the Boot and Shoe establishment of William Tawse, Day's Block, Market Square.

union organizations. Its membership consisted of the skilled journeymen shoemakers of Guelph who worked in the many shoemaking establishments. Its primary function was to maintain a pension and welfare fund for its members, inform them of job opportunities and unfair employers throughout North America, and to supervise wages and employment conditions. Since its membership, as skilled workmen, viewed themselves as responsible members of society, they preferred to boycott unfair employers rather than strike—a weapon used only as a last resort. As time passed, other skilled workmen such as carpenters, iron molders and coopers formed similar unions, but none were particularly active.

In the economic crisis of 1896-1897, local employers attempted to maintain the profitability of their enterprises by a reduction in wages. The *Mercury* outlined the events at one of these plants, the Bell Organ and Piano Company:

A crisis was threatened at the Bell Organ and Piano Company on Friday, September 24, 1897, when trouble which had been brewing between the employees and management for some time threatened to develop into something of a more serious nature. The cause of the trouble was an eight per cent cut in wages all round, and the employees after making appeals to Mr. Bell, the then general manager, was referred to the old country board [i.e., the Board of Directors of the British Head Office], but the onus was placed on the management, and with this decision the men decided that they would receive their old wages or walk out on strike. Mr. Bell refused to make any concessions after receiving a document signed by 200 of the workers, and the men, with the exception of the varnishers and polishers, decided to remain at work until October 3.[60]

In the end the men capitulated and accepted Bell's terms.

The failure of the various trade unions in Guelph to prevent reductions in wages did, however, have one concrete result: it brought about the establishment of a Trades and Labour Council in Guelph in 1898. In 1912 that body summarized their activities as follows:

The above Council came into being in the year 1898, securing its charter from the Dominion Trades and Labor Congress, there being thirteen local unions affiliated. Bro. E.J. Corman, of the Iron Molders' Union was its first President, his successors being: Edward Powers, 1899; C.W. Dawson, 1900; Joseph Dandeno, 1901-2; A.A. Anderson, 1903; Wm. Drever, 1904; O.R. Wallace, 1905; J.C. McKenzie, 1906; Frank Howard, 1907; Thos. Hall, 1908-9-10; Harry Thatcher, 1911; Wm. Parker, 1912.

Since its inception the Council has more than justified its existence, having taken an active interest in all matters appertaining to the welfare of the wage-worker. Its activities have not been confined to the betterment of the organized worker only; but have been freely given to all movements stretching out for the public good.[61]

Nor were these claims exaggerated. As Guelph's newspapers showed, the local Trades and Labor Council, as the voice of labour, was active not only in matters relating to working conditions, but in political, commercial and cultural matters as well.

In the period 1902 to 1914 leading unionists hoped to persuade both the growing number of industrial employees, and the public at large, to support unions through the purchase of "union label" goods. E.W.A. O'Dell, Canadian representative of the Boot and Shoe Workers' Union explained this policy to a *Mercury* reporter in October, 1902:

Mr. O'Dell reports business is very good in the boot and shoe line and states that there is a growing demand for union stamped shoes in Canada. The policy of the Boot and Shoe Workers' Union, Mr.

*A view of the Bank of Montreal showing the Guelph Co-operative
Association stores on Quebec Street at the left.*

O'Dell says, is meeting with great favor. In the drawing up of agreements between the firms and the union this organization has practically made strikes and lockouts an impossibility in union shops. "When we grant the use of our stamp to a manufacturer", he says, "we enter into an agreement by a signed contract that there shall be no strike or lockout, and that all questions of labor which cannot be settled by mutual agreement shall be submitted to a board of arbitration, and the decision of this board shall be final and binding upon the employer, the union and the employees." The union is steadily growing Mr. O'Dell states. . . .

It might just be mentioned here that the President, John F. Tobin, and Secretary Charles Bain, of the Boot and Shoe Workers' Union, are both old Guelph boys, the President being born and raised here.[62]

The second major result of trade union activity in Guelph was the creation of the Guelph Co-operative Association in 1902. Two years after this association was formed, it began its own retail operations, and quickly attracted members from all walks of life. In fact, by 1908, it could no longer be described as a "union" activity. The *Guelph Mercury Industrial Souvenir*, of 1908, gave this description of the co-operative store's management and success:

Under this system the necessities and luxuries of life

Piano and Organ Workers Union No. 34, organized March 21st, 1902.
TOP ROW: *W. Triggs, Bert Foltz, C. Hodgkins.* MIDDLE ROW: *W. Lansing, B. Howse, W. Stephens, J. Smith.* BOTTOM
ROW: *Alex. Cross, Treas., J.F. Mann, Vice Pres., C.L.J. Camidge, President, G. Cutting, Rec. Sec., W. Drever, Fin. Sec.*
The first Piano Makers Union organized in Canada. The members of this Union were all employees of the Bell Piano
and Organ Co. Makers of the famous "Bell" Piano. "Built to last a life-time."

are secured at a trifle over cost to the shareholders, as the goods are bought in large quantities from first hands, thus avoiding the middleman and saving his profits. The Guelph Co-operative Association, Limited, was organized in 1904, and is composed of between 300 and 400 shareholders, wage earners of the City. They own and operate two large stores at 39 and 41 Quebec Street, in each of which they occupy three floors.[63]

The "Co-op" did much to reduce the cost of living for Guelph's residents and to ensure price competition among Guelph's merchants.

The platform of the T.L.C. in 1912 shows the breadth of interest it had developed in just fourteen years:

[T.L.C.] Platform of Principles

1. Free compulsory education.
2. Legal working day of eight hours, and six days to a week.
3. Government inspection of all industries.
4. The abolition of the contract system on all public works.
5. A minimum living wage, based on local conditions.
6. Public ownership of all franchises, such as railways, telegraphs, telephones, water-works, lighting, etc.
7. Tax reform, by lessening taxation on industry and increasing it on land values.
8. Abolition of the Dominion Senate.
9. Exclusion of all Orientals.

10. The Union Label to be placed on all manufactured goods, where practicable, and on all government and municipal supplies.
11. Abolition of child labor by children under fourteen years of age; and of female labor in all branches of industrial life, such as mines, workshops, factories, etc.
12. Abolition of property qualification for all public offices.
13. Voluntary arbitration of labor disputes.
14. Proportional representation with grouped constituencies and abolition of municipal wards.
15. Direct legislation through the initiative and referendum.
16. Prohibition of prison labor in competition with free labor.[64]

Although some of these principles were dropped, many still remain the goals of the trade union movement.

From 1900 on, as a series of confrontations developed between local unions and factory owners, the Guelph T.L.C. became actively involved in politics both at the municipal and national level. Delegations appeared regularly at City Council meetings to give labour's point of view and to request concessions for "working people." Among the most active of the political leaders of the local T.L.C. were a number of self-proclaimed "Socialists" who, as time went on, achieved considerable influence.

Until World War I the newspapers in Guelph took a rather tolerant, if suspicious view of the Socialists, but with the outbreak of war, this attitude changed. One of the Socialists' demands was that Canada refrain from entering the war (a view shared by the *Christian Guardian*, a leading Methodist newspaper.) When the local Socialists continued to oppose Canada's deepening war involvement, feelings in Guelph against them ran high. The *Mercury* reported on such an incident in 1917:

There were some lively doings on the streets of Guelph on the night of June 1, 1917, following an anti-conscription meeting, held in the Trades and Labor Hall. The members of the 64th Battery, and some of the returned soldiers, together with many civilians, decided that the Socialists should be further entertained. A number of them were accordingly lined up at the head of the procession, and made to lead the parade up Wyndham Street. When the Opera House was reached, a move was made to take possession of the House, and place the Socialists on the stage, so that everybody could get a good view of them. The idea did not altogether appeal to the manager of the theatre, and he and the police prevailed upon the soldiers not to do this. The march was then begun back down town. At the front of the King Edward Hotel, a large blanket was produced, and three of the most prominent leaders of the Socialists were introduced into the delightful little game of being tossed high in the air from the blanket. At the conclusion of this. . . . they were also forced to give "three cheers for conscription."[65]

With the Socialists intimidated by such displays, local attention was drawn to the Jesuit Novitiate situated some three miles north of the City.

When the Military Service Act (Conscription Act)[66] was given Royal assent on August 29, 1917, one clause caused considerable resentment. According to the Act theological students were liable for conscription, whereas "Clergy, including members of any recognized order of an exclusively religious character. . . .,"[67] were not. Thus, as novice Jesuits were members of such an order, they were not liable for military service. This "injustice" disturbed local Protestants and strong protests against the Act were made to the Government.

More seriously, rumours began to circulate that a number of Catholics who would otherwise have been liable for service had entered Novitiates to escape military duty, and that one of these was Marcus Doherty, son of Charles Doherty, the Minister of Justice and the only Catholic in the Borden Cabinet.[68] As time passed, these rumours became even more exaggerated. One Guelph resident claimed that he had seen cannons and munitions being brought into the Novitiate, while others claimed that the Jesuits had constructed a network of tunnels into the City proper.[69] In this climate of suspicion, the military authorities decided to stage an inspection of such institutions.

On the night of June 7, 1918, an armed unit of Dominion and Military Police from London, Ontario, under the leadership of Inspector Minard and Assistant Provost Marshal A.C. Macauley raided the Novitiate and detained and questioned three novices including Marcus Doherty. At this time, Macauley had, by telephone, been ordered to leave the premises by Doherty's father, the Justice Minister, but had refused. Recognizing that such a raid might create a national uproar and revive religious antagonisms between Prostestants and Catholics, Charles Doherty ordered that strict censorship be imposed.[70] In an attempt to prevent ill feeling amongst Catholics, Macauley and his superior, Colonel Godson-Godson, were ordered to go to the Novitiate and apologize to Father Bourque, while General Mewburn, the Minister of Militia wrote:

Words can't express to you my deep regret of the action taken by the Deputy Provost Marshal, Capt. Macauley, on the evening of the 7th.

My attention was called to this matter on my arrival in Ottawa this a.m., and I find that my A.G. has taken immediate action for a most thorough investigation, and if the facts are as stated in your letter, which, of course, I do not doubt, I can assure you that the error in judgment committed by this officer will be dealt with in a proper way, as I will

Lieut. George A. Drew, Mayor, Guelph 1925.

not tolerate any such action on the part of any military officer so far as the operation of the Military Service Act is concerned.[71]

On June twentieth, in order to reduce tension, Captain Macauley was transferred to Winnipeg.[72]

Meanwhile, the Guelph Ministerial Association, led by Reverend W.D. Spence, the president, believing that the publication ban was a tactic to protect Catholic draft evaders from exposure and Charles Doherty from embarrassment, decided to breach the ban. When Doherty imposed the news blackout, the Reverend Spence sent this telegram to him:

Protestant ministers of Guelph have learned from the authorities all details pertaining to the visit of the soldiers to the Guelph Novitiate. We also learn that the censor has forbidden publication of the facts. We do not propose submitting to any such Kaiserism and intend to hold public meetings and make known all the facts, expose the names, and demand justice.[73]

On the following Sunday, the matter was discussed from the pulpits of many Protestant churches,[74] and strong attacks made upon the "preferential" treatment of the Jesuit novices. Faced with this opposition, the Government lifted the publication ban on June twentieth.[75]

When the news of the raid was made public it created a national sensation. Journalists flocked to Guelph and major newspapers everywhere made it headline news. Within days, however, although the Guelph Ministerial Association continued to hint at "revelations" still to come, it became clear that all the rumours and fears had been unfounded. None of the novices were liable for military service and no laws had been broken.

In an effort to reduce tension Prime Minister Borden removed Doherty from the sensitive Justice post to the Post Office[76] and General Mewburn was sent overseas. The Jesuit Order replaced Father Bourque with a new rector, Reverend Joseph Leachy.[77] Finally a public enquiry was ordered, and by the end of summer only an occasional reference could be found.

In September, 1919, the promised public hearing was held, but by now it was of little public importance. After making headlines for a few days, the hearings terminated quietly with the complete exoneration of everyone except Captain Macauley who, it was claimed, had exceeded his orders.[78]

For Guelph's residents, the affair of the raid had been both painful and embarrassing. However, with the return of prosperity in the early nineteen twenties, tensions lessened, and civic calm returned. It had been a difficult period, but the memories of conflict and bitterness faded as the City approached its one-hundredth birthday.

Curling on the Speed River near Allan's Dam,
from an oil painting by Evan Macdonald. (Courtesy Guelph Curling Club)

XIV

Reflections on the First Century

With the Armistice of November 11, 1918, ending World War I, and the Centennial of the City's founding approaching, it was a time of reflection upon the past and the reasserting of values. This renewed interest in the past and its meaning to Guelph's residents took many forms. Long time residents were tracked down and asked to write their memoirs for the Centennial Edition of the *Mercury*, famous sons such as Edward Johnson,[1] the internationally known tenor, were eulogized, and historic buildings were identified and documented. The Priory, Guelph's first major building, however, had a sad ending.

After the departure of John Galt, the Priory continued to serve as an office and temporary living quarters for the Canada Company and its officials until 1831. In that year it was taken over by Captain Strange, who lived there until 1838, when ownership passed to William Allan, proprietor of the adjacent mill, and in turn to his son, David. In 1878, Allan's Mill and the Priory were taken over by David Spence, and finally in 1887 the Priory was converted into a station for the Guelph Junction Railway.[2]

Concern about the preservation of the

Lieutenant-Colonel John McCrae, soldier-poet-physician.

Priory as a link to Guelph's past had been shown as early as 1877, when Robert Thompson had pointed out in his history of Guelph that only four of the 1827 buildings remained.[3] As the Priory fell increasingly into disrepair, public opinion appears to have been divided as to its future. While some voiced concern about the loss of this obvious link to John Galt and Guelph's past, others fearful that passengers disembarking from the C.P.R. trains would receive a poor impression of Guelph, felt that the building should be demolished and replaced with a more modern structure.

When the C.P.R. built the Guelph to Goderich extension of the Guelph Junction Railway, it was proposed that the Priory should be torn down and replaced by a brick and stone building costing some $40,000.[4] Although the project was not undertaken at that time, the prospect that the Priory might be razed drew a response from as far away as Glasgow, Scotland. In October, 1905, Guelph's Mayor, George Sleeman, received the following communication:

As a townsman of John Galt, Canadian Pioneer and Novelist, I have been interested in a report which has reached Scotland that Galt's house at Guelph is about to be demolished. Can you inform me if this is true? and if so, will you kindly supply me with any available information on the subject. It would be a further obligement if you could let me have a picture of Galt's threatened Guelph house. In return I will be glad to send a photograph of the house in which Galt was born in Irvine, Scotland.[5]

The *Mercury*, on printing this letter, remarked that Mayor Sleeman was "one of the many citizens who hope that the old landmark will not be disturbed."[6]

Although nothing came of the original proposal to replace the Priory with a modern station, pressure began to be placed upon the

C.P.R. to carry out its promise. This came to a head in May, 1908:

An important conference was held yesterday afternoon between the members of the Ry. and Manufacturing Committee [of City Council], Mr. Wm. Bell and Col. Macdonald, of the Guelph Junction Board, and Mr. G.B. Ryan, chairman of the Ry. Committee of the Board of Trade. The important matter discussed was the possibility of improvements in the service and accommodation of the C.P.R. As a result of deliberations, a committee to interview the head officials of the C.P.R. was selected as follows: Messrs. Bell, Macdonald and J. Kennedy, for the Guelph Junction Board; Mr. H.C. Scholfield, G.B. Ryan and Lindsay Torrance, for the Board of Trade; Mayor Newstead, Ald. Simpson and Ald. Penfold for the Council. . . . The deputation will urge upon the officials that the service should be improved. . ., [and] that the C.P.R. should carry out its promise and erect a new station here. In case this is done, the deputation will give assurance of a very large increase in business.[7]

The C.P.R. decided to comply with Guelph's wishes, and by October, 1910, workmen had commenced the building of the new station near the Eramosa Road bridge.[8] As the time approached for the Priory to be demolished, a few of Guelph's residents, led by George Sleeman, tried to save the building. Unfortunately, neither the C.P.R. nor the City were interested and it appeared that the building was doomed. At this point, after protracted negotiations, ex-Mayor George Sleeman purchased the building from the C.P.R., and moved the two wings to his home on Waterloo Avenue. He also persuaded the City to allow him to move the main structure to a vacant lot close to its original site until a permanent home could be found. This move was completed in November, 1911.[9] The Priory stood on this site until 1926.

Although there appeared to be little general

The Priory, when used as the Canadian Pacific Railway Company station, circa 1905.

The new Canadian Pacific Railway Company station in Trafalgar Square.

interest in preserving the Priory, from time to time there was evidence that the building and its significance had not been forgotten. Immediately after World War I two major proposals were put forward, but neither of these gained widespread support. The first, from President G.E. Creelman of the Ontario Agricultural College, suggested that if public support were forthcoming, the Priory could be moved to the O.A.C. grounds, where it would be turned into a museum.[10] The second proposal was put forward by the Guelph Horticultural Society, but there again the main problem was money:

At a meeting of the Horticultural Society held last evening. . .there was considerable discussion regarding the old Priory Building, better known as the first house in Guelph. The Society are willing to undertake all the work in connection with fixing the old building up if the citizens will back them up with the funds. The Horticultural Society is not a wealthy organization but they feel it is up to them to take this matter in hand, and with some financial assistance from the citizens, could convert the old log cabin into a picturesque building surrounded by beauty. The President, Mr. H. Occomore, will interview Mr. Geo. Sleeman, the owner of the building regarding the proposed plans.[11]

Although Sleeman was enthusiastic, none of the more influential civic groups offered to assist and the project quickly died.

By 1922, the dilapidated state of the Priory began to draw the attention of other centres. In May of that year the *London Advertiser* (Ontario) made this wry comment:

Guelph has one spot that is dear to its heart, and that is an old log house that tradition says is the first place erected in that snug little city. . . .It was going to get the deuce a few years ago but kindlier minds prevailed and the cry of "Spare that Shanty" won out, but its last days have not been its proudest. . . .It's tough when an old log house lives to be real old to have to get shunted off on a side street and never have folks come around to say "Oh, look at that". . .Cruel, that's what it is. Cruel.[12]

Deeply stung by this ridicule of Guelph's lack of concern for its historical beginnings, both the *Guelph Mercury* and some of the residents began to reconsider their previous indifference to the fate of the Priory. A few weeks after the *London Advertiser*'s article appeared, the *Mercury* made this editorial comment:

A Large Donation:—Announcement is made this morning that a splendid donation of a check for $250.00 has been received from Mr. Wm. Higinbotham, the former well known Guelphite, to be used in connection with the restoration of the old Priory Building, Guelph's first house. Mr. Higinbotham is keenly interested in preserving this historical relic of the Royal City, and states that as preparations will soon be under way for the celebration of Guelph's Centennial, it would not be complete unless the old Building was properly restored for the event.[13]

With both the *Mercury* and men of the status of Mr. Higinbotham supporting the restoration of the Priory, City Council again considered the matter, but no action was taken. Left unattended, the rain soon penetrated the roof and much of the structure rotted. In February, 1926, the City Building Inspector, concerned that someone might be injured, condemned the building. The *Mercury* commented:

Now that the Building Inspector has condemned the Old Priory Building, it has been suggested that some of the material in the structure be utilized in making a miniature replica of the building and that it be placed in one of the parks as a memento of the founder of the City, John Galt, who erected it. Inspector Scroggie states that there are a few of the logs that are still fairly sound, the rafters are still fit for use and the window casings and two of the doors are not beyond repair. The building as it stands is dangerous and will have to be torn down.[14]

Immediately a committee composed of W.A. Cowan, Doctor N. Wallace, Sheriff Allan and Roswell Goldie was struck in a last attempt to save the building, but it was in vain. In 1957 Cowan described his efforts:

We had quite a few meetings, some in the City Hall and others in the County Court House. . . ., and our committee had even a contractor named Ibbotson who was picked out to rebuild the Priory. . . .

We knew where there was a stand of elm trees that seemed suitable to use in replacing the original logs. However, we found that the Priory had been constructed of rock elm. The other elm trees didn't seem suitable and were no longer considered. Still, we were hopeful of rebuilding. . . .[15]

Mr. Cowan did, however, make extensive drawings of the old Priory, and his sons, David and Walter, under their father's supervision, constructed a replica which stood for many years in Riverside Park.[16]

For some time after the Priory was torn down, Ed. Stewart stored the good logs, hoping against hope that funds would be found to reconstruct the building. Finally, in the nineteen-thirties, the logs were moved to Riverside Park where they lay unwanted until they were cut up and used as fuel by men on relief.[17] Eventually, the wings which had been retained by George Sleeman were donated to Doon Pioneer Village.[18]

Even that voice of "progress", the *Mercury*, found occasion to mourn the lack of an appreciation for the City's rich historical and architectural heritage. In 1914 one writer remarked that "the historical instinct does not appear as one of the marked possessions of our people. We have spasms of it from time to time, but only spasms."[19]

In reflecting upon the past the *Mercury* in their Centennial Issue[20] made clear there was much about which the residents of Guelph could be justly proud. In the sphere of sport there were very real and significant achievements to report. Many of Guelph's residents had been active and skilful sportsmen. Although for the first few years individual sporting activities such as hunting, fishing, swimming and hiking were predominant, with the immigration of the well-to-do English families in 1832, more elaborate forms of organized sport were initiated.

The first of the club sports to be established was cricket. While both 1832 and 1833 have been given as the date of the beginning of the cricket club, the more extensive accounts normally give the second date.[21] The origins of the Guelph Cricket Club were described as follows by one early historian:

The Guelph Cricket Club was organized in 1833. Mr. J.C.W. Daly, then agent for the Canada Co., got a grant of $20 from the commissioners to level the ground, which was on the Market square. He presented the club with a set of balls and bats, and cricket became the standard amusement. Among the players of the early days are mentioned Messrs. John and James Wilson, two brothers named Thompson, Messrs. Walter King, Barnard, James Salter, Hodgert, King, Nichols, Marsh, Smith, Reeves, James Howard, William Wilson and Murton.[22]

As early as 1834 a team from Guelph was reported to have taken part in a tournament in Hamilton.[23] The same writer described the club's activities in the early eighteen-forties as follows:

This club in those days could put up a fine team, and hold its own with any team in the province; once, indeed, about 1841, at Hamilton, they played a team picked from all the province. Practice was held about three afternoons each week, first on the

Square, and later on the old cricket ground, near Goldie's mill. Matches were played almost annually with Toronto. The club, numbering about thirteen or fourteen men went down in an open wagon through the woods. The journey to Toronto occupied two days, for the men did not hurry themselves unduly; another two days would be spent in the match—an innings each—and, as the journey home required two days, the whole time required for the match was a week. Mr. [Geo.] Wilson generally drove the team down. The following are the eleven that went to Toronto in 1840: Messrs. Wilson, John Wilson, Wm. Thompson, E. Thompson, Walter King, George King,—[probably George] Murton, J.W. Colson, Barnard, Nichols, Jas. Salter: S. Neeves, spare man: Terry Marsh, umpire; Jas. Hodges, scorer. Other places with which the Guelph Club competed were Woodstock, Brantford, Paris, London and Galt.[24]

The *Guelph Herald* of September 30, 1847, gives this account of a cricket match with Hamilton:

Cricket—Guelph Against Hamilton.—The return game of the match between the clubs of the places named, commenced on the Hamilton ground, on Thursday morning, and terminated yesterday at noon. . . .The Hamilton club having won the toss, put their opponents in. The batting of the Guelph gentlemen was excellent—the wonder is how with the magnificent bowling and fielding which they had to encounter, they managed to score 95 in their first innings. . . .

At the close of the innings, the party partook of lunch on the ground, after which Messrs. Sadlier and Hamilton took the bats, on behalf of the Hamilton club. The bowling, although passably good, bore no comparison with that of Messrs. Sharpe, Hamilton and Gillesby, which in some measure will account for the very large score made by the Hamiltonians, 121. The Guelph club went in for their second innings, but the day was so far advanced that the game could not possible to finish [*sic*] before nightfall. In consequence an adjournment took place, after five wickets had gone down. The clubs dined together at Roach's Hotel, and yesterday

The Guelph Cricket Club, Colonel White at far right, circa 1907.

morning came to scratch again, the game being finally won by the Hamilton club, with nine wickets to go down. Everything went off pleasantly, and the most cordial feeling existed throughout the game.[25]

As the Town of Guelph began to grow rapidly after 1850, membership in the Guelph Cricket Club grew as well. In 1873 the *Town of Guelph Directory* carried this note:

The Guelph Cricket Club is one of the oldest institutions of the Town, having been organized in 1833—forty years ago. It has always been fortunate in securing good material, and though not exempt from occasional defeat, yet its records show it to have been more uniformly successful than most of its contemporaries..It now numbers over 70 members, and ranks second to none in the cricket scale. The officers are: President [Judge] F.J. Chadwick; Vice-President, Geo. Murton, Jr.; Secretary and Treasurer, Mr. Fitzgerald.[26]

In 1907 a major step was taken with the formation of the Western Ontario Cricket League. As this story from the *Mercury* notes:

It was apparently in 1907 that the first Cricket Association in this district was formed, for the records show that a "meeting was held in Galt on April 11th, for the formation of a Cricket Association. . . .in an effort to revive Cricket in this part of the Province." This Association was named "The Western Ontario Cricket League," and is still [in 1927] in existence. From 1907 to 1923, with the exception of the years 1917 to 1919, during which there was no competition, Guelph was a regular participant in the league, and won the championship on six occasions, three times, in 1907-8-9, successively. The local club then went under the title of Guelph and O.A.C. Cricket Club, and it was not until 1924 that it was renamed Guelph C.C.[27]

The second club sport to be organized in Guelph was curling. In the winters of 1827-1830, Doctor William Dunlop and several other residents apparently had curled on the local ponds, but on an informal basis.[28] According to E.C. Guillet, Adam Fergusson organized the first curling club in the area at Fergus in 1834. Similar associations were established in Galt and Guelph in 1838.[29] In spite of its popularity, this association, the Union Curling Club, apparently became inactive for a time in the early eighteen-fifties.

It was not until the winter of 1857-1858 that the sport was reorganized under the leadership of William Congalton:

Mr. William Congalton, father of Mr. Alex. Congalton, was chiefly responsible for the renewal of the game. He had come to Guelph during the year 1855 and could not bear to pass a winter without curling. So he set to work, made some stones of granite boulders and the game was started on Allan's dam. Mr. Adam Robertson, Sr., made handles for the curling stones. Among the first to take an active part in the game were Messrs. Wm. Congalton, Adam Robertson, Alex. Congalton, Thos. McCrae, Chas. Davidson, Alex. Emslie, Colonel Webster, Geo. A. Bruce. . ., Adam Robertson, Jr., David Kennedy, Thos. Dobbie and Jas. Barclay, of Ayr. This first year no matches were played with outside clubs. In the following year the club was regularly organized, and matches began to be played with Fergus, Elora, Galt and other surrounding towns. Before stones were secured, wooden blocks were used. . . .In the early days, of course, play was carried on entirely on outside ice. Games took place on Allan's dam, Goldie's dam, down by the Dundas bridge, at Sleeman's—in fact, wherever ice suitable could be secured.[30]

In September, 1868, a group of citizens became incorporated to build Guelph's first covered rink. According to David Allan:

Those interested at the time, were John Hogg, Thomas Dobbie, Col. N. Higinbotham, William Allan, Alex. Congalton and several other enthusiastic curlers. This rink was a plain wooden building and used for both curling and skating. At the end facing Huskisson Street, were dressing rooms on ei-

*Guelph Curling Society, reorganized
Feb.y 9th 1858.—*

Minutes.

Feb.y 9. According to public announcement, a meeting of Curlers was held in M.r Armstrongs Saloon, for the purpose of reorganizing the Curling Society, when George Pirie Esq. was called to the chair, and M.r Stewart acted as Secretary. It was moved —

1.   That James Webster Esq. be Patron of the Club.
                                      Carried.
2.   That George Pirie Esq. be President.   do.
3.   That Peter Gow Esq be Vice President — do.
4   That James Ferguson be Sec.y and Treasurer. do.

The following gentlemen were appointed a Committee of Management viz,
Messrs. A. Robertson, A Emslie, G. Lapraik, D. Murray, and C. Davidson, three to form a quorum.

It was next resolved that there should be six rinks of curlers, and that the following gentlemen be Skips, viz,
Mess.rs Robertson, Lapraik, Gow, Ferguson, Congalton, and Davidson

It was also resolved that each member should pay. 2/6. or 50 cents of entrance fee,

Next meeting to morrow evening in M.r Armstrongs. to choose players for the different rinks, and to make further arrangements connected with the reorganization of the Club,

Minutes of Guelph Curling Society, formed 1858.

*The Peter Gow trophy and old iron
curling stone. (Guelph Curling Club)*

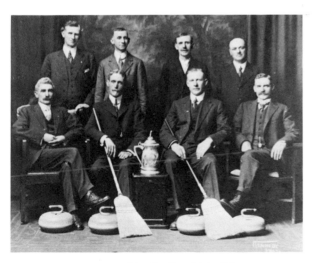

*Guelph Royal City Curling Club. Winners
Ontario Tankard, 1918.* BACK ROW: *W.A. Mahoney, Lead.
F.H. Barber, Second. Fred'k Smith, Second.
E.H. Johns, Lead.* FRONT ROW: *H. Mahoney,
Vice-Skip. C.R. Crowe, Skip. R. Dillon, Skip.
R. Mahoney, Vice-Skip.*

ther side of the entrance. It was situated at the corner of Huskisson and Wellington Streets, it stood for several years, and was a profitable venture for the owner.[31]

In 1869, when the rink was completed, the Union Curling Club joined the Provincial Association, and the Honourable Peter Gow, a resident of Guelph, was named that association's first president.[32]

The City of Guelph Directory for 1882-1883 carried this description of the curling club:

Guelph Union Curling Club was organized in 1838. C. Davidson, Patron; Mrs. C. Davidson, Patroness; D. Stirton, President; D. Kennedy, Vice-President; Geo. Murton, Sec.-Treas.; Wm. Mitchell and A. Robertson, Representative Members; Rev. J.C. Smith, Chaplain. There are 50 members.[33]

In 1885, Peter Gow donated a cup bearing his name for the City championship, and the trophy was won in its first year by a rink skipped by Alex. Congalton.[34] The Union Curling Club produced some outstanding rinks over the years, most notable being one foursome who were runners up for the Ontario Tankard in 1887, and a second who won the Governor-General's Cup in 1920.[35]

In 1888, a second Guelph curling club, the Royal, was organized, with George Sleeman as its first president. Of that organization, the *Mercury* said:

Younger in years, but none the less strong and widely known for that, is the Royal City Club, formed in 1888. In the same year the organization affiliated with the Ontario Association, and from then on has had a splendid record. In any tournaments in which they took part, members of this club made their presence felt, but it was not until 1918 that they became champions, winning the Province's highest curling honor, the Ontario Tankard.[36]

During March, 1889, a group of Guelph residents decided to construct a new commercial arena. To this end a committee composed of George Sleeman, R. Mitchell, A.B. Petrie and J.A. Mowat was established to solicit subscriptions and gather information.[37] In 1892 their efforts resulted in the construction of Victoria Rink on Baker Street behind Knox Presbyterian Church. This rink was used by the Royal Curling Club and for ice skating in the winter, and roller skating in the summer.[38] In 1894 the second of Guelph's major curling prizes, the Sleeman Trophy was donated by George Sleeman.[39] In 1926, the two clubs united to form the Guelph Curling Club.

Our first records of horse racing as an organized sport date from July, August and September, 1847, when the Reverend Arthur Palmer of St. George's Anglican Church discovered to his horror, that part of the parsonage grounds was being used as a race course. On July twentieth he complained bitterly in a letter to John Comb Wilson:

Dear Sir,—I have learned with much regret that arrangements are in progress for converting the grounds of the Parsonage into a Race Course, during the continuance of my lease to you. I was not aware of the intention of holding races on these grounds last year, in time to offer any remonstrance upon the subject, and I did hope that the occurrence would not again take place. But finding that fresh arrangements are now being made, I cannot any longer forbear expressing the strong feeling I entertain on the subject. . . .

I consider then, that any pleasure that may be derived from the trial of the speed of a few horses, or any supposed advantage in regard to the improvement of their breed, is dearly purchased by the demoralizing effects produced by horse racing, in gambling, swearing and drunkenness that it generates in the number of thoughtless and unprincipled persons it attracts to a place, and in the general spirit and habits which it diffuses; a spirit the very opposite of a sober or religious one, and habits

specially ill suited to Canadian life. . . .It cannot but be most painful and repugnant to my feelings, that the Parsonage ground should be used for the purpose above referred to. It was cleared and improved by myself, it was my home for many years as Clergyman of this place, and was afterwards leased to you *as a farm*, during my occupancy of your house in Town, and could I have foreseen that it would have been used as a race ground it should never have passed out of my hands.

I am aware that you have re-let the Parsonage to another, [Mr. Buckland] and I am sure that had it remained in your hands, you would not have allowed it to be used as it now is, without paying me the respect of consulting my feelings on the subject.[40]

In spite of Reverend Palmer's protests, the races took place.

Horse races in Guelph in 1847 ranged, apparently, from rather informal "pickup" matches between local favourites to well organized and widely advertised events sponsored by the Wellington District Turf Club. The *Guelph Herald* reported one such "pickup" match in 1847:

Racing.—A very prettily contested Match came off on Saturday last, between Mr. Sheriff Grange's Mare "Dudu" and Mr. Richard Jackson's Horse "Why not," which created quite a flare-up in the sporting circles here, and drew to the ground a large concourse of people of both sexes, among whom we noticed a goodly number of the beauty and fashion of the Town.—The distance run was one mile. Mr. Grange's "Dudu" took the lead and came in gallantly to the winning Post heading "Why not" about a neck or thereabouts.

The second Match was between Judge Powell's chesnut [sic] Mare and Mr. Grange's "Dudu," Mr. Powell's Mare winning by a considerable distance. . . .[41]

The main races of the year 1847, sponsored by the Turf Club, were held on September fifteenth and sixteenth. According to the advertisement, the stewards were Richard Jackson, Esq., Alexander Harvey, Esq., James Wilson, Esq., and James Hodgert, Secretary and Treasurer.[42] The races advertised were:

Wednesday, 15th Sept., 1847
1st. The Innkeeper's Purse of Ten Pounds, added to a Sweepstakes of Ten Shillings, open for horses the property of Residents in the Township of Guelph, and owned by them three months previous to the first day of the Races. 4 years old, to carry 10 stone—5 years, 10 stone 8 lbs.—6 years and aged—11 stone—two mile heats [fifteen minutes were allowed between each of three heats].
2nd.—The Tradesmen's Purse of £5, added to a Sweepstakes of 10s for Hacks, owned in the District—Catch weights—Heats—Once round the

course. The winner to be sold for £12.10s. if demanded in the usual way.
3rd.—The Ladies Purse of £7.10s., added to a Sweepstakes of £1, for horses owned in the District, 4 years old, to carry 9 stone—5 years 9 stone 8 lbs.—6 and aged, to 11—mile heats.[43]

On the second day of the meet there was a race open to any horse owned in the district, a Hurdle race, and a Pony race. The officials of the Turf Club elected in 1864 were:

President of the Guelph Turf Club. . .was Hon. A.J. Fergusson Blair. Mr. Sheriff Grange was vice-president and the stewards were William Clarke, Mayor of Guelph; Hon. W.H. Dickson, T.S. Parker, M.P.P.; Arthur Hogge, J.J. Kingsmill, C.E. Romain, Richard Jackson, George Palmer and G. McK. Stewart. Judges were Hon. A.J. Fergusson Blair, Hon. W.H. Dickson and Richard Jackson.[44]

The highlight of the Guelph Spring Meet in 1864 was the running of the Queen's Plate at the mile track at Gray's Inn on Eramosa Road (the old Newstead farm). Held on the first day of a three day meet, July 6, 1864, the race was run in three heats. The *Guelph Mercury* of July 8, 1864, communicated the excitement of the day in its report of that event:

Guelph was alive on Tuesday. Between noon and two o'clock a constant stream of vehicles of all kinds—carriages, buggies, wagons, dog-carts, shandry-dans—in fact, everything that could be rigged on wheels, were on the road. Clouds of dust were raised as these passed each other, and pedestrians panted up hill and down dale, still the stream showed no diminution for hours, and the whole picture showed as truthful a representation of the "Derby" on a small scale as was possible to get up in Canada. Arrived at the ground the people got a mouthful of fresh air; but even there it was hot, and as every carriage passed another dust bath had to be endured. The crowd on the race course and around the stands was motley enough. The "fancy" was well represented, but we believed they did not reap a great harvest.

Guelph Fall Races Program, Sept. 26, 1872.

Fast young men with white turbans, the latest of "peg-tops", and the latest slang talk were in abundance. There was quite a sprinkling of the older sporting "gents"—veterans in horse racing—who only bet when they are sure to win and know, or pretend to know, much more about the horses that are to run than anybody else. There was also a sprinkling of young ladies who seemd to have doubts in their own minds as to whether they should be there or not; besides a scattering of old dowagers who evidently felt that their presence there was sufficient to make the affair fashionable. It was a grand collection of characters beginning of the lowest strata of the blackleg and mounting up by easy graduations to the honest man. One commendable feature we noticed—the entire absence of gamblers who ply their arts on the roulette table, and make money out of the "greenhorns" by other knavish devices. A few peep shows were on the grounds, but they lacked customers. The drinking booths were well patronized. Attempts were made to get up a fight or two, but they were nipped in the bud.[45]

"Brunetta", owned by a Doctor Morton won two of the three heats and the purse of fifty sovereigns.[46]

Not only did the Guelph Turf Club continue to carry out successful meets, but in July, 1896, the Guelph Trotting Association was formed to carry on harness racing as well.[47] Moreover, the quality of locally-foaled Standard Bred horses appears to have been high. The *Mercury* of October 9, 1909, carried this story of the career of one such horse:

One of the greatest harness horses ever turned out of Canada is now doing big things on the American Turf: It is Darky Hal the former black Guelph mare.

Darky Hal did her first racing in Guelph as the property of Mr. Walter Herod and was sold two years ago for about as many hundreds as she is now worth in thousands, to John Swartz of Wingham, Ont., her present owner.

The mare paced two heats in remarkably fast

time defeating Mayor Brino at the New York State Fair.[48]

The continued popularity of horse racing in Guelph was attested to by a crowd of between five and six thousand which attended a Civic Holiday meet at the Guelph Exhibition Park in August, 1919.[49]

Robert C. Dunbar of the Toronto *Globe* gave this account of the origin of baseball in Guelph:

Baseball was first introduced into Guelph... by A.S. Feast....He came from Hamilton, where a successful team, the Maple Leafs, was then in existence. The new game took well with the Guelph people, and in 1861 a club was formed, called after the Hamilton club—the Maple Leafs. The membership fee was twelve and a half cents, or as it was then called, sixpence. The membership was large, the first president being J.W. Coulson...The first match played by the new club was against the Flamboro' club, and resulted in a tie—27 to 27. Neither the umpire nor the teams knew that it was permissible to play ten innings, if nine were not sufficient to decide the match. The Guelph battery on this occasion was W[alter] Sunley....and Jas. T. Nicholls of Walkerton. The next year the Hamilton Maple Leafs visited Guelph, and were defeated by 15 to 13; but, later in the season more than balanced this score. Sunley and Nicholls were again the battery, and among the Guelph team were John Coulson and his son; William Dyson..., R. Howard..., and A.S. Feast.[50]

By 1865 the Maple Leafs had developed sufficiently to be a serious challenge for the Canadian championship, and all of Guelph's residents were caught up in the enthusiasm. Dunbar says:

During the next few years the Leafs met principally local teams with good success. They made a number of unsuccessful attempts to wrest the championship from Woodstock, and the interest that was taken in the game is shown by the fact that for one match 500 people and a brass band accompanied the team from Guelph to Woodstock to see the game. 1868 was the year when the Guelph people first became real baseball enthusiasts. In that season 1,500 people went to Woodstock to see a championship game. The Leafs lost, but the game was an exciting one, and caused a great free fight between the supporters of the two teams.[51]

In 1869, the Maple Leafs' attempts to become Canadian champions were crowned with success when they won a three-day tournament at London. In the tournament they defeated Ingersoll by a margin of forty-four runs, and Woodstock by the score of 30 to 17. For

their efforts they won the "Silver Ball" and a purse of $150 in gold pieces. A few weeks later they turned back a challenge by the London club, and were generally acknowledged as champions.[52]

For the next two years the Guelph club defeated every challenge to their Canadian championship, and looking farther afield undertook, in 1870, a tour of several American cities where they achieved considerable success, defeating Rochester "Flower City" twice, Oswego "Ontario's" once and losing to a "picked nine" from Syracuse. On the season

H. Myers (First Base).   J. Smith (Right Field).   C. Maddock (Catcher).   W. Smith (Pitcher).   H. Spence (Third Base).

The Maple Leaf Baseball Club of Guelph, from Harper's Weekly, September 12, 1874.

they outscored their opposition by 374 runs to 146.

By now the Maple Leafs had decided to become semi-professionals—that is—although no salaries were paid, at the end of the season the team members split whatever surplus had been accumulated. In 1871, in order to improve their income, a series of crack professional American teams were invited to include Guelph as a stop on their tour, and although the Guelph team lost every game to the professionals, they gave a good account of themselves. In spite of these losses the Maple Leafs retained the "Silver Ball" against Canadian opposition, and in 1872 gained permanent possession of it by a third successful defence.

In 1874 the Maple Leafs reached the high point of their success. George Sleeman later reminisced about that event:

I was always a member of the Maple Leaf team, from the time it was formed in 1861 by A.S. Feast, who came from Hamilton, but in 1874 they elected me President. The first year of my presidency we succeeded in winning the semi-professional championship of the United States and Canada, at Watertown, N.Y. . . .

A man, named Col. Fowler, who lived in Watertown, N.Y., got up the tournament. It was open to all semi-professional clubs of Canada and the United States. We had played the Boston League team, in Brantford, on the 30th of June, 1874, and on the 1st of July we played them here, and had the largest crowd which ever attended a baseball match in Guelph. It was estimated there were 10,000 people on the ground that day.

We left, the same night, for Watertown, and entered the Maple Leafs for the tournament. The first club we played against was the Klu-Klux, of Oneida, N.Y. The game was 13-4 in our favor. The next club we played was Nassau, and we defeated them 13-8. Finally it was a contest between Easton, Pa., and the Maple Leafs. We beat them 13 to 10. . . .Thus we won the first prize of $500 and the championship of America in the non-professional class.[53]

From 1875 to 1891 baseball declined in popularity as some of the best talent retired and quarrels among the teams in the various leagues prevented any continuity or development. Competing amateur teams such as the Silver Creek Club and the Guelph Beavers were founded, but generally did not last for very long as semi-professional teams lured away their best players. Moreover there were several attempts to form a professional team as well.

In 1886, George Sleeman imported a strong professional team to play in the Canadian League, but when the Toronto and Hamilton teams joined the International League, Sleeman's team lost money and consequently disbanded.[54] In spite of these problems some noteworthy achievements were recorded. In 1876, the Maple Leafs defeated the St. Louis Browns in an exhibition match,[55] and in 1878 were awarded the professional championship of Canada.[56] In the early eighteen-eighties one local player, Fred Dyson, played as a professional for the Grand Rapids and Buffalo clubs.[57]

Baseball Ticket, 1876

In 1892, baseball fever returned to Guelph as the Maple Leafs were reorganized under a new board of officers. The popularity of the sport is demonstrated by this account of that year:

To say that they have been well supported by the people of the City would be a mild way of putting it. When the team played at home the business of the City was practically suspended during the game. For some of the matches the men employed in the factories, started work at 4 o'clock in the morning in order that they might attend the ball game. All classes of the population have been equally enthusiastic in their support of the club, from the small boys who climb over the fences. . .to the leading and professional and business men of the City, who would on no account miss seeing a baseball match. The management of the club charged a low rate of admission, 15 cents, but even then were able to give more to visiting clubs than they received. At every match many ladies were present, and it might almost be said that they were more enthusiastic admirers of the Maple Leafs than their fathers, brothers, etc. . . .[58]

This team reached its peak in 1894 when it won the semi-professional championship of Canada. The 1894 team, James Hough, Bill Dyson, George Chamberlain, Daddy Downes, D.E. Macdonald, Joseph P. Downey, George Bradford, Frank Snyder, Billy Congalton, Bob Benzie, Jim McCracken, Mickey Powers and Billy McElroy, was considered by many to have been the best ever to represent Guelph.[59] After 1894 the club deteriorated and for some years interest in baseball waned.

After World War I, the Maple Leafs were reorganized and from 1919 to 1927 were strong contenders in the newly formed Intercounty League. In 1919, 1920 and 1921 they won the regular season pennant, but were defeated in the play-offs. From 1922 to 1927 (with the exception of 1925) they reached the final series but were defeated in the play-offs.[60]

Aside from cricket, curling, and baseball, other team sports in Guelph did not achieve a great deal of prominence before 1927. A lacrosse club was formed in 1878, Association Football (soccer) was played from 1887 on, and a hockey club was organized in 1897.

The one really bright spot on the hockey scene before 1927 was the championship season of 1903. In that year the Guelph "Wellington" and the "Victoria" clubs joined forces to play in the Western Ontario Hockey Association intermediate series. Among the stars of that team was Bert Lindsay who later became a first rate professional with Pembroke, Victoria and the Montreal Wanderers. In the finals, the Guelph team defeated Preston to give Guelph its first hockey title.

Although soccer enjoyed considerable success in local play-downs, the sport never managed to capture the public's fancy. In 1887, the first year that organized soccer was played in the City, Guelph's team was composed of several well-known Guelph residents, including Alderman Harry Mahoney, Charles Raymond, Ben and Jim Mooney, Art Gibbs and Herb Pass. The championship, as it turned out, was to be decided at a "field day" in Elmira, with Galt and Guelph meeting in the semi-finals, and the winner to meet the Elmira team in the finals. As the *Mercury* told the story, the games produced an unusual aftermath:

The important day arrived and there were at least one thousand buggies and carry-alls around the scene of the struggles, when the first game, between Guelph and Galt, was started. The rivalry between these cities was just as keen in those days as it is. . .today.

However, Guelph won, and qualified to meet Elmira in the final for the cup.

Fresh from their victory in the morning, the

Guelph team set about their task of winning the final with such fixity of purpose that at the conclusion of the game the championship was theirs.

Some one, claiming an official connection with the Elmira team, asked for the loan of the cup which was now Guelph's by virtue of conquest, and unsuspectingly the request was granted.

But that was the last ever seen of the trophy. A search was conducted, but no cup could be found and the Guelph team, believing themselves to be victimized, decided to show their disapproval of the incident in a novel manner.

Waiting their opportunity, the cup winners quietly tied a number of the harnessed horses together and then some one started the tied steeds on the move. It requires but a little imagination to picture the havoc and destruction wrought before the stampede was finally halted.

Needless to say, the Guelph lads did not stay to offer an explanation of their action.[61]

The failure of soccer to develop as a major spectator sport in Guelph was a phenomenon that attracted the attention of local sports writers. From time to time, strong clubs were organized, such as the Guelph Nationals teams of 1902-1904, but according to the *Mercury* the main problem arose from the lack of local player development:

The development of soccer has been gradual.

Lawn Bowling Tournament at Victoria Rink Gardens circa 1910.

Throughout the forty years [1887-1927] since the game was first introduced here, until the present year, there have been periods when soccer attracted as many followers as any other sport here. In 1914 it appeared as though the game would establish itself as the principal outdoor sport in the Province.

But the Great War intervened, and with ninety per cent of the players having joined the forces, to return home at the conclusion of the war broken in health, a lowering of the standard of play, and consequently a lessening of the attendance was inevitable. . .

One matter causes regret. Too little attention is being paid towards the development of young native born players. Young players of today are the officials and the spectators of tomorrow, and a broad policy embracing this phase of the development of the game is necessary, for the greater future which many keen judges predict for soccer.[62]

With a constant supply of mature players coming from England and Scotland, local club owners saw little reason to develop a strong junior team program with all its attendant expenses. Unfortunately, this attitude was short sighted, and soccer therefore never gained great popularity among native-born Canadians.

The sports discussed here in some detail were by no means the only ones played in Guelph. From time to time almost every imaginable sport has had a degree of popularity. Boating, shooting, speed skating, long distance running, walking, snowshoeing, quoits, cycling, tennis, lawn bowling, golf, carpet ball, bowling, etc., all had their enthusiasts, and several Guelph residents achieved national prominence in their specialities. As a sports centre, Guelph took second place to none.

In the realm of literature, Guelph has had a long tradition of prose and poetry writing which was shared by all levels of Guelph's society. Whether or not it had been John Galt who provided the inspiration, local residents displayed a remarkable inclination to distinguish themselves in print. Although several local writers had published books, most notably John McLean's[63] *Notes of a Twenty-Five Years' Service in the Hudson's Bay Company*, written while he lived at 21 Nottingham Street, and published in London in 1849; Acton Burrows' *Annals of the Town of Guelph*, published in Guelph in 1877; Mary Leslie's *Cromaboo Mail Carrier*, published in Guelph in 1878; and David Kennedy, whose *Incidents of Pioneer Days at Guelph and the County of Bruce* was published in Toronto in 1903;[64] the main focus of local literary effort was poetry.

Country Dancing.
(Courtesy Public Archives of Canada)

Perhaps the first poem composed in the Guelph area.was "The Paisley Block Ball" written on October 4, 1836, by John Taylor, the original settler on Lot 13, Concession 1, Division B, Guelph Township. It was sung to the air of "The Wearing of the Green":

PAISLEY BLOCK BALL[65]

Think of Great Columbus, that man of worth and fame,
Who found out this great continent that should have borne his name.
In his voyage of discovery no dangers did appal,
    Or we might not now be singing at a
        Paisley Block Ball.

    Chorus – At a Paisley Block Ball,
        At a Paisley Block Ball,
        Or we might not now be singing
        At a Paisley Block Ball.

Our old Mother Country, the land of the brave,
So deeply sunk in debt, the sponge can only save;
The thought of a civil war we did not like at all,
For fighting's not so pleasant as a Paisley Block Ball.

    Chorus – At a Paisley Block Ball,
        At a Paisley Block Ball,
        For fighting's not so pleasant
        At a Paisley Block Ball.

So we left our native land and those we dearly love,
The tears did flow in torrents, while the vessel off did move;
We trusted to the ocean, whatever did befall,
So here we are rejoicing at a Paisley Block Ball.

    Chorus – At a Paisley Block Ball,
        At a Paisley Block Ball,
        So here we are rejoicing
        At a Paisley Block Ball.

Our friends and relations that we did leave behind,
Relief from their burdens we hope they soon will find;
That they are happy, we wish them one and all,
We are here with mirth and glee at the Paisley Block Ball.

    Chorus – At a Paisley Block Ball,
        At a Paisley Block Ball,
        As we are here with mirth and glee

        At the Paisley Block Ball.
When we came to the wild land all covered with wood,
We soon made a clearance where mighty timber stood;
By steady perseverance, we made many a tree to fall,
Which led us on to comforts and a Paisley Block Ball.

    Chorus – And a Paisley Block Ball,
        And a Paisley Block Ball,
        Which led us on to comforts
        And a Paisley Block Ball.

We turned the forest into fertile fields to support ourselves and stock,
We have comfortable homes within the Paisley Block;
As in Lebanon of old, we cut cedars straight and tall,
So let us now enjoy ourselves at the Paisley Block Ball.

    Chorus – At a Paisley Block Ball,
        At a Paisley Block Ball,
        So let us now enjoy ourselves
        At a Paisley Block Ball.

Now to the ladies, the partners of our lives,
We wish every comfort to sweethearts and wives;
They're like as many stars all shining in the hall,
And move about most gracefully at the Paisley Block Ball.

    Chorus – At a Paisley Block Ball,
        At a Paisley Block Ball,
        And move about most gracefully
        At the Paisley Block Ball.

From all the ills of life, we wish they may be free,
Without them the place a wilderness would be,
We'll drink to the ladies' healths, I know you join me shall,
For their beauty is the lustre of the Paisley Block Ball.

    Chorus – Of the Paisley Block Ball,
        Of the Paisley Block Ball,
        For their beauty is the lustre
        Of the Paisley Block Ball.

We have horses, cows and pigs, we have poultry and sheep,
We have produce for to sell and plenty still to keep;

We have instruments to cut, and cattle for to haul,
So we'll toast our noble selves at the Paisley Block
Ball.
>   *Chorus –* At a Paisley Block Ball,
>   At a Paisley Block Ball,
>   So we'll toast our noble selves
>   At the Paisley Block Ball.

Now to conclude, your patience I will praise,
And thank you for your chorus unto my humble
lays;
Though my song it be but homespun, and but a
silly scrawl,
It may set wiser heads to work for next Paisley
Block Ball.
>   *Chorus –* For next Paisley Block Ball,
>   For next Paisley Block Ball,
>   It may set wiser heads to work
>   For next Paisley Block Ball.

One suspects that it required more than one long pull of William Allan's strong Guelph whisky to reach the last hearty chorus.

The Paisley Block produced several writers and poets, the most prolific of which was Thomas Laidlaw, who was born in Roxburghshire, Scotland, in 1825, and came as a child to the Paisley Block in 1831. He was Bard of the Guelph St. Andrews and Caledonian Societies for many years, and among his writings were two books of verse, *Sprigs of Heather* and *In the Long Ago*, as well as a book of prose and poems, *The Old Concession Road*, first published in Guelph in 1892. The following stanzas provide the introduction to the 1899 edition of this work:

>   To love we would the task resign
>   And from oblivion wrest
>   Scenes of the old concession line,
>   When first by traffic prest.
>
>   Ah! he who sings was then a boy
>   Bareheaded and unshod
>   And sees in age with chastened joy
>   The Old Concession Road.

The pioneer experience, of course, was the focus of many such poems. Robert Boyd, another of the early "Paisley Block" settlers, arrived in 1830 from Ayrshire, Scotland. "While he frequently contributed to the press, as well as occupying the honorary position of Bard of the St. Andrews and Caledonian Societies, he published several creditable books."[66] One of the best known of his poems was "The Batchelor in his Shanty":[67]

>   Tis somewhat strange a chiel like me
>   Should frae his native country flee,
>   And leave his friends o' social glee–
>   And loves sae dear,
>   And cross the braid Atlantic sea
>   In quest o' gear.
>
>   To come to this strange land o' trees,
>   This vile abode o' frogs and fleas,
>   Wi' no ane near to sympathise,
>   Or yet to hate us;
>   Devoured alive by slow degrees
>   By curs'd mosquitoes.
>
>   To tremble 'neath the ague's power,
>   Cauld and het, hour after hour,
>   Drinkin' vile Peruvian stour
>   And Ironwood sass,
>   Wi' mony ither auld wife's cure—
>   Wud kill an ass!
>
>   Roasted by the summer's heat—
>   Till life's weak pulse can scarcely beat,
>   Half-drown'd in streams o' creeshy sweat
>   That gem my beard,
>   As thick as morning's dewy weet,
>   On flow'ry sward!
>
>   Follow'd by Winter's biting breeze—
>   That tears the mantle off the trees,
>   Nips a' the flow'rs — kills a' the fleas
>   Wi' savage sway;
>   And ilka birdie frighten'd flees,
>   to th' South away. . . .

The poem continued for twenty-four more verses, describing eloquently and with genuine humour the troubles and annoyances to which the early settler was subjected.

Alexander Blyth, another early Guelph area poet, was born in Glasgow, Scotland, in 1807, and came to the Scotch Block, (Elora Road) in 1833. He opened the first hotel in that part of Guelph Township, and later built the hotel at Marden. He and his wife, Janet McDonald (one of the La Guayran settlers) "operated a hotel in the Township for thirty-eight years, and their hostelry was noted far and wide for its excellence."[68] The following are a few stanzas of his poem "Alma Heights" which first appeared in the *Guelph Mercury* of 1870:

Here's a health to the land that has sent her
sons forth,
To fight for Old England's rights;
From hill, dale and glen came the men of the
    North,
And their tartans first crowned Alma heights.
Accustomed to roam Scotia's mountains at large,
They ascended the heights like the deer;
Then with shouther to shouther they form'd to the
    charge,
Then dash'd on with a true British cheer.
                    Chorus.
Then here's to the bonnet, the plume and the hose,
To the sporan, the kilt and the plaid;
To the jacket so smart, and the broad buckled
    shoes;
Make the garb of the true highland lad.

Here's a health to the land that claims Sir Colin
    the bold,
Stern and rugged her clifts they may be;
But of sterner stuff and ruggeder mold,
Are her sons with the kilt to the knee.
Then intrenchments and batteries, last the re-
    doubts,
Each were carried and won with a cheer;
When Sir Colin look'd round, and the old Lion's
    shouts
Lads there's nane but our ain highland bonnets
    seen here. . . .
                Chorus – Then here's to, etc.

This poem is a commemorative one, dealing with incidents in the Crimean War.

Poetry, for Guelph's residents, was above all a lively art. The following two poems were part of a lengthy exchange between George Pirie, editor of the *Guelph Herald* and John Smith, editor of the Guelph *Advertiser*. Indeed, as a result of Smith's reply to "A Song for the Times", Pirie challenged Smith to a duel. Here are two of the poems in that exchange, printed in January, 1851:

A SONG FOR THE TIMES[69]
S.T.T. (George Pirie)

Wee Johnnie S—cam' to our town,
    A *muckle* sheet to print:
Resolved, whatever it might cost
    That he wad swell his mint.

The paper and the types were got,
    The rollers and the press
But what to write, or what to print,
    Wee Johnnie couldna guess.

He didna wish to gie offence
    To either Rad or Tory.
Because the loss of *either*'s pence
    Wad mak' him very sorry.

When Johnnie asked the Tory lads
    If they would buy his paper,
No party man was he at all
    No *enemy* to "Draper."

His winning manner, witching words
    And smirking bonnie face
Made honest folk believe wee John
    Could not be a "hard case."

He hadna printed very long
    Before his greed of pelf
Was visible, and folks began
    To watch the little elf.

He tried to please both parties weel
    Wi' soft soap editorial
(Which mongrel "loose fish" politics
    Are Johnnie's sad memorial.)

The Tories they wad not be gull'd,
(Those sly discerning lads,)
And Johnnie, as a last resource,
Cried, "Hurrah for the Rads!"

Puir simple souls, they took the bait—
And Johnnie then began
In vanity and self-deceit
To set up for a MAN!!!

Unsparingly he plied the taws
To simple Austin's back,
Till "Liberals" were satisfied
Wee Johnnie was no quack.
[Austin was the first editor of the *Herald*]

The scene it changed! a sick'ning change
Which made his prospects eerie
As henceforth he wad have to fight
Wi' far-famed "Poor old Pirie."

He struggled hard—wi' *foreign aid*
His page was often fired,
Till quite unequal to the task,
He POMPOUSLY retired.

Determined that he'd ne'er oppose
What's the prevailing passion,
(Even Johnnie was a Temperance man
Where that was a' the fashion.)

Did Johnnie, wi' his press and types
E're rectify abuses?
We answer, NO! But then—but then—
He biggit twa bra houses!
Postscript
His mantle, it has fall'n on one
Wha at the Fates did fret
Because a single *liberal* type
His fingers never set.

Deplorable condition this
For any "man of feeling,"
If you'd be happy, "cut and run"
I pray thee, G.M.K.——g!

[G.M. Keeling, temporarily editor of the *Advertiser* and founding editor of the *Mercury*]

John Smith's reply was not long in coming:

For the Guelph Advertiser

ANOTHER SONG FOR THE TIMES[70]

Written after reading the "Song for the times" published in last "*Herald*"

by. S.T.T.'s Mother

When Georgie P—e cam' to town
A *muckle* sheet to print;
Resolved, if possible, that he'd
Recruit his bankrupt "mint,"

Some paper and some types were got.
An *tick*, as you may guess,
An straightway Georgie cam' to be
A "gemman of the Press."

Now, how to write or how to print,
Poor Georgie did not know;
So off he went to old friend John,
To ask him what to do.

Said John, "You shouldna gie offence
To either Rad or Tory,
Be very smooth to one and all–
To saints—or sinners hoary;

And when you "write," you should *uphold*
The *Honor* of your Order,—
Be bland to all, and keep on hand
Plenty of good soft-sawder.

And then your principles,—if any
Principles you've got—
Keep shady—bottle them—or pr'aps
Your types may go to pot.

Soap everybody—that's the way
To catch the people's pence;
If e'er you *speak your mind* you'r sure
To give some sad offence.

Well Georgie went to work, but soon
His precious greed o'pelf
Spoiled all the sawder that he gave
To others or himself;

He tried to please all parties weel
Wi' soft soap editorial
And mongrel "loose fish" politics,
Stale and undignitorial;

He soaped the folks, and many gull'd
    With finely—and cooked up stories
'Bout how he'd put the taverns down
    And whip'd some drunken Tories,—

Puir simple souls, they took the bait,
    And Georgie then began
In vanitie and "self-consate"
    To set up for a *Man!*

Not only *that*, he set up for
    The first Reeve's chair to fill—
But gosh!—that's slipped him, and he's had
    To gulp a bitter pill!

His hopes were at the top o' the poll,
    Which made him blithe and cheery;
But now they're smashed, and he's no *Reeve*
    Nor aught but "*Poor old Pirie.*"

                Postscript

Dear "Advertiser" now I've got
    Some good advice to give,—
Stand by your *colours* and your *friends*
    As long as you shall live;

Your chosen banner keep unfurl'd,
    Stick to it to the last;
And IF it e'er in danger be,
    Nail, NAIL IT TO THE MAST!

But *danger!* lor! you've no stern foe
    To meet in contest weary;
Your foe he's not a *Man*—What then?
    Why, he is POOR OLD PIRIE!

Never deny your colours like
    That poor old coon has done;
But to 'em stick,—and we'll yet see
    That covy "cut and run."

From time to time, the poetic muse was put to commercial use, as these two advertisements from 1850 and 1855 show:

            LOOK HERE![71]

A splendid Town Lot still in Guelph may be got,
    If anyone wishes to buy it;
It is level and square, and for business stands fair,—

I think there is none to deny it.

Besides in the ground there is stone may be found,
    Enough to build dwellings all round it;
That on some future day to a friend you might say—
    "I think I did well when I found it!"

This Lot so complete is in Nottingham Street,
    Close behind Mr. Stephen's dwelling;
For particulars to know, apply to *John Crowe*,
    For he is inclined to be selling!

Guelph, May 29, 1850.

                ABERFOYLE
                (Brock Road)

        CARRIAGE, WAGON, AND SLEIGH
                MANUFACTORY[72]
                PAUL ROSS

Good day, my friends! I've come at last,
To thank you all for favors past,
And hope when you the Brock Road travel,
That fine Macadamize and gravel,
At Aberfoyle you'll surely stop,
And come and view my carriage shop
I'll make or mend your ploughs and harrows,
Your gigs, your carts, and your wheelbarrows,
And carriages of all descriptions,
In them I'll warrent no deceptions.
And buggies, too, the very best,
There's none can beat them in the west.
In this great age of *Railroad* speed,
My friends you will a carriage *need.*
Your *wives* and *daughters* labor hard,
'Tis fit they should have some reward.
And you who lead a single life,
Come, buy one ere you seek a *wife*;
For when that you your produce sell,
You get more cash than you can tell,
Bring it along, give me a call,
I'm sure that I can suit you all.
No more your time and labor waste,
I'll please the most fastidious taste;
For I've the best and latest style,
At my old stand in Aberfoyle.
                        May 8, 1855.

On other occasions, the use of poetry was not limited to advertisements. Witness this poem which gloats of the victory of the Wellington, Grey and Bruce over the Toronto, Grey and Bruce in 1869:

IN MEMORIAM[73]

Hurrah! Hurrah! for Wellington,
  Hurrah! for Bruce and Grey;
And give three cheers for Hamilton,
  For they have won the day.
Toronto, backed with all the lies
  Its papers could produce,
Has been "stamped out" in Wellington,
  And beat in Grey and Bruce.

As Greek meets Greek, so Hamilton
  Toronto met in fight;
Then came the tug of war, to see
  If might would vanquish right.
Though Laidlaw used the basest means
  He found himself undone,
And had to crouch beneath the lash
  Of Brown of Hamilton.

Still thick as locusts on they came,
  (But 'twas to meet their doom);
And then from them arose a shout,
  Room for our speakers! room!
Some frothy orator, would then
  Belch forth his fulsome stuff,
Till Hamilton rushed to the front
  And cried, "Lay on Macduff."

"I think there are six Laidlaws,
  In the field," Brown said, "to-day,
I've slain red five, and now there comes
  Another one to slay;
But though there were a thousand more,
  Still onward let them come,
We'll meet the schemers face to face,
  And beat them backward home.

"Now Brant, now Carrick, forward all!
  The day will soon be ours,
The enemy must needs give way
  When White leads forth his Powers.
See how our gallant north men fight,

Their foes before them flee;
And from the ranks of Stirton comes
  The shout of victory."

Now "Laidlaw's gang" may gnaw a file
  And chew the cud of grief
Until they hatch some other scheme
  To bring their minds relief.
In sack cloth now they weep and wail,
  Their heads in sorrow hung,
"But let the galled jade wince," say we,
  "Our withers are unrung."

The *Telegraph*, may telegraph
  "False tidings" far and near:
The *Leader* still *mislead* its friends
  By being insincere.
But "truth though crushed will rise again,"
  While error wounded lies
And they will buried be, beneath
  A pyramid of lies.

"Blow winds and crack your cheeks with rage,"
  And howl Toronto's doom;
For "busted" is their narrow-gauge,
  Its up beyond the moon.
Toronto shall not dare again,
  With us to break a lance;
They, *like a crab, shall backward go*,
  While we will still "Advance."

O, York, thou greedy, grasping knave,
  Thy hands are on the stretch;
And ready aye to grab at all
  That comes within thy reach.
Thou cut-purse of common weal,
  Thy pilfering now give o'er;
Go mend thy ways, thou renegade
  And henceforth sin no more.

Other poets spoke of the more melancholy aspects of life. The following stanzas by James McGrogan appeared in the *Herald* in October, 1847:

LINES WRITTEN ON THE DEATH OF ELIZABETH MCGROGAN[74] BY HER SON, JAMES.

O, cruel Death what hast thou done,

Why wast thou so severe;
Oh! why so soon her glass was run,
    My tender mother dear.

She nurtur'd me when I was young,
    But now she is no more;
From her to many estates I sprung,
    Then must I not deplore.

For nature binds the human heart,
    And I must here repine;
From my dear mother I must part,
    She'll be no longer mine.

Her children dear must weep and wail,
    They lost a mother kind;
But on her grave they'll shed a tear,
    For nature does them bind.

But still there is a heavenly hope,
    Her soul is soar'd above;
There to enjoy the boundless scope
    Of Christ's redeeming love.

In whose redemption made complete,
    She'll join the mighty throng;
Where ransom'd Jew and Gentile meet,
    To sing Salvation's song.

Then let us cease to heave a sigh,
    Though death did sternly call;
But trust her Spirit reigns on high,
    Where God is all in all.

That hope shall make us cease to mourn,
    For why should we despair;
To earth our mother won't return,
    But we shall meet her there.

But still her mould'ring dust must lie,
    Enclosed in Cranfield tomb;
Till judgment seals in yonder sky,
    Her last eternal doom.

                            James McGrogan

Not surprisingly, given Guelph's strong military tradition, many of the City's residents wrote glorifying the bravery and daring of Canada's militia and soldiers. This poem, written by George Pirie, appeared in April, 1866:

THE VOLUNTEERS
OF CANADA[75]

The Volunteers of Canada, right loyal men are
    they,
Requiting love with loving deeds, but fearless of the
    fray;
Their hearts made strong by honest thoughts, their
    hands by honest toil,
The franklins of the bench and forge, the yeomen of
    the soil.

The Volunteers of Canada a gallant lineage claim,
The annals of the olden time are radiant with their
    fame;
Wherever foot of man has trod or galley spread a
    sail,
They've left the record of their might—the Saxon
    and the Gael.

The Volunteers of Canada are no degenerate race,
The flag 'neath which their fathers fought, they
    never will disgrace.
O'er tower and town, o'er tented field, above our
    inland seas,
That flag shall brave as it has braved, "the battle
    and the breeze."

The Volunteers of Canada have heard the bugle
    call,
And they are rushing to the front from hamlet and
    from hall;
To guard the leal hearts that make rich each fair
    Canadian home,
To fend their faith and father-land, the altar and
    the throne.

The Volunteers of Canada—a wealth of love is
    theirs—
A nation's heart goes forth with them—a nation's
    hopes and prayers;
For them the grey-haired patriarch pleads, the
    maiden mid her tears,
And infant lips have learned to lisp, "God bless our
    volunteers!"

The Volunteers of Canada—God speed the noble
    band
That girdle with a band of steel our free, fair for-
    est-land;

A noble cause prompts noble deeds, no fears for
   them we feel—
But woe betide the braggart loons that meet their
   levelled steel!

The Volunteers of Canada, the soldiers of the line,
Whose banners tell of battles won in many a hostile
   clime—
The Fenian fray, if come it may, they'll meet with
   British cheers;
Hurrah, for England's hearts of oak and our brave
   volunteers!

Colonel John McCrae, Guelph's soldier-poet, wrote in this tradition when he composed his famous "In Flanders Fields." This poem by McCrae, was published in 1917:

THE ANXIOUS DEAD[76]

Guns, fall silent till the dead men hear
Above their heads the Legions pressing on;
(These fought their fight in time of bitter fear
And died, not knowing how the day had gone.)

O, flashing muzzles, pause and let them see,
The coming dawn that streaks the sky afar;
Then let your mighty chorus witness be
To them, and CAESAR, that we still make war.

Tell them, O guns, that we have heard their call,
That we have sworn, and will not turn aside,
That we will onward till we win or fall,
That we will keep the faith for which they died.

From time to time Guelph's residents praised the accomplishments of their forefathers in the building of the City. This poem was written in celebration of Guelph's fiftieth anniversary in 1877:

GUELPH'S FIFTIETH ANNIVERSARY[77]

Just fifty years ago to-day,
   Noble Galt and Dunlop stood—
With brandy flask and powder horn—
   Within a pathless wood:
An Indian cabin nestled there,
   Offering shelter from the storm;

Gladly they sought its humble shade,
   To rest each weary'd form.

Galt struck the monarch of the wilds,
   With strong manhood's earnest might;
Dunlop, Prior and the wood men fell'd
   It, on that thrice-honoured night:
For good King George, our patron saint,
   Made it famous in his day—
When chivalry and brave knighthood
   Held firm undisputed sway.

Great Shakespeare, the prince of poets,
   Entered this blooming world;
On that same day, in after years—
   His life in death was furled,
Galt gave England's royal honoured name
   To the then far distant town:
Never let ignoble acts or deeds
   Tarnish its bright renown.

Let us take a retrospective glance
   Over the then and now;
Then forests, Indians and wild beasts,
   Alone crown'd nature's brow;
Guelph of to-day in honour stands—
   A bright imperial gem,
Which our Queen need ne'er blush to own
   As a star in her diadem.

Her Churches, gems of modern art,
   With their lofty sparkling spires,
Leads one to hope that Christian grace,
   Noble thoughts and deeds inspire;
Her Hospitals are doing a noble work—
   Where her sick meet tender care
From the sisters and nurses—woman's hands
   Render loving duties there.

Her schools, magnificent structures, stand
   Wherein intelligence and grace
Are cultured by an efficient band,
   Bright ornaments in any place;
Her Agricultural College, the farmer's pride—
   There her sons are wisely taught
The science of tilling dear old Earth,
   With such wealth and beauty fraught.

A home for the aged and the maim,
   Will shortly lift its head—

An asylum for distress and pain,
    There the helpless may have bread;
Her Ministers, gentle Christian men,
    Working in their Master's name;
Striving to lift poor straying souls
    From the depths of sin and shame.

Her Doctors, men of scientific skill,
    Stand foremost in the ranks,
For this, their gentle healing art,
    We yield them warmest thanks.
Her lawyers, men of scholastic lore,
    Winning laurels and renown;
From our Senate Halls, we hear the voice
    Of a resident of our Town.

Her Editorial staff are managed by
    Brilliant minds and willing hands,
Assisted by telegraphs and steam engines,
    Bringing in news from foreign lands.
Her Courts and Councils are govern'd well,
    By men of good common sense
Who give their influence and time,
    Her means and justice to dispense.

Her Merchants, kindly courteous men,
    Stand ready, with bows and smiles,
To lead us gently through the maze
    Of subtle fashion's changing wiles.
Her Mechanics, men of honest worth,
    A mighty bulwark stand,
With gifted minds and simple faith
    A tower of strength in our land.

Her Farmers, sturdy sons of toil—
    To them we yield the palm
For independence and sweet peace,
    And fair primeval calm.
Her brave Volunteers—God bless them!
    Stand ready to defend
Their homes at a moment's warning,
    And their Queen—the people's friend.

Her Daughters fill an honoured place—
    Fair maidens and blooming wives
And mothers; Heaven's blessing rest
    On their self-sacrificing lives.
Then come forth, ye aged veterans,
    Ye early settlers come,

Enjoy the peace and pleasure
    Flowing from each pleasant home.

Many friends have fallen in our midst—
    This is the lot of man;
To love, to labour, and to die—
    Life is such a little span.
Brave Galt, the founder of our Town,
    Now sleeps on Scotia's shore;
His kind colleagues of those early days
    Are known on earth no more.

Thus our retrospect is sadly tinged
    By changes and dire decay;
Who will be here, of this vast crowd,
    To greet Guelph's Centennial day?
Fling sadness aside, let each glad heart
    Rejoice in laughter and song;
Let kind good will and merry cheer—
    The joyous hours prolong.

Three cheers for our beloved Queen!
    Three cheers for our patron saint!
And three times three for dear old Guelph,
    May her brave hearts never faint!
To God let each glad homage bring
    On this bright auspicious day,
Long may it in our memories ring,
    Fragrant as the breath of May.

                                        Anonymous.

Before leaving Guelph's literary tradition, special reference must be made to James Gay, carpenter, tavern-keeper, (one time proprietor of the Bull Frog Inn), watch repairman, and Canada's self-proclaimed "Poet Laureate." A genuine character, Gay wandered the streets of Guelph with his flute and his printed verses, lightening the hearts of all he met with a song, a story or a poem.[78] Gay's language even in ordinary conversation was "poetic"—"Nice day—good day—James Gay—here today—soon away," etc.[79] Typical of Gay's poetry were the following verses inset in a longer work entitled *The Great Exhibition*:[80]

> The greatest wonder for four days
> To be seen at the stall of the poet Gay's,
> His two headed Colt so tall and thin,
> The greatest sight that ever was seen.
>
> Come one, come all, as well you may,
> Ten cents will only be the pay,
> Gay's five-cent poems will all surprise,
> Both farmers and their loving wives.
>
> Then rally, strangers, from day to day,
> To hear the flute the poet play,
> Come forward, gents, both stout and tall,
> As fifteen cents will pay for all.

And yet, as peculiar as Gay's self-praise may appear, as the subject of his own poetry, in many ways it exemplified what was best about the spirit of Guelph society. By 1927, Hamilton and Toronto had vastly outstripped the City in economic growth, Kingston and London may have created more prestigious intellectual institutions, but all that had been ac-

James Gay, Guelph's "Poet Laureate."

The Bull Frog Inn on Eramosa Road, as it appeared in 1975.

complished in building the City had been done by Guelph's own residents against enormous odds. Thus a spirit of pride, identity and self-sacrifice had to be maintained among all residents if Guelph was to survive as a major city. The *Mercury* of 1927 was as dedicated to that survival, and the creation and the maintenance of that spirit, as James Gay and the Anonymous author had been half a decade before.

❧

Guelph, at its Centenary in 1927, found itself faced with many of the same underlying problems and pressures that had accompanied its founding a century before. Moreover, these problems being endemic to Canadian society, would be solved, when they were solved, by temporary measures at best. But to this task, the City's residents brought a will to work and a confidence in their own abilities. If the problems and conflicts were part of life, the will to overcome these challenges was equally part of Guelph's approach to them. Guelph's experiences, although unique in detail, represent in miniature one facet of what it means to be Canadian.

The arch erected for Guelph's Centennial Celebrations in 1927.
At the right of City Hall is the old Provincial Winter Fair Building.

Notes

Chapter I

1. See, for example, the map in Canada, *Sessional Papers* (1847), Appendix T "Report on the Indians of Canada...."; also, the map in Gilbert Paterson, "Land Settlement in Upper Canada 1783-1840," *Seventeenth Report of the Department of Archives for the Province of Ontario* (Toronto, 1921), p. 220.

2. John Galt, *Autobiography* (London, 1833) Vol. I, pp. 277-9. For a succinct summary see W.H. Graham, *The Tiger of Canada West* (Toronto, 1962), pp. 41-2.

3. Lillian F. Gates, *Land Policies of Upper Canada* (Toronto, 1968), p. 167; Jennie W. Aberdeen, *John Galt* (London, 1936), p. 134.

4. Paterson, p. 198.

5. Quoted in the *Guelph Evening Mercury*, July 20, 1927.

6. *Ibid.*

7. Gates, pp. 168-170; Paterson, pp. 198-205.

8. John Galt to William Dunlop, March 19, 1827, quoted in the *Guelph Evening Mercury*, July 20, 1927. While Galt consistently uses "Prior" as in this letter, some authorities use "Pryor".

9. Ancaster *Gore Gazette*, April 14, 1827, typescript in W. Tyson, "Scrapbook A", Guelph Historical Society.

10. Galt, *Autobiography* I, p. 54.

11. Robert Thompson, *A Brief Sketch of the Early History of Guelph* (Guelph Mercury Steam Printing House, 1877), p. I.

12. Galt, *Autobiography* II, pp. 57-58.

13. *Ibid*, pp. 58-59.

14. *Ibid.*

15. *Ibid*, pp. 90-91; also quoted in W.H. Smith, *Canada, Past Present and Future* (Toronto, 1852) Vol. II, pp. 93-99.

16. Galt, *Autobiography* II, p. 60.

17. *Ibid*, pp. 60-61.

18. Robert Thompson, p. 2.

19. This description is taken from the *Guelph Evening Mercury*, April 23, 1955, Higinbotham Scrapbook #3, Guelph Public Library.

20. Galt, *Autobiography* II, pp. 115.

21. *Ibid*, pp. 64-65.

22. Reprinted in the *Guelph Evening Mercury*, July 20, 1927, p. 7. Gilkison is also spelled Gilkinson in several sources.

23. *Guelph Evening Mercury*, July 20, 1927, p. 112.

24. Quoted in *ibid.*

25. Acton Burrows, *Annals of the Town of Guelph*, (Guelph, 1877), p. 22.

26. *Ibid*, pp. 14-15.

27. Galt to Moir, August 1, 1827, quoted in the *Guelph Evening Mercury*, July 20, 1927.

28. Burrows, pp. 16-17.

29. See, for example, Mrs. B.S. Kennedy's reminiscences in the *Guelph Evening Mercury*, July 20, 1927. p. 13.

30. *Ibid.*

31. Galt, *Autobiography* II, p. 97.

32. Quoted in the *Guelph Evening Mercury*, July 20, 1927.

33. *Ibid.*

34. *Ibid.*

35. *Ibid.*

36. Galt, *Autobiography* II, pp. 98-99.

37. *Guelph Evening Mercury*, July 20, 1927.

38. James Innes, "...History of Guelph..." Published in instalments in the *Guelph Weekly Mercury*, starting January 11, 1866. This excerpt is from the issue dated February 8, 1866. (Instalment VIII, 1963 reprint).

39. Thompson, p. 7.

Chapter II

1. Acton Burrows, p. 28.

2. *Ibid*, p. 30.

3. Quoted in *Guelph Evening Mercury*, July 20, 1927, p. 7.

4. Canada Company circular, February 1, 1828, copy in the archives of the Guelph Historical Society.

5. *Ibid*.

6. *Ibid*.

7. Innes, February 15, 1866. (Instalment IX, 1963 reprint.)

8. Population data is from "Provincial Secretary's Papers", P.A.C., R.G.5, B. 26, vols. 1-7; and *Journals of the Legislative Assembly of Upper Canada*, 1823-1842, Appendices, P.A.O. (microfilm).

9. Innes, April 19, 1866. (Instalment XXIII, 1963 reprint).

10. Thompson, pp. 7-8, in addition to those whom Thompson listed as still living in 1877, he names the following as having been resident in Guelph during the winter of 1827-1828, but who were no longer living in Guelph:
Chas. Armstrong, D.D. Akins, Chas. Boyington, Thos. Baker, Chas. Burns, Jack Bilerd, John Clark, James Coleman, Robert Clark, Ed. Carroll, James Cornfoot, Daniel Dougan, Wm. Delimore, James Elliott, Robert Elder, John Foster, John Farrell, Wm. Gregg, David Gibbs, Edward Gilmore, Daniel Hill, Louis Howard, John Hall, John Herreld, George Henry, Thomas Johnson, Thomas Kelly, Wm. Kemley, Enoch Kenyon, Uriah Lampart, John Lennox, Thomas Lee, Malcolm Livingston, James McCartney, Michael Mullen, Wm. McCrae, John McDonald, James McGarr, John McLeod, McLaren & Miller, John McNeil, Hugh McDonald, Peter Butchard, Alex Rose, John Gaffney, John Smith, Geo. Wallace, Alex Reid, Wm. Johnson, Richard Johnson, Alex. McTavish, J. Oliver, Henry Pennybaker, Thomas Stewart, Thomas Smith, Fenton Molloy, John Barnes, Joseph. Milloy, Robert McCuen, John McNulty, James Thompson, John Thompson, John Taft, W.W. Wright, John Wilson, Matthias Wert, James Yates, John Mitchell, Andrew Ritchie.

11. See Galt's mention of the "Khan" in Galt to Moir, August 1, 1827, reprinted in the *Guelph Evening Mercury*, July 20, 1927.

12. Adam Fergusson, *Tour in Canada. . . .in 1831* (London, 1833), pp. 281-3.

13. Innes, April 12, 1866. (Instalment XXII, 1963 reprint).

14. Canada Company circular, February 1, 1828.

15. Innes, April 12, 1866. (Instalment XXII, 1963 reprint).

16. Thompson, p. 4.

17. *Ibid*, pp. 4-5.

18. Galt, *Autobiography* II, p. 99.

19. *Ibid*, pp. 99-101.

20. *Ibid*, pp. 115-119.

21. *Ibid*, p. 119 ff. Also Acton Burrows, pp. 31-2.

22. Acton Burrows, pp. 30-32.

23. Galt, *Autobiography* II, pp. 131-136, and A.W. Drummond, *Guelph, The Royal City*, (Guelph, 1924), pp. 27-8.

24. Robert Troup to Lord Alloway, April 20, 1829, quoted in Acton Burrows, p. 36.

25. Reprinted in the *Guelph Evening Mercury*, July 20, 1927.

26. Quoted in W.H. Graham, *The Tiger of Canada West*, (Toronto, 1965), p. 60, paperback.

27. Galt, *Autobiography* II, p. 163; Acton Burrows, pp. 41-2; Graham, pp. 60-1.

28. Proceedings, *Court of Directors*, 2 July 1829, (C.C.P., P.A.O.).

29. Galt, *Autobiography* II, pp. 61-2.

30. David Allan, Higinbotham Scrapbook #2, p. 13.

31. Galt, *Autobiography* II, p. 119.

32. From a speech by James Hodgert, November 30, 1850, reported in the *Guelph Advertiser*, December 5, 1850, microfilm, P.A.O.

33. Reminiscences of J.C.W. Daly, reprinted in the *Guelph Evening Mercury*, July 20, 1927.

34. *Ibid*.

35. Quoted in the *Guelph Evening Mercury*, July 20, 1927.

36. *Wellington County Historical Society*, vol. 1, 1932, pp. 5-6.

37. Agricultural data is from "Provincial Secretary's Papers", P.A.C., R.G.5, B.26, vols. 1-7; and *Journals of the Legislative Assembly of Upper Canada*, 1823-1842, Appendices, P.A.O. (microfilm).

38. *Ibid*.

39. *Ibid*.

40. *Ibid*.

41. *Ibid*.

42. *Ibid*.

43. This figure is from W.H. Smith, *Smith's Canadian Gazetteer* (Toronto, 1846), pp. 72-3.

44. Fergusson, pp. 161-2.

45. "Statistical Sketches of Upper Canada. . .by a Back-Woodsman", (William Dunlop) (London, 1832), reprinted in *Tiger Dunlop's Upper Canada*, with an introduction by Carl F. Klinck (Toronto, 1967), pp. 132-3.

46. *Ibid*, p. 70.

47. William Cattermole, *Emigration. . . .* (London, 1831), pp. 29-32.

48. Anonymous to J. Corbett in *ibid*, pp. 167-8.

49. William Lyon Mackenzie, *Sketches of Canada. . . .* (London, 1833), p. 249.

50. David Allan, "The Milling Industry Guelph and Vicinity", *Wellington County Historical Society*, vol. 1, 1932, pp. 3-4. It would appear from the assessment records that the "Red

Mill" was operated initially as a sawmill, and only later was converted to a grist mill. See Table VIII.

51. Dunlop to Canada Company Commissioners, 29 May, 1829, quoted in Graham, p. 64.

52. Acton Burrows, pp. 47-8.

53. James Hodgert, *op. cit.*

54. "Provincial Secretary"s Papers", P.A.C., R.G.5, B.26, vols. 1-7; and *Journals of the Legislative Assembly of Upper Canada,* 1823-1842, Appendices, P.A.O. (microfilm).

55. *Ibid.*

56. *Historical Atlas of Wellington County,* (Toronto, 1906), p. 11.

57. Quoted in the *Guelph Evening Mercury,* July 20, 1927, p. 112.

58. Quoted in James Innes, March 15, 1866 (Instalment XV, 1963 reprint).

59. Fergusson, pp. 279-80.

60. *Guelph Evening Mercury,* July 20, 1927.

61. Innes, March 15, 1866. (Instalment XV, 1963 reprint).

62. Donald McDonald, *Plan of the Town of Guelph,* October, 1847, Archives of the Guelph Historical Society.

63. Acton Burrows, pp. 50-1.

64. Quoted in Innes, March 8, 1866. (Instalment XV, 1963 reprint).

65. *Ibid.*

66. *Guelph Daily Mercury,* April 19, 1902.

67. Innes, March 8, 1866. (Instalment XV, 1963 reprint).

68. See Statutes of Upper Canada, 7 William IV, cap 79 and 1 Victoria, cap. 32.

69. Statutes of Upper Canada, 7 Victoria, cap. 33.

70. *Ibid,* 9 Victoria, cap. XCVIII

Chapter III

1. A.E. Byerly, *The Beginning of Things in Wellington and Waterloo Counties* (Guelph, 1935), pp. 8-9.

2. The "Tory" party mentioned was the "Family Compact" party. For more discussion on political differences at that time see Gerald M. Craig, *Upper Canada—The Formative Years 1784-1841* (Toronto, 1963).

3. Susanna Moodie; *Roughing it in the Bush* (Toronto, 1871); Coles reprint edition, 1974, pp. 248ff.

4. William Lyon Mackenzie, *Sketches of Canada and the United States* (London, 1833), p. 249.

5. Innes, March 1, 1866; (Instalment XII, 1963 reprint).

6. Acton Burrows, p. 51.

7. For a description of this event see Hazel B. Mathews, *Oakville and the Sixteen* (Toronto, 1953), p. 145.

8. Acton Burrows, pp. 52-53.

9. *Ibid,* p. 53.

10. Innes, March 1, 1866; (Instalment XIII, 1963 reprint).

11. Acton Burrows, p. 53.

12. Newspaper clipping, N.D., Higinbotham Scrapbook No. 2, p. 3.

13. See E.C. Guillet, *Early Life in Upper Canada* (Toronto, 1933), p. 676.

14. Innes, June 7, 1866; (Instalment XXXV, 1963 reprint).

15. Newspaper clipping N.D., N.P., Higinbotham Scrapbook no. 3, p. 123. This clipping is likely from one of the missing instalments of Innes' history of Guelph.

16. *Ibid.*

17. Innes, June 7, 1866; (Instalment XXXIV, 1963 reprint).

18. *Ibid.*

19. *Ibid.* June 7, 1866; (Instalment XXXV, 1963 reprint).

20. Acton Burrows, pp. 52-53.

21. 33 George III, cap. 2.

22. The best work on the evolution of local government is J.H. Aitchison, "The Development of Local Government in Upper Canada", 2 vols., Ph. D. Thesis, University of Toronto, 1953. Other useful works are C.W.R. Biggar. *Municipal Manual.* Toronto, 1901: J. McEvoy. "The Ontario Township," *University of Toronto Studies in Political Science.* I, no. 1 (1889): Adam Shortt. "Municipal Government in Ontario," *University of Toronto Studies, History and Economics.* II, no. 2 (1903).

23. 33 George III, cap. 2.

24. Biggar, p. 5.

25. Acton Burrows, pp. 22-23.

26. Innes, March 8, 1866; (Instalment XIV, 1963 reprint).

27. "Journals and Proceedings of the House of Assembly of Upper Canada, 1792." P.A.C., Q. vol. 279-1, pp. 87 ff.

28. P.A.C., Q. vol. 279-2, pp. 335ff.

29. McEvoy gives an excellent description of the duties of each of these officers.

30. Innes, March 1, 1866; (Instalment XIII, 1963 reprint).

31. *Ibid.*

32. Innes, March 8, 1866; (Instalment XIV, 1963 reprint).

33. Acton Burrows, p. 54.

34. Byerly, p. 3.

35. *Ibid.*

36. *Guelph Evening Mercury,* July 20, 1927, Page 20. Note—There is some question as to the actual Architect for the Jail and Court House. While the *Mercury* states that Thomas Young was the Architect, other references say that the Architect was David Allan, son of Wm. Allan, the contractor, who built the Court House. It is interesting to note that a Wm. Day was also the contractor for the Goderich jail which was completed in 1843.

37. Byerly, p. 12.

38. *Guelph Evening Mercury*, July 20, 1927, Page 20.

39. C.P. Lucas, ed., *Lord Durham's Report on the Affairs of British North America*, (Oxford, 1912), p. 238.

40. Quoted in Paul Knaplund, *Letters from Lord Sydenham to Lord John Russell* (London, 1931), p. 75.

41. 4-5 Victoria, cap. 10.

42. Compiled from the *Records and Bylaws of the. . .Country of Wellington* (Guelph, 1922), pp. 7-14.

43. 4-5 Victoria, cap. 10, sec. 50.

44. Data for 1840, 1843 and 1845 is from "Provincial Secretary's Papers," P.A.C., R.G.5, B.26, Vols. 1-7; *and Journals of the Legislative Assembly of Canada* 1842-1849. Data for 1848 is from W.H. Smith, *Canada Past, Present and Future*, vol. II (Toronto, 1852), p. 126.

45. The district council was ordered, by the statute, to meet on the second Tuesday of February, May, August and November. No meeting was to last longer than six days (Sunday excepted). Extraordinary meetings could be held only by the express permission of the Governor. See 4-5 Victoria, cap. 10, secs. XXII. and XXIII.

46. *Guelph and Galt Advertiser*, November 30, 1848.

47. *Ibid.*

48. 12 Victoria, cap. 81.

49. 12 Victoria, cap. 81, Schedule A.

50. *Ibid*, Schedule B.

51. *Ibid*, Schedule C.

52. *Ibid*, section CC 11.

53. 13-14 Victoria, cap. 64.

54. Letter, Hiram Capron, Paris, to Robert Baldwin, December 14, 1848; Baldwin (R) Papers, Vol. 38, no. 74, Metropolitan Toronto Reference Library.

55. *Guelph and Galt Advertiser*, November 30, 1848.

56. *Ibid*, December 28, 1848.

57. *Ibid.*

58. *Ibid*, November 29, 1849.

59. *Ibid*, December 28, 1848.

60. *Ibid.*

61. *Ibid*, January 20, 1849.

62. See the accounts of the "Committee against the dismemberment of the Wellington District," *Guelph Advertiser*, November 29, 1849.

63. *Hamilton Spectator*, January 20, 1849, quoting the *Guelph Herald*.

64. *Guelph and Galt Advertiser*, March 8, 1849.

65. *Ibid*, April 26, 1849.

Chapter IV

1. Figures are taken from "Provincial Secretary's Papers," op. cit.

2. *Ibid*. The figure for Puslinch, 1843, is arrived at by pro-rating the data for 1840 and 1845.

3. *Ibid*.

4. *Guelph and Galt Advertiser*, March 12, 1847.

5. *Canada Census*, 1852-3, Calculations are my own. The estimate for the acres cultivated is a minimum figure arrived at by deducting ten cultivated acres for each occupied holding, twenty acres and under. The acreage of wheat and bushels of wheat figures are maximums, no amount being deducted for occupied holdings under twenty acres. Because of the small number of holdings of under twenty acres, maximum error is estimated to be less than one percent.

6. W.L. Smith, *The Pioneers of Old Ontario* (Toronto, 1923), p. 190.

7. Donald McDonald, Map of Guelph, October, 1847, Guelph Historical Society Archives.

8. *City of Toronto and Home District Registry*, 1837 (Toronto, George Walton, 1837), second section, p. 40.

9. Acton Burrows, p. 54.

10. 7 William IV, Cap. 79.

11. Clipping from the Toronto *Examiner* (undated) in the "Toronto and Lake Huron Railway Papers", M.G. 24, E8, Vol. II, P.A.C.

12. 1 Victoria, Cap. 32.

13. 3 Victoria, Cap. 33.

14. 9 Victoria (2), Cap. XCVIII. See the description of this road in Hazel B. Mathews, *Oakville and the Sixteen* (Toronto, 1953), pp. 193-194.

15. *Guelph Herald*, October 7, 1847.

16. 6 William IV, Cap. 5.

17. 6 William IV, Cap. 7.

18. *Guelph and Galt Advertiser*, January 15, 1847.

19. *Ibid*, February 26, 1847.

20. 10-11 Victoria, Cap. 88.

21. 10-11 Victoria, Cap. 91. See also the *Guelph and Galt Advertiser*, September 3, 1847.

22. *Guelph Herald*, September 2, 1847.

23. *Guelph and Galt Advertiser*, September 3, 1847.

24. *Guelph and Galt Advertiser*, October 22, 1847.

25. *Ibid*.

26. *Ibid*.

27. *Ibid*.

28. *Guelph and Galt Advertiser*, October 15, 1847.

29. *Dundas Warder*, N.D., quoted in the *Guelph and Galt Advertiser*, October 29, 1847.

30. *Guelph Herald*, November 9, 1847.

31. *Ibid.* January 18, 1848.

32. Calculated from the Waterloo County Accounts in the *Guelph Advertiser*, March 6, 1851.

33. *Guelph Advertiser*, January 31, 1850.

34. *Ibid*, January 17, 1850.

35. *Guelph Herald*, January 4, 1848.

36. *Ibid*, March 7, 1848.

37. *Guelph and Galt Advertiser*, April 21, 1848.

38. *Ibid*, July 13, 1848.

39. *Ibid*, July 27, 1848.

40. *Ibid*, July 19, 1849.

41. See *ibid*, October 12, 1849; and the *Hamilton Spectator*, January 24, 1849.

42. In 1976 a large proportion of the original printing remained in the vault of the Wellington County building, still unissued.

43. 13 and 14 Victoria, Cap. CXXXII.

44. *Guelph Advertiser*, September 5, 1850.

45. *Journals of Waterloo County*, minutes, December 11, 1850.

46. *Guelph Advertiser*, January 23, 1851.

47. *Ibid*, January 30, 1851.

48. *Ibid*, March 6, 1851.

49. *Ibid*, June 12, 1851.

50. *Journals of Waterloo County*, 1852, Appendix.

51. *Ibid.*

52. "Minutes", Town of Guelph, June 18, 1852.

53. *Guelph Advertiser*, June 24, 1852.

54. Reported in *ibid*, June 17, 1852.

55. Ibid.

56. Ibid.

57. *Ibid*, April 3, 1851, and July 1, 1852.

58. *Ibid*, July 1, 1852.

59. *Ibid*, July 29, 1852.

60. *Ibid.*

61. *Ibid*, July 15, 1852.

62. *Ibid.*

63. *Ibid*, July 22, 1852.

64. *Ibid*, August 5, 1852.

65. *Ibid.*

66. The County accounts for 1853 show that only £657. 4s. 8d. were collected in that year. See *Journals of Wellington County*, Appendix, 1854.

67. *Ibid*, 1855 and 1857.

68. *Guelph and Galt Advertiser*, August 10, 1848.

69. *Guelph and Galt Advertiser*, September 17, 1847.

70. *Ibid*, October 8, 1847.

71. *Guelph Herald*, November 16, 1847.

72. *Guelph and Galt Advertiser*, December 10, 1847.

73. *Guelph Herald*, February 8, 1848.

74. *Guelph and Galt Advertiser*, October 26, 1848.

75. *Ibid*, August 2, 1849.

76. *Journals of Wellington County*, Appendix, January 1859.

77. *Guelph and Galt Advertiser*, June 8 and December 7, 1848.

78. *Guelph Advertiser*, March 28, 1850.

79. *Ibid*, May 2, 1850, Minutes of the Guelph and Arthur Road Company.

80. *Ibid.*

81. *Journals of Waterloo County*, Minutes, January 29, 1851; and *Guelph Advertiser*, April 10, 1851.

82. *Journal of Wellington County*, Appendix 1857, "Report of the Special Committee of the Memorial of the Guelph and Arthur Road Company", January 28, 1864.

83. *Ibid*, Appendix, By-law No. 102, December 6, 1864.

84. *Guelph Advertiser*, June 30, 1853.

Chapter V

1. See the letter Dr. Alling to the Commissioners of the Canada Company, December 16, 1840, reprinted in the *Guelph Evening Mercury*, July 20, 1927.

2. W.H. Smith, *Gazetteer*, (Toronto, 1846), pp. 72-3.

3. Canada, *Census*, 1852-1853.

4. *Ibid*. Calculations are my own.

5. Innes, January 25, 1866. (Instalment V1, 1963 reprint).

6. Acton Burrows, pp. 34-35.

7. *Guelph Evening Mercury*, July 20, 1927 and May 8, 1952.

8. *Guelph Evening Mercury*, Souvenir edition, 1908.

9. Higinbotham Scrapbook, typescript, Guelph Public Library.

10. *Guelph Evening Mercury*, July 20, 1927.

11. David Allan, *St. Andrew's Presbyterian Church—A Centenary Memoir—1832-1932*, Published 1932.

12. *Guelph Evening Mercury*, Souvenir edition, 1908.

13. *Guelph Historical Society Publications*, Vol. I., No. 7.

14. *Guelph Evening Mercury*, July 20, 1927, pp. 50-51.

15. *Ibid.*
16. A.E. Byerly, *One Hundred Years at Knox Presbyterian Church*, Guelph 1944, pp. 9 & 22.
17. Acton Burrows, pp. 21-22.
18. Galt II, p. 61.
19. Byerly, *Beginning of Things*, p. 95.
20. *Guelph Daily Mercury*, Jan. 21, 1967.
21. *Guelph Historical Society Publications*, Vol. I, No. 8, 1961-62.
22. E.M. Lenore Cutten, *St. George's Parish, Guelph, 1832-1932*, Gummer Press, (Guelph, 1932), p. 4.
23. Acton Burrows, p. 49.
24. Strachan Papers, "Proclamation by Sir John Colborne", June 21, 1836, P.A.O. (microfilm).
25. *Ibid*, "Proclamation by George Jehoshaphat, Bishop Mountain", Sept. 10, 1838, P.A.O. (microfilm).
26. E.M. Lenore Cutten, *St. George's Parish, Guelph, 1832-1932*, Gummer Press, (Guelph, 1932), p. 14.
27. W.H. Smith, *Gazetteer*, p. 72.
28. Ivan Muller, "Baptist Churches in Guelph", *Guelph Historical Society Publications*, Vol. 1, No. 9, 1961.
29. Greta M. Shutt, "History of the Guelph Congregational Church", *Ontario History*, LIV, No. 3, p. 206.
30. George H. Knighton, "A Brief Statement of the Main Facts in the History of the Guelph Congregational Church", typescript, Goldie Scrapbook, Guelph Public Library.
31. *Ibid.*
32. *Centenary Souvenir, Norfolk United Church*, (Guelph, 1936).
33. Data is from the Appendices, *Journals of the Legislative Assembly of Canada*, 1843; and Canada *Census*, 1851-52.
34. For a history of Orangeism in the British Isles during this period, see Hereward Senior, *Orangeism in Ireland and Britain 1795-1836* (Toronto, 1966), pp. 235-273.
35. Doctor Henry Orton, "The Memoirs of Henry Orton, M.D.", typescript, Guelph Historical Society, Archives, p. 13.
36. *Ibid*, pp. 15-16.
37. *Ibid*, p. 16.
38. *Ibid*, p. 16.
39. *Ibid*, p. 17.
40. *Ibid*, p. 24.
41. See the *Guelph Evening Mercury*, "History is Recalled By Our Lady's Parish", Jan. 21, 1967.
42. Toronto, *British Colonist*, November 15, 1844.
43. C. Acton Burrows in the *Annals of the Town of Guelph*, 1877, p. 49, gave a somewhat different version, "This Church (St. Patrick's) stood until 1846, when on the night when the news was received of the liberation of Daniel O'Connell, the Irish residents became so enthusiastic, that they lighted large bonfires on the hill, and some of the sparks falling on the roof, the church was burned down.".
44. Acton Burrows, pp. 57-58.
45. *Hamilton Spectator*, August 7, 1847.
46. *Guelph and Galt Advertiser*, April 2, 1847.
47. *Ibid*, April 2, 1847.
48. *Ibid*, June 4, 1847.
49. *Ibid.*
50. *Ibid*, June 18, 1847.
51. See letters by William Richardson and Sheriff George J. Grange in *ibid*, July 23, 1847; and by James Clarvise in *ibid*, August 6, 1847.
52. *Ibid*, July 2, 1847.
53. *Ibid.*
54. *Ibid.*
55. *Ibid.*
56. See comments in *ibid*, July 23, 1847.
57. *Ibid.*
58. *Ibid*, July 9, 1847.
59. *Ibid*, July 23, 1847.
60. *Ibid.*
61. *Ibid*, July 9, 1847.
62. *Ibid*, July 23, 1847.
63. *Ibid.*
64. *Ibid*, August 6, 1847.
65. *Guelph Herald*, August 12, 1847.
66. *Ibid.*
67. *Ibid.*
68. *Ibid*, September 2, 1847.
69. *Guelph and Galt Advertiser*, August 13, 1847.

Chapter VI

1. 47 George III, cap. 6.
2. 4 George IV, Session 2, cap. 8.
3. Acton Burrows, pp. 15-16.
4. Galt to Dr. Moir, August 1, 1827, reprinted in *Guelph Evening Mercury*, July 20, 1927.
5. Innes, January 25, 1866 (Instalment VI, 1963 reprint).
6. *Guelph Evening Mercury*, July 20, 1927.
7. *Ibid.*
8. *Ibid.*

9. Byerly, *Beginning of Things*, p. 100.

10. Greta M. Shutt, *The High Schools of Guelph* (Toronto, 1961), p. 32.

11. *Ibid*, p. 22.

12. *Guelph and Galt Advertiser*, April 2, 1847.

13. *Guelph Herald*, August 26, 1847.

14. 4-5 Victoria, cap. XVIII.

15. Innes, March 8, 1866, (Instalment XV, 1963 reprint).

16. 7 Victoria, cap. XXIX.

17. Acton Burrows, p. 56.

18. By-laws of the District of Wellington, No. 2, Fifth Session, February 18, 1843.

19. Higinbotham Scrapbook No. 2, p. 3.

20. *Guelph Herald*, May 23, 1848.

21. *Guelph and Galt Advertiser*, March 12, 1847.

22. *Ibid*, January 4, 1850.

23. "Minutes of Waterloo County Council," June 11, 1851, in the *Guelph Advertiser*, June 19, 1851.

24. Letter to the editor from H. Orton, June 26, 1851, in the *Guelph Advertiser*, July 3, 1851. William Wetherald's school referred to in this quote was the Rockwood Academy, attended by many Guelph boys, a number of whom became famous.

25. *Ibid*.

26. Byerly, p. 83.

27. Shutt, pp. 18-19.

28. "Minutes of the Guelph Town Council," March 5, 1852.

29. Report of the Board of Trustees, N.D., published in the *Guelph Advertiser*, February 12, 1852.

30. Acton Burrows, pp. 56-57, places the date of the founding of the Wellington District Benevolent Association in 1843. Speakers at the Annual Meeting of that body in 1848 and 1849 placed it in 1845. See *Guelph and Galt Advertiser*, May 25, 1848, and May 31, 1849.

31. *Guelph and Galt Advertiser*, May 31, 1849.

32. *Ibid*, May 28, 1847.

33. *Ibid*.

34. *Ibid*.

35. *Ibid*, May 28, 1847; May 25, 1848; May 31, 1849.

36. *Guelph Advertiser*, May 29, 1851.

37. *Ibid*.

38. *Ibid*, May 30, 1850.

39. "Minutes of the Town of Guelph," February 11, 1851.

40. *Guelph Advertiser*, May 27, 1852.

41. David Allan, *Guelph and its Early Days*, pp. 24 and 32.

42. *Guelph Herald*, August 5, 1847.

43. *Ibid*, January 25, 1848.

44. Acton Burrows, p. 63.

45. *Ibid*, January 4, 1850.

46. *Ibid*, January 17, 1850.

47. Acton Burrows, p. 63.

48. *Guelph Advertiser*, January 31, 1850.

49. Minutes of Farmers' and Mechanics' Institute, March 1, 1850.

50. *Guelph Advertiser*, March 14, 1850.

51. *Ibid*, April 18, 1850.

52. *Ibid*, January 19, 1854.

53. This information was obtained from the Minutes of the Mechanics' Institute, and was given in a talk to the Guelph Historical Society on March 7, 1974, by Mr. John Snell, Chief Librarian, Guelph Public Library. A tape recording of this talk is on file in the Archives of the Guelph Historical Society.

54. *Ibid*.

55. John Snell, *Guelph Daily Mercury*, March 19, 1974.

56. *Ibid*.

57. City of Guelph By-law No. 89, January 15, 1883.

58. *Ibid*.

59. City of Guelph By-law No. 99, April 16, 1883.

60. *Guelph Evening Mercury*, April 24, 1903, p. 1.

61. *Ibid*.

Chapter VII

1. For a penetrating analysis of the "philosophy of railroads" as expressed by T.C. Keefer, see the introduction by H.V. Nelles in T.C. Keefer, *Philosophy of Railroads and other Essays*, Toronto, 1972. This essay was published in Montreal in 1850.

2. Editorials in the *Advertiser* supporting the Toronto and Guelph Railway frequently paraphrased Keefer's arguments. See the editorial and accompanying letter by John Smith, the owner of the *Advertiser*, published June 26, 1851.

3. Keefer, *Philosophy....*, pp. 7-8.

4. *Acton Burrows*, p. 59.

5. *Guelph Advertiser*, June 26, 1851.

6. *Ibid*. Letter to the editor dated June 25, 1851.

7. *Ibid*, "Signs of Vitality". June 26, 1851.

8. *Ibid*, July 3, 1851.

9. *Ibid*.

10. *Ibid.*

11. *Ibid*, July 10, 1851, reporting the *Toronto Patriot*, July 7, 1851.

12. *Ibid.*

13. 14-15 Victoria, cap. CXLVIII.

14. *Guelph Advertiser*, July 24, 1851.

15. *Ibid*, July 31, 1851.

16. *Ibid*, August 28, 1851.

17. *Toronto Patriot*, abridged and reprinted in the *Guelph Advertiser*, September 4, 1851.

18. *Guelph Advertiser*, September 11, 1851.

19. *Ibid.*

20. *Ibid*, September 25, 1851.

21. *Ibid*, October 9, 1851.

22. *Ibid.*

23. *Ibid*, October 16, 1851.

24. *Ibid*, October 9, 1851.

25. Toronto *Globe* quoted in *ibid*, November 27, 1851.

26. *Guelph Herald* reprinted in the *Hamilton Spectator*, November 26, 1851.

27. *Guelph Advertiser*, November 27, 1851. *Hamilton Spectator*, November 26, 1851.

28. *Guelph Advertiser*, November 27, 1851.

29. *Ibid.*

30. *Guelph Advertiser*, December 11, 1851.

31. *Ibid*, December 18, 1851. The official count of the vote reported to the Guelph Town Council was 112 in favour, 6 against and 72 not polled; "Minutes of the Town of Guelph," December 15, 1851: The official count in Guelph Township was 105 in favour, 2 against out of a total of 550 electors. "Minutes of the Township of Guelph," December 22, 1851.

32. *Guelph Advertiser*, January 22, 1852.

33. *Ibid*, March 4, 1852; Letter to the editor signed "An Eramosa Rate-Payer."

34. *Ibid*, "The Railroad", October 28, 1852.

35. *Ibid*, January 29, 1852, "Minutes of the Town Council," January 26, 1852.

36. *Journals of Waterloo County*, January 28, 1852.

37. See the *Guelph Advertiser*, April 15 and 29, 1852.

38. Report by J.G. Bowes, Chairman of the Provisional Directors, printed in the *Guelph Advertiser*, April 8, 1852.

39. *Guelph Advertiser*, April 1, 1852.

40. *Ibid*, April 8, 1852.

41. *Ibid.*

42. *Ibid*, January 6, 1853.

43. *Ibid.*

44. *Ibid*, May 27, 1852.

45. 16 Victoria, cap. XXXVII.

46. *Guelph Advertiser*, November 25, 1852.

47. 16 Victoria, cap. XXXIX.

48. 16 Victoria, cap. XLI.

49. See the comment by Lieutenant-Governor Sir George Arthur, June 7, 1837, in E.A. Cruikshank, *The Arthur Papers*, Vol. I. no. 197, p. 193.

50. *Guelph Advertiser*, November 11, 1852.

51. *Ibid.*

52. Macdonald was apparently a partner in the Port Sarnia land deal with the Gzowski firm. See the *Globe*, June 12, 1851.

53. *Globe*, June 12, 1851.

54. *Ibid.*

55. *Guelph Advertiser*, February 24, 1853.

56. *Ibid*, April 14, 1853.

57. Byerly (A.E.) Papers, PAO, 1853; The Town of Guelph letter is printed in the Council Minutes, May 6, 1853.

58. *Guelph Advertiser*, May 12, 1853.

59. *Ibid*, May 19, 1853.

60. Reprinted in *ibid*, June 2, 1853.

61. *Ibid*, July 7, 1853.

62. *Ibid*, July 14, 1853.

63. *Ibid*, August 4, 1853.

64. 16 Victoria, cap. XLII.

65. *Ibid.*

66. *Guelph Advertiser*, June 30, 1853.

67. *Ibid.*

68. *Ibid*, April 21, 1853.

69. *Ibid.*

70. "Minutes of the Town of Guelph," August 19, 1853.

71. *Guelph Advertiser*, August 25, 1853.

72. *Ibid.*

73. *Ibid.*

74. *Ibid.* Acton Burrows (p. 72) and others appear to have been in error when they stated that McCracken was a resident of Preston. The City Hotel referred to was not the Preston house of that name, but a similarly named hotel in Hamilton. See the *Guelph Advertiser*, July 10, 1854.

75. *Ibid*, August 25, 1853.

76. *Ibid.*

77. Reprinted in *ibid*, July 10, 1854.

78. *Ibid.*

79. *Ibid*, September 15, 1853.

80. *Ibid*, September 22, 1853.

81. See the various references in *ibid*, March 7, 1855; *Guelph Daily Mercury*, "Souvenir Issue" 1908, p. 28; *Guelph Evening Mercury*, July 20, 1927. Although Henry Hough in his remi-

niscences believed that George M. Keeling had emigrated to Guelph in 1853, a belief that most subsequent historians have shared, it is certain that he came to Guelph several years earlier. Keeling served as editor of the *Advertiser* from July 11, 1850, to September 23, 1852. See the *Advertiser* of those dates for editorials concerning his editorial policies.

82. Toronto *Globe*, March 2, 1879. Most historians use the phrase "early in 1854" in discussing the founding of the *Mercury*. The earlier date is more likely to be correct.

83. *Guelph Advertiser*, September 29, 1853.

84. *Ibid*, October 20, 1853.

85. *Ibid*, October 1 and November 24, 1853.

86. *Ibid*, September 22, 1853.

87. *Ibid*.

88. *Ibid*, February 23, 1854.

89. *Ibid*, October 27, 1853.

90. *Ibid*.

91. *Ibid*, March 31; 1853.

92. Reprinted in the *Galt Reformer*, January 18, 1854, General Clarke was an American who had been a major contractor on the Great Western.

93. *Ibid*.

94. *Guelph Advertiser*, March 30, 1854.

95. *Dumfries Reformer*, May 17, 1854.

96. *Guelph Advertiser*, June 19, 1854.

97. *Ibid*, June 12, 1854.

98. *Ibid*, August 7 and 14, 1854. The formal opening actually took place on August twenty-first: *ibid*, August 28, 1854.

99. See the description of Jacob Hespeler's manoeuvrings in Preston, *ibid*, August 7, 1854.

100. *Galt Reformer*, November 25, 1854.

101. *Guelph Advertiser*, January 19, 1855.

102. *Ibid*, February 26, 1855.

103. *Ibid*.

104. See the Minutes of the Annual Meetings of the Galt and Guelph and the Great Western, and the ensuing discussions in the *Guelph Advertiser*, February 24; March 7, 14, 19, 20, 23, 28; and June 4, 1855.

105. "Town Council Minutes," June 4, 1855, in *ibid*, June 6, 1855.

106. *Ibid*.

107. *Guelph Advertiser*, June 6, 22, 25 and 29, 1855.

108. Town of Guelph, By-law No. 47, August 1, 1855. Eventually, Guelph ended up owning:

Village of Preston Debentures	£2,400.
City of Hamilton Debentures	2,500.
Township of Guelph Debentures	2,600.
Galt and Guelph Railway Stock	7,500.
	£15,000.

In addition, the Town retained £5,000 of its own debentures that it had previously voted to give to the Railway, plus it continued to own its original £10,000 worth of shares; *Guelph Advertiser*, February 21, 1856.

109. *Guelph Advertiser*, November 10, 1853; August 7, 1854; March 7, 1856.

110. Quoted in the *Guelph Advertiser*, August 7, 1854.

111. *Guelph Advertiser*, November 10, 1853 and March 7, 1856.

112. See Grange's advertisement in the *Guelph Advertiser*, April 2, 1856.

113. "Guelph Town Council Minutes," March 12, 1856, in *Guelph Advertiser*, March 20, 1856.

114. *Ibid*.

115. *Ibid*.

116. *Guelph Advertiser*, February 7, 1856.

117. *Ibid*, June 16, 1856.

118. *Ibid*, extra edition, June 14, 1856, reprinted in *ibid*, June 16, 1856.

119. *Ibid*.

120. Toronto *Leader*, June 14, 1856, quoted in the *Guelph Advertiser*, June 16, 1856.

121. *Guelph Advertiser*, June 16, 1852.

122. Acton Burrows, pp. 87-8.

123. Quoted in *ibid*.

124. Quoted in *ibid*. See also the *Guelph Advertiser*, June 16, 1856.

Chapter VIII

1. *Guelph Advertiser*, September 23, 1852.

2. *Ibid*, June 3, 1852.

3. *Ibid*, April 28, 1853.

4. *Ibid*, September 15, 1853.

5. *Ibid*, September 22, 1853. For an excellent introduction to the rise of the "Idea of Progress," see R.V. Sampson, *Progress in the Age of Reason*, Cambridge, Mass., 1956. For a useful introduction to the Idea's background in Canada, see L.S. Fallis, "The Idea of Progress in the Province of Canada: 1841-1867" (Ph.D. Thesis, U. of Michigan, 1966).

6. The *Leader*, reprinted in the *Guelph Advertiser*, February 2, 1854.

7. *Guelph Advertiser Tri-Weekly*, May 26, 1854.

8. *Ibid*, June 30, 1854, advertisement.

9. *Ibid*, July 31, 1854.

10. *Consolidated By-Laws of the City of Guelph* (Guelph, 1923), pp. 3-4.

11. *Guelph Advertiser Tri-Weekly*, April 2, 1856.

12. Not all of these streets were settled immediately.

13. *Guelph Advertiser*, February 14, 1855.

14. *Ibid*, May 28, 1855.

15. *Guelph Advertiser*, December 6, 1855.

16. *Ibid*. A curious aspect of this sale has been the manner in which historians have recorded it—leaving the impression that the whole sale's profits had gone to John A. Macdonald. For example, Acton Burrows says:
Hon. (now Sir) John Macdonald, owner of the property, was present, and was warmly greeted by gentlemen on both sides of politics. At noon a sumptuous lunch was partaken of at the British Hotel, after which the party adjourned to the Macdonald property, when the sale commenced,—some of the property sold that day bringing as much as £10,000 per acre, corner lots on the Market Square reaching £2,000, and square lots fetching £20 per foot frontage, exclusive of the building.
See Acton Burrows, *op cit*, p. 82. This version of events has generally been repeated without question, by subsequent historians.

17. *Ibid*, May 15, 1856.

18. *Ibid*, May 22, 1856.

19. *Guelph Advertiser Tri-Weekly*, June 13, 1856.

20. *Guelph Advertiser*, May 8, 1856.

21. *Guelph Herald*, October 7, 1847.

22. *Ibid*.

23. *Ibid*.

24. *Ibid*.

25. *Ibid*.

26. *Ibid*.

27. *Canada Directory*, 1851, pp. 92-94.

28. *Canada Directory*, 1853.

29. See the story about the "Mechanics Soiree" and its emphasis upon the "respectability" of those who attended, *Guelph Advertiser*, May 27, 1852.

30. Byerly, pp. 99-100; Allan, p. 25. Upon Dr. Alling's death in 1848, his place as agent for the Bank of Montreal was taken by his son-in-law, Frederick Marcon. He was succeeded in 1851 by John McLean.

31. *Guelph and Galt Advertiser*, November 9, 1848.

32. *Guelph Advertiser*, April 11, 1850.

33. "Annual Report of the County of Waterloo Building Society", May 29, 1852, in *Guelph Advertiser*, July 1, 1852.

34. "Rules of the County of Waterloo Building Society," *Guelph Advertiser*, May 9, 1850.

35. *Guelph Advertiser*, May 2, 1850.

36. *Ibid*, May 9, 1850.

37. *Guelph Advertiser*, February 9, 1854.

38. *Ibid*, March 16, 1854.

39. *Ibid*, March 30, 1854.

40. *Ibid*, April 4, 1855.

41. *Ibid*.

42. Acton Burrows, pp. 79-80.

43. *Ibid*.

44. *Ibid*, pp. 80-82.

45. *Ibid*, pp. 83-84.

46. *Ibid*, p. 68.

47. *Guelph Advertiser*, February 13, 1851.

48. "Guelph Town Council: Minutes", March 8, 1851, in *ibid*, March 13, 1851.

49. See Mr. Carrol's remarks in the Town Council debate. In fact, if later experience means anything, its cost would likely have exceeded £3,000.

50. "Guelph Town Council: Minutes," March 8, 1851, in the *Guelph Advertiser*, March 13, 1851.

51. *Guelph Advertiser*, March 27, 1851.

52. Letter to the editor by "Will Watch" in *ibid*.

53. *Guelph Advertiser*, March 27, 1851.

54. "Guelph Town Council: Minutes" June 2, 1851, in *ibid*, June 5, 1851.

55. "Guelph Town Council: Minutes," May 10, 1851, in *Guelph Advertiser*, May 15, 1851.

56. "Guelph Town Council: Minutes," June 2, 1851, in *ibid*, June 5, 1851.

57. Acton Burrows, p. 69.

58. *Ibid*, pp. 70-71.

59. *Guelph Advertiser*, March 16, 1854.

60. "Guelph Town Council: Minutes," *Guelph Advertiser*, April 10, 1856.

61. "Guelph Town Council: Minutes," May 7, 1856, in *ibid*, May 8, 1856.

62. *Guelph Advertiser*, May 22, 1856.

63. *Ibid*, May 29, 1856.

64. *Ibid*.

65. *Ibid*.

66. *Guelph Advertiser*, June 6, 1856.

67. Acton Burrows, pp. 92-93.

68. *Ibid*.

69. *Ibid*, p. 93.

70. *Guelph Advertiser*, November 27, 1856.

71. In addition to the £6000 voted in 1856, a second by-law (No. 67) was passed on July 6, 1857, authorizing an additional

---

£5000 "for completing the Market House." *Consolidated By-Laws*, 1923, p. 25.

72. See the debate concerning the tax rate in 1858 and 1859 in "Guelph Town Council: Minutes."

73. Robert W. Mackay, *Canada Directory* [Supplement to 1851] (Montreal, 1853), pp. 76-78; and John Lovell, *Canada Directory, 1857-8* (Montreal, 1858).

74. Reprinted in the *Guelph Advertiser*, September 11, 1856.

75. Quoted in Acton Burrows, pp. 94-95.

76. Reprinted in the *Guelph Advertiser*, September 11, 1856.

28. *Ibid*, June 11, 1866.

29. *Monetary Times*, October 10, 1867.

30. *Hamilton Evening Times*, May 27, 1868.

31. *Monetary Times*, November 28, 1867.

32. Ontario, 31 Vict. cap. XL.

33. *Hamilton Evening Times*, March 26, 1868.

34. Hugh Templin, *Fergus* (Fergus, 1933), p. 187.

35. *Guelph Evening Mercury*, Dec. 2, 1870, p. 1.

36. J.M. and Edward Trout, *The Railways of Canada* (Toronto, 1871), p. 153.

37. *Guelph Advertiser*, March 4, 1852.

Chapter IX

1. *Galt and Guelph Advertiser*, November 26, 1847.

2. *Ibid*, July 9, 1847.

3. *Ibid*.

4. *Guelph and Galt Advertiser*, November 9, 1848.

5. David Allan, "Early Industrial Life. . .," p. 11.

6. Reprinted in the *Guelph Advertiser*, September 20, 1854.

7. *Ibid*.

8. *Guelph Advertiser*, June 30, 1853.

9. *Ibid*, September 30, 1854.

10. *Guelph Advertiser*, November 27, 1856.

11. David Allan, "The Milling Industry, Guelph and Vicinity," *Wellington County Historical Society*, vol. 1, 1932, pp. 6-7.

12. *Ibid*.

13. Acton Burrows, p. 130.

14. *Guelph Evening Mercury*, June 23, 1894.

15. N.D., Goldie Scrapbook.

16. *Ibid*.

17. *Canadian Biographical Dictionary* (Toronto, 1880), pp. 320-322.

18. G.H. Hacking, *Town of Guelph Directory*, 1873, p. 94.

19. George M. Rose, *Cyclopedia of Canadian Biography*, Rose Publishing Co. (Toronto, 1886), p. 139.

20. *Ibid*.

21. "Higinbotham Scrapbook—No. 1" G.P.L., p. 25. N.D.

22. "Journals of Wellington County," Minutes, June 4, 1858.

23. Toronto *Globe*, February 15, 1862.

24. 27-28 Victoria, cap. XCIII, June 30, 1864.

25. *Hamilton Evening Times*, April 30, 1864.

26. *Guelph Herald*, May 29, 1866.

27. *Hamilton Evening Times*, May 30, 1866.

Chapter X

1. Canada *Census*, 1851, 1861, 1871, 1881.

2. *Guelph Daily Mercury*, Jan. 21, 1967.

3. *Canada Directory*, 1853; "Guelph".

4. "St. Joseph's Home Scrapbook", clipping, n.d.

5. *Guelph Evening Mercury*, July 20, 1927.

6. *Charlton's Directory of the Town of Guelph, 1875-6-7*, p. 20.

7. William W. Evans, *City of Guelph Directory, 1882-1883*, (Guelph, 1883), p. 10.

8. Acton Burrows, pp. 128-129.

9. *Guelph Daily Mercury*, Jan. 21, 1967.

10. *Guelph Evening Mercury*, July 20, 1927, pp. 50 and 123.

11. Wm. W. Evans, *Guelph City Directory, 1885-86*, (Toronto, 1884), pp. 37-38.

12. *Guelph Evening Mercury*, July 20, 1927, p. 50.

13. Acton Burrows, p. 68.

14. *Ibid*, p. 102.

15. *Ibid*, p. 128.

16. *Ibid*, p. 149.

17. E.M. Lenore Cutten—*St. George's Parish, Guelph, 1832-1932*, p. 19.

18. Guelph Town By-law No. 230, passed March 18, 1873.

19. *Town of Guelph Directory*, 1873, p. 21.

20. *Guelph Evening Mercury*, June 5, August 22 and September 8, 1905; *Guelph Evening Mercury*, July 20, 1927, p. 123.

21. Wm. W. Evans, *Guelph City Directory, 1885-86*, p. 39.

22. David Allan—*St. Andrew's Church, Guelph, 1832-1932*.

23. Acton Burrows, p. 101; *Wellington County Historical Society*, vol. 3, 1934, p. 8.

24. *Ibid*, p. 143.

25. *Town of Guelph Directory, 1873*, p. 22.

26. Acton Burrows, p. 143.

27. *Guelph Evening Mercury*, July 20, 1927, p. 122.

28. *Town of Guelph Directory, 1873*, p. 22.

29. Rev. D.G. Paton, *Chalmers Church History* (Guelph, 1968), p. 8.

30. *Guelph Evening Mercury*, July 12, 1905.

31. *Guelph Evening Mercury*, July 20, 1927.

32. *Town of Guelph Directory, 1873*, p. 23.

33. *Guelph Evening Mercury*, July 20, 1927.

34. Acton Burrows, pp. 78-79.

35. *Town of Guelph Directory, 1873*, p. 21.

36. Acton Burrows, p. 154.

37. *Guelph Herald*, Nov. 1, 1876.

38. *Town of Guelph Directory, 1873*, p. 23.

39. *Guelph Evening Mercury*, July 20, 1927, p. 50.

40. Acton Burrows, p. 138.

41. *City of Guelph Directory, 1885-86*, p. 38.

42. Ivan Muller, "Baptist Churches in Guelph", *Guelph Historical Society Publications*, vol. I, no. 9.

43. *Guelph Evening Mercury*, July 20, 1927.

44. Ivan Muller, op cit.

45. *Town of Guelph Directory, 1873*, pp. 23-24.

46. *City of Guelph Directory, 1885-86*, p. 37.

47. Acton Burrows, p. 98.

48. *Town of Guelph Directory, 1873*, p. 21.

49. David Allan, *History of Guelph*, p. 29.

50. *Guelph Evening Mercury*, July 20, 1927, p. 50.

51. *City of Guelph Directory, 1882-83*, p. 40.

52. *Town of Guelph Directory, 1873*, p. 24.

53. *City of Guelph Directory, 1885-86*, p. 38.

54. Canada *Census*, 1881.

55. *City of Guelph Directory, 1885-86*, p. 39.

56. *Guelph Weekly Mercury*, March 13, 1884.

57. Anonymous, *Guelph Historical Society Publications*, vol. 1, no. 11.

58. *Guelph Evening Mercury*, July 20, 1927, p. 52.

59. *Guelph Advertiser*, February 17, 1851, describes the meeting of that year as "The Fifteenth Annual Meeting".

60. *Guelph and Galt Advertiser*, February 25, 1848.

61. *Guelph Advertiser*, February 27, 1851.

62. *Town of Guelph Directory, 1873*, p. 31.

63. *Guelph and Galt Advertiser*, March 10, 1848.

64. *Guelph Advertiser*, January 30, 1851.

65. Guelph City By-law, manuscripts, in Guelph City Hall.

66. *Ibid.*

67. At the County level, By-law no. 69 "for the better preservation of Public Morals within the County of Wellington", performed the same function. See *Journals of Wellington County*, Appendix, October 24, 1861.

68. *City of Guelph Directory, 1885-86*, pp. 30-35.

69. Mary McIntosh, "Guelph General Hospital", *Guelph Evening Mercury*, July 20, 1927, p. 85.

70. *Ibid.*

71. H. Kirby and M. Cosyn, *A Century of Care and Concern—Guelph General Hospital*, Woodstock, 1975.

72. Dr. John Roaf, letter to the editor, Toronto *Globe*, February 5, 1852.

73. *Guelph Advertiser*, December 26, 1850.

74. E. Ryerson, "Papers by the Chief Superintendent of Education, 1852", J.G. Hodgins, ed., *Historical and other Papers and Documents. . .of the Educational System of Ontario* (Toronto, 1911), IV, p. 89.

75. Letter to the editor by John Kirkland, November 23, 1852, in *Guelph Advertiser*, January 27, 1853.

76. *Ibid*, January 19, 1854.

77. Greta Shutt, *The High Schools of Guelph*, p. 34. David Allan's *History of Guelph*, p. 5.

78. *Guelph Advertiser Triweekly*, February 7, 1855.

79. Acton Burrows, p. 78.

80. *Guelph Advertiser Triweekly*, April 25, 1855.

81. *Guelph Advertiser*, February 19, 1857.

82. *Ibid.*

83. Canada, *Sessional Papers*, 1862, vol. 5, no. 36; *ibid*, 1866, vol. 4, no. 45; Ontario, *Sessional Papers*, 1871-2, vol. 1, no. 4; *ibid*, 1881, vol. 2, no. 5.

84. For more discussion on this action see my *History of Ontario County 1615-1875* (Whitby, 1973), pp. 268-271.

85. Acton Burrows, p. 133.

86. Toronto *Globe*, Jan. 30, 1851.

87. *Guelph Advertiser*, February 19, 1857.

88. *Guelph Historical Society Publications*, vol. I, no. 4, 1961.

89. *Guelph Herald*, November 1, 1876.

90. *Ibid.*

91. For an excellent description of the development of the Ontario Agricultural College, see Alexander M. Ross, *The College on the Hill* (Toronto, 1974).

92. *Guelph Evening Mercury*, July 20, 1927, p. 65.

93. *Ibid.*

94. *Ibid.*

95. *Guelph Daily Mercury*, November 30, 1965, p. 8.

96. *Guelph Evening Mercury*, July 20, 1927, p. 65.

Chapter XI

1. *Town of Guelph Directory, 1873* (Guelph, 1873), p. 20.

2. *Guelph Evening Mercury*, November 29, 1870, p. 1.

3. These occupations are from either the *Wellington County Directory*, 1867, or the *Town of Guelph Directory, 1873*. Only in James Hazelton's case was there any disagreement in occupational description.

4. *Guelph Evening Mercury*, November 29, 1870, p. 2.

5. *Guelph Herald*, November 1, 1876; *Globe Weekly*, January 26, 1877.

6. *Guelph Evening Mercury*, July 20, 1927, p. 88.

7. David Allan, "Early Industrial Life of Guelph," *Wellington County Historical Society*, vol. 3, 1934, p. 13.

8. *Guelph Evening Mercury*, July 29, 1870, p. 1.

9. *Ibid*, August 24, 1870, p. 1.

10. Town of Guelph, By-law 200, manuscript, City Hall, Guelph.

11. *Guelph Evening Mercury*, August 27, 1870.

12. Acton Burrows, p. 148.

13. *Guelph Evening Mercury*, July 20, 1927.

14. These names are drawn from newspaper items, old local histories, directories, etc. It is certain that they are not a complete list.

15. *County of Wellington Directory*, 1867, p. 119.

16. *Monetary Times*, September 10, 1869.

17. Wm. W. Evans, *Guelph Directory*, 1882-1883, p. 230.

18. See footnote no. 14.

19. Population for years ending in figure 1 are from Canada *Census*. Others are from Guelph Directories of 1873 and 1875/6/7.

20. *Toronto Telegraph* reprinted in the *Guelph Evening Mercury*, August 3, 1870, p. 1.

21. *Guelph Evening Mercury*, October 7, 1870.

22. *Ibid*, November 22, 1870.

23. *Guelph Weekly Mercury*, February 22, 1877.

24. *Guelph Evening Mercury*, October 7, 1870.

25. Quoted anonymously in the *Guelph Evening Mercury*, October 7, 1870.

26. *Guelph Weekly Mercury*, February 22, 1877.

27. *Guelph Evening Mercury*, April 3, 1877.

28. *Ibid*, December 27, 1878.

29. Macdonald Papers, no. 31293-31295, P.A.C.; letter, John Horsman to the Right Honorable Sir John Macdonald, dated Guelph, 24 March, 1879.

30. For a description of Lord Lorne's visit to Guelph, see the *Guelph Evening Mercury*, July 20, 1927, p. 106.

31. Reprinted in the *Guelph Evening Mercury*, October 9, 1886.

32. *Ibid*.

33. Macdonald's National Policy included the use of protective tariffs, the building of the transcontinental railway and settlement of Western Canada to stimulate the economy. For more information on this subject see Heath Macquarrie—*The Conservative Party*, Toronto, 1965, pp. 42 and 43. In this connection it is interesting to note that C. Acton Burrows was present when the National Policy was drawn up. He was 24 years old when he became editor of the *Guelph Herald* in 1874 and his *Annals of the Town of Guelph* was published in 1877. The following quotation is from *Renegade in Power: The Diefenbaker Years*, Toronto, 1963, p. 186, by Peter C. Newman and is reprinted with permission of the Canadian Publishers, McClelland and Stewart Limited. "The most valuable item in the collection was a copy, in Macdonald's own handwriting of the original National Policy, drawn up on January 16, 1878, at a political meeting in Toronto's Shaftesbury Hall. The recording secretary at the meeting was a young reporter for the Guelph *Herald*, called Acton Burrows, later Manitoba's first Deputy Minister of Agriculture. He willed the document to his son Aubrey, a Toronto publisher who, just before he died in 1957, sent it to Diefenbaker."

34. *Guelph Weekly Mercury*, February 22, 1877.

35. 42 Victoria, cap. 41.

36. *Guelph Weekly Herald*, May 1, 1879.

37. *Ibid*.

38. *Ibid*.

39. *Ibid*.

40. *Ibid*.

41. *Ibid*.

42. *Guelph Evening Mercury*, April 3, 1886.

43. City of Guelph, By-law no. 29, June 21, 1880.

44. *Ibid*,
   By-law No. 43, January 4, 1881; Wicks, McNaughton & Co.; Cutlery.
   By-law No. 54, May 2, 1881; David McCrae; Textiles, Fabrics.
   By-law No. 62, September 5, 1881; William Bell; Cabinet Organs.
   By-law No. 64, November 21, 1881; Guelph Carriage Goods Co.; Carriage Goods.
   By-law No. 76, May 15, 1882; Burr and Skinner; Furniture.
   By-law No. 156, April 19, 1886; Burr Bros.; Chairs.
   By-law No. 224, September 10, 1889; Williams, Green and Rome; Shirts, Collars, Cuffs.
   By-law No. 227, December 23, 1889; James Hough, Jr.; Paper Boxes, Stationery.
   By-law No. 254, July 20, 1891; Thomas Griffin; Stoves.
   By-law No. 305, October 9, 1893; The Curtain and Upholstering Mfg. Co.; Chenille Curtains, Covers, Upholstery Goods.

By-law No. 313, June 4, 1894; Rachael Crawford's Mfg. Est.; Shoddy Yarns.

By-law No. 325, March 18, 1895; Laughlin Hough Drawing Table Co.; Drawing Tables, Architect and School Supplies.

By-law No. 326, April 1, 1895; Guelph Norway Iron and Steel Co.; Rolling Mill for Iron & Steel.

By-law No. 335, November 4, 1895; Charles Raymond; Sewing Machines, Cash Registers.

By-law No. 365, August 16, 1897; Wallace and McAdoe; Pork Packing, Bacon.

By-law No. 371, September 19, 1898; Guelph Carpet Mills; Carpets.

By-law No. 383, May 15, 1899; Guelph Iron and Steel; Iron & Steel Products.

By-law No. 387, December 18, 1899; A.R. Woodyatt & Co.; Lawnmowers, etc.

45. Canada, *Sessional Papers*, 1885, no. 37, pp. 12 and 18.

46. *Guelph City Directory*, 1885-1886, p. 12.

47. *Hamilton Evening Times*, October 19, 1867.

48. *Guelph Evening Mercury*, July 20, 1927, p. 24.

49. *Ibid*, p. 24.

50. For an uncritical sketch of the Credit Valley Railway see James Filley, *Credit Valley Railway "The Third Giant"*, Boston Mills Press, Cheltenham, Ontario, 1974.

51. Macdonald Papers, P.A.C., no. 58581-58583, James Goldie, Guelph, to Sir John A. Macdonald, May 29, 1886.

52. *Guelph Evening Mercury*, January 13, 1885.

53. The *Brantford Expositor* reprinted in the *Guelph Evening Mercury*, May 8, 1884.

54. Canada, XLVII Victoria, cap. 79.

55. *Ibid.*

56. *Guelph Evening Mercury*, July 20, 1927, p. 26.

57. *Ibid*, December 17, 1885.

58. *Ibid*, December 24, 1885.

59. *Ibid.*

60. *Ibid*, July 20, 1927, p. 26.

61. Dr. Marvin W. Farrell, *The Guelph Junction Railway 1884-1950*. Ontario Agricultural College, Guelph, July 1951.

62. *Guelph Evening Mercury*, October 13, 1886.

63. *Ibid*, July 20, 1927, p. 26.

64. *Ibid*, April 20, 1886.

65. *Ibid*, July 2, 1886.

66. *Ibid*, November 29, 1886.

67. *Ibid*, advertisement.

68. *Ibid.*

69. *Ibid*, Letter to the Editor by Walter Macdonald.

70. *Ibid*, December 3, 1886.

71. Originally the subsidy was $48,600, but because some of the construction was of poor quality (e.g. the use of wood instead of stone for culverts), the subsidy was reduced. *Guelph Evening Mercury*, July 20, 1927, p. 26.

72. *Ibid*. See also Guelph City By-law no. 216.

73. *Guelph Weekly Mercury*, May 9, 1889, p. 1.

74. *Ibid*, July 25, 1889, p. 2.

75. *Ibid*, December 12, 1889, p. 3.

76. *Ibid*, January 23, 1890.

Chapter XII

1. Canada *Census*, 1881, 1901, 1911, 1921.

2. *Guelph Evening Mercury*, July 20, 1927.

3. Guelph Town By-law, no. 315, October 21, 1878.

4. *Guelph Evening Mercury*, March 13, 1909, p. 11.

5. *Ibid.*

6. *City of Guelph Directory*, 1882-3, p. 2.

7. *Guelph Herald*, October 6, 1887.

8. *Guelph Weekly Mercury*, January 24, 1889.

9. *Ibid*, June 23, 1894.

10. *Guelph Evening Mercury*, April 24, 1902.

11. *Ibid*, May 3, 1902.

12. *Ibid*, May 6, 1902.

13. *Ibid*, August 20, 1902.

14. *Ibid*, August 27, 1902.

15. *Ibid*, September 11, 1902.

16. *Ibid*, December 8, 1903.

17. *Ibid*, March 23, 1907.

18. *Ibid*, February 14, 1907.

19. Guelph City By-law no. 590, January 14, 1907. The first Water Commission had been removed in 1884 and the waterworks placed under a committee of Council. In 1906 the Board of Trade took up an agitation to establish an "independent" elected Commission. This was done by By-law 590.

20. *Guelph Evening Mercury*, March 13, 1909, p. 13.

21. *Ibid.*

22. *Ibid*, July 20, 1927.

23. *Ibid*, May 4, 1914.

24. David Allan, *Guelph and Its Early Days*, pp. 27-8.

25. *Guelph Herald*, May 15, 1866.

26. Guelph Town By-law no. 200, August 26, 1870.

27. *Guelph Weekly Mercury*, January 19, 1888.
28. *Ibid*, November 24, 1891.
29. *Guelph Evening Mercury*, October 21, 1902.
30. *Ibid*, February 14, 1903, p. 1.
31. W.R. Plewman, *Adam Beck and the Ontario Hydro* (Toronto, 1947), p. 29.
32. *Guelph Evening Mercury*, June 17, 1902.
33. *Ibid*.
34. 62 Victoria (2) Cap. 26.
35. *Guelph Evening Mercury*, June 17, 1902, p. 1.
36. *Ibid*, October 21, 1902.
37. *Ibid*.
38. *Ibid*.
39. Letter to the editor by Alderman S. Carter, *Guelph Evening Mercury*, February 24, 1903.
40. *Ibid*, March 2, 1903.
41. Guelph City By-law no. 455, February 9, 1903.
42. *Guelph Evening Mercury*, January 26, 1903.
43. W.R. Plewman, pp. 34-50.
44. *Ibid*, pp. 50-53.
45. *Guelph Evening Mercury*, September 5, 1906.
46. *Ibid*, November 21, 1906.
47. *Ibid*, November 28, 1906.
48. *Ibid*, November 29, 1906.
49. *Ibid*, December 28, 1906.
50. Guelph City By-law no. 592, January 14, 1907.
51. W.R. Plewman, p. 51.
52. *Ibid*, pp. 52-3.
53. Guelph City By-law no. 533, July 17, 1905.
54. Guelph City By-law no. 644, January 20, 1908.
55. *Guelph Evening Mercury*, March 2, 1909.
56. *Ibid*, November 12, 1909.
57. *Ibid*, October 26, 1910.
58. *Guelph Historical Society Publications*, volume XIV, nos. 2 and 3.
59. Agreement between George Sleeman and the City of Guelph signed August 7, 1894 (typescript), Guelph City Hall.
60. *Ibid*.
61. The By-law confirming this agreement, Guelph City By-law no. 321, was read all three times and passed on August 7, 1894.
62. *Guelph Evening Mercury*, July 20, 1927, p. 126.
63. *Ibid*, May 21, 1903.
64. *Ibid*, April 29, 1903.
65. *Ibid*, May 14, 1903.
66. *Ibid*, May 21, 1903.
67. *Ibid*, May 26, 1903.
68. *Ibid*, October 1, 1903.
69. *Ibid*, January 23, 1903.
70. *Ibid*, December 14, 1899.
71. *Ibid*, February 14, 1903.
72. *Ibid*, July 9, 1903.
73. *Ibid*, October 1, 1903.
74. *Ibid*, November 24, 1904.
75. The *Guelph Evening Mercury* of May 22, 1908, lists the following as having become naturalized citizens: Carere Domenio, Guiseppe Nocaro, Angelo Albanese, Franco Galarso, Salvatore Silevestro, Grovinzzo Guiseppe, Pezzno Vincenzo, Salvatore Pezzno, Giovinzzo Mickele, Salvatore Roso, Vincezzo Torrenti, Mickele Valorioto, Carrere Giorgio, Aleviano Arceagolo, Valrioto Salvatore, Antonnio Tromonto, Michelino Agostino, Francesco Carere, Guiseppe Ammendolia, Felici Mairo, Thomas Belmont, Georgio Tedisco, Spataro Mimo, Domenico Roso, Nelisco Luigo, Mammolti Antono, Coseno Carere, Domenio Piccolo; Addario Francesco, Domenico Cardona, Lonzo Francesco, Addaco Guiseppe. The same paper gives another application for citizenship signed by Col. White listing the following names: Magnolio Francesco, Michele Carere, Agostino Salvatore, Tidesco Guiseppe, Raso Dominico, Antonio Grovenazzo, Agostino Guiseppe.
76. *Guelph Daily Mercury*, September 9, 1955.
77. Quoted in the *Guelph Evening Mercury*, September 27, 1909.
78. Quoted in *ibid*, October 8, 1903.
79. *Guelph Weekly Mercury*, September 29, 1910.

Chapter XIII

1. *Guelph Evening Mercury*, September 30, 1902.
2. *Ibid*, November 10, 1906.
3. *Ibid*, January 24, 1907.
4. *Ibid*, December 20, 1909.
5. *Ibid*, January 29, 1914.
6. *Ontario Provincial Fair Review*, (Guelph, 1919), p. 27.
7. See the list of major amalgamations in Canada compiled in *Monetary Times*, January 6, 1912.
8. *Guelph Evening Mercury*, April 26, 1916.
9. *Ibid*.
10. David Allan, *Guelph and its Early Days*, p. 22.

11. *Guelph Daily Mercury*, December 23, 1950, p. 104.

12. *Ibid*, Commercial Industrial Progressive Edition, 1916, p. 1.

13. This and subsequent personal information comes form his memoirs, a typescript of which is in possession of the Guelph Historical Society.

14. *Ibid*, p. 33.

15. *Guelph Evening Mercury*, May 4, 1914.

16. *Ibid*, May 5, 1914.

17. *Ibid*, June 22, 1914.

18. *Ibid*, July 3, 1915.

19. *Ibid*, July 15, 1915.

20. There are innumerable articles debating these issues in the *Mercury* between 1914 and 1916.

21. *Guelph Evening Mercury*, December 16, 1919.

22. *Guelph Evening Mercury*, July 20, 1927, p. 110.

23. *Galt and Guelph Advertiser*, June 25, 1847.

24. *Ibid*, November 8, 1848.

25. *Ibid*, June 28, 1849.

26. *Guelph Historical Society Publications*, vol. I, no. 6, 1961.

27. Acton Burrows, p. 96.

28. *Ibid*, p. 122.

29. *Ibid*.

30. *Ibid*.

31. David Stirton to John A. Macdonald, December 24, 1864, Macdonald Papers, vol. 338, pt. 2, Nos. 154687-154689, P.A.C.

32. See the accounts in Acton Burrows, pp. 135-6, *Guelph Evening Mercury*, March 15, 1926, *ibid*, July 20, 1927, p. 110.

33. Acton Burrows, p. 136.

34. *Guelph Evening Mercury*, July 20, 1927, p. 110.

35. *Ibid*.

36. Acton Burrows, pp. 134-135.

37. *Town of Guelph Directory*, 1873, p. 28.

38. *Guelph Daily Mercury*, June 23, 1894.

39. Higinbotham Scrapbook No. 3, N.D.

40. *Guelph Evening Mercury*, July 20, 1927, p. 110.

41. *Ibid*, February 28, 1948.

42. *Ibid*, July 20, 1927, p. 110.

43. *Ibid*, December 17, 1909.

44. *Ibid*, February 28, 1948.

45. *Ibid*, July 20, 1927, p. 54.

46. *Ibid*, August 14, 1914.

47. *Ibid*, August 11, 1914.

48. *Ibid*, December 1, 1916, p. 9.

49. *Ibid*, July 20, 1927, p. 129.

50. *Ibid*, p. 60.

51. *The Canadian Patriotic Fund*, compiled and edited by Philip H. Morris (N.D., N.P.), p. 10.

52. *Ibid*, p. 219.

53. *Guelph Evening Mercury*, July 20, 1927, p. 62.

54. Letter from George A. Drew in the *Guelph Evening Mercury*, December 31, 1921, p. 2.

55. *Guelph Evening Mercury*, November 27, 1923, p. 1.

56. *Ibid*, December 28, 1926, p. 6.

57. *Guelph Advertiser*, May 26, 1853.

58. *Guelph Advertiser Triweekly*, January 15, 1855.

59. Although some 2,000 persons attended the rally to discuss the nine-hours movement in 1872, and a resolution was passed in favour of such an innovation, no strong action was taken to ensure its implementation. See Acton Burrows, p. 151.

60. *Guelph Evening Mercury*, July 20, 1927, p. 38.

61. Guelph Trades and Labour Council, *Souvenir Booklet*, TLC 28th Annual Convention, at Guelph, September, 1912.

62. *Guelph Evening Mercury*, October 3, 1902.

63. *Ibid, Industrial Souvenir*, 1908, p. 11.

64. T.L.C. *Convention Souvenir Booklet*, 1912.

65. *Guelph Evening Mercury*, July 20, 1927, p. 60.

66. 7-8 George V, cap. 19.

67. *Ibid*, Schedule, Section 6.

68. *Guelph Evening Mercury*, June 24, 1918; see also, *Orange Sentinel*, June 27, 1918.

69. *Toronto Star*, June 22, 1918.

70. *Guelph Evening Mercury*, June 20 and 24, 1918.

71. Toronto *Globe*, June 21, 1918.

72. *Ibid*.

73. *Ibid*.

74. *Guelph Evening Mercury*, June 24, 1918.

75. *Ibid*, June 20, 1918.

76. Toronto *Globe*, July 16, 1918.

77. *Ibid*, July 6, 1918.

78. *Ibid*, September 9, 10, 11, 12 and 13, 1919.

Chapter XIV

1. For the story of Edward Johnson, see Ruby Mercer, *The Tenor of his Time*, (Toronto, 1976).

2. David Allan, *Guelph Evening Mercury*, July 20, 1927, p. 19.

3. Of the four reported by Thompson, only two still remained in good condition in 1927. One was used as the office of a coal yard on Waterloo Street (owned by M.F. Cray), and the other, a residence on Quebec Street was occupied by L.N.E. Lafontaine. *Guelph Evening Mercury*, February 1, 1927.

4. *Guelph Evening Mercury*, August 1, 1905.

5. Gilbert Campbell, Glasgow, to Mayor [George] Sleeman, October 4, 1905, reprinted in the *Guelph Evening Mercury*, October 16, 1905.

6. *Ibid*.

7. *Ibid*, May 29, 1908.

8. *Ibid*, October 25, 1910.

9. *Ibid*, November 21, 1911.

10. *Ibid*, April 15, 1919.

11. *Ibid*, March 10, 1920.

12. Reprinted in *ibid*, May 11, 1922.

13. *Ibid*, June 20, 1922.

14. *Ibid*, March 4, 1926.

15. *Ibid*, December 10, 1957.

16. When the City rebuilt the model of the Priory early in 1970, a board was found under the roof with the following inscription in W.A. Cowan's handwriting: "This is a replica of the first house built in Guelph in 1827 by John Galt. It is built to a scale of 1½ inches to the foot by David and Walter Cowan, sons of W.A. Cowan, Building Contractor. The measurements for the work were taken from the original building prior to demolition on May 6th and 7th, 1926. The occasion on which this replica is used is Guelph's Centennial Celebration, August 1-6, 1927." (David was 17 when this model was built, and Walter 15).

17. *Guelph Evening Mercury*, December 10, 1957.

18. *Ibid*, undated article by Vern McIlwraith in Goldie Scrapbook "A".

19. *Guelph Evening Mercury*, May 23, 1914.

20. *Ibid*, July 20, 1927, contains the special "Centennial Issue."

21. *Ibid*, July 20, 1927, gives 1832, but both James Innes (Instalment XII) and a detailed account in the *Mercury* of April 19, 1902, gives 1833.

22. *Ibid*, April 19, 1902.

23. *Ibid*, July 20, 1927, p. 92.

24. *Ibid*, April 19, 1902.

25. *Guelph Herald*, September 30, 1847.

26. *Directory of the Town of Guelph*, 1873, p. 27.

27. *Guelph Evening Mercury*, July 20, 1927.

28. *Ibid*, April 19, 1902.

29. Edwin C. Guillet, *Early Life in Upper Canada* (Toronto, 1933), p. 343.

30. *Guelph Evening Mercury*, April 19, 1902. This article was reprinted in the *Guelph Historical Society Publications*, Vol. II, no. 2, 1962.

31. David Allan, *Guelph and its Early Days*, p. 43.

32. *Guelph Evening Mercury*, July 20, 1927, p. 93.

33. *City of Guelph Directory*, 1882-3, p. 36.

34. *Guelph Evening Mercury*, January 13, 1915.

35. *Ibid*, July 20, 1927, p. 93.

36. *Ibid*.

37. *Guelph Weekly Mercury*, March 14, 1889.

38. David Allan, p. 44.

39. *Guelph Evening Mercury*, June 23, 1894.

40. *Guelph Herald*, July 29, 1847.

41. *Ibid*, August 5, 1847.

42. *Ibid*, August 26, 1847.

43. *Ibid*.

44. *Guelph Evening Mercury*, column by Findlay Weaver, N.D. in Walter Tyson's Scrapbook "A". Guelph Historical Society Collection.

45. *Ibid*, July 20, 1927, p. 91.

46. *Ibid*.

47. *Ibid*, p. 126.

48. *Ibid*, October 9, 1909.

49. *Ibid*, August 5, 1919.

50. *Reprinted* in the *Guelph Daily Mercury*, March 4, 1942. The story was originally written in 1892. Other sources place the date of actual formation of the club as 1863.

51. *Ibid*.

52. *Ibid*.

53. Higinbotham Scrapbook no. 3, Guelph Public Library, newspaper clipping, N.D.

54. *Guelph Daily Mercury*, March 21, 1942.

55. *Guelph Evening Mercury*, July 20, 1927, p. 123.

56. *Ibid*, p. 124.

57. *Ibid*.

58. *Guelph Daily Mercury*, March 21, 1942.

59. *Ibid*, February 28, 1948.

60. *Guelph Evening Mercury*, July 20, 1927, p. 89.

61. *Ibid*, p. 91.

62. *Ibid*.

63. *Guelph Historical Society Publications*, Vol. XIII, no. 8, 1973-4.

64. Byerly, *Beginning of Things*, p. 72.

65. *Guelph Evening Mercury*, July 20, 1927, p. 73.

66. *Historical Atlas of Wellington County*, (Toronto, 1906), p. 16.

67. *Guelph Evening Mercury*, July 20, 1927, p. 7.

68. *Ibid*, October 18, 1916.

69. *Guelph Herald*, January 7, 1851.

70. *Guelph Advertiser*, January 9, 1851.

71. *Ibid*, June 27, 1850.

72. *Guelph Herald*, July 10, 1855.

73. Anonymous poem, N.D., N.P. in files of Guelph Historical Society.

74. *Guelph Herald*, October 12, 1847.

75. Reprinted in the Galt *Reporter*, April 27, 1866.

76. *Guelph Evening Mercury*, August 8, 1917, reprinted from the Spectator, June 30, 1917.

77. Anonymous, a hand-written copy is in the Hugh Douglass Collection, Guelph Public Library.

78. For some interesting commentary on James Gay, see William Arthur Deacon, *The Four James*, (Ottawa, 1927).

79. *Ibid*

80. *Guelph Historical Society Publications*, Vol. I, no. 2, 1961.

Appendices

Appendix A

MAYORS, REEVES, ALDERMEN AND COUNCILLORS, 1851-1927. *

MEMBERS OF THE TOWN COUNCIL, 1851 TO 1855, INCLUSIVE

Year	REEVE	COUNCILLORS			
1851	Samuel Smith	Wm. Stevenson	John Thorp	Edward Carroll	Edwin Hubbard
1852	William Clarke	W. S. G. Knowles	John Smith	George Sunley	Henry Orton
1853	William Clarke	W. S. G. Knowles	John Pipe	George Sunley	Henry Orton
1854	W. S. G. Knowles	Wm. Clarke	John Pipe	John Harris	Wm. Stevenson
1855	John Smith	John Pipe	John Watt	John Harris	Peter Gow

1855—John Pipe resigned in May and Frederick George was elected in his place.

MEMBERS OF THE TOWN COUNCIL, 1856 TO 1870, INCLUSIVE

Year	MAYOR	COUNCILLORS			
		East Ward	North Ward	West Ward	South Ward
1856	John Smith	J. C. Presant Evan Macdonald Robert Thompson	John Thorp Frederick George Adam Robertson	John Smith George Elliott George Sunley	William Day Peter Gow William Atkins
1857	George Sunley	Evan Macdonald Robert Thompson George P. Tatham	Frederick George John Harvey James Armstrong	George Sunley Samuel Smith George Elliott	William Day Peter Gow W. S. G. Knowles

1856—The Council elected John Smith Mayor, George Sunley Reeve, and Peter Gow Deputy-Reeve.
1857—The Council elected George Sunley Mayor, Peter Gow Reeve, and James Armstrong Deputy-Reeve. The Mayor died in March and Samuel Smith was elected for the remainder of the year, and Wm. J. Brown was elected to fill the vacancy.

* Appendices have not been indexed.

MEMBERS OF THE TOWN COUNCIL (Continued)

Year	MAYOR	COUNCILLORS			
		East Ward	North Ward	West Ward	South Ward
1858	George Elliott	John Harris Charles Davidson James Murphy	John Harvey Fred George James Armstrong	George Elliott George Bruce, Sr. G. M. Keeling	Wm. Day Peter Gow John Kirkland
1859	James Webster	John Harris Charles Adsett James Murphy	John Harvey James Armstrong Fred George	G. M. Keeling C. J. Buckland Robert Melvin	John Kirkland John Stevens Robert Thompson
1860	John Harvey	Charles Davidson N. Higinbotham David Allan	James Armstrong Fred George G. S. Herod	George Elliott C. J. Buckland G. M. Keeling	T. S. Parker Thomas Holliday John Kirkland
1861	T. S. Parker	Charles Davidson N. Higinbotham George Hood	John Harvey G. S. Herod Wm. Clarke	Thomas Gowdy C. J. Buckland G. M. Keeling	H. W. Peterson John Kirkland Thomas Holliday
1862	George Palmer	Charles Davidson George Hood Robert Melvin	John Harvey Adam Robertson Francis Evatt	C. J. Buckland Henry Hatch F. W. Galbraith	H. W. Peterson Thomas Holliday T. S. Parker
1863	H. W. Peterson	George Hood George Palmer Robert Melvin	John Harvey Adam Robertson Richard Mitchell	George Elliott Henry Hatch F. W. Galbraith	Peter Gow T. S. Parker Edward Carroll
1864	Wm. Clarke	George Palmer George Hood Robert Melvin	John Harvey Adam Robertson Richard Mitchell	George Elliott Henry Hatch Richard Hampson	H. W. Peterson Peter Gow John A. Lamprey
1865	Wm. Clarke	George Hood N Higinbotham John Harris	John Harvey Adam Robertson Richard Mitchell	George Elliott Henry Hatch James Massie	H. W. Peterson Peter Gow C E. Romaine
1866	Peter Gow	N. Higinbotham Robert Melvin Thomas Sayers	John Harvey Richard Mitchell G. S. Herod	George Elliott Henry Hatch James Massie	H. W. Peterson Thomas Holliday Wm. Day
1867	Peter Gow	F. J. Chadwick Patrick McCurry Thomas Sayers	John Harvey G. S. Herod James Mays	F. W. Galbraith James Massie Alex. Thomson	Wm. Day Thomas Holliday Wm. Hockin

1858—The Council elected George Elliott Mayor, James Armstrong Reeve, and John Harvey Deputy-Reeve.
1858—Fred George resigned in February, and George S. Herod was elected in his place.
1859—By amendment of the Municipal law the Mayor was elected by the people, and the Council elected John Harvey Reeve, and John Kirkland Deputy-Reeve.
1859—G. M. Keeling's seat was declared vacant 21st March, and George Bruce, Sr., was elected to fill his place.
1860—The Council elected George Elliott Reeve, and Charles Davidson Deputy-Reeve.
1860—Fred George resigned May 7th, and Wm. Clarke was elected to fill the vacancy.
1861—The Council elected John Harvey Reeve, and John Kirkland Deputy-Reeve.
1861—Dr. Clarke resigned August 5th, and George Palmer was elected to fill the vacancy.
1861—G. M. Keeling died in October, and John Keller was elected to fill his place.
1862—The Council elected Dr. Parker Reeve, and Charles Davidson Deputy-Reeve.
1863—The Council elected George Palmer Reeve and George Elliott Deputy-Reeve.
1864—The Council elected George Palmer Reeve and Adam Robertson Deputy-Reeve.
1864—John A. Lamprey's seat became vacant in October and C. E. Romaine was elected to fill the place.
1865—The Council elected H. W. Peterson Reeve and James Elliott Deputy-Reeve.
1866—The Council elected H. W. Peterson Reeve and James Massie Deputy-Reeve.
1866—Henry Hatch resigned on July 2nd and Alexander Thompson was elected in his place.
1867—Elected by the people:—Robert Melvin, Reeve. H. W. Peterson and Richard Mitchell Deputy-Reeves.
1867—Wm. Hockin resigned in January and T. A. Heffernan was elected in his place.

MEMBERS OF THE TOWN COUNCIL (Continued)

Year	MAYOR	COUNCILLORS			
		East Ward	North Ward	West Ward	South Ward
1868	N. Higinbotham	F. J. Chadwick	John Harvey	James Massie	Wm. Day
		Thomas Sayers	G. S. Herod	Alex. Thompson	Thomas Holliday
		Patrick McCurry	James Mays	George Howard	Thos. A. Heffernan
1869	G. S. Herod	F. J. Chadwick	John Harvey	G. A. Bruce	Thos. A. Heffernan
		Wm. Allan	Robert Mitchell	George Howard	Thomas Holliday
		Thomas Sayers	John A .Wood	Alex. Thomson	Wm. Day
1870	G. S. Herod	Thomas Sayers	John A. Wood	G. A. Bruce	Thos. A. Heffernan
		Wm. Allan	Adam Robertson	George Howard	Thomas Holliday
		David McCrae	Robert Mitchell	John McNeil	Wm. Day
1871	Richard Mitchell	Wm. Allan	Adam Robertson	G. A. Bruce	Thos. A. Heffernan
		John Stewart	Robert Mitchell	John McNeil	Thomas Holliday
		David McCrae	Charles Walker	Henry Hatch	David Kennedy
1872	Richard Mitchell	Wm. Allan	Adam Robertson	John McNeil	Wm. Stevenson
		John Stewart	Robert Mitchell	R. W. Bell	Michael Snider
		J. P. MacMillan	John Hogg	John Crowe	David Kennedy
1873	Adam Robertson	John Horsman	Richard Mitchell	George Elliott	Thos. A. Heffernan
		Dennis Coffee	John Hogg	J. C. McLagan	Thos. Holliday
		William Bell	Robert Mitchell	John Crowe	David Kennedy
1874	John Harris	Charles Davidson	Adam Robertson	George Elliott	A. B. Petrie
		Dennis Coffee	Wm. H. Mills	George Bruce	J. W. Hall
		David McCrae	Edmund Harvey	John Crowe	T. A. Heffernan
1875	Robert Melvin	Thomas Sayers	Adam Robertson	George Bruce	A. B. Petrie
		Charles Davidson	Caleb Chase	George Murton	Thos. A. Heffernan
		Dennis Coffee	Wm. H. Mills	John Crowe	J. P. MacMillan
1876	Robert Melvin	Thomas Sayers	G. S. Herod	J. C. McLagan	A. B. Petrie
		J. B. Armstrong	Wm. H. Mills	George Bruce	George Sleeman
		Daniel Kribs	Caleb Chase	Wm. Hart	J. P. MacMillan
1877	F. J. Chadwick	Dennis Coffee	Fred Biscoe	George Elliott	John A. Lamprey
		Joseph Heffernan	Wm. H. Mills	Thomas Gowdy	Francis Gauhan
		Alex. Dunbar	Wm. Hearn	J. C. McLagan	J. T. Cunningham

1868—Robert Melvin Reeve, H. W. Peterson and Richard Mitchell Deputy-Reeves. H. W. Peterson resigned in March; James Massie resigned his councillorship and was elected a Deputy Reeve, and J. C. Buckland was elected councillor in James Massie's place.
1869—Richard Mitchell Reeve. Patrick McCurry and James Goldie Deputy-Reeves.
1869—John Harvey resigned his seat, and A. Robertson was elected to fill his place.
1870—Richard Mitchell Reeve, F. J. Chadwick and Henry Hatch Deputy-Reeves.
1871—James Massie Reeve, N. Higinbotham and George Howard Deputy-Reeves.
1872—James Massie Reeve, George Howard and G. A. Bruce Deputy-Reeves.
1872—John Stewart died and Dennis Coffee was elected in his place.
1872—J. McNeil resigned and George Elliott was elected in his place.
1873—James Massie Reeve, F. J. Chadwick and George Howard Deputy-Reeves.
1873—In July William Bell resigned and C. Davidson was elected in his place.
1874—George Howard Reeve, Charles Raymond 1st Deputy-Reeve, George Hood 2nd Deputy-Reeve.
1875—George Howard Reeve, Charles Raymond 1st Deputy-Reeve; David McCrae, 2nd Deputy-Reeve.
1876—George Howard Reeve, David McCrae 1st Deputy-Reeve, David Kennedy 2nd Deputy-Reeve, George Hood 3rd Deputy-Reeve.
1877—George Hood Reeve, William Hart 1st Deputy-Reeve, George Sleeman 2nd Deputy-Reeve, J. P. MacMillan 3rd Deputy-Reeve.
1877—A. Dunbar resigned and G. B. Fraser was elected in his place.
1877—W. H. Mills resigned and Dr. Clarke was elected in his place.
1877—T. Gowdy resigned and H. Hatch was elected in his place.

MEMBERS OF THE TOWN COUNCIL (Continued)

Year	MAYOR	COUNCILLORS			
		East Ward	North Ward	West Ward	South Ward
1878	George Howard	M. J. Doran Robert Melvin F. J. Chubb	Fred Biscoe Wm. Hearn Robert Mitchell	E. W. McGuire George Bruce Thomas Gowdy	John Roche Daniel Ray Francis Gauhan

1878—George Elliott Reeve, George Sleeman 1st Deputy-Reeve, Richard Mitchell 2nd Deputy-Reeve, Cabel Chase 3rd Deputy Reeve.
1878—F. J. Chubb resigned and D. Coffee was elected to fill his place.
1878—F. Gauhan was unseated and J. P. MacMillan was elected to fill his place.

Year	MAYOR	COUNCILLORS					
		St. Patrick	St. George	St. John	St. David	St. Andrew	St. James
1879	Geo. Howard	Dennis Coffee Thos. Dobbie	E. W. McGuire W. Stevenson	Wm. Hearn Robt. Mitchell	James Hewer John Tyson	George Bruce John Roche	Daniel Day T. Holliday

MEMBERS OF THE CITY COUNCIL
ALDERMEN

1880	Geo. Sleeman	F. J. Chadwick Dennis Coffee M. J. Doran	E. W. McGuire W. Stevenson Fred Biscoe	A. Robertson John Hall W. J. Fairbank	Wm. Hart James Hewer John Tyson	George Bruce Thos. Gowdy J. C. McLagan	G. S. Grange J. A. Lamprey J. P. McMillan
1881	Geo. Sleeman	F. J. Chadwick Walter Laing Jas. Paterson	Fred Biscoe C. Davidson W. Stevenson	John Hall John Read A. Robertson	Thos. Goldie James Hewer G. H. Skinner	Geo. Bruce Geo. Elliott Thos. Gowdy	F. J. Chadwick Jno. A. Lamprey D. Kennedy
1882	Geo. Sleeman	D. Coffee Ed. O'Connor Wm. Russell	C. Davidson W. Stevenson F. B. Skinner	John Hall John Read A. Robertson	James Hewer S. Hodgskin G. H. Skinner	Geo. Bruce Thos. Gowdy R. F. Maddock	N. Burns F. Gauhan J. A. Lamprey
1883	Caleb Chase	D. Coffee Walter Laing Ed. O'Connor	C. Davidson F. B. Skinner W. Stevenson	Wm. Hearn John Read Chas. Walker	Thos. Goldie James Hewer G. H. Skinner	Thos. Gowdy R. F. Maddock Wm. Russell	N. Burns James Keough J. A. Lamprey
1884	Caleb Chase	D. Coffee J. H. Finlay Ed. O'Connor	A. H. Macdonald F. B. Skinner W. Stevenson	James T. Brill John Hall Chas. Walker	Henry Hatch David N. Hogg Thos. Goldie	Geo Bruce R. F. Maddock John Roche	N. Burns Jas. Cormack J. A. Lamprey
1885	W. Stevenson	Wm. Carter Wm. Hortop Geo. W. Stull	W. N. Husband A. H. Macdonald F. B. Skinner	James T. Brill John Read Chas. Walker	T. Goldie Wm. Hearn Wm. G. Smith	Geo. Bruce R. F. Maddock W. F. Barber	N. Burns James Keough J. A. Lamprey
1886	W. Stevenson	Wm. Carter Thos. P. Coffee James Wells	J. H. Hamilton W. N. Husband F. B. Skinner	Joseph Carter John Hall John Read	Wm. Hearn James Hewer W. G. Smith	Geo. Bruce W. H. Cutten R. F. Maddock	F. J. Chadwick James Keough J. A. Lamprey

1879—Caleb Chase Reeve, George Sleeman 1st Deputy-Reeve, J. P. McMillan 2nd Deputy-Reeve, and Fred Biscoe 3rd Deputy-Reeve.
1879—Wm. Hearn resigned and W. J. Fairbank was elected in his place.
1879—Daniel Day resigned and Francis Gauhan was elected in his place.
1880—George S. Grange resigned in March and Nicholas Burns was elected to fill the vacancy.
1881—F. J. Chadwick was elected for St. Patrick's and for St. James' Wards; he disclaimed St. James' Ward, and Robert Morrison was elected for St. James' Ward. F. J. Chadwick also disclaimed St. Patrick's Ward and was re-elected; he was then unseated and was succeeded by William Russell.
1881—George Elliott disclaimed St. Andrew's Ward, and R. F. Maddock was elected to fill the vacancy.
1886—James Wells resigned his seat in March, and Wm. Hortop was elected in his place.
1886—John Hall died in March and Charles Raymond was elected in his place.
1886—F. J. Chadwick resigned in June, and Dennis Coffee was elected in his place.

MEMBERS OF THE CITY COUNCIL (Continued)

Year	MAYOR	ALDERMEN					
		St. Patrick	St. George	St. John	St. David	St. Andrew	St. James
1887	A. H. Macdonald	Henry Hatch T. P. Coffee John Kennedy	Geo. Howard W. N. Husband J. H. Hamilton	John Read Joseph Carter J. W. Kilgour	Wm. Hearn James Hewer W. G. Smith	R. F. Maddock Thos. Gowdy D. Scroggie	J. A. Lamprey T. Holliday D. Kennedy
1888	A. H. Macdonald	Dennis Coffee John Kennedy Thos. Pepper	J. H. Hamilton Geo. Howard C. Kloepfer	J. W. Kilgour John Read C. S. Walker	Robert Barber James Hewer W. G. Smith	W. H. Cutten R. F. Maddock D. Scroggie	P. Hartnett J. A. Lamprey Wm. Russell
1889	Thos. Gowdy	Henry Hatch Jno. Kennedy Thos. Pepper	Geo. Howard Henry Howitt C. Kloepfer	Solomon Dawson W. B. Kennedy S. J. Taylor	Robt. Barber Jonathan Kelly J. W. Kilgour	Peter Kerr David Scroggie W. H. Wardrope	P. Hartnett J. A. Lamprey Wm. Russell
1890	Thos. Gowdy	M. J. Duignan John Kennedy Thos. Pepper	Frank Dowler Geo. Howard C. Kloepfer	Thos. Goldie J. Hugo Reed S. J. Taylor	Robt. Barber Jonathan Kelly J. A. Mowat	Peter Kerr Jas. Palmer David Scroggie	J. B. Fischer P. Hartnett J. A. Lamprey
1891	Thos. Goldie	Thos. P. Coffee Jas. Hough, Jr. David Little	Frank Dowler James Hewer C. Kloepfer	J. H. Hamilton J Hugo Reed S. J. Taylor	Robt. Barber Jonathan Kelly W. H. Wardrope	Peter Kerr James Palmer David Scroggie	P. Hartnett J. A. Lamprey S. J. Laughlin
1892	Thos. Goldie Geo. Sleeman	Thos. P. Coffee James Hough David Little	James Hewer C. Kloepfer A. J. Little	J. H. Hamilton R. E. Nelson S. J. Taylor	Robt. Barber Thos. Moffatt J. G. Sully	W. G. Smith James Palmer David Scroggie	J. A. Lamprey Wm. Slater J. B. Fischer
1893	W. G. Smith	T. P. Coffee John Kennedy David Little	Jas. Hewer C. Kloepfer Philip Spragge	W. B. Kennedy R. E. Nelson G. B. Ryan	Jonathan Kelly D. L. Schultz J. G. Sully	R. F. Maddock James Palmer David Scroggie	Wm. Carter P. Hartnett S. J. Laughlin
1894	W. G. Smith	T. P. Coffee James Hough David Little	Jas. Hewer C. Kloepfer Philip Spragge	S. J. Taylor W. B. Kennedy R. E. Nelson	John Newstead J. G. Sully D. L. Schultz	R. F. Maddock David Scroggie John J. Mahoney	L. O. Barber P. Hartnett Clayton Peterson
1895	Jno. A. Lamprey	T. P. Coffee John McHardy G. W. Stull	James Hewer D. E. Macdonald E. Parkinson	Andrew Crosbie Robt. Dowrie S. J. Taylor	John Newstead D. L. Schultz J. G. Sully	Fred Hendley J. J. Mahoney David Scroggie	L. O. Barber P. Hartnett C. Peterson
1896	Jno. A. Lamprey	T. P. Coffee Jno. Kennedy Geo. Penfold	H. A. B. Calvert R. E. Nelson E. Parkinson	Andrew Crosbie Robt. Dowrie S. J. Taylor	John Newstead D. L. Schultz J. G. Sully	R. F. Maddock J. J. Mahoney David Scroggie	P. Hartnett J. A. McHardy C. Peterson
1897	James Hewer	Geo. Penfold G. W. Stull Robt. McDonald	H. A. B. Calvert R. E. Nelson W. W. White	And. Crosbie J. H. Hamilton John A. McLean	Geo. Howard J Newstead Albert Wicks	H. Walker W. F. Clarke J. J. Mahoney	P. Hartnett Wm. Hearn C. Peterson
1898	James Hewer	John Kennedy Geo. Penfold G. W. Stull	R. E. Nelson E. Parkinson W. W. White	And. Crosbie J. H. Hamilton J. W. Mann	Robt. Barber Geo. Howard John Newstead	W. F. Clarke H. Walker J. J. Mahoney	Wm. Hearn C. Peterson P. Hartnett
1899	R. E. Nelson	G. J. Thorp J. Kennedy L. Nunan	T. O'Connor W. W. White Wm. Dyson	J. J. Drew J. H. Hamilton Robt. Dowrie	Robt. Barber Geo. Howard G. H. Skinner	W. F. Barber James Ryan H. Walker	C. Peterson R. C. Kennedy W. R. Kee

1888—Ald. Cutten resigned on February 6th, 1888, and Thos. Gowdy was elected to fill the vacancy.
1889—In November, 1889, M. J. Duignan was elected Alderman in place of Henry Hatch, whose seat was declared vacant through absence.
1891—On February 2nd, 1891, Ald. Wardrope resigned and J. G. Sully was elected to fill the vacancy.
1892—Mayor Goldie died in February, 1892, and Geo. Sleeman was elected to fill the vacancy.
1893—On February 14th, John Kennedy resigned and James Hough was elected to fill the vacancy.
1895—Ald. L. O. Barber died in April and Wm. Hearn was elected to fill the vacancy.
1897—Robt. McDonald was unseated and John Kennedy was elected to fill his place.
1897—Albert Wicks disclaimed, but elected again; unseated and Robert Barber elected to fill his place.
1897—New election rendered necessary by Ald. Calvert being absent more than three months without leave, and Alex B. Petrie elected.
1899—G. H. Skinner resigned, and W. T. Tanner was elected to fill the vacancy.

MEMBERS OF THE CITY COUNCIL (Continued)

Year	MAYOR	ALDERMEN					
		St. Patrick	St. George	St. John	St. David	St. Andrew	St. James
1900	R. E. Nelson	Geo. Penfold John Kennedy Geo. J. Thorp	A. B. Petrie T. O'Connor W. W. White	J. J. Drew G. A. Barker J. H. Hamilton	S. Carter J. W. Kilgour Robt. Barber	C. L. Dunbar Hugh Walker Geo. Hastings	J. Newstead C. Peterson G. J. Brill
1901	John Kennedy	H. H. O. Stull W. E. Taylor G. J. Thorp	Jas. E. Day A. B. Petrie W. W. White	G. A. Barker J. H. Hamilton S. Carter	Robt. Barber J. W. Kilgour J. A. Scott	C. L. Dunbar Geo. Hastings Jas. Ryan	Jas. Anderson R. Crowe Wm. Slater
1902	John Kennedy	J. Newstead H H. O. Stull W. E. Taylor	J. J. Drew J. E. Day W. W. White	G. A. Barker S. Carter J. H. Hamilton	Robt. Barber J. W. Kilgour J. A. Scott	W. F. Barber G. Hastings J. J. Mahoney	R. H. Crowe T. Irvine Wm. Slater

In each of the years 1903, 1904, 1905 and 1906 eleven Aldermen were elected by general vote pursuant to a vote of the ratepayers at the 1902 election.

Year	MAYOR	St. Patrick	St. George	St. John	St. David	St. Andrew	St. James
1903	John H. Hamilton	Geo. A. Barker Samuel Carter	R. H. Crowe Robt. Johnston	John J. Mahoney Hugh Malone	John Newstead W. W. White	Asa Rumford John A. Scott	H. H. O. Stull
1904	John H. Hamilton	Robt. Barber Geo. A. Barker	Samuel Carter R. H. Crowe	Geo. Hastings G. L. Higgins	J. J. Mahoney J. Newstead	Geo. Penfold John A. Scott	J. M. Struthers
1905	George Sleeman	John Newstead G. L. Higgins	M. F. Cray Geo. Penfold	T. H. Gemmell Geo. A. Barker	Robt. Barber Wm. F. Barber	J. M. Struthers Jno. Cunningham	J. H. Hamilton
1906	George Sleeman	D. E. Macdonald James W. Lyon	R. E. Nelson J. Newstead	Geo. Penfold Chas. E. Howitt	J. A. McCrea M. F. Cray	Geo. B. Ryan G. L. Higgins	Alex. Stewart

In each of the years 1907, 1908 and 1909 the Aldermen were elected by Wards pursuant to a vote of the electors at the 1906 election.

Year	MAYOR	St. Patrick	St. George	St. John	St. David	St. Andrew	St. James
1907	John Newstead	D. E. Rudd G. J. Thorp John Kennedy	J. W. Lyon Jas. Hewer R. E. Nelson	J. H. Hamilton G. L. Higgins J. Denyes	Robt. Simpson J. A. McCrea D. Messenger	W. F. Barber R. McMillan J. M. Struthers	Jno. Cunningham John McAteer J. E. Carter
1908	John Newstead	E. J. Bennett G. J. Thorp Geo. Penfold	Jas. Hewer R. E. Nelson John Kennedy	I. H. Hamilton J. Pequegnat J. Denyes	H. B. Callandar H. Mahoney R. Simpson	R. D. Stewart Jas. Ryan R. McMillan	John McAteer R. Humphries I. E. Carter
1909	Geo. Hastings	Jas. Johnston D. E. Rudd W. E. Taylor	R. L. Mackinnon S. Calvert F. Waters	C W. Kelly J. Pequegnat S. Rundle	H. B. Callandar H. Mahoney J. A. McCrea	Jas. Ryan T. C. Rogers C. Yeates	Albert Barber Matt. Cheevers Jos. Shaw

In each of the years 1910, 1911, 1912, 1913, 1914, 1915, 1916, 1917 and 1918 eleven Aldermen were elected by general vote, pursuant to a vote of the electors at the 1909 election.

Year	MAYOR	St. Patrick	St. George	St. John	St. David	St. Andrew	St. James
1910	George Hastings	D. E. Rudd G. J. Thorp	J. E. Carter H. Mahoney	W. E. Taylor J. W. Pequegnat	C. W. Kelly R. McMillan	S. Rundle M. Cheevers	S. Penfold
1911	Geo. John Thorp	J. E. Carter R. E. Nelson	J. W. Pequegnat J. Kelly	F. Howard H. Occomore	C. W. Kelly H. C. McLean	H. Mahoney S. Penfold	S. Calvert
1912	Geo. John Thorp	J Lawson J. Kelly	J. E. Carter R. H. Brydon	S. Penfold S. Calvert	H. Mahoney J. Pequegnat	F. Howard H. Occomore	H. C. McLean
1913	Samuel Carter	D. H. Barlow R. H. Brydon	J. E. Carter W. T. Doughty	T. J. Hannigan Robt. McMillan	I. Newstead H. Occomore	W. B. Parker S. Penfold	H. C. Steele

1902—J. J. Drew resigned and Hugh Walker was elected to fill the vacancy.
1903—Robert Johnston died and W. F. Barber succeeded him.
1903—W. W. White resigned and J. M. Struthers succeeded him.
1904—R. H. Crowe resigned and W. F. Barber succeeded him.
1905—Geo. A. Barker resigned and Geo. Howard succeeded him.
1906—George Penfold disclaimed, and O. E. Rowen succeeded him.
1907—D. Messenger resigned and H. B. Callendar was elected.
1907—John Cunningham was unseated and R. W. Humphries was elected.
1908—James Hewer resigned, and O. E. Rowen was elected.
1909—James Johnston resigned, and John Newstead was elected.
1912—H. C. McLean resigned in September, and R. McMillan succeeded.
1913—Robt. McMillan resigned in March, and T. H. Gemmell succeeded.

MEMBERS OF THE CITY COUNCIL (Continued)

Year	MAYOR	ALDERMEN					
1914	Samuel Carter	D. H. Barlow R. H. Brydon	C. H. Burgess W. T. Doughty	T. J. Hannigan H. Mahoney	J. Newstead H. Occomore	S. Penfold Jas. Ryan	H. C. Steele
1915	Harry Mahoney	S. Rundle H. C. Steele	D. Martin G. Dunbar	E. Crawford S. Calvert	H. H. O. Stull J. E. Carter	Jas. Hewer J. Newstead	O. E. Rowen
1916	Harry Mahoney	D. H. Barlow R. H. Brydon	G. Dunbar G. M. Henry	J. R. Howitt J. Lawson	D. Martin O. E. Rowen	S. Rundle H. C. Steele	H. Westoby
1917	John Newstead	A. A. Buchner Geo. Dunbar	G. M. Henry F. Howard	H. J. McHugh R. A. Payne	O. E. Rowen S. Rundle	H. C. Steele Wm. Stratton	H Westoby
1918	John Newstead	A. A. Buchner S. R. Rundle	Wm. Stratton F. Howard	H. J. McHugh R. A. Payne	G. M. Henry S. Penfold	E. Crawford D. H. Barlow	W. A. Cowan

Pursuant to 1918 Ontario Statute, C. 62, in each of the years 1919, 1920, 1921, 1922 and 1923, the Council consisted of eighteen Aldermen, elected by general vote. The six who obtained the highest number of votes at the election for the year 1919 held office for three years; the six who obtained the next highest number of votes held office for two years; and the six who obtained the next highest number of votes held office for one year. In each year thereafter one-third of the said eighteen Aldermen were elected for three years. The Council elected annually one of its members, Mayor.

Year	Mayor	Elected for three year term in year shown		two year term remaining		one year term remaining	
1919	J. E. Carter	E. A. Macdonald J. E. Carter John Newstead	Wm. Stephens R. H. Brydon W. G. Hood	T. J. Hannigan Chas. Burgess H. Westoby	G. M. Henry W. A. Cowan J. H. Simpson	H. Quarmby D. H. Barlow F. Howard	J. B. Hoover G. W. Walker S. Penfold
1920	H. Westoby	S. Penfold F. Howard D. H. Barlow	R. H. Wing A. A. Buckner H. Quarmby	E. A. Macdonald J. E. Carter John Newstead	Wm. Stephens R. H. Brydon W. G. Hood	T. J. Hannigan Chas Burgess H. Westoby	G. M. Henry W. A. Cowan J. H. Simpson
1921	C. H. Burgess	C. H. Burgess F. C. Grenside A. W. Tyson	W. P. Evans H. J. McElroy Chas. Yeates	S. Penfold F. Howard D. H. Barlow	R. H. Wing A. A. Buckner H. Quarmby	E. A. Macdonald J. E. Carter H. Mahoney	Wm. Stephens R. H. Brydon W. G. Hood
1922	F. Howard	Alex. Jaffray Geo. A. Drew Wm. Stephens	A. E. Baldwin H. Mahoney J. W. Oakes	C. H. Burgess F. C. Grenside A. W. Tyson	W. P. Evans H. J. McElroy Chas. Yeates	S. Penfold F. Howard D. H. Barlow	R. H. Wing A. A. Buckner H. Quarmby
1923	Wm. Stephens	F. Howard S. Penfold J. Armstrong	R. H. Brydon M. Coady J. A. Finnie	Alex. Jaffray Geo. A. Drew Wm. Stephens	A. E. Baldwin H. Mahoney J. W. Oakes	C. H. Burgess F. C. Grenside A. W. Tyson	W. P. Evans H. J. McElroy Chas. Yeates

Chapter 65 of the 1923 Ontario Statutes provides that the Council shall consist of a Mayor and eighteen Aldermen. The Aldermen are elected as for 1919 to 1923 inclusive but the Mayor is elected annually by the general vote of the electors.

Year	Mayor						
1924	Wm. Stephens	W. P. Evans Alex. Bain H. J. McElroy	C. W. Dempsey R. Bev. Robson L. Cunningham	F. Howard S. Penfold J. Armstrong	R. H. Brydon M. Coady J. A. Finnie	Alex. Jaffray Geo. A. Drew G. E. Meldrum	A. E. Baldwin H. Mahoney J. W. Oakes
1925	Geo. A. Drew	H. Mahoney Alex. Jaffray D. H. Barlow	A. E. Baldwin D. Bentley W. W. Stuart	W. P. Evans Alex. Bain H. J. McElroy	C. W. Dempsey R. Bev. Robson L. Cunningham	F. Howard S. Penfold J. A. Armstrong	R. H. Brydon M. Coady J. A. Finnie
1926	R. Bev. Robson	S. Penfold A. McNiven L. M. Stuart	R H. Grundy Sam. Rundle Ben. Howden	H. Mahoney Alex. Jaffray D. H. Barlow	G. E. Meldrum D. Bentley W. W. Stuart	W. P. Evans Alex. Bain H. J. McElroy	C. W. Dempsey M. Coady L. Cunningham

1920 — T. J. Hannigan resigned and David Martin succeeded.
1920 — John Newstead died in May, and Harry Mahoney succeeded.
1924 — G. E. Meldrum completed term of Wm. Stephens when Stephens was elected Mayor.
1925 — A. E. Baldwin resigned in December and George J. Meldrum succeeded for balance of his term.
1926 — M. Coady completed term of R. Bev. Robson when Robson was elected Mayor.

MEMBERS OF THE CITY COUNCIL (Continued)

Year	MAYOR	ALDERMEN					
		Elected for three year term in year shown		two year term remaining		one year term remaining	
1927	R. Bev. Robson	Alex. Bain	L. Brown	S. Penfold	R. H. Grundy	H. Mahoney	G. E. Meldrum
		F. C. Grenside	R. H. Wing	A. McNiven	Sam. Rundle	Alex. Jaffray	D. Bentley
		F. R. Ramsey	L. Cunningham	L. M. Stuart	Ben. Howden	D. H. Barlow	W. W. Stuart

P.S. — James Hough was appointed Clerk and Treasurer at the organization of the first council in 1851, and on his retirement in 1869 John Harvey was appointed. On the death of Mr. Harvey in 1884, the offices were separated, Richard Mitchell being appointed Clerk, and Edmund Harvey, Treasurer. David Scroggie succeeded E. Harvey in 1897. On the appointment of Mr. Mitchell as Police Court Clerk in 1908, Thomas J. Moore was appointed City Clerk. In 1909 Joseph Orr Rose succeeded Mr. Scroggie as Treasurer, and on the death of Mr. Moore in 1920, H. J. B. Leadley was appointed Clerk. Russell Stephens succeeded Joseph Orr Rose as Treasurer on June 6, 1927.

Appendix B

GUELPH HISTORICAL SOCIETY EXECUTIVE 1973-1977.

The Executive of the Guelph Historical Society during the period in which this History was in preparation included the following: Ruth Pollard, Pres.; Greta Shutt, Past Pres.; Alfred D. Hales, John Snell, Wm. S. Steele, Vice-Pres.; Evelyn Graham, Rec. Secy.; Eber A. Pollard, Treas.; Shirley and Dennis Mooney, Joan Smith, Social Convenors; James L. Baker, Yvette Davis, Tom O. Graham, Clifford Hall, Wm. Harris, Rowena and Harold Koch, Irene Matthews, Norma Neudoerffer, E. Root, E. Rae Stuart, Dorothy and Wm. Waines.

Appendix C

GUELPH HISTORY WORKSHOP MEMBERS.

In addition to the research done by Leo Johnson, the following members of the Guelph Historical Society assisted in making up the research cards used in the writing of this History: Georgina and Jim Baker, Ruth Bennett, Patricia Craven, Wilma Cheesman, Yvette Davis, Evelyn and Tom Graham, Lura Gillies, Marrian Grindlay, Alfred Hales, Wm. Harris, Clifford Hall, John Keleher, Rowena and Harold Koch, Ursula Mark, Irene Matthews, Verne McIlwraith, Doreen Murdock, Ruth and Eber Pollard, Don Smith, Wm. Steele, Dorothy and Wm. Waines. Typing of the manuscript was done by: Wilma Cheesman, Margaret Christie, Pat. Craven, Grace Gargett, Marrian Grindlay and Ruth Pollard. Following editing and typing, the manuscript was read by Hugh Guthrie and Alfred Hales. Photographic assistance was provided by Clifford Hall and Wm. Steele.

Appendix D

MEMBERS OF GUELPH CITY COUNCIL 1973-1977.

Members of Guelph City Council during this period included the following: Mayor—Norm Jary; Aldermen—Peter Brazolot, Mel Cochrane, Anne Godfrey, Kenneth O. Hammill, C.M. Hammond, Carl Hamilton, Patrick F. Hanlon, James Howitt, Les Love, David Kendrick, Margaret Mackinnon, Clara Marett, Robert Scammell, D.M. Valeriote. City Clerk—W. Gord Hall; City Treasurer—Milton Sather; City Administrator—Fred M. Woods.

Appendix E

SUBSCRIBERS

Ackerman, Gwen A. Heming
Allan, Leslie G.
Allen, Mrs. A.W.
Amèrica, Linda
Armstrong, Norman & Anne
Baker, Georgina
Baker, James L.
Bennett, Ruth K.
Blyth, Colin R.
Blyth, Don & Joyce
Bodlick, Eleanor M.
Borden, Dr. H.A.
Brooke, John & Terricia
Bull, Mr. & Mrs. John
Bunce, Maureen
Canadian Imperial Bank of Commerce
Caspers, Anthony & Nancy
Cheesman, Wilma F.
City of Guelph Clerk
City of Guelph Mayor
Clark, Dorothy Anne
Coady, Reg & Ruth
Coulman, Donald E.
Cowan, Dr. & Mrs. Robert F.
Craven, Patricia
Crosbie, Margaret
Crowley, T.A.
Currell, Lloyd W.
Dadd, Leonard & Betty
Dahms, Dr. F.A.

Davis, Yvette
Davis, William
Day, Fred & Margaret
Dearing, A.W.
Doyle, June & Bernie
Dryden, Elizabeth
Ecott, Ms. Janice
Ecott, Ms. Lynda G.
Ecott, Ron & Hazel
Edwards, Lorna J.
Entwistle, Harold & Gladys
Ernst, E.B.
Farmer, Dr. & Mrs. H.F.
Fearnall, Mr. & Mrs. W.F.
Ferrier, Mr. Vernon
Forler, June
Fowke, Ronald & Wilhelmina
Galt, Mrs. George M.
Gargett, Grace
Gilchrist, Jack M.
Gilchrist, Teri L.
Goheen, Alice P.
Goring, Mrs. Norma F.
Graham, Evelyn
Graham, Tom O.
Grindlay, Marrian
Guelph Collegiate Vocational Institute
Guthrie, Hugh & Lorna
Guthrie, Mrs. Hugh C.
Guthrie, Joy

Hales, Alfred & Mary
Hall, Clifford & Margaret
Hall, Emerson M.
Hall, Lloyd C.
Hall, William Gordon
Hamilton, Ald. Carl
Hammill, Mrs. Kenneth O.
Harris, William
Harrison, Gordon
Harrison, Viona
Harvey, Donald & Diane
Hawkins, Dr. N.A.
Heming, Frank B.
Heming, Ogilvy T.
Heming, Robert O.
Hewer, Elsie B.
Hill, Archdeacon & Mrs. Allen
Howlett, Eva B.
Hulland, Tom & Eleanore
Hutchinson, Helen L.
Jackson, Mr. & Mrs. David J.
Jarrett, William
Jary, Mayor & Mrs. Norm
Johnson, Mrs. Estelle
Jordan, Richard
Keleher, John W.
Kennedy, Darrel E.
Killan, Dr. Gerald
Kirk, Audrey L., UE
Kloepfer, Mr. & Mrs. Wm. A.

Koch, Harold E.
Koch, Rowena E.
Kostal, Thomas Joseph
Lavoie, Paul
Leger, Governor General & Madame J.
Lewis, Steve
Long, Mrs. H.B.
Maddaford, F. Catharine
Mann, Gordon
Marett, Ald. Clara M.
Marshall, Dr. & Mrs. John U.
Matthews, Irene J.
McCall, Elva B.
McCraw, Dr. & Mrs. Bruce M.
McDonald, Dr. & Mrs. R.J.
McFarlane, A. Eleanor
McGibbon, Lieutenant Governor P.
McIlwraith, Vernon
McKeough, Edward & Ethel
Mercer, Paul & Edna
Milne, Mr. & Mrs. K.
Mitchell, Edward R.
Mitchell, Mary E.
Mooney, Dennis & Shirley

Morrison, Christina Downey
Muller, Mrs. Margaret E.
Murdock, Doreen
Mutrie, Dr. & Mrs. Eric T.
Myhill, Margaret H.
Naismith, John & Ruth
Nash, Dr. & Mrs. F.C.
Newson, Clarence & Patricia
Paddison, Terry
Peachell, Laura
Peter, Marg & Joe
Peterson, Clayton Ross
Peterson, Clayton T.
Peterson, Douglass Roberet
Pollard, Eber A.
Pollard, Ruth
Robinson, Jack & Helen
Sansom, Ron & Jane
Saunders, Guy L.
Saunders, Mrs. Marjorie
Savoie, David Michael Galt
Scott, Roderick & Lourene
Smart, Eric & Irene
Smith, Donald A.

Smith, Mr. & Mrs. Norman J.
Snell, John D.
Steele, William & Mary
Stephenson, Don & Joan
Stevens, Robert A.
Stewart, Robert Alan Maclean
Stortz, Thomas Gerald John
Sutherland, Donald
Swanson, D.L.
Theaker, Archie & Rita
Tolton, William G.
Trapnell, Louise
Trowbridge, Kenneth & Alva
Trudeau, Prime Minister Pierre E.
Verspagen, Peter & Madelyn
Waines, Dr. & Mrs. W.J.
Waterston, Douglas & Elizabeth
Whitaker, Edward L.A.
Wilburn, David
Wilburn, Mr. & Mrs. John H.
Wood, W.C. Company Limited
Woods, Fred & Victoria

Index